CLASSICAL FORM

Classical Form

A Theory of Formal Functions
for the Instrumental Music
of Haydn, Mozart, and Beethoven

WILLIAM E. CAPLIN

OXFORD
UNIVERSITY PRESS

Oxford University Press

Oxford New York
Athens Auckland Bangkok Bogotá Buenos Aires Calcutta
Cape Town Chennai Dar es Salaam Delhi Florence Hong Kong Istanbul
Karachi Kuala Lumpur Madrid Melbourne Mexico City Mumbai
Nairobi Paris São Paulo Shanghai Singapore Taipei Tokyo Toronto Warsaw

and associated companies in
Berlin Ibadan

Library of Congress Cataloging-in-Publication Data
Caplin, William Earl, 1948–
    Classical form : a theory of formal functions for the instrumental music of Haydn,
Mozart, and Beethoven / William E. Caplin.
        p. cm.
    Includes bibliographical references and index.
    ISBN 978-0-19-510480-6; 978-0-19-514399-7 (pbk.)
        1. Musical form.   2. Instrumental music—18th century—Analysis, appreciation.
3. Instrumental music—19th century—Analysis, appreciation.   4. Musical analysis.
5. Classicism in music.   6. Music—Theory—20th century.
7. Haydn, Joseph, 1732–1809—Criticism and interpretation.
8. Mozart, Wolfgang Amadeus, 1756–1791—Criticism and interpretation.
9. Beethoven, Ludwig van, 1770–1827—Criticism and interpretation.   I. Title.
MT58.C37   1997   97-25561

To my parents,
ARTHUR AND NATALIE CAPLIN

PREFACE

This project owes its origins to a specific curricular requirement of all music students at McGill University. Shortly after my arrival here in 1978, I was asked to teach a semester course on form that was restricted to music in the classical style. I soon discovered that the standard textbooks, which surveyed a much broader stylistic field, did not address many issues particularly associated with the music of Haydn, Mozart, and Beethoven. I thus turned back to material that I had first encountered several years earlier in a seminar on musical form given by Carl Dahlhaus at the Berlin Technical University, in which the principal reference work was Erwin Ratz's *Einführung in die musikalische Formenlehre*. I began incorporating into my course at McGill some ideas from this treatise, as well as similar material from *Fundamentals of Musical Composition* by Arnold Schoenberg, with whom Ratz had studied.

My own expansion of these concepts of form reached a sufficient stage of development to begin writing this book during a sabbatical leave in 1984–85. In subsequent years, earlier drafts of this book were used as a reference text in a variety of classes at McGill, as well as at Yale University, the University of Ottawa, and the Université de Sherbrooke. Although I have written this book as a comprehensive theoretical treatise, the reader will quickly discern a distinct pedagogical tone, betraying its origins in the interactive experience of classroom instruction.

AMONG THE MANY PEOPLE who helped me realize this project, I must first mention the considerable stimulus and encouragement offered by Janet Schmalfeldt, with whom I have had a continuing dialogue on almost every topic treated in this book. Her work with me at times approached a collaborative effort, and her teaching of this material helped me shape the diverse collection of ideas and concerns into a systematic theoretical–analytical approach. At various stages of the project I also received significant help and support from Brian Alegant, Bo Alphonce, Elliot Asarnow, Wallace Berry, Richard Braley, William Drabkin, Michelle Fillion, Ingeborg Pfingsten Gürsching, Steven Huebner, Patricia Kerridge, Cynthia Leive, Donald McLean, Leonard B. Meyer, Christopher Reynolds, Lewis Rowell, Norma Sherman, Peter Schubert, and Elaine Sisman. In addition, I owe much gratitude to the many students at McGill whose response to my teaching stimulated many new ideas and helped keep me honest. I particularly want to acknowledge the efforts of Patrick McCreless, William Rothstein, and M. Evan Bonds, who read substantial portions of the book and offered numerous suggestions for its improvement. All remaining errors and misinterpretations are, of course, entirely my responsibility.

The musical examples were prepared with the help of Peter von Holtzendorff, Cathrine McKinley, Suzanne Davies, William Brock, François de Médicis, and James Wright; I thank Keith Hamel for allowing me to use early versions of his music notation program NoteWriter II. I also thank Maribeth Payne and her colleagues Soo Mee Kwon and Cynthia Garver at Oxford University Press for their interest in my work and for their many suggestions on how to make it a viable publication. Finally, my wife, Marsha, has sustained me throughout my endeavors to bring this work to completion; for her patience and encouragement I am especially grateful.

Research for this project was generously supported by grants from the Social Sciences and Humanities Research Council of Canada and from the Faculty of Graduate Studies and Research, McGill University.

Portions of this book have appeared earlier in article form. I want to thank the publishers for permission to incorporate material from the following articles:

"The 'Expanded Cadential Progression': A Category for the Analysis of Classical Form," *Journal of Musicological Research* 7 (1987): 215–57.

"Hybrid Themes: Toward a Refinement in the Classification of Classical Theme Types," *Beethoven Forum* 3 (1994): 151–65.

"Funktionale Komponenten im achttaktigen Satz," *Musiktheorie* 1 (1986): 239–60.

"Structural Expansion in Beethoven's Symphonic Forms," in *Beethoven's Compositional Process*, ed. William Kinderman, 27–54. Lincoln: University of Nebraska Press, 1991.

Montreal   W. E. C.
March 1997

NOTE ON THE MUSICAL EXAMPLES

I have used as many musical examples as feasible to illustrate the theoretical issues presented in this book. In order to draw maximum efficiency from the examples, I have often used single examples to illustrate multiple theoretical issues. As a result, the book contains numerous cross references to examples within and between chapters. Thus I ask the reader to refer to earlier appearing examples and even, though much less often, to look ahead to examples that appear later than their mention in the text. In a number of cases, I have broken up a relatively long musical passage into individual examples, so that the music may be located near its discussion. Starting with part II, the example discussions, which illustrate the immediately preceding points of theory, are printed in reduced type so that they may be distinguished from the flow of the general theoretical presentation.

To save space, I have reset all the examples as "reduction transcriptions," in which the texture is compressed into a single staff. This procedure often resulted in my shifting the various voices into different octaves and inverting the inner parts. In addition, I sometimes rewrote orchestral accompanimental figurations in order to make them easier to play at the piano. I tried to keep the melody and bass line as close to the original as possible. The added harmonic analyses are based on the complete texture of the original sources and thus may sometimes not correspond exactly to the transcriptions (e.g., a II$^{6}_{5}$ label may be used where the transcription merely shows a II^6 chord).

Works by Beethoven are labeled by opus numbers. Works by Mozart are identified by their original Köchel numbers as well as by a revised number, where necessary, from the sixth edition of the Köchel catalogue (e.g., K. 250/248b). Haydn's symphonies are numbered according to Hoboken group I; his string quartets are labeled by their traditional opus number; and his other works are given complete Hoboken numbers. The reference to "piano" in any work citation or caption is generic for the appropriate keyboard instrument.

CONTENTS

CLASSICAL FORM

Watch the harmony;
watch the root progressions;
watch the bass line.

Schoenberg, *Fundamentals of*
Musical Composition

INTRODUCTION

The time is ripe for a new theory of classical form. Despite many recent, distinguished studies devoted to the instrumental works of Haydn, Mozart, and Beethoven,[1] most writers continue to describe the formal organization of this music using ill-defined concepts and ambiguous terminology derived from theories that have long fallen into disrepute. Once a venerable subdiscipline of music theory, the traditional *Formenlehre* ("teaching of form," often by means of comprehensive treatises) has largely been abandoned by theorists and historians, for many reasons. These include the influence of Heinrich Schenker's critique of form as a foreground manifestation of more fundamental contrapuntal–harmonic processes; the acceptance of a historicist attitude that eighteenth-century music is best analyzed by eighteenth-century theories; and the mistrust by the "new musicology" of systematic, classificatory models of musical organization.

This book is intended to revive the *Formenlehre* tradition by establishing it on more secure and sophisticated foundations. The theory here formulates coherent principles and proposes clear terminology to serve as theoretical tools for analyzing form at all hierarchical levels in a single movement.[2] An extensive set of annotated musical examples drawn from the standard instrumental genres illustrates the theoretical concepts and provides models of formal analysis.[3]

The immediate sources of inspiration for this study are the principles of form introduced by Arnold Schoenberg early in this century and eventually published in his *Fundamentals of Musical Composition*.[4] Schoenberg's ideas were then developed by his student Erwin Ratz in *Einführung in die musikalische Formenlehre*. Central to the concern of these theorists is the notion that the formal units of a work play specific roles in articulating its overall structure. Ratz, in particular, proposed a fundamental model (*Urform*) of five "formal functions."[5] Whereas his model generally operates at a single, relatively background level of a given composition, the theory developed here identifies a multitude of functions discernible at all levels in a classical movement. Thus this study strives to realize ideals implicit in the writings of Schoenberg and Ratz by formulating a comprehensive theory of formal functions.[6]

Like most theories of form, the various procedures and techniques are investigated in increasing order of complexity, thus following somewhat the hierarchy of an individual movement from the local to the global. To give the reader a general orientation to the theory before plunging into more detailed examinations of specific formal types, the opening chapter of part I ("Preliminaries") surveys the basic precepts of the theory; the second chapter then defines the fundamental harmonic progressions that play such crucial roles in establishing formal functions. Part II ("Tight-Knit Themes") describes the principal forms characteristic of main themes—sentence, period, hybrids, small ternary, and small binary. Part III ("Looser Formal Regions") discusses the formal organization of broader expanses within a movement—subordinate theme, transition, development, recapitulation, and coda. Part IV ("Full-Movement Forms") examines the large-scale formal designs of entire movements—sonata, sonata without development, large ternary, theme and variations, minuet/trio, rondo, and concerto.

The following points highlight features of the theory that distinguish it from earlier theories of musical form in general and classical form in particular.

The theory is based on music of a single style. My investigation is limited to the instrumental music of Haydn, Mozart, and Beethoven as representing the core repertory of the high Viennese classical style (ca. 1780–1810).[7] This restriction is due as much to theoretical as to practical considerations. Though extraordinarily individualistic in melody, rhythm, and dramatic expression, works in this style are grounded in a highly sophisticated set of compositional conventions, what are identified here as formal functions. Indeed, a good deal of the aesthetic pleasure that we gain from listening to this music involves the interaction of our (often unconscious) understanding of functional norms with their particular manifestations in a given work. Although tonal music from earlier and later periods (baroque, early classical, romantic, and late romantic) also exhibits formal functionality in a variety of ways, form in these periods is considerably less conventional, thus frustrating the establishment of general principles. In classical music, how-

3

ever, formal functions can be defined and illustrated with much greater clarity.

The theory emphasizes the role of local harmonic progression as a determinant of form. Theorists and historians widely recognize that the form of a classical work is determined in large part by its pitch organization. Most current discussions, however, have centered on how the succession of various tonal regions or keys within the home tonality is responsible for creating relatively high level formal designs.[8] Less attention has been paid to how formal functionality at a movement's lower levels is defined by specific progressions of harmonies in a given tonal center, be it the home key (tonic) or related keys (dominant, mediant, etc.). In my theory, local harmonic progression is held to be the most important factor in expressing formal functions in themes (or themelike units). This detailed study of the ways in which surface harmonies and their progressions relate to form distinguishes my approach from virtually all previous theories.

The theory clearly distinguishes formal function from grouping structure. To the extent that traditional theories of form employ labels indicating formal functionality (like antecedent, consequent, main theme, transition, exposition, and coda), such identifications usually correspond directly to a work's "grouping structure"—that is, to the variety of discrete time spans organized hierarchically in a work.[9] In other words, a given musical group (unit, part, section) is assigned a single functional label, and, conversely, a given function is understood to take place within the confines of a single group. In the theory presented here, on the contrary, formal functionality arises from harmonic, melodic, and rhythmic processes that are not necessarily the same as those that create the work's grouping structure. Function and group are often congruent, but this need not always be the case. In some situations, a group may express more than one function simultaneously; for example, continuation and cadential functions may fuse together in a single four-measure phrase (see chap. 3). At other times, several consecutive groups may express the same formal function, such as when a number of distinct phrases with highly contrasting melodic–motivic material are supported by one expanded cadential progression (see chap. 8). Finally, a given group can at first be understood as expressing a particular function but then be reinterpreted as another function (e.g., codettas of postcadential function are frequently understood retrospectively as an initiating function).[10] Thus in this theory, grouping structure and formal function are conceived as different, yet interactive, dimensions of musical form.

The theory minimizes motivic content as a criterion of formal function. Most theories of form rely heavily on the identification of melodic and motivic relationships for determining a work's formal organization. To be sure, the grouping structure of a given piece is often based on similarities and dissimilarities of melodic–motivic material. But contrary to common opinion, the formal function of an individual group does not depend on its motivic content. The appearance of a particular melodic motive—leaving aside its implied harmony—rarely determines its formal expression. In fact, a single motive can saturate a musical composition without obscuring the form, precisely because motives carry little in the way of functional implications.[11] Given that this theory minimizes motivic relationships as a criterion of formal functionality, it largely sets aside, ironically, Schoenberg's own preoccupation with *Grundgestalt* and "developing variation."[12]

The theory establishes strict formal categories but applies them flexibly in analyses. One reason that the traditional *Formenlehre* has fallen out of favor with many historians and theorists is their belief that the use of rigid, abstract categories of form results too often in procrustean analyses that obscure diversities in style and distort the individuality of the musical work. Yet forsaking categories would make it almost impossible to generalize about formal organization, and such a situation runs counter to most musicians' intuitions that classical form features regularly recurring patterns of conventionalized procedures. Alternatively, broadening the categories to accommodate virtually all formal instances would seriously undermine the general theoretical framework, throw into doubt the meaning of the categories, and obscure the line between what is, or is not, an exemplification of a given formal procedure.

In this book, categories of form are defined in as precise and restricted a manner as possible. These categories are comparable to what Carl Dahlhaus, following Max Weber, calls "ideal types" (*Idealtypen*) and thus represent abstractions based on generalized compositional tendencies in the classical repertory. A category is not necessarily meant to reflect frequency of occurrence in a statistical sense: it is often the case that relatively few instances in the repertory correspond identically to the complete definition of a given category. Nor are categories meant to represent standards of aesthetic judgment, such that passages deviating from the norm are devalued in any respect.

By strictly defining categories of form, it is possible to apply them in analysis with considerable flexibility. Although many situations can easily be seen as exemplars of a given category or procedure, many others defy simple classification. In such cases, one can present the range of options and identify which individual characteristics of the musical passage conform to, and depart from, the definitions of established formal conventions.

It is important from the outset that certain limitations of the theory be clearly spelled out.

The theory is not a comprehensive account of "form" in music. Many of the phenomena and issues broadly associated with "musical form" are not treated here. For example, the role of motivic development in delineating form is, as already discussed, largely downplayed in this study. The notion of form as "durational proportions" is not explored except to the extent that relatively symmetrical phrase groupings (4 + 4, 8 + 8) are contrasted with asymmetrical ones as more or less appropriate to certain formal situations.[13] The ways in which the "dynamic curve" of a work helps define its form are discussed in a number of contexts but are not studied exhaustively.[14] The relationship of formal function to Schenker's conception of form and to other approaches influenced by him are barely touched on.[15] Finally, many traditional *Formenlehren* include considerable material on the various genres of musical composition. Matters pertaining to genre arise now and then in this book, but much information has been omitted because of its ready accessibility in the standard sources (*New Harvard Dictionary, New Grove*).

The theory does not include late-eighteenth- and early-nineteenth-century accounts of form. Much of the recent work on classical form has been inspired by a renewed interest in the authority of theorists contemporary to classical composers.[16] Some music historians are thus likely to be disappointed that the theory presented here makes little reference to earlier writings on form. This omission is largely motivated by the goal of developing a modern theory, one that permits an unfettered rethinking of formal issues while taking advantage of the full history of music-theoretical thought (which certainly includes the work of theorists postdating the classical period). As fascinating and suggestive as contemporary writings may be, their ideas on musical form are limited by a rudimentary theory of harmony (which understands little about harmonic progression at multiple levels) and a lack of familiarity with the huge classical repertory that we have at our fingertips today. An investigation of the extent to which late-eighteenth- and early-nineteenth-century theory incorporates form-functional observations would be highly revealing, but it must be postponed for a later study.

The theory is empirical and descriptive, not deductive and prescriptive. The account of classical form given here is a "theory" only in an informal sense (though no less rigorous in intent). Principles are derived from empirical observation and are largely descriptive. No attempt is made to ground the concepts in some broader system of mathematics, logic, cognition, or the like, and no proof is offered for the many assertions made. For some scholars, what is presented here would indeed not even count as a legitimate theory. I reject the notion that a humanistic theory must resemble a scientific, axiomatic system, but I welcome any future attempt to formalize the observations and principles proposed in what follows.

I

PRELIMINARIES

Some Basic Formal Functions:
An Overview

Most musicians have a general notion of what constitutes musical form. If asked, they would probably respond that form concerns itself with how the various parts of a composition are arranged and ordered; how standard patterns of repeated material appear in works; how different sections of a work are organized into themes; and how the themes themselves break down into smaller phrases and motives.[1] Indeed, this general understanding of form is a fairly accurate one and can be used as the basis of a more detailed investigation into how the parts of a musical work are defined and distinguished from one another.

More technically, the form of a musical work can be described minimally as a hierarchical arrangement of discrete, perceptually significant time spans, what has been termed the *grouping structure* of the work.[2] Each *group*—a self-contained "chunk" of music (as psychologists would say) at one level of the hierarchy—can be identified most neutrally in terms of its measure length. Thus we speak of a two-measure idea grouping with another two-measure idea to form a four-measure phrase, which in turn may group with another phrase of the same length to form an eight-measure theme, and so on. (Grouping structures are not always so symmetrical, of course.)

Such identifications by measure length have limited value, since they say nothing about the content of the groups or how they relate to one another (except in regard to duration). Thus, most of the traditional theories of form identify some groups with labels, such as letters of the alphabet, which indicate whether the musical content of a group is the same as, similar to, or different from, another group (e.g., A–A′, A–B–A′). Even more precise are labels that specify the *formal function* of the group—that is, the more definite role that the group plays in the formal organization of the work. For example, a given four-measure group may stand as an "antecedent" phrase in relation to a following "consequent"; an eight-measure group may serve as the "main theme" of a minuet; or a seventy-three-measure group may function as the "development section" in a sonata.

The theory presented here develops a comprehensive set of such functions with the goal of analyzing classical form more precisely than it has been before. In addition, the the-

ory defines a set of formal *processes* (e.g., repetition, fragmentation, extension, expansion) and a set of formal *types* (e.g., sentence, period, small ternary, sonata, rondo). Along the way, a host of concepts associated with harmony, tonality, and cadence are introduced and examined. The purpose of this chapter is to present some fundamental principles of the theory by way of selected excerpts from the Viennese classical repertory. Since what follows in this chapter is merely introductory, many of the ideas are only partially explained. The reader thus may wish at times to look ahead to later chapters, in which all the concepts are fully developed and illustrated and more complete references to the scholarly literature are cited.

I begin by illustrating the concept of formal function in connection with the three most important theme-types of classical instrumental music—the sentence, the period, and the small ternary. Each contains a conventional set of formal functions that operate in the structural boundaries of the theme. Next I examine some additional functions that frame the boundaries of these themes. Finally, I consider how themes themselves can acquire unique formal functions at a higher level of structure, namely, the exposition section of sonata form.

SENTENCE

Example 1.1, the main theme from the first movement of Beethoven's Piano Sonata in F Minor, Op. 2/1, presents perhaps the most archetypal manifestation of the *sentence* form in the entire classical repertory. Indeed, this passage was used by Arnold Schoenberg (the virtual discoverer of the sentence as a distinct theme-type) for his initial example of the form, and his student Erwin Ratz followed suit in the introductory chapter of his treatise.[3]

The sentence is normatively an eight-measure structure.[4] It begins with a two-measure *basic idea*, which brings in the fundamental melodic material of the theme. The basic idea frequently contains several distinct *motives*, which often are developed in the course of the theme (or later in the movement).

EXAMPLE 1.1 Beethoven, Piano Sonata in F Minor, Op. 2/1, i, 1–8

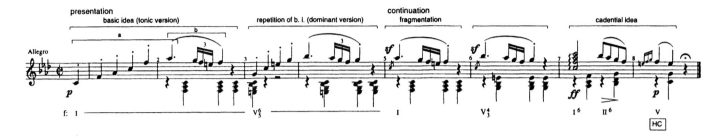

EXAMPLE 1.2 Beethoven, String Quartet in F, Op. 135, iii, 3–10

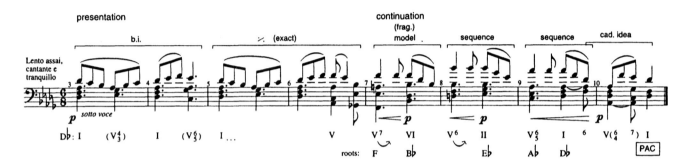

We can readily identify two motives ("a" and "b") in this basic idea. But because Beethoven gives them to us in the form of a single gesture, we should thus regard the basic idea, not the individual motive, as the fundamental building block of the theme. Beethoven uses specific compositional devices later in the theme to highlight more clearly the motivic duality of the basic idea.

The basic idea is repeated in measures 3–4. This repetition has a number of significant effects, two of which can be mentioned at this point. First, repeating the basic idea helps the listener learn and remember the principal melodic–motivic material of the theme. Second, repetition plays an important role in demarcating the actual boundaries of the idea: although the quarter-note rest at the end of measure 2 suggests that the basic idea has ended, the sense of ending is confirmed when we perceive the idea starting over again in measure 3. As a result of repetition, the basic idea has been unequivocally "presented" to the listener, and so we can speak of this music fulfilling *presentation* function and label the first four measures a *presentation phrase*.[5]

Let us now consider the harmonic context in which the basic idea and its repetition are presented, for the underlying harmony of a passage is an essential criterion of its formal function. The basic idea expresses the root-position tonic of F minor (the home key), and the repetition expresses the dominant. The basic idea is thus given originally in a *tonic version*, also termed a *statement*, and the repetition in a *dominant version* or *response*; such an arrangement results in a *statement–response repetition* of the idea.

When the V^6_5 of measures 3–4 resolves to I on the downbeat of measure 5, we can characterize the resulting harmonic progression as *tonic prolongational*. As a general rule, all presentation phrases have tonic harmony at their basis. This tonic may be extended literally for four measures or, more frequently, be expressed by a prolongational progression featuring neighboring or passing chords. A presentation is thus defined not only by its melodic–motivic content but also by its harmonic organization.

At this point we can observe a third significant effect of repeating a basic idea. Immediate repetition within a presentation has the result of separating the individual ideas from each other. At the end of the phrase, we do not have the impression that thematic closure (or "cadence") has been achieved. On the contrary, the strongly ongoing quality created by a presentation generates demand for a *continuation phrase*, one that will directly follow, and draw consequences from, the presentation.

The formal function of *continuation* has two outstanding characteristics: *fragmentation*, a reduction in the size of the units; and *harmonic acceleration*, an increase in the rate of harmonic change. Both characteristics are manifest in this sonata theme.[6]

In the presentation phrase, the size of the constituent units (i.e., the basic idea) is two measures. At the beginning of the continuation phrase, the units are reduced by a half. As in the presentation, the immediate repetition of the units helps clarify their size. When we hear the material of measure 5 starting over again in measure 6, we realize that the unit is only one measure long. In this example, the fragments derive motivically from the preceding ideas. But such a motivic connection need not occur, for the concept of fragmentation exclusively concerns the *length* of the musical units, not necessarily their motivic content.

In the presentation phrase, the harmony changes every two measures. In the continuation, there is a steady acceleration in the harmonic rhythm. It is a particular feature of this theme that each of the component units through measure 6 contains a single harmony, and therefore fragmentation and harmonic acceleration go hand in hand. In many cases, however, these processes are not congruent. We will encounter examples in which the units decrease in size within a uniform harmonic rhythm or, conversely, in which an increase in the rate of harmonic change occurs without any corresponding fragmentation of the units.

Let us now briefly examine the motivic organization of the continuation phrase. We have already seen that the fragmented units derive from the basic idea. To create the fragmentation, Beethoven simply detaches motive "b" from the basic idea, thus giving that motive special attention. Another way of understanding this process is to say that motive "a" has been largely eliminated, that all that remains is the leaping grace note of measures 5–6 and the arpeggiated chord in measure 7. In that same measure, the sixteenth-note triplet, the most prominent rhythmic idea of motive "b," is abandoned, and the melodic descent occurs via eighth notes instead. This systematic elimination of characteristic motives is termed *liquidation*. Fragmentation and liquidation frequently work together, as in this example. In principle, however, they are different compositional processes: fragmentation concerns the lengths of units, and liquidation concerns the melodic–motivic content of units.

The continuation phrase of this sentence ends with a *half cadence (HC)*, which effects closure for the entire theme. *Cadential* function is the third formal function—beside presentation and continuation—in the sentence theme-type.[7] A cadential idea contains not only a conventionalized harmonic progression but also a conventionalized melodic formula, usually of falling contour. The melody is *conventional* because it lacks motivic features that would specifically associate it with a particular theme. In this sense, the cadential idea stands opposed to the basic idea, whose *characteristic* motives are used precisely to define the uniqueness of the theme. When we hear measures 1–2, we immediately identify them as belonging to a specific piano sonata by Beethoven, but when we hear measures 7–8 alone, we could well imagine them closing any number of themes from different works.

We can now understand that the purpose of motivic liquidation is to strip the basic idea of its characteristic features, thus leaving the merely conventional ones for the cadence. Not all themes feature liquidation, and when they do not, the composer achieves the same end by simply abandoning material from the basic idea and writing a cadential melody that is not directly derived from the earlier idea.

Although continuation and cadential are separate functions, we can observe that the cadential idea of measures 7–8 grows naturally out of the preceding measures. The processes of fragmentation, harmonic acceleration, and liquidation begun in measure 5 extend all the way to measure 8, and thus the cadential material here seems to be genuinely a part of the continuation process as well. Indeed, the two functions of continuation and cadential normally *fuse* into a single "continuation phrase" in the eight-measure sentence. (We will see later in this chapter, in connection with a subordinate theme, that the two functions can occupy individual phrases of entirely different melodic–motivic content.)

A second example illustrates again the main features of the eight-measure sentence and also reveals some additional characteristics of the basic functions already introduced. Example 1.2 forms the opening theme of the slow movement from Beethoven's final published work, the String Quartet in F, Op. 135. (The theme proper begins in measure 3; it is preceded by a two-measure introduction, to be discussed in connection with ex. 1.5.) Measures 3–4 bring a basic idea whose repetition in the following two measures creates a presentation phrase. The subsequent continuation features fragmentation of the two-measure idea into one-measure units and concludes with a *perfect authentic cadence (PAC)* in measure 10.[8]

Let us now examine some details that distinguish this sentence from the preceding one. As before, the presentation phrase prolongs tonic harmony in root position.[9] But whereas example 1.1 contains a statement–response repetition of tonic and dominant versions, the repetition in this example brings no fundamental change of harmony. Such a repetition is termed *exact*, even when there are ornamental differences in melody or harmony.

Another difference between the examples concerns the content of the fragmented units. In the piano sonata, the fragments retain a motive from the basic idea. In the quartet, they bring entirely different melodic material. Yet structural fragmentation can still be identified there despite the lack of motivic connection between the basic idea and the shorter units of the continuation phrase. The fragmented units of this example also display a new, third type of repetition, in which the entire fragment in measure 7 is transposed to different scale-degrees in measures 8–9. This *sequential repetition* is particularly characteristic of continuation function. By convention, we refer to the initial unit as a *model* and each unit of repetition as its *sequence*. Thus sequential repetition can also be termed *model–sequence technique*.

At the harmonic basis of sequential repetition is a *sequential progression* of the harmonies—that is, chords whose roots are organized according to a systematic intervallic

EXAMPLE 1.3 Mozart, *Eine kleine Nachtmusik*, K. 525, ii, 1–8

pattern. In the example here, the roots progress by a series of descending fifths (F, B♭, E♭, A♭, D♭). Harmonic sequence is an important characteristic of a continuation. The ongoing quality of such a progression—its projection of harmonic mobility—coordinates perfectly with the forward impetus to a goal associated with this formal function.

At this point we may inquire whether the continuation phrase of this excerpt brings about an acceleration of harmonic rhythm, another trait of continuation function. The foreground harmonies progress at a fairly consistent rate of two chords per measure, hence, no acceleration. But this level of harmonic activity does not necessarily conform to our listening experience. The dominant seventh chords that prolong the tonic in the basic idea and its repetition seem not to represent genuine harmonies in their own right; thus we perceive a kind of harmonic stasis throughout the presentation phrase.[10] In comparison, the sequential progression of the continuation phrase brings a palpable sense of harmonic motion and increased activity. We see, therefore, that an analysis of harmonic acceleration can be problematic and requires careful judgment about the relative structural importance of the constituent chords in the progressions.

As in the sonata example, the fragmented units of the quartet lead directly into a cadential figure to close the theme. Here, however, the perfect authentic cadence creates a greater sense of closure than does the half cadence of the previous example.

PERIOD

The two themes from Beethoven just examined exemplify the principal features of the sentence, although they express the main functions of the form in diverse ways. Most fundamentally, the themes differ with respect to their cadential closure. Whereas the sonata theme remains structurally incomplete because of its ending with a half cadence, the quartet theme fully completes its essential harmonic and melodic processes by means of a perfect authentic cadence.

That formal units can express varying degrees of cadential closure allows for the possibility of creating thematic organization based largely on such cadential differentiation. If an initial unit ending with a weak cadence is repeated and brought to a fuller cadential close, then we can say, following traditional usage, that the first unit is an *antecedent* to the following *consequent*. Together, the two functions of antecedent and consequent combine to create the theme-type normally termed *period*.

Like the sentence, the period is normatively an eight-measure structure divided into two four-measure phrases.[11] Example 1.3, the opening of the slow movement of Mozart's *Eine kleine Nachtmusik*, K. 525, illustrates the model period form. Like the presentation of a sentence, the antecedent phrase of a period begins with a two-measure basic idea. The same features of a basic idea discussed in connection with the sentence apply to the period as well. Instead of immediately repeating the basic idea, however, measures 3–4 of the antecedent phrase bring a *contrasting idea* that leads to a weak cadence of some kind.

The notion of a "contrasting" idea must be understood in the sense of its being "not-a-repetition." The extent to which a contrasting idea differs from a basic idea may be striking, as in the example here. At other times, however, the contrast may be minimal. Nevertheless, the idea in measures 3–4 of an antecedent phrase must be sufficiently distinct from the basic idea that we do not perceive it to be a repetition, for if it were, we might very well believe that a presentation was in the making.

It is difficult to generalize about the nature of a contrasting idea, but we can say that it often features characteristics of continuation function such as fragmentation, an increased rate of harmonic change, harmonic sequence, and a conventionalized melodic formula for the cadence. In Mozart's theme, measures 3–4 (including the upbeat) reveal obvious fragmentation and a degree of harmonic acceleration.

The consequent phrase of the period repeats the antecedent but concludes with a stronger cadence. More specifically, the basic idea *returns* in measures 5–6 and then leads to a contrasting idea, which may or may not be based on that of the antecedent.[12] In example 1.3, measures 7–8 bring a distinctly different melody for the contrasting idea of the consequent. Most important, of course, the contrasting idea must end with a cadence stronger than the one closing the antecedent, usually a perfect authentic cadence.

SMALL TERNARY

A third fundamental theme-type, the *small ternary*, embraces a new set of formal functions. Two basic notions lie at the heart of this three-part design: (1) a relatively closed thematic unit is juxtaposed with a structurally open unit of contrasting content and formal organization, and (2) the original unit is brought back, but in a manner that ensures complete closure of the theme.

This formal scheme is traditionally indicated in letter notation as *A–B–A'*, and for convenience we can continue to use this nomenclature for the small ternary form. Such letter designations, however, are preferably supplemented by descriptive labels that specify more precisely the formal function of the three sections. Thus, the initial section is termed an *exposition*; the later return of that section, a *recapitulation*; and the section that stands between these two, a *contrasting middle*.[13]

The exposition (A) of the small ternary form is frequently built as one of the conventional theme-types already discussed—namely, a sentence or a period. Less conventional thematic designs are occasionally found there as well.[14] As for its tonal plan, the section may remain throughout in its initial tonality, the *home key*, or else the section may modulate to a closely related *subordinate key* (usually the dominant region if the home key is major, or the mediant if the home key is minor). In either case, the exposition confirms that key with a perfect authentic cadence, thus creating sufficient closure to render the exposition a structurally independent section. We could say, indeed, that the A section emphasizes tonic, since its closing chord and (almost always) its opening one express this harmony.[15]

The contrasting middle (B) of the small ternary achieves its contrast foremost through harmonic means—namely, by an emphasis on dominant. The final harmony of the section is almost always the dominant of the home key, and frequently the section opens with this harmony as well. In the simplest case, the B section consists entirely of a *standing on the dominant*, a passage supported exclusively by a dominant prolongation.

This harmonic contrast is usually associated with new melodic and rhythmic material. In addition, the section may feature changes in texture, instrumentation, and accompanimental patterns. Contrary to popular belief, however, contrasts of this sort are of secondary importance and are not required of the form. The contrasting middle of many a small ternary is based entirely on the motivic and textural content of the exposition.

Finally, a word must be said about the general phrase-structural organization of the B section. Compared with the exposition, the contrasting middle is less often composed as a conventional theme-type (indeed, the period form is never found). Rather, the B section has a *loose* organization in relation to the more *tight-knit* A section. Although the distinction between tight-knit and loose organization has an important role in this book, these expressions are first introduced as vague metaphors whose meaning in relation to strictly musical phenomena must eventually be clarified. For the present, I will not attempt to define these notions; rather, I will gradually demonstrate their significance in connection with specific examples and the formal issues they generate.[16]

The recapitulation (A') of the small ternary has two main functions: to complete the harmonic–melodic processes left open at the end of the B section (and by a modulating A section) and to create a semblance of formal symmetry by providing a return of the exposition. In order to realize these two functions, the A' section is required, at the very least, to begin with the basic idea of the A section and to close with a perfect authentic cadence in the home key. On occasion, the recapitulation brings back the entire exposition unchanged. More frequently, however, the A' section eliminates unnecessary repetitions or further develops motives from the A section. If the exposition has modulated to a subordinate key, the recapitulation must be *adjusted* to remain in the home key so as to provide tonal unity to the theme.

Example 1.4 shows the main theme of the second movement of Beethoven's Piano Concerto No. 1 in C, Op. 15. The A section (mm. 1–8) is a fully conventional period: a two-measure basic idea is followed by a two-measure contrasting idea, leading to a weak, half cadence in measure 4; a consequent phrase then repeats the material of the antecedent and closes with a stronger, perfect authentic cadence in measure 8.

The B section (mm. 9–14) achieves its contrasting character most obviously by new motivic content. More significantly, however, it contrasts with the exposition by emphasizing dominant harmony. The section not only opens with this harmony but also concludes with a half cadence in measure 12. The cadential dominant is further intensified by its own dominant (V$^6_5$/V), both preceding and following the cadence. From the upbeat to measure 9 through the beginning of measure 10, the dominant scale-degree also is emphasized when the bass line leaps down to the low E♭s on the second half of each beat.[17] All this dominant emphasis generates considerable harmonic tension, which is eventually resolved in the recapitulation.

Let us now examine in detail the formal organization of this contrasting middle. The section begins with a new two-measure idea. Like the basic idea of a sentence or period form, this idea is essentially grounded in tonic harmony despite its literal beginning with a dominant. The idea begins to sound again, in the form of an exact repetition, which, if realized, would create a normal presentation phrase. But in

EXAMPLE 1.4 Beethoven, Piano Concerto No. 1 in C, Op. 15, ii, 1–18

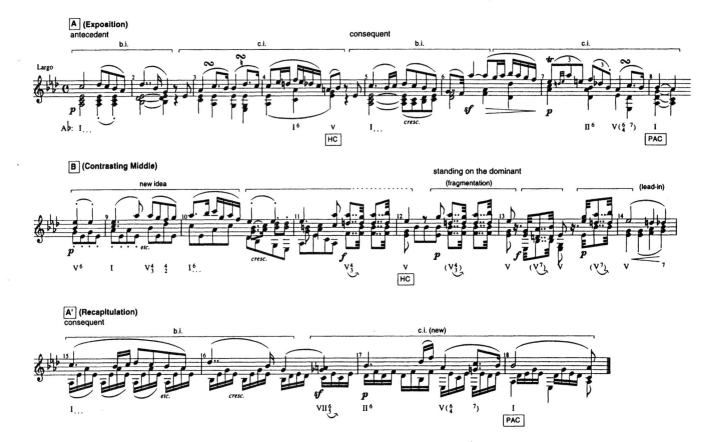

the second half of measure 11, the harmony is substantially altered, and the passage arrives on dominant harmony for the half cadence. Following the cadence, measures 12–14 function as a standing on the dominant, within which the unit size is fragmented in measures 12 and 13.

How can we understand the overall phrase structure of this B section? If we focus exclusively on the disposition of its melodic–motivic content, we might be tempted to recognize a sentence form (i.e., a two-measure idea that is repeated and subsequently fragmented). Such a view, however, ignores the fundamental harmonic and cadential organization of the passage and thus misinterprets its form-functional behavior.

First, the opening four measures do not prolong tonic harmony, and thus we cannot speak of a genuine presentation phrase. Moreover, the presence of a cadence at the end of this phrase rules out a presentation, since this function, in principle, does not end with a cadence. The possibility of a sentence is further weakened when we recognize that measure 12 brings the only cadential moment in the passage. Thus unlike a real sentence, the fragmentation of the basic idea follows, rather than precedes, the harmonic–melodic goal. As a result, the conclusion of the harmonic process of

the section (as marked by the half cadence in m. 12) does not coincide with the conclusion of the broader grouping process (end of m. 14), which sees the establishment of an idea, its repetition, and its ultimate fragmentation.[18]

Since the sentence model is not applicable to an analysis of the B section, we might wish to consider whether the period model offers any help instead. In particular, the presence of a half cadence at the end of a four-measure phrase suggests an antecedent function. This interpretation is not convincing, however, because measures 11–12 (with upbeat) seem to be more a repetition of the basic idea than a contrasting idea, as expected by an antecedent phrase.

We can thus conclude that the contrasting middle section acquires a nonconventional form as a result of two main features: (1) the initial four-measure phrase is neither a genuine presentation nor an antecedent (although it has elements of both), and (2) the half cadence does not come at the end of the fragmentation but, rather, precedes it. Both these nonconventional aspects yield a significantly looser organization in relation to the more tightly knit periodic design of the preceding exposition.

Let us now turn to the A' section (mm. 15–18). In comparison to the exposition, the recapitulation is significantly reduced in size and content. Its four measures consist of a restatement of the basic idea from measures 1–2 and a new contrasting idea (i.e., one not found in the A section), which leads to a perfect authentic cadence. In effect, the A' is built exclusively as a consequent. And this phrase alone fulfills the two primary conditions of recapitulation function—opening with the basic idea from the A section and closing with a perfect authentic cadence in the home key.

It is easy to understand why Beethoven does not simply restate the entire period of the A section, for the music that he has eliminated is structurally superfluous. It is unnecessary to bring yet another half cadence (as in mm. 3–4), especially after the dominant emphasis of the B section, and it is redundant to repeat the basic idea (as in mm. 5–6), since the listener is by now familiar enough with this material. A single consequent phrase is thus sufficient to give the impression of recapitulating the essential content of the A section.

FRAMING FUNCTIONS

Up to this point we have been discussing the form-functional constituents of the three principal theme-types: presentation, continuation, and cadential for the sentence; antecedent and consequent for the period; and exposition (A), contrasting middle (B), and recapitulation (A') for the small ternary. All these functions occur within the boundaries of the themes as defined by their structural beginning and end.

Some themes contain music standing outside these boundaries—material that functions as a "before-the-beginning" or an "after-the-end." These seemingly paradoxical functions can perhaps be made clearer by analogy to a running race. The beginning of the race is literally marked by the opening gun; the end, by the moment when each runner crosses the finish line. But the full experience of the race also includes the time preceding and following these temporal boundaries. The period of time when the runners set themselves up in the starting blocks and wait for the officials to fire the gun is filled with a sense of accumulating tension, which is temporarily released when the race finally gets under way. What happens after the runners cross the finish line belongs to the complete experience of the race as well. The runners do not merely stop cold, but instead they gradually release their physical and psychical energy by slowing down into a sprint, followed by some brief walking.

A musical theme contains similar temporal phases. The theme's structural beginning is articulated by the start of its basic idea; its end is defined by the moment of cadential arrival. Occasionally, the theme is framed by material that precedes and follows these structural limits. Such *framing functions* are termed *introduction* and *postcadential*, respectively.

Introduction

An introduction to a theme (or *thematic introduction*, as it may more technically be called) is generally short, two to four measures at most.[19] Sometimes one or two chords alone suffice, such as at the start of Beethoven's *Eroica* Symphony. The melodic–motivic component of such an introduction is either weakly defined or entirely absent, so that the expression of a genuine basic idea can be saved for the structural beginning of the theme. Thematic introductions usually emphasize tonic harmony, although in certain situations (such as at the beginning of a subordinate theme), dominant harmony may be employed.

Introduction function is well illustrated by example 1.5, which immediately precedes the Beethoven quartet theme discussed in example 1.2. This two-measure introduction presents a gradual establishment of the tonic triad through the staggered entrance of each of the four instruments. Even on first hearing, we would not likely mistake these measures for the beginning of the theme, since they possess no distinct melodic profile. Our impression that they serve an introductory function is confirmed with the arrival of the true basic idea in measures 3–4, marking the structural beginning of the theme.

Despite the lack of motivic material and harmonic progression, these measures institute a distinct *dynamic* process. The term dynamic is used here in a broader sense than merely "intensity of sound" (i.e., loud or soft, crescendo or decrescendo). Rather, dynamic activity involves the systematic growing or diminishing of tension and excitement created by a variety of musical means, including changes of intensity. As a general rule, a thematic introduction features what Wallace Berry terms a *progressive dynamic*—one in which there is an increasing buildup of energy and anticipation.[20] From a rhythmic point of view, this dynamic growth is usually described as an "anacrusis," an upbeat, whose corresponding "thesis," a downbeat, is the structural beginning of the theme.

A progressive dynamic is clearly manifest in this example, not only by the actual crescendo but also by the accumulating texture. In fact, the analogy of runners taking their place in the starting blocks is particularly appropriate here, where each instrument enters one after the next. Moreover, the lack of melodic material creates an anticipation for the appearance of a distinctive melody at the beginning of the theme. A definite anacrustic quality is also present in these measures. When the downbeat at measure 3 arrives, it is interesting to observe how Beethoven suddenly pulls back the intensity level (*sotto voce*). This change in intensity should not be entirely surprising, since the moment of beginning, the downbeat, has sufficient structural weight not to require any additional emphasis.

EXAMPLE 1.5 Beethoven, String Quartet in F, Op. 135, iii, 1–4

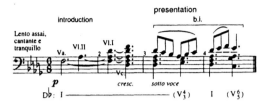

EXAMPLE 1.6 Beethoven, String Quartet in F, Op. 135, iii, 10–13

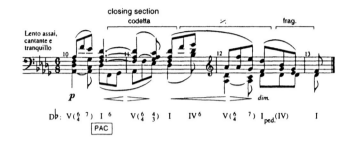

Postcadential Function

Introductions to themes are relatively rare, as most themes literally start with their structural beginning. More frequently, a theme may include postcadential material, music that follows the point of cadential arrival. In general, postcadential functions appear in two main varieties, depending on the type of cadence closing the theme. A perfect authentic cadence can be followed by a *closing section* containing *codettas*; a half cadence can be followed by a *standing on the dominant*, a phrase type already discussed in connection with example 1.4 (mm. 12–14).[21]

Both types of postcadential function prolong the final harmony of their preceding cadence. In addition, both tend to feature a *recessive dynamic*, in which the energy accumulated in the motion toward the cadential goal is dissipated.[22]

Closing section, codettas. A closing section to a theme consists of a series of codettas; rarely does a closing section contain a single codetta. In most cases the initial codetta is repeated, after which fragmentation brings reduced versions of the same codetta or else entirely new ones. The grouping structure of an extensive closing section can therefore resemble a sentence.

An individual codetta can be as short as a single chord or as long as a full four-measure phrase. Codettas usually contain melodic–motivic material different from that found in the theme itself, though, at times, material from the opening basic idea or from the closing cadential idea may be reused within the codetta. As a general rule, melodic activity tends to center on the tonic scale-degree in order to preserve the melodic closure achieved by the cadence and to prevent the codetta from sounding like a new beginning.

Harmonically, a codetta prolongs the root-position tonic of the cadence. This prolongation can take a variety of forms. In some cases, a tonic pedal in the bass voice underlies the entire codetta; at other times, tonic and dominant harmonies alternate with each other (the dominant thus functioning as a neighboring or passing chord). Frequently, the tonic prolongation features a local tonicization of subdominant harmony.[23]

A codetta occasionally has a cadential progression at its

basis. This fact has resulted in some serious misunderstandings about the nature of cadence and codetta. When some theorists or historians refer to the closing section as a "cadential area" or a "cadence phrase," they are suggesting that the music has a cadential function. But only the material leading to the cadential arrival—the point that marks the structural end of the theme—can truly be said to fulfill cadential function. A closing section (and its constituent codettas), on the contrary, plays an entirely different role, namely, a postcadential one. Thus, whereas an individual codetta may indeed resemble a cadential idea, these two units of musical form remain conceptually (and experientially) distinct.

The Beethoven quartet theme (see ex. 1.2) includes a brief closing section, shown here in example 1.6, which consists of codettas based on the cadential idea of the theme.[24] Following the cadence in measure 10, Beethoven writes a one-measure codetta by shifting the cadential melody into the bass voice (played by the cello). He then repeats the codetta in the second half of measure 11 by transferring the idea back to its original location in the upper voice. The passage concludes with a single, short codetta built over a tonic pedal (and including a neighboring subdominant). This final half-measure codetta represents fragmentation in relation to the preceding one-measure codettas.

Standing on the dominant. When a theme (or a portion thereof) ends with a half cadence, the final harmony can be prolonged by means of a postcadential standing on the dominant. We have already seen an instance of this procedure in the Beethoven concerto theme (see ex. 1.4). The B section reaches its harmonic goal with a half cadence on the downbeat of measure 12. The dominant is then prolonged to the end of measure 14 through the use of its own dominant (V/V) as neighboring chords. In this example, the postcadential area is based on material of the half cadence itself. Such a procedure recalls how the quartet theme uses the cadential idea for the codettas. More often than not, however, the melodic–motivic content of a standing on the dominant is entirely new.

INTERTHEMATIC FUNCTIONS: A SONATA EXPOSITION

Up to this point we have been focusing on the functional constituents of individual themes—that is, on the formal properties of the various phrases or sections associated with a single thematic unit. These *intrathematic functions*, as they may be termed, are linked together in a specified order and thus establish a kind of "syntax" of formal organization. Thus, a typically syntactical sequence of functions—presentation, continuation, cadential, and closing section—creates a theme conforming to the formal conventions of music in the classical style. Conversely, the following succession of functions—continuation, closing section, cadential, presentation, and introduction—is entirely nonsyntactic and unstylistic.

Just as the component parts of themes are functionally differentiated, so, too, are the various themes (or themelike units) in movements. Moreover, these *interthematic functions* also occur in a conventionalized order (depending on the full-movement form) and thus give rise to a higher-level formal syntax. To conclude this opening chapter, let us briefly consider the nature of interthematic functionality in connection with the three principal functions of an exposition section of sonata form—main theme, transition, and subordinate theme.

As discussed, the definition of intrathematic formal functions depends largely on their underlying harmonic progressions in a given key. For the interthematic functions, issues of tonality—relations among various keys—come more to the fore. Inasmuch as most complete movements contain multiple themes, tonal monotony would result if all of the themes were to reside in the same key. Consequently, most movements feature a prominent modulation away from the initial home key to a new subordinate key, one that is closely related to, and ultimately dependent on, the home key. Eventually, the home key returns (often after the music has explored additional related keys) and is fully confirmed in order to provide tonal unity to the movement as a whole.

The various themes and themelike units of a movement directly participate in expressing this tonal design; hence, their formal functions are fundamentally based on their relationship to tonality. In a sonata-form exposition, the *main theme* expresses the home key through cadential closure. Likewise, a later-occurring *subordinate theme* confirms the subordinate key. Standing between these two functions is the *transition*, a themelike unit that destabilizes the home key and (usually) modulates to the subordinate key.

Tonal considerations are thus central to the functional distinctions among themes and themelike units. But tonality alone does not account for the differing phrase-structural designs manifested by these functions. Rather, we can invoke again the distinction between tight-knit and loose to help characterize the varying formal organization of the in-

terthematic functions. As a general rule, the main theme is the most tight-knit unit in a sonata exposition, whereas the transition and subordinate theme are distinctly looser in structure.[25]

As mentioned, tight knit and loose are metaphors that defy simple definition. Yet I can now offer some general observations about which musical factors help create one or the other type of formal expression. Tight-knit organization is characterized by harmonic–tonal stability, cadential confirmation, unity of melodic–motivic material, efficiency of functional expression, and symmetrical phrase groupings. Loose organization is characterized by harmonic–tonal instability, evasion or omission of cadence, diversity of melodic–motivic material, inefficiency or ambiguity of functional expression, and asymmetrical phrase groupings (arising through extensions, expansions, compressions, and interpolations). These distinctions are well illustrated by the exposition from the first movement of Beethoven's Piano Sonata in F Minor, Op. 2/1, whose main theme served as the initial example of this chapter.

Main Theme

As already discussed, the main theme of this exposition is a model sentence form (see ex. 1.1). Tight-knit organization is expressed in a number of ways. Harmonic and tonal stability are created by both the clear establishment of the home-key tonic in the presentation phrase and the cadential confirmation of that key at the end of the continuation. (Greater harmonic stability and a correspondingly tighter form would result if the theme closed with an authentic cadence rather than a half cadence.) The melodic material is unified through the use of motives derived exclusively from the basic idea, and the grouping of this material into two four-measure phrases is highly symmetrical. Finally, the constituent functions (presentation, continuation, and cadential) are presented in the most compact and efficient manner possible. Every detail of the musical organization contributes to the functional expression, and nothing can be eliminated without obscuring an aspect of that functionality.

Transition

The transition, shown in example 1.7, begins in measure 9 and stretches to measure 20. The section begins with a restatement of the main theme's basic idea in the lower voice. The appearance of this idea in a C-minor harmony throws the prevailing tonal context into doubt, for this minor harmony would not normally be interpreted as dominant in the home key of F minor. (A genuine dominant harmony contains the leading-tone of the key.) Instead, these measures suggest tonic in C minor, analogous to the harmonic–tonal context at the beginning of the main theme (see ex. 1.1, mm. 1–2).

EXAMPLE 1.7 Beethoven, Piano Sonata in F Minor, Op. 2/1, i, 9–20

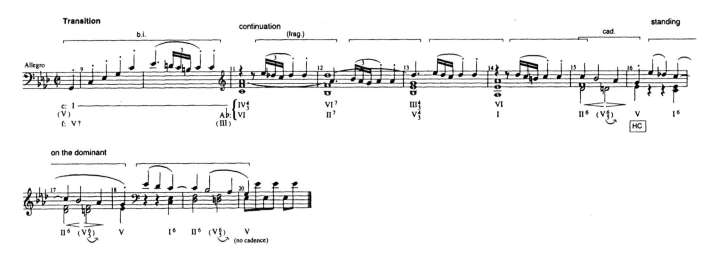

EXAMPLE 1.8 Beethoven, Piano Sonata in F Minor, Op. 2/1, i, 21–48

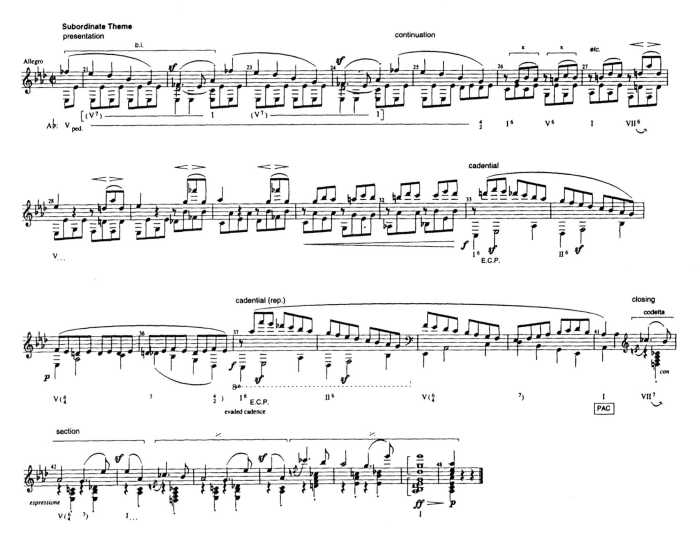

The basic idea is neither repeated (as in a presentation phrase) nor juxtaposed with a contrasting idea (in the manner of an antecedent). Rather, it is followed by four measures that display features of continuation function: fragmentation into one-measure units (cf. mm. 5–6 of the main theme), acceleration of harmonic rhythm, and a descending fifth sequential progression.[26] In measures 15–16, the tonal context is finally clarified when the continuation phrase concludes with a half cadence in the subordinate key of A♭ major. Beethoven then extends the sense of arrival by twice repeating the half-cadence idea, thus creating a postcadential standing on the dominant for four measures.

How does this transition express a looser organization? Most obviously by its harmonic and tonal instability in relation to the main theme. At first, the sense of home key is disrupted by the C-minor harmony, which seems to function as a new tonic. But the key of C minor never receives cadential confirmation, nor is its tonic even prolonged by a dominant (as in mm. 3–4 of the main theme). The subsequent move to A♭, the genuine subordinate key, renders the transition modulatory. Additional harmonic instability is imparted by the sequential progression and by the dominant emphasis of the postcadential area.

In additional to harmonic–tonal means, the transition acquires a looser organization by virtue of its asymmetrical grouping structure—2 mm. (basic idea) + 6 mm. (continuation) + 4 mm. (standing on the dominant). Moreover, the formal functions of these groups, though fully identifiable, are not as efficiently expressed or as clearly defined as are those in the main theme. For example, the continuation is *extended* by two measures over its typical four-measure length in a tight-knit sentence.[27] Since these two measures are not essential for establishing continuation function, their presence creates a degree of redundancy that loosens the functional expression. Moreover, the moment of cadential arrival at measure 16 is somewhat obscured by the repetition of the half-cadence gesture within the standing on the dominant (which dominant chord—m. 16, m. 18, or m. 20—represents the real cadence?). Finally, the lack of a full presentation phrase renders the transition's beginning less solid, and so looser in expression, than the opening of the main theme.

With respect to this last point, the absence of a presentation must not be seen to reflect a compositional weakness. An additional statement of the basic idea is hardly necessary in light of its firm establishment in the presentation of the main theme. Likewise, the foregoing observations on functional inefficiency and cadential obscurity are not meant to imply a faulty structure of any kind. On the contrary, these loosening techniques are entirely appropriate to the transition's fundamental functions—namely, to destabilize the home key, to effect a modulation to the subordinate key, and to motivate the appearance of the subordinate theme, which will eventually confirm the new key.

Subordinate Theme

The subordinate theme, shown in example 1.8, begins with a new two-measure basic idea. (This "new idea" is actually an inverted variant of the main theme's basic idea; see ex. 1.1, mm. 1–2.) With the repetition of this basic idea in measures 23–24, the melodic–motivic requirement for presentation function is fulfilled; however, we may wonder whether the harmonic requirement—the presence of a tonic prolongation—is satisfied as well.

At first glance, measures 21–24 would seem to prolong dominant harmony (of A♭ major) as a result of the bass pedal. But temporarily ignoring the pedal, we can also hear a tonic prolongation, since the goal of the melody, the A♭ on the third beat of measure 22 (and m. 24), demands to be supported by this harmonic function.[28] In this latter interpretation, the tonic is not merely a neighboring chord to the preceding and following dominant; rather, the dominant is subordinate to the tonic. We can thus recognize two levels of harmonic activity in this phrase: (1) a surface level containing the tonic prolongation, which satisfies the harmonic requirement of presentation function, and (2) a deeper level containing the dominant prolongation (created by the bass pedal), which undermines, but does not obliterate from our perception, the lower-level tonic prolongation.[29]

A continuation phrase starts in measure 25. The basic idea begins to be repeated again, but before reaching completion, the melodic line leads abruptly into a new eighth-note motive ("x"). The continuation develops this motive, fragments the preceding two-measure units of the presentation phrase into half-measure segments, and accelerates the harmonic rhythm.

The continuation reaches a climax at measure 33 with a prominent arrival on I⁶. At this point, too, the melodic and rhythmic material changes when motive "x" gives way to a long, descending scale passage. The resulting four-measure phrase is then repeated (beginning in m. 37) and extended by an extra measure in order to bring a perfect authentic cadence on the downbeat of measure 41. To understand the formal function of this new phrase (and its repetition), it is necessary to carefully examine its underlying harmonic organization.

The repeated phrase (mm. 37–41) features a complete authentic cadential progression: I⁶–II⁶–V(⁶₄ ⁷)–I. The initial phrase (mm. 33–36) is also based on this progression, but the promised cadence is *evaded* when the bass descends stepwise (through a V⁶₄ chord) onto the I⁶ in measure 37, which initiates the repetition of the phrase.

In all the themes that we have looked at so far, the authentic cadential progression is a relatively short harmonic formula constituting the last part of a continuation or consequent phrase. In this example, however, the cadential progression is expanded to the extent that it supports an entire phrase, one whose melodic–motivic content fully distinguishes it from the preceding continuation. A phrase built exclusively on such an *expanded cadential progression (E.C.P.)* can be said to have a uniquely cadential formal function.

Following the authentic cadence in measure 41 comes a section made up of three short codettas (mm. 42–48). In traditional theories of sonata form, such a passage is often termed a "closing theme" or even a "cadence theme." Since these codettas do not constitute a genuine theme in the sense developed in this study and since they are clearly postcadential in function, we can label these measures a closing section, as defined earlier in this chapter.

Let us now interpret the structure of the subordinate theme (including its closing section) in terms of the criteria for tight-knit and loose formal organization that I have developed thus far. In comparison to the eight-measure main theme, the subordinate theme distinguishes itself most obviously by its greater length—twenty-eight measures. Within its temporal boundaries, the subordinate theme consists of the same formal functions found in the main theme: presentation, continuation, and cadential. However, these functions assume a distinctly looser form. In the tight-knit sentence of the main theme, continuation and cadential functions are fused into a single four-measure continuation phrase. The entire theme thus acquires a symmetrical 4 + 4 grouping structure. The subordinate theme, on the contrary, becomes considerably looser when the continuation and cadential functions are given their own distinct phrases that possess a different melodic–motivic content and harmonic progression. Moreover, these functions are both extended and expanded to create an asymmetrical 4 + 8 + 4 + 5 grouping structure for the theme proper. Adding seven measures of the closing section (grouped 2 + 2 + 3) further lengthens the theme and renders it all the more asymmetrical.

Distinguishing between processes of extension and expansion is useful and important, especially since this subordinate theme features both loosening devices.[30] *Extension* results from "adding on" material to stretch out a particular formal function in time. Continuation phrases are frequently extended when more units of fragmentation are included in the phrase than are necessary to express the function. It usually takes only two measures of fragmentation to make the continuation function evident to the listener; thus the sense of continuation is fully manifest in this subordinate theme by the end of measure 27. But Beethoven then extends the phrase by five more measures of fragmented material (mm. 28–32) and thereby significantly loosens the functional expression of the phrase.[31]

Extension can also occur with cadential function. In that case, an implied cadence fails to materialize, and the function is repeated in order to achieve the cadential goal. The subordinate theme could have closed with an authentic cadence in measure 37, but the cadential evasion motivates a repetition of the entire cadential phrase that substantially

extends the function. Delaying the expected cadence makes its eventual arrival seem all the more powerful, thus dramatically reinforcing the subordinate theme's primary function of confirming the subordinate key.

Whereas extension occurs after a function has already been expressed, *expansion* arises in the process of establishing the function. Expansion involves the internal lengthening of component members of the function over their normative size in tight-knit themes. This loosening technique is most commonly associated with cadential function, in which the individual harmonies of the cadential progression are lengthened compared with their relatively compressed appearance (usually in two measures) at the end of a tight-knit phrase.[32] Expansion thus resembles the rhythmic technique of."augmentation," in which the durational values of the individual notes of an idea are systematically increased so that the original proportional relations among the durations is retained (i.e., doubled or quadrupled). In this subordinate theme, the component harmonies of the cadential progression are twice the length of those in the main theme (cf. ex. 1.1, mm. 7–8). But expansion technique does not require that the durational proportions of the normative form be strictly maintained. A single harmony of the cadential progression, for example, can become highly expanded in relation to the other harmonies (a procedure exemplified in the discussion of subordinate theme organization in chap. 8).

We have seen how extension and expansion significantly loosen the continuation and cadential areas of this subordinate theme. The presentation is loosely organized as well, although it achieves its looser form not by phrase-structural means but by harmonic ones, namely, its underlying dominant pedal. As pointed out, the foreground harmony of the passage projects a tonic prolongation, but this inherent harmonic stability—particularly appropriate to the expression of a structural beginning—is undermined by the destabilizing dominant prolongation, a progression more naturally associated with an after-the-end, postcadential function (or sometimes a structural middle, as in small ternary form).[33] Consequently, the harmonic situation at the opening of this subordinate theme is not entirely supportive of an initiating formal function, and a looser organization is created from the resulting functional ambiguity (is the phrase still part of the preceding standing on the dominant, or is it a new beginning?).

If the subordinate theme is distinctly looser than the main theme, how does the former stand in relation to the transition section, which also features a looser organization? In general, it is difficult to compare degrees of loosening between transitions and subordinate themes, since both functions use many of the same loosening techniques. Nevertheless, somewhat different devices tend to be emphasized by the two functions. In this exposition, the transition is rendered loose by harmonic, tonal, and cadential means, whereas the subordinate theme acquires its looser form from extensions and expansions of the grouping structure.

Although it may be difficult to judge whether in a sonata exposition a given transition is more or less loose than a subordinate theme, the subsequent development section is almost always distinctly looser than any of the interthematic functions in the exposition. Indeed, a development combines harmonic–tonal instability with phrase-structural extensions and expansions to create the most loosely organized part of an entire sonata movement.[34]

Fundamental Progressions of Harmony

The important role of harmony in defining formal functions should be evident from the preceding chapter. The intrathematic functions (such as presentation, continuation, and cadential) are especially contingent on specific types of local harmonic progression. Thus one of the earliest tasks in any formal analysis—indeed, perhaps the first task—is to determine the underlying harmony of a given passage. This chapter, a kind of brief *Harmonielehre*, systematically presents the fundamental harmonic progressions used by the classical composers to articulate formal functions. For ease of comparison, the progressions are exemplified as simple paradigms in the key of C major.[1]

HARMONIC FUNCTIONS

Before dealing directly with progressions of harmonies, we must first define the individual *harmonic functions* that make up a progression. Chapter 1 illustrated the concept of functionality with respect to formal organization. Traditionally, however, the concept has been associated more with harmony than with form. In the last quarter of the nineteenth century, Hugo Riemann developed an extensive theory of harmonic functions (*Funktionstheorie*),[2] which he offered in opposition to the prevailing theory of scale-degree progressions (*Stufentheorie*, "step theory").[3] Although Riemann's ideas continue to dominate modern German thinking, harmonic theory in North America is largely rooted in the scale-degree tradition. Aspects of the functional approach have nevertheless made themselves felt on this continent,[4] and, accordingly, this book, too, incorporates notions of harmonic functionality in a general scale-degree theory of harmony.

The strict scale-degree theory recognizes seven distinct and independent harmonies in a given tonality. These harmonies are identified by roman numerals denoting the scale-degrees on which the roots (or fundamentals) of the harmonies stand. The functional theory rejects the notion of seven independent harmonies and instead recognizes three fundamental functions, which embrace all harmonic formations in a key. These functions form a logical progression that serves to express tonality. The most important function is *tonic*, the central harmony of a key, the one to which all others ultimately relate and derive their meaning. The second function includes harmonies whose primary role is to progress to the tonic. These are *dominant* functioning harmonies, all of which contain the leading-tone. The third fundamental function comprises a variety of harmonies whose primary purpose is to lead to the dominant. Traditional functional theory speaks of a "subdominant" function in this connection, but the alternative term *predominant* is used here because this function includes a number of harmonic formations not directly related to the harmony built on the fourth degree of the scale.[5]

The harmonic theory employed throughout this study combines features from both the scale-degree and the functional theories. Since the former is widely known, it need not be discussed any further. The latter, however, requires more elaboration to specify how the various harmonies and chords of a key are classified in relation to the three fundamental functions.[6]

1. *Tonic function*. Tonic function is usually represented by the major or minor triad built on the first scale-degree (tonic) of a key. In certain contexts, the triad built on the submediant (VI) degree of the scale has a tonic function and can frequently "substitute" for an expected I chord, especially when following a root-position V (the "deceptive resolution" of the dominant).

2. *Dominant function*. Dominant function is most often represented by a major triad or a major–minor seventh chord built on the fifth scale-degree. The leading-tone diminished triad in first inversion (VII⁶) and the leading-tone seventh chord (VII⁷ and its three inversions) also have a dominant function when they resolve to a tonic harmony. These leading-tone chords are not considered dominants when in some sequential situations, they progress to nontonic harmonies (such as III).

3. *Pre-dominant function*. The large number of predominant harmonies in a key generally relate to one of two main types—those built above the fourth degree of the scale and those derived from the dominant of the dominant (V/V).

EXAMPLE 2.1 Prolongational progressions—pedal point

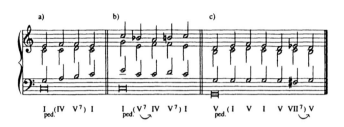

EXAMPLE 2.2 Prolongational progressions—neighboring chords

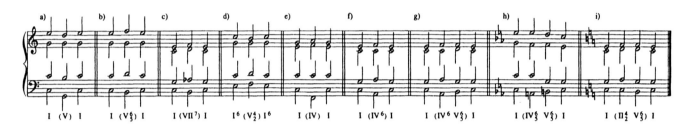

EXAMPLE 2.3 Prolongational progressions—passing chords

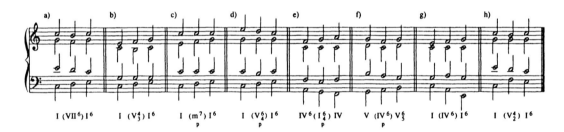

Many harmony texts suggest that the subdominant triad leads most typically to the dominant. An examination of the classical literature reveals, however, that the supertonic triad in first inversion (II⁶) is the more characteristic predominant. Both II⁶ and IV can be enriched through the addition of dissonant sevenths, and even greater variety can be gained by means of *modal mixture* (or modal borrowing), in which chords containing notes from the minor scale are used in major-mode contexts, or vice versa. The "Neapolitan" or "phrygian" harmony in first inversion (♭II⁶) is another important pre-dominant, especially in minor.

One group of pre-dominants features the chromatically raised fourth scale-degree, which functions as the leading-tone of the dominant. The significance of the raised fourth degree is highlighted by its normally being placed in the bass voice, so that its motion to the root of the following dominant is all the more enhanced. The most typical pre-dominant of this type is the diminished seventh VII⁷/V; the less dissonant V⁶/V and V⁴₃/V are also regularly encountered.

The three varieties of augmented sixth chords—the so-called Italian, German, and French sixths—are an important subclass of pre-dominant harmonies. They are usually built over the sixth degree of the natural minor scale. On occasion, however, they are also found over the raised fourth degree, thus revealing their kinship to secondary dominants of V.

HARMONIC PROGRESSIONS

Let us now consider how the functions just described can be arranged to make progressions of harmonies. Most progressions can be classified into one of three categories—prolongational, cadential, and sequential. Each category pertains to specific roles that progressions can play in the pitch organization of a particular musical passage: a *prolongational* progression sustains in time an individual harmony (within an implied tonality); a *cadential* progression confirms a tonal center; and a *sequential* progression projects a melodic–contrapuntal pattern independent of harmonic functionality.[7]

Prolongational Progressions

A harmonic prolongation is created when a single harmonic entity is perceived in the listener's imagination to be sustained through time, despite the presence of an intervening chord (or chords) of different harmonic meaning. The *prolonged harmony* thus "remains in effect without being literally represented at every moment" throughout the progression.[8] The intervening chord can be considered a *subordinate harmony* because it remains under the influence and control of the prolonged harmony. Prolongation thus entails two levels of harmonic activity: a local level that contains the succession of prolonged and subordinate harmonies and a deeper level that contains the prolonged harmony alone.

For the listener to sense that an individual harmony is being prolonged, the subordinate harmony must form a strong functional connection to the prolonged harmony. Failing that, the progression must feature a conventional contrapuntal process that establishes an intimate voice-leading bond among all the chords. Both these conditions are often met within a prolongational progression.

The many different prolongational progressions can be grouped into four main types according to the compositional technique associated with the prolongation. These techniques include the use of (1) a pedal point, (2) neighboring chords, (3) passing chords, and (4) substitute chords. Most of the progressions discussed and illustrated here prolong tonic harmony, although many of them can prolong harmonies on other scale-degrees as well.

Pedal point. The most perceptually forceful way of prolonging a harmony is by means of a *pedal point*. The pedal, which lies in the bass voice throughout the progression, contains the root of the prolonged harmony (ex. 2.1).[9] In most cases, this harmony appears at the beginning and end of the progression. The bass note of the subordinate harmonies is replaced by the pedal note, thus significantly reducing the structural status of these harmonies; hence, they always are placed in parentheses in the analysis located below the music.[10] Since the missing bass often makes it impossible to determine the position of the subordinate chords, they are indicated in root position unless a specific inversion is implied by the context in which the progression arises. Prolongations featuring pedal points are prominently employed in connection with postcadential function. Example 2.1b, with its tonicized subdominant, is frequently used in codettas, example 2.1c is typical of a standing on the dominant.

Neighboring chords. An individual harmony is prolonged by one or more *neighboring chords* when the prolonged har-

mony remains in the same position (root position or inversions) from the beginning to the end of the progression. In such cases, a melodic neighbor-tone motion is usually (but not necessarily) present in one or more of the voices (ex. 2.2).

Example 2.2a resembles the cadence formula described by many harmony textbooks. This progression can indeed be classified as cadential according to criteria to be developed in the next section. In actual compositional practice, however, the simple I–V–I progression is often better understood as prolongational.

Passing chords. A given harmony is prolonged by one or more *passing chords* when the prolonged harmony changes position from the beginning to the end of the progression. Such prolongations usually see a passing tone in the bass voice lying between the root-position and first-inversion forms of the prolonged harmony. A variety of chords can be built over this passing tone, as shown in example 2.3a–f. Another common prolongation finds an ascending passing motion in the soprano (usually $\hat{3}$–$\hat{4}$–$\hat{5}$) against a bass that leaps in contrary motion (ex. 2.3g). A passing chord may arise, however, without any of the voices literally displaying passing motion (ex. 2.3h).

In some prolongational progressions, the passing chord is not an independent harmony because of its unstable six–four position or its weak functional relation to the prolonged harmony. Such passing chords are placed in parentheses in the analysis at all times and are given an added label, p (passing), to show that they arise primarily from contrapuntal processes and only minimally from harmonic ones. The passing chord in example 2.3c arises entirely out of the counterpoint and thus should not be analyzed as a II[7] harmony. Not only is the progression I–II[7]–I nonfunctional, but also the "seventh" (C) is doubled and incorrectly resolved, thus violating the fundamental voice-leading for chordal sevenths. For these reasons, the symbol m[7] (minor seventh chord) is used in place of a roman numeral.

Substitute chords. Some chords can participate in prolonging a given harmony because they express the same fundamental function as does the prolonged harmony. In such cases, the original and substitute harmonies have two chord-tones in common, which largely accounts for their functional similarity (ex. 2.4a–c). Passing chords can be introduced between the original and substitute harmonies to form even more complex prolongations (ex. 2.4d–e).[11]

In the preceding examples, the root of the substitute chord lies a third below the original harmony. In some situations, a chord lying a third above participates in the prolongation (ex. 2.4f–g). Here, the substitute chord is understood to arise out of passing motion in the soprano voice with the simultaneous elimination of the root (ex. 2.4h; cf. ex. 2.4f).

EXAMPLE 2.4 Prolongational progressions—substitute chords

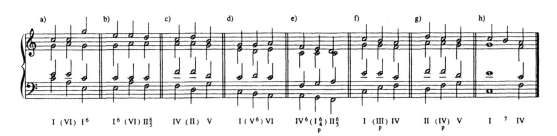

I (VI) I⁶   I⁶ (VI) II⁶₃   IV (II) V   I (V⁶) VI   IV⁶(I⁶₄) II⁶₃   I (III) IV   II (IV) V   I ⁷ IV
                                                              p   p   p

EXAMPLE 2.5 Authentic cadential progressions—basic

EXAMPLE 2.6 Authentic cadential progressions—dominant embellishment

I⁶ II⁶ V ⁷ I   I⁶ IV V I

I⁶ II⁶ V(⁶₄ ⁷) I

EXAMPLE 2.7 Authentic cadential progressions—pre-dominant embellishment

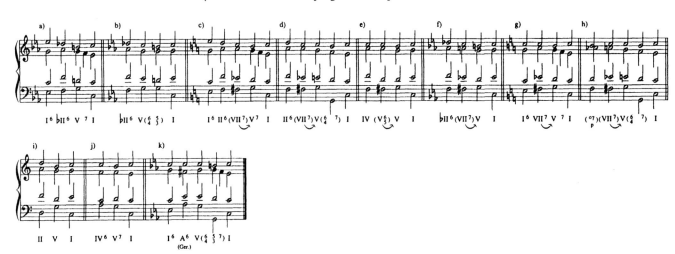

I⁶ ♭II⁶ V ⁷ I   ♭II⁶ V(⁶₄ ⁵₃) I   I⁶ II⁶(VII⁷)V⁷ I   II⁶(VII⁷)V(⁶₄ ⁷) I   IV (V⁶₃) V I   ♭II⁶(VII⁷)V I   I⁶ VII⁷ V ⁷ I   (°⁷)(VII⁷)V(⁶₄ ⁷) I
                                                                                                                                              p

II V I   IV⁶ V⁷ I   I⁶ A⁶ V(⁶₄ ⁵₃ ⁷) I
                              (Ger.)

EXAMPLE 2.8 Authentic cadential progressions—initial tonic embellishment

I II⁶ V(⁶₄ ⁷) I   V⁴₂ I⁶ II⁶ V ⁷ I   V⁶₅ IV V ⁷ I   VII⁶₅ II⁶ V⁷ I

26

Cadential Progressions

The harmonic progressions just discussed involve the prolongation of an individual harmony irrespective of the function that it may ultimately serve in a given tonality. As soon as we assign a specific function to the prolonged harmony —be it tonic, dominant, or pre-dominant—then a tonal center of some kind is logically assumed. Thus a given progression can prolong a "C-major harmony," but this harmony can be understood not only as tonic in the key of C major but also as dominant in F major or even pre-dominant in G. The task of confirming that an implied tonality is indeed the actual tonality of the musical passage in question falls to a second category of progressions—*cadential progressions*.[12] The strongest tonal confirmation is achieved by an *authentic cadential progression*; a weaker confirmation, by a *half-cadential progression*.

Authentic cadential progressions. A *complete* cadential progression is made up of the fundamental harmonic functions in the following temporal sequence—tonic, predominant, dominant, and tonic. (The two cadential tonics are distinguished as *initial* and *final* tonics, respectively.) An *incomplete* cadential progression occurs when the initial tonic or pre-dominant (or both) is omitted.

For the authentic cadential progression to possess sufficient harmonic strength to confirm a tonality, both the dominant and the final tonic must be in root position, their most stable form. The fundamental-bass motion of a descending fifth (or ascending fourth) is exposed in the bass voice so that the sense of a strong harmonic progression can be projected most powerfully. If the dominant were inverted, then the move to the tonic would necessarily result in a stepwise motion in the bass, thus usurping the melodic function of the upper voices and undermining the bass's own role as bearer of the harmonic fundamentals. If the final tonic is inverted (or otherwise altered harmonically) then a *deceptive* cadential progression is created (a variant type to be discussed in connection with ex. 2.9).

Pre-dominant function within an authentic cadential progression is built most often over the fourth scale-degree in the bass, although it is occasionally found over the second or sixth degrees as well.[13] The initial tonic is usually placed in first inversion, probably so as not to anticipate (and thus spoil) the solid effect of the final root-position tonic.[14]

The basic form of the authentic cadential progression is shown in example 2.5a. Note that the pre-dominant harmony above the fourth scale-degree is not the subdominant triad, as many textbooks suggest but, rather, the first-inversion supertonic triad. To be sure, the IV chord is regularly encountered (ex. 2.5b), but the version with II⁶ is more typical of the classical style.[15]

As already mentioned, either the initial tonic or the pre-dominant may be omitted, thus yielding an incomplete cadential progression. In such cases, the initial tonic is left out more often than the pre-dominant is, for eliminating the latter results in the loss of a fundamental harmonic function. Excluding both of these harmonies occurs infrequently in the literature.

Let us now examine how each of the three harmonies that precede the final root-position tonic triad can be varied and embellished, beginning with the dominant and moving backward through the pre-dominant to the initial tonic. We can then consider how altering the final tonic leads to a deceptive cadential progression.[16]

1. *Dominant embellishments.* The principal embellishment of dominant harmony (besides adding a seventh, of course) occurs through the use of a "cadential six–four" chord constructed over the fifth scale-degree (ex. 2.6).[17] The frequent use of the cadential six–four helps clarify, perhaps, why II⁶ is preferred to IV as the main pre-dominant harmony in cadential progressions. If we compare example 2.5a with 2.5b, we see that the II⁶ in the former creates a more active and directed melodic line, in which the motion from the second scale-degree to the leading-tone can be filled in by a passing tone, supported by the cadential six–four (ex. 2.6). When the IV chord is used instead (ex. 2.5b), the melody tends to be static, and adding a six–four embellishment would further emphasize the tonic scale-degree.

2. *Pre-dominant embellishments.* The pre-dominant function in an authentic cadential progression can take a variety of forms. In addition to the common use of II⁶ and IV, the "Neapolitan" or "phrygian" sixth chord (♭II⁶) is occasionally found above the fourth scale-degree, usually in minor-mode contexts (ex. 2.7a–b).

The most frequently employed embellishment of pre-dominant function appears over a chromatic passing tone lying between the fourth and fifth scale-degrees in the bass voice (ex. 2.7c–h). In some cases, two consecutive diminished seventh chords prolong pre-dominant harmony (ex. 2.7h): the first diminished seventh is built on the regular fourth scale-degree, and the second, on the raised fourth degree. Although the first chord is spelled like VII⁷, it does not have a dominant function but instead serves in this context as a replacement for the pre-dominant II⁶₅ (from the minor mode).[18]

Pre-dominants can also be built on the second and sixth degrees of the scale by changing the position of the harmonies (ex. 2.7i–k).

3. *Initial tonic embellishments.* As already pointed out, the initial tonic occurs most frequently in first inversion, but the root-position form occasionally appears as well (ex. 2.8a). The initial tonic can be embellished, especially in expanded cadential progressions, by a neighboring V⁶₄ (ex. 2.8b). Various chromatic alterations can convert the initial

EXAMPLE 2.9 Deceptive cadential progressions

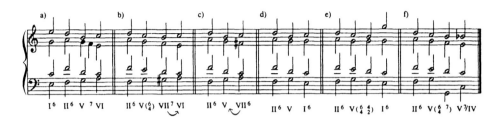

I⁶ II⁶ V ⁷VI   II⁶ V(⁶₄) VII⁷VI   II⁶ V ⌣ VII⁶   II⁶ V I⁶   II⁶ V(⁶ ⁴₄ ₂) I⁶   II⁶ V(⁶₄ ⁷) V⁷/IV

EXAMPLE 2.10 Half-cadential progressions

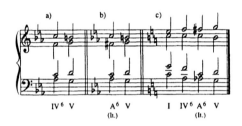

IV⁶ V   A⁶ V   I IV⁶ A⁶ V
         (It.)   (It.)

EXAMPLE 2.11 Sequential progressions — descending fifth

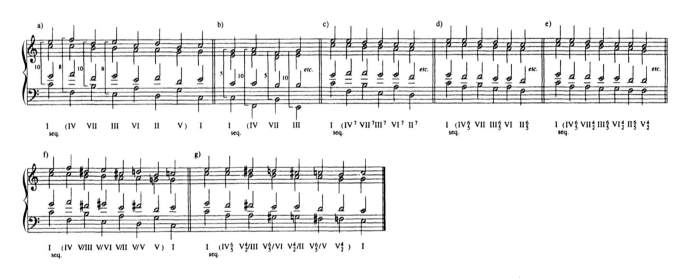

I   (IV VII III VI II   V)   I   I   (IV VII III   I   (IV⁷ VII⁷III⁷ VI⁷ II⁷   I   (IV⁶₅ VII III⁶₅ VI II⁶₅   I   (IV⁶₅ VII⁴₂ III⁶₅ VI⁴₂ II⁶₅ V⁴₂
 seq.   seq.   seq.   etc.   seq.   etc.   seq.   etc.

I   (IV V/III V/VI V/II V/V   V)   I   I   (IV⁶₅ V⁴₂/III V⁶₅/VI V⁴₂/II V⁶₅/V V⁴₂)   I
 seq.   seq.

28

tonic into a secondary dominant of IV or II, thus emphasizing motion into the pre-dominant (ex. 2.8c–d).

4. *Deceptive cadential progressions.* The deceptive cadential progression is created when the final tonic of the authentic cadential progression is replaced by a related harmony.[19] The most common form of this progression sees the bass ascend stepwise from the fifth scale-degree to the sixth, which supports a submediant substituting for the implied final tonic (ex. 2.9a). This progression can be embellished by a passing secondary dominant of VI (ex. 2.9b). Further variants arise when different harmonies are built over the sixth degree in the bass voice (ex. 2.9c).

In less frequently encountered instances of the deceptive cadential progression, the dominant leads to a first-inversion tonic rather than to the expected root-position form (ex. 2.9d). In order to make the move to I⁶ more compelling, a passing V⁴₃ is frequently inserted following the root-position dominant, which itself often contains the six–four embellishment (ex. 2.9e).[20] A more dramatic deception can be achieved by converting the final tonic into a secondary dominant seventh of the subdominant (ex. 2.9f); the addition of a chordal dissonance makes the tonic too unstable for cadential articulation.[21]

Half-cadential progressions. In the authentic cadential progression, the final tonic is the harmonic goal of the progression. The dominant occupies the *penultimate* position and thus creates a powerful dynamic impulse into the final tonic.

In the half-cadential progression, the dominant itself becomes the goal harmony and so occupies the *ultimate* position. To be sure, this dominant usually resolves to tonic, one that normally initiates a new harmonic progression, but within the boundaries of the half-cadential progression itself, the dominant possesses enough stability to represent a harmonic end.

To acquire the requisite stability for an ending harmony, the dominant of the half-cadential progression must take the form of a root-position triad. Adding a dissonant seventh—appropriate to the penultimate position in an authentic cadential progression—would overly destabilize the ultimate dominant of a half-cadential progression.

Except for omitting a final tonic and ensuring that the dominant is a consonant triad, half-cadential progressions can contain the same harmonies as authentic cadential ones do. Complete progressions include an initial tonic and a pre-dominant; incomplete versions omit one of these functions. All the authentic cadential paradigms (with the adjustments just mentioned) thus apply to the half-cadential progression as well. Several other paradigms, in which the ultimate dominant is approached by descending motion from the sixth degree (usually lowered), are especially associated with that progression (ex. 2.10).

Sequential Progressions

Sequential progressions involve harmonies arranged according to a consistent intervallic pattern among the individual voices of the chords (e.g., a 5–6 soprano–bass pattern).[22] Although some sequential progressions exhibit a degree of harmonic functionality among their constituent chords, this aspect of the progression is secondary to the fundamental purpose they are meant to serve—to move the music away from, or return it to, a particular harmonic function or tonal center. Thus sequential progressions are especially suitable for destabilizing harmonic activity in a given key or for modulating from one key to another.

A sequential progression normally begins with a chord that has a definite harmonic function within a key. The subsequent chords are linked together according to a particular melodic–contrapuntal pattern and consistent root motion, and the final chord restores a clear functional meaning in either the initial key or, in the case of modulating sequences, a new key.[23]

Sequential progressions can express a large number of melodic–contrapuntal patterns. Moreover, the same progression of harmonies can yield different patterns depending on how the individual notes of the chords are distributed among the voices. As a result, sequential progressions are most easily classified on the basis of the interval generated by the roots of the component chords.

Sequential progressions can feature consistent root motion by descending or ascending fifths, thirds, or seconds, thus yielding six categories of sequential progression.[24] The following discussion treats each category by focusing on the conventional contrapuntal patterns associated with the progressions, as well as the degree of harmonic functionality that they express.

Descending fifth. The most commonly used sequential progression features chords whose roots are organized into a series of descending fifths (or ascending fourths) (ex. 2.11a–b). This "circle-of-fifths" progression (as it is frequently called) can be varied in manifold ways through chord inversion, chromatic alteration, and added dissonances (ex. 2.11c–g).

Compared to the other categories of sequential progressions, the descending fifth pattern features the strongest harmonic–functional expression. Since the root motion of a descending fifth lies at the basis of every dominant-to-tonic progression, this functional relation is implied, by analogy, at each link in the sequential chain (e.g., VI–II, or III–VI), even if the "dominant" does not actually contain the leading tone of the "tonic."[25]

Despite the prominent sense of harmonic functionality inherent in the descending fifth progression, its use nevertheless promotes a weakening of the harmonic–tonal envi-

EXAMPLE 2.12 Sequential progressions—ascending fifth

I (V   II   VI) IV   I⁶
seq.

EXAMPLE 2.13 Sequential progressions—descending third

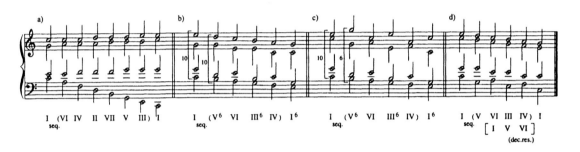

a) I (VI IV II VII V III) I   b) I (V⁶ VI III⁶ IV) I⁶   c) I (V⁶ VI III⁶ IV) I⁶   d) I (V VI III IV) I
   seq.   seq.   seq.   seq. [I V VI]
                                                                                                    (dec.res.)

EXAMPLE 2.14 Sequential progressions—ascending third

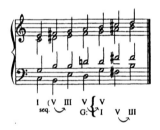

I (V III V ⌠ V
seq.   ⌡ G: I IV III

EXAMPLE 2.15 Sequential progressions—descending second

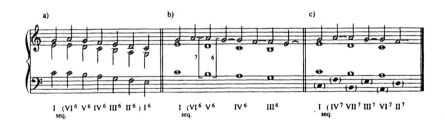

a) I (VI⁶ V⁶ IV⁶ III⁶ II⁶) I⁶   b) I (VI⁶ V⁶   IV⁶   III⁶   c) I (IV⁷ VII⁷ III⁷ VI⁷ II⁷
   seq.   seq.   seq.

EXAMPLE 2.16 Sequential progressions—ascending second

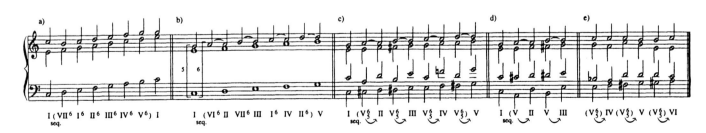

a) I (VII⁶ I⁶ II⁶ III⁶ IV⁶ V⁶) I   b) I (VI⁶ II VII⁶ III I⁶ IV II⁶) V   c) I (V⁶₅ II V⁶₅ III V⁶₅ IV V⁶₅) V   d) I (V II V III   e) (V⁶₃) IV (V⁶₃) V (V⁶₃) VI
   seq.   seq.   seq.   seq.

30

ronment. Whereas each link may be functionally related, the overall direction of the progression remains somewhat in doubt until it is completed. To be sure, many sequential progressions have conventional ending points (indeed, the descending fifths progression normally concludes with tonic harmony). But in relation to prolongational or cadential progressions, which strongly imply their final harmony, sequential progressions are more open-ended and often conclude with an unexpected harmony or in a different tonality.

Ascending fifth. The strong functional drive exhibited by the descending fifth pattern is entirely absent in sequential progressions by ascending fifths. Most such sequences begin with tonic harmony and progress to the submediant (ex. 2.12), at which point the sequential chain is broken and the music proceeds to pre-dominant harmony (usually IV).

Descending third. The unembellished form of descending third progressions is illustrated in example 2.13a. More often, however, the leap in the bass voice is filled in by stepwise motion, which produces intervening passing chords in first inversion (ex. 2.13b–c).

The passing chords introduce a degree of harmonic functionality. Since each root-position harmony is followed by a passing chord whose fundamental is a fifth above (or a fourth below), the latter stands as a "dominant" in relation to the former. When the root-position harmony is a tonic, then the passing chord is its literal dominant, and when the root-position harmony is another scale-degree, then the passing chord is a dominant "by analogy." These dominant-like passing chords then resolve deceptively to the next root-position chord, which can be understood as a tonic substitute.[26] This functional interpretation is made even more evident when the passing chords themselves are placed in root position (ex. 2.13d).

Ascending third. The ascending third progression is the least frequently used sequential pattern in the classical repertory. Its unembellished form is rarely, if ever, found. A version employing passing chords is more viable (ex. 2.14). Each passing chord is the "dominant" of the following main harmony of the sequence, and thus a degree of functionality accrues to the progression. Yet even this pattern seldom appears in the literature.[27]

Descending second. Sequential progressions by descending seconds pose a potential problem of voice-leading:[28] if the chords appear in root position, then parallel fifths can easily arise. Therefore, the unembellished form of the descending stepwise progression finds all the chords in first inversion (ex. 2.15a), thereby eliminating any interval of a fifth against the bass. The progression is frequently embellished by a series of 7–6 suspensions (ex. 2.15b). Sequential progressions of this category express little, if any, sense of harmonic functionality, since there is no syntactical relationship between harmonies whose roots move in a stepwise descent.[29]

Ascending second. The potential problem of faulty parallels encountered with the descending second progression applies to ascending ones as well. Using first-inversion triads can eliminate the difficulty (ex. 2.16a), although this version occurs infrequently in the literature. Instead, the stepwise ascent usually remains in root position while the parallel fifths are broken up by means of a 5–6 pattern formed by one of the upper voices against the bass (ex. 2.16b).

This contrapuntal procedure generates intervening first-inversion chords that stand, by analogy, in a dominant–tonic relationship to the succeeding root-position chords. This functional implication can be made even more explicit through chromatic alterations in the bass, so that each six–three chord becomes a genuine secondary dominant (ex. 2.16c). Finally, a more emphatic dominant-to-tonic expression is produced when the intervening chords themselves are placed in root position (ex. 2.16d).

Like descending second progressions, ascending second ones have little inherent functionality. Nevertheless, the passing chords that tonicize each member of the sequence (either literally or by analogy) and the ascending motion of every voice help propel the progression forward and create a powerful tension-building effect.

One form of the ascending stepwise progression resembles an embellished version of the deceptive cadential progression (ex. 2.16e).[30] The potential ambiguity of this progression can be effectively exploited by composers who wish to make obscure whether a particular formal unit has a continuation function (as supported by a sequential progression) or a cadential function (as supported by a deceptive cadential progression).[31]

II

TIGHT-KNIT THEMES

Sentence

The sentence is an eight-measure theme built out of two four-measure phrases.[1] In this grouping structure, which Ratz indicates as (2 × 2) + 4,[2] the theme expresses three formal functions—presentation, continuation, and cadential.[3] The opening phrase contains the first of these functions and thus is termed a presentation phrase. The second phrase incorporates the remaining two functions. For the sake of simplicity (if not absolute theoretical consistency), this unit is normally termed a continuation phrase.[4]

Before proceeding further, it is necessary to clarify the meaning of "measure" in the definition and description of formal units. All musicians are taught early in their training that a measure is the unit of time defined by the "bar lines" placed throughout a composition. But what a listener perceives as "one full measure" of music does not necessarily correspond to the notated bar lines of the score. We thus need to distinguish between a *real*, experiential measure and a *notated* measure. The former, which may or may not correspond to the latter, is the only valid measure for an analysis of form based on our musical experience.

The distinction between real and notated measures arises when the composer adds or deletes bar lines to facilitate reading the score of movements whose tempo is very slow or very fast. In an adagio movement, for example, we may perceive that a single real measure actually occupies only one half of the notated measure. In such cases, we can use the formula $R = \frac{1}{2}N$ as a shortcut for indicating the relationship of real (R) to notated (N) measures. Triple-meter scherzo movements, conversely, typically feature real measures that embrace two notated measures, thus $R = 2N$. A fast first or last movement may also be notated in this way.[5]

Unfortunately, it is impossible to specify just how much musical content makes up a real measure of music. But the following general guidelines may help us determine whether the notated measures of a given work correspond to our sense of the real measures. First, it helps us to recognize that the notational scheme does not change during the course of a given movement, unless the tempo changes at some point.[6] We must be careful not to make an initial hypothesis about the status of the notated measures based on the work's opening ideas, only to discover that we must

change our interpretation in light of new material later in the movement. Second, we can be guided by our knowledge of formal conventions in the classical style, as the following examples illustrate.

EXAMPLE 3.1: In this Adagio movement, each notated measure seems to hold two real measures, and thus we can recognize the presence of an eight-measure sentence notated in four measures. We might question why this passage could not be analyzed as a simple four-measure antecedent phrase of an eight-measure period, so that $R = N$. Further examination of the movement reveals these opening measures to be the complete main theme, with the transition beginning immediately at measure 5. As a general rule, a main theme lasts at least eight real measures. Moreover, few main themes in the repertory are composed of a single antecedent phrase. Thus our original interpretation of an eight-measure sentence ($R = \frac{1}{2}N$) is supported (though by no means fully validated) by the norms of classical form.

EXAMPLE 3.2: This famous theme is an eight-measure sentence notated as sixteen measures ($R = 2N$).[7] If we believe that $R = N$, then we meet with a basic idea lasting four real measures, which runs counter to our knowledge that the basic idea of most main themes is two real measures in length. Our familiarity with classical norms, combined with our intuitive sense that each notated measure does not contain sufficient material for a real measure of music, helps confirm our interpretation that $R = 2N$.

The definitions of formal units presented in this book are given in terms of real measures. Thus the sentence form discussed in this chapter contains eight real measures, whether or not the theme is notated as four, eight, or sixteen measures.[8]

PRESENTATION PHRASE

The eight-measure sentence begins with a four-measure *presentation phrase*, consisting of a repeated two-measure basic idea in the context of a tonic prolongational progression.[9] The presentation functions to create a solid structural beginning for the theme by establishing its melodic–motivic content in a stable harmonic–tonal environment.

EXAMPLE 3.1 Mozart, Piano Sonata in F, K. 332/300k, ii, 1–4

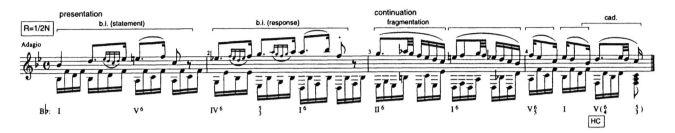

EXAMPLE 3.2 Beethoven, Symphony No. 5 in C Minor, Op. 67, i, 6–21

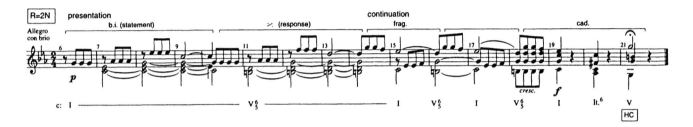

EXAMPLE 3.3 (a) Mozart, Piano Sonata in G, K. 283/189h, i, 1–10; (b) rewritten version of mm. 7–10

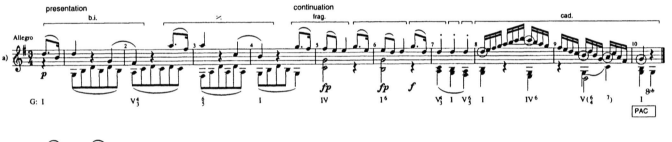

EXAMPLE 3.4 Beethoven, Piano Sonata in G, Op. 14/2, i, 1–8

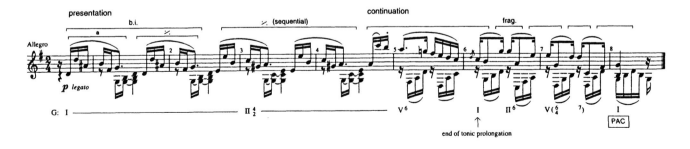

The initial statement of the basic idea sets forth the fundamental material of the theme, and the immediate repetition of the idea fully "presents" it as such to the listener. The tonic prolongational progression provides the requisite harmonic stability.

Basic Idea

Many books on musical form begin by discussing the very smallest units of formal organization, a collection of several notes usually termed a *motive*.[10] (The terms "cell" and "germ" are frequently encountered as well.) The textbooks then show how these motives group into larger units, which in turn combine to form even larger units, and so forth. The impression is that a composition is constructed out of tiny building blocks (often just a single interval formed by two notes), which represent the fundamental units of formal structure for the work.

This view of form has some merits (particularly for late romantic compositions by Brahms, for example), but it does not apply well to classical compositions. Admittedly, a work in this style features the grouping of lower-level units into higher-level ones during the course of its unfolding. But the smallest motives should not be construed as the fundamental building blocks. Rather, the classical work initially groups together several motives into a single gesture, a larger idea lasting two real measures. This *basic idea* is small enough to group with other ideas into phrases and themes but large enough to be broken down (fragmented) in order to develop its constituent motives.[11] Indeed, the opening material of a classical theme typically is integrated into larger formal units as well as disintegrated into smaller motivic elements. The two-measure basic idea is just the right size to act as the starting point for both these processes.[12]

As a general rule, the initial statement of a basic idea emphasizes tonic harmony, usually in root position. In the vast majority of cases, the idea begins directly with the tonic, which often literally prevails throughout the entire idea, as in example 3.2.[13] Subsequent statements of the basic idea may be supported by different harmonies.

The melodic content of a basic idea can often be described as *characteristic*, as opposed to *conventional*. A characteristic melody uniquely defines a theme as an individual, one different from other themes. A conventional melody, on the contrary, is interchangeable from piece to piece. Whereas a characteristic melody normally appears at the very beginning of a thematic unit, a conventional melody is typically used for interior passage-work and cadential closure.[14] A basic idea acquires its characteristic quality by the nature of its constituent melodic and rhythmic motives. A diversity of intervallic content (combinations of leaps, steps, and directional changes) and a variety of durational patterning help bestow individuality on the idea. Conversely, conventional ideas tend to feature consistent stepwise or arpeggiated motion within a series of uniform durational values.

Appropriate to its function as the initiator of a theme, a basic idea often projects the character of a melodic "opening up." (By contrast, a cadential idea generally results in a melodic "closing down.") An opening-up quality is created most simply by a distinctly ascending gesture. A sense of melodic opening can also be achieved by immediately sounding (and subsequently embellishing) the third or fifth scale-degrees, thus motivating an eventual descent to the tonic at the cadence. In cases in which the initial basic idea expresses a weak degree of opening up, the immediate repetition of the idea usually occurs at a higher pitch level, thus producing a rising contour at a deeper level of melodic structure.

EXAMPLE 3.3: The two-measure basic idea initially elaborates the fifth scale-degree but then drops down to the tonic and leading-tone, thus creating a closing gesture. The subsequent repetition of the idea significantly expands the melodic space by leaping to the high A, opening up a melodic gap that is filled in stepwise by the continuation phrase. (Example 3.3b is discussed toward the end of the chapter.)

The melodic end of a basic idea is often marked by silence, which sets off the idea from subsequent material (see ex. 3.1). A similar effect is created when the final note of the idea is relatively longer than those that precede and follow it (see ex. 3.2). Determining the exact boundaries of the basic idea can be difficult at times. Articulation signs, especially slurs, sometimes help clarify its limits, but these signs can also be misleading and must be ignored in the face of the analyst's intuitions about the grouping structure of the idea.[15]

A potentially confusing situation arises when the two-measure basic idea is itself built out of a repeated one-measure idea. Although it might be tempting in such cases to consider the one-measure unit as the real basic idea, such an interpretation usually results in a misleading analysis of the overall theme.

EXAMPLE 3.4: The initial one-measure gesture ("a") is repeated exactly in the next bar, which might suggest the expression of presentation function. But then the entire two-measure unit is repeated sequentially to create the true four-measure presentation phrase for the complete eight-measure sentence.[16]

Repetition of the Basic Idea

Most repetitions fall into one of three main categories — exact, statement-response, and sequential. These categories are based on the harmonic context in which the repetition occurs, not on any melodic considerations. An *exact repetition* of an idea retains the same basic harmony of the original version. *Statement–response repetition* brings an ini-

EXAMPLE 3.5 Mozart, Piano Sonata in C, K. 330/300h, i, 1–8

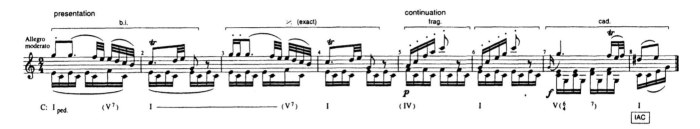

EXAMPLE 3.6 Haydn, Piano Sonata in B-flat, Hob. XVI:41, ii, 1–8

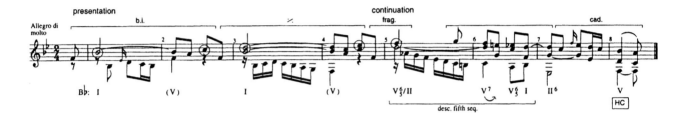

EXAMPLE 3.7 Haydn, Piano Sonata in G, Hob. XVI:27, ii, 1–8

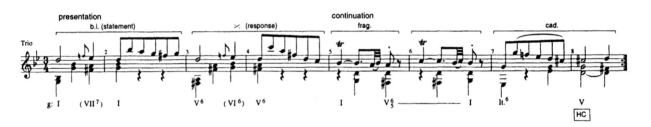

EXAMPLE 3.8 Mozart, String Quartet in C ("Dissonance"), K. 465, i, 23–30

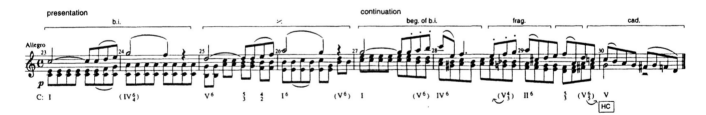

tial *tonic version* of the idea followed by a *dominant version*. *Sequential repetition* involves transposing a complete idea (both melody and harmony) to a different scale-degree. Since a presentation phrase is supported in principle by a tonic prolongational progression, not a sequential one, the category of sequential repetition receives only minimal treatment at this time.[17]

Exact repetition. A basic idea is repeated exactly when it is harmonized like its original statement. Although the notion of "exact" applies essentially to the harmonic component, the repetition usually retains the idea's fundamental melodic shape, although it may become ornamented in some way or another.

EXAMPLE 3.5: The opening two-measure basic idea, firmly set in tonic harmony, is repeated in measures 3–4 with the same harmonic support. The melodic content of this exact repetition is identical except for the slight rhythmic ornamentation at its beginning.

At times, the melody is transposed to a different scale-degree while the harmony remains the same. Such cases are classified as exact repetitions, despite the obvious change to the melodic component.

EXAMPLE 3.6: The basic idea and its repetition are supported entirely by tonic harmony (with neighboring dominants). Because the harmonic context remains the same, we can identify an exact repetition here even though the melody of the repeated version lies a third higher than the original version. Taken together, the two forms of the basic idea create an ascending stepwise melodic progression, a Schenkerian *Anstieg* (see circled notes), that is complemented by a descending progression in the continuation phrase.[18]

Statement–response repetition. The *statement* of a basic idea receives a *response* when an original version supported primarily by tonic harmony is answered by a repeated version supported by dominant harmony. A variety of harmonic patterns can create tonic and dominant versions of an idea. The simplest case arises when the statement is built entirely out of tonic and the response is built out of dominant (see ex. 3.2).[19] A richer harmonization results if each of these fundamental harmonies is prolonged by neighboring or passing chords.

EXAMPLE 3.7: The basic idea is initially supported by tonic harmony with a neighboring dominant. The repetition takes the form of a response, whose basic dominant support is slightly embellished by a neighboring VI[6] chord on the third beat of measure 3.

One important type of statement–response repetition involves the motion away from tonic to dominant (I–V) in the statement and a return from the dominant to the tonic

(V–I) in the response (see ex. 3.3a, mm. 1–4).[20] In such cases, the *initial* harmony of the idea is responsible for expressing the sense of the tonic and dominant versions. In a variation on this pattern, a pre-dominant harmony of some kind (II[6], IV, V/V) precedes the dominant that appears at the beginning of the response.

EXAMPLE 3.8: The presentation phrase features a statement–response repetition of the basic idea. But rather than having the tonic move directly to the dominant to signal the response, Mozart inserts an embellishing pre-dominant (IV$^6_4$) in the second half of the statement (m. 2).[21]

A statement–response repetition also is created when the repeated idea is supported exclusively by subdominant harmony.[22] A more complicated version of a subdominant response appears in example 3.1. The initial chords of each idea are tonic and subdominant, respectively, and these harmonies are further embellished by their own dominants in first inversion (the I[6] on the second half of m. 2 being a "dominant" of IV). The overall progression, however, remains tonic prolongational (I–I[6]).

Most statement–response repetitions involve transposing the melody to a different scale-degree in order to accommodate the change in harmonization. As seen in the examples just discussed, the transposition is usually stepwise,[23] except when the melody in both versions circles about the fifth scale-degree, a tone common to I and V (as in ex. 3.7)

Sequential repetition. A basic idea is repeated sequentially if its entire melodic–harmonic content is transposed to a different scale-degree. In sequential repetition, both the melody and its harmonic support are transposed by the same interval, such as in example 3.4 in which the idea ascends by a step.[24] A single sequential repetition, as in a presentation phrase, does not necessarily produce a sequential harmonic progression. For instance, the move from I to II$^6_5$ in example 3.4 takes place in a broader tonic prolongation, as will be discussed shortly.

Sequential repetition and statement–response repetition can easily be mistaken for each other if only the melodic line is considered. As we have already seen, the melody of a response is usually transposed stepwise, thus superficially resembling a sequential repetition of the kind found in example 3.4. But the harmony of the response is transposed up a fifth. A genuine sequential repetition transposes both harmony and melody by the same interval. The concept of "melodic sequence," frequently cited in elementary texts, has no form-functional import.

Tonic Prolongation

According to my definition, a presentation phrase prolongs tonic harmony. The prolongation is often contained in the

EXAMPLE 3.9 **(a)** Mozart, Symphony No. 40 in G Minor, K. 550, iii, 1–14; **(b)** rewritten version of mm. 1–6

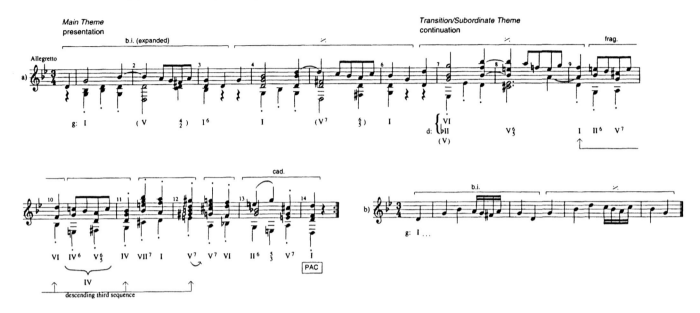

EXAMPLE 3.10 Mozart, Violin Sonata in A, K. 402/385e, i, 1–8

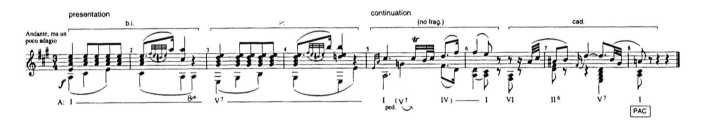

boundaries of the phrase (see exs. 3.1 and 3.5). Frequently, though, a response version of the basic idea ends with dominant harmony, and thus the progression is not actually completed until the arrival of the tonic at the beginning of the continuation phrase (as in exs. 3.2 and 3.7). In exceptional cases, the tonic prolongation concludes after the continuation phrase has already begun. In example 3.4, the prolongation ends on the downbeat of measure 6.

Deviations from the Norm

Presentation phrases in a tight-knit sentence rarely depart from the norms just described.[25] The few deviations that do occur usually result from *expanding* the component basic ideas beyond their normative two-measure size.[26]

EXAMPLE 3.9: The basic idea is internally enlarged to three measures by augmenting the durational values of the second and third notes of the melody. The repetition of the basic idea thus results in a six-measure presentation.[27] Example 3.9b reconstructs a normative version of the basic idea showing how its essential motivic

content could have been easily accommodated to the normal two-measure length.[28]

CONTINUATION PHRASE

The second phrase of the sentence combines the formal functions of continuation and cadential. *Continuation* function destabilizes the prevailing phrase-structural, rhythmic, and harmonic context (as defined by the presentation) and features a breaking down of the structural units (fragmentation), an increase in rhythmic activity (acceleration of harmonic change and shorter surface durations), and a weakening of harmonic functionality (sequential progression). *Cadential* function brings closure to the theme and is characterized by tonal confirmation (cadential progression) and the conversion of characteristic motives into conventional ones (liquidation).

Following the lead of Schoenberg, the second four-measure unit of the sentence form is termed a *continuation phrase*.[29] Needless to say, this choice of terminology is problematical because it fails to specify any cadential function in the phrase. But for the sake of simplicity, a single-word expression (analogous to presentation, antecedent, and consequent) seems preferable. Labeling the phrase according to only one of its constituent functions is motivated by the fact that the continuation function is usually more salient throughout the entire phrase than is the cadential function, which does not normally appear until later in the phrase.[30]

Continuation Function

The presentation of a sentence establishes the fundamental content of the theme in a relatively stable phrase-structural and harmonic context: the units of structure are clearly defined as two measures in length, and the tonic prolongational progression creates harmonic solidity. In the presentation, moreover, the effect of repetition combined with the absence of any cadential closure sets up strong expectations for ensuing material that will bring something new, something that will permit the theme to acquire momentum and drive. It is precisely the function of the continuation to destabilize the formal context established by the presentation and to give the theme greater mobility.

Continuation function is characterized by the following four compositional devices: (1) phrase-structural fragmentation, (2) acceleration in the rate of harmonic change, (3) increase in surface rhythmic activity, and (4) sequential harmonies. Although often closely related to one another in a given continuation, these are distinct and independent processes. Moreover, none of them is a necessary condition of the function.

Fragmentation. The most common characteristic of continuation function is the immediate breaking down of the two-measure unit size (established in the presentation) into smaller segments. This process of shortening the units is termed *fragmentation.*[31] The smaller segments are *fragmented units* or, more simply, *fragments.*

Just as the presentation uses repetition to define unequivocally the size of the constituent units, so, too, is the shortening of the units usually confirmed by a repetition of the fragments. Consequently, a continuation phrase most often begins with a one-measure idea, which is immediately repeated in the following measure (as in ex. 3.5; see also exs. 3.1, 3.2, and 3.7).

Sometimes fragmentation does not occur until after the continuation phrase has already begun (see ex. 3.4). Often in such cases, the continuation starts as though it were going to restate the entire basic idea for a third time, but before reaching its conclusion, the idea leads into new material that effects the fragmentation (see ex. 3.8).

The process of fragmentation exclusively concerns the *length* of the musical units, regardless of how the melodic content of the fragments relates to the preceding mater-

ial. To be sure, there are many cases in which the fragmented units contain motives derived from the basic idea (see ex. 3.8; see also exs. 3.2, 3.7, and 3.9), but it is just as possible for the melodic material to change significantly at the beginning of the continuation phrase (see ex. 3.1; see also ex. 3.5).

Structural fragmentation has significant consequences for the higher-level rhythm of a theme. The systematic shortening of the constituent units results in a marked rhythmic acceleration. The greater activity thus achieved is important for creating the impression of mobility essential to continuation function.

Acceleration of harmonic rhythm. Another important component of a theme's large-scale rhythm is the rate of change of its supporting harmonies. The continuation function typically features *harmonic acceleration* in relation to the presentation.

An analysis of harmonic rhythm can sometimes prove difficult, owing to the hierarchical nature of harmony. Since each level of harmonic succession in a theme has its own durational patterning, there can often be more than one description of the theme's harmonic rhythm. The problem is one of determining exactly which chords belong to a given level, but once they are identified, it is simple to describe the harmonic rhythm.

As a general rule, the level of harmonic activity most important to projecting the continuation function is the level most directly associated with the basic idea, its repetition, and its fragmented units. We can refer to this as the "level of the *idea unit.*" In the simplest cases, such as example 1.1 (shown on p. 10), a single harmony supports each idea unit (i.e., one chord per basic idea and fragment), and thus it is easy to demonstrate harmonic acceleration on this level of formal organization.

When an idea unit is harmonized by several chords, it is more difficult to decide whether every one of these chords belongs to the level of the idea unit—that is, whether they all participate in the primary harmonic rhythm of the theme. Sometimes, individual chords are merely ornamental and thus play no role in creating a sense of harmonic change. At other times, the subordinate chords in an idea unit have sufficient importance to be included in the analysis of the harmonic rhythm.

EXAMPLE 3.10: The new melodic–motivic material at the beginning of the continuation phrase is organized into a two-measure unit (mm. 5–6), thus maintaining the unit size already given by the presentation. To compensate for the absence of fragmentation, Mozart accelerates the harmonic rhythm in these measures. To be sure, the IV chord introduced on the third beat of measure 5 (and preceded by its own dominant) is a neighboring chord in a root-position tonic prolongation. Nevertheless, compared with the lack of any ornamental chords at the level of the idea unit in the presentation, this embellishing of the tonic in the continuation creates a

EXAMPLE 3.11 Mozart, Piano Sonata in D, K. 311/284c, iii, 1–8

sense of greater harmonic activity. Simply to ignore the subdominant harmony of measures 5–6 in an analysis of the harmonic rhythm is to miss an important way in which the composer expresses the continuation function despite the lack of fragmentation.

Increase in surface rhythmic activity. The two principal characteristics (fragmentation and harmonic acceleration) of continuation function involve rhythmic activity at a relatively high structural level in a theme. But rhythmic acceleration can also be projected by events lying at the very surface of the musical texture. The durational patterns formed by the attack points of every note in a passage create varying rates of activity. In comparison to the presentation, the continuation function frequently features shorter note values, hence an increased animation in the surface rhythm. Increasing surface rhythmic activity is particularly effective in the absence of harmonic acceleration.

EXAMPLE 3.11: The root-position tonic from the end of the presentation (m. 4) is maintained throughout the first two measures of the continuation, thus slowing down the harmonic rhythm. To counterbalance this deceleration, Mozart introduces a flurry of sixteenth notes, which increases toward the approach to the half cadence.[32]

Harmonic sequence. In most of the preceding examples, the continuation function is initially supported by a tonic prolongational progression. If the tonic remains in root position throughout the prolongation, then the harmonic stability established in the presentation is maintained in the continuation, as in example 3.10 (see also exs. 3.2, 3.5, and 3.7). But if the tonic is allowed to change from root position to first inversion, then the harmonic texture of the continuation is made less weighty and more mobile (see ex. 1.1).

Sequential progressions create even greater harmonic mobility within a continuation. Their inherent instability make them especially suited for continuation function, one of whose primary goals is to destabilize the harmonic context established by the presentation.

EXAMPLE 3.6: The presentation features a standard tonic prolongation created by neighboring dominant chords. On the downbeat of measure 5, the two notes in the upper voices (D and F) represent the expected tonic, which would complete the prolongation. The

missing root of the tonic harmony (B♭) does not actually sound in the bass part, as it did analogously after the downbeats in measures 1 and 3. Instead, the lower line of measure 5 expresses a V$^6_5$/II, which initiates a short descending fifth sequential progression, one that continues in the following measure. The subsequent half-cadential progression in measures 7–8 brings the theme to a close.[33]

To be sure, the sequential progression of the preceding example hardly represents a radical overthrow of the prevailing tonic. Indeed, the descending fifth pattern is the most harmonically functional of all the sequential progressions, and here it leads quickly back to the tonic. It is entirely appropriate in this case that the use of sequential harmonies does not overly threaten the tonic's stability. After all, this sentence serves as a sonata-form main theme, which, in principle, should retain a strong, tight-knit organization. For this reason, main themes do not normally exhibit significant sequential activity.

In fact, the use of sequence is rare in sentences that conform to the eight-measure model, no matter where they may occur within a movement. Because of the restricted time span between the end of the presentation's tonic prolongation and the beginning of the requisite cadential progression at the close of the theme, there is little room for including enough harmonies to make palpable the sense of sequence. For this reason, sequential progressions occur most often in a continuation when that function is extended beyond its conventional four-measure limits, as in example 3.9, which is discussed later in this chapter in connection with deviations from the norm.

Cadential Function

Music in the classical style is often characterized as highly goal directed, and many of the principal goals in a composition are the cadences marking the ends of themes and theme-like units. Identifying the cadences is thus a critical objective of any formal analysis. Unfortunately, traditional ideas of cadence are riddled with misconceptions that stand in the way of a truer understanding of this important compositional phenomenon.[34] The following discussion attempts to clear the air of some erroneous notions and to begin laying the foundations for a more complete and accurate concept of cadence than that found in most theories of musical form. Additional issues of cadence will be raised in later chapters as they pertain to formal situations other than the sentence.

Fundamental concepts of cadence.   To begin, let us differentiate three usages of the term *cadence* (and its adjectival form, *cadential*). The first refers to the *cadential arrival*, the specific moment in time that marks the structural end of a thematic region. More simply, this is "the cadence," the point at which a symbol such as PAC (perfect authentic cadence) would be placed in the analysis.

The second usage refers to the time span leading up to this point of arrival, that is, the idea or phrase in the theme that communicates to the listener that "the cadence" is forthcoming. This passage of music can be said to have a *cadential function* because it creates the requisite conditions for thematic closure by means of specific harmonic, melodic, and phrase-structural devices.

The third sense of cadence refers to the particular type of harmonic progression used to confirm a tonality. This *cadential progression* (which was extensively treated in the previous chapter) is most often associated with cadential function. But it can also provide harmonic support for other formal functions, especially codettas.

With these distinctions in mind, we can now define the concept of cadential function in greater detail. As a general rule, the boundaries of the function are limited by its underlying cadential progression. Thus, the initial harmony of the progression marks the beginning of cadential material (be it a short idea or a full phrase), and the onset of the final harmony articulates the point of cadential arrival.

Whereas the presence of a cadential progression is a necessary condition for cadential function, it is not a sufficient one. The general formal context in which the passage is located plays a significant role as well. A cadence essentially represents the structural *end* of broader harmonic, melodic, and phrase-structural processes. Thus cadential function implies the presence of prior material—for example, presentational or continuational—on which the cadential function follows in order to effect thematic closure. We must be careful not to identify a passage as cadential unless we can demonstrate that it logically ensues from previous *initiating* or *medial* functions.[35]

In addition to its requisite harmonic component, a cadential function often contains a distinctive melodic profile, a highly conventionalized formula that occurs frequently in works in the classical style. This cadential melody normally has a falling contour, which conveys the sense of "closing down" a melodic process. The cadential idea thus contrasts with the basic idea at the beginning of the theme, which, as pointed out, features a characteristic melody, one that "opens up" the melodic line.[36]

Put somewhat differently, cadential material often arises when the composer systematically eliminates characteristic melodic and rhythmic motives introduced in the basic idea, a technique termed motivic *liquidation*. Strictly speaking, any elimination of a characteristic motive represents liquidation, and thus in cases in which the continuation phrase begins with material that contrasts with the presentation, complete liquidation takes place immediately. But liquidation is more palpable as a process when the elimination is gradual, reaching its completion in the cadential function.[37]

Classification of cadences.   Cadences are classified into two main types based on the final harmony of the underlying cadential progression. If the goal of the progression is tonic, an *authentic cadence* is created; if the harmonic goal is dominant, a *half cadence (HC)* is created.

Authentic cadences are further subdivided according to the extent of melodic closure achieved at the cadential arrival.[38] In a *perfect authentic cadence (PAC)*, the melody reaches the tonic scale-degree in conjunction with the onset of the final tonic harmony. In an *imperfect authentic cadence (IAC)*, the melody is left open on the third scale-degree (or, very rarely, the fifth degree). The half cadence is not subject to further subdivision based on any such melodic criterion.

These three cadences—perfect authentic, imperfect authentic, and half—are the only genuine cadences in music in the classical style. I must offer additional cadential labels, however, to cover situations in which an expected authentic cadence fails to materialize. For example, if the final tonic of the cadential progression is replaced by a different harmony (or occasionally by a tonic in first inversion), we recognize that a *deceptive cadence* has appeared in lieu of the authentic cadence.[39] Following the deceptive cadence, the composer normally repeats the material leading up to the unrealized cadence and closes it with the authentic cadence originally promised.

EXAMPLE 3.12: The theme heads toward closure with an authentic cadence at the downbeat of measure 8, but, instead, the dominant scale-degree in the bass is chromatically raised, and the subsequent resolution to VI in the second half of the measure creates a deceptive cadence. Haydn then repeats the entire continuation phrase, finally allowing it to reach a true authentic-cadential closure in measure 12.[40]

So far, I have not mentioned any cadence featuring the progression from subdominant to tonic, the "plagal cadence" described by virtually every theory text. An examination of the classical repertory reveals that such a cadence rarely exists—if it indeed can be said to exist at all.[41] Inasmuch as the progression IV–I cannot confirm a tonality (it lacks any leading-tone resolution), it cannot articulate formal closure in the sense developed in this book. Rather, this progression is normally part of a tonic prolongation serving a variety of formal functions—not, however, a cadential

EXAMPLE 3.12 Haydn, Piano Trio in C, Hob. XV:27, i, 1–12

EXAMPLE 3.13 Beethoven, Piano Sonata in C, Op. 2/3, i, 1–13

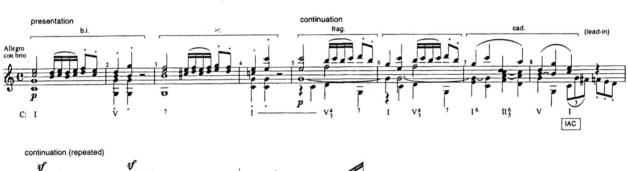

one. Most examples of plagal cadences given in textbooks actually represent a postcadential codetta function: that is, the IV–I progression follows an authentic cadence but does not in itself create genuine cadential closure.[42]

Cadence in the sentence form.   As defined here, cadential function begins with the onset of the cadential progression, which, in the case of the sentence form, usually occurs around the middle of the continuation phrase, either at the downbeat of measure 7 or at the preceding upbeat. If the ultimate dominant of a half-cadential progression is preceded by a single chord (thus resulting in an incomplete progression), the cadential function may begin as late as the upbeat to measure 8 (see ex. 3.1, m. 4, beats 2 and 3, where R = ½N; see also ahead ex. 5.9, mm. 7–8).

Sometimes the cadential progression supports a distinctly new melodic idea of marked cadential character, a melody that is clearly different from the preceding material associated with an exclusive continuation function, as in examples 3.6 and 3.12 (see also exs. 3.5 and 3.7, in which the cadential idea derives from the basic idea). Frequently, though, the cadential idea grows directly out of the melodic–motivic content of the continuation, as in examples 3.2 and 3.11.

Any one of the three main cadence types may be used to close a sentence. The form frequently ends with a half cadence, even though that cadence does not create full closure of the melodic–harmonic processes that arise in the theme.[43] If a sentence ends with an imperfect authentic cadence, the continuation phrase, or a portion thereof, is often repeated in order to provide greater melodic closure by means of a perfect authentic cadence.

EXAMPLE 3.13: The initial sentence closes with an imperfect authentic cadence at measure 8. The weaker cadence motivates a repetition of the continuation phrase, which, after a degree of cadential expansion, closes with a perfect authentic cadence on the downbeat of measure 13. Rhythmic continuity between the two continuation phrases is achieved by means of the triplet *lead-in* at measure 8.[44]

Now that the concept of cadence has been somewhat clarified, it is possible to confront an issue pertaining to the presentation phrase of a sentence that could not be adequately raised in the earlier discussion of that function. Since many traditional theories teach that every "phrase" must end with a cadence, we may be tempted to identify cadential closure at the end of some presentation phrases. This analytical mistake can be circumvented when we understand more clearly why a presentation, in principle, never closes with a cadence.

The absence of a supporting cadential progression in most presentation phrases automatically prohibits us from identifying cadential closure in those cases. Occasionally,

however, a presentation contains a prolongation that ends with a root-position dominant resolving to a root-position tonic, as in example 3.13, measures 3–4. Here, the possibility of a cadence is at least suggested. But Beethoven leaves the melodic line open at the end of the phrase, thus helping to counteract the cadential implications given by the harmony.

But there is no cadence at the end of this phrase, or any other presentation, for a more fundamental reason. Inasmuch as the basic idea itself functions to *begin* a theme, a repetition of that idea must also express a similar function of beginning. Indeed, repeating an opening idea actually reinforces the sense of formal initiation. Conversely, to effect thematic closure, a basic idea must be followed by different material, a "contrasting idea," that has the appropriate harmonic content to express cadential function.

An analogy to natural language may help clarify the difference between a basic idea and a cadence in music. A grammatically complete sentence (in language) must normally contain a subject followed by a predicate. Similarly, a basic idea is a kind of "subject" for a musical sentence; hence, a presentation phrase is analogous to a compound subject. For example, the subject phrase "the man and his dog" does not form a complete sentence but, rather, sets up expectations for an ensuing predicate, such as "ran together across the street." Similarly, a presentation phrase by itself does not bring about thematic closure but, instead, sets up strong expectations for further material that will ultimately close the theme. Thus, to continue the analogy, the "predicate" of a musical sentence is fulfilled by the continuation and cadential functions that follow the presentation.

Additional Features

Continuation ⇒ cadential.   As defined at the opening of this chapter, the second half of the eight-measure sentence combines continuation and cadential functions into one four-measure phrase. The presence of two different functions in a single group can more technically be termed form-functional *fusion.* Fusion poses a problem of terminology because formal units are preferably labeled according to their primary functional expression. The decision to call the second half of a sentence a *continuation phrase* reflects the fact that in the majority of cases, continuation function is more prominently displayed than cadential function is. Not only does the phrase begin with continuation function, but also the processes of fragmentation, harmonic acceleration, and increased surface rhythm often carry on into the cadential material.

In some cases, however, the cadential component vies for equal expression with the continuation function, or even surpasses it. Cadential function acquires this greater status when the phrase begins directly with the cadential progression, which is then expanded to support the entire phrase.

EXAMPLE 3.14 Haydn, String Quartet in D Minor, Op. 42, i, 1–8

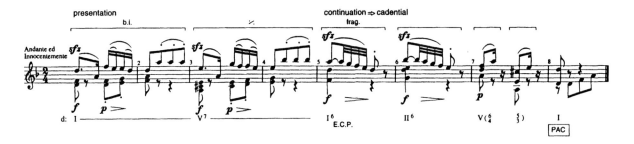

EXAMPLE 3.15 Mozart, String Quartet in A, K. 464, ii, 1–8

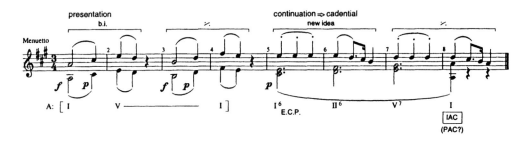

EXAMPLE 3.16 (a) Beethoven, Piano Trio in G, Op. 1/2, ii, 1–9; (b) rewritten version of mm. 7–9

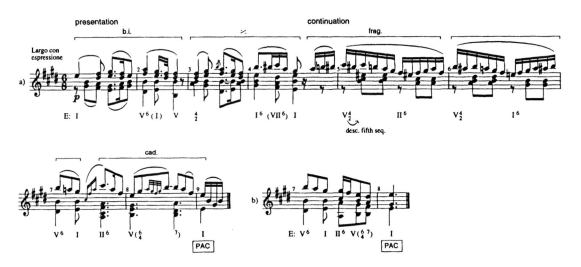

In more loosely organized phrase-structural contexts (such as a subordinate theme), a phrase built on such an *expanded cadential progression (E.C.P.)* usually has an exclusive cadential function. This *cadential phrase* would normally follow a continuation phrase devoted entirely to that function. The two functions would thus receive individual phrases of their own.[45]

In an eight-measure sentence, a phrase supported by an expanded cadential progression normally features both continuation and cadential functions, just like a standard continuation phrase. Once again, though, the form-functional fusion in the phrase poses a problem of terminology. To call the unit a *continuation phrase* fails to give sufficient weight to its underlying cadential progression. But to call it a *cadential phrase* slights the obvious continuational features so characteristic of the sentence form.

Thus for this particular case, it seems reasonable (albeit somewhat cumbersome) to indicate both functions by labeling the phrase in the following way: *continuation⇒cadential*. The symbol ⇒ stands for "becomes" and denotes a retrospective reinterpretation of formal function.[46] In other words, what we expect to be a continuation phrase (following, as it does, a presentation) is understood retrospectively to be a cadential phrase based on an expanded cadential progression, a phrase that nevertheless contains continuational characteristics.

EXAMPLE 3.14: The theme begins with a regular four-measure presentation featuring a statement–response repetition of the basic idea. We now expect a continuation phrase that will likely fragment the unit size and increase the rate of harmonic change. These continuational traits are clearly manifest in measures 5 and 6 of the theme. Indeed, fragmentation carries on into measure 7 as well. The motion from I^6 to II^6 in measures 5 and 6 suggests the presence of a cadential progression. But since this interpretation is not fully confirmed until the arrival of the root-position dominant in measure 7, it is only then that we can understand retrospectively that the cadential function was actually initiated at the very start of the phrase.[47]

EXAMPLE 3.15: The continuation function is not nearly so well expressed in this continuation⇒cadential phrase, owing to the lack of fragmentation. Instead of reducing the size of the units, measures 5–6 bring a new two-measure idea, which is repeated in measures 7–8. A sense of continuation function is nonetheless projected by the slight increase in harmonic and surface-rhythm activity.[48]

Modulating sentence.   All the themes referred to thus far (with the exception of ex. 3.9) close in the key in which they begin. Occasionally, though, the continuation phrase modulates to a new, closely related key. Most often the new key is the dominant region of the opening key, although the mediant ("relative major") is frequently used if the opening key is minor. In all modulating sentences, the final cadence

is authentic, for a half cadence is too weak to confirm a new tonality, especially one that lacks its own tonic prolongation associated with the presentation function.

A modulating sentence rarely stands alone as an independent formal unit. Rather, it tends to link up with other units to form a larger-scale theme, one that ultimately returns to the original key and closes there with a perfect authentic cadence. Modulating sentences thus are found most often in the first part of small ternary or small binary forms (see ahead ex. 7.3).[49]

Deviations from the Norm

The continuation phrase of the sentence frequently deviates from its four-measure norm, and almost always so if the presentation deviates as well. Indeed, the continuation is likely to be altered more often than the presentation is, whose four-measure length sets the standard against which subsequent phrase irregularities can make their effect.[50] The following examples are typical of the ways in which a continuation phrase departs from the norm.

Extension of continuation function.   Additional units of fragmentation and a thorough sequential progression are typical means of extending continuation function.[51]

EXAMPLE 3.9: The expanded presentation (discussed earlier) motivates an even more extended continuation. Mozart first states the basic idea a third time (mm. 7–9). Ordinarily, such an additional repetition would be a part of an extended presentation, but since the supporting harmony no longer prolongs the initial tonic (introducing instead a modulation to the dominant region), the repeated idea is better seen as belonging to the continuation. The upbeat to measure 10 brings fragmentation of the second motive of the basic idea in a descending third sequence, which further extends the function. The theme closes with a conventional perfect authentic cadence to confirm the new key.[52]

Expansion of cadential function.

EXAMPLE 3.16: The extra measure of this nine-measure theme is created by a small expansion of the cadential progression. (Schoenberg speaks of similar situations as a "written-out ritardando.")[53] A reconstructed normative ending to this theme is shown in example 3.16b, in which the cadential progression represents the final stage in the harmonic acceleration. (See also ex. 3.13, mm. 11–13.)[54]

EXAMPLE 3.3: The second phrase of the theme stretches to six measures, and the two "extra" measures are created by an extension of the continuation (m. 7) and an expansion of the cadence (mm. 8–9, representing a single measure). Measures 5 and 6 of the continuation, featuring fragmentation into one-measure units, are regular enough. According to the model form, measure 7 would then bring a cadential progression ending on the downbeat of measure 8; indeed, Mozart could easily have written a "galant" cadence formula, as shown in example 3.3b. Instead, the composer

EXAMPLE 3.17 Haydn, String Quartet in B-flat, Op. 50/1, ii, 1–6

allows the melody to hold itself insistently on the fifth scale-degree (ex. 3.3a, m. 7), giving the impression of even more fragmentation (into one-beat units). At the same time, the cadential function is delayed by means of further tonic prolongation (m. 7 to the downbeat of m. 8). The pent-up energy created by frustrating expectations of melodic and harmonic closure is finally released in a flurry of sixteenth notes (mm. 8–10). This three-measure cadential unit brings a melodic descent (somewhat disguised by register transfer and passing notes; see circled notes) over a cadential progression expanded by means of rhythmic augmentation.

Compression of the continuation phrase.

EXAMPLE 3.17: The continuation phrase is reduced in scope to just two measures. Yet we can still recognize the basic functional components of the phrase: measure 5 brings both the fragmentation (into half-measure units) and the harmonic acceleration typical of continuation function, and measure 6 contains the half-cadence formula to close the theme.[55]

Period

The most common tight-knit theme-type in instrumental music of the classical style is the eight-measure *period*. The period is divided into two, four-measure phrases fulfilling *antecedent* and *consequent functions*, respectively. The *antecedent phrase* begins with a two-measure basic idea, which is followed by a two-measure contrasting idea leading to a weak cadence. The *consequent phrase* repeats the antecedent but alters the contrasting idea in order to create a stronger cadence to close the theme.[1]

Essential to the concept of the period is the idea that a musical unit of partial cadential closure is repeated so as to produce a stronger cadential closure. As a result, the two units group tightly together to form a higher-level whole, a relatively complete structure in itself. The formal and aesthetic effect of antecedent–consequent repetition thus differs significantly from the repetition found within the presentation phrase of a sentence. There, a repeated open-ended unit (a basic idea) yields an unclosed structure that generates powerful tendencies for continuation.

The general principle of periodic formation just described can operate at a variety of levels within a musical work. For example, the two parts of the small binary form can sometimes result in a kind of antecedent–consequent relationship. A similar situation can obtain between the two parts of the full-movement sonata without development form. In this book, however, I limit the concept of period to two tight-knit theme-types—the eight-measure period (treated here) and the sixteen-measure period (treated in chap. 5).

ANTECEDENT PHRASE

The antecedent phrase of an eight-measure period begins with a two-measure basic idea. All the characteristics of a basic idea discussed in connection with the presentation of a sentence also apply to the antecedent of a period. By itself, a given basic idea does not indicate whether it will open a sentence or a period.[2] Which form results from a given basic idea depends largely on the following two bars of music. In a sentence, the basic idea is immediately repeated,

but in a period, the basic idea is juxtaposed with a contrasting idea, one that brings a weak cadence.

Contrasting idea. The *contrasting idea* of an antecedent achieves its "contrast" with the basic idea most obviously by means of melodic–motivic content. In the clearest cases, the contrasting idea introduces motives distinctly different from those of the basic idea.

A contrast between the two ideas of an antecedent phrase may also be achieved, or at least supported, by secondary features such as texture, dynamics, and articulation.

EXAMPLE 4.1: The arpeggiated ascent projected by the basic idea is complemented by the scalar descent of the contrasting idea. (The final upward leap of a third at the end of each idea, however, projects a slight sense of repetition rather than contrast.)

EXAMPLE 4.2: The motivic content of the contrasting idea is entirely different with respect to durational values, harmonic pacing, and overall melodic countour compared with that of the basic idea. Unlike the preceding example, the antecedent phrase here ends with the less common imperfect authentic cadence.

EXAMPLE 4.3: The basic idea is soft and legato. The very start of the contrasting idea at measure 3 brings a sudden change to a forte dynamic and staccato articulation.

More significantly, however, the basic idea and contrasting idea differ with respect to their fundamental harmonic organization. The basic idea is usually supported by a tonic prolongational progression, and the contrasting idea must close with a cadential progression. In cases in which the contrasting idea seems to resemble the basic idea because of shared motives, the different underlying harmonies distinguish one idea from the other.

EXAMPLE 4.4: The basic idea opens with a one-measure rhythmic motive, one that Mozart used to start a number of his piano concertos.[3] The beginning of the next idea at measure 3 brings back this same motive, which might lead the listener to suspect that the basic idea is being repeated in the manner of a presentation phrase. But the motive is supported by a completely different harmonic

EXAMPLE 4.1 Haydn, Piano Trio in C, Hob. XV:27, iii, 1–8

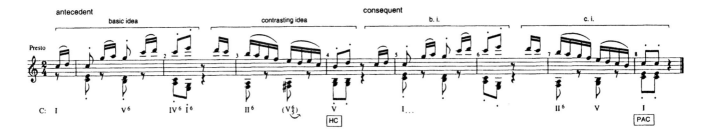

EXAMPLE 4.2 Mozart, Piano Sonata in B-flat, K. 281/189f, i, 1–8

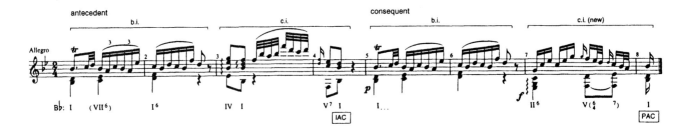

EXAMPLE 4.3 Mozart, Piano Sonata in D, K. 311/284c, ii, 1–8

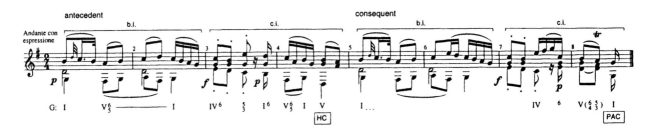

EXAMPLE 4.4 Mozart, Piano Concerto in F, K. 459, i, 1–8

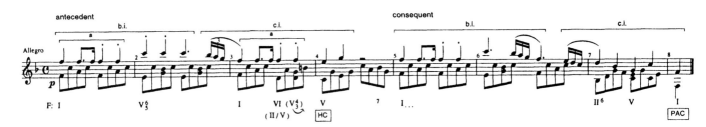

EXAMPLE 4.5 Haydn, Symphony No. 100 in G ("Military"), iv, 1–8

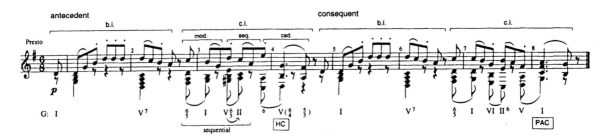

progression, one that brings a half cadence to end the contrasting idea of an antecedent phrase. The return of the motive again at measure 5, now supported by its original harmonization, signals the true restatement of the basic idea, which functions to initiate the consequent phrase.

A contrasting idea often contains characteristics of continuation function, such as fragmentation, an accelerated harmonic or surface rhythm (or both), and even a hint of sequential harmonies.

EXAMPLE 4.5: The two-measure contrasting idea (mm. 3–4) displays most of the characteristics of a full four-measure continuation phrase—fragmentation (into half-measure units), marked harmonic acceleration, a stepwise ascending sequence, and a concluding half-cadential progression.

The notion of the contrasting idea as continuational becomes even more apparent when the basic idea itself is composed of a one-measure motive that is imediately repeated, in the manner of a "small presentation." The entire antecedent then resembles the sentence theme-type. It is more useful for a comprehensive theory of form, however, if we distinguish between a *sentence-like* (or *sentential*) structure and a genuine sentence, the latter being a specific tight-knit theme with the characteristics described in the previous chapter. In many cases throughout this book, we recognize the presence of sentential characteristics without wanting to say that the resulting structure is a sentence proper.

EXAMPLE 4.6: The entire antecedent phrase has a miniature sentential design. The basic idea itself contains a one-measure statement that is immediately repeated as a response, thus suggesting presentation function. The contrasting idea (mm. 3–4) features fragmentation, harmonic acceleration, and cadential closure, like a continuation. It would be inappropriate, however, to consider this four-measure unit a genuine sentence, since it does not contain sufficient musical content to make up a full eight-measure theme.[4]

Weak cadential closure. A basic idea followed by a contrasting idea does not in itself constitute an antecedent. Essential to this function is the presence of a weak cadence that effects partial closure of the phrase. When defining antecedent function, both the half cadence and the imperfect authentic cadence can be considered weak because each leaves unclosed some harmonic or melodic process. Of the two, the half cadence, with its combination of harmonic and melodic incompleteness, is decidedly weaker than the imperfect authentic cadence, which results in melodic incompleteness alone.[5] The vast majority of antecedent phrases end with a half cadence, no doubt to magnify the sense of cadential differentiation. The perfect authentic cadence cannot be used to close an antecedent phrase, since this strong cadence achieves complete harmonic and melodic closure.[6]

"Stop" versus "end." The notion of cadence has often been associated with the "cessation of musical activity." For many musicians, cadence refers to a *stop* in the rhythmical motion of the phrase. To be sure, cadences in the classical literature often occur at points where the surface rhythm comes to a temporary halt. But this is not invariably so: many cadences see the rhythmic motion continuing through to the next formal unit, and sometimes a melodic lead-in also helps maintain rhythmic continuity.

EXAMPLE 4.7: The end of the antecedent phrase is characterized by a sudden increase in activity, such that the flurry of eighth-note runs carries this momentum on through the half cadence (downbeat of m. 7) to the beginning of the consequent at measure 9. The phrase thus "ends" with a half cadence, but the rhythmic motion does not "stop" with that cadence.[7]

Although a rhythmic stop may be associated with a given cadence, a cessation of activity is not essential to the concept of cadence. Moreover, rhythmic motion can come to a halt at places that are clearly noncadential.

EXAMPLE 4.3: The only place where the musical motion completely stops is in the middle of measure 3, a moment that does not project any sense of cadence. On the contrary, this point is the most unstable moment in the phrase.

If cadence does not necessarily entail a stopping of rhythmic activity, it nonetheless does embody the notion of structural closure, the marking of a formal *end*. A rhythmic stop and a formal end are entirely different musical phenomena: although they often operate together, they are conceptually (and perceptually) distinct.[8]

Nonelision of antecedent with consequent. When measure 4 of the antecedent phrase maintains rhythmic continuity all the way until measure 5, we might be tempted to say that rather than ending with a half cadence, the antecedent closes with an authentic cadence, one that *elides* with the beginning of the consequent; that is, measure 5 would be seen to function as both the last measure of the antecedent and the first measure of the consequent.[9] Such an interpretation, however, usually proves to be faulty. In most cases, there are specific harmonic reasons that the beginning of measure 5 cannot be considered a cadence. More important, however, the sense of a formal "goal" in an antecedent almost always precedes the sense of a new beginning for the consequent. It seems that the perception of repeating a unit of weak closure with one of stronger closure is obscured if the boundaries between the units are not clear. An examination of the classical repertory reveals that an antecedent phrase rarely, if ever, elides with a consequent phrase.[10]

EXAMPLE 4.6 Mozart, Piano Sonata in A, K. 331/300i, i, 1–8

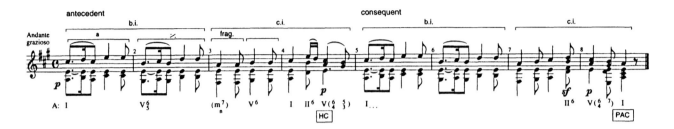

EXAMPLE 4.7 Haydn, Piano Trio in E-flat, Hob. XV:30, iii, 1–16

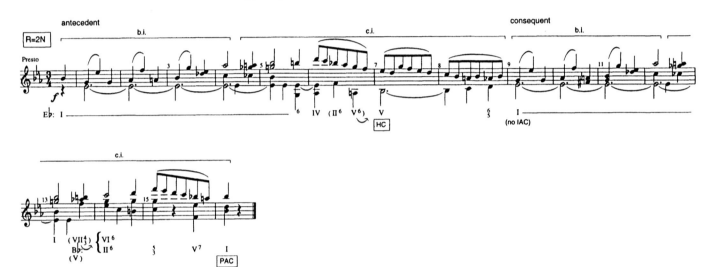

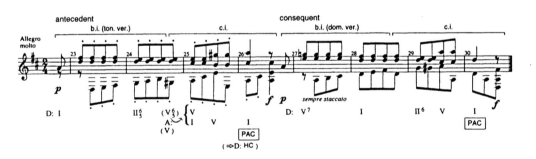

EXAMPLE 4.8 Beethoven, Serenade for Violin, Viola, and Cello in D, Op. 8, iv, 23–30

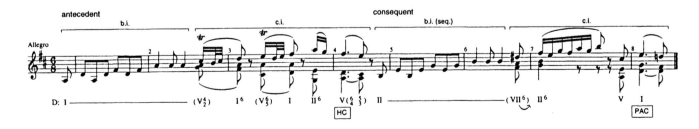

EXAMPLE 4.9 Mozart, Piano Sonata in D, K. 576, i, 1–8

EXAMPLE 4.7: Because of the continuous rhythmic motion into the downbeat of measure 9, we might be tempted to hear an imperfect authentic cadence closing the antecedent at that point. But the bass note B♭ in measure 7 is filled in with stepwise motion leading up to the E♭ in measure 9, and the resulting change to the ⁶₄ position on the third beat of measure 8 undermines the potential for the dominant to function as the penultimate harmony of an authentic cadential progression. Instead, the dominant (in root position) on the downbeat of measure 7 must be construed as an ultimate dominant ending a half-cadential progression. Thus antecedent and consequent do not elide, despite the rhythmic continuity into the latter phrase.

CONSEQUENT PHRASE

The consequent repeats and alters the antecedent so as to achieve greater closure by means of a stronger cadence. With few exceptions, a consequent ends with a perfect authentic cadence, thus fully completing the harmonic and melodic processes of the theme. If the antecedent has closed with a half cadence, the consequent may end with an imperfect authentic cadence, although this weaker form of closure rarely occurs.[11]

To create the impression of repeating the antecedent phrase, the consequent must begin with a restatement of the initial basic idea. The consequent then closes with a contrasting idea leading to the cadence. The contrasting idea of the consequent usually resembles that of the antecedent, although it can also be built out of entirely new melodic–motivic material (see ex. 4.2).

Harmonic organization. In most periods, the basic idea of the consequent is supported by the same harmony as in the antecedent—that is, most often by a firm root-position tonic prolongation. On occasion, the basic idea of the consequent is a dominant version, in relation to a tonic version of the antecedent. The overall harmonic design of the period thus takes on a statement–response character (ant.: I–V, cons.: V–I).

EXAMPLE 4.8: The basic idea of measures 1–2 clearly returns to begin the consequent phrase at measure 5. But the idea's new harmonic support creates a dominant version, compared with the tonic version at the beginning of the antecedent. Indeed, it would be possible to place measures 5–6 directly after measures 1–2 to make a standard presentation phrase featuring a statement–response repetition of the basic idea. (The unusual cadential close of the antecedent phrase is explained toward the end of this chapter.)[12]

A looser harmonic expression is created when the basic idea of the antecedent is restated sequentially in the consequent, usually by being transposed up a step into the supertonic region.

EXAMPLE 4.9: The consequent phrase begins by sequencing the initial basic idea one step higher supported by II. This sequential restatement of the main theme's basic idea proves to have interesting consequences later in the movement for the subordinate theme of the exposition and that of the recapitulation, as discussed in connection with examples 8.1 and 11.12, respectively.[13]

The cadential progression of the consequent often begins earlier in the phrase than in the antecedent, especially if the latter ends with a half cadence (which is usually the case). Since the final harmonies of both phrases normally occupy analogous positions (e.g., downbeats of mm. 4 and 8), the penultimate dominant of the consequent must be shifted backward in relation to the ultimate dominant of the antecedent. In addition, the initial tonic or pre-dominant (or both) appears earlier in the consequent than in the antecedent. The contrasting idea of the consequent may even be supported entirely by the cadential progression and thus resemble the cadential idea closing a sentence.[14] As a result of these various alterations, the consequent phrase acquires a more powerful cadential expression relative to the antecedent, owing to not only the type of cadence but also the greater temporal weight accorded to the cadential progression.

EXAMPLE 4.4: The cadential progression of the antecedent begins with the VI chord (functioning as a pre-dominant II/V) in the second half of measure 3. In the consequent, the pre-dominant II⁶ is shifted back to the beginning of measure 7 to accommodate the penultimate dominant in the second half of that measure. The contrasting idea of the consequent is thus supported entirely by an authentic cadential progression. (See also exs. 4.6 and 4.9.)

Modulating consequent, cadential strength. Most periods conclude in the key in which they begin. Often, however, the consequent phrase modulates, and the theme closes with a perfect authentic cadence in a related tonality. Like the modulating sentence, the modulating period rarely stands alone as an independent theme but, rather, constitutes the first part of a larger thematic unit, such as a small ternary or small binary (see ahead ex. 6.11). In such cases, it might be asked how a subordinate-key cadence closing the consequent phrase can be considered stronger than a home-key cadence closing the antecedent phrase.

We can answer the question by distinguishing between two types of pitch closure in a composition: one type involves the degree of *harmonic–melodic* closure achieved within a key (or several keys), and the other type, operating at a higher structural level, involves the degree of *tonal* closure exhibited by a succession of keys in relation to the home key. The relative strength of cadences is established on the basis of the first type of closure. When the antecedent phrase ends with a weak cadence, we perceive that a harmonic or melodic process in the home key remains somewhat open. But when the consequent phrase modulates and

EXAMPLE 4.10 (a) Haydn, String Quartet in G, Op. 54/1, iii, 1–10; (b) rewritten version of mm. 1–10

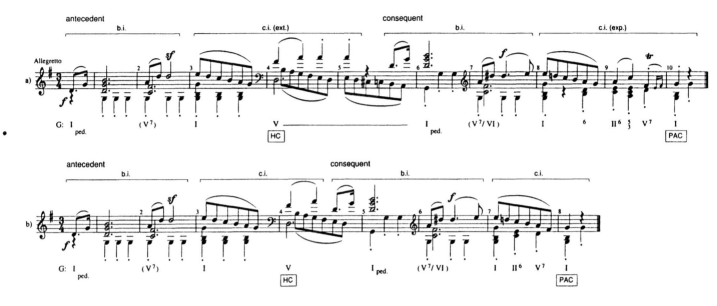

EXAMPLE 4.11 (a) Mozart, Piano Concerto in F, K. 459, ii, 1–10; (b) rewritten version of mm. 1–10

54

establishes a subordinate key by means of a perfect authentic cadence, we perceive that full harmonic–melodic closure *in that new key* has been achieved. In relation to the openness of the antecedent, the fuller closure of the consequent is achieved by a stronger cadence.

As regards the tonal organization of a modulating period, the consequent phrase is more open than the antecedent, since the latter resides in a subordinate key. This tonal instability has important consequences for the rest of the composition, for the music must eventually return to the home key (either shortly thereafter or later in the movement) to achieve tonal closure. Such considerations of tonality, however, have no direct bearing on the strength of cadences, whose degrees of closure relate to harmonic–melodic processes within the various keys of the composition.

Unlike the consequent, which is free to modulate to a related tonal region, an antecedent phrase always closes in the same key in which it begins. (One major exception to this rule will be discussed shortly.) If the antecedent phrase were to modulate (and the consequent to remain entirely in the subordinate key), then the home key, expressed only by the tonic prolongation supporting the initial basic idea, could not compete in prominence with the subordinate key. Thus for the period to attain sufficient tonal stability, it must first confirm its opening key with a cadence (albeit a weak one) before modulating and confirming a new key (with a stronger cadence).

DEVIATIONS FROM THE NORM

Deviations from the model period form occur frequently throughout the classical repertory. Many of these periods employ the same techniques of extension, expansion, and compression discussed earlier in regard to the sentence form. In the case of the period, however, it is useful to distinguish further whether a deviation yields a symmetrical or an asymmetrical grouping structure, for quite different aesthetic effects obtain thereby. In addition to these phrase-structural alterations, deviant periodic forms can arise because of irregular cadential formations.

Symmetrical Deviations

Like the sentence, the period is divided into two, four-measure phrases. But even more than the sentence, the 4 + 4 grouping structure of the period suggests a symmetrical organization, since the consequent phrase repeats the antecedent rather than bringing something essentially new (as does the continuation phrase of the sentence). For this reason, alterations to the normative phrase lengths of the period frequently take place in a way that maintains this sense of equilibrium between the phrases. As a general rule, if the antecedent is altered from its four-measure

norm, then the consequent will be changed to restore the sense of symmetry.[15]

EXAMPLE 4.10: The ten measures of this period exhibit a symmetrical 5 + 5 grouping structure. A reconstructed normative version (ex. 4.10b) reveals that the theme has undergone two alterations. First, the half cadence ending the antecedent is extended by an extra measure of dominant harmony. Second, the contrasting idea of the consequent is expanded by an additional measure, thus establishing a symmetrical grouping structure by matching the length of the antecedent. Moreover, this second change allows the descending eighth-note motive of the contrasting idea to maintain its original tonic support (mm. 3 and 8) and also permits the new cadential melody (mm. 9–10) to correspond rhythmically to that of the half-cadential extension (mm. 4–5). Despite the apparent symmetry in grouping structure (5 + 5), a certain asymmetrical quality is projected by the 4 + 6 pattern as defined by the cadence points.[16]

The preceding example illustrates well the difference between extension and expansion. On the one hand, the structural end of the antecedent's contrasting idea, as articulated by the half cadence, occurs in its normative place—the downbeat of measure 4. Thus the formal functions of antecedent, contrasting idea, and cadence are fully established by that point. Measure 5 merely stretches out these functions in time. On the other hand, the consequent's contrasting idea is not fully expressed until the cadence finally arrives at measure 10. The phrase is thus lengthened as a result of an internal expansion of its component members, which occurs in the course of establishing the formal functions.

The next example features a new type of phrase alteration—*interpolation*.[17] An interpolation can be defined as musical material that is inserted between two logically succeeding formal functions, yet seeming not to belong to either function. An interpolation is distinguished from an extension largely through the absence of a motivic connection between the interpolated material and its preceding function, so that this function does not appear to be stretched out in time. (An extension, on the contrary, usually has an intimate motivic connection with the material that it is extending.) An interpolation can easily be eliminated in order to restore a more normative grouping structure.

EXAMPLE 4.11: The antecedent phrase is expanded to five measures by an interpolated rising eighth-note idea entering in the second half of measure 2. (The consequent phrase is similarly expanded.) This brief figure seems entirely unrelated to its preceding basic idea, yet it also does not belong to the contrasting idea (despite some obvious motivic connections). Moreover, the interpolated figure does not give the impression of extending the basic idea, which is clearly over by the beginning of measure 2. Finally, both interpolations can easily be excised in order to create a normative eight-measure period (ex. 4.11b).

Closer examination reveals that the interpolated lines play a

EXAMPLE 4.12 Beethoven, String Quartet in G, Op. 18/2, ii, 1–6

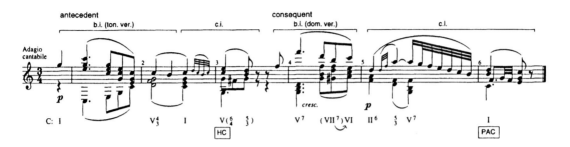

EXAMPLE 4.13 Mozart, Piano Sonata in C, K. 279/189d, iii, 1–10

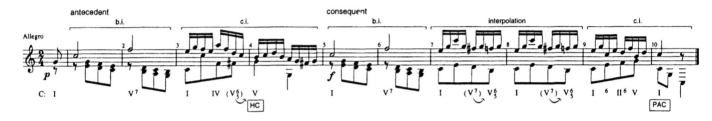

EXAMPLE 4.14 Mozart, Piano Sonata in A Minor, K. 310/300d, iii, 1–20

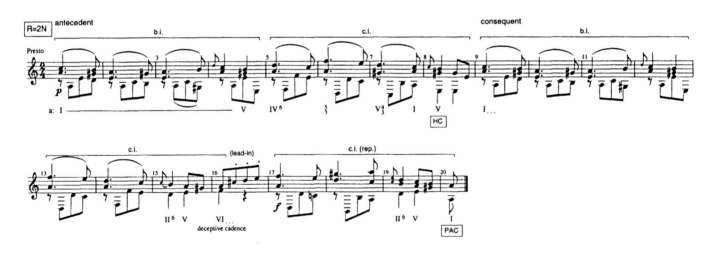

56

more important role in articulating formal functionality than might originally be thought. Note, first of all, that the basic idea has a strong cadential character: after the initial leap from E up to G, the melody "closes down" to the tonic scale-degree while being supported by a V–I progression. The interpolated figure then helps project an "opening up" of the melodic process by filling in stepwise the E to G leap, thus reasserting the initiating character so abruptly cut short by the end of the basic idea. The contrasting idea brings a further stepwise ascent to the high A, at which point the melody suddenly drops down for the half cadence. The gap left hanging by the high A is then filled in by a short lead-in, which inverts the chromatic line of the earlier interpolation. Following the restatement of the basic idea at the beginning of the consequent, the interpolated figure restores the high A abandoned at the end of the antecedent and continues the line, completing it up to C. The new contrasting idea begins with C (now an octave lower) and once more carries the stepwise ascent up to A, which then resolves back to G before leaping down again for the final cadence. Thus, rather than being merely incidental, the interpolations significantly participate in important melodic processes within the theme.

A symmetrically altered period can also result from the technique of phrase-structural compression.

EXAMPLE 4.12: Both the antecedent and consequent are compressed into three-measure phrases. The antecedent begins regularly enough with a two-measure basic idea, but the contrasting idea consists of a one-measure half cadence, thus resulting in a 2 + 1 grouping structure for the antecedent. The basic idea begins to be repeated at the start of the consequent, but this idea is broken off at the end of measure 4 when the melody suddenly leaps down a seventh from C to D. The remaining two measures then make up a normal contrasting idea, supported harmonically by an authentic cadential progression. The sudden change of dynamic level back to piano at the beginning of measure 5 further supports this 1 + 2 grouping structure. The 3 + 3 symmetry at the level of the phrase is thus complemented by a more subtle, less symmetrical 2 + 1, 1 + 2 structure at the level of the idea unit.

Asymmetrical Deviations

In the preceding examples, the consequent phrase was altered to match a deviation already present in the antecedent phrase and, in so doing, to preserve the inherent symmetry of the form. A different aesthetic effect occurs when the antecedent assumes its regular four-measure length, thus promising a normative period, but the consequent is altered to create an asymmetrical deviation. The asymmetry usually arises from an expansion of the consequent, but sometimes that function is extended when an expected perfect authentic cadence fails to appear for some reason or another, and the phrase (or portion thereof) is repeated in order to bring true cadential closure.

EXAMPLE 4.13: The consequent phrase lasts six measures because of the interpolation of measures 7–8. These two measures, which belong to neither the preceding basic idea nor the following con-

trasting idea, can easily be eliminated without disrupting the formal, harmonic, or melodic syntax of the theme. Although it is not obvious why Mozart inserted these extra measures, we can speculate that he wanted to achieve a greater rhythmic drive to the cadence than what a single measure (m. 9) could have provided. Moreover, the transition section immediately following this main theme features running sixteenth notes. This rhythm is better "prepared" by Mozart's asymmetrical period than by a hypothetical version that eliminates measures 7–8.[18]

EXAMPLE 4.14: The consequent promises to end in measure 16, but a deceptive cadence instead motivates an extension of the phrase. The cadential idea is repeated (with an important melodic variant, one that allows the line to reach a climax on the high A), and the theme achieves closure with the perfect authentic cadence at measure 20.

Irregular Closure of Antecedent Phrase

Reinterpreted half cadence. That an antecedent must close with a weak cadence is fundamental to the definition of the function. In some cases, however, this cadence appears to be irregular, yet we still want to recognize the presence of an antecedent. One common irregularity occurs when a presumed antecedent appears to modulate to the dominant region, closing there with a perfect authentic cadence, as in example 4.8, measures 3–4. Two principles of antecedent function are thus violated—that it close with a weak cadence and that it not modulate. Nonetheless, when the home key is immediately reinstituted at the beginning of the consequent phrase, the sense of modulation is instantly canceled, and we recognize instead that the antecedent has closed with a *reinterpreted half cadence*, as this commonly occurring cadential formation can be termed.

EXAMPLE 4.15: The opening four-measure phrase consists of a basic idea followed by a contrasting idea leading to a cadence. As the opening phrase of a theme, it sounds very much like an antecedent. Yet we also recognize that at the very surface of the harmonic activity, measure 3 brings a quick modulation to D major, the dominant region of the home key, G. The cadential formation at the end of the phrase is therefore a perfect authentic cadence. There is even the sense of a brief codetta in the second and third beats of measure 4 to confirm that cadential arrival. Yet when the music returns emphatically to G major at the beginning of the consequent phrase, it is easy to hear that the D-major harmony at the end of the antecedent marks a reinterpreted half cadence in the home key. It must be emphasized that the cadential formation in measures 3–4 of this example (as well as ex. 4.8) is literally a perfect authentic cadence. Only in the broader context of antecedent–consequent functionality does it become a reinterpreted half cadence.[19]

Melodic ambiguity. Another (potential) irregularity in the cadential closure of an antecedent phrase arises in connection with the definition of an imperfect authentic cadence. As a general rule, this type of cadence occurs when the final

EXAMPLE 4.15 Haydn, String Quartet in G, Op. 64/4, i, 1–8

EXAMPLE 4.16 Beethoven, Bagatelle in D, Op. 33/6, 1–8

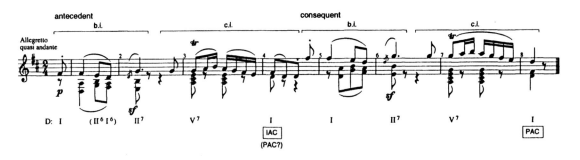

note in the melody remains open on the third scale-degree. In cases of an ornamented melody, however, it can sometimes be difficult to say exactly which note is the "final note" for purposes of this definition. On occasion, the last note of the melody appears to ornament the more fundamental melodic line, whose final note remains open on the third degree (see again chap. 3, n. 48).

EXAMPLE 4.16: Does the opening phrase end with a perfect or an imperfect authentic cadence? The decision depends on which note—the very final D or the preceding F♯ on the downbeat of the measure—is taken as the true structural end of the melody. Since an opening four-measure phrase of a theme does not normally end with full harmonic and melodic closure, we are inclined to believe that this phrase is an antecedent ending with an imperfect authentic cadence. When we perceive that the next phrase is a genuine consequent, closing unambiguously with a perfect authentic cadence, our initial hypothesis of a period design is confirmed. The final D of the antecedent is thus understood to be an embellishment (a "chordal skip") of the more fundamental melodic note, F♯.[20]

Hybrid Themes and Compound Themes

The sentence and period are presented by Schoenberg and his followers as fundamentally opposing theme-types. Indeed, Ratz regards the two forms as distinct not only structurally but also aesthetically:

> In the case of the period we have a symmetrical structure that has a certain "repose in itself" owing to the balance of its two halves, which are more or less equal. . . . The eight-measure sentence, however, contains a certain forward-striving character because of the increased activity and compression in its continuation phrase, making it fundamentally different in construction from the symmetrical organization of the period.[1]

This distinction between two fundamental theme-types notwithstanding, the actual compositional practice is considerably more complex.[2] Many themes are difficult to classify within the sentence/period model. To be sure, some bear little relation to either form;[3] however, a sizable number combine features of both types. These latter themes have received little theoretical discussion. At best, someone familiar with Schoenberg's ideas might observe that a given theme is "more like a sentence than a period" (or vice versa) but could not describe precisely how the theme fits into a theoretical framework consisting exclusively of two fundamental types.

This chapter develops more fully the idea that an individual theme can exhibit both sentential and periodic characteristics. The first part treats simple, eight-measure *hybrid themes*, as these mixed forms can be termed. The second part discusses the sixteen-measure period and the sixteen-measure sentence; these *compound themes* are dealt with here because they also typically combine form-functional traits of the sentence and period.

HYBRID THEMES

A hybrid theme, like a sentence or period, is normally constructed as an eight-measure unit divided into two phrases of four measures each. Four categories of hybrids can be identified based on the internal organization of these phrases.

Hybrid 1: antecedent + continuation. Many hybrid themes begin like a period but end like a sentence; that is, they are composed of a four-measure antecedent followed by a four-measure continuation.

EXAMPLE 5.1: The first phrase is a standard antecedent—a two-measure basic idea followed by a contrasting idea ending with a half cadence. The second phrase begins with new material and modulates to the dominant region. Since the basic idea does not return, the phrase cannot be considered a consequent. Rather, the phrase projects the most typical feature of continuation function—namely, fragmentation of the preceding two-measure ideas into one-measure units.[4]

If the second phrase of hybrid type 1 does not feature fragmentation, then the sense of continuation is somewhat weakened. Such cases, however, usually bring a perceptible increase in the rate of harmonic change so that the continuation function is sufficiently expressed.

EXAMPLE 5.2: Following a normal antecedent, the second phrase brings a new two-measure idea at measure 5 and closes with a simple cadential figure. This second phrase cannot be considered a consequent because the opening basic idea is not restated. Due to the lack of fragmentation, the phrase is not obviously continuational. Yet that function is nonetheless expressed by an increased harmonic rhythm and a considerably more active bass line (in comparison to the antecedent).

In the examples just discussed, the first phrase can be considered a genuine antecedent, despite its not being followed by a consequent. Although the pair antecedent/consequent creates a logical succession, the two functions need not be linked together in all formal situations, and their mutual presence is not a necessary condition for their individual expression. The same independence holds for presentation and continuation phrases as well. Intrathematic functions in general need not be confined to the standard theme-types with which they are conventionally associated (i.e., period, sentence). Not all combinations of phrases make up a syntactical arrangement of functions, however: a consequent followed by a presentation, for ex-

EXAMPLE 5.1 Mozart, Piano Sonata in C, K. 330/300h, ii, 1–8

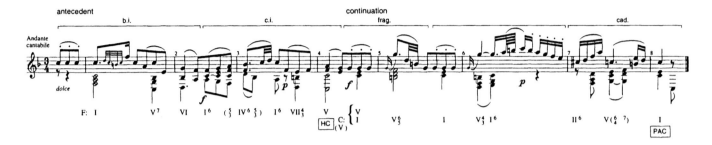

EXAMPLE 5.2 Beethoven, Symphony No. 2 in D, Op. 36, ii, 1–8

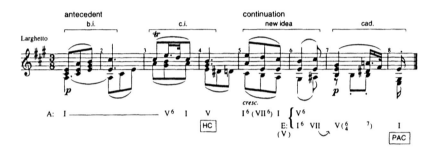

EXAMPLE 5.3 Beethoven, Violin Sonata in D, Op. 12/1, iii, 1–8

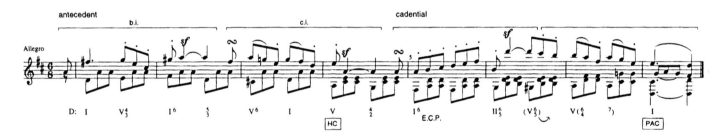

EXAMPLE 5.4 Haydn, String Quartet in G, Op. 64/4, ii, 1–8

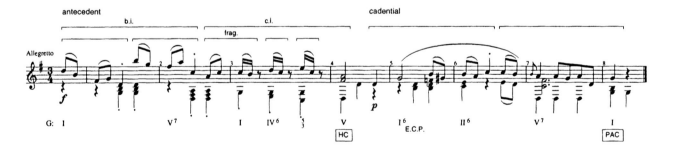

ample, would be functionally illogical. The hybrid type antecedent + continuation, on the contrary, is entirely logical, because an initiating function (antecedent) is followed by medial and concluding functions (continuation and cadential, fused into a single continuation phrase). The other hybrid types also conform to this logical arrangement of general form-functional elements.

Hybrid 2: antecedent + cadential.   A second hybrid type features an antecedent followed by a phrase built exclusively on an expanded cadential progression. In the context of a sentence, this latter phrase is termed continuation⇒ cadential because we expect a presentation to lead to a continuation and because the phrase usually does contain traits of this function. But in the context of an implied period, as suggested by an initial antecedent, the situation is different: not only do we not expect an ensuing continuation, but the phrase supported by the expanded cadential progression often displays few, if any, continuational characteristics. Thus following an antecedent, the second phrase of this hybrid type can be considered exclusively cadential in function.

EXAMPLE 5.3: The first phrase is a regular antecedent closing with a half cadence in measure 4. The next phrase brings new material built over an expanded cadential progression. Since the music continues to group itself into two-measure units, like the antecedent, there is no sense of fragmentation; neither is there any acceleration of harmonic rhythm. (In fact, the harmonies slow down somewhat.) Due to the lack of any continuational features, the phrase is best labeled cadential.

EXAMPLE 5.4: The antecedent phrase itself is sentential: the basic idea is made up of two, one-measure motives (like a miniature presentation), and the contrasting idea has manifest continuational traits. The following phrase is exclusively cadential, for it does not suggest a continuation function in the least: the new two-measure melody projects no sense of fragmentation, and the rate of harmonic change diminishes considerably.[5]

Hybrid 3: compound basic idea + continuation.   By definition, an antecedent contains a basic idea followed by a contrasting idea leading to a weak cadence. If a cadence does not appear at the end of the phrase, then an essential component of antecedent function has been lost. What is the function of such a phrase? Inasmuch as the lack of cadential closure creates a sense of open-endedness, the phrase takes on the character and function of a higher-level basic idea. Thus the term *compound basic idea* can be applied to a phrase consisting of a simple basic idea and a contrasting idea that does not close with a cadence.[6] By virtue of its melodic–motivic content, a compound basic idea resembles an antecedent. In light of its underlying harmony, which is usually (but not always) tonic prolongational, a compound basic idea resembles a presentation. Thus the four-measure phrase itself represents a hybrid of antecedent and presentation functions.

EXAMPLE 5.5: At first glance, the opening phrase might seem to be a regular antecedent: a basic idea is followed by a contrasting idea ending with a dominant triad in measure 4. But since that dominant first appears in measure 3 to support the entire contrasting idea, we cannot identify a specific progression to create a half cadence in the final measure of the phrase. Indeed, the phrase contains a single I–V[7] tonic prolongation. Because of the lack of cadence, the opening phrase must be defined as a compound basic idea. The following phrase is a typical continuation featuring fragmentation and harmonic acceleration and closing with a perfect authentic cadence.[7]

If the phrase following a compound basic idea is built over an expanded cadential progression, then its function may be simply cadential or, more often, continuation⇒ cadential (the latter being appropriate if the phrase contains continuational characteristics).

EXAMPLE 5.6: The first phrase is a compound basic idea because the underlying tonic pedal destroys any potential for cadential closure. The following phrase has an expanded cadential progression at its basis. Since it also features marked acceleration in harmonic rhythm, the phrase is best labeled continuation⇒cadential. (The final cadence is most likely an imperfect authentic cadence, the final C being an "overhang"; see chap. 3, n. 48).[8]

Hybrid 4: compound basic idea + consequent.   In this fourth, and final, category of hybrid themes, a compound basic idea is followed by a consequent rather than a continuation, as in the previous category. Thus, the opening basic idea returns in measures 5 and 6, and the theme ends with a perfect authentic cadence. Hybrids of this type differ from periods in only one respect: they lack the weak cadence in the fourth measure of the theme.

EXAMPLE 5.7: The first phrase is a compound basic idea; the absence of any harmonic motion into measure 24 prohibits us from recognizing any cadence there. The second phrase brings back the initial basic idea (now supported by dominant harmony), and the subsequent contrasting idea brings an emphatic perfect authentic cadence to close the theme.[9]

When a compound basic idea is supported by a tonic prolongational progression, as is usually the case, the harmonic organization of the phrase resembles a presentation. As discussed in chapter 3, the tonic prolongation of a presentation may not reach completion until after the continuation has begun (see ex. 3.4). The same situation may occur in connection with a compound basic idea and its following phrase (be it a continuation or a consequent).

EXAMPLE 5.8: The contrasting idea of the compound basic idea is supported by II, which continues on into the following phrase

EXAMPLE 5.5 Haydn, Piano Sonata in C, Hob. XVI:35, i, 1–8

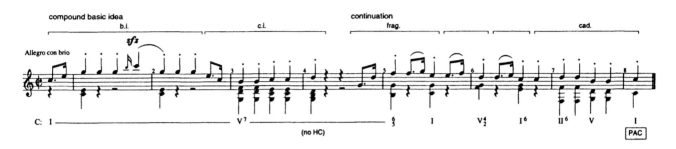

EXAMPLE 5.6 Haydn, Symphony No. 95 in C Minor, iii, 1–8

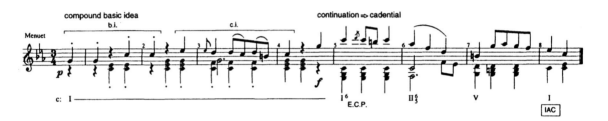

EXAMPLE 5.7 Beethoven, String Quartet in G, Op. 18/2, iv, 21–28

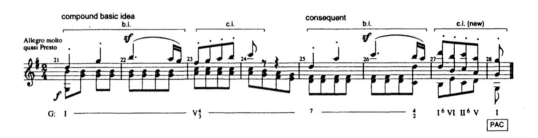

EXAMPLE 5.8 Haydn, Symphony No. 87 in A, iii, 1–8

sentence	hybrid 3	hybrid 1	hybrid 2	hybrid 4	period
pres. + cont.	c.b.i. + cont.	ant. + cont.	ant. + cad.	c.b.i. + cons.	ant. + cons.

FIGURE 5.1 Relation of the hybrids to the sentence and the period.

until the arrival of V⁷-I in measures 6-7. Thus a single tonic prolongation underlies the first seven measures of the theme, which then closes with a simple cadential progression. (The absence of pre-dominant in this cadential progression is due not only to lack of space but also to the earlier prominence of supertonic harmony in measures 3-5.)

The second phrase has a consequent function, as marked by the return of the basic idea. Note, however, that the increased harmonic activity in this phrase imparts a degree of continuational expression as well. Indeed, the consequent phrase in this hybrid category frequently accelerates the harmonic rhythm in comparison to the preceding compound basic idea, whose tonic prolongation generally brings a relatively slow rate of harmonic change.

Additional issues. Inasmuch as hybrid themes combine functional elements from both the sentence and period, it is possible to situate the four hybrid categories within a spectrum of formal possibilities, where the sentence and period occupy the two extreme positions (see figure 5.1). Hybrid 3 (compound basic idea + continuation) is very much like a sentence, except that the basic idea is not repeated. Hybrid 4 (compound basic idea + consequent) closely resembles a period. Hybrid 1 (antecedent + continuation) contains aspects of the sentence and period in equal measure, and hybrid 2 (antecedent + cadential) is somewhat more periodic, since continuational traits are missing.

Of the logically possible ways in which the various phrases of the sentence and period can be combined to make a hybrid, one pattern is conspicuously absent—a theme that begins with a presentation and ends with a consequent. As shown in figure 5.2, such an arrangement of phrases brings a threefold statement of the basic idea. The resulting redundancy of material within an excessive tonic prolongation likely explains why this potential type of hybrid seldom occurs in the repertory.

At this point we might inquire why hybrid themes appear regularly throughout classical compositions. An obvious answer, of course, is that they offer more options beyond the sentence or period for shaping a logically satisfying theme. But they also offer something more: the latent ambiguity of a hybrid—is it more like a sentence or more

like a period?—renders it especially suitable for assimilating itself to a higher-level unit of more conventional thematic design, such as the sixteen-measure period, the small ternary, or the small binary. To be sure, some hybrids stand entirely alone, although most form part of a larger thematic whole.[10]

Aside from the general sense of structural ambiguity latent in all hybrid themes, a more specific technical feature in the first three categories of hybrids helps explain their tendency to be used in larger forms. With the exception of hybrid 4 (compound basic idea + consequent), the basic idea of a hybrid is stated only once in the theme. This situation is different from both the sentence and the period, in which the basic idea appears twice, either immediately repeated (as in the sentence) or following an intervening contrasting idea (as in the period). Such hybrid themes are thus useful in certain larger-scale contexts when it is desirable that the basic idea *not* reappear within the eight-measure scope of the theme. One such formal context involves the sixteen-measure period, a compound theme to be considered next.[11]

Hybrid themes containing a single statement of the basic idea are also useful as the first section of a small ternary or small binary when that section modulates to a related region (usually the dominant). In such cases, a hybrid can often be more effective than a period in consolidating the sense of the new key. With the period, the consequent phrase usually brings tonic harmony of the home key in measures 5 and 6 of the theme in order to support the restated basic idea. As a result, there is little room left in the eight-measure span of the theme for the modulation to take place. In the case of a hybrid, however, the use of a continuation (or cadential) phrase provides more space in which to effect the change of key.

COMPOUND THEMES

The simple sentence and period are defined as normative eight-measure themes whose constituent phrases may be

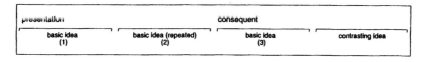

presentation		consequent	
basic idea (1)	basic idea (repeated) (2)	basic idea (3)	contrasting idea

FIGURE 5.2 Uncommon hybrid type—presentation + consequent.

EXAMPLE 5.9 Beethoven, Piano Concerto No. 2 in B-flat, Op. 19, iii, 1–17

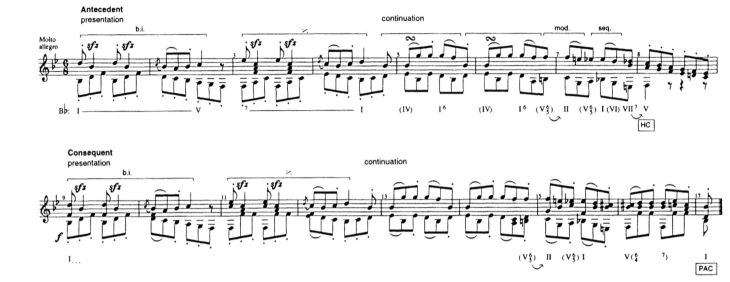

EXAMPLE 5.10 Beethoven, Piano Sonata in C Minor, Op. 10/1, ii, 1–16

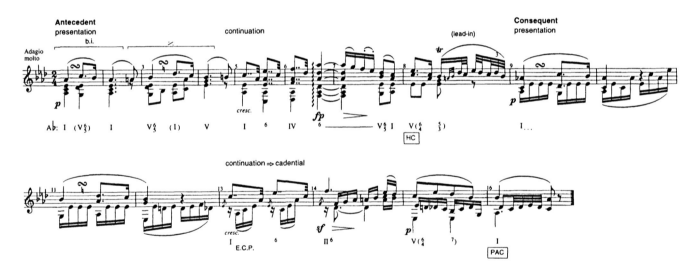

shortened or lengthened by standard alteration techniques (extension, expansion, compression, and interpolation). More complex versions of these two forms appear regularly in the classical repertory. Such *compound themes* are defined as structures containing sixteen real measures.[12] The compound sixteen-measure period consists of an eight-measure antecedent followed by an eight-measure consequent; the compound sixteen-measure sentence consists of an eight-measure presentation followed by an eight-measure continuation (fusing continuation and cadential functions).[13] Like simple eight-measure themes, the length of a compound theme may be altered by extension, compression, and so forth.

Sixteen-Measure Period

The sixteen-measure period is constructed out of two eight-measure themes. The first theme (built as either a simple sentence or a hybrid) acquires an antecedent function by closing with a weak cadence, normally a half cadence but also possibly an imperfect authentic cadence.[14] The second theme (also a sentence or a hybrid) becomes a consequent by repeating the first theme but concluding with the stronger perfect authentic cadence. Thus the essential features of repetition and cadence that define antecedent and consequent functions for the eight-measure period apply to the sixteen-measure period as well.[15]

The major difference between simple and compound periods lies in the internal organization of the antecedent and consequent units. In the eight-measure period, the four-measure antecedent (and consequent) phrase is built out of a two-measure basic idea and a two-measure contrasting idea. In the sixteen-measure period, the corresponding "ideas" of the large antecedent (and consequent) are four-measure *phrases*, some of which are themselves composed of simple basic or contrasting ideas. The phrase functions making up the large antecedent and consequent units are drawn from those associated with simple themes. The first half of each unit can be built as a presentation, antecedent, or compound basic idea, and the second half is most always a continuation (or else a continuation⇒cadential). A four-measure consequent is not normally found within a sixteen-measure period.[16]

Most sixteen-measure periods can be assigned to one of three categories on the basis of these phrase combinations. Since the eight-measure antecedent is repeated in the subsequent consequent, the following categories are labeled with reference to the organization of the antecedent alone.

Antecedent = presentation + continuation. A compound period from this category is made up of two eight-measure sentences: the first sentence ends with a weak cadence, and the second, a repetition of the first, ends with a perfect authentic cadence. This type of compound period represents the full-fledged development of the simple period whose four-measure antecedent has a miniature sentential design (see ex. 4.6).

EXAMPLE 5.9: Both the antecedent and consequent units display the main characteristics of the sentence: a presentation with statement–response repetition; a continuation with fragmentation, harmonic acceleration, model–sequence technique; and a concluding cadence (slightly expanded in the consequent to permit the final tonic to appear on a metrically strong beat).[17]

Like the simple sentence, the phrase following the presentation may be based on an expanded cadential progression and thus acquire continuation⇒cadential function.

EXAMPLE 5.10: The antecedent unit contains regular presentation and continuation phrases. The consequent restates the original presentation but alters the expected continuation so as to be supported by a single expanded cadential progression; hence the phrase is appropriately labeled continuation⇒cadential. Such cadential expansion, lasting an entire phrase in the context of a compound period, is analogous to a cadential progression that supports the complete two-measure contrasting idea in a simple period.

This example illustrates another aspect of periodic structure, which was examined earlier in connection with the simple period—namely, the tendency for the cadential progression of the consequent to be more expanded than that of the antecedent. Here, the antecedent closes with a brief half-cadential progression from the very end of measure 7 to measure 8; the consequent expands the progression to four measures (mm. 13–16). (In retrospect, we can observe that the continuation of the large-scale antecedent also begins with a potential expanded cadential progression in measures 5–6, one that is abandoned with the move to V^6_5 in the middle of measure 7.)[18]

Antecedent = compound basic idea + continuation. In this category, the large antecedent (and consequent) is constructed as a hybrid theme of type 3 (compound basic idea + continuation). The term compound basic idea gains in appropriateness more in the context of compound themes than in the simple hybrids, where it was first introduced. A four-measure compound basic idea occupies the same hierarchical position in a sixteen-measure period as a two-measure basic idea does in an eight-measure period.

EXAMPLE 5.11: Traditional theory would perhaps identify a "plagal" cadence at the end of the first phrase. But the subdominant in measure 4 simply embellishes the tonic prolongation that supports the compound basic idea. Just as the two contrasting ideas in a simple period need not contain the same material, so may the two continuation phrases in a sixteen-measure period also exhibit diverse melodic–motivic content, as in this example.[19]

EXAMPLE 5.12: The second phrase of the antecedent (mm. 7–10) has continuation⇒cadential function: the expanded cadential progression brings a manifest harmonic acceleration in relation to the

EXAMPLE 5.11 Mozart, Piano Concerto in A, K. 488, i, 1–16

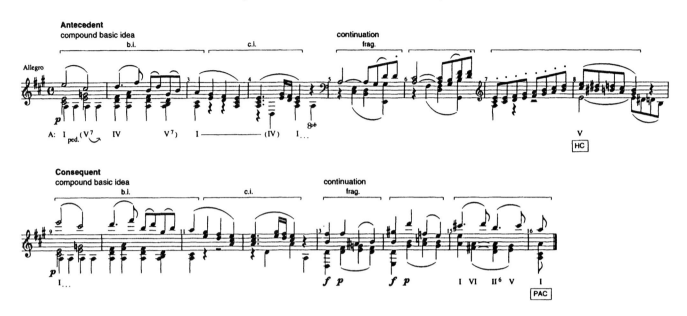

EXAMPLE 5.12 Haydn, String Quartet in C, Op. 74/1, i, 3–18

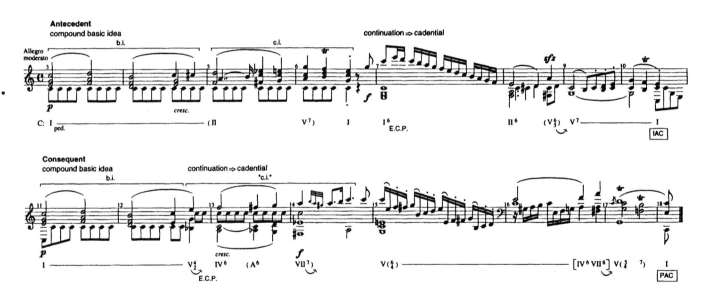

EXAMPLE 5.13 Beethoven, Piano Sonata in A-flat, Op. 26, i, 1–16

tonic pedal of the compound basic idea (mm. 3–6). The sudden flurry of sixteenth notes at measure 7 also adds continuational character to the phrase.

The consequent is significantly altered in relation to the antecedent, especially with respect to harmonic organization. The last beat of measure 12 initiates a move away from the tonic pedal of the basic idea. The new contrasting idea is then supported by a variety of pre-dominant harmonies. The dominant finally arrives at measure 15 and is prolonged (with the help of neighboring chords in m. 16) until the final tonic of the perfect authentic cadence. A large expanded cadential progression is thus created, beginning with V⁷/IV (as the initial tonic) and continuing for the remaining six measures of the theme.

Because of the underlying harmony, cadential function in the consequent must be seen to begin in measure 13, but a definite continuational quality is expressed at this point as well, since compared with the static tonic pedal of the basic idea, the bass line in measures 13–14 projects a significant increase in rhythmic activity. The consequent phrase thus consists of a two-measure basic idea followed by a six-measure continuation⇒cadential phrase. This formal arrangement is markedly different, of course, from that of the antecedent. Nevertheless, from the point of view of melodic organization, we still recognize formal remnants of the earlier section: measures 11–14 clearly suggest a compound basic idea, and the sixteenth-note flurry in measure 15 corresponds to the analogous moment in the antecedent (m. 7).

This theme presents an interesting variant on the technique of expanding the cadential function in the consequent relative to the antecedent (as discussed in connection with ex. 5.10). Since the antecedent already featured an expanded cadential progression of four measures, the cadential progression of the consequent is even further expanded to six measures. To accommodate this greater expansion within the eight-measure norm, Haydn uses the contrasting idea of what would have been a compound basic idea as the starting point of the continuation⇒cadential phrase.[20]

Antecedent = antecedent + continuation. This category features hybrid type 1 as the basis of both antecedent and consequent units.

EXAMPLE 5.13: This passage illustrates well the model form. The initial four-measure antecedent is followed by a continuation featuring fragmentation into two-beat units (which develop the upward fourth leap at the beginning of the basic idea), a marked acceleration of the harmony, and a second half cadence to close the eight-measure antecedent. The return of the basic idea is saved for measures 9–10 to signal the large-scale consequent.[21]

The use of a four-measure antecedent as the first part of an eight-measure antecedent implies the idea of a "period within a period" or a "double period" (see n. 15). However, the appearance of a continuation instead of a consequent undermines genuine periodic expression at the lower level. Indeed, the classical composers rarely use a simple period to build the antecedent and consequent units of a compound period.[22] Their avoidance of such a double period has a logical aesthetic explanation: the return of the basic idea in measures 9–10 of the theme (required for marking the higher-level consequent) would be preempted, and hence spoiled in its effect, if the basic idea were to reappear in measures 5–6 in order to project a lower-level consequent. For the same reason, hybrid type 4 (compound basic idea + consequent) is not used in a sixteen-measure period because the appearance of the basic idea to signal the lower-level consequent would poorly anticipate the higher-level consequent. This problem is circumvented if the large antecedent is built as a sentence or as hybrid types 1 or 3. In the case of the sentence, the basic idea is immediately repeated, but it does not return until the beginning of the higher-

EXAMPLE 5.14 Haydn, Symphony No. 93 in D, iv, 1–16

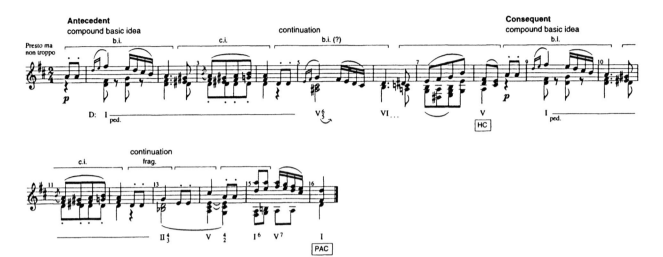

EXAMPLE 5.15 Beethoven, Piano Concerto No. 3 in C Minor, Op. 37, i, 1–16

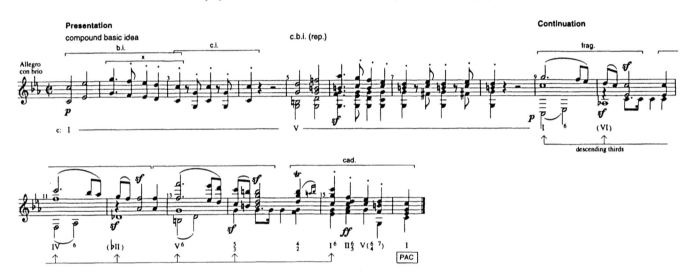

EXAMPLE 5.16 Haydn, String Quartet in G, Op.77/1, i, 1–14

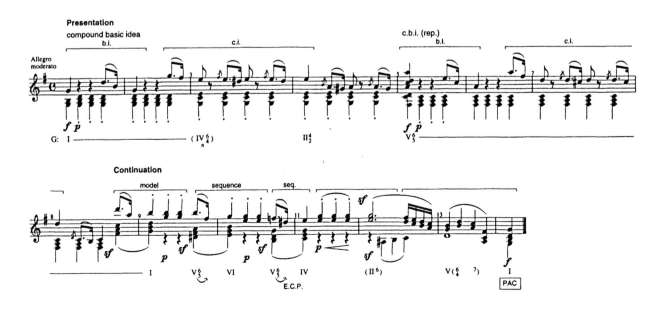

level consequent. With either of the hybrids, the basic idea appears in the larger antecedent just once and returns only in measures 9–10 of the compound theme.[23]

At first glance, some themes in the repertory seem to violate the general principle just enunciated, inasmuch as measures 5–6 bring melodic–motivic material resembling the basic idea, thus suggesting a lower-level consequent. But a closer look at this "basic idea" reveals that it is supported by different harmonies and that it returns with its original harmonic support only in measure 9, which marks the beginning of the higher-level consequent.

EXAMPLE 5.14: The theme opens with a compound basic idea built over a tonic pedal. The next phrase appears to bring back the basic idea in the manner of a consequent, but the supporting harmonies, which are entirely different from those of the opening basic idea, accelerate the harmonic rhythm and thus suggest a continuation function. A more exact restatement of the basic idea in measures 9–10, with its initial harmonization, signals the real consequent of this theme. The last phrase (mm. 13–16) brings an unambiguous continuation expressed foremost by fragmentation.[24]

Sixteen-Measure Sentence

Model form. The model sixteen-measure sentence consists of an eight-measure presentation followed by an eight-measure continuation. The presentation contains a compound basic idea and its immediate repetition, both supported by a tonic prolongational progression.[25] The continuation is characterized by fragmentation, harmonic acceleration, sequential harmonies, or increased surface rhythm. The cadential progression is usually expanded to support the final four-measure phrase. The sixteen-measure sentence most often closes with a perfect authentic cadence; a concluding half cadence is rare (but see ex. 5.18, discussed shortly in the next section).

EXAMPLE 5.15: The presentation features statement–response repetition of a compound basic idea. The continuation develops the second motive ("x") from the initial two-measure basic idea in the context of phrase-structural fragmentation and harmonic acceleration. (The opening motive from the basic idea is also present in the bass voice.) Although the underlying harmony of the continuation is quite functional, I–IV–V–I⁶, the use of substitute chords (VI and ♭II) and the choice of bass notes on the downbeats of each measure strongly suggest a descending third sequential progression.[26]

Compressed continuation. Whereas it is in the nature of the period to maintain a balance between its antecedent and consequent functions, the sentence, with its forward-striving character, has less need to preserve a symmetrical phrase structure. In particular, the formal functions of continuation and cadence can often be fully expressed in fewer than the eight measures offered by the model form. Thus, many compound sentences compress their continuation and cadential functions into a single four-measure continuation or continuation⇒cadential phrase, like that of a simple sentence. Even when the continuation is compressed, however, the composer may restore a semblance of symmetrical organization by repeating the continuation phrase or by adding a postcadential extension, thus stretching the theme back to its normative sixteen-measure length.

EXAMPLE 5.16: In the model form, the continuation usually fragments the preceding four-measure compound basic ideas into two-measure segments (see the preceding example). This procedure results in a 2:1 ratio between the original unit and the fragment.[27] Further fragmentation may then produce one-measure segments, which again yields a 2:1 ratio. In this example, the beginning of the continuation suddenly reduces the unit size from four measures (in the presentation) to a single measure, which results in a compressed continuation of six measures. Underlying the fragmentation is a descending third sequential progression, whose last link, V⁶₅/IV–IV, also marks the beginning of an expanded cadential progression.[28]

EXAMPLE 5.17: The presentation is followed by a four-measure continuation⇒cadential phrase ending with a deceptive cadence in measure 12. The failure to realize a genuine cadence motivates a repetition of the phrase, which brings the expected perfect authentic cadence. The repetition also reestablishes phrase-structural symmetry when eight measures of continuation and cadential function now match the preceding eight-measure presentation.[29]

EXAMPLE 5.18: A compressed continuation leads to a half cadence in measure 12. Although the theme has technically ended at this point, a subsequent four-measure standing on the dominant extends the passage to sixteen measures, thus restoring a sense of balance with the presentation.

The preceding discussion has focused on the compressed continuation because this deviation technique is most characteristic of the sixteen-measure sentence. Other methods of altering the model form are also employed by the classical composers, including the use of extension, expansion, and interpolation, devices sufficiently exemplified in previous discussion to not warrant further attention here.

EXAMPLE 5.17 Mozart, Clarinet Trio in E-flat, K. 498, i, 1–16

EXAMPLE 5.18 Haydn, Symphony No. 83 in G Minor ("The Hen"), i, 1–16

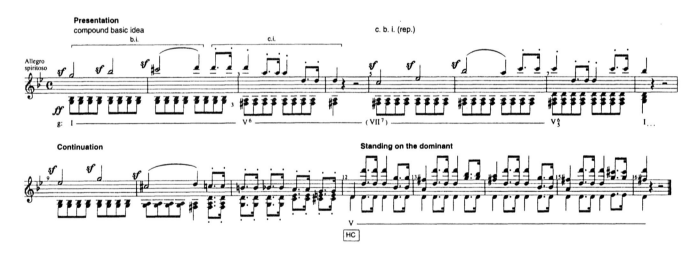

6

Small Ternary

The small ternary is one of the most important forms in all of classical instrumental music.[1] As a theme-type in its own right, the small ternary can constitute the main theme of any full-movement form (sonata, rondo, concerto, etc.). The theme of most theme and variations movements is built as a small ternary. And the form, at times highly modified, can make up all three sections of the slow-movement large ternary form, as well as an interior theme of a rondo form.[2] In addition to functioning as an individual thematic unit, the small ternary can replicate the basic formal and tonal plan found in the full-movement minuet and sonata forms. Thus, more than any other theme-type, the small ternary raises issues of musical form that transcend the scope of simple thematic organization.

The small ternary consists of three main sections, which express the formal functions of exposition (A), contrasting middle (B), and recapitulation (A'). The exposition is constructed as a tight-knit theme,[3] most often a period, but also possibly a sentence, hybrid, or even a nonconventional design. This theme ends with a perfect authentic cadence in either the home key or, in the case of a modulating A section, a closely related, subordinate key.[4] The exposition occasionally ends with a brief closing section that consists of one or more codettas.

The contrasting middle section achieves its sense of contrast primarily by harmonic and phrase-structural means and only secondarily by melodic–motivic means. Whereas the exposition emphasizes tonic harmony (by beginning and ending with this harmonic function), the contrasting middle emphasizes dominant harmony. The harmonic goal of the section is, with rare exceptions, the dominant of the home key, and this harmony is frequently found at the very beginning of the section as well. The phrase structure of the B section is looser and usually less conventional in its thematic design than the preceding A section is.

The recapitulation represents a return, either complete or partial, of the exposition. The section must begin with the basic idea from the exposition and close in the home key with a perfect authentic cadence. If the A section has modulated, the A' section must be adjusted to remain entirely in the home key.

Many small ternaries are built unequivocally out of three discrete sections, fully distinguished from one another by marked changes in musical content and formal organization. The form appears more often, however, in a way that somewhat obscures its tripartite organization. In these cases, the A section is immediately repeated before the onset of the B section, and then, following the end of the A' section, B and A' together are repeated. The composer usually indicates this structure by repeat signs, although the repeated sections are occasionally written out in order to introduce ornamental changes. Since these repetitions produce a distinctly two-part design, many theorists and historians have labeled this a "binary" form. More specifically, the term "rounded binary" has been employed in recognition of the return of material from the opening of the first part later in the second part.

One of the most vigorous debates in the history of theory concerns whether the simple form under consideration here (as well as its more expanded manifestation, the sonata) consists essentially of two or three parts. Advocates of the binary view argue from a number of positions. They observe, for example, that the two sections are often similar in length and thus display a kind of symmetrical balance. Some theorists point to the repetition scheme, noting that the so-called middle section (of the ternary view) is structurally dependent on the subsequent A' section and, hence, cannot be repeated in its own right. Finally, supporters of the binary view stress that when the first part modulates, the overall tonal process—the movement away from, and ultimate return to, the home key—expresses a fundamentally bipartite shape, to which the more tripartite melodic organization is merely secondary.

Supporters of the ternary position argue that the binary view minimizes two significant aspects of formal expression—the notion of a truly contrasting middle, and the idea of recapitulating the opening material. These are, of course, two of the functional components of the form emphasized in our discussion up to now.

When the arguments of both sides are sorted out, the theoretical conflict would seem to disappear, since the opposing positions are incompatible neither with each other

EXAMPLE 6.1 Mozart, String Quartet in D Minor, K. 421/417b, ii, 1–26

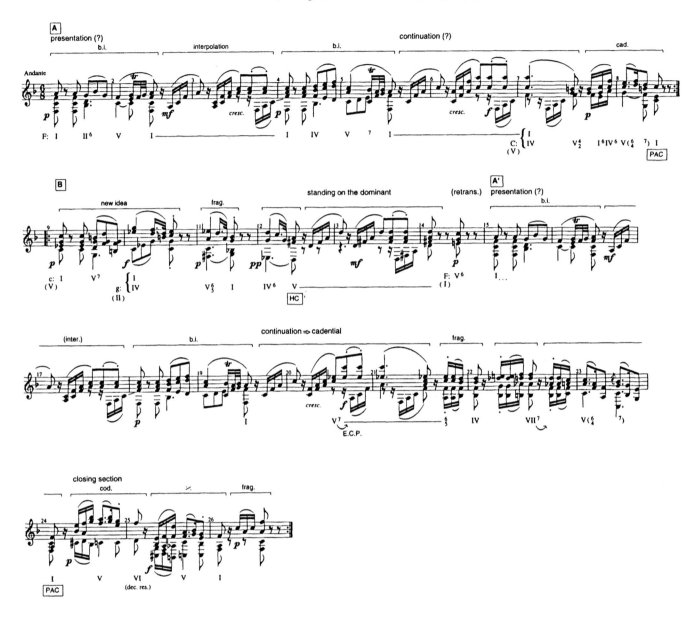

nor with the empirical facts presented by the music. Both views say something important about formal organization in this theme-type, and there is no reason to completely reject one or the other.

It should be clear that this book emphasizes the ternary approach because of its greater compatibility with issues of formal functionality. Nevertheless, notions of a more specifically binary theme prove useful in two differing contexts. First, another theme-type—the *small binary*—is defined as functionally distinct from the small ternary (chap. 7). Second, the term *rounded binary* can be used in cases in which the two-part character of the small ternary form is given prominence through the repetition of the sections. The small ternary and rounded binary must be understood, nonetheless, as essentially the same form; that is, they both contain the three functions of exposition, contrasting middle, and recapitulation.

EXPOSITION

The exposition section of a small ternary (rounded binary) is built as a relatively tight knit, self-contained theme, one whose internal harmonic and melodic processes are brought to a close by means of a perfect authentic cadence, in either the home key or a subordinate key.[5] All the conventional theme-types discussed in the previous chapters (sentence, period, hybrid) can be used to construct an exposition.

Model forms. Most often the A section consists of an eight-measure period or an eight-measure hybrid with periodic characteristics (antecedent + continuation or compound basic idea + consequent). If the period remains in the home key, it has the potential of functioning alone as a complete main theme, followed by some other thematic unit (such as a transition, subordinate theme, or interior theme). When a contrasting middle and recapitulation ensue instead, the listener understands in retrospect that the initial period functions as the exposition of a small ternary.[6] Conversely, if the exposition modulates to a new key, the change of key will set up powerful expectations for a following B section, because a modulating theme cannot function by itself as a main theme, a formal function that must always close in the home key.[7] The eight-measure sentence and the sentential hybrid (compound basic idea + continuation) are used less frequently as the basis of an exposition,[8] and compound themes are even more rarely encountered.[9]

Nonconventional forms. The exposition can also be constructed in a nonconventional manner, although a sense of tight-knit organization (symmetrical grouping structure, emphases on tonic harmony, unity of melodic–motivic material) is usually expressed nonetheless. A nonconventional exposition may contain, for example, multiple thematic units,[10] or it may consist of a single phrase, thus resulting in an incomplete theme.[11] At other times, the exposition includes material that only remotely relates to one of the conventional theme-types.

EXAMPLE 6.1: The constituent elements of this exposition are difficult to interpret functionally. The opening two-measure idea can be viewed as a basic idea, although its supporting harmonies and melodic contour (save the final upward turn) are entirely cadential in nature. A contrasting idea seems to start in measure 3, only to be cut short by a return of the "basic idea" in measures 4–5.[12] As a result, measure 3 can be understood instead as an interpolation, whose marked change in texture and lack of harmonic progression give it the impression of not entirely belonging to the prevailing functional unfolding.[13] Two functional interpretations have emerged thus far in the theme: first, the passage can be understood as beginning with an antecedent, whose contrasting idea has been interrupted by a return of the basic idea (to mark a consequent); or, second, the passage can be regarded as a presentation, whose restatement of the basic idea is interrupted by an interpolation. In light of what happens in the rest of the theme, the second interpretation of a sentential scheme is perhaps preferable to the first interpretation of a periodic one.

The material of measure 3 returns at measure 6. But since this music is now extended to bring about a modulation to the subordinate key (V), it seems to have a greater functional significance than before, when it simply prolonged the tonic harmony from the end of the basic idea. Moreover, following as it does on a presentation of sorts (assuming the second interpretation), the material now forms itself into a definite continuation, which ultimately ends with a one-measure cadential idea that confirms the new key. To summarize, the theme is probably best interpreted in terms of the sentential functions, yet it also distributes its material in a decidedly periodic fashion (alternating basic and contrasting ideas). Since the theme cannot be classified as one of the regular hybrids, it must ultimately be seen as nonconventional in form.

Despite its lack of conventional organization, this exposition embodies some distinctly tight-knit characteristics. Until the point of modulation, the home-key tonic is emphasized by means of two cadential progressions and further tonic prolongation in measures 3 and 6. And although the internal grouping structure is obviously asymmetrical, the exposition as a whole fills a conventional eight-measure mold. Finally, the A section proves to be more tightly knit than either of the following B and A' sections, whose decidedly loose organization is discussed later.

Closing section. The exposition of a small ternary occasionally concludes with a postcadential closing section consisting of one or more codettas. As discussed in chapter 1, a codetta prolongs the tonic at the end of an authentic cadence, often within the context of a recessive dynamic that helps dispel the energy built up in achieving the cadence.

EXAMPLE 6.2: Following a modulating eight-measure period, the exposition ends with a brief closing section, which consists of a one-measure codetta that is immediately repeated. The final fortissimo

EXAMPLE 6.2 Haydn, Piano Sonata in G, Hob. XVI:40, ii, 1–24

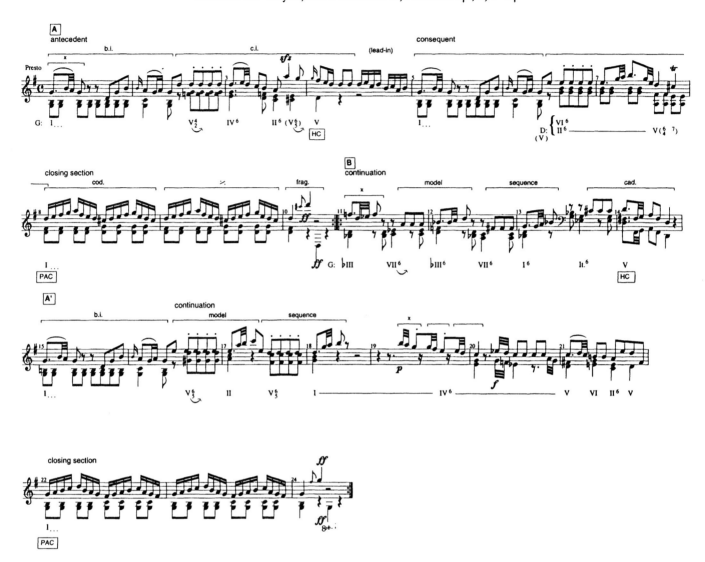

EXAMPLE 6.3 Mozart, *Eine kleine Nachtmusik*, K. 525, ii, 9–16

Ds in measure 10 should also be regarded as a codetta, thus bringing about fragmentation in relation to the preceding codettas. Although the flurry of running sixteenth notes in measures 8-9 might appear to counter a sense of recessive dynamic, their placement immediately following the cadential figure in measure 7 has a definite recessive effect nonetheless. It is as though a spring was wound up in measure 7 and finally released in the closing section, thus dissipating the accumulated energy of the theme.[14]

CONTRASTING MIDDLE

The contrasting middle of the small ternary is more loosely organized than the preceding exposition. This looser organization is achieved by a variety of means, foremost among them being harmonic. Whereas the exposition expresses the stability of tonic harmony (the section normally begins with tonic and closes with an authentic cadential progression), the contrasting middle expresses the instability of dominant harmony. The B section often starts on the home-key dominant and, with few exceptions, concludes with that harmony. (In some cases, the section consists entirely of a standing on the dominant.) Prominent sequential progressions can reinforce this harmonic instability all the more.[15]

The contrasting middle also achieves a looser organization through phrase-structural means. The B section is usually less symmetrical than the A section and frequently undergoes expansions, compressions, interpolations, and the like. Although intrathematic functions associated with tight-knit forms are often found in the contrasting middle, they do not usually organize themselves into a conventional thematic design. Occasionally, the B section contains an eight-measure sentence ending with a half cadence, but the period form is rarely (if ever) used.[16]

Whereas the B section contrasts with the A section primarily by means of harmony and phrase structure, the appearance of new melodic–motivic material can create contrast as well. The B section may also feature prominent changes in dynamics, articulation, texture, and accompanimental figuration. The use of polyphonic devices, especially motivic imitation among the voices, often distinguishes the contrasting middle from the exposition, which is usually more homophonic in texture.[17]

An examination of the classical repertory reveals that the contrasting middle never elides with the exposition. That is, the final measure of the A section cannot at the same time be construed as the first measure of the B section. Rather, the contrasting middle always begins in the measure following the end of the exposition. Likewise, the B and A' sections do not normally elide. This lack of elision has both historical and theoretical explanations. Historically, the classical small ternary derives from various baroque binary forms whose two parts were invariably repeated. Such a repetition could not take place if the end of the first section

(analogous to a ternary A section) elided structurally with the beginning of the second section (analogous to a B section). Theoretically, the sense of a distinctly contrasting "middle" would presumably be weakened if that middle were to be directly attached to the end of the exposition or to the beginning of the recapitulation.

Unlike the exposition, the contrasting middle never closes with an authentic cadence in the home key. Rather, the B section most often ends with a simple home-key half cadence. The section may occasionally conclude with an authentic cadence in the dominant region. In such cases, the tonic of the subordinate key is often converted into the dominant of the home key through the addition of a dissonant seventh. At times, however, cadential closure may not occur at all. If the section consists exclusively of a standing on the dominant, then the lack of a cadential progression will exclude the presence of a formal cadence. Moreover, even though the section contains a definite harmonic progression that concludes with dominant harmony, we sometimes may be reluctant to speak of a genuine cadence at that point, because the dominant takes the form of a seventh chord or because the onset of the dominant seems not to mark the actual end of the melodic, rhythmic, and phrase-structural processes. I thus term such a situation a *dominant arrival* in order to distinguish it from a genuine half cadence.

Standing on the dominant. In the simplest cases, the B section is supported exclusively by dominant harmony (either literally or prolonged). Typically a new two-measure idea is introduced and repeated; fragmentation and liquidation may then ensue. (Since the opening two-measure idea essentially expresses dominant harmony, it should not be considered a "basic idea," which, in principle, is initially supported by tonic harmony.) The formal function of this passage can more technically be termed a *standing on the dominant*.[18] Unlike those cases in which a standing on the dominant directly follows a half cadence and thereby expresses a postcadential function (see ex. 1.4, mm. 12–14, and ex. 5.18, mm. 12–16), a standing on the dominant that follows on an authentic cadence ending an exposition expresses the general sense of functional initiation—namely, initiating the new contrasting middle. I later examine B sections that contain a true postcadential standing on the dominant (following a half cadence).

EXAMPLE 6.3: The A section of this small ternary, a nonmodulating period, was described in connection with example 1.3. The B section, shown here, begins with a new two-measure idea at the upbeat to measure 9, and then the idea is repeated in the following two measures. Since the new idea and its repetition are supported by a dominant prolongational progression, the entire contrasting middle can be said to consist of a standing on the dominant.

For the purposes of the formal analysis, measures 11–12 are

EXAMPLE 6.4 Beethoven, Piano Sonata in E-flat, Op. 7, ii, 1–24

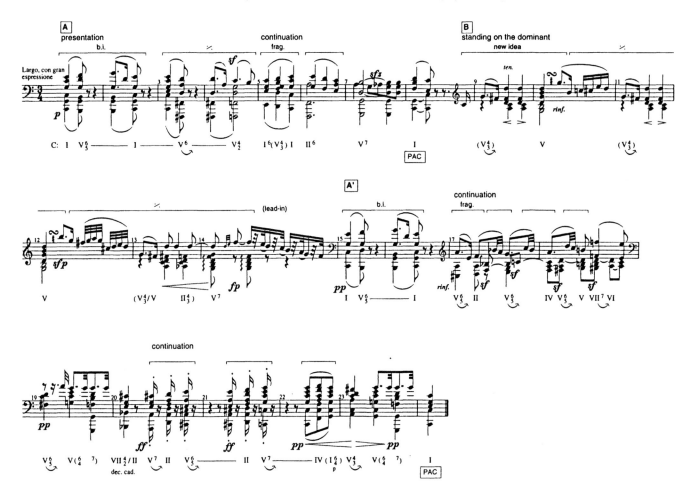

EXAMPLE 6.5 Beethoven, Piano Sonata in G Minor, Op. 49/1, ii, 1–16

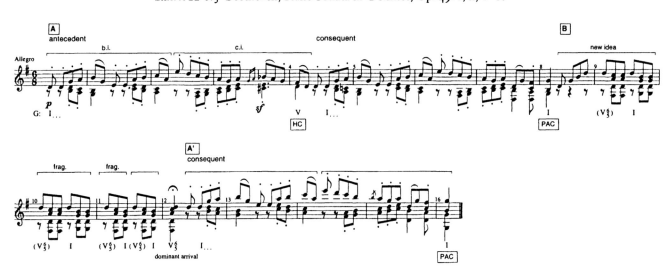

considered an exact repetition of measures 9–10. However, we should not overlook the important melodic and harmonic variants in the repeated form of the idea. First, the melodic line reaches up to a climactic C in the middle of measure 11. Second, a greater sense of finality is created when the melody ends on the dominant scale-degree, preceded by its own leading-tone and harmonized by its own dominant (VII⁶/V).[19]

EXAMPLE 6.4: The standing on the dominant (mm. 9–14) comprises three varied statements of a new two-measure idea.[20] The dominant prolongation is achieved by neighboring V⁴₃/V chords, which temporarily convert the dominant into a local tonic. (There is no modulation, however, since the dominant region is not confirmed cadentially.) The addition of the dissonant seventh in measure 14 reestablishes the G harmony unambiguously as dominant of the home key, in preparation for the initial tonic of the recapitulation.

A contrasting middle section may begin and end with a dominant without necessarily being supported by a prolongation of that harmony. The initial dominant may function instead as a subordinate chord within a tonic prolongation. In a series of alternating dominant and tonic harmonies, it is sometimes difficult to decide which is the primary, prolonged harmony and which is the subordinate harmony. The particular melodic–rhythmic context alone helps determine the correct harmonic analysis.

EXAMPLE 6.5: The B section appears at first glance to be a simple standing on the dominant. Yet the V⁶₅ chords on the downbeats of each measure have a strong tendency to resolve to the following tonics. Since the dominants are thus subordinate to the tonic, and not vice versa, we can conclude that the B section is actually supported by a tonic prolongation until the very final chord (m. 12). We must therefore reject our initial interpretation of a standing on the dominant. Nevertheless, dominant harmony receives considerable emphasis in the section. Not only are the initial and final harmonies dominant in function, but also this harmony falls on metrically strong positions in the measures. Melodic stasis on the fifth scale-degree further emphasizes the sense of dominant. As noted later in this chapter, the section ends with a dominant arrival rather than a half cadence.[21]

Model–sequence technique. The contrasting middle of a small ternary frequently brings (especially at its beginning) prominent sequential repetitions or, to use an alternative expression, *model–sequence technique.* With this procedure, an idea (the model) is repeated (as a sequence) on differing scale-degrees. The sequential harmonic progression supporting model–sequence technique expresses a definite sense of harmonic instability, which is especially appropriate for creating a more loosely organized section. If a short sequential passage is followed by a half cadence, then the entire B section may resemble a continuation phrase, such as might be found in a sentence.

EXAMPLE 6.2: The melody of the B section immediately suggests model–sequence technique, although the organization of the sequential repetition is rather subtle. The material might appear to group into one-measure units as defined by the bar lines, yet the actual model does not begin until the middle of measure 11. The sequence then appears a third lower in measures 12–13. Hence, the first half of measure 11, which brings the opening motive ("x") from the original basic idea, does not actually participate in the sequential plan.

The model would seem to be sequenced again in measures 13–14, but Haydn breaks the descending third pattern and starts the idea a fourth lower instead. Moreover, whereas the harmony on the third quarter of measure 13 would have been a VII⁶/V (in order to maintain the sequence a fourth lower), the bass note has been chromatically lowered to E♭ so that it can descend to D rather than ascend to F♮ (again, according to the sequence). All these alterations to the original model ultimately convert it into a conventional half-cadence idea, which brings the B section to a close. The resulting four-measure unit has all the characteristics of a continuation phrase and may be so labeled in the analysis.[22]

Looser sentential form. Because the contrasting middle of the small ternary is more loosely organized than the preceding exposition, conventional theme-types infrequently appear in the B section. Indeed, the period and its most closely related hybrid (compound basic idea + consequent) are never found there. Occasionally, however, the contrasting middle is distinctly sentential in design. In such cases, the supporting harmonies are made less stable or the grouping structure less symmetrical than in the regular tight-knit form. The resulting looser organization is particularly suitable for a contrasting middle.

EXAMPLE 6.6: The B section is built as an eight-measure sentence. Note how the underlying harmonies significantly loosen the form. First, the presentation prolongs tonic in first inversion (rather than in the more stable root position); moreover, the opening harmony is a dominant seventh. Second, the continuation phrase features an extensive stepwise-descending sequential progression, which continues to prolong the I⁶ of the presentation, leading ultimately to a half cadence. Compared with the hybrid theme of the A section, with its six-measure tonic pedal and perfect authentic cadence, the sentence of the B section has a distinctly looser formal expression. (The second phrase of the exposition might be labeled "continuation⇒cadential" if the harmony of measure 5 is already thought to represent a pre-dominant—IV with a raised fifth—in the new key, in which case an expanded cadential progression could be seen to begin at that measure.)[23]

Postcadential standing on the dominant. We have already examined cases in which a contrasting middle consists entirely of a standing on the dominant. Frequently, however, that phrase function appears toward the end of a B section, directly following the half cadence that marks its structural close. This postcadential standing on the dominant builds up powerful expectations for harmonic resolution to

EXAMPLE 6.6 Haydn, Piano Sonata in E-flat, Hob. XVI:49, iii, 1–24

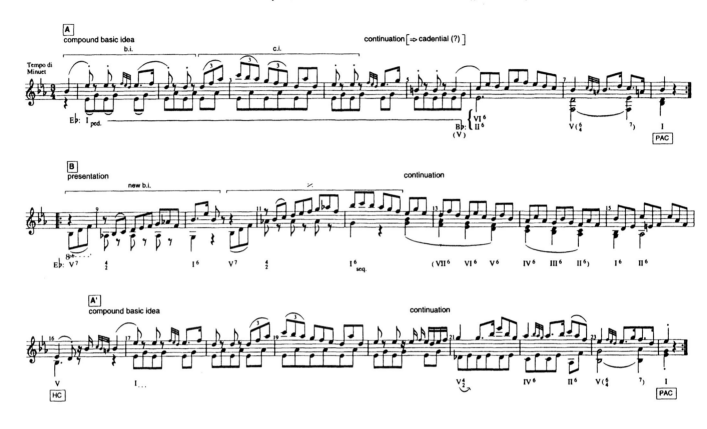

EXAMPLE 6.7 Mozart, String Quartet in E-flat, K. 428/421b, iv, 1–34

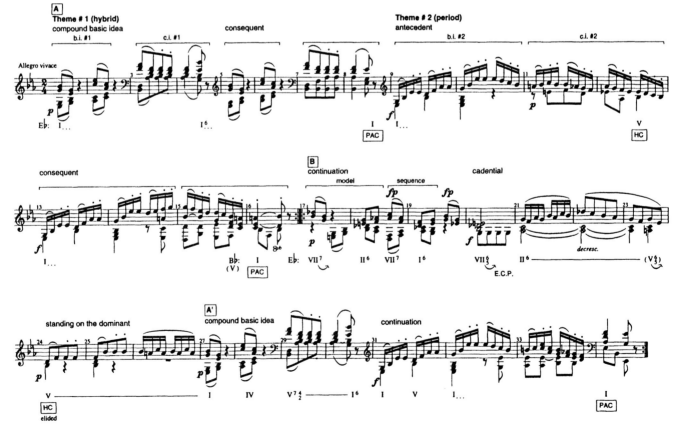

the tonic at the beginning of the recapitulation. Often in a standing on the dominant, the texture is systematically reduced (even to a single voice), and motives from the basic idea are gradually reintroduced. Both these techniques help prepare for the imminent return of the basic idea.

EXAMPLE 6.7: The B section begins in measure 17 with model–sequence technique built out of imitations of the basic idea's opening motive. (The organization of this model–sequence technique is not straightforward: the model itself lasts a measure and a half, and the sequence compresses the model by bringing simultaneously the motive of the violins with its inverted version in the viola and cello.) There follows an expanded cadential progression leading to a half cadence on the downbeat of measure 24. The cadential arrival elides with a three-measure standing on the dominant. The dissolution of texture throughout this postcadential passage "clears the air," so to speak, for the return of fuller four-part writing at the beginning of the recapitulation. In addition, the first two measures of the standing on the dominant anticipate the motive of the contrasting idea (mm. 29–30). Motives from the basic idea are not used here (as would often be the case), perhaps because they had already appeared prominently in the preceding model–sequence passage (mm. 17–19).[24]

Subordinate key, retransition. A contrasting middle can emphasize dominant even more by confirming that region as a genuine subordinate key through authentic-cadential closure. A contrasting middle that modulates to the dominant usually follows on an exposition that has remained in the home key. (A nonmodulating A section, however, need not result in a modulating B section.) If the A section modulates to the dominant, then the B section either moves off to other related regions or returns quickly to the home key.[25]

After an authentic cadence in the dominant key, the composer may add a dissonant seventh to the new "tonic" in order to convert that harmony into the dominant of the home key, thus motivating a resolution to the tonic at the start of the recapitulation.[26] The function of this chord can be termed *retransition* because it effects a remodulation to the home key. Sometimes the composer writes a more extended passage, up to a full four-measure phrase or more, whose function is more specifically to effect the remodulation. This passage, also termed a retransition, typically contains model–sequence technique leading to a home-key dominant, in either the form of a half cadence or a dominant arrival (to be discussed shortly). A reduction in texture and an anticipation of motives from the basic idea may also occur in a retransition, just as in a postcadential standing on the dominant.

EXAMPLE 6.8: Following a nonmodulating A section, the B section opens directly in the dominant region with an eight-measure hybrid. Measures 9–12 bring a compound basic idea prolonging I⁶ (of the subordinate key), after which a cadential phrase confirms

the new key with a perfect authentic cadence in measure 16. (The melodic idea in the bass part of measures 11–12 has strong motivic connections with the basic idea, yet the different melodic contour and harmonic support render this two-measure unit a contrasting idea rather than a repetition of the basic idea.) The next four-measure phrase has a retransition function. A brief model–sequence in measures 17–18 leads to a home-key half cadence at measure 20.

(The two-part texture of this B section makes it difficult to analyze the harmony with certainty. In particular, the identification of VI and A⁶ in the expanded cadential progression of measures 13–16 is based on the analogous reading in measures 19–20 of the retransition, in which the augmented sixth chord is explicitly present.)[27]

If the exposition has already modulated to the dominant region, the B section usually returns quickly to the home key but sometimes modulates to yet another related region and confirms it as a key with a cadence (either half or authentic). Here, too, a retransition of some kind—be it a full phrase or simply a single chord—brings back the home-key dominant for the literal end of the section.

EXAMPLE 6.1: Because the exposition has already modulated to the dominant region, Mozart allows the tonality of the contrasting middle to wander even further afield. The section begins in measure 9 by tonicizing the minor dominant region with a new two-measure idea (based on motives from the original basic idea). Two measures of fragmentation lead to a half cadence (m. 12), which establishes the supertonic as a new key within the theme. An additional measure and a half of a postcadential standing on the dominant further emphasizes V/II. Finally, this dominant resolves irregularly to V⁶ of the home key (as a single retransitional chord) to link smoothly to the recapitulation.[28]

Noncadential ending, dominant arrival. As pointed out, the entire B section of a small ternary can be supported by a single dominant prolongation. In such cases, the section does not close with a cadence, because there is no independent harmonic progression to mark a cadential arrival. Even if a contrasting middle displays greater harmonic activity, it can conclude without a cadence if the final dominant is inverted or else contains a dissonant seventh, for the dominant would then be too unstable to function as a cadential goal. In such cases, the formal articulation created by this final harmony can be labeled a *dominant arrival*, in contrast to a genuine half cadence.[29]

EXAMPLE 6.5: Following a tonic prolongation (with dominant emphasis, as noted earlier), the move to dominant harmony at the end of the section (m. 12) cannot be construed as a half cadence because the dominant is inverted and contains a dissonant seventh; the last V⁶ therefore marks a dominant arrival. Note that by adding a fermata over this final chord of the section, Beethoven prompts us to hear this dominant as an "ending" harmony despite its noncadential status.[30]

EXAMPLE 6.8 Haydn, Symphony No. 101 in D ("The Clock"), iv, 1–22

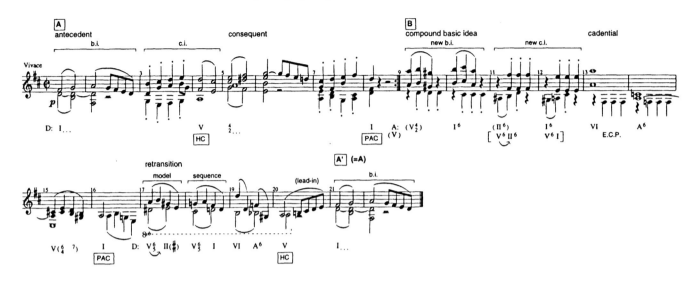

EXAMPLE 6.9 Beethoven, Symphony No. 7 in A, Op. 92, i, 67–96

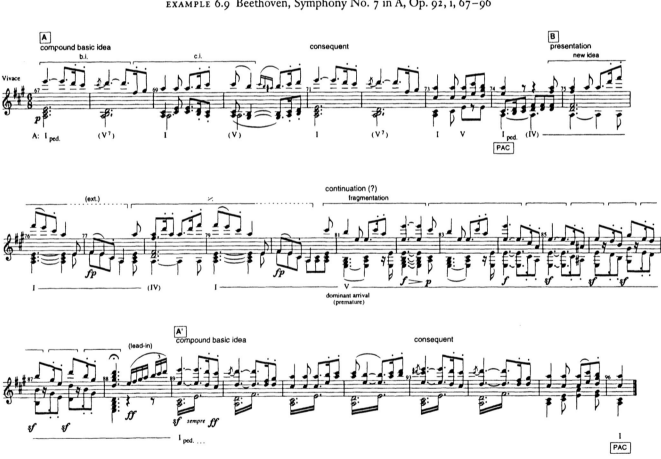

A contrasting middle can also conclude noncadentially if its final dominant precedes the moment in time that represents the end of the prevailing melodic, rhythmic, and grouping processes. Because the final harmony appears before the section's "structural" end, the expression *premature dominant arrival* seems apt for characterizing the formal articulation achieved by this dominant.

EXAMPLE 6.9: The B section begins with a new two-measure idea, which is then extended by an additional measure. The idea is next repeated to yield a six-measure presentation supported by a tonic prolongation. Measure 81 brings a new two-measure idea, now supported by dominant harmony. The reduction in unit size from three to two measures represents the first stage in a process of fragmentation that extends to the end of the section (m. 88). As a result of the fragmentation, this unit, supported entirely by dominant harmony, takes on the character of a continuation phrase, thus suggesting an overall sentential design for the B section.

We cannot speak of a genuine sentence, however, unless we can identify a closing cadence. But a quick look reveals that the entire B section is supported by a single I–V progression and that the V harmony, the "final" dominant, arrives considerably before the end of the section. Indeed, the harmony at measure 81 marks not an end but, rather, a middle—the onset of the fragmentation process. The moment of the real phrase-structural end, the fermata in measure 88, cannot be considered a half cadence because of the lack of genuine harmonic progression into the downbeat of that measure. Thus the harmonic goal of the B section is, according to the norm, a dominant (m. 81), but its appearance marks a premature dominant arrival, and the section ultimately ends without cadential closure.[31]

EXAMPLE 6.10: The contrasting middle opens in measure 10 with a new two-measure idea, which is then repeated in the following two measures. Despite the unison texture, the idea clearly implies V⁷/VI. The following two measures see the root of this dominant, C, repeated as a dotted-rhythm figure within a *poco ritardando*. This gesture suggests that the section is coming to a close and sets up strong expectations for a root-position F harmony to mark the beginning of something new. From what we have heard so far, we might believe that the entire section has been constructed as a standing on the dominant, not of the home key but of the submediant.[32]

But in measures 16–17 Beethoven surprises the listener (and at the same time concedes that he has indeed brought the "wrong" dominant) by resuming the original tempo and shifting the dotted-rhythm figure up to D♭, the seventh of the home-key dominant, which is arpeggiated in measures 18–19. That the fermata over the dominant E♭ marks the literal end of the B section is confirmed in the following measure when the basic idea from the A section returns to mark the beginning of the recapitulation.[33]

Although the B section conforms to the norm by closing with the dominant of the home key, this final harmony is not associated with any cadence. The E♭ fermata in measure 19 cannot be a half cadence because no harmonic progression leads into the downbeat of this measure. Just where the dominant harmony actually arrives is not immediately evident on first hearing, although in retrospect we can identify the repeated D♭s in measure 16 as the onset of that

harmony. Yet this measure possesses no cadential quality since it does not represent a phrase-structural end. Inasmuch as the harmonic goal of the B section fails to coincide with its melodic and phrase-structural goal, we can speak of a premature dominant arrival at measure 16 and recognize that the contrasting middle concludes without a cadence.

RECAPITULATION

The recapitulation of the small ternary brings back the fundamental melodic–motivic material of the exposition and reconfirms the home key with a perfect authentic cadence. Sometimes the A' section restates the A section exactly. More often than not, however, the structure of the earlier section is significantly altered, usually by eliminating functionally redundant material or by further developing motives from the preceding sections. At the very least, the recapitulation must begin with the basic idea from the A section in the home key and end with a perfect authentic cadence confirming that key. Like the exposition, the final cadence can be followed by a closing section that further prolongs the final tonic. When the exposition modulates to a subordinate key, the recapitulation must be tonally adjusted to remain entirely in the home key.

Although the dominant harmony at the end of the contrasting middle clearly resolves to the tonic harmony at the beginning of the recapitulation, this harmonic resolution must not be construed as marking an authentic cadence. The resolving tonic represents exclusively the harmonic initiation of the A' section, not the harmonic goal of the B section (this latter function being fulfilled by a half cadence or dominant arrival).

Recapitulation = exposition. Many recapitulations are an exact restatement of the exposition. In such cases, the A' section brings back the melodic–motivic material of the A section in the same harmonic, tonal, and phrase-structural scheme. Even with an exact restatement, however, the music is often not identical, for the recapitulation may feature changes in accompanimental figuration, texture, and instrumentation, as well as introduce embellishments of harmony and melody.

EXAMPLES 6.8 AND 6.10: The recapitulations are the same as the expositions except for added lead-ins to provide greater rhythmic continuity into the A' sections. (To save space, the music of these sections has not been reproduced.) In example 6.10, the lead-in is particularly effective in reviving the rhythmic momentum brought to a halt by the fermata at the end of the B section.

EXAMPLE 6.9: The recapitulation is sounded by the full orchestra, compared with the thinner instrumentation of the exposition section (woodwind sonorities punctuated by string accompanimental patterns). As so often is the case, the change in orchestration serves

EXAMPLE 6.10 Beethoven, Piano Sonata in E-flat, Op. 31/3, ii, 1–20

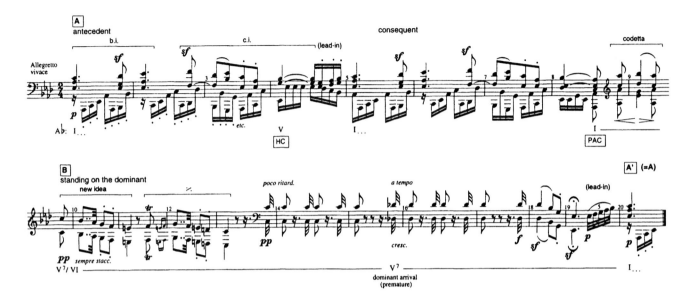

EXAMPLE 6.11 Haydn, Symphony No. 99 in E-flat, iv, 1–20

a particular aesthetic aim. Here, the recapitulation achieves the climax of an instrumentational and dynamic crescendo that grows from the very opening measures of the theme. (Indeed, the ternary itself is preceded by a thematic introduction [mm. 63–66; not shown] featuring a systematic increase of instruments, chord elements, and intensity level.)

Tonal adjustment. If the exposition of the small ternary modulates to a subordinate key, then the recapitulation must be *adjusted* to end in the home key, thus establishing tonal unity for the entire theme.

EXAMPLE 6.6: The recapitulation is adjusted by turning toward the subdominant of the home key (mm. 21–22) at the point in the exposition where the tonic moves to a pre-dominant harmony of the subordinate key (mm. 5–6). Except for the tonal adjustment, the A′ section is closely modeled on the A section.[34]

Change in formal function. In the examples treated thus far, the melodic material of the exposition is recapitulated in the context of the same formal functions. Often, however, the composer changes the recapitulation in such a way as to introduce a different set of functions. In the following examples, the new functional arrangements do not affect the size of the A′ section relative to the A section. Frequently, however, the alteration of functions results in a compressed or expanded recapitulation, as explained in separate sections later.

EXAMPLE 6.11: The recapitulation transfers the original basic idea to the bass voice. But instead of being followed by a contrasting idea to create an antecedent, as in the A section, the basic idea is repeated to make a four-measure presentation. Another version of the basic idea finally appears in the upper voice, and the theme closes with a two-measure cadential idea.

Since the second phrase begins with a variant of the basic idea (mm. 17–18), we might be tempted to label this phrase a consequent (as in the exposition). Yet the preceding phrase is clearly presentational, which implies instead a subsequent continuation. And so Haydn fulfills our expectations by significantly increasing the rate of harmonic activity in measures 17–18. Thus despite the lack of structural fragmentation and the presence of a third statement of the basic idea, the second phrase is perhaps better understood as a continuation rather than a consequent, so that the recapitulation acquires a sentential form. With this example, we see that the same basic idea can serve as the opening gesture for both a period and a sentence.

EXAMPLE 6.2: The recapitulation begins in measure 15 with the basic idea from the exposition. Immediately thereafter, the contrasting idea begins to sound, although it now receives a different harmonic support from that of the exposition. Rather than ending this idea with a weak cadence to make an antecedent phrase, Haydn instead initiates fragmentation by repeating sequentially the first motive of the contrasting idea (upbeat to m. 18). He then suddenly stops the rhythmic motion with one of his famous midphrase pauses, leaving the listener with a heightened sense of ex-

pectation for further continuation and ultimate cadence. Indeed, fragmentation continues in the following measures as the composer develops the characteristic dotted-rhythm motive ("x") from the very opening of the theme. Measure 20 brings a pre-dominant IV⁶, which initiates the first of two cadential progressions, one resolving deceptively on the second quarter of measure 21, the second effecting a perfect authentic cadence in the next measure. (It is also easy to hear a single cadential progression here, in which the motion to VI and II⁶ in measure 21 can be understood as a double-neighbor embellishment of V.)

The six measures following the single statement of the basic idea have all the characteristics of a developmental continuation phrase. Here, the continuation is extended beyond its normative four measures in order to create a recapitulation whose eight-measure length matches that of the exposition. Haydn reinforces the correspondence between the A and A′ sections by bringing back the closing section from the exposition, transposed into the home key, of course.[35]

Compressed recapitulation. The recapitulation of a small ternary is frequently compressed in relation to the exposition. The shorter length is usually achieved by eliminating material that is functionally redundant in the A′ section (although essential to the structure of the A section). A compressed recapitulation can also bring about a change in formal functions in relation to the exposition.

If the exposition is built as an eight-measure period, then a compressed recapitulation typically eliminates both the interior half cadence and the second statement of the basic idea. Since the A′ section itself is directly preceded by an important dominant harmony at the end of the B section, the additional dominant emphasis created by a half cadence in the A′ section is generally dispensable. A second appearance of the basic idea can also be omitted because this idea has by now been sufficiently established in the listener's memory not to require any further restatement. As a result of these deletions, the recapitulation is reduced to a single four-measure consequent phrase. This phrase is sometimes identical to the second half of the original period, but at other times, the phrase resembles more the linking together of the basic idea from measures 1–2 with the contrasting idea from measures 7–8. It is even possible for the new consequent to bring a contrasting idea unrelated to any from the exposition (see ex. 1.4, mm. 17–18).

EXAMPLE 6.5: The recapitulation is made up of the consequent phrase from the exposition transposed one octave higher.[36]

EXAMPLE 6.3: The A′ section is a single consequent phrase based on, but not identical to, material of the A section (see ex. 1.3). The basic idea, which had been supported by a firm tonic pedal in the exposition, now receives harmonic intensification through a brief descending fifth sequential progression. The contrasting idea, whose version resembles that of measures 7–8 of the exposition, is given a more active harmonic setting to match that of the basic idea. The resulting consequent phrase is not directly related to either one of the constituent phrases of the exposition. In his use of dynamic markings, however, Mozart suggests that the piano basic idea refers to the original antecedent phrase (mm. 1–4) and that the forte contrasting idea refers to the original consequent (mm. 5–8). In this way, the four-measure recapitulation embodies elements of the entire eight-measure exposition.[37]

EXAMPLE 6.7: The exposition section contains two complete themes, each possessing a different structure. The first theme (mm. 1–8) is a nonmodulating hybrid (compound basic idea + consequent), and the second theme (mm. 9–16) is a period, which modulates to the subordinate key (V). For the recapitulation, Mozart eliminates redundant material by combining the compound basic idea from the first theme with the consequent phrase from the second theme, now adjusted to remain in the home key. In the new context of the recapitulation, however, this second phrase no longer has a consequent function. First, the phrase does not restate the basic idea of the section (mm. 27–28), and second, the harmonic and surface-rhythm activity of the phrase is significantly increased in relation to the preceding compound basic idea. For these reasons, material that once functioned as a consequent in the A section now functions as a continuation in the A' section.

Expanded recapitulation. Since a contrasting middle is functionally analogous to a development section of sonata form, one might believe that the "development" of melodic-motivic material in a small ternary is most appropriately confined to its B section. Some of the examples already discussed reveal, however, that the A' section can also significantly develop earlier ideas (see exs. 6.2 and 6.11). Melodic-motivic development of this kind usually takes place in a new continuation added to the recapitulation and often generates an expansion relative to the exposition. The A' section can also be lengthened by interpolations, expanded cadential progressions, and evaded cadences. Even further expansion may result from adding a closing section not found in the exposition.

EXAMPLE 6.1: The first five measures of the recapitulation follow the same path as the exposition. At the upbeat to measure 20, the tonic begins to be prolonged (as in the A section), but quickly changes into a secondary dominant of IV, thus effecting the tonal adjustment. With the upbeat to measure 22, Mozart fragments the unit size by developing the sixteenth-note anacrusis motive within the harmonic context of a cadential progression. A definite continuation function is thereby created, one that now fully realizes the incipient continuation of the exposition. (It is difficult to locate exactly the onset of the cadential progression. Although it could be understood to begin at the upbeat to measure 20, it is perhaps more convincingly located two measures later, analogous to the cadential idea of the exposition.)

The perfect authentic cadence finally arrives in measure 24, after which Mozart expands the recapitulation even further by adding a new closing section. The codettas are derived from the cadential idea of the A section (m. 8), which had to be abandoned in the recapitulation because of the motivic development. Mozart thus uses the codettas to "recapitulate" an idea that otherwise would not find a place in the internal structure of the A' section.

EXAMPLE 6.4: The recapitulation begins in measure 15 with a return of the basic idea from the opening of the movement. Rather than repeating the idea, as in the exposition, Beethoven immediately introduces a new continuation phrase. He can eliminate a second statement of the basic idea (with its resulting melodic-motivic redundancy) and still preserve a strong sense of tonic prolongation because a complete I–V–I motion is accomplished in the basic idea, rather than in the complete four-measure presentation, as is so often the case.[38]

The continuation phrase of the recapitulation is entirely different from that of the exposition. Rather than developing the stepwise motive from the basic idea, the new continuation develops the leaping dotted-rhythm motive by means of fragmentation into one-beat units in an ascending-stepwise sequential progression.[39] Measure 19 brings the cadential progression, which leads to a deceptive cadence when the dominant resolves to the mysterious VII♭⁷/II.

A second continuation then begins in measure 20, which, like the exposition, develops the first motive of the basic idea, but now with massive fortissimo chords in a highly dramatic outburst. The sudden pianissimo at the upbeat to measure 23 signals a return to the cadential idea of measure 19, and the following perfect authentic cadence brings closure to the theme as a whole. In this example, we see how the composer draws entirely new consequences from the melodic–motivic material of the basic idea and thus creates a recapitulation whose structure and character differ markedly from that of the exposition.[40]

TIGHT-KNIT VERSUS LOOSE ORGANIZATION

Using some of the examples in this chapter, it is now possible to describe in greater detail the relative degree of tight-knit and loose organization represented by the various sections of the small ternary form. First, however, let me summarize the criteria developed thus far for classifying formal units (of any size or function) in the tight-knit/loose continuum.

1. *Tonality.* From the point of view of tonality, a unit is most tightly knit if it begins and ends in the home key. It is less tightly knit if it opens and closes in a subordinate key. An even looser expression is achieved if a unit modulates.
2. *Cadence.* The notion of "cadential weight" correlates directly with the distinction between tight knit and loose. Closing a unit with a perfect authentic cadence contributes to an overall tight-knit expression; an imperfect authentic cadence makes for a less tightly knit unit; and a half cadence is responsible for a looser organization. The lack of cadential closure, due to a premature dominant arrival, for example, results in a significantly looser form.

3. *Harmony.* The extent to which the underlying harmony of a given unit is functionally stable or unstable affects its tight-knit or loose organization. Authentic cadential progressions and tonic prolongational progressions have the most tightly knit harmonic expression, whereas dominant prolongations create a looser expression. Sequential progressions also are loose, especially to the extent that the individual links in the sequential chain of chords are harmonically nonfunctional. The more a progression is chromatically altered, the more tonally destabilizing it will be, and hence the looser it will become.

4. *Grouping structure.* Symmetrical grouping structures are relatively tight knit in formal organization. Conversely, the more asymmetrical the grouping is, the looser the form will be. Symmetries based exclusively on exponentials of two (e.g., 2 + 2, 4 + 4, 8 + 8, 16 + 16) are more tightly knit than those based on three, five, and combinations of these with two (e.g., 3 + 3, 5 + 5, 6 + 6).

5. *Functional efficiency.* Formal units that express their component functionality in an efficient manner are more tightly knit than are those whose functions obtain a degree of redundancy through repetitions, extensions, expansions, and interpolations. An ambiguity of formal function, of course, also gives rise to a looser organization.

6. *Motivic uniformity.* The presence of uniform melodic–motivic and accompanimental material contributes to a unit's tight-knit organization. A unit filled with diverse motives and frequently changing accompanimental patterns acquires a looser expression.

7. *Formal conventionality.* Conventional formal types (period, sentence, hybrid) are more tightly knit than nonconventional designs. Among the conventional types, the period is the most tightly knit; the sentence is the least tightly knit; and hybrids are more or less tightly knit to the extent that they resemble the period or sentence.

These criteria can obviously interact with one another in a wide variety of ways. At times, they may work together to create an unequivocally tight knit or loose expression. At other times, they may conflict with one another so that some factors contribute to a tight-knit organization while others make for a looser one. The latter situation renders comparison particularly difficult, and at times, it may not be possible to determine, say, which of two units is looser than the other, because different criteria are responsible for the formal loosening.

In light of these considerations, comparing the three sections of the small ternary as tight knit or loose often proves challenging. Some generalizations can be offered nonetheless:

1. *Exposition versus contrasting middle.* In virtually all small ternaries, the exposition is relatively tight knit, and the contrasting middle distinctly looser in expression.

2. *Exposition versus recapitulation.* If the outer sections of the small ternary are constructed identically, they will possess the same degree of tight-knit expression.[41] If the two sections differ in form, however, the recapitulation is usually organized more loosely than the exposition. The techniques used to compress or expand a recapitulation are generally associated with formal loosening, and if the recapitulation receives a different set of formal functions, the new functional arrangement most often is looser.

There is one principal exception to the rule that an altered recapitulation is looser than its corresponding exposition. If the A section is modulatory and the A' section is identical in organization except for being tonally adjusted to remain in the home key, the latter section will appear to be more tightly knit than the former section (according to the criterion of tonality).

3. *Contrasting middle versus recapitulation.* If it is modeled closely on the exposition, a recapitulation usually retains its tight-knit expression relative to the immediately preceding contrasting middle. If, however, the recapitulation is manifestly looser than the exposition, then both the contrasting middle and the recapitulation will appear loosely organized. In some cases it is possible to say with some degree of certainty that one section is looser than the other. In many cases, however, the comparison proves problematic, and we profit more by analyzing the specific loosening techniques associated with each section rather than by trying to decide which is looser.

Let us now apply these criteria to some of the examples discussed in this chapter and attempt to characterize their component sections as relatively tight knit or loose.

EXAMPLE 6.3: The exposition (see again ex. 1.3) contains a fully symmetrical period, one that begins and ends in the home key and thus expresses a very tightly knit organization. The contrasting middle is distinctly looser: the section is supported exclusively by a dominant prolongation; its thematic design is nonconventional (it is not a period, a sentence, or a hybrid); and it closes without a cadence.

The recapitulation is more difficult to classify. On the one hand, it lies entirely in the home key and efficiently expresses its functional requirements (i.e., a restatement of the basic idea and the confirmation of that key by an authentic cadence). For this reason, the recapitulation represents a relatively tight knit structure, especially in relation to the contrasting middle. But, on the other hand, compared with the exposition, the recapitulation is somewhat looser in expression because it does not contain a conventional thematic design (its consequent phrase being only one-half a period) and because of the slight chromatic inflection and loss of tonic pedal supporting the basic idea. The A′ section thus stands between the two extremes of tight knit and loose as defined by the A and B sections, respectively.

EXAMPLE 6.1: The contrasting middle is obviously the most loosely organized section of the ternary. Comparing the outer sections with each other is more difficult, however, for both feature significant loosening techniques—nonconventional thematic organization, asymmetrical grouping structure, and ambiguous functional expression. As regards tonal organization, the modulatory exposition is looser than the nonmodulating recapitulation. But the grouping structure of the eight-measure exposition would seem to be somewhat more balanced, and thus tight knit, in relation to the more expansive recapitulation (including its closing section). Thus, different factors are responsible for rendering the A and A′ sections somewhat loose, and it is not clear that we can judge which section is looser. In any case, both sections are significantly more tightly knit than the contrasting middle, and thus the fundamental norms of small ternary organization are preserved.

EXAMPLE 6.6: We have already examined the looser sentential form of the contrasting middle. The exposition and recapitulation have the same basic formal structure—a tight-knit hybrid. But owing to its modulatory tonal organization, the A section is rendered somewhat looser compared with the A′ section, which remains in the home key throughout. Here, then, is one instance in which the recapitulation is distinctly more tightly knit than the exposition.

EXAMPLE 6.4: The exposition is unquestionably the most tightly knit section of this ternary form. The recapitulation—with its phrase-structural asymmetry, prominent sequences, extensive chromatic enrichment, and cadential deception—is markedly looser in formal expression. It is more difficult to compare this loose recapitulation with its preceding contrasting middle, which also has a loose expression because of an emphasis on dominant harmony, a lack of cadential closure, and a nonconventional thematic design. But compared with the A′ section, the B section is relatively more unified in its melodic–motivic material, has a greater symmetry of phrase structure (3 × 2), and is decidedly less chromatic. Thus the contrasting middle is not obviously looser than the recapitulation, as is usually the case. In fact, the former section may well be interpreted as somewhat more tightly knit than the latter section.

Small Binary

Traditional theories of form posit a variety of binary structures. Little consensus has been achieved, however, on the fundamental attributes that permit a theme to be classified among these various binary types or even for it to be distinguished from ternary forms.[1] As pointed out in the previous chapter, one type of traditional binary, the "rounded" binary, is better understood as a version of the small ternary. Not all binaries, however, should be assimilated to ternary forms. There exists a specific main theme-type that is appropriately termed *small binary* because its functional characteristics are sufficiently distinct to permit it to be defined independent of the small ternary form.[2]

As its name makes clear, the small binary consists of two *parts*. Each is normatively eight measures long and is usually repeated, by means of either repetition signs or a written-out version that introduces ornamental variations. In its external shape, the small binary resembles the rounded binary version of the small ternary form. However, the small binary distinguishes itself from the rounded binary primarily through its lack of genuine recapitulation—the second part does not bring back the opening basic idea in the home-key tonic.

In addition, the two forms generally differ on melodic–motivic grounds. The second part of the small binary usually begins with material that directly relates to the beginning of the first part. Such a motivic connection helps project the sense of bipartite structure as well as dampen expectations for a subsequent recapitulation of the basic idea. The rounded binary, on the contrary, usually begins its contrasting middle with material that differs from the opening idea of the theme.

Finally, the two forms can sometimes be distinguished on how their first parts conclude. Whereas the A section of the rounded binary is a relatively self-contained unit closing with a perfect authentic cadence,[3] the first part of the small binary frequently ends with a half cadence and thus can remain structurally incomplete.

The small binary tends to be used in movements that feature multiple recurrences of a theme, such as a rondo or a theme and variations. By using this formal type, the composer can minimize an overexposure of the basic idea, since

it will not be recapitulated in the course of the theme itself. The small binary is especially suitable for variation forms, in which the return of the basic idea can be reserved to mark the beginning of each variation.[4]

Unlike the small ternary, whose three sections have unique and well-defined formal functions, the two parts of the small binary have less distinct overall functional meanings. Since it is difficult to propose specific terminology for the constituent parts of the form, they are identified instead by the relatively neutral terms *first part* and *second part*.[5] In each part, however, it is often possible to identify specific functional components conventionally associated with the sentence, period, or small ternary.

More than any other theme-type, the small binary emphasizes a sense of structural symmetry by regularly appearing in its normative length of sixteen real measures (8 + 8). Thus the standard phrase alterations of extension, compression, and the like are infrequently found in the form.[6]

FIRST PART

The first part of a small binary is usually constructed as an eight-measure theme of conventional organization (sentence, period, or hybrid). This theme may remain in the home key or modulate to a subordinate key, and it may close with any of the three cadential types—half, perfect authentic, or (rarely) imperfect authentic. When ending with a perfect authentic cadence (in any key), the first part of a small binary cannot be distinguished from the exposition of a small ternary. Only when the next part closes without recapitulating the initial basic idea can we be sure of the small-binary interpretation.[7]

If the first part of a small binary closes with a half cadence, then a potential small ternary is not implied, since the exposition of that form rarely ends with weak cadential closure.[8] When the first part begins to be repeated, the listener might believe that the consequent of a sixteen-measure period is in the making. But when the part again ends with the same half cadence, the period interpretation fails, and a small binary form is strongly suggested instead. Among the

EXAMPLE 7.1 Haydn, Piano Sonata in E, Hob. XVI:31, iii, 1–16

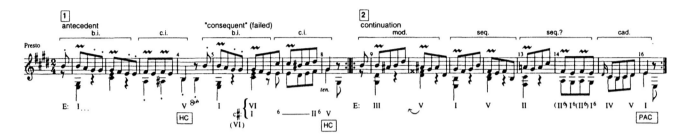

EXAMPLE 7.2 Beethoven, Violin Sonata in A, Op. 30/1, iii, 1–32

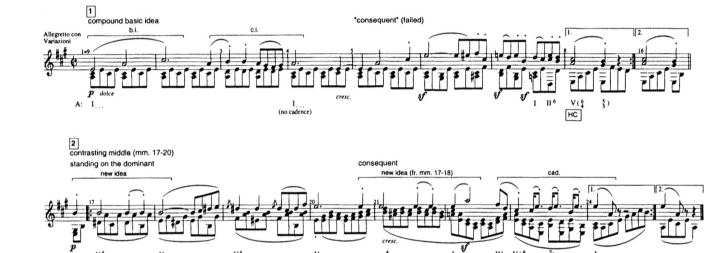

EXAMPLE 7.3 Haydn, Piano Trio in A-flat, Hob. XV:14, ii, 1–16

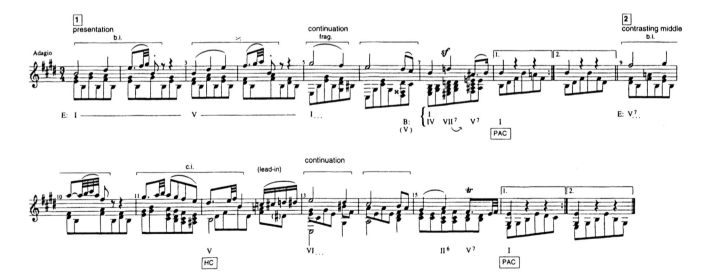

conventional theme-types, only the sentence and the sentential hybrid (compound basic idea + continuation) tend to end with a half cadence. The period and the periodic hybrids normally conclude with an authentic cadence.[9] The first part of a small binary can nevertheless express a sense of periodic organization yet still end with a half cadence. In this case, the resultant form is nonconventional.

EXAMPLE 7.1: This small binary begins with a regular antecedent phrase. The second phrase restates the basic idea in the manner of a consequent and quickly modulates to the submediant region. But rather than closing with an authentic cadence, as would be expected, the phrase ends instead with another half cadence, thus denying the implied period form. Although we might be tempted to label this phrase an antecedent because of its weak cadential closure, we must recall that a true antecedent is nonmodulatory. The second phrase is thus better seen as a *failed consequent*.

EXAMPLE 7.2: This small binary opens with a compound basic idea. The following phrase begins with a variant of the opening basic idea, thus implying a consequent phrase to make hybrid type 4. But a half-cadential closure in measure 8 disallows this interpretation, and the theme acquires a nonconventional form, albeit one with prominent periodic qualities.

The melodic *close* of the two phrases suggests a kind of "reversed" or "inverted" period—a consequent followed by an antecedent. This functional implication is offset, however, by the melodic *beginning* of the phrases, in which the second phrase opens up the melodic space farther than the first phrase. From this perspective, the two phrases are appropriately placed in relation to each other.

SECOND PART

The second part of the small binary begins, in the majority of cases, with a four-measure unit identical in organization to a contrasting middle (B section) of the small ternary.[10] The material that follows the B section can express a variety of functions (though not a recapitulation): some are entirely conventional, such as continuation, cadential, or consequent, whereas others cannot be described with simple labels. Less frequently, the second part of a small binary contains no contrasting middle and is constructed instead as a single themelike unit, often having sentential or periodic characteristics. No matter how the second part is constructed, it always concludes with a perfect authentic cadence in the home key.

The melodic material opening the second part usually derives from the basic idea of the first part. The reasons for this motivic connection are twofold. First, the overall bipartite design of the form is projected in a more cogent way, and second, there is less motivation for a recapitulation of the basic idea, which would transform the binary into a ternary. The second part of some binaries, however, begins with contrasting material.[11] Thus a motivic correspondence

between the first and second parts is not required of the form.

Presence of a Contrasting Middle

Contrasting middle + continuation. The second part of a small binary often consists of a four-measure contrasting middle followed by a four-measure unit displaying continuational traits. This continuation phrase may refer back to a similar continuation from the first part, or it may be constructed out of entirely different material.

EXAMPLE 7.3: Following the modulation, the second part returns to the home key with a two-measure idea, one relating to the basic idea but emphasizing dominant harmony instead. A subsequent contrasting idea leads to a half cadence. These four measures are typical of a contrasting middle, and if a recapitulation were to appear next, an overall rounded binary would be realized. Instead, the subsequent four-measure phrase is a version of the continuation from the first part but now is tonally adjusted to remain in the home key.[12]

If Haydn had wanted to compose a small ternary in connection with the preceding example, he would not have found it easy to retain its symmetrical 8 + 8 grouping structure. When an exposition section is built as a sentence (or sentential hybrid), it is difficult to construct a four-measure recapitulation that includes the essential materials of the original sentence. Unlike the period, in which composers can choose to recapitulate the four-measure antecedent or consequent (or some combination of the two), the eight-measure sentence cannot be compressed so easily into four measures.[13] When the exposition of a small ternary takes the form of a sentence, the A' section usually brings back the A section unchanged (see ex. 6.6, a sentential hybrid), or else the basic idea appears only once, followed by a full continuation of some kind (see ex. 6.4). In either case, the recapitulation usually exceeds four measures, thus stretching the small ternary beyond sixteen measures. Should composers wish to write a symmetrical 8 + 8 theme beginning with an eight-measure sentence, they will most likely choose the small binary form, as in example 7.3.

Contrasting middle + cadential. The phrase following the contrasting middle may be built over an expanded cadential progression.

EXAMPLE 7.4: The second part of this binary begins with a contrasting middle consisting entirely of a standing on the dominant. The following phrase (mm. 78–81) brings back material that resembles the basic idea, but with its new harmonic support, the phrase acquires a cadential rather than a recapitulation function.

The grouping structure of this second part resembles a sentence (2 × 2) + 4. But the first four-measure phrase is not a real presentation, for it is supported by a dominant prolongation (as

EXAMPLE 7.4 Beethoven, Fifteen Variations for Piano in E-flat, Op. 35, 66–81

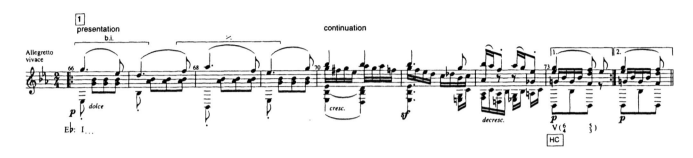

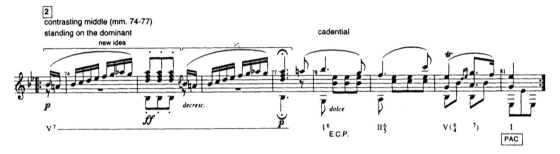

EXAMPLE 7.5 Mozart, String Quartet in D Minor, K. 421/417b, iv, 1–24

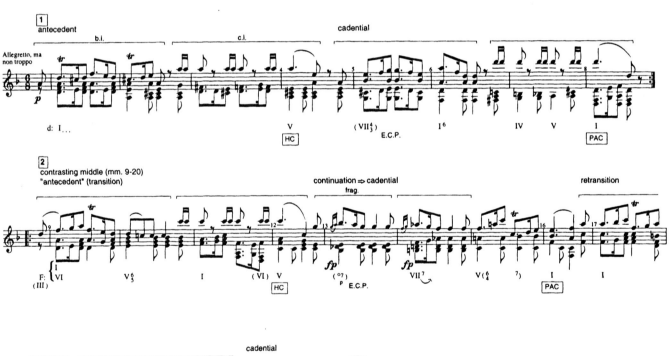

befits a B section), and thus a true sentence does not emerge. Nonetheless, since both parts have a similar grouping structure and since the first ends with a weaker cadence than the second does, the idea of an overall sixteen-measure period is suggested. But this interpretation, too, cannot be sustained, because the second part does not open with a return of the basic idea and thus cannot be considered a consequent.[14]

EXAMPLE 7.5: The first part of this binary can be viewed has hybrid type 2 (antecedent + cadential), although this analysis is not entirely straightforward. The cadential character of measures 5–8 is weakly expressed because the appearance of I⁶, which usually signals the onset of cadential function, is delayed until measure 6, because of the embellishing VII♯ in the preceding measure.

The second part features an elaborate contrasting middle, which modulates to the III region as confirmed by the perfect authentic cadence in measure 16. The first phrase of the B section is antecedent-like but, because of its modulating structure, is better understood as a *transition* leading to the dominant of the relative major. The following continuation⇒cadential phrase (mm. 13–16) reinforces F major and fully confirms it as a genuine subordinate key through authentic cadential closure. Measures 17–20 function as a retransition, which brings the music back to the dominant of the home key, thus marking the end of the contrasting middle. Had the following phrase brought a return of the initial basic idea, a small ternary would have resulted. Instead, Mozart introduces entirely new material built over an expanded cadential progression to conclude the second part of the small binary.

It is interesting to observe how Mozart increasingly intensifies the cadential quality of the phrases following the various half cadences in this theme (mm. 4, 12, 20). The relatively weak cadential expression of measures 5–8 (due to the delayed cadential I⁶) has already been discussed. In the continuation⇒cadential phrase (mm. 13–16), the bass line projects a standard authentic cadence formula, but the harmony in measure 13 is a diminished seventh chord, which substitutes for a more regular pre-dominant built over the fourth scale-degree.[15] Moreover, continuation function vies for expression in this phrase through the fragmentation into one-measure units. It is not until measures 21–24 that Mozart brings a decisive and exclusively cadential phrase, one that emphasizes the Neapolitan as pre-dominant.

Another noteworthy feature of this example is the relatively symmetrical grouping structure arising from the regular alternation of half and authentic cadences at the end of each four-measure phrase. The resulting 3 × 8 structure is noncongruent with the grouping structure arising from the form-functional analysis: 8 (A) + 12 (B) + 4 (cad.).

Contrasting middle + consequent. The final phrase of a small binary can sometimes be built out of a new two-measure idea followed by a contrasting idea that leads to a perfect authentic cadence. If this two-measure idea were identical to the basic idea opening the first part (instead of being new), the phrase would function as a consequent, and an overall small ternary form would result (such as with exs. 6.3 and 6.5). But when this final phrase brings a different two-measure idea, there is no sense of recapitulation, and the theme acquires a small binary form. What, then, is the function of the final phrase? Although there is no corresponding antecedent from the first part, the phrase can still be labeled a consequent, since its internal characteristics are identical to that formal function.

EXAMPLE 7.2: The second part of this binary begins in measure 17 with a four-measure contrasting middle featuring a standing on the dominant. The following phrase (mm. 21–24) brings a two-measure idea followed by a contrasting idea, which itself closes with a perfect authentic cadence. The phrase has no continuational characteristics, and unlike a cadential phrase, its supporting harmonies do not make up an expanded cadential progression. Instead, the phrase is best described as a consequent, even though it has no immediately preceding antecedent. Nonetheless, the two-measure idea beginning this consequent is clearly derived from the opening measures of the standing on the dominant, and thus within the second part, a period-like relation obtains between the B section and the following consequent. (In addition, this consequent completes the melodic descent to the tonic scale-degree left incomplete at the end of the second phrase of part 1.)[16]

Contrasting middle + further dominant prolongation. Another common procedure for constructing the second part is to prolong the goal dominant of the B section well into the subsequent phrase. Frequently, the dominant resolves deceptively to VI, after which a perfect authentic cadence closes the theme. In such cases, the resulting phrase cannot be easily described using any of the labels for the conventional formal functions.

EXAMPLE 7.6: The opening phrase of the second part makes up a normal contrasting middle, closing with a half cadence in the home key. The following phrase, unlike most of those examined up to now, does not begin with the tonic to resolve the dominant ending the previous B section. Instead, the dominant continues to be prolonged, only to resolve deceptively on the last beat of measure 14. The last two measures bring the concluding perfect authentic cadence. Inasmuch as the final phrase features a new idea (mm. 13–14) followed by a cadential idea, we might be tempted to consider it a consequent phrase. But the lack of tonic support for the new idea at the beginning of the phrase weakens the sense of consequent function.[17]

Absence of a Contrasting Middle

The second part of a small binary is sometimes built without a clearly discernible contrasting middle. Instead, the second part may be organized along the lines of a conventional theme-type (most often a sentence, rarely a period).[18] At other times, a distinctly looser structure may result, one that brings continuation or cadential functions exclusively. Even though the second part may not contain a complete contrasting middle (with its ending on the home-key dominant), the beginning of the part may strongly suggest that function, such as emphasizing dominant harmony or immediately bringing model–sequence technique.

EXAMPLE 7.6 Haydn, Piano Sonata in E, Hob. XVI:22, iii, 1–16

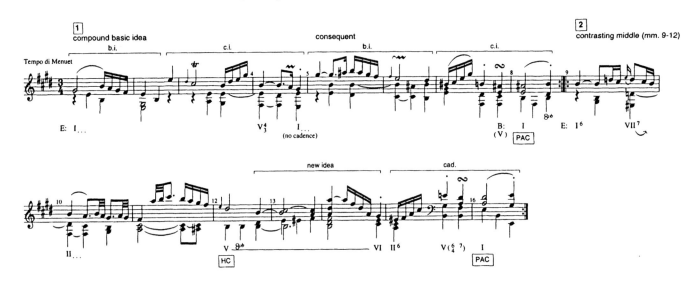

EXAMPLE 7.7 Beethoven, String Quartet in C-sharp Minor, Op. 131, iv, 1–32

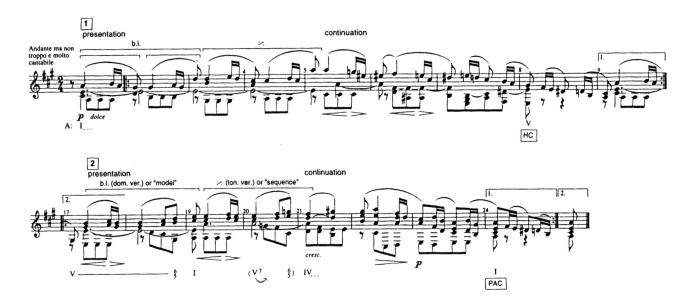

EXAMPLE 7.8 Beethoven, Violin Sonata in A, Op. 12/2, ii, 1–32

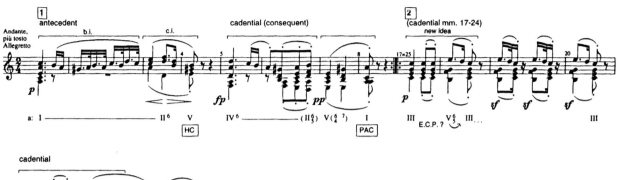

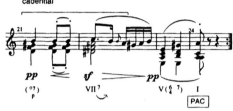

EXAMPLE 7.7: The second part of this binary begins in measure 17 with material derived from the initial basic idea, but now in a distinctly dominant version. A following tonic version (mm. 19–20) creates a presentation phrase, and the subsequent continuation closes with a perfect authentic cadence. Thus the second part, like the first, takes the form of a sentence.

Instead of viewing this theme as a small binary, we might be tempted to consider it a sixteen-measure period, on several accounts. The two parts of the theme feature cadential differentiation typical of a period (half cadence followed by a perfect authentic cadence). Moreover, both parts have a sentential design based on a similar basic idea. This interpretation seems plausible enough, but it ignores aspects of the theme better explained by the small binary model. First, the notion that the consequent repeats the antecedent—central to the concept of period—is significantly weakened when the antecedent itself is repeated before the consequent appears. Thus, as we saw earlier in connection with the first part, the music beginning at measure 9 implies a potential consequent, but when the section ends again with a half cadence, we realize that the consequent function remains unrealized. Even though what follows at measure 17 resembles the original basic idea, the music no longer sounds like a repeated antecedent, since measures 9–10 already achieved that repetition.

Second, whereas the first part (the "antecedent") begins with a stable statement–response repetition of the basic idea (mm. 1–4), the second part reverses this pattern and brings the loose arrangement of a response followed by the statement (mm. 17–20). In fact, an even looser sequential repetition is suggested when the music leads from V to I (mm. 17–19) and then from I to IV (mm.

19–21) to begin the continuation. As a result, measures 17–20 lack the stability of initiation usually associated with a consequent function, yet they are perfectly suited to serve as the beginning of a second part of a small binary, with their suggestion of a contrasting middle.

EXAMPLE 7.1: The grouping structure of the second part resembles a sentence (2 × 2) + 4, but the initial four measures display model–sequence technique, and the resulting lack of tonic prolongation prohibits us from speaking of a true presentation phrase. The entire second part thus functions as a large eight-measure continuation (such as that found in the second half of a sixteen-measure sentence). (The incomplete texture in measures 14–16 makes it difficult to interpret the supporting harmonies and thus to determine whether the model is repeated sequentially a second time in measures 13–14.)[19]

EXAMPLE 7.8: The first part of this binary can be viewed as hybrid type 2 (antecedent + cadential), although the second phrase could also be considered a consequent because measures 5 and 6 bring back material sufficiently similar to the basic idea. The second part begins (m. 17) with a four-measure phrase prolonging III. The following phrase is clearly cadential, beginning with a pre-dominant diminished seventh chord, which substitutes for a more conventional II⁶ (or IV) (see n. 15). From a broader perspective, the second part as a whole can be seen to be supported by a highly expanded cadential progression, in which the prolonged III (mm. 17–20) substitutes for the more conventional initial tonic in first inversion.

III

LOOSER FORMAL REGIONS

8

Subordinate Theme

To avoid tonal monotony, almost every movement of a classical instrumental work establishes a subsidiary tonal area, a subordinate key, that contrasts with, yet is closely related to, the home key.[1] One outstanding feature of the classical style (compared with the earlier baroque practice) is the articulation, indeed, the dramatization,[2] of this subordinate key through a distinct *subordinate theme*.[3] More than just a new melody, this theme is an integral unit of form containing a syntactical succession of formal functions and a concluding authentic cadence.

Just as the subordinate key contrasts with the home key, so too does the subordinate theme contrast with the main theme. The contrasting nature of these themes has long been discussed by theorists and historians. Today, of course, we generally reject the typical nineteenth-century position, which, by focusing on melodic–motivic design, held that a dynamic, "masculine" main theme stands in opposition to a lyrical, "feminine" subordinate theme.[4] In fact, the frequent absence of such contrasting melodies in works of the classical composers, especially those of Haydn, has led most theorists to abandon melodic dualism as an essential element of classical form.

In recent years, scholars have tended to locate the source of contrast principally in the realm of harmony and tonality (while still acknowledging that other musical factors can also create thematic contrast).[5] In this view, the subordinate theme (usually identified as the "second key area") distinguishes itself from the main theme ("first key area") primarily by residing in a contrasting tonal region, one that engenders large-scale dissonance with the home key.[6] Although this view is valid enough, it does not address the fundamental differences in phrase-structural organization routinely evidenced by these themes.

A more comprehensive approach is offered by Schoenberg and Ratz, who view the subordinate theme as loosely organized in relation to a relatively tight-knit main theme.[7] As discussed earlier in connection with the small ternary, the metaphors tight knit and loose summarize a wide variety of musical forces responsible for varying formal expressions (see the last section of chap. 6). Thus the position of Schoenberg and Ratz is advantageous because it embraces

not only issues of harmony and tonality but also those of formal function, grouping structure, melodic–motivic content, and the like. Moreover, the view is fully confirmed by the empirical evidence: in the classical repertory, subordinate themes are, with rare exceptions, more loosely organized than their preceding main themes.

A subordinate theme is normally thought of as a formal unit in a sonata exposition (or recapitulation). In line with the fundamental precepts of this book, however, a subordinate theme refers not only to a thematic unit but also to a definite formal function. And like most other functions, subordinate-theme function need not be tied to a specific grouping structure or to any one formal type. To be sure, the function is especially associated with sonata form, but it is also expressed in many other classical forms, such as rondo, concerto, minuet, and various slow-movement forms.[8]

Subordinate themes are usually constructed out of the intrathematic functions associated with tight-knit main themes, albeit in a significantly looser manner. Thus the constituent phrases of a subordinate theme frequently express an *initiating* function of some kind (antecedent, presentation, or compound basic idea), a *medial* function (continuation), and a *concluding* function (cadential or, more rarely, consequent). Framing functions, such as introduction, codetta, and standing on the dominant are frequently associated with the theme as well. A major exception pertains to the small ternary form, as the three functions of exposition, contrasting middle, and recapitulation, rarely appear in a subordinate theme.[9]

Unlike a main theme, which may close with any one of the three standard cadence types, a subordinate theme ends with a perfect authentic cadence in the subordinate key. Exceptions to this principle are rare.[10] This stricter cadential requirement is dependent on one of the theme's principal functions: confirming the subordinate key. For that key to acquire sufficient weight to vie for prominence with the home key (and thus to create the dramatic conflict of tonalities so central to the classical aesthetic), the subordinate key must be fully confirmed by a perfect authentic cadence. The home key must also be so confirmed, if not at the end of the main theme (because of its closing with a half

EXAMPLE 8.1 Mozart, Piano Sonata in D, K. 576, i, 28–58

98

cadence), then at least later in the movement, usually in the tonally adjusted subordinate theme of the recapitulation.

The subordinate key is often articulated by two or more themes forming a *subordinate-theme group*.[11] Each theme in the group ends with a perfect authentic cadence. One of the themes, usually the first, may be constructed as a tight-knit theme-type. This situation might seem to violate the requirement that a subordinate theme be more loosely constructed than its preceding main theme. But the general principle relating main and subordinate themes is sustained if the entire subordinate-theme group, rather than any one theme, is taken into account when comparing the relative degree of tight-knit or loose organization with respect to the main theme (or main-theme group).

The final cadence of the subordinate theme (or group of themes) is almost always followed by a closing section consisting of codettas. The closing section itself may then lead into a retransition, which modulates back to the home key, usually for a return of the main theme.

LOOSER SENTENTIAL FUNCTIONS

Most subordinate themes are constructed out of the three sentential functions—presentation, continuation, and cadential. One or more of these functions usually acquires a loose organization by means of various compositional techniques, many of which are described in the following sections.

Presentation Function

Additional repetition of the basic idea. A presentation phrase can be extended by repeating the opening basic idea once again. This third statement of the idea makes the grouping structure somewhat asymmetrical (2×3) and promotes a degree of functional redundancy—two criteria for loose organization.

EXAMPLE 8.1: The first of two subordinate themes begins in measure 28 with a varied, canonic statement of the basic idea found in the opening measures of the movement (see ex. 4.9, mm. 1–2). The idea is then sequenced a step higher into the supertonic region. (This sequence in II matches a similar one at the beginning of the consequent phrase in the main theme, ex. 4.9, mm. 5–6.) But this sequential repetition now creates a harmonic–formal predicament: because II does not normally function as a neighboring chord to I or as a passing chord to I⁶, the music cannot easily progress to tonic at measure 32 to form a regular four-measure presentation. So Mozart repeats the basic idea once again, this time within dominant harmony, and the return to I on the downbeat of measure 34 completes the tonic prolongation.[12]

Repetition of the presentation phrase. Another way of loosening the presentation is to repeat the entire phrase before the continuation begins.

EXAMPLE 8.2: The second subordinate theme begins with a presentation in measures 92–95 that is repeated in the following four measures. The resulting functional redundancy contributes to a sense of formal loosening.[13] Note that the rhythmic continuity is enhanced when the end of the repeated presentation elides with the beginning of the continuation (m. 99). (A single four-measure presentation phrase, by contrast, rarely elides with its continuation.)

A repeated four-measure presentation itself gives rise to an even larger, eight-measure presentation, thus suggesting the onset of a sixteen-measure sentence. But the presentation of a true compound sentence consists of a repeated compound basic idea, not a repeated presentation. The difference between these two situations is significant: with a repeated compound basic idea, the two-measure basic idea appears twice, but with a repeated presentation, the basic idea appears four times. Thus the former situation has a distinctly tighter and more integrated expression than does the latter, whose looser organization is especially appropriate to subordinate themes (and, for that reason, is seldom found with main themes).

Weakening of the tonic prolongation. Presentation function can acquire a loose expression if its supporting tonic prolongation is weakened or destabilized. The strongest, most stable prolongation features the tonic in root position, with subordinate harmonies located on weak metrical positions. A tonic prolongation can be weakened by inverting the prolonged harmony, by placing the subordinate harmonies on metrically accented positions, or by undermining the prolongation with a dominant pedal.

EXAMPLE 8.3: The presentation phrase prolongs tonic in first inversion by means of subordinate dominant seventh chords in third inversion. Thus the resulting prolongation is less stable than that found at the very opening of the main theme (ex. 8.3b), which features a root-position tonic pedal.[14]

A tonic prolongation can be significantly weakened if all the constituent harmonies of the progression are placed over a dominant pedal (in the bass voice), one that continues on from the end of the preceding transition. In such situations, the listener can experience the sense of two different prolongations, each on a different hierarchical level of the work—a tonic prolongation at the lower (foreground) level and a dominant prolongation at the higher (background) level. An instance of this technique was illustrated in connection with example 1.8, mm. 21–24 (p. 19).[15]

Continuation Function

In tight-knit main-theme forms, the continuation function is usually fused with the cadential function to make a single continuation phrase. In the context of a subordinate theme,

EXAMPLE 8.2 Beethoven, Piano Sonata in A, Op. 2/2, i, 92–116

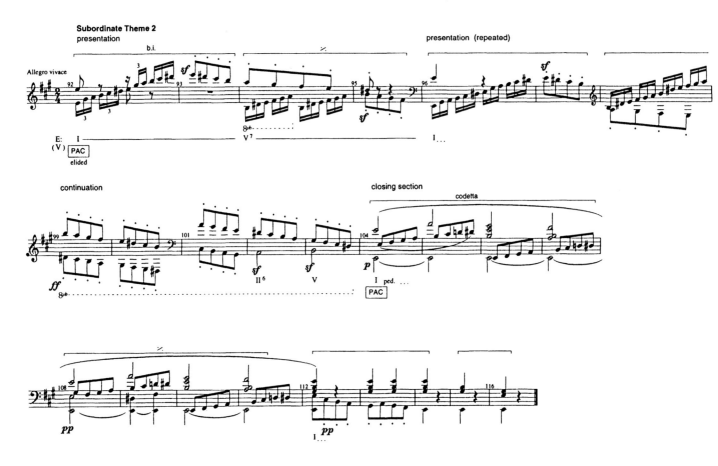

the same form-functional fusion may take place.[16] More typically, however, the functions of continuation and cadential are accorded their own distinct groups, as defined by their melodic–motivic content, rhythmic patterning, accompanimental figuration, and so forth. Thus a continuation phrase (or group of phrases) in a subordinate theme often does not end with a cadence, which is saved for a phrase (or group of phrases) of uniquely cadential function.[17]

Continuation function achieves its looser expression primarily by means of extension; that is, the constituent units (usually fragments) are repeated a greater number of times than would be necessary to express the function. Model-sequence technique is especially suitable for extending continuation function, since a sequential harmonic progression, in principle, has no definite ending point.[18]

EXAMPLE 8.3: The continuation begins in measure 18 with fragmentation and model–sequence technique. In a tight-knit sentence, the fragmented units usually appear in measures 5 and 6 of the theme, because a single repetition of the fragment is all that is needed to project the sense of continuation function. In the looser context of this subordinate theme, fragmentation is extended for an additional two measures (through m. 21) in order to realize a complete circle-of-fifths progression. There can be no talk of a ca-

dence at the end of this four-measure continuation phrase because the goal tonic is approached by an inverted dominant. The following four-measure phrase produces cadential function.[19]

Another way for the composer to extend continuation function is to delay fragmentation by creating units of repetition that are initially the same size as those found in the presentation. In the absence of fragmentation, the sense of continuation must be expressed by other characteristics, such as an acceleration of harmonic change, quicker surface rhythms, or a harmonic sequence. Fragmentation can then appear somewhat later in the theme, sometimes in the context of another distinct phrase, thus extending the continuation function.

EXAMPLE 8.1: The continuation begins at measure 34 with a new two-measure idea, which is then repeated exactly. Because the prevailing two-measure unit size is not reduced, we cannot speak of fragmentation at the beginning of the continuation. Compared with the presentation, however, the continuation immediately accelerates both the rate of harmonic change and the surface rhythm. Fragmentation eventually occurs with the change of material at measure 38, and thus the continuation function is extended into this new phrase. At the same time, measure 38 marks the onset of a cadential progression, and so the new phrase is best interpreted as continuation⇒cadential. Thus in the theme as a whole, continuation function is sufficiently extensive to embrace two distinct phrases, the final one serving cadential function as well.[20]

Cadential Function

Cadential function is subject to a variety of loosening devices, most of which fall into one of two categories: (1) extending the function through the failure to realize an implied perfect authentic cadence, and (2) expanding the function by allowing it to occupy one or more complete phrases, each of which is supported by an expanded cadential progression. Often a number of devices operate together to create a cadential area of enormous scope.

Especially in connection with cadential function, the notion of formal "loosening" must not be equated with formal "weakening" of any kind. Extensions and expansions of the cadence do not make that function any less effective. On the contrary, the moment of cadential arrival is often highly intensified by being withheld considerably longer than might be expected (compared with a tight-knit context).

Cadential extension. Most cadential extensions occur when a promised perfect authentic cadence fails to materialize, thus motivating the appearance of one or more cadential units to make the requisite closure. The expected perfect authentic cadence can remain unfulfilled when in its place, the composer writes an imperfect authentic cadence, a deceptive cadence, an evaded cadence, or an abandoned cadence. On few occasions, the initially promised authentic cadence does appear, yet the cadential function is extended simply by repeating the prior phrase and bringing the same cadence once again.

Although the techniques described in this section may involve extending the cadential function only, continuational materials are frequently implicated as well. Following the failure to realize the implied cadence, the subsequent music may bring back a prior continuation, or even introduce a new continuation, before leading to the cadential material, which will again attempt to close the theme.[21]

1. *Imperfect authentic cadence.* Since subordinate themes almost always close with a perfect authentic cadence, the appearance of an imperfect authentic cadence signals that the theme has not yet reached its true end. Typically in such cases, the preceding phrase (be it a continuation, cadential, or continuation⇒cadential phrase) is repeated, leading this time to a perfect authentic cadence.[22]

EXAMPLE 8.4: A second subordinate theme (following the first subordinate theme, shown ahead in ex. 8.9) is organized as an eight-measure sentence, whose continuation is extended by one measure to close with an imperfect authentic cadence at measure 110. The continuation is then repeated, in a way that creates a stronger cadential dominant, and ends with a perfect authentic cadence in measure 114.[23]

When a phrase ending with an imperfect authentic cadence is repeated and then closed by a perfect authentic cadence, a sense of antecedent–consequent functionality is expressed. The resulting structure should not normally be considered a period, however, since the passage in question does not function as a self-contained, tight-knit theme and seldom contains other characteristics of a true antecedent or consequent phrase, such as a clear two-measure basic idea followed by a two-measure contrasting idea. Moreover, the phrase ending with the imperfect authentic cadence sometimes elides with the beginning of the following phrase (as in the previous example, m. 110), a situation that does not obtain with a genuine period.

2. *Deceptive cadence.* As pointed out in chapter 2, an authentic cadential progression can be changed into a deceptive cadential progression if the final tonic is replaced by a related harmony, one usually built over the sixth scale-degree in the bass. If the arrival point of that substitute harmony truly groups with the preceding material and thus represents its melodic and harmonic goal, we can speak of a *deceptive cadence* bringing partial closure to the theme.[24] The theme then continues in some way (usually by repeating the previous idea or phrase) in order to reach full closure through a perfect authentic cadence.

The sense of partial closure associated with the deceptive cadence is projected largely through the motion of the soprano voice as the harmony moves from the cadential dominant to the substitute for the final tonic. And depending on how the melody closes, the resulting deceptive cadence can be considered a substitute for an authentic cadence that is either perfect (if the melody ends on the first scale-degree) or, more seldom, imperfect (if the melody ends on the third scale-degree).[25]

EXAMPLE 8.5: Following a long standing on the dominant, a deceptive cadential progression begins in measure 42 and concludes two measures later on VI. Since the descending scale in the upper line ends with the tonic scale-degree, the resulting deceptive cadence replaces a potential perfect authentic cadence. The idea is repeated, with the melody beginning a third higher, but once again ends with the same deceptive cadence. A third statement, beginning even higher, finally achieves perfect authentic closure when the cadential dominant resolves to tonic at measure 48.

3. *Evaded cadence.* The most common way of extending cadential function in a subordinate theme is through the use of an *evaded cadence*, in which the prevailing harmonic and melodic processes (often accompanied by distinct rhythmic and textural processes) fail to reach their projected goal.[26] More specifically, the musical event that directly follows the cadential dominant is perceived to group with subsequent material, not with the material leading up to that dominant. The event that appears when the cadential dominant progresses to another harmony does not sound like a structural end but, rather, like a new beginning

EXAMPLE 8.3 **(a)** Mozart, Piano Sonata in C, K. 545, i, 13–28; **(b)** mm. 1–4

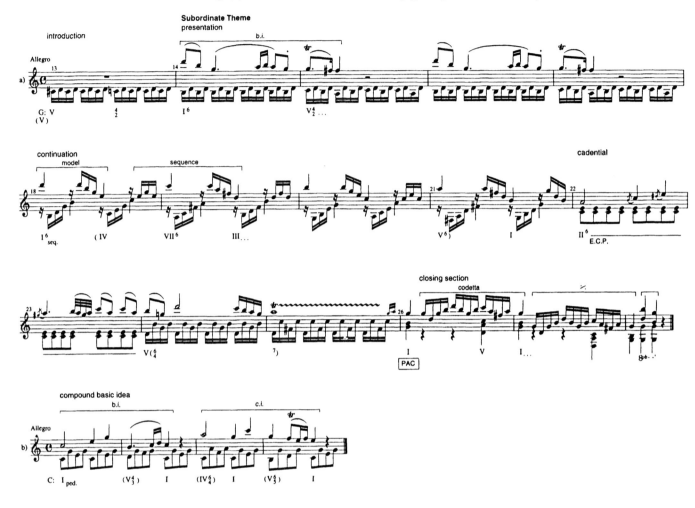

EXAMPLE 8.4 Beethoven, Overture to *Coriolanus*, Op. 62, 102–18

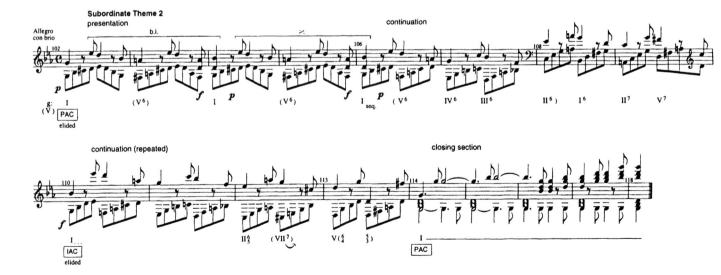

EXAMPLE 8.5 Beethoven, Piano Sonata in A-flat, Op. 26, iv, 27–49

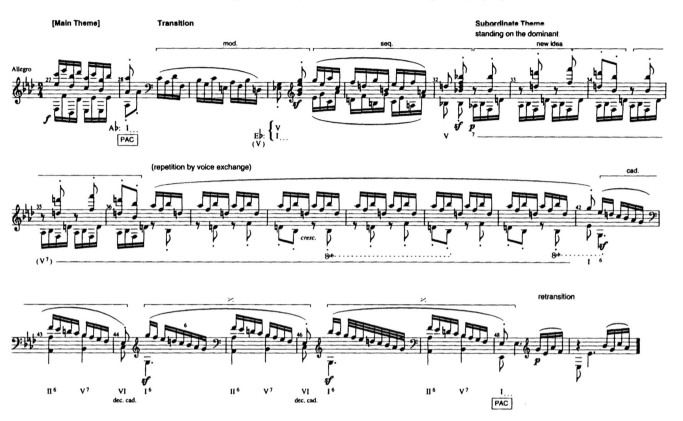

(or even, sometimes, a new middle). The music supported by the cadential dominant is thus left "hanging in the air" without a sense of formal resolution (although the dominant may receive a harmonic resolution).

The sense of cadential evasion can be projected by many different factors. For example, a distinct change in texture, dynamics, and accompanimental patterning often helps mark a new beginning. Moreover, the melodic line is usually interrupted in its projected resolution to the tonic (or, rarely, third) scale-degree. Indeed, the melody often leaps back up to the fifth scale-degree in order to start another descent toward the tonic in subsequent cadential passages. At other times, the melody moves to the tonic degree, but one that lies in a different register, so that the normal stepwise resolution is avoided. Even if the melody appears to resolve as expected, the sense of evaded cadence may still be projected by a variety of other musical forces.[27]

In most evaded cadences, the cadential dominant moves to I⁶, which is appropriate because the inverted form of the tonic prohibits the listener from construing a true cadence at that point. Moreover, the I⁶ can then easily function as the beginning of another cadential progression, one that may be evaded again or finally bring an actual cadence.[28] To lead more smoothly into the I⁶, the cadential dominant may move to V⁴₃ just before the cadential evasion.[29]

EXAMPLE 8.6: Measure 25 sees the appearance of a short cadential progression to close a second subordinate theme, which began at measure 20. (The first subordinate theme is shown ahead in ex. 8.15.) Both the melody and bass lines are clearly heading for the tonic scale-degree at the downbeat of measure 26. But the cadence is evaded when the bass leaps down to the third scale-degree to bring the tonic in first inversion. The dramatic change of dynamics and texture, combined with the sudden shift to the minor mode, creates the impression of a new beginning, despite the melodic resolution to the tonic scale-degree.

The material following an evaded cadence is sometimes new, as in the preceding example. Frequently, however, the composer repeats previously heard ideas and leads them again to a potential cadence. Another evasion may occur, or else genuine cadential closure finally results. Janet Schmalfeldt colloquially terms this particular type of cadential evasion the *"one more time" technique*, since the composer backs the music up, so to speak, in order for the listener to hear the impending cadential arrival one more time.[30]

EXAMPLE 8.7: A cadential idea beginning in measure 58 is evaded at the downbeat of measure 60. The subsequent material obviously represents a return to the beginning of measure 58 to run through the cadential idea "one more time." The perfect authentic cadence is eventually achieved on the downbeat of measure 62.

EXAMPLE 8.6 Haydn, String Quartet in B Minor, Op. 64/2, i, 19–40

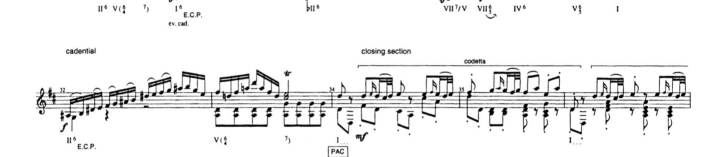

EXAMPLE 8.7 Haydn, Piano Sonata in C, Hob. XVI:35, i, 36–67

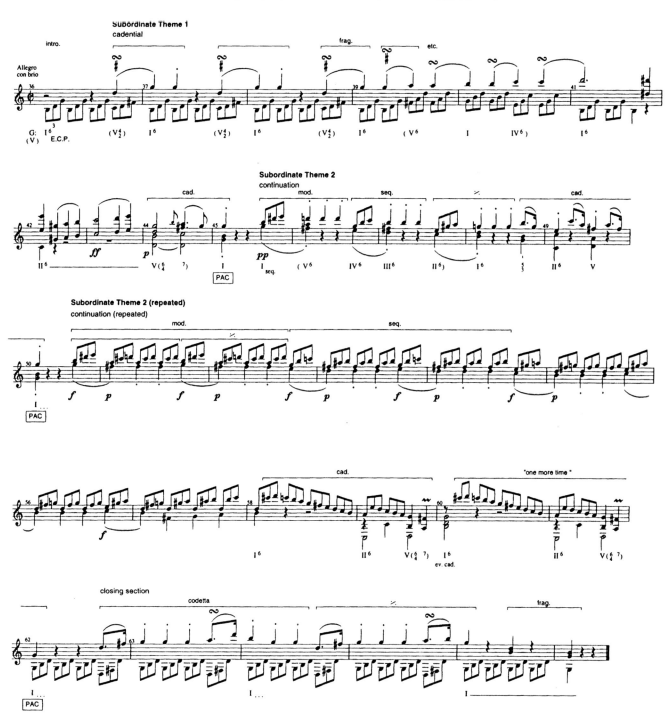

EXAMPLE 8.8 Mozart, Violin Concerto in A, K. 219, i, 98–112

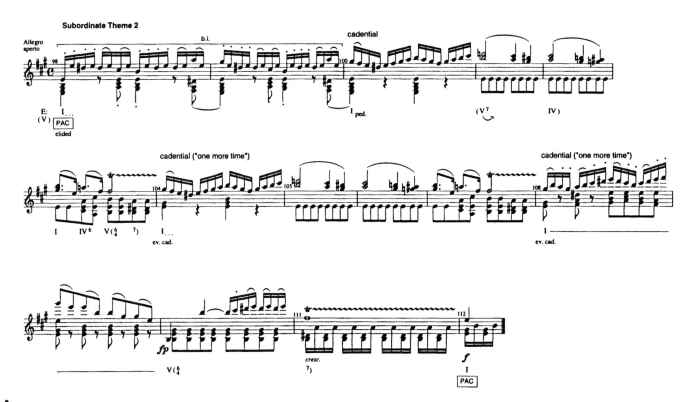

A situation that is related to, but is essentially different from, the "one more time" technique arises when the material following a genuine authentic cadence or a deceptive cadence repeats the previous idea or phrase. In example 8.4, for instance, the music following the imperfect authentic cadence at measure 110 restates once again the prior continuation phrase. Likewise, in example 8.5, each deceptive cadence (mm. 44 and 46) immediately brings back the same cadential idea. Neither of these cases, however, should be considered examples of the "one more time" technique, since they do not involve any cadential evasion. In other words, the aesthetic effect of the "one more time" technique depends on our hearing that a structural goal is approached but not achieved, after which the attempt toward the goal is made once again using the same musical material. In the case of an imperfect authentic cadence or a deceptive cadence, a definite goal has been reached, even if that goal is not the final one.

Most cadential evasions employ a I[6] to thwart the expected resolution of the cadential dominant. But an evaded cadence can also result if that dominant is followed by other harmonies, including some built on the sixth degree of the scale (VI, IV[6], and even VII[6]/V). A cadential evasion can occur even if the cadential dominant moves to a root-position tonic, as long as there is a sufficient disruption of melody, texture, dynamic, register, and so on to counter our

perceiving a structural end when the I chord appears. In such cases, the "one more time" technique can sometimes be helpful in projecting the sense of cadential evasion. As soon as we hear previous cadential material starting over again, we realize that cadential arrival has not yet occurred.

EXAMPLE 8.8: At first glance, measure 104 might seem to be an imperfect authentic cadence, with the following measure representing a repetition of the cadential phrase to bring the expected perfect authentic cadence. But when we hear that measure 104 corresponds exactly to measure 100, we sense instead that the cadence has actually been evaded and that the cadential idea is being restated one more time. An additional cadential evasion then occurs at measure 108, and another repetition of the cadential phrase, now with a somewhat expanded dominant harmony, finally brings cadential closure at measure 112.[31]

4. *Abandoned cadence.* For both deceptive and evaded cadences, the failure to realize the implied cadential arrival involves either altering harmonically or omitting entirely the formal event associated with the final tonic of the authentic cadential progression. With a deceptive cadence, the final cadential tonic is replaced by another harmony (usually VI). With an evaded cadence, the tonic is effectively eliminated (the harmony following the dominant, say, I[6], does not really belong to the prevailing cadential progression but instead introduces a new progression). In both cases, how-

ever, the cadential dominant in root position remains intact to provide an anchor for the subsequent failure to realize a true cadential arrival.[32]

Another way of averting a genuine cadence is altering, or even eliminating, the cadential dominant itself. In other words, the composer initiates what seems to be a cadential progression but then "abandons" the progression by either inverting the cadential dominant or allowing the progression to bypass that dominant entirely. The resulting cadential situation can thus be termed an *abandoned cadence*.[33] Cadential function can be abandoned in a number of ways. Sometimes the dominant may be placed in root position but then may become inverted (usually to the $\frac{6}{4}$ position) before resolving to I. Another possibility is for the dominant to appear at first in inversion. Finally, dominant harmony may be omitted. Following an abandoned cadence, the music typically expresses a continuation function. At some point, however, a new cadential progression appears, which eventually leads to a perfect authentic cadence.

EXAMPLE 8.6: Following the evaded cadence on the downbeat of measure 26, an expanded cadential progression begins with I[6] and leads to a pre-dominant Neapolitan sixth. The radical reduction of texture at measure 28 makes a precise harmonic analysis difficult, but this measure can likely be construed as VII[7]/ V (the notated A♭ is heard enharmonically as G♯), thus continuing to prolong pre-dominant harmony. The following measure (likely interpreted as VII$\frac{6}{5}$/IV) breaks away from the cadential progression, and by the time harmonic clarity is restored at measure 31, the dominant seventh appears in first inversion and thus cannot function as a cadential harmony. Thus the cadential function initiated with I[6] at measure 26 is abandoned and is restored only with the appearance of the pre-dominant II[6] at measure 32. Then a new expanded cadential progression finally reaches closure on the downbeat of measure 34.

EXAMPLE 8.9: Toward the end of an immense modulating subordinate theme (analyzed in greater detail later in this chapter), the expanded Neapolitan sixth at measure 92 implies the beginning of a cadential progression to close the theme. But the sense of impending cadence is abandoned at measure 96 when the pre-dominant moves to dominant in the form of a diminished seventh in second inversion (VII$\frac{4}{3}$). The subsequent harmonic sequence yields a new continuation, and the abandoned cadential function is not recovered until measure 99, when the pre-dominant IV[6] initiates a brief cadential progression to close the theme at measure 102.[34]

5. *Perfect authentic cadence.* In the situations discussed up to now, cadential extension has been achieved by delaying the perfect authentic cadence that marks the true end of the theme. Sometimes, however, this cadence, including the phrase leading up to it, is repeated, which extends the cadential (and possibly the continuation) function. Such a situation creates a formal dilemma: which of the two cadences marks the end of the subordinate theme? If the first cadence is seen as decisive, then the second cadential unit would rep-

resent an appendage of sorts, one not belonging to the theme proper. If the second cadence is taken as genuine, then the first cadence must be downgraded in structural importance; it may even be reinterpreted as an evaded cadence. Because the use of two cadential units, each ending with a perfect authentic cadence, tends to obscure the formal articulation, this situation seldom occurs in the repertory.

EXAMPLE 8.10: The second part of the first subordinate theme, beginning in measure 81 (shown ahead in ex. 8.17), is constructed as a sixteen-measure sentence, whose continuation brings a perfect authentic cadence in measure 94. The final four measures of the continuation are then repeated exactly, thus again producing the same cadence in measure 98. Since the cadences in measures 94 and 98 are identical, we might ask which one closes the theme. On the one hand, measure 94 could be considered the genuine end, with the subsequent phrase functioning as a codetta. On the other hand, the rising tonic arpeggio in measure 94 can be seen to keep the melody somewhat open, thus helping motivate a repetition of the phrase, whose cadence at measure 98 would represent the true close of the theme. This second interpretation is probably preferable, since a codetta following a subordinate theme is not normally made up of the same material used for the preceding continuation and cadential functions.

6. *Aesthetic effect of cadential extension.* Now that the various techniques of cadential extension have been defined and illustrated, we can compare and contrast the differing aesthetic effects that result from their use. The situation just discussed of a repeated perfect authentic cadence is probably the least effective (and hence least used) means of extending cadential function, for not only does it result in a certain degree of cadential redundancy but it also poses the question of which cadence truly effects thematic closure.

The use of an imperfect authentic cadence, followed by a perfect authentic cadence, is also somewhat redundant. But the open-ended quality of the former cadence effectively motivates the latter one. Even greater motivation arises from a deceptive cadence, for the lack of harmonic closure is more palpable than the melodic incompleteness of the imperfect authentic cadence.

Of the various techniques used to extend cadential function, the evaded cadence is unquestionably the most dramatic: the imminent closure of the theme is thwarted at the last second and then quickly reattempted. The lack of any event representing formal closure, combined with the breaking off of a highly goal-directed process just before its completion, arouses a powerful expectation for further cadential action. This effect is particularly well suited to subordinate themes, since dramatizing the subordinate key is a principal aesthetic objective of the classical style. The goal of establishing that key as a foil to the home key is made all the more effective if the struggle to gain its cadential confirmation is hard won. But the need for dramatic articulation of the home key early in a movement is not pressing, and

EXAMPLE 8.9 Beethoven, Overture to *Coriolanus*, Op. 62, 46–102

EXAMPLE 8.10 Mozart, Violin Concerto in A, K. 219, i, 88–98

thus evaded cadences seldom appear in main themes, as the techniques of partial closure (use of an imperfect authentic cadence or a deceptive cadence) are more typical modes of cadential extension.

The aesthetic impression imparted by the abandoned cadence is entirely different, for a partial cadential goal is neither achieved (as with the deceptive cadence) nor even immediately promised (as with the evaded cadence). If the abandoned cadence is less dramatic, it nonetheless promotes a significant formal loosening, since the cadential progression loses its sense of direction and the music tends to wander off somewhere else before returning on track toward another cadence. Cadential abandonment is thus particularly appropriate to the formal conventions of a subordinate theme.

Cadential expansion. Cadential function in a subordinate theme can be enlarged by means of an *expanded cadential progression*, which supports one or more complete phrases in the theme, phrases marked by distinct melodic ideas and accompanimental textures. Such phrases are most often exclusively cadential, since continuation function is usually featured in the preceding phrase.[35] The majority of expanded cadential progressions contain all four harmonic functions (initial tonic, pre-dominant, dominant, and final tonic). Occasionally the preceding continuation concludes with tonic harmony and the cadential phrase thus begins with a pre-dominant (see ex. 8.3, m. 22).

In many simple expanded progressions, no one harmony is given special emphasis over the others (see ex. 8.1, mm. 38–41, and ex. 8.3, mm. 22–26). Often, however, one of the harmonies leading to the final tonic is prominently expanded in relation to the others. If the cadential expansion is sufficiently large, the entire progression may provide the

harmonic support for several phrases, each having its own distinct melodic–motivic content.[36]

1. *Expansion of the dominant.* The most easily recognizable case of prominent cadential expansion occurs when the dominant is considerably lengthened, thereby delaying as long as possible its resolution to the tonic. In most cases, the dominant is first sounded with its six–four embellishment, and this "dissonant" sonority usually receives the greatest expansion in the phrase, thus raising powerful expectations for resolution to the five–three sonority.[37] The heightened dramatic expression inherent in this gesture makes it ideal for use in operatic and concerto genres, but it is often found in the symphonic, chamber, and solo-sonata repertories as well.

EXAMPLE 8.11: The second subordinate theme concludes with an unusual expanded cadential progression beginning at measure 58. (The details of this progression are examined later in this chapter.) When the dominant arrives at measure 61, it initially takes the form of a cadential six–four. The harmony is stretched out for three measures before leading to the dominant seventh proper in measure 64 and resolving to the tonic in the following measure. In this four-measure dominant expansion, the music acquires a marked acceleration in rhythmic activity and displays virtuosic passage-work for the clarinet and upper strings. The culminating trill confirms the concerto-like style that Mozart adopted for a chamber work featuring a solo woodwind part.[38]

2. *Expansion of the pre-dominant.* The pre-dominant may, on occasion, achieve prominence in an expanded cadential progression. In such cases, the composer typically employs a variety of pre-dominant harmonics in a single progression. But this harmonic function does not normally sustain the kinds of enormous expansions frequently found with the dominant or initial tonic.[39]

EXAMPLE 8.11 (a) Mozart, Clarinet Quintet in A, K. 581, i, 42–79; (b) rearrangement of harmonies in mm. 58–61

3. *Expansion of the initial tonic.* The initial tonic of an expanded cadential progression is usually placed in first inversion. Indeed, the classical composers often use the prominent arrival on I⁶ as a cue or "conventionalized sign" for the onset of an expanded cadential progression.⁴⁰ When expanded, this initial tonic is frequently embellished by a neighboring dominant seventh in third inversion. This use of V⁴₂ works especially well because of the voice-leading rule demanding its resolution to I⁶.

EXAMPLE 8.7: The first subordinate theme begins with a large expansion of the first-inversion tonic. I⁶ is initially prolonged by conventional V⁴₂ chords (mm. 36–39) and then is further expanded by a more complex succession of neighboring harmonies in measures 39–40. The fundamental progression continues with the appearance of the pre-dominant II⁶ in measures 42–43 and concludes with root-position dominant resolving to tonic at measure 45. The overall harmonic support for the theme is therefore cadential. Of the component harmonies making up this large cadential progression, the initial tonic receives the greatest expansion. (The notion that this subordinate theme begins directly with a cadential progression, thus expressing cadential function at the very start of the theme, is discussed later in the section on "beginning with cadential function.")⁴¹

If the initial tonic of an expanded cadential progression is prolonged for four measures and supports at the same time a new two-measure basic idea and its repetition, a phrase with presentation function will be created. A continuation could then bring the remaining harmonies of the cadence, thereby forming an eight-measure sentence.⁴²

ADDITIONAL LOOSENING TECHNIQUES

Expanded Periodic Design

Antecedent and consequent functions occur less frequently in subordinate-theme construction than do the sentential functions of presentation, continuation, and cadential just considered. When periodic functions do appear, the antecedent usually retains its conventional size of four or eight measures, but the consequent is often expanded in order to create a looser organization.

A period is rarely found if the exposition contains just a single subordinate theme. But in cases of multiple subordinate themes, one of the themes (usually the first but occasionally the last) may assume this tight-knit form.

EXAMPLE 8.1: A second subordinate theme begins at the upbeat to measure 42 with a four-measure antecedent phrase. The following consequent is expanded by means of the expanded cadential progression in measures 48–53. Note that the opening motive of the new basic idea beginning this theme is derived from the contrasting idea of the main theme (see ex. 4.9, mm. 3–4). Although the

pitches and rhythm are identical, the new tonal context changes the scale-degree functions and thus obscures our hearing a direct connection between these ideas.⁴³

Omission of an Initiating Function

A subordinate theme can acquire formal loosening by giving the impression of starting in medias res. In other words, the theme begins with a continuation or cadential function instead of a standard initiating function (such as a basic idea or presentation). Another possibility is for the initiating function to be replaced with a standing on the dominant built over that harmony from the end of the transition.

The notion of a theme "beginning" with a medial or concluding function poses a theoretical conundrum. How can a passage be a continuation if it is not preceded by some other material that it "continues"? How can a phrase appearing at the beginning of a theme be cadential if there is no other earlier phrase that is being "closed"? Since formal functionality essentially involves the way in which music expresses its logical location in a temporal spectrum consisting fundamentally of beginnings, middles, and ends, the idea that a middle (continuation) or an end (cadential) can serve to articulate a structural beginning seems, on the surface, absurd.

Yet one of the special properties of classical instrumental music is the capacity for a passage to express the sense of beginning, middle, or end independent of the passage's actual temporal location. Because formal functions are so conventionalized, because they are so well defined by specific characteristics, we can sometimes identify a given function without necessarily taking into account its position in a theme.⁴⁴ Thus the appearance of model–sequence technique alone can signal the sense of continuation function, or the presence of a cadential progression may in itself be sufficient to project a cadential function. To be sure, if a given function is actually placed differently from its expressed temporal position—if a medial function appears as a beginning, for example—a kind of formal "dissonance" will result. If that dissonance is carefully controlled, it may be suitable for expressing a loose organization. Too great a formal dissonance, however, can produce an illogical succession of formal functions.⁴⁵

Beginning with continuation function. The most effective way of expressing continuation function at the start of a theme is by means of sequential harmonic progressions, usually in connection with model–sequence technique. Since the other continuational characteristics (fragmentation, harmonic acceleration, increased surface rhythm) create their most palpable effect in relation to an immediately preceding initiating function, they are rarely used by themselves to begin a theme. They may, however, accompany the presence of sequential harmony.

EXAMPLE 8.12 Beethoven, Piano Sonata in A, Op. 2/2, i, 58–92

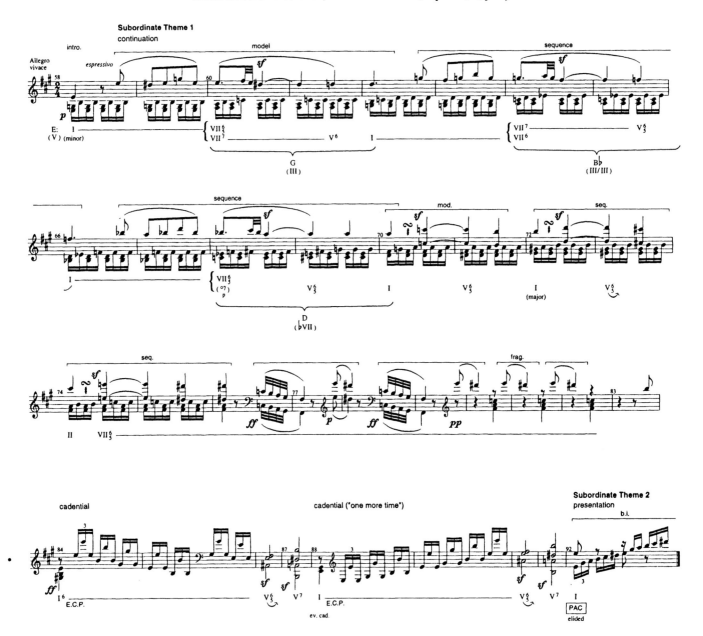

A continuation function replaces a true structural beginning most often with a second or third subordinate theme of a group. In this way, the start of the new theme at least can be understood to "continue" the subordinate group as a whole.

EXAMPLE 8.7: A perfect authentic cadence in measure 45 closes the first of two subordinate themes. (The structure of this first subordinate theme is examined shortly.) The second theme begins directly with a one-measure model, which is sequenced by descending thirds. The one-measure size of the model creates fragmentation in relation to the preceding two-measure cadential idea (mm. 44–45). The theme can thus be said to begin with a continuation function, bypassing a more conventional presentation (or other initiating function).

With the upbeat to measure 49, a brief cadential idea brings the theme to a close. Such an abrupt ending to a subordinate theme suggests that more is to come, and indeed, the theme begins to be repeated immediately. This time, however, it is more loosely organized, for the model and each subsequent sequence is extended by means of internal repetition. In addition, the cadential idea is evaded in measure 60 and repeated with "one more time" technique to bring a perfect authentic cadence in measure 62.

EXAMPLE 8.12: The first of two subordinate themes begins with a shift to the minor mode (itself a loosening device discussed later in this chapter) and introduces a three-measure model, which is then sequenced twice by the interval of an ascending minor third. (Although the sequential repetitions take place a third higher each time, the underlying sequential progression is actually stepwise ascending, with its characteristic 5–6 melody–bass counterpoint; see ex. 2.16b for the basic diatonic model.) A new two-measure model (mm. 70–71) is then sequenced by ascending steps.

All this harmonic and phrase-structural instability is highly indicative of continuation function. Here, the effect of beginning with a continuation is especially bold because the function begins the *first* of two subordinate themes, and thus the theme group as a whole lacks a sense of structural initiation. As discussed earlier in this chapter, the second subordinate theme (see ex. 8.2, mm. 92–104) emphasizes its own presentation function and therefore compensates for the lack of formal initiation in the first subordinate theme.[46]

Beginning with cadential function.   A subordinate theme occasionally begins directly with a cadential progression and thus projects a sense of that function, despite the lack of any previous material that the cadence would bring to a close.

EXAMPLE 8.7: As already discussed, the first of two subordinate themes is supported by a single expanded cadential progression, and so one functional label—cadential—can be assigned to the theme as a whole. It must be admitted, of course, that the expanded I⁶ starting this theme possesses a degree of harmonic stability. Therefore in an overall cadential function, the opening measures project a sense of structural beginning. Nonetheless, the five-measure unit supported by the I⁶ cannot easily be identified as a conventional initiating function. Instead, the grouping structure more resembles a continuation than either a presentation or a compound basic idea.[47]

EXAMPLE 8.13: The subordinate theme starts with tonic harmony in first inversion and progresses quickly to IV two measures later (m. 48). The pre-dominant harmony is further prolonged by subordinate chords in the following measure, after which dominant harmony underlies measures 50–51. Thus from its start, the theme is supported by an expanded cadential progression, and we can experience the sense of a cadential function replacing a more standard initiation. Before reaching its end, the progression leads deceptively to VI at measure 52, after which a highly compressed cadence formula brings the theme to a close.

Beethoven's decision to begin this theme with cadential function was surely related to his adopting the same procedure for the main theme, shown in example 8.13b. Starting a subordinate theme with cadential function, though relatively unusual, nevertheless conforms to the classical goal of loosening the form, and Beethoven could find precedents already with Mozart and Haydn (see the previous example). In the case of a main theme, however, Beethoven is breaking new ground. Starting a classical sonata with the pre-dominant harmony of a cadential progression is a radical procedure, one that looks forward to the romantic style, especially that of Schumann.[48]

Beginning with standing on the dominant.   As I discuss in the following chapter, the subordinate theme of an exposition is preceded by a transition whose harmonic goal is normally dominant of the subordinate key. Most often, a subsequent standing on the dominant marks the final stage of the transition, after which the beginning of the subordinate theme is articulated by new melodic–motivic material supported by tonic harmony (of the new key).

At times, the boundary between the transition and the subordinate theme becomes blurred when the dominant from the end of the transition is held over to provide harmonic support for a standing on the dominant at the beginning of the subordinate theme proper.[49] The standing on the dominant is then followed by either a continuation or a cadential function, leading eventually to the close of the theme. A standing on the dominant would not lead to one of the standard initiating functions (presentation, compound basic idea), for we would then have the impression that the standing on the dominant belongs to the end of the transition and that the initiating function is the true structural beginning of the subordinate theme.

In most cases when a subordinate theme begins with a standing on the dominant, a marked change of melodic–motivic material helps indicate where the transition ends and the subordinate theme begins. Even so, the listener's first impression when hearing the standing on the dominant is that it belongs to the transition. When a continuation or a cadential function subsequently appears, we understand that an initiating function for the theme has been bypassed, and we retrospectively reinterpret the standing on the dominant as the real start of the subordinate theme.[50]

EXAMPLE 8.13 (a) Beethoven, Piano Sonata in E-flat, Op. 31/3, i, 46–53; (b) mm. 1–8

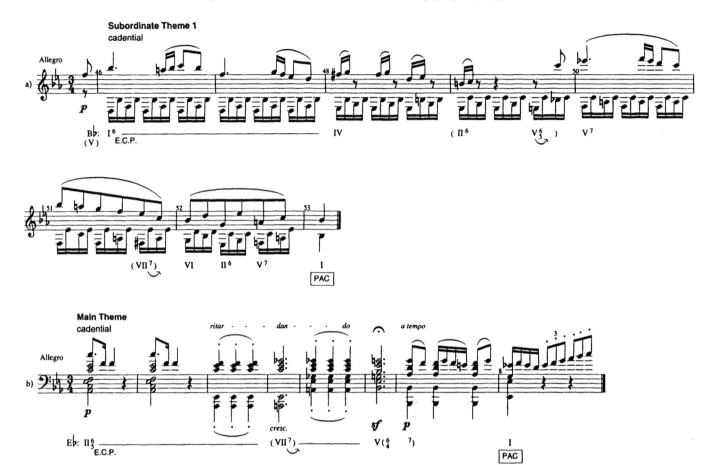

EXAMPLE 8.5: The main theme of this rondo exposition closes with a perfect authentic cadence in measure 28. A brief transition brings a two-measure model, which is sequenced up a fifth to close on the dominant of the subordinate key in measure 32. This harmony is then extended for nine measures to support a standing on the dominant, in which appears a new two-measure idea (mm. 33–34), which is immediately repeated. At measure 36, the previous four-measure unit is repeated (with an exchange of voices) and is extended by an extra bar. The dominant finally resolves to root-position tonic on the downbeat of measure 42, but the immediate change to I⁶ (with *sforzando*) signals the beginning of a cadential progression. Deceptive cadences in measures 44 and 46 allow the cadential function to extend as far as the perfect authentic cadence in measure 48.

In the context of the passage as a whole, it seems only reasonable to regard the second half of measure 32 as the beginning of the subordinate theme. The change in musical material and dynamic level (from forte at measure 27 to piano at measure 32) supports this interpretation as well.[51]

EXAMPLE 8.14: The transition leads to dominant harmony of the subordinate key (E♭ major) on the downbeat of measure 36, but the motivic material of the transition continues to be heard in the standing on the dominant of measures 36–37. The following mea-sure brings the typical dissolution of texture that so frequently marks the end of a transition. A new idea at measure 39 signals the beginning of the subordinate theme, but the underlying harmony retains the dominant from the end of the transition. The idea is repeated twice in measures 41–44, still supported by dominant harmony, and then is extended for an additional bar as the dominant finally resolves to tonic. Measure 46 sees the beginning of a continuation phrase that features model–sequence technique, and measure 50 begins a cadential phrase to close the theme in measure 54.[52]

EXAMPLE 8.15: The beginning of this subordinate theme is especially difficult to determine because little in the way of any rhythmic, textural, or dynamic change helps articulate the boundary between the transition and the subordinate theme.[53] After the transition arrives on the dominant of the subordinate key (downbeat of m. 15), a new melodic idea, featuring a chromatic stepwise descent, prolongs the half cadence by means of another half-cadential progression. This idea begins to be repeated at the upbeat to measure 17 and is further extended by fragmentation and descending six–three chords in a way that suggests continuation function. A brief cadential idea then closes the theme with a perfect authentic cadence at measure 20. The only viable beginning point for the subordinate theme is the standing on the dominant starting in the middle of measure 15.

EXAMPLE 8.14 Mozart, Symphony No. 39 in E-flat, K. 543, ii, 35–55

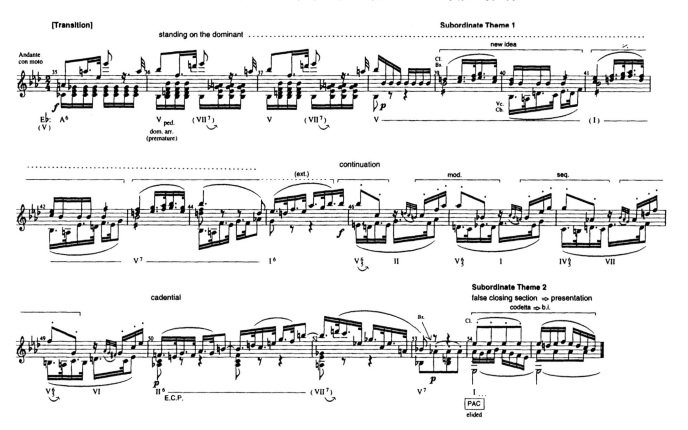

When considering subordinate themes that begin with a dominant pedal, it is necessary to distinguish cases of a genuine standing on the dominant, as seen in the three previous examples, from those in which the dominant is used to undermine what is otherwise a prolongation of tonic harmony. This latter situation was considered in connection with weakening the tonic prolongation of a presentation phrase (see ex. 1.8, mm. 21–24). The essential difference between the two situations lies in the nature of the prolongation implied by the melodic–motivic material. If the material implies a tonic prolongation, we can speak of a presentation that becomes looser as a result of the dominant pedal; if the material implies a dominant prolongation, we can speak of a theme that begins with a standing on the dominant (in place of a presentation or other initiating function).

Internal Half Cadence (Dominant Arrival)

As stated at the opening of this chapter, a subordinate theme ends with an authentic cadence in order to fulfill one of its primary functions—to confirm the subordinate key. Sometimes, a subordinate theme seems instead to end with either a half cadence or a dominant arrival.[54] The goal dominant may be further prolonged by a postcadential standing on the dominant. Although we recognize a certain sense of ending to the theme, we also know that a more conclusive authentic cadence must eventually follow. Since more subordinate-theme material will invariably be heard, we can speak of an *internal half cadence* (or internal dominant arrival) in a single subordinate theme.[55]

The appearance of an internal half cadence is most often motivated by how the transition ends. Most transitions modulate to the subordinate key and conclude there with a half cadence followed by a standing on the dominant, which builds up strong expectations for tonic resolution at the start of the subordinate theme. Sometimes, however, the transition does not modulate and closes instead on the dominant of the home key; the subordinate theme then begins directly in the subordinate key. In such cases, the absence of an emphasized subordinate-key dominant at the end of the transition is often rectified by an internal half cadence within the subordinate theme.

There are two main strategies for how the subordinate theme proceeds following an internal half cadence: (1) a resumption of continuation or cadential function, which eventually leads to a perfect authentic cadence to close the theme, or (2) the introduction of a new basic idea in the context of an initiating function (usually a presentation phrase) to begin a second part of the subordinate theme.

EXAMPLE 8.15 Haydn, String Quartet in B Minor, Op. 64/2, i, 13–22

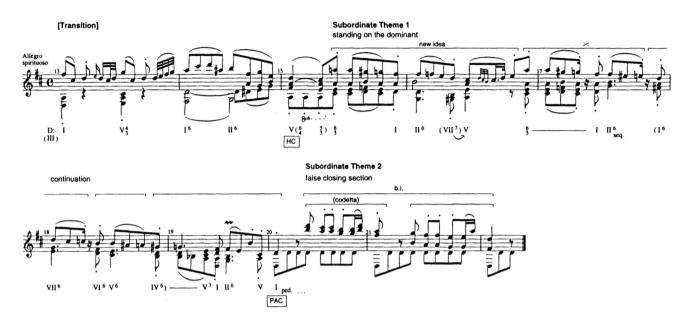

EXAMPLE 8.16 Mozart, Piano Sonata in D, K. 576, iii, 22–50

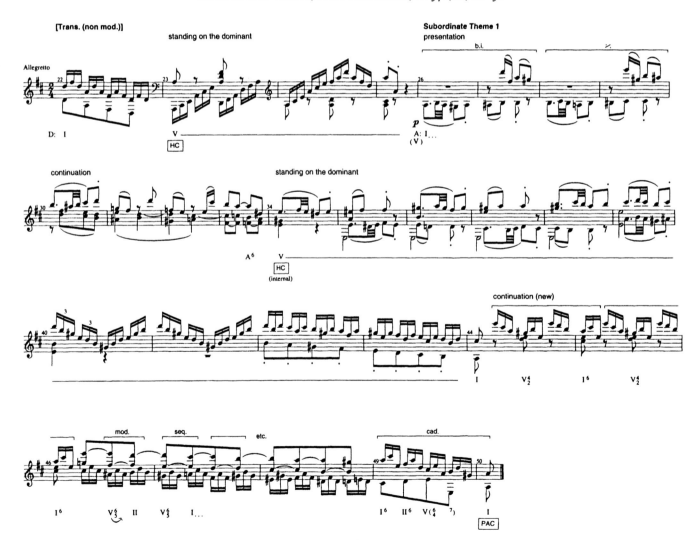

Resumption of continuation or cadential function. The idea of a half cadence "internal" to a single subordinate theme is well expressed when the dominant is followed by further continuation. In the absence of any new initiating idea, there is little sense that another theme is beginning. The continuation eventually leads to a cadential unit of some kind to close the theme. In some cases, a continuation is bypassed, and the internal half cadence may be followed directly by a cadential function (see ahead ex. 10.7b, m. 68).[56]

EXAMPLE 8.16: A nonmodulating transition ends with a half cadence (m. 23) of the home key, D major, and a three-measure standing on the dominant ensues. The subordinate theme then begins directly in the subordinate key of A major with the basic idea from the main theme sounding in the left-hand part. The repetition of the idea in the following two measures creates a presentation phrase, whose subsequent continuation leads to an internal half cadence at measure 34 and ten measures of standing on the dominant.

When the dominant finally resolves to tonic at measure 44, the material that follows has more the character of a continuation than of a new beginning. The ideas are brought in one-measure units; the prolonged tonic is placed in the less stable first-inversion position alternating with V^4_3; and the triplets maintain the same rhythmic figures introduced in the second part of the standing on the dominant. Sequential activity beginning in measure 46 further expresses continuation function, which culminates in the cadential idea of measures 49–50.[57]

New initiating function, two-part subordinate theme. When a subordinate theme leads to a half cadence, which is then followed by a new initiating function (presentation, compound basic idea), the listener may well believe that an entirely different subordinate theme has begun (and that the first subordinate theme has ended with a half cadence). Such a view is not unreasonable. But if we want to maintain the idea that a subordinate theme must end with a perfect authentic cadence—and there are many good reasons for doing so—then the interpretation of two different subordinate themes for the situation just described must be modified.[58] In its place, the notion of a *two-part subordinate theme* may be introduced and defined as follows: in a two-part subordinate theme, the first part ends with a half cadence, which may be followed by a standing on the dominant; the second part begins with a new basic idea, which is usually incorporated into a presentation or a compound basic idea and which eventually leads to perfect authentic closure for the entire theme.

EXAMPLE 8.17: After a nonmodulating transition ending with a half cadence in the home key, the subordinate-theme group begins on the second beat of measure 71 in the subordinate key of E major. A normal presentation phrase leads to a compressed continuation ending with a half cadence in measure 80. (Here, the internal half cadence is, exceptionally, not followed by a standing on the dominant.) A completely new basic idea then initiates a second

part to this subordinate theme. This part is organized as a sixteen-measure sentence, whose compressed continuation phrase ends with a perfect authentic cadence in measure 94 (see ex. 8.10). The cadential component is then repeated to bring the theme to a close in measure 98.

The way in which the cadential endings of the two parts relate to each other clearly creates a certain "antecedent–consequent" expression (i.e., half cadence in m. 80, perfect authentic cadence in mm. 94 and 98). Yet to regard the overall structure of the subordinate theme as a period of any kind would do violence to the fundamental definition of this theme-type: too many other characteristics of periodic organization are lacking, especially the notion that the consequent "repeats" the antecedent (by beginning with the same basic idea).

Following traditional notions of form, some analysts might see the true "second subject" as beginning in measure 81 because of the catchier tune and because that idea was also found in the opening ritornello (m. 20).[59] But this view ignores the fact that measures 74–80 reside entirely in the new key. Thus for tonal reasons, as well as phrase-structural ones, this passage is consistent with the definition of a subordinate theme (first part) and should not be regarded as belonging to the transition. (See also the discussion of this example in chap. 17).[60]

Not every passage involving an expansion of dominant harmony in a subordinate theme can be considered an internal half cadence and standing on the dominant. For example, the dominant of an expanded cadential progression (such as ex. 8.11, mm. 61–64) functions as the penultimate harmony of the progression, not the ultimate harmony, as is the case with a half cadence. Other dominant expansions, not belonging to a cadential progression, may arise without necessarily representing an internal half cadence and standing on the dominant.

EXAMPLE 8.12: The harmony in the second half of measure 74 is the dominant-functioning VII^6_5. This harmony is then expanded for nine additional measures, after which the I^6 of measure 84 signals the onset of the cadential progression. Does the diminished seventh chord of measure 74 mark a dominant arrival, and is the subsequent prolongation of that harmony a standing on the dominant? No, because measure 74 does not represent the harmonic goal of the previous progression. In a broad stepwise-ascending pattern in the bass (which starts at the very beginning of the subordinate theme), the VII^6_5 functions as a passing chord between I (m. 72) and I^6 (m. 84).

The highly dramatic gesture associated with this expanded diminished seventh chord cannot go unnoticed. The harmonic stasis on a dissonant sonority, combined with violent disruptions of dynamics and register, sets up powerful expectations for resolution, which is provided by the sixteenth-note flurry of the expanded cadential progression (mm. 84–85).

Introduction to a Subordinate Theme

As we saw in chapter 1, a main theme is sometimes preceded by a brief introduction. The principal characteristics

EXAMPLE 8.17 Mozart, Violin Concerto in A, K. 219, i, 71–89

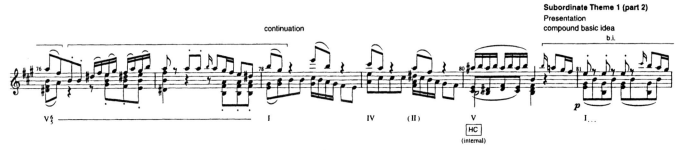

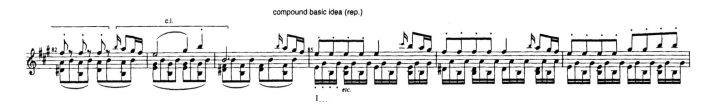

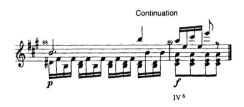

of this function are a prolongation of tonic harmony, an absence of melodic profile (so as not to imply a basic idea), and a progressive dynamic. The beginning of a subordinate theme can also be preceded by a short introduction. Typically, however, the underlying harmony is dominant, which is prolonged from the end of the transition and resolved to the tonic at the beginning of the subordinate theme. The opening measure of example 8.3 illustrates well the use of dominant prolongation at the basis of a thematic introduction. In such cases, the composer usually separates the end of the transition from the introduction to the subordinate theme through such means as rests or marked dynamic and textural changes. Sometimes the dominant at the end of the transition resolves to tonic, which forms the basis of an introduction to the subordinate theme.[61]

One type of introduction typical of subordinate themes is created when tonic harmony and new accompanimental patterns start on the downbeat of the measure following the end of the transition; the basic idea then begins later in that measure, so that the downbeat of the next measure must be seen as the actual "first" measure of the theme. The openings of examples 8.7, 8.11, and 8.12 illustrate this technique. It is interesting to observe that this type of thematic introduction is rarely encountered with main themes, although the opening of Mozart's Symphony No. 40 in G Minor, K. 550, is a notable exception.[62]

Modal Shift

Almost all subordinate themes reside in the major mode; even in minor-mode movements, the subordinate theme usually lies in the relative major. Nonetheless, a change from major to minor is frequently encountered within a subordinate theme (or theme group).[63] Such a *modal shift* introduces a broader spectrum of pitches and pitch relationships and, similar to the use of chromaticism, creates a looser formal expression. That this modal shift can be considered a loosening device is confirmed by the general absence of this technique in tight-knit main themes.[64]

Except at the final cadence of the theme (or theme group), a modal shift can take place anywhere in a subordinate theme; however, the technique tends to occur in connection with continuation function. Among the examples discussed in this chapter, modal shifts can be found at the initial tonic of an expanded cadential progression (see ex. 8.6, m. 26) and at the beginning of a second subordinate theme (see ex. 8.11, m. 50).[65] A modal shift is particularly dramatic when it occurs at the beginning of the subordinate theme (or theme group) (see ex. 8.12).[66] No matter where the modal shift takes place, the major modality is ultimately restored, at least by the final cadence of the theme (or in the case of a theme group, by the cadence of the last theme).[67]

Tonicization of Remote Regions

A shift to minor mode in the subordinate theme brings into play tonal regions, such as ♭III, ♭VI, ♭VII, and ♭II, that would otherwise be considered remote in a strictly major-mode context. The prominent tonicization of these regions is another loosening device typical of subordinate themes (but not of main themes).

EXAMPLE 8.11: The second subordinate theme begins at the upbeat to measure 50 with a shift to the minor mode. An initiating phrase, which could be analyzed as either a compound basic idea or a presentation (see the circled notes), is followed by a continuation, whose descending fifth sequential progression leads the music into the ♭VI region. The following passage, beginning at measure 58, consists of an ingenious variation to an expanded cadential progression, in which the typical bass-line ascent is actually found in the tenor voice (see the circled notes). A rewritten version of this progression (ex. 8.11b) inverts the chords to make the bass line more conventional. In this form, the augmented triad in measure 58 can be understood as a chromatic variant of the initial cadential tonic. The following diminished seventh sonority substitutes for the pre-dominant built over the fourth degree in the bass. In Mozart's actual placement of these chords (ex. 8.11a), we perceive that the sustained C♮ in the bass voice implies a prolongation of ♭VI throughout measures 58–59, thus reinforcing the tonicization of that region. The diminished seventh VII♯/V of measure 60 obscures any further sense of C major, but it is not until the arrival of the cadential six–four in the following measure that the music regains its tonal bearings firmly in the subordinate key of E major. (See also ex. 8.9, mm. 92–95, and ex. 8.12, mm. 60–70.)

Modulating Subordinate Theme, "Three-Key Exposition"

The most radical loosening of a subordinate theme by means of harmonic–tonal devices occurs when the theme begins in a key other than that in which it ends. Examples of such a *modulating subordinate theme*[68] are seen most often in Beethoven and reflect this composer's greater use of more far-reaching tonal relationships than those employed by Haydn and Mozart.[69]

In all cases of modulating subordinate themes, the goal subordinate key, that in which the theme closes with a perfect authentic cadence, is the dominant region of the home key. The key in which the theme begins can vary, but the submediant region in major-mode movements and the mediant (relative major) in minor-mode ones are usually favored. This initial key is already established by its dominant at the end of the transition.

Some writers have recently adopted the expression *three-key exposition* to characterize such procedures.[70] But this term is somewhat of a misnomer. In the classical style, the "second" key, the one beginning the subordinate theme, is rarely confirmed as such by cadential closure.[71] Rather, this initial key functions more as an emphasized tonal region in

EXAMPLE 8.18 Beethoven, Piano Sonata in E-flat, Op. 31/3, ii, 31–63

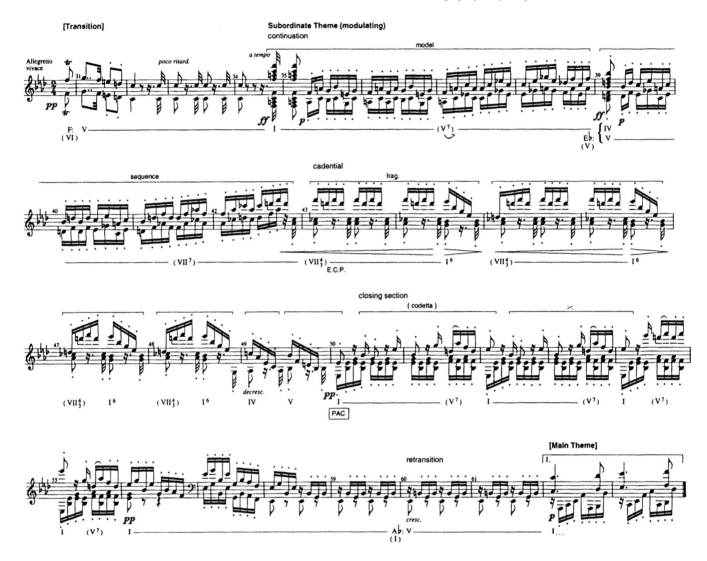

the broader modulatory process from the home key to the true subordinate key (dominant).[72]

EXAMPLE 8.18: A very brief transition (shown in full in ex. 9.8) leads to the dominant of F (VI of the home key, Ab). A sudden fortissimo outburst heralds a surprising shift to the major mode and initiates a four-measure model to begin the subordinate theme. The model is sequenced down a fifth into Bb (IV of VI), which functions as the pivot harmony (V) for the modulation to the true subordinate key, Eb. The fragmentation in measures 43–48 is supported by an expanded cadential I⁶. The rest of the cadential progression in measures 49–50 brings the concluding perfect authentic cadence. Beethoven then writes a long closing section (mm. 50–59) emphasizing root-position tonic. In so doing, he compensates for the complete absence of that harmony—and its attendant initiating function—within the structural boundaries of the modulating subordinate theme.

EXAMPLE 8.9: The transition ends with a dominant arrival of Eb, the relative major of the home key and the normal subordinate key for works in the minor mode. The subordinate theme begins in measure 52 with a compound basic idea that is immediately repeated to make a presentation. The idea begins to be repeated again but veers off instead to the supertonic region, where at measure 64 the previous eight measures are sequenced one step higher. At measure 72 the music arrives on G minor (the mediant of Eb) with a single statement of the original basic idea. The following music is fully continuational and leads to an internal half cadence and standing on the dominant of G minor, the true subordinate key.

The motivation for this internal half cadence is evident: because of the theme's modulatory structure and of how the subordinate key was approached, the dominant of the new key received no prior emphasis.[73] From measure 84 onward, Beethoven adopts both the strategies typically found after an internal half cadence. On the one hand, a new presentation phrase (mm. 84–87) suggests the beginning of a second part to the theme. On the other hand, this presentation immediately functions as a model for sequential repetition a fifth lower in measures 88–91, thus also expressing a resumption of continuation function.[74]

MULTIPLE SUBORDINATE THEMES

The exposition section of a large-scale movement—one usually written in sonata, rondo, or concerto form—often features a *group* of subordinate themes. Conforming to the stylistic norms, each one of these themes ends with a perfect authentic cadence in the subordinate key.[75] The use of multiple subordinate themes is one of the principal means for the classical composer to enlarge the formal dimensions of the musical composition, for a greater number of loosening techniques can be employed there than would be possible in the confines of a single theme. Indeed, the way in which such techniques are dispersed among the various themes of the group is usually of significant analytical interest.[76]

The functional relationship among multiple subordinate themes is difficult to define, since the individual themes can exhibit such a wide range of formal expression. Therefore, an entirely neutral scheme of identifying the themes in a group is adopted here, in which they are simply numbered according to their order of appearance (i.e., first subordinate theme, second subordinate theme). A more functional characterization of the various subordinate themes of a group awaits further research.

To maintain rhythmic continuity among multiple subordinate themes, the end of one theme may elide with the beginning of the next theme. More precisely, the final tonic of the perfect authentic cadence functions simultaneously as the initial tonic of the subsequent theme. (Subordinate theme groups from this chapter featuring elision between themes can be seen in ex. 8.9, m. 102; ex. 8.10, m. 98; and ex. 8.12, m. 92.)[77] Such elision must be distinguished from what may be called *accompanimental overlap*, in which the moment of cadential arrival brings with it the new accompanimental figuration of the next theme, but the first true downbeat of that theme does not occur until the beginning of the following measure.[78] (An accompanimental overlap can be seen in ex. 8.11, m. 49.)

In some situations, it is not possible to characterize the individual themes making up a group as more or less loose in relation to one another. They simply contain a different set of loosening techniques. Frequently, however, one of the themes is distinctly more tight knit. This tight-knit theme often occurs in the first position within the group (especially in Mozart) but also may occupy a medial or final position.[79]

EXAMPLE 8.11: The first of two subordinate themes is constructed as a tight-knit sentence, whose continuation is compressed into three measures. The second subordinate theme begins in measure 50 with the clarinet taking up the basic idea of the previous theme, but the change to the minor mode signals a looser organization. The music moves off in measure 54 toward a prominent tonicization of bVI and significant cadential expansion.[80]

EXAMPLE 8.2: As discussed, the second subordinate theme begins in measure 92 with a four-measure presentation whose repetition elides with the continuation, which closes with a perfect authentic cadence in measure 104. Although repeating the presentation makes this theme somewhat looser than a simple eight-measure sentence, the resulting formal organization is significantly more tightly knit than the first subordinate theme (see ex. 8.12), with its chromatic sequences and cadential evasions. Indeed, emphasizing the presentation in the second subordinate theme compensates for the lack of an initiating function in the first subordinate theme.

EXAMPLE 8.4: Following a very loose modulating theme (shown in ex. 8.9), a considerably more tightly knit second subordinate theme helps provide stability and further confirmation of the true subordinate key, G minor. The theme takes the form of an eight-measure sentence, whose continuation phrase is repeated.[81]

EXAMPLE 8.19 Mozart, Symphony No. 39 in E-flat, K. 543, ii, 53–69

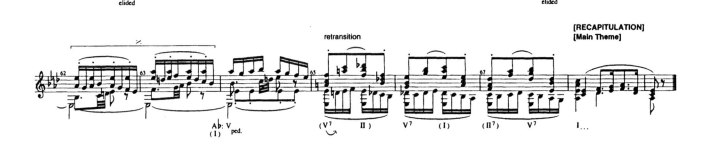

CLOSING SECTION

Traditional theories of form refer to a "closing theme," which directly follows the "second subject" and brings the exposition to a close. Unfortunately, the concept of closing theme is usually not defined with any precision, and the term tends to be applied indiscriminately to a wide range of formal contexts.[82] In light of the categories established in this study, what is traditionally called a closing theme can most often be identified as either a true subordinate theme (usually the last of a group) or a collection of codettas following the final subordinate theme.[83] Indeed, it is not normally possible to identify a specific theme-type that should be considered a closing theme, as opposed to a subordinate theme.[84] For this reason, the notion of a specific closing "theme" is not adopted here; rather, the term *closing section* is used more specifically to label a group of codettas, just as this term is used elsewhere in this book.[85]

In movements containing a single subordinate theme, a postcadential closing section almost always follows the perfect authentic cadence ending that theme. In movements containing a subordinate-theme group, the closing section follows the cadence ending the last theme of the group. Rarely is a closing section omitted from an exposition.[86] In this respect, subordinate themes differ from main themes, which only occasionally include a closing section. This difference is the result of the greater energy built up in the course of achieving the cadential goal of a subordinate theme, compared with that typically generated by a main theme. Thus a subordinate theme almost always demands a postcadential passage either to dissipate the accumulated energy or, sometimes, to sustain that energy even further beyond the actual moment of cadential closure.

A closing section usually contains several different codettas.[87] Typically, the first codetta is repeated and then followed by a second codetta, which may or may not be repeated; a third codetta may then also appear. In such cases, the subsequent codetta is usually shorter than the previous one, thus creating phrase-structural fragmentation within the closing section. Indeed, a general sense of compression of musical material is usually expressed in a closing section, whereas expansions of ideas are rare.[88]

The melodic content of most closing sections contrasts markedly with the cadential ideas closing the theme. The material usually consists of conventionalized scalar or arpeggiated patterns. On occasion, however, the codettas can establish more significant motivic references, especially when ideas from the main theme return to round out the whole exposition.

EXAMPLE 8.7: The closing section begins at the upbeat to measure 63 with a two-measure codetta clearly derived from the basic idea of the main theme (see ex. 5.5). The codetta is immediately repeated, after which fragmentation brings a new one-measure codetta devoid of motivic content.

Retransition

The final codetta of the closing section is sometimes followed by a *retransition*, a passage that functions to modulate back to the home key and to lead smoothly to a repeat of the exposition. The material of the retransition sometimes grows directly out of the final codetta (see ex. 8.18, mm. 60–61; see also ahead ex. 8.19, mm. 65–67). At other times, the content of the retransition is quite different from the closing section. On occasion, the retransition anticipates main-theme motives in order to prepare for the repeated exposition.

False Closing Section

Within a subordinate-theme group, a true closing section appears only after the final theme of the group. The perfect authentic cadences of any of the prior themes, however, may be followed by material with the prominent characteristics of a codetta (i.e., tonic pedal, prolongation of tonic scale-degree in the soprano voice, a generally recessive dynamic). The subsequent development of this material, however, is revealed retrospectively to function as the beginning of a new subordinate theme. In most cases, the codetta-like idea can be reinterpreted as a basic idea, whose repetition creates a presentation phrase. In such situations, we can say that the new theme begins with a *false closing section*.

EXAMPLE 8.19: The cadence of the subordinate theme at measure 54 elides with material of obvious codetta character. But the passage proves to be a false closing section, because a genuine theme-type (an eight-measure sentence, compressed by one measure) emerges as a second subordinate theme. When the theme begins to be repeated at measure 60, Mozart shows that these same ideas can indeed function as codettas of a real closing section.

(Given the highly imitative texture, it is difficult to say which of the various lines define the grouping structure of the second subordinate theme: the clearest pattern is found in the first clarinet part, which projects a four-measure presentation phrase. This same melodic fragment also begins the real closing section that follows the theme.)

EXAMPLE 8.6: The first subordinate theme (shown in ex. 8.15) ends with a perfect authentic cadence in measure 20. The following idea has the character of a codetta, as expressed by the tonic pedal and octave descent from the tonic scale-degree in the melody. Subsequent fragmentation over the tonic pedal further suggests a closing section. When the bass line starts to become more active in the second half of measure 23, however, we realize that a more fully developed thematic unit is in the making, and the evaded cadence at measure 26 destroys any lingering sense of a closing section.

As just shown, the local phrase-structural context in measures 20–21 suggests a closing section, even though subsequent events reveal it to be the beginning of another subordinate theme. But by taking a broader view, the listener might have predicted from the start that the closing section would prove false. A true closing section at measure 20 would have yielded a subordinate theme (see ex.

8.15) that is shorter than the main theme, a violation of classical norms. Moreover, the subordinate theme would not have witnessed any cadential extension or expansion. Indeed, the material that follows the false closing section provides just this significant cadential emphasis.

DYNAMIC CURVE OF SUBORDINATE THEME

A subordinate theme (or theme group) usually features a *dynamic curve* involving a fluctuation of progressive and recessive dynamics, with a distinct climax at some point in the theme.[89] As a general rule, the theme begins in a state of relative calm. Example 8.18 is exceptional, beginning as it does with the surprising fortissimo chords.[90] In cases in which there is considerable rhythmic activity from the very start of the theme, the intensity is still usually soft (see exs. 8.12 and 8.13).

Most themes then feature a progressive dynamic leading to some high point near the end of the theme or even at the very moment of the cadential arrival.[91] Indeed, the major climax of the entire subordinate-theme area is usually associated with an expanded cadential progression. In concerto movements especially, the climax occurs where the increasing rhythmic activity reaches its highest state with the trill in the solo part just before the cadential arrival (see ex. 8.8, m. 111). This device is also found in other genres, where its appearance signals a concerto style (as in ex. 8.11, m. 64).

The closing section can exhibit a variety of dynamic states. Most often, a recessive dynamic dissipates the energy built up for the cadential arrival (see ex. 8.2, mm. 104–16). In cases in which the closing section is relatively calm, the very final measures might suddenly return to forte in order to mark a decisive conclusion for the exposition (see ex. 8.11, mm. 78–79). Another, somewhat less common, possibility is for the closing section to sustain the intensity achieved by the climax in the preceding cadential area, thus remaining highly charged to the very end of the exposition (see ex. 8.4, mm. 114–18). In the case of a false closing section, the music usually begins with a recessive dynamic, which helps give the impression that it is a closing section. However, as the music proceeds and we learn that it is actually organized as another subordinate theme, a progressive dynamic takes over, and another climax is usually reached by the end of the theme (see ex. 8.6, mm. 32–34).

9

Transition

At the heart of the tonal drama in the exposition of a full-movement form (sonata, concerto, rondo, etc.) lies the conflict between the home key and its rival subordinate key. The formal functions of main theme and subordinate theme are responsible for establishing and confirming these tonalities. Standing between these functions is the *transition*, which serves to destabilize the home key so that the subordinate key can emerge as a competing tonality in the exposition.[1] In addition, the transition loosens the form established by the tight-knit main theme, imparts greater rhythmic continuity and momentum to the movement, and, especially toward its end, liquidates the characteristic melodic–motivic material in order to "clear the stage" for the entrance of the subordinate theme.

Most often, the transition destabilizes the home key through the process of modulation, so that the home key is eventually given up and replaced by the subordinate key. But the transition need not modulate: if the main theme has tonic as its harmonic goal (by closing with an authentic cadence), the transition may undermine this tonal stability simply by leading to the home-key dominant, a decidedly weaker harmonic goal. These two tonal procedures characterize the main categories of transition, termed *modulating* and *nonmodulating*, respectively. A third category combines these two types into a single *two-part transition*.

The harmonic goal of a transition is normally dominant—of the subordinate key, in the case of a modulating transition, or of the home key, in the case of a nonmodulating one. This dominant may be articulated by a half cadence but may also appear in ways that are noncadential. The transition thus closes somewhat like the B section of a small ternary.[2] Unlike main and subordinate themes, a transition need not end with a cadence. For this reason, it is not considered a genuine theme but, rather, a *themelike unit* within the exposition.

As an integral unit of form, a transition is constructed out of the same intrathematic functions associated with main and subordinate themes. The sentential functions of presentation, continuation, and cadential are most commonly employed. The periodic function of antecedent occurs now and then,[3] but a true consequent (which by its very nature must lead to a tonic goal, an authentic cadence) is seldom found. Although introductions are rare, a postcadential standing on the dominant appears at the end of most transitions. As in the case of subordinate themes, the ternary functions of exposition, contrasting middle, and recapitulation are not used in transitions (see chap. 8, n. 9).

A transition is more loosely organized than its preceding main theme.[4] Many of the devices of formal loosening described in the previous chapter are applicable to transitions—extended continuation, omission of initiating function, modal shift, tonicization of remote regions, and expanded cadential progressions. Some of the loosening techniques associated with subordinate themes, however, are not appropriate to transitions. For example, a transition seldom begins with a standing on the dominant, since most main themes close with tonic harmony, which is usually continued into the beginning of the transition.[5] (Even when the main theme ends with dominant harmony, the transition most always begins with tonic.) A string of evaded cadences, so common with subordinate themes, rarely is found in transitions, since this technique is connected with an impending authentic cadence, not with a half cadence ending a transition. Finally, transitions are often quite short, sometimes lasting as little as four measures.[6] The massive expansions of form typical of subordinate themes are seldom encountered with transitions.

In comparison with main themes, transitions less often contain melodic material that would be characterized as tuneful (except, of course, when beginning with the preceding main-theme material).[7] Rather, they frequently feature "passage-work"—arpeggiations and scale patterns projecting a "brilliant style."[8] Transitions are often the first place in the movement where a continuous rhythmic accompaniment (such as an "Alberti" bass) is employed. Furthermore, a transition is typically characterized by a significant increase in dynamic intensity and forward drive. Indeed, the beginning of the transition is often the moment when the movement seems to be "getting under way." The frequent use of structural elision with the end of the main theme and a sudden change from piano to forte also helps create the impression of high energy at the beginning of the transition.

EXAMPLE 9.1 Mozart, Violin Sonata in C, K. 403/385c, i, 1–9

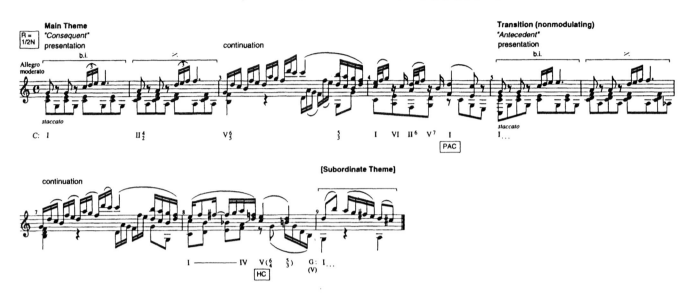

EXAMPLE 9.2 (a) Haydn, Piano Sonata in C, Hob. XVI:21, ii, 7–12; (b) mm. 1–4

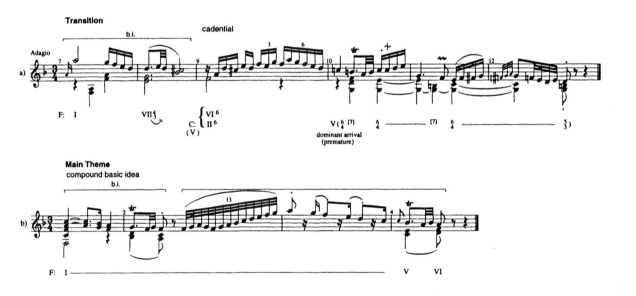

MODULATING VERSUS NONMODULATING TRANSITION

Most transitions can be divided into two main categories based on their underlying tonal structure. The majority of transitions modulate from the home key to the subordinate key, although a significant minority remain in the home key. Both types end with dominant harmony and feature similar loosening techniques. (Two-part transitions, which combine a nonmodulating and modulating transition, make up a third category, described at the end of this chapter.)

Modulating Transition

The most thorough way of destabilizing the home key is to abandon it entirely by modulating to the subordinate key. Each movement finds its own specific way of modulating, but some general procedures are regularly encountered.[9]

In major-mode movements, the subordinate key (almost always the dominant region of the home key) is usually reached by means of a *pivot-chord* modulation. A simple pivot sees the home-key tonic becoming the subdominant of the subordinate key, which then can move easily to the dominant.[10] Often, there is a prominent move to VI, which pivots to become a pre-dominant II in the subordinate key.[11] Sequential progressions also are effective in creating a smooth modulation to the new key.[12]

In minor-mode movements, the modulation to the relative major (the conventional subordinate key) frequently involves reinterpreting VI as IV, which then progresses to V. Another common pivot sees IV in the home key becoming II in the new key.[13] If the subordinate key is the minor dominant, then the modulation usually takes place along lines similar to major-mode movements.

Nonmodulating Transition

The primary function of a transition—to destabilize the home key—can be achieved without necessarily abandoning that key. If the main theme ends with tonic harmony of an authentic cadence, the home key can still be significantly weakened by allowing the transition to conclude on dominant harmony. The subordinate theme then begins directly in the subordinate key.[14] Nonmodulating transitions are found most often in major-mode movements, since the final dominant can simply be sustained as the tonic of the new key.[15]

EXAMPLE 9.1: The main theme, built as an eight-measure sentence (R = ½N), ends with a perfect authentic cadence in measure 4. The theme begins to be repeated in the following measures, but when the sentence closes instead with a half cadence, we perceive a distinct weakening of the home key in a manner that suggests transition function. The G-major harmony from the end of measure 8

is continued at the start of the next thematic unit, but this harmony now is fully interpreted as tonic of the subordinate key. We can thus hear this new unit as a subordinate theme and confirm our suspicions that the preceding unit is a nonmodulating transition. (The possibility of hearing measures 1–8 as a "reversed period"—a consequent followed by an antecedent—is considered shortly in connection with transitions that begin with main theme material.)[16]

If the main theme closes with a half cadence, a nonmodulating transition is not normally used: a second ending on the dominant of the home key would not, in itself, represent a destabilization of that key.[17]

Because a nonmodulating transition does not bring the dominant of the new key before the beginning of the subordinate theme, an internal half cadence and standing on the dominant often appear in the subordinate theme proper (see chap. 8).

BEGINNING THE TRANSITION

Most transitions open in one of four main ways: with new material supported by the home-key tonic, with the opening material of the main theme, with a false closing section made up of codettas to the main theme, or with a sudden shift to a nontonic region of the home key. The first two procedures account for the majority of transitions; the third and fourth procedures are less common. The choice of beginning depends to some extent on the structure of the preceding main theme (group), especially how it ends.

New material. Many transitions in the classical literature begin with new material supported by the home-key tonic. This opening is commonly used after the main theme has closed with a perfect authentic cadence, less often after a half cadence. At first, the listener cannot be sure whether the new material represents a transition or possibly a second main theme, for only the subsequent modulation to the new key or a goal dominant in the home key can confirm that a transition has indeed been under way. (A second main theme would close with another perfect authentic cadence in the home key.)[18]

EXAMPLE 9.2: The transition opens in measures 7–8 with a new two-measure basic idea. To be sure, this "new" idea clearly derives from the opening basic idea (ex. 9.2b, mm. 1–2), in that it consists of a scalar descent and closes with the same rhythmic gesture. Yet the melodic scale-degrees, the harmonic support, and the accompanimental setting of measures 7–8 (ex. 9.2a) are sufficiently different to project the sense of a new beginning (of the transition) rather than a repetition (of the main theme).[19]

Main-theme material. This opening is typically employed when the main theme ends with a half cadence. In

EXAMPLE 9.3 Beethoven, Piano Sonata in G Minor, Op. 49/1, i, 1–17

EXAMPLE 9.4 Haydn, Piano Trio in E-flat, Hob. XV:30, i, 15–44

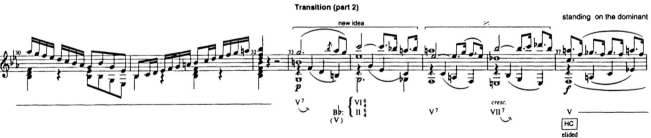

such cases, we have the initial impression that the main theme is not yet over. Since the half cadence can be heard to close an antecedent unit, the return of the opening basic idea implies the start of a consequent. When the music no longer corresponds to the antecedent and modulates to the new key, we understand in retrospect that the return of the basic idea marked the beginning of the transition and that the half cadence truly closed the main theme.[20]

EXAMPLE 9.3: The half cadence in measure 8 closes a simple sentence. The sentence begins to be repeated, thus suggesting the formation of a sixteen-measure period. But the modulation at measure 12 and the ending with another half cadence at measure 15 prompt the listener to reinterpret the first sentence as a main theme and the second sentence as a transition.

Analysts might be tempted to locate the beginning of the transition at measure 12, the moment when the "consequent" of the main theme departs from its course and the modulation takes place. To be sure, this moment marks the end of main-theme material, but from a more strictly formal point of view, this moment represents neither an end (of the main theme) nor a beginning (of the transition). Rather, measure 12 stands very much in the middle of a formal process, one that clearly begins at measure 9.[21]

The strategy of beginning the transition like a repetition of the main theme can also be used when the latter has closed with an authentic cadence. Frequently in such cases, the beginning of the transition elides with the end of the main theme.[22] If the transition is nonmodulatory, the combined main theme and transition can sometimes give the impression of being a kind of "reversed period" (i.e., a consequent followed by an antecedent).[23]

EXAMPLE 9.1: As discussed, the opening four measures are constructed as a sentence (R = ¼N) ending with a perfect authentic cadence. The sentence is repeated in the following four measures but ends this time with a half cadence in measure 8. The overall structure suggests a sixteen-measure period whose constituent functions have been reversed. This use of *phrase* functional labels is fine as far as it goes, but it leaves open the question of how logical it can be for the composer simply to reverse syntactical units. When we recognize that the two units have specific *thematic* functions, namely that of a main theme followed by a nonmodulating transition, then the formal syntax becomes more convincing. Some details of pitch structure in this example suggest that "re-reversing" the units into a normative antecedent–consequent succession would not be entirely satisfactory. Note that the second unit introduces a number of chromatic embellishments (the A♭ at the end of m. 6; the F♯ and B♭ in m. 7). This chromatically inflected antecedent would unlikely be followed by a purely diatonic consequent of a regular period. Thematically, however, the chromaticism contributes to destabilizing the home key, thus helping to fulfill one of the central functions of a transition.[24]

False closing section.   A main theme that ends with a perfect authentic cadence can be followed by a closing section consisting of codettas. When this occurs, the end of the closing section and the subsequent beginning of the transition usually are separated by a distinct break in rhythmic motion.[25] On occasion, however, such codettas merge directly into material that no longer seems part of a closing section but, rather, is more typical of a transition. In these cases, the codettas appear at first to have a postcadential function in relation to the main theme, but they are then understood retrospectively to initiate (usually as a presentation) the transition proper. We can thus speak of the codettas forming a false closing section, as defined in the previous chapter in connection with subordinate themes.

EXAMPLE 9.4: The main theme closes with a perfect authentic cadence on the downbeat of measure 16. At this same moment, the violin sounds a new two-measure idea of obvious codetta character and repeats it in measures 18–19. The piano then takes over the same music in a somewhat embellished manner at measure 20. Just before reaching completion, however, the music moves off to VI (m. 24), which signals that the preceding passage, which seemed like a closing section to the main theme, functions instead as the beginning of the transition.[26]

It sometimes is difficult to determine whether codetta material forms a genuine closing section to the main theme or a false closing section to begin the transition. In such cases, an analysis of the grouping structure can be helpful. As a general rule, the structural beginning of a thematic unit brings a moderate-size unit (two to four measures in length). However, the presence of small, fragmented units normally represents a thematic continuation, rarely a new beginning. Therefore, if the codettas in question are followed by a larger unit, they probably belong to a separate closing section independent of the transition, whose beginning is articulated by the new, larger group. But if the codettas are followed by a smaller unit, they probably form a false closing section to begin the transition.

EXAMPLE 9.5: The end of the main theme on the downbeat of measure 8 leads directly into material that has the standard characteristics of a codetta, including a typical pedal-point prolongation of the tonic that emphasizes the subdominant (cf. the paradigm in ex. 2.1b). The resulting four-measure closing section can, however, be reinterpreted as a presentation phrase to begin the transition when, at measure 12, the fragmentation into one-measure units and the sudden acceleration of surface rhythm clearly express continuation function.

Nontonic region.   Most transitions begin with tonic of the home key to provide a firm footing for the later destabilization of tonality. In some compositional contexts, however, harmonic stability at the opening of the transition might be unnecessary or even redundant. If the main-theme area strongly emphasizes tonic harmony—through the use of a

EXAMPLE 9.5 Beethoven, Piano Sonata in C Minor, Op. 10/1, iii, 8–18

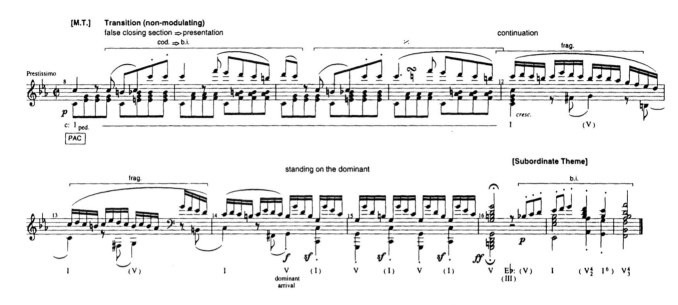

EXAMPLE 9.6 Mozart, Piano Sonata in F, K. 332/300k, i, 19–27

EXAMPLE 9.7 Haydn, String Quartet in B-flat, Op. 50/1, iv, 13–34

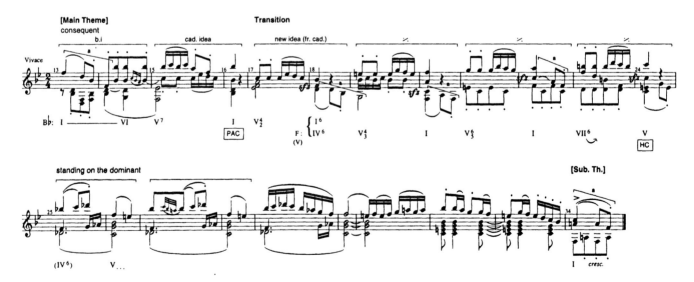

closing section or multiple main themes (or both)—the transition may begin directly in a nontonic region of the home key in order to advance the process of tonal destabilization.

The nontonic region used in the majority of cases is the submediant. This harmony is particularly effective because it creates an immediate modal contrast and can easily function as a pivot to the new key. Yet at the same time, VI continues to function as a tonic substitute, thus making it an appropriate harmony to project a sense of formal initiation for the transition.

EXAMPLE 9.6: The main-theme group consists of two themes, each ending with a perfect authentic cadence. Moreover, the cadence of the second main theme (mm. 19–20) is followed by two codettas of one measure each. As a result of this emphasis on the home-key tonic, it is not surprising that the transition starts with VI at measure 23. That this moment represents a new beginning is made clear by the change from one-measure codettas (mm. 21–22) to a four-measure compound basic idea (mm. 23–26) and by the abrupt shift to forte dynamic and *Sturm und Drang* style.[27]

Unusual Beginnings. Whereas the majority of transitions begin in the ways just described, some different procedures are employed now and then. Three, in particular, occur frequently enough to warrant illustration.

1. Beginning with the cadential idea of the main theme.

EXAMPLE 9.7: The main theme closes with a perfect authentic cadence in measure 16; the true melodic line lies in the second violin (the alto voice in mm. 15–16). (The first violin plays a newly added subsidiary idea.) The transition begins by repeating the cadential gesture in measures 17–18 and develops this idea all the way until the half cadence at measure 24. The accompanying voices sound the head motive "a" from the basic idea of the main theme.[28]

2. Beginning like a previous B section.

EXAMPLE 9.8: The main theme is constructed as a small ternary (see ex. 6.10). The upbeat to measure 29 brings back music from the beginning of the contrasting middle (one octave higher) and thus suggests that the B and A' sections might be repeated, as sometimes happens in the rounded binary version of the small ternary form. But the supporting V[7]/VI harmony, which gave the impression of being the "wrong" dominant back at measures 10–15, now serves as the "real" (and only!) harmony of the transition.

The use of a single harmony in a transition is most unusual. Beethoven compensates for the lack of harmonic progression by writing a subordinate theme that, as discussed in the previous chapter, creates a more definite sense of modulation (see ex. 8.18). In this respect, the modulating subordinate theme also possesses a degree of transition function.[29]

3. Beginning like an A' section.

EXAMPLE 9.9: Measures 1–8 and 9–18 make up the exposition and contrasting middle of a small ternary. (The internal organization of the exposition is most unconventional, especially since it is not even clear that it closes with a perfect authentic cadence; in light of what follows, however, the opening eight measures must be interpreted as an A section.) The return to the basic idea at measure 19 signals an obvious recapitulation, one that would normally bring an authentic cadence to close the main theme. But the melodic D# in measure 22 steers the music toward the subordinate key, and the section closes instead with a half cadence in measure 29. The recapitulation of the ternary is thus left incomplete, and we understand retrospectively that the functional beginning of a modulating transition occurs at measure 19.[30]

ENDING THE TRANSITION

The close of the transition is often marked by a liquidation of melodic–motivic material, a reduction in texture, and sometimes (but not always) a break in rhythmic activity to set off the entrance of the subordinate theme. The final harmony is a dominant—of either the subordinate key or the home key. Most often this dominant arises in a half-cadential progression, and the appearance of that harmony creates a genuine half cadence. Sometimes the dominant cannot be considered cadential because it is inverted, contains a dissonant seventh, or does not correspond to the "end" of the prevailing phrase-structural processes. At other times, the final dominant does not even belong to a recognizable cadential progression but comes instead as the last link of a sequential chain. In very few cases, the dominant, by resolving quickly and without interruption to the tonic at the beginning of the subordinate theme, is not perceived as an "arrival" of any kind.

The final dominant of the transition is usually given temporal emphasis in order to arouse the listener's expectation for a tonic resolution. A number of techniques can be used to stretch out the dominant in time. Most often a standing on the dominant bringing new melodic–motivic material either follows, or elides with, the half cadence. A somewhat different way of creating a standing on the dominant consists of repeating the half-cadence idea several times in succession. In those instances when the final dominant is not created out of a half-cadential progression, the dominant is often elongated (sometimes with a fermata) relative to the prior harmonies in order to give an impression of being an "ending" harmony nonetheless.

The following discussion of transition endings is organized along a continuum of possibilities from the clearest half-cadential articulation at one extreme to the complete absence of a concluding function at the other extreme.

EXAMPLE 9.8 Beethoven, Piano Sonata in E-flat, Op. 31/3, ii, 28–35

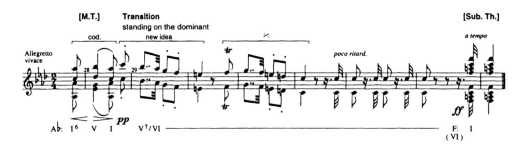

EXAMPLE 9.9 Beethoven, Piano Sonata in C, Op. 2/3, iv, 1–29

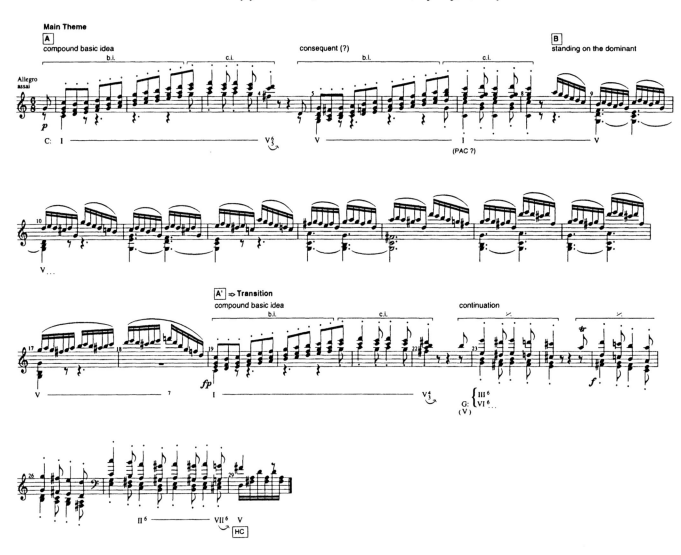

Half Cadence

A transition can be concluded most definitively by means of a half cadence. According to the rule, the dominant of a half cadence must initially appear as a triad in root position. A subsequent prolongation, however, may introduce a dissonant seventh and invert the harmony. The half cadence closing a transition is usually followed by a postcadential standing on the dominant, one that may become highly extended. Sometimes, and especially in slow movements, a standing on the dominant is omitted, and the subordinate theme immediately follows the half cadence (see ex. 9.1, m. 8, and ex. 9.3, m. 15).

EXAMPLE 9.7: The transition closes with a half cadence in measure 24. The subsequent standing on the dominant features accented neighboring chords built over the lowered sixth degree of the new key. Although the melodic line at the end of the transition leads decisively to a tonic harmony at measure 34, this moment must not be interpreted as an imperfect authentic cadence. The harmony prolonged from measure 24 on is the *ultimate* dominant of a half-cadential progression, not a *penultimate* dominant of an authentic cadential progression.

EXAMPLE 9.10: The modulation to F major occurs immediately at the start of the transition, and the new key is confirmed by the half-cadential progression beginning with I6 in measure 20. The half cadence at measure 22 is then followed by a multiphrase standing on the dominant. The first phrase (mm. 22–25) consists of two repetitions of the cadential idea itself. The second phrase (mm. 26–29) features a change to triplet rhythm in the upper part and the use of neighboring secondary dominants. The final phrase (mm. 30–32) further accelerates the rhythm by means of sixteenth notes and introduces the dissonant seventh.

Because the cadential arrival at measure 22 is immediately followed by repetitions of the half-cadential idea, the sense of an ending at that measure is somewhat weakened. Indeed, the listener who focuses primarily on melodic and textural content might well believe that the change of material at measure 26 marks the structural close of the transition. But the harmonic content clearly points to measure 22 as the true cadence establishing closure. This discrepancy between the cadential arrival and a melodic–motivic change is a loosening trait typical of transition sections. Even more obvious discrepancies of this kind are considered shortly in connection with premature dominant arrivals.

One might object to the reading of a cadence in measure 22 by comparing these repeated half-cadence ideas with the "one more time technique," a situation in which a true authentic cadence does not occur until the final repetition. But the latter technique involves cadential evasion, in which the final harmony of the cadential progression is not understood to arrive (and thus to define cadential closure) until the last repetition. In the case of the repeated half-cadence ideas of this transition, the dominant harmony on the downbeat of measure 22 is perceived as the final harmony of the progression (and not at all as an initial harmony), thus marking a cadential arrival at that point. (See also ex. 1.7, mm. 16–20.)[31]

Dominant Arrival

Unlike a main theme or a subordinate theme, a transition need not necessarily end with a cadence. In some cases, a half-cadential progression is present, but for a variety of reasons, the appearance of the final dominant fails to create a true cadence. In other cases, a cadential progression is absent, yet the final dominant still gives the impression of being an ending harmony. As explained earlier in chapter 6, the term *dominant arrival* distinguishes such situations from actual half cadences.

Presence of a cadential progression. Various factors can obscure, or even destroy, true cadential closure even when a half-cadential progression is present at the end of the transition.

EXAMPLE 9.2: A pre-dominant II6 in measure 9 leads in the following measure to a cadential six–four. In a typical half cadence, the six–four would resolve quickly to a five–three, and the moment of cadential arrival is easily associated with the entrance of the root of the dominant in the bass voice (i.e., with the appearance of the six–four chord) (see ex. 9.1, m. 8). In this example, the six–four chord is itself prolonged (by neighboring dominant sevenths) for more than two measures before resolving to the five–three position on the second beat of measure 12. The resulting noncongruence of the harmonic arrival (m. 10) and the melodic–motivic arrival (m. 12) obscures the sense of half cadence, and since the dominant harmony appears before the end of the phrase unit, we can speak of a *premature* dominant arrival in measure 10. (See also ex. 8.14, m. 36.)

EXAMPLE 9.5: A half-cadential progression may sometimes consist simply of I moving directly to V (as in ex. 4.3, m. 4). The very end of the transition (m. 16) brings such a progression, and so we might be tempted to recognize a half cadence at that point. But the preceding music, from as early as measure 12, also contains a series of I–V progressions, and accordingly, we might ask whether they create half cadences as well. Since the chords in the second half of measures 12 and 13 clearly function as subordinate harmonies that help prolong tonic from the beginning of the transition, these dominants cannot represent moments of half cadence. The same could initially be said for the dominant on the third quarter-note beat of measure 14. But the following tonic, coming as it does "too early" in comparison with the pattern of alternating harmonies set up thus far, seems to be subordinate in a dominant prolongation continuing into measures 15 and 16. The dominants in these measures have the potential of being final chords of a half cadence, but none can claim any special cadential status over the others. On the contrary, the music in these measures sounds like a standing on the dominant. According to this interpretation, a half cadence would appear with the dominant on the second half of measure 14. But as we observed, this dominant sounds like a primary harmony only in retrospect, for on its first appearance, it seems subordinate to a tonic prolongation. The change in melodic–motivic material at this moment, however, at least supports the notion of a dominant arrival, if not a clear-cut half cadence.[32]

EXAMPLE 9.10 Mozart, Piano Trio in B-flat, K. 502, iii, 18–32

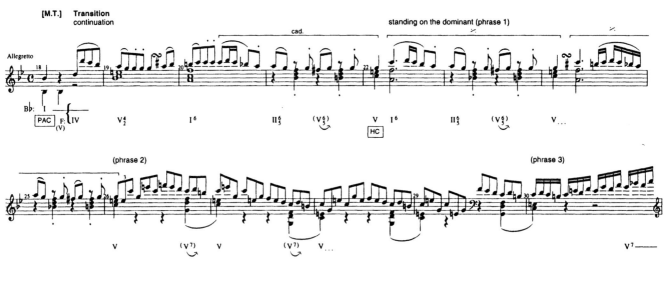

EXAMPLE 9.11 (a) Beethoven, Symphony No. 2 in D, Op. 36, i, 57–63; (b) mm. 34–41

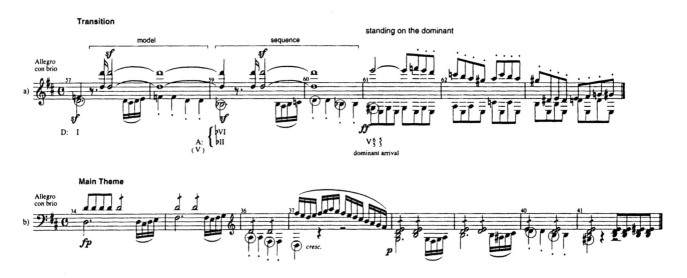

Absence of a cadential progression. The final dominant of a transition is not always achieved by a genuine half-cadential progression. Sometimes the progression is in the making but fails to be fully realized because the final dominant includes a dissonant seventh.[33] At other times, a cadential progression is not even implied when the final dominant appears. In both cases, the dominant can appear to be an ending harmony nonetheless, because (among other possibilities) it may mark what sounds like the beginning of a standing on the dominant, it may feature liquidation and a reduction in texture, or it may be especially elongated relative to its preceding harmonies.

EXAMPLE 9.11: The goal dominant of the transition arrives at measure 61 in a noncadential manner by appearing in first inversion. Immediately thereafter, the bass takes up the root of the harmony, which is prolonged for eleven measures (only three of which are shown in the example). The complete change of musical material following the dominant arrival gives the impression of being a typical standing on the dominant, despite the lack of cadential articulation.

Note that the dominant initially appears in first inversion, for specific motivic reasons. The main theme (ex. 9.11b) features a prominent descending third motive in measures 36–37 (see circled notes), which is repeated in measures 40–41. The latter version is then chromatically altered in measures 60–61 of the transition (ex. 9.11a). Moreover, this same motivic pattern is also played out at a higher level, shown by the circled downbeats of measures 57, 59, and 61.

EXAMPLE 9.12: The downbeat of measure 89 is initially heard as I, which completes the tonic prolongation of the presentation begun at measure 81. (The transition of this movement starts earlier at m. 65 and consists largely of new material supported by extensive tonic prolongations.) The rest of measure 89 is interpreted as II$\frac{6}{5}$/III (in the new key of F major), and this harmony initiates a descending fifth progression, which supports model–sequence technique (somewhat modified) in measures 89–92. The last harmonic link in the sequential progression is the dominant of the subordinate key at measure 92, which then emerges as the final, noncadential harmony of the transition. The ongoing melodic activity, however, is not concluded until measure 95, after which new material appears for the standing on the dominant. Since the harmonic goal precedes the melodic goal, we can speak of a premature dominant arrival at measure 92.[34]

Omission of Concluding Function

Now and then, the final dominant of a transition gives no sense of being an ending harmony whatsoever. The dominant does not appear to be the goal of the progression; it receives no emphasis; and it resolves directly to tonic at the beginning of the subordinate theme with little or no rhythmic break. With a minimal sense of functional end for the transition, it can be difficult sometimes to determine just where the subordinate theme begins. Usually, however, the

composer provides some means of expressing a beginning, such as the appearance of a new basic idea in the context of a presentation phrase.[35]

EXAMPLE 9.13: Most of the transition consists of brilliant passage-work prolonging the tonic of the home key. (Note the unusual use of three different presentation phrases to project this lengthy prolongation.) At measure 28, the move to VI provides a pivot for modulating to the subordinate key, whose dominant appears one measure later. This dominant does not seem to mark any kind of "ending" whatsoever as it moves directly to the tonic in the following measure. At that point, the basic idea from the main theme returns in the lower voice, supported by a solid tonic prolongation in the new key. Listeners familiar with Haydn's practice of beginning subordinate-theme groups with a transposed version of the main theme's basic idea could likely believe this to be the case here, even though the transition lacks a specific concluding function. And indeed this interpretation would be correct, since at no later point in the exposition can a stronger sense of structural beginning for the subordinate theme be found.[36]

The lack of a concluding function for a transition may produce a subordinate theme containing an internal half cadence and a subsequent standing on the dominant. The dominant emphasis missing from the end of the transition is thus regained in the subordinate theme itself.

EXAMPLE 9.14: The transition begins in measure 19 with a two-measure idea from the opening of the main theme. The idea is then repeated in the bass voice, now supported by the dominant of the subordinate key. By the end of measure 22, the listener does not expect this dominant to be the goal harmony of the transition: there is no cadential articulation, no standing on the dominant, and no temporal extension. Moreover, a repetition of a two-measure idea (mm. 21–22) tends to reinforce formal initiation, not create formal closure. Nevertheless, the following material clearly expresses the sense of a new beginning by bringing a presentation phrase supported by a root-position tonic in the subordinate key. There is no reason, therefore, not to consider measure 23 the start of the subordinate theme, even though the transition lacks a functional end. Since the transition accords no emphasis to the dominant of the subordinate key, we are not surprised to find the continuation of the subordinate theme leading to an internal half cadence at measure 30. The second part of the subordinate theme then begins at measure 36 with a new idea, now supported by the less stable I^6.[37]

TWO-PART TRANSITION

The process of tonal destabilization sometimes takes place in two distinct stages, thus yielding a *two-part transition*. Following a main theme ending with a perfect authentic cadence, the first part of the transition leads to a half cadence (or dominant arrival) in the home key, just as in a single nonmodulating transition; the second part then modulates to the subordinate key.

EXAMPLE 9.12 Beethoven, Symphony No. 4 in B-flat, Op. 60, i, 81–108

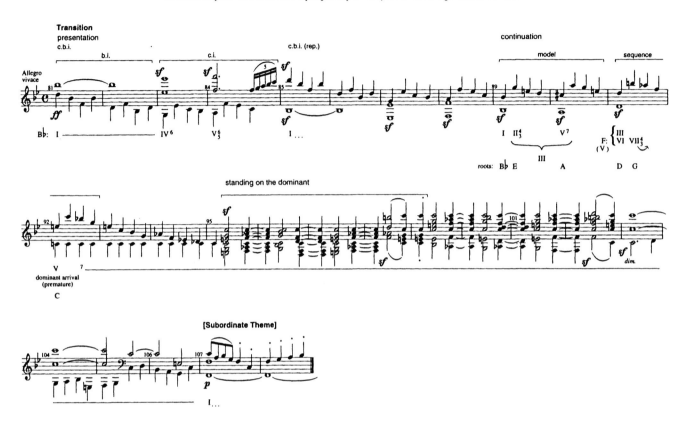

EXAMPLE 9.13 Haydn, Symphony No. 90 in C, iv, 16–35

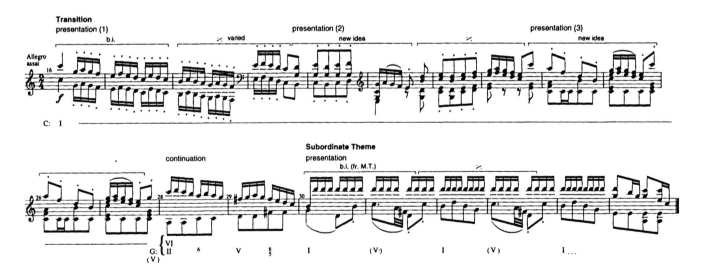

EXAMPLE 9.14 Mozart, Piano Sonata in C Minor, K. 457, i, 17–37

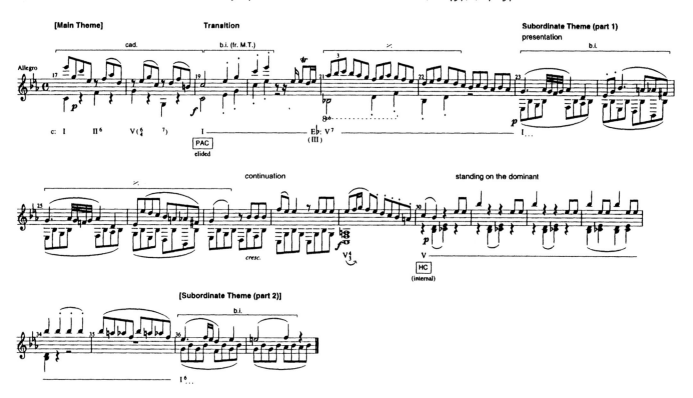

EXAMPLE 9.4: The first part of the transition begins with a false closing section to the main theme and leads to a half cadence in the home key at measure 26. A second part then begins at measure 33 with V⁷/VI, whose resolution pivots to tonicize II of the subordinate key. The transition then ends at measure 37 with a half cadence, which elides with a standing on the dominant.[38]

Frequently, the second part of a two-part transition begins with the basic idea of the main theme supported by the home-key tonic. The resulting structure then resembles the case in which what seems to be a small-ternary recapitulation is retrospectively understood as the beginning of the transition (see the discussion of ex. 9.9). The fundamental difference between these two situations depends on whether the passage leading to the dominant of the home key is understood as a contrasting middle or as the first part of a transition. In many cases, the former interpretation must be ruled out because of the fundamental principle prohibiting a B section from eliding with its preceding A section.

EXAMPLE 9.15: Measure 16 brings a perfect authentic cadence to close the main theme. The following unit begins with a false

closing section and leads to a half cadence in the home key (m. 24) and a long standing on the dominant. Measure 32 brings back the basic idea of the main theme (see ex. 9.15b), but rather than following it with a contrasting idea, the basic idea is repeated twice (ex. 9.15a, mm. 32–35). (Two additional statements of the idea appear through imitation, shown in the lower set of brackets.) New material at measure 37 effects the modulation, and the transition closes at measure 42 with a half cadence in the subordinate key, followed by a five-measure standing on the dominant.

The return of the basic idea at measure 32 might lead us to consider this moment as the beginning of an A' section (which would then be reinterpreted retrospectively as the start of the transition). But to view the main theme as an incomplete small ternary form would be incorrect, as the material following the perfect authentic cadence at measure 16 sounds like a closing section, not the beginning of a contrasting middle, which usually emphasizes dominant harmony. Moreover, measure 16 both closes the sixteen-measure period and begins the next unit leading to the home-key half cadence in measure 24. As a result of this structural elision, we may not speak of a contrasting middle here, and the notion of a recapitulatory function at measure 32 must also be abandoned. We therefore understand the main theme to end at measure 16, at which point begins a two-part transition.[39]

EXAMPLE 9.15 (a) Mozart, Piano Trio in D Minor, K. 442, iii, 15–48; (b) mm. 1–4

▣ 10

Development

A number of the most important full-movement forms—sonata, sonata–rondo, and concerto—include a central section traditionally termed *development*.[1] Like other formal labels employed in this study, development can refer to both a particular section of a movement and a distinct formal function.[2] As a formal unit, a development stands between an exposition and a recapitulation. As a formal function, a development generates the greatest degree of tonal and phrase-structural instability in the movement and thus motivates a restoration of stability (to be accomplished by the recapitulation).

In light of its formal placement and function, a development is a higher-level analogue to the contrasting middle of the small ternary form. Like a contrasting middle, a development features a looser organization than its preceding section, an emphasis on sequential progressions, an avoidance of authentic cadential closure in the home key, and an ending on dominant harmony (normally of the home key). Indeed, the central section of some slow movements can be labeled just as easily a contrasting middle as a development (see the discussion in chap. 14 of ex. 14.3).

Normally, however, a development is distinguished from a contrasting middle by its greater length and complexity of organization. Whereas a contrasting middle is a relatively short unit (the longest B section illustrated in chap. 6 is fourteen measures, see ex. 6.9), a development can sometimes exceed the size of the entire exposition. A contrasting middle rarely consists of more than a single thematic unit (i.e., a set of intrathematic functions expressing a beginning, middle, and end). Conversely, a development usually contains multiple themelike units. A contrasting middle often remains entirely in the home key or else brings a brief modulation to the dominant region. A development section, however, regularly explores other tonal regions in the home key.

The melodic–motivic material of a development normally derives from that of the exposition. This material is often subjected to significant variation, transformation, and recombination. But new ideas may also appear. Mozart, in particular, likes to introduce melodies that have no obvious connection to the exposition. Haydn, by contrast, generally restricts his developments to motivic and accompanimental patterns from the exposition. Moreover, he sometimes brings back expositional material in the development in an order similar to that of the earlier section.[3] Because there is enough theoretical literature devoted to the ways in which motives from the exposition are transformed and recombined in the development,[4] I do not consider this topic in detail in this book. Instead, I look primarily at the tonal, phrase-structural, and form-functional contexts in which the various motivic manipulations arise.

TONAL ORGANIZATION

In traditional theories of form, the tonal organization of the development section is often characterized as a somewhat haphazard succession of remote modulations. According to this view, composers are free to indulge in flights of harmonic fancy unrestricted by the kinds of tonal conventions imposed by an exposition or recapitulation. More recently, we have come to understand that a clear and logical plan usually underlies the various tonal regions explored in a development. Schenker, for example, shows how most developments prolong the home-key dominant at a deep structural level, with other tonal regions emerging only through a strictly organized contrapuntal scheme within this dominant prolongation.[5]

Unlike the exposition, the specific tonal organization of a development cannot be predicted in advance. Nonetheless, certain tonal regions regularly appear, depending on the modality of the home key. In major-mode movements, the development usually explores the submediant, mediant, or supertonic. In minor-mode movements, the subdominant or dominant often is used. Note that all these are minor-mode regions in the home key.[6] This emphasis on minor modality in the development contrasts with the exposition, which resides predominantly in the major mode, even in cases in which the home key is minor (because the subordinate key is the relative major).

Tonal hierarchy. Inasmuch as the study of development sections raises issues of tonal organization more complex than that of an exposition, we need a way to differentiate the structural importance of the various regions of the home key, especially in their relation to specific formal contexts. The following scheme does not represent a comprehensive theory of classical tonality, but it does provide some working concepts and terminology for the analysis of classical form.

First, this scheme differentiates two kinds of change in tonal focus—*modulation* and *tonicization*. Both procedures create the perception of a new tonic harmony, but they differ on whether this new tonic seems to represent the focal point of a new key, displacing the previous tonic from our primary attention, or whether this tonic is perceived as a more localized tonal emphasis within a prevailing key. More technically, the difference between modulation and tonicization depends on whether or not this new tonic is associated with a cadential function. In other words, we can speak of a modulation to a new key if the new tonic is confirmed by a cadential progression in a formal context that functions to end a thematic process. By contrast, a new tonic disassociated from cadential articulation is better understood to represent the tonicization of a region in the prevailing key. This difference between modulation and tonicization can, of course, be challenged on a number of theoretical grounds. (It is largely untenable in a strictly Schenkerian view of tonal organization, for example.)[7] Nevertheless, it seems to have some basis in experiential reality, and for purposes of formal analysis, it is manifestly pragmatic to distinguish key from region and, thus, modulation from tonicization.

Let us now consider the structural hierarchy of the keys and tonal regions in a movement. At the very top of the hierarchy lies the *home key*, the tonality to which all the other keys and regions ultimately relate. The home key is confirmed by a cadence (of any kind) early in the movement and eventually receives authentic cadential confirmation by its end. The home key is associated formally with the main theme and the beginning of the transition in an exposition and with the entire recapitulation and coda.

Next down the hierarchy (and thus of lesser structural importance) lies the *subordinate key*. Like the home key, the subordinate key must ultimately be confirmed by an authentic cadence. This key is primarily associated with the subordinate theme of the exposition and also with the last part of the transition. The subordinate key may appear briefly in the main theme (when built as a small ternary or binary) and is frequently extended into the beginning of the development. Once abandoned, though, the subordinate key rarely returns in the work.

Of lower structural rank are keys that do not require authentic cadential confirmation. Since such keys usually arise in the context of a development section, they may be referred to as *development keys*. Although development keys may at times be confirmed by an authentic cadence, more often than not, a half cadence or a dominant arrival provides their minimal confirmation. On occasion, an authentic cadence may be implied, but a deceptive, evaded, or abandoned cadence occurs instead, without any further cadential articulation. (For this reason, the notion of cadential confirmation refers to the presence of a cadential "function," not necessarily a cadential "arrival.")

If multiple development keys appear in a movement, it is sometimes helpful to distinguish one as *primary* and the other(s) as *secondary*. The primary development key generally receives the strongest cadential articulation on a scale leading from an authentic cadence, through half cadence and dominant arrival, to the lack of a cadential arrival (deceptive, evaded, and abandoned cadences). The primary development key is usually the final key of the development section, often obtaining the most durational, dynamic, and textural emphasis. Secondary development keys are associated with weaker cadential articulation and tend to appear earlier in the development.

On the lower rungs of the tonal hierarchy reside various *tonicized regions*, which, by definition, do not receive cadential confirmation. Although it lacks a cadence, a region can still acquire considerable structural importance if it is associated with an initiating formal function, such as a basic idea, a presentation, or a compound basic idea. If a new theme (or themelike unit) begins in a tonal region as yet unconfirmed as a key, we recognize the potential of the prolonged tonic supporting that function to become confirmed cadentially as the tonal center of a true key. But if the music then takes a different tonal direction, this *initiating region*, as the region of the opening tonic prolongation can be termed, must ultimately be understood as a tonicization in some other key.

Less structurally important are tonicized regions arising from sequential activity in a continuation phrase or a developmental core (to be defined shortly). Since such regions participate in a broader, ongoing process of tonal change, they have less potential than do initiating regions for receiving cadential confirmation. (The final region of a sequence, of course, is often confirmed by a cadential function.)

At the bottom of the tonal hierarchy lie the very local tonicizations that introduce varying degrees of chromatic inflections in a solidly prevailing key. Although such tonicizations have little to do with intrathematic functionality, they can nonetheless contribute to an overall loosening of the harmonic–tonal context and thus can help support the expression of a particular interthematic function (such as a transition or subordinate theme).

Development keys. As mentioned earlier, one or more minor-mode regions of the home key are likely to be confirmed as development keys in the course of a development section. The listener cannot predict which development keys will be employed but can anticipate certain possibilities, depending on the overall modality of the movement.

When the home key is major, the development key is likely to be the submediant, the most closely related minor-mode region.[8] Also frequently used is the mediant, which, though more remote than VI, is the relative minor of the subordinate key (the dominant). The supertonic appears as a development key less often than does either VI or III. If more than one of these regions is cadentially confirmed, then VI usually emerges as the primary development key, with III or II as secondary.

The subdominant rarely functions as a primary development key because it does not provide modal contrast with the major-mode keys of the exposition. Moreover, since a development key is frequently emphasized by its dominant harmony, the use of V/IV toward the end of the development would poorly anticipate the home-key tonic (at the beginning of the recapitulation), given that both harmonies have at their basis a major triad built on the first scale-degree. If the subdominant has a prominent place in the development, it is normally found as a secondary development key early in the section and is usually confirmed by an authentic cadence.[9] Otherwise, the subdominant is tonicized as an initiating region leading to some other development key (or perhaps the home key).[10]

The number of tonal regions available for use as development keys increases with modal borrowing. Beethoven, who more than Haydn and Mozart expands the tonal spectrum in his works, often employs development keys borrowed from the parallel minor of the home key, such as ♭VI, ♭III, and minV.[11] Although ♭VI and ♭III are "major-mode regions," their close relationship to the parallel minor creates sufficient contrast with the keys of the exposition.

When the home key is minor, the two minor-mode regions of subdominant and dominant are used as development keys with approximately the same degree of frequency.

Tonicized regions in the development. Not every development section confirms a development key. Relatively short developments often have insufficient scope both to establish a new key and to emphasize the home-key dominant in preparation for the recapitulation. In such cases, tonal contrast with the exposition is achieved by tonicizing the same regions that typically appear as development keys (e.g., VI and III in major, IV and V in minor).[12]

Even in larger developments featuring one or more development keys, other regions can be prominently emphasized by tonicization. In major-mode movements, both the subdominant and the lowered submediant are frequently employed as initiating regions.[13] In addition, the extensive sequential organization typically found in developments usually results in tonicizations of regions that can be understood in relation to a prevailing development key or to the home key.

End of the development. The final harmony of the development is normally the dominant of the home key. This harmony best prepares for the recapitulation, which almost always begins with the home-key tonic. The dominant usually appears as the final harmony of a half-cadential progression and represents the goal of the last themelike unit of the development. The harmony is typically prolonged by a substantial standing on the dominant in order to reinforce expectations for its resolution to tonic.

Two exceptional situations can motivate a different harmony at the end of the development.[14] First, if the recapitulation does not begin with the home-key tonic, the final harmony of the development is usually one that leads most naturally into the recapitulation's opening harmony.

EXAMPLE 10.1: The recapitulation begins in measure 125 with the dominant seventh of the home key, just as at the start of the exposition (m. 21). In order to set up this unusual beginning, Haydn closes the development with the pre-dominant VII⁷/V.[15]

A second exception arises when the composer ends the development with a harmony that can function as a substitute for the normal home-key dominant, such as V/VI, but also V/III. Both these harmonies contain the leading-tone of the home key, a necessary condition for dominant functionality. In order to mitigate an abrupt resolution to the tonic (due to a cross-relation between the harmonies), the texture at the very end of the development is usually reduced to a single voice.[16]

EXAMPLE 10.2: The development ends with V/VI, which resolves directly to I at the beginning of the recapitulation. The potentially offensive cross-relation of C♯ (in V/VI) and C♮ (in I) is avoided by the reduction in texture just before the recapitulation.[17]

PRE-CORE/CORE TECHNIQUE

The phrase-structural technique most characteristic of a development involves the establishment of a relatively large model, which is repeated sequentially one or more times. Subsequent fragmentation leads to a half cadence (or dominant arrival) of either the home key or a development key, after which a standing on the dominant typically appears. Ratz calls the entire unit defined by this process the "core of the development" (*Kern der Durchführung*).[18] The *core* is usually preceded by a *pre-core*, whose characteristics are described in greater detail later in this chapter. Lengthy development sections are likely to contain two different cores: the first normally confirms a development key, and the second leads to the dominant of the home key to prepare for the recapitulation.[19] Pre-core/core technique is pervasive in works by Mozart and Beethoven, but it appears much less often in Haydn.

EXAMPLE 10.1 Haydn, Symphony No. 92 in G ("Oxford"), i, 121–30

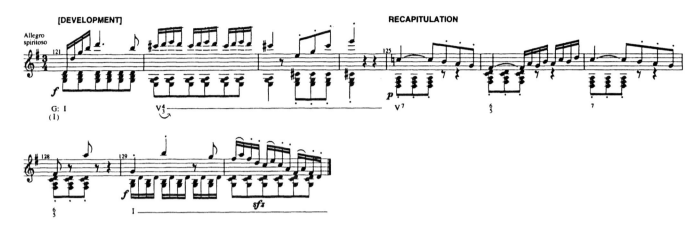

EXAMPLE 10.2 Beethoven, Violin Sonata in F ("Spring"), Op. 24, i, 118–27

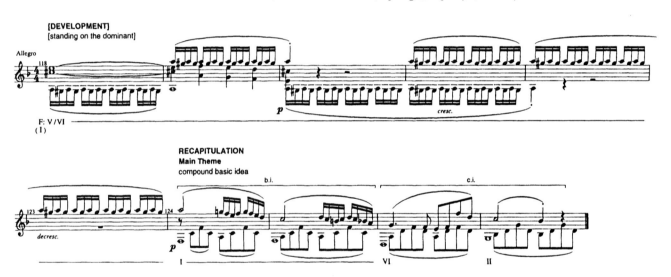

Core

The core of the development typically projects an emotional quality of instability, restlessness, and dramatic conflict. The dynamic level is usually forte, and the general character is often one of *Sturm und Drang*. The core normally brings a marked increase in rhythmic activity projected by conventionalized accompanimental patterns.[20] Polyphonic devices—imitation, canon, fugal entries—can contribute further to the complexity of the musical texture. In short, the core is that part of the development in which the traditional aesthetic sense of a "working out" of the material is most prominently expressed.

EXAMPLE 10.3: The core begins at measure 58 by eliding with the end of the pre-core. A four-measure model of *Sturm und Drang* character, built over dominant harmony of the development key, E minor (HK: V), is established in measures 58–61. The model is sequenced twice down a perfect fifth (mm. 62–65 and 66–69).

Fragmentation occurs at measure 70 with a new one-measure idea, which itself becomes a model for sequential repetition, now by stepwise descent. (Although the pattern of sequential repetition changes, the underlying harmonic progression continues to be that of descending fifths.) Measure 73 sees further fragmentation into one-beat units, and a cadential progression brings a home-key half cadence in the following measure. A postcadential standing on the dominant ensues, leading eventually to the recapitulation at measure 80.

Model.   The model of a core is constructed as a relatively long unit, normally four to eight measures. The model must be sufficiently large to project a sense of structural beginning, as well as to permit extensive fragmentation. The model itself may contain repeated material, but because of the need to sequence the entire model, these internal repetitions cannot always be easily classified according to the standard types (i.e., exact, statement–response, and sequential). In the case of sequential repetition within the model

EXAMPLE 10.3 Mozart, Piano Sonata in A Minor, K. 310/300d, i, 57–81

143

EXAMPLE 10.4 Haydn, Piano Sonata in E-flat, Hob. XVI:49, i, 84–107

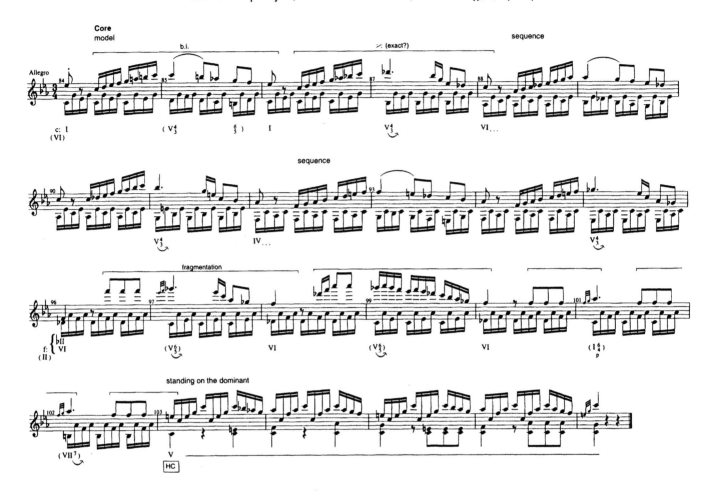

itself, the composer must make sure that the larger-scale sequencing of the full model remains distinctly perceptible.

The melodic–motivic content of a model may be drawn from any previous material of the movement, or it may be new. If the model is quite long, it may contain a variety of ideas taking up a number of distinct phrases of differing formal function.

Sequence. Following its initial statement, the model is sequenced one or more times. Although a single sequential pattern may be used throughout (such as a descending fifth or an ascending second), the pattern often changes in the course of the core. The supporting sequential progressions either create a true modulation or introduce a variety of tonicized regions.

The structure of the model is normally retained in its sequenced version (see ex. 10.3, m. 62). Sometimes, however, the sequence alters the model, especially if it consists of several phrases. In such cases, the first phrase usually conforms to the original model, but subsequent phrases may be changed or even eliminated.

Fragmentation. Most cores produce an extensive process of fragmentation, which breaks down the grouping structure defined by the model (and its sequences) and eventually motivates a formal close to the core. The passage of fragmentation may continue to employ ideas from the model or may bring about a change in musical content. The fragmentation itself may even establish a new model for sequential repetition. Now and then, however, the sequential process becomes exhausted at the onset of fragmentation (or sometime after that point), and the rest of the core is supported instead by prolongational progressions of the kind found in a regular continuation phrase.

Concluding function, standing on the dominant. The great majority of cores have as their harmonic goal a dominant of either the home key or a development key. A core thus tends to end along the lines of a transition. Most often, the fragmentation leads to a half cadence. Frequently, though, a genuine cadence fails to materialize, and a dominant arrival, sometimes a premature one, results instead. On rare occasions, the core leads to a distinctly new section

EXAMPLE 10.5 Mozart, String Quartet in G, K. 387, i, 72–87

(another core or a retransition) without being closed by any concluding function.[21]

Sometimes a core ends with an authentic cadential progression in a development key. An actual authentic cadence may arise, or it may be evaded or abandoned, in which case cadential closure may never be achieved.

The half cadence (or dominant arrival) closing a core is usually followed by a standing on the dominant.[22] This postcadential unit is often highly extended by means of several distinct sections, each with its own melodic–motivic content. If the standing on the dominant occurs at the end of the development, then anticipatory motives derived from the basic idea of the exposition's main theme often appear to help prepare for the beginning of the recapitulation.

The following examples illustrate the points just discussed.

EXAMPLE 10.4: The core starts with a four-measure model beginning on the second beat of measure 84; the model is sequenced twice by descending thirds. The model itself consists of a repeated two-measure idea that is first supported by a simple tonic prolongation (mm. 84–86). In the manner of an exact repetition, the idea starts again on the local tonic, but measure 87 replaces an implied V⁶₅ with V⁶₅/VI in order to effect the descending third sequence.

The final sequence of the model concludes at measure 96 on ♭II of the original development key (C minor), which pivots to become VI in the new development key of F minor (HK: II). A

broad process of fragmentation then begins with a reduction of the previous four-measure model into a new two-measure unit (mm. 97–98) and a further reduction to one-measure segments starting at measure 101. The beginning of the fragmentation also ends the sequential activity, and the rest of the core is supported by prolongational progressions eventually leading to a half cadence (in F minor) at measure 103.[23]

EXAMPLE 10.5: The core begins at measure 72 with a two-measure idea, whose melody and harmonic support are then transposed a third lower. On hearing this descending third sequence, we might assume that the model is two measures long. But the sequential pattern is broken when the next appearance of the idea (m. 76) is transposed a fourth higher, followed again by a descending third. A more consistent pattern of repetition emerges when we recognize the ascending stepwise sequence of a four-measure model. (Ex. 2.16c shows the harmonic paradigm of this sequence.) Note that when the melody of the two-measure idea descends a third at measures 74 and 78, the bass line ascends by a half step, thus blurring somewhat the sense of sequence at this level of structure. As a result, the broader ascending-stepwise sequence of the true model emerges with greater clarity.[24]

Following the augmented sixth chord in measure 80, the dominant of E minor (HK: VI) has the potential of being the goal harmony of the core. But the music presses on, and the tonic at measure 82 marks the beginning of a compressed cadential progression. The deceptive resolution of the dominant in measure 83 leads to

EXAMPLE 10.6 Mozart, String Quintet in E-flat, K. 614, i, 87–109

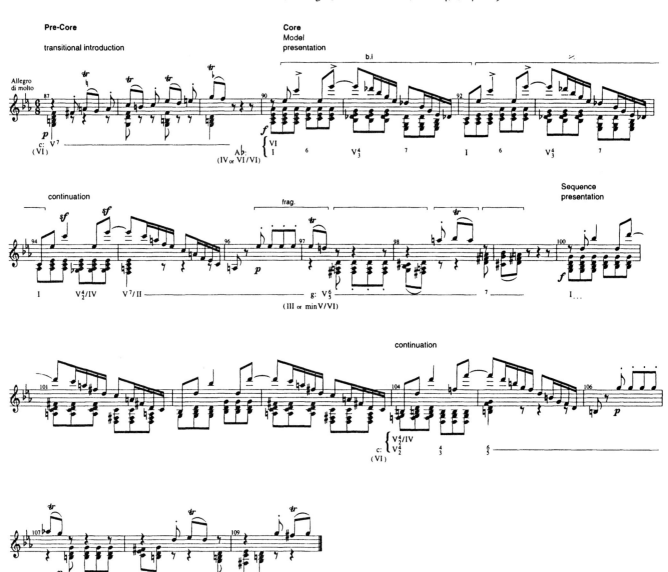

146

another try at the cadence, which is then evaded when measure 84 brings back ("one more time") the same material as measures 82–83. The cadence is finally achieved on the downbeat of measure 86.[25] A brief closing section made up of codettas follows. All this cadential and postcadential activity is typical of a subordinate theme, except, of course, that it takes place in a minor-mode development key rather than the subordinate key of the movement.

EXAMPLE 10.6: The model begins in measure 90 with an entirely new two-measure basic idea in the initiating region of A♭ major (HK: IV).[26] The idea is then repeated exactly to create a presentation phrase. A second repetition (m. 94) begins, but the idea is suddenly liquidated as the harmony departs from the tonic prolongation (of A♭). As a result, continuation function is clearly expressed. This function is further reinforced at the upbeat to measure 97 by fragmentation involving motives from the opening of the movement. The newly supporting V⁶₅ eventually resolves at measure 100 to bring a stepwise-descending sequence of the entire ten-measure model, one that has a decidedly sentential organization.[27] The presentation phrase of the model is sequenced a step lower at measures 100–3. The harmonic plan is then altered in measures 104–6 so that the continuation (mm. 107–9) is transposed down a fifth in relation to the original model.[28]

EXAMPLE 10.7: The pre-core ends at measure 128 with a perfect authentic cadence in the development key of A minor (HK: VI). The model of the core (based on the retransition at the end of the exposition, mm. 119–22) then begins with an extended upbeat that maintains tonic harmony (of A minor). The rest of the model tonicizes IV in that key (mm. 130–33). In the repetition, the bulk of the model is sequenced down a step to tonicize III (in A minor) (mm. 135–38). The extended upbeat (mm. 133–34), however, does not follow the sequential pattern. An exact sequence of this upbeat would have taken place in a G-minor harmony, a step lower than the A minor of the model. But the appearance of G minor at this point would be awkward following directly on the D minor of the model. (The awkwardness would result because the D-minor harmony would sound like a "minor dominant" in relation to the following G-minor harmony.) Instead, Mozart retains the D-minor harmony from the end of the model into the beginning of the repetition and brings an implied G harmony (VII⁶₅/III) first at measure 135. (Ex. 10.7b is discussed later in this chapter.)

EXAMPLE 10.8: The eight-measure model is based on material from the opening of the subordinate theme (see ex. 1.8). With the upbeat to measure 64, the model begins to be sequenced up a step. But the sequence remains incomplete when the continuation phrase of the model is eliminated, and in its place, a new two-measure model is established at measure 68.[29] Fragmentation then occurs when this model is sequenced down a step in measures 70–71. The model begins to be sequenced again when it unexpectedly leads into yet another two-measure model (mm. 73–74).[30] Further fragmentation occurs at measure 79, at which point one-measure segments prepare for the half cadence.

The half cadence in measure 81 is followed by a standing on the dominant made up of two different parts (mm. 81–94 and 95–100). The second part signals the imminent return of the main theme by reintroducing the sixteenth-note triplet figure (motive "b") from the opening basic idea.

EXAMPLE 10.9: The core begins in measure 81 with a five-measure model that is sequenced down a step at measure 86. Fragmentation occurs at measure 91 when the final idea of the model is itself repeated sequentially. A further sequence begins at measure 93 supported by the dominant of E♭ major (HK: ♭VI). This harmony is then extended all the way to the fermata at measure 98, which marks the end of the core. In retrospect, we understand that the V at measure 93 is the harmonic goal of the core and thus marks a premature dominant arrival.[31]

EXAMPLE 10.10: The core approaches its end by completely liquidating the orchestral texture, leaving the solo piano alone. An authentic cadence in the development key of G minor (HK: V) is promised for measure 329. But the cadence is dramatically evaded when the orchestral tutti reenters with V⁶₅/IV (in that key). This moment then marks the beginning of a second core, whose new four-measure model is sequenced a fourth higher at measure 333. The first core, therefore, never receives the authentic cadential closure anticipated by the progression in measure 328.

Pre-Core

A development section does not normally start with a core,[32] as the dramatic character projected by a core usually requires it to be set up by material of lesser emotional intensity. Ratz refers to this opening passage as an "introduction" (*Einleitung*), but his usage is problematic.[33] *Introduction* has a relatively restricted form-functional meaning in my theory, and thus its use is not applicable to the many different formal procedures that can precede a core. Since no single functional label adequately covers the initial part of a development, I use the neutral term *pre-core* instead.

The pre-core typically begins with tonic of the subordinate key, thus retaining the harmony from the end of the exposition. The pre-core may then remain entirely in that key or, more frequently, modulate to a development key (or to some initiating region in a development key) for the beginning of the core.

Sometimes the pre-core begins immediately in a different key (or region). In such cases, the opening harmony is often dominant, and the music takes on the character of an upbeat unit to the resolving tonic of the new key. This tonic then supports a new initiating function of some kind (e.g., basic idea, presentation). The formal function of this upbeat gesture is rather complex and thus presents a terminological dilemma. On the one hand, it gives the impression of appearing "before-the-beginning" and therefore seems to function as an introduction. On the other hand, its underlying dominant harmony makes a transition from the subordinate key to the new development key. The rather clumsy expression *transitional introduction* perhaps best describes what happens.[34]

Unlike the core's character of ongoing restlessness, the pre-core is generally more relaxed yet also somewhat hesitant and anticipatory. The dynamic level tends to be soft,

EXAMPLE 10.7 (a) Mozart, Symphony No. 36 in C ("Linz"), K. 425, i, 119–38; (b) mm. 62–71

EXAMPLE 10.8 Beethoven, Piano Sonata in F Minor, Op. 2/1, i, 55–102

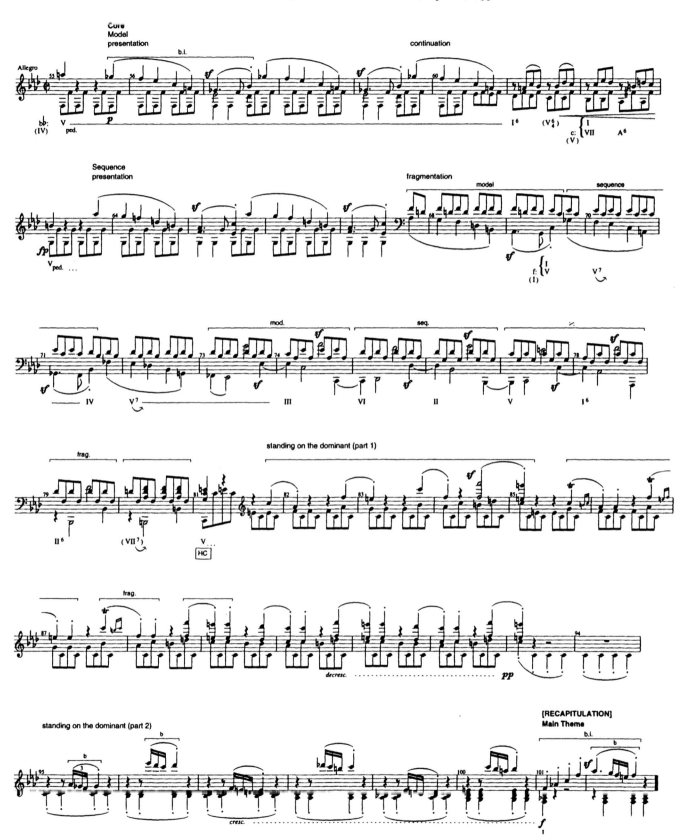

EXAMPLE 10.9 Beethoven, Piano Sonata in G, Op. 14/2, i, 80–100

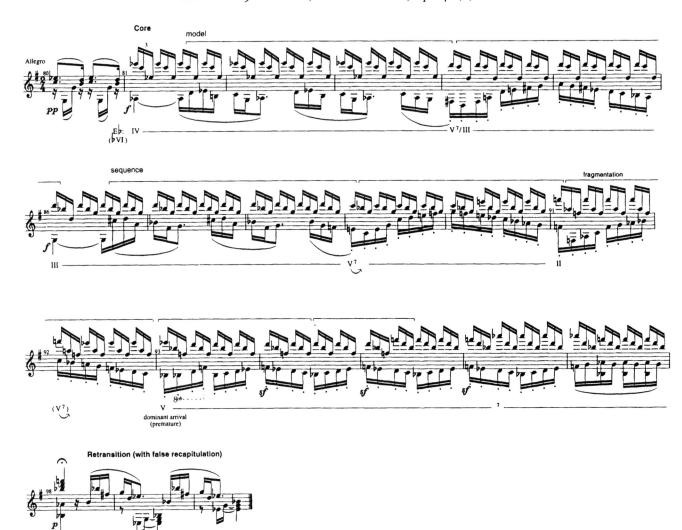

EXAMPLE 10.10 Mozart, Piano Concerto in C Minor, K. 491, i, 324–35

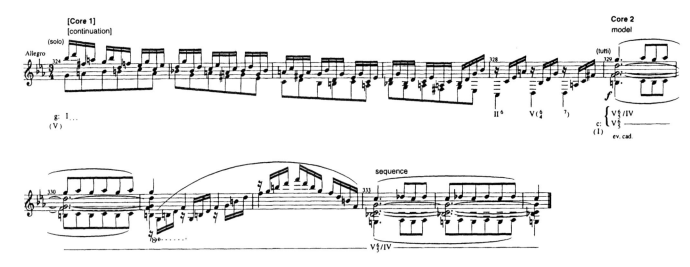

EXAMPLE 10.11 Beethoven, Piano Sonata in G, Op. 14/2, i, 64–82

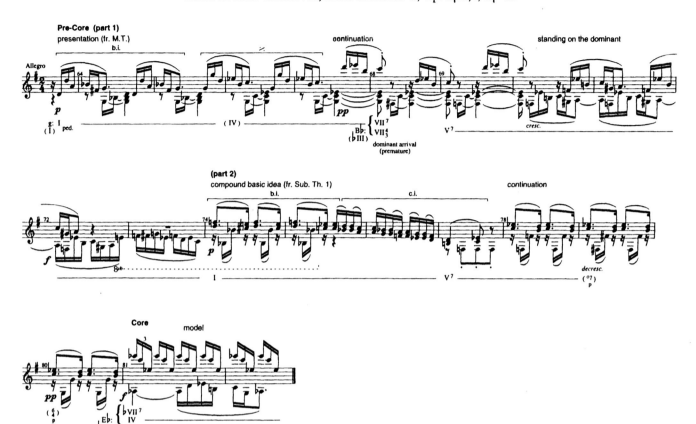

and the rhythmic motion is frequently discontinuous (or at least less active than the subsequent core). If the core often bursts out with *Sturm und Drang*, the pre-core can be likened to the calm before the storm.

Beginning the pre-core. Whereas the core may draw on any ideas from the prior exposition, the opening of the pre-core is usually restricted to material derived from the basic idea of the main theme or from the closing section of the exposition. Rarely does it refer directly to the transition or subordinate-theme group (ex. 10.7 is an exception explained later in this chapter). Like the core, the pre-core may also introduce entirely new material.

1. *Main theme's basic idea.* In a sonata-form movement, the repetition of the exposition before the onset of the development forges a link between the end of the exposition and the beginning of the main theme. An effective variation on this original link can be created when the pre-core refers again to the main theme's basic idea, this time, of course, in a different tonal (and often textural) context.

EXAMPLE 10.11: The return of the main theme's basic idea (see ex. 3.4) at the beginning of the pre-core is marked by a change of mode. Our first impression is that the music has been shifted into

the parallel minor of the home key. As the pre-core continues, however, we can better understand the G-minor region as VI in the development key of Bb (HK: bIII).[35]

2. *Closing section material.* Beginning the pre-core with material from the closing section of the exposition promotes the continuity of motive, rhythm, and texture from the end of that section into the beginning of the development.

EXAMPLE 10.12: The pre-core develops the treble motive ("x") in measure 62 of the closing section, thus creating an effective link between the exposition and the development. Yet the motive sounds quite different because it is metrically displaced to enter one beat earlier.[36]

3. *New material.* The beginning of the pre-core may feature material that is not obviously related to anything appearing earlier in the movement. Mozart particularly favors this approach, one rarely used by Haydn and Beethoven.[37] Although the pre-core may give the initial appearance of being new, its motivic material may often be understood to derive from earlier ideas through motivic transformation.

Unlike the two options previously discussed, a direct continuity between the exposition and the development is

EXAMPLE 10.12 Haydn, Piano Sonata in E-flat, Hob. XVI:49, i, 60–86

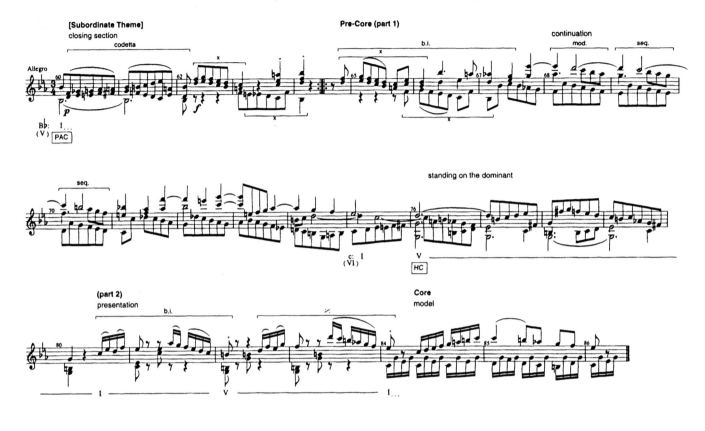

EXAMPLE 10.13 Mozart, Piano Sonata in B-flat, K. 333/315c, i, 64–71

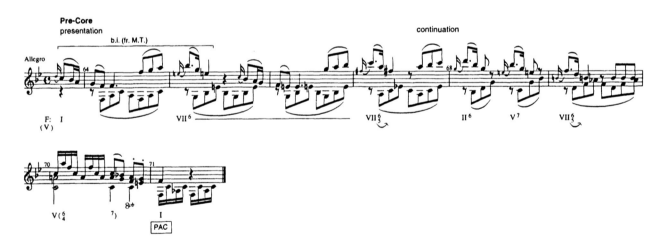

not established when the pre-core begins with new material. This technique can be compositionally appropriate nonetheless, because the new material acts as a foil for the subsequent manipulation of more familiar ideas as the development section continues.[38]

Phrase-structural organization. Pre-cores can be structured in a wide variety of ways, employing many different kinds of formal functions. For the sake of classification, pre-cores can be differentiated at first as *complete* or *incomplete* thematic units. A pre-core is formally complete if it contains a full complement of initiating, medial, and concluding intrathematic functions. Some pre-cores of this type resemble a new main theme because of their tight-knit construction; others resemble a transition because of their looser, modulating organization.[39] An incomplete pre-core is made up of one or two intrathematic functions and usually lacks a concluding function of some kind. A more complex pre-core can be constructed out of multiple thematic units, which themselves may be complete or incomplete.

1. *Complete thematic unit: tight-knit pre-core.* The pre-core may take the form of a relatively tight knit sentence, period, or hybrid. By virtue of its placement at the very beginning of the development, a tight-knit pre-core is analogous to a main theme. Indeed, such a pre-core is often based on material from the actual main theme of the exposition. In that case, the formal organization of the pre-core usually is somewhat looser than that of the main theme. The essential difference between the two units, however, is tonal: whereas the main theme resides in the home key, the pre-core either continues the subordinate key or is set in a development key. A tight-knit pre-core is particularly common in the works of Mozart, but it appears in Haydn and Beethoven as well.

EXAMPLE 10.13: The pre-core begins in the subordinate key with material derived from the basic idea of the main theme. This material, together with the remainder of the pre-core, forms an eight-measure sentence ending with a perfect authentic cadence in measure 71. Although this theme is relatively tight knit with respect to grouping structure and functional efficiency, its greater use of chromaticism makes it looser than the original main theme, whose presentation phrase is shown ahead in example 10.19, measures 94–97. (For reasons of melodic contour, the opening phrase of the main theme may also be considered a compound basic idea.)[40]

2. *Complete thematic unit: transition-like pre-core.* A pre-core can be formed in a way that resembles a transition. The organization is usually sentential, and the harmonic goal is the dominant of a development key. Like most transitions, this type of pre-core is modulatory. Sequential progressions are often found here, but if they are used to support model–sequence technique, the model must be sufficiently small so as not to suggest the beginning of the core proper.

EXAMPLE 10.12: A pre-core of polyphonic texture (Ratner's "strict" or "learned" style)[41] begins in the subordinate key with a basic idea extended to three measures (mm. 65–67). A large continuation featuring model–sequence technique eventually leads to a half cadence (m. 76) and a standing on the dominant of the development key, C minor (HK: VI).[42] Notice that the one-measure model and sequences contained in this continuation do not give the impression of a core, since their unit size is too small to mark the beginning of a new section.[43]

EXAMPLE 10.14: From the point of view of motive and grouping structure, the pre-core is organized like an extended eight-measure sentence, one that modulates from the subordinate key to the dominant of the development key, E minor (HK: V). In this sense, the pre-core is transition-like. Some interesting details of harmony, however, do not entirely support this interpretation. First, the tonic prolongation of the presentation is disrupted by a move to the dominant of IV (appearing first at m. 53 as VII⁵/IV). Second, the "continuation" phrase starts by prolonging this harmony but then reinterprets it enharmonically as an augmented sixth chord of E minor. A more global view of the pre-core would see its being supported by a single harmony (until its very end), one whose root is C and whose initial function as dominant of F (HK: IV) becomes transformed at the last moment into the predominant of the new development key. As such, the entire pre-core could be considered a transitional introduction and thus categorized as an incomplete thematic unit.

3. *Incomplete thematic unit.* A pre-core can be constructed out of one or more intrathematic functions that, taken as a whole, do not constitute a complete thematic unit. A concluding function is usually missing, although the lack of an initiation may also give rise to the thematic incompleteness. Pre-cores of this type tend to be relatively short.

EXAMPLE 10.6: The pre-core begins directly with dominant harmony of the development key, C minor (HK: VI). The single phrase making up this pre-core is best labeled as a transitional introduction. The core begins when the dominant resolves deceptively at measure 90.

EXAMPLE 10.15: The main theme's basic idea returns in the subordinate key for the beginning of the pre-core. The idea is then extended by an extra measure. A dominant version of the basic idea appears, but its corresponding extension leads the music to the dominant of the development key, B♭ minor (HK: IV) at measure 55. The progression from the augmented sixth to the dominant suggests a half cadence, but this interpretation is questionable, since measure 54 seems to group more with its preceding two measures (as an extension) than with measure 55. As a result, the lack of a clear cadence renders the pre-core structurally incomplete.[44]

EXAMPLE 10.7: The pre-core begins in an unusual manner, for it uses material from the cadential area of the first subordinate theme (ex. 10.7b). There, an internal half cadence at measure 66 is prolonged by a standing on the dominant for two measures, after which a cadential phrase brings the theme to a close. This same

EXAMPLE 10.14 Mozart, Piano Sonata in A Minor, K. 310/300d, i, 50–58

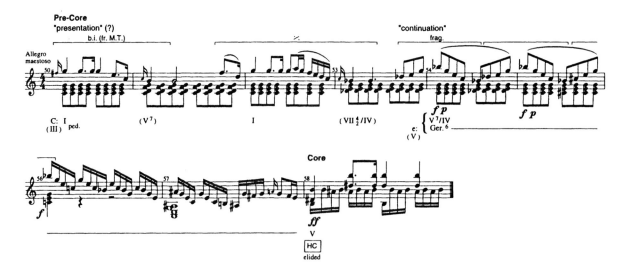

EXAMPLE 10.15 Beethoven, Piano Sonata in F Minor, Op. 2/1, i, 49–55

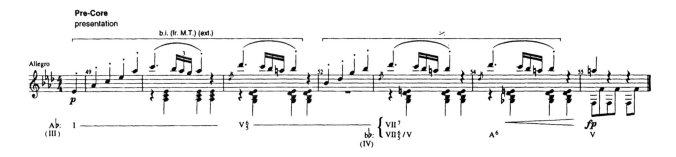

EXAMPLE 10.16 Mozart, Piano Sonata in B-flat, K. 333/315c, i, 71–86

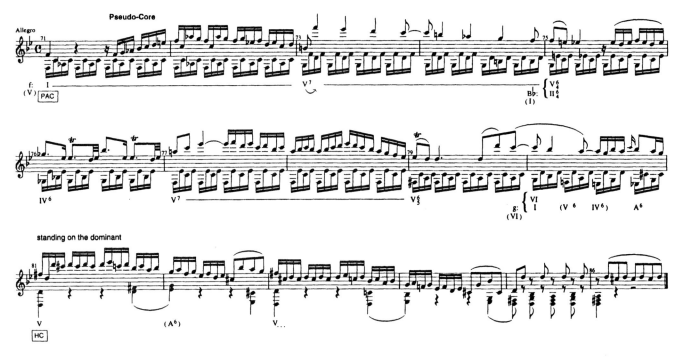

material is brought back at the beginning of the pre-core (ex. 10.7a) and transposed into the development key, A minor (HK: VI). The prolonged dominant of measures 123–24 now functions as a transitional introduction, not to an initiating unit but to a cadential phrase. The lack of functional beginning thus renders this pre-core thematically incomplete.

4. *Multiple thematic units.* A small number of relatively large pre-cores are constructed out of two thematic units. One of these units is usually incomplete.

EXAMPLE 10.11: The pre-core consists of two parts: the first is complete, and the second is incomplete. The first part opens like the main theme (see ex. 3.4) but, rather than closing with a cadence, ends with a premature dominant arrival (m. 68) and a subsequent standing on the dominant of Bb (HK: bIII). The second part begins at measure 74 by bringing back the compound basic idea from the first subordinate theme of the exposition. The idea begins to be repeated (m. 78), but the chromatically rising bass line already creates a continuation that leads to the sudden outburst at measure 81, marking the beginning of the core. The second part of the pre-core is thus left without structural closure.[45]

EXAMPLE 10.12: What was described earlier as a transition-like pre-core (mm. 65–80) is actually the first part of the complete precore. The resolution to the tonic (of C minor) at the upbeat to measure 81 brings a second part, which consists of only a presentation phrase based on the beginning of the first subordinate theme. The core (shown in ex. 10.4) then begins at the extended upbeat to measure 85.

Although the presentation in measures 81–84 belongs by definition to the pre-core (in that it still precedes the beginning of the core), this phrase undoubtedly groups more intimately with the core than with the first part of the pre-core. Indeed, the opening two measures of the model (mm. 85–86) appeared earlier in the first subordinate theme as the beginning of a continuation phrase following this same presentation. Here in the development, the core is a kind of magnified continuation (with its extensive sequential activity), which logically succeeds an initiating presentation.[46]

DEVELOPMENT SECTIONS WITHOUT A CORE

Many classical development sections are not organized in the ways just described. Such developments may indeed begin with a unit structured like a pre-core, and they usually end with an extensive standing on the dominant of the home key. But missing is a genuine core, a well-articulated process of model, sequence, and fragmentation. Haydn, in general, constructs his development sections without a core, whereas Mozart and Beethoven omit the core only now and then.

In place of a core, a variety of phrase-structural options may be employed. Sometimes there appears a pseudo-core, a unit whose dynamics, rhythm, texture, and emotional character strongly resemble those of a core but whose ma-

terial is not organized by model–sequence technique. At other times, the development consists of themelike units formed along the lines of a transition or a subordinate theme. Frequently enough, of course, the development is organized in unique ways that do not permit ready classification. Even in these cases, however, it is often possible to find hints of pre-core/core technique or the kinds of themelike units just mentioned.

Pseudo-core. As described earlier, the core of a development typically expresses restlessness, instability, and *Sturm und Drang*, as well as bringing a relatively loud dynamic, thicker textures, and continuous rhythmic activity. The appearance of these traits strongly suggests a core, even when the musical material is not organized by processes of model, sequence, and fragmentation. Such a *pseudo-core*, as this unit can be termed, sometimes features a prominent sequential organization of the harmonies, but they are not used to support the extensive model–sequence technique typical of a core. At other times, the pseudo-core appears to lack harmonic definition and takes on the improvisatory style of a "fantasia" or "toccata." In such cases, a prominent linear progression in the bass may help achieve coherence amid the seeming harmonic rambling. A pseudo-core is usually preceded by a unit that functions as a pre-core and generally closes with a half cadence (or dominant arrival) followed by a standing on the dominant.

EXAMPLE 10.16: At the final cadence of the tight-knit pre-core, the music suddenly shifts into the minor mode and introduces a continuous Alberti-bass accompaniment supporting a restless melody of running sixteenth notes and syncopated quarter notes. The character of the music leading up to the half cadence in G minor (HK: VI) at measure 81 is highly suggestive of a core. Yet at no point can we identify a model that is sequentially repeated. Even the harmonic progressions suggest little in the way of sequential organization.[47] Instead, they seem more tightly controlled by the bass line, which oscillates chromatically between F and G (until the descent to D at m. 81).[48]

Transition-like unit. In place of a core, the central section of the development may be occupied by a thematic unit whose tonal and phrase-structural organization resembles a transition. This transition-like *core substitute* (not to be confused with a transition-like *pre-core*) usually begins in one key with a standard initiating function (presentation, compound basic idea), modulates to some other key (development or home), and closes with a half cadence or dominant arrival. Model–sequence technique of limited scope may appear somewhere in this unit (usually in connection with a continuation function), but not in a way that gives rise to a genuine core.

EXAMPLE 10.17: A new themelike unit begins at measure 36 immediately after the pre-core closes in Ab (HK: bIII). A basic idea and

EXAMPLE 10.17 Haydn, Symphony No. 102 in B-flat, ii, 33–46

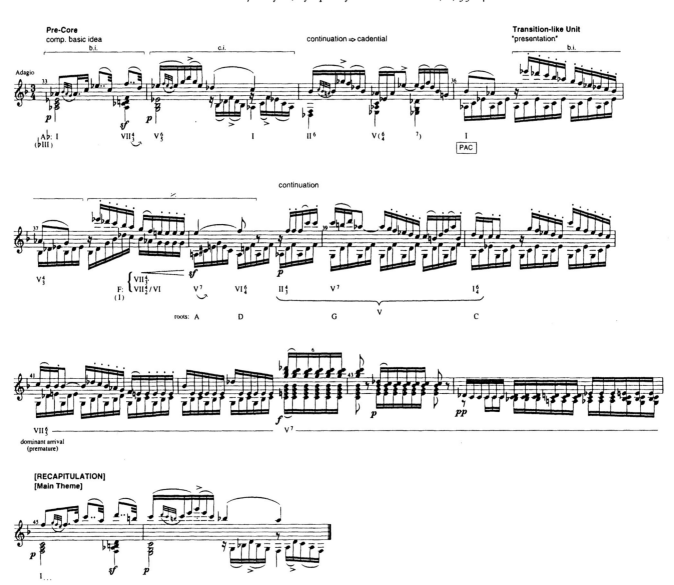

its varied repetition create presentation function.[49] The subsequent continuation (upbeat to m. 39) contains a sequential progression (but no model–sequence technique) as the music modulates back to the home key. The move to VII⁵ at measure 41 brings a premature dominant arrival to mark the end of harmonic activity for this transition-like unit. The rest of the development plays itself out over a prolonged dominant of the home key.[50]

EXAMPLE 10.18: This development section consists of four parts. The first part (mm. 56–67) begins with a four-measure transitional introduction to a relatively tight knit theme, based on material from the main theme (see mm. 97–98) but now set in the development key, E♭ (HK: IV). This part is thus comparable to a pre-core, despite the absence of a genuine core in what follows. The second part (mm. 68–76) begins with a compound basic idea, whose initial harmony is heard as tonic in E♭ but which, by the end of the idea in measure 71, is easily reinterpreted as IV in the home key. A brief cadential idea leads to a half cadence at measure 73. Because of its modulating structure (from E♭ to B♭) and its ending on dominant harmony, the formal organization of this second part resembles a transition.

At this point in the form, we might be led to consider this return to the home-key dominant as marking the end of the development, except that the section would be rather short and it would be unusual for there to have been no exploration of a minor-mode region. So it is not entirely surprising when the home-key dominant moves to the dominant of G minor (HK: VI), the primary development key, which is fully confirmed in the third part of the development, to be discussed shortly. (The earlier key of E♭ [HK: IV] thus becomes a secondary development key within the movement.)

Subordinate themelike unit. A unit in a development can resemble a subordinate theme if its harmonic goal is an authentic cadence of a development key and if it features loosening devices such as an extended continuation, an expanded cadential progression, and evaded, deceptive, or abandoned cadences. Unlike a genuine subordinate theme, which must always close with a perfect authentic cadence, a themelike unit of the development can promise authentic cadential closure but never achieve a true cadential arrival. Frequently, the unit begins in one tonal region or key and modulates to another key where it receives authentic cadential closure (or the promise of such closure).[51]

EXAMPLE 10.18: The third part (mm. 77–85) of this development begins with a two-measure basic idea in the development key, G minor (HK: VI). The following two measures can be seen as a varied repeat, thus creating a presentation phrase. At the same time, however, measure 80 also initiates a continuation, as expressed by fragmentation and increased rhythmic activity. An expanded cadential progression begins at measure 82 but is momentarily abandoned on the downbeat of measure 84.[52] A subsequent compressed cadential progression in the same measure finally confirms the development key. The concluding perfect authentic cadence is followed by a brief closing section (mm. 85–86). (This closing section eventually is understood as false, since, as I explain shortly, it functions to open the fourth part of the development, the retransi-

tion.) The themelike unit thus resembles a loosely organized subordinate theme because of the obscuring of functional boundaries (in m. 80), the expanded cadential progression, and the abandoned cadence.

In a number of respects, the first three parts of this development model the organization of an exposition: the pre-core is tight knit like a main theme; the second part resembles a transition; and the third part is suggestive of a subordinate theme. In fact, this relationship of development to exposition is also supported by the melodic–motivic material. The pre-core is based on ideas from the exposition's main theme; the second part draws on the continuation phrase of the first part of the subordinate theme (mm. 25–34); and the third part is based on the second part of the subordinate theme (mm. 35–42).[53]

RETRANSITION

In this book, I have used the term *retransition* for those passages that modulate back to the home key in preparation for the return of some previous opening material. I identified retransitions with reference to the end of the contrasting middle of a small ternary and the end of a closing section following a subordinate theme. Traditional theories of form normally recognize a retransition at the end of most development sections, especially in connection with what I have termed here a standing on the dominant.[54] There is a problem with this traditional usage, however. By the time the standing on the dominant begins, the home key has already been achieved, as confirmed by the half cadence (or dominant arrival). If the term retransition is to be used with most development sections, it should be applied before the standing on the dominant, presumably at that moment when the modulation to the home key takes place.

Although most developments express a general retransition function, in that they all eventually return from a subordinate or development key to the home key, only some developments include a specific passage whose primary function is retransitional. It would seem preferable, therefore, to restrict the term to those passages in particular.[55] Most typically, a retransition is a complete phrase, or even a full themelike unit, that follows the cadential articulation of a development key. At times, the retransition may consist of the home-key dominant exclusively, but only when that harmony directly follows the dominant of the preceding development key.

EXAMPLE 10.18: The fourth part of the development section (mm. 85–96) begins with what at first sounds like codettas to the third part but that are retrospectively understood as a false closing section to initiate this retransition. The modulation back to the home key occurs at measure 87, and the subsequent half cadence at measure 91 confirms the tonal return. The retransition ends with a postcadential standing on the dominant (mm. 91–96).[56]

EXAMPLE 10.18 Haydn, Piano Sonata in B-flat, Hob. XVI:41, i, 56–99

EXAMPLE 10.19 Mozart, Piano Sonata in B-flat, K. 333/315c, i, 86–97

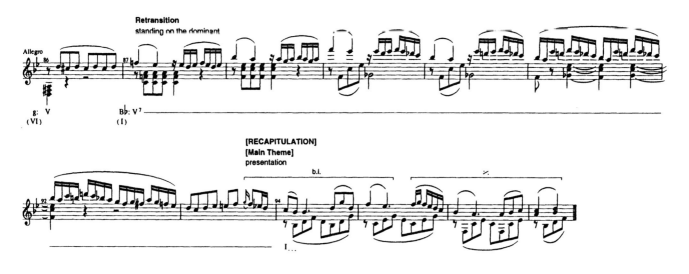

EXAMPLE 10.20 Beethoven, Piano Sonata in G, Op. 14/2, i, 98–108

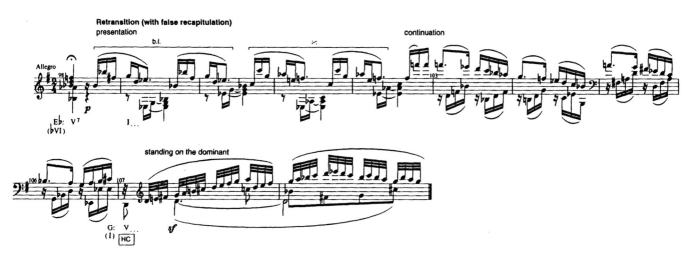

EXAMPLE 10.19: Immediately following the standing on the dominant of VI, which ends the pseudo-core (see ex. 10.16), Mozart reintroduces the dominant of the home-key at measure 87 and writes a standing on the dominant of this key for the remainder of the development. Although this passage contains just a single harmony, it can nonetheless be considered a distinct retransition, for it seems not to belong to the preceding pseudo-core, whose formal processes have played themselves out by the end of measure 86.[57]

A retransition sometimes starts with reference to the opening material from the main theme, usually in the development key just confirmed by a prior half cadence. This effect can be characterized as a *false recapitulation*.[58]

Eventually, the music returns to the home key for the true recapitulation.

EXAMPLE 10.20: As discussed in connection with example 10.9, the core concludes on the dominant of B♭ (HK: ♭VI). Following the fermata at measure 98, a new part begins just like the main theme (ex. 3.4) but still in the prevailing development key. Although the gesture is recapitulatory, the tonal requirements of a genuine recapitulation are not met. Therefore, following the opening presentation, the music modulates back to the home key, as confirmed by the half cadence in measure 107 and a substantial standing on the dominant (most of which is not shown). The real recapitulation begins at measure 125 (not shown). The music from the beginning of the false recapitulation to the real recapitulation thus functions as a retransition.[59]

Recapitulation

The full-movement sonata form and its allied forms (concerto, sonata–rondo, and sonata without development) contain a *recapitulation*, a large section that brings back, usually in modified form, an earlier exposition.[1] The recapitulation functions to resolve the principal tonal and melodic processes left incomplete in earlier sections and to provide symmetry and balance to the overall form by restating the melodic–motivic material of the exposition.

These formal functions are analogous to those of the recapitulation of the small ternary. Like an A' section, a large-scale recapitulation minimally realizes its functions by beginning in the home key with the basic idea of the main theme, by adjusting the following material so that it remains in the home key, and by confirming that key with a concluding perfect authentic cadence.[2] Also like an A' section, the recapitulation frequently modifies the formal organization of the exposition by eliminating functional redundancies and developing earlier motivic material.

When comparing a given recapitulation with its corresponding exposition, we can distinguish between two general kinds of changes. One kind involves dynamics, instrumentation, register, texture, accompanimental figuration, melodic embellishments, and the like.[3] These *ornamental changes* are motivated by general aesthetic concerns for variety and by the particular expressive values that the composer wishes to convey in the movement. A second kind of change involves harmonic–tonal organization, melodic-motivic material, grouping structure, and formal functions. These *structural changes* are motivated primarily by fundamental differences in the function of the recapitulation, as compared with the exposition. In addition, structural changes can be prompted by the content and organization of the development section (e.g., the elimination of a certain idea from the recapitulation because of its extensive use in the development).

Inasmuch as the recapitulation restates the material of the exposition in roughly the same order as it earlier appeared, it is conventional practice to label the constituent parts of the recapitulation with the same terms employed for the exposition: main theme, transition, and subordinate theme (including the closing section).[4] As convenient as this practice may be—and for the sake of tradition, it is maintained here—this labeling scheme obscures the significantly different formal functions that these units serve in the recapitulation.

Main theme. The main theme of the exposition has three major functions: to introduce and fix in the mind of the listener the principal melodic–motivic ideas of the movement; to establish and confirm the home key by means of a cadence (usually authentic but possibly half); and to define the degree of tight-knit organization with which the more loosely organized units in the movement can be compared.

At the beginning of the recapitulation, these functions are no longer required or even necessarily appropriate. The melodic–motivic material is well known by this point in the movement. The home key was reestablished toward the end of the development and will definitely receive ultimate confirmation later in the recapitulation (in the subordinate-theme area), and a defining tight-knit organization need not be expressed yet again. Instead, the main theme of the recapitulation functions primarily to signal the sense of "return." In addition, the theme's beginning on a home-key tonic harmonically resolves (at a local level) the dominant expressed at the end of the development.[5]

Transition. In the exposition, the transition functions to destabilize the home key in order to establish a contrasting subordinate key and to loosen the form (as defined by the main theme). In the recapitulation, the transition continues to fulfill these general functions, but the home key is destabilized for completely different reasons—to permit the subordinate theme to sound fresh when transposed into the home key and to prevent the recapitulation from becoming tonally monotonous.

Subordinate theme. The subordinate theme of the exposition provides the formal means of confirming the subordinate key as the tonal antagonist of the home key. The subordinate theme also functions to loosen the formal organization, primarily by means of extensions and expansions, so that the rival key acquires sufficient temporal weight to

EXAMPLE 11.1 Beethoven, Piano Sonata in A, Op. 2/2, i, 242–52

EXAMPLE 11.2 Mozart, Piano Sonata in G, K. 283/189h, i, 72–85

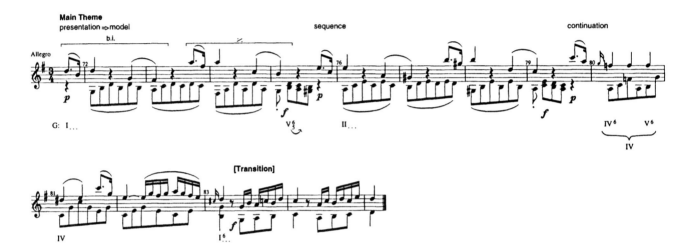

EXAMPLE 11.3 Beethoven, Symphony No. 7 in A, Op. 92, i, 297–308

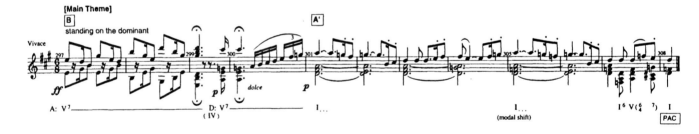

counterbalance its inherent structural subordination. The recapitulation resolves this fundamental conflict of tonalities when the subordinate theme is transposed back into the home key. The subordinate theme retains its loose organization, but now its expansiveness serves to endow the home key with the greatest power of expression in the movement.

The functional differences just described account for many of the structural changes that typically take place in a given recapitulation. The remainder of this chapter systematically examines such changes as well as those motivated by the preceding development section. Ornamental changes are observed and explained as they arise in the individual examples.

MAIN THEME

In many recapitulations, the main theme is organized just as it was in the exposition, although ornamental changes may be included. Frequently, however, the main theme undergoes some of the following structural changes because of its new formal function in the recapitulation.

Deletion of thematic restatements. Since the main theme's melodic–motivic material is by now quite familiar to the listener, a restatement of ideas, which was appropriate in the exposition (in which the material is heard for the first time), is often eliminated in the recapitulation, especially if those ideas were prominently exploited in the development section. If the entire main theme was repeated in the exposition, the recapitulation usually states the theme just once.[6] If the main theme was originally constructed as a small ternary, then the A (or A') section alone is likely to be used in the recapitulation.[7]

Additional model–sequence technique. In the main theme of the recapitulation, the composer may throw new light on some old ideas (especially those not treated in the development) by means of a newly composed passage using model–sequence technique. Charles Rosen speaks in this connection of a *secondary development*.[8]

Emphasis on "flat" tonal regions. The harmonic plan of the main theme is sometimes altered in a way that emphasizes the "flat" side of the tonal spectrum—regions that introduce chromatically lowered scale-degrees, such as the subdominant, the lowered mediant, the lowered submediant, and the Neapolitan.[9]

Deletion of the home-key cadence. Since there is ample opportunity to confirm the home key later in the recapitulation (in the subordinate theme), a cadence to end the main theme is dispensable in the recapitulation. A subsequent closing section may also be omitted because the home key hardly requires reinforcement at this point in the form.

The following examples illustrate these techniques.

EXAMPLE 11.1: The main theme in the exposition (shown in ex. 13.6) has a decidedly loose organization. (To follow better the changes that occur in the recapitulation, the reader may wish to consult the discussion of the main theme in chap. 13, p. 201.) The recapitulation opens with the same antecedent-like unit (ex. 13.6, mm. 1–20; not reproduced in ex. 11.1). But rather than continuing as in the exposition, the final phrase is sequenced down a step (m. 244) into the "flat" region of D major and then is sequenced again up a fifth (m. 248) in order to end the main theme on the home-key tonic. Besides adding this brief secondary development, Beethoven eliminates a restatement of the initial basic idea (as in mm. 21–22 of the exposition) and the final cadence.

EXAMPLE 11.2: The initial presentation phrase is sequenced up a step (mm. 76–79) and is then followed by a new continuation (cf. ex. 3.3). The appearance of a sequential passage is particularly appropriate here, since it compensates for the lack of a core in the preceding development section.[10] The new continuation (mm. 80–83) ends on I^6, after which the transition immediately follows. As a result, the main theme receives no cadential closure.

EXAMPLE 11.3: The main theme in the recapitulation follows the same course as the exposition (see ex. 6.9) until the end of the B section, in which the fermata over V^7 (m. 299) is followed by another fermata over V^7/IV. The subsequent music corresponds to the original A' section but is now transposed into the subdominant region. The change to minor at measure 305 shifts the music even further to the flat side. The theme closes with a cadence, but in the subdominant minor, not in the home key.

TRANSITION

The transition is the section of the recapitulation most likely to be altered in relation to the exposition. If the original transition is modulatory, then the one in the recapitulation must be tonally *adjusted* to remain in the home key. The adjustment can be accomplished by any number of harmonic and phrase-structural means and can occur at any place in the transition. Frequently, the subdominant region is tonicized, thus promoting (in the sense of a pre-dominant) a logical succession to the dominant to end the transition. If the original transition is nonmodulatory, a tonal adjustment is not necessary, and the transition may even retain its original structure.[11]

In addition to changes brought about by tonal adjustment, certain other alterations are regularly encountered, some of which are similar to those discussed for the main theme.

Deletions and compressions. The transition in the recapitulation often deletes or compresses a substantial portion

EXAMPLE 11.4 Beethoven, Symphony No. 4 in B-flat, Op. 60, i, 351–70

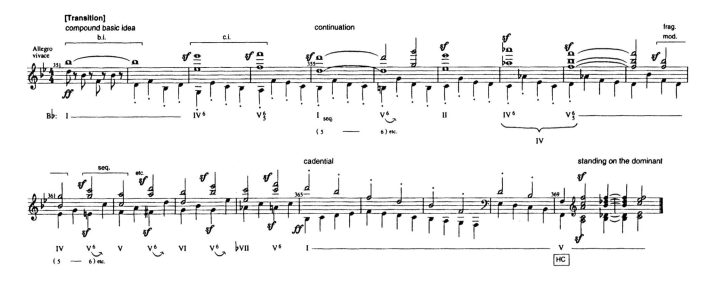

EXAMPLE 11.5 Mozart, Violin Sonata in C, K. 403/385c, i, 39–46

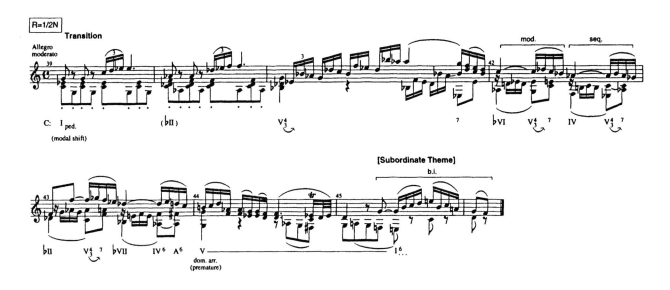

EXAMPLE 11.6 Mozart, Piano Sonata in C Minor, K. 457, i, 117–32

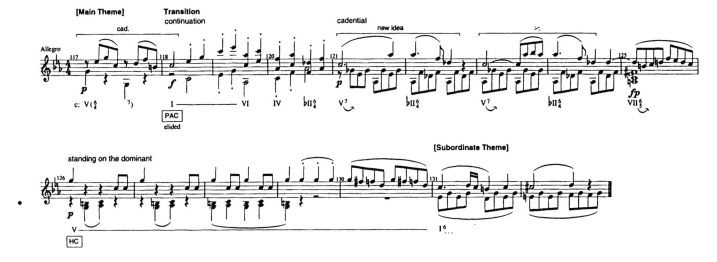

of material used in the exposition. (In the most extreme case, the entire transition may be eliminated.)[12] The deleted passages are usually taken from the beginning of the transition, where they generally function to prolong home-key tonic. Extensive tonic prolongation is needed in the exposition in order to reinforce the home key before modulating. Conversely, such a prolongation can easily be omitted in the recapitulation because the upcoming subordinate theme provides abundant tonic emphasis.

If the exposition contains a two-part transition, the composer usually deletes some material from each part (especially the modulating passages from the second part) so that the transition in the recapitulation is compressed into a one-part, nonmodulating structure.[13]

Additional model–sequence technique. The transition in the recapitulation often includes passages that do not correspond directly to the exposition. These passages, which usually extend an existing continuation (or create a new one) normally employ model–sequence technique in the sense of Rosen's secondary development.[14] Indeed, motives not prominently featured in the development section proper are frequently given special treatment here.

Emphasis on "flat" regions. Since both the main and the subordinate themes of the recapitulation generally stress diatonic harmonies in the home key, the transition offers the best opportunity for composers to create a significant harmonic–tonal contrast in the recapitulation. To that end, they typically tonicize the "flat" side of the tonal spectrum, particularly if they leave the main theme relatively unaltered (and thus focused on the home-key tonic). This move in the flat direction is especially appropriate to the transition because the subsequent return to diatonic progressions of the home key at the beginning of the subordinate theme shifts the music back to the "sharp" side, a tonal change that corresponds to the move from the home key to the subordinate key in the exposition. In the recapitulation, the return from flat regions to the diatonicism of the home key helps make the tonal context of the subordinate theme sound fresh and revitalized.

The following examples illustrate these techniques.

EXAMPLE 11.4: The transition in the recapitulation opens with a compound basic idea (mm. 351–54) taken from the middle of the transition in the exposition (see ex. 9.12, mm. 81–84). Thus, an enormous passage built over a tonic pedal (mm. 65–80, not shown in ex. 9.12) is deleted in the recapitulation. Also deleted is the repetition of the compound basic idea (mm. 85–88), so that measure 355 brings a new, highly extended continuation featuring motivic play and an ascending-stepwise sequence in the sense of a secondary development. At measure 369, the transition conforms again to that of the exposition by concluding with the same standing on the dominant (ex. 9.12, mm. 95–106).

EXAMPLE 11.5: The sudden appearance of the home-key parallel minor at the very beginning of the transition marks a shift to the "flat" side of the tonal spectrum (cf. ex. 9.1, m. 5). The music then moves even further in that direction by tonicizing A♭ major, the lowered submediant. Measure 42 sees the beginning of a new model–sequence passage, which does not correspond to anything in the exposition. The transition ends with a premature dominant arrival of the home key on the downbeat of measure 44. Both tonal and modal balance is finally restored at the beginning of the subordinate theme, when the music shifts in the "sharp" direction to project a more palpable sense of C major as the home key.

EXAMPLE 11.6: The transition begins at measure 118 with a canonic variation of the exposition's basic idea (ex. 9.14, mm. 19–20) and then moves quickly to introduce new material in a tonicized ♭II region (mm. 121–24). This Neapolitan then functions as an expanded pre-dominant (which also embraces the following VII$^{6}_{5}$/V) in order to achieve the home-key half cadence in measure 126. (The remainder of the transition is examined in connection with the subordinate theme.)

EXAMPLE 11.7: The opening seven measures of the transition are the same as those of the exposition (cf. ex. 9.4, mm. 16–22). The change of mode at measure 158 initiates a new passage, one not found in the earlier section. The music leads eventually to a half cadence and a standing on the dominant of the home key (m. 164), corresponding to the end of the transition in the exposition (ex. 9.4, mm. 37–41). Haydn has thus compressed what was originally a two-part transition in the exposition into a single unit. He does so by eliminating material from the exposition that would be either redundant or functionally inappropriate in the recapitulation—namely, most of the first part (containing additional tonic prolongations and another home-key standing on the dominant) and the beginning of the second part (containing main-theme material and the modulation to the new key).[15]

FUSION OF MAIN THEME AND TRANSITION

The main theme and transition usually remain discrete units in the recapitulation, just as they were in the exposition. Now and then, however, they *fuse* into a single thematic structure.[16] This formal compression is usually brought about by eliminating the end of the main theme and the beginning of the transition and by attaching the close of the latter to what remains of the former. In some cases, the entire transition from the exposition is eliminated, and the main theme, which closed with an authentic cadence in the exposition, ends instead with a half cadence.

This form-functional fusion is often accompanied by the same alteration techniques used for both main themes and transitions, such as deleting unnecessary repetitions, adding new model–sequence technique, and emphasizing the "flat" tonal regions.

EXAMPLE 11.7 Haydn, Piano Trio in E-flat, Hob. XV:30, i, 152–70

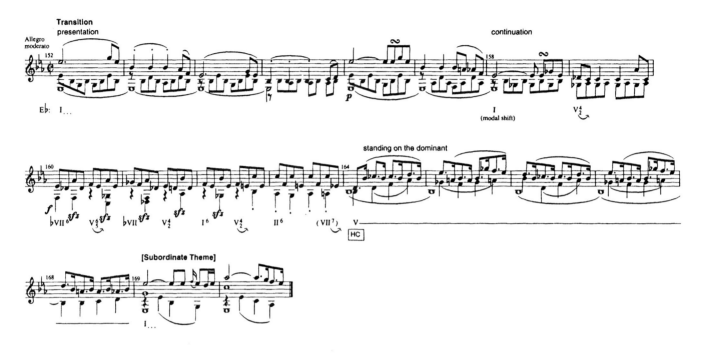

EXAMPLE 11.8 Beethoven, Piano Concerto No. 3 in C Minor, Op. 37, i, 317–30

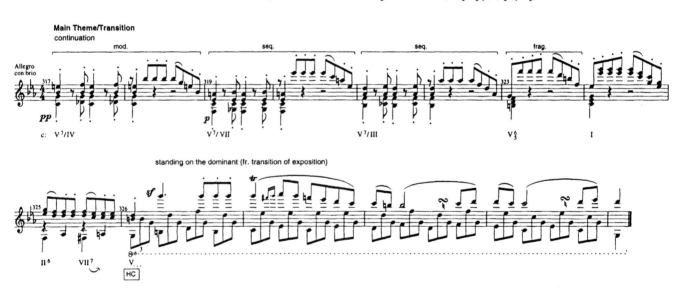

EXAMPLE 11.9 Haydn, Piano Sonata in C, Hob. XVI:21, ii, 40–50

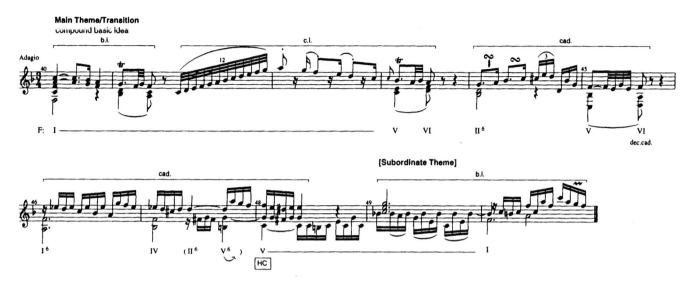

EXAMPLE 11.8: The main theme and transition in the exposition occupy two distinct sections. (Ex. 5.15 gives the main theme version found in the opening ritornello of this concerto, but the main theme of the solo exposition has the identical form.) The recapitulation begins with the same eight-measure presentation (mm. 309–16, not shown) but then introduces an entirely new continuation (mm. 317–26), which sequentially develops the final motive of the compound basic idea. Rather than ending with an authentic cadence, as in the exposition, the continuation leads to a half cadence at measure 326, and the subsequent standing on the dominant corresponds to that found at the end of the transition in the exposition.[17]

EXAMPLE 11.9: The opening six measures of the recapitulation are essentially the same as the main theme of the exposition, except that the final chord is VI rather than I. Thus instead of closing with a perfect authentic cadence, the theme brings a deceptive cadence in measure 45. The following cadential phrase leads not to the expected authentic cadence but to a home-key half cadence (m. 48) in preparation for the subordinate theme. The complete transition from the exposition (see ex. 9.2) is deleted, and the final cadential phrase of the recapitulation's main theme takes over transition function.[18]

SUBORDINATE THEME (GROUP)

As a general rule, the subordinate theme (or theme group) returns as it had originally appeared in the exposition, except for being tonally adjusted into the home key. Mozart and Beethoven follow this practice as a matter of course. Only occasionally do their subordinate themes exhibit significant structural changes. Haydn, on the contrary, regularly alters this area in the recapitulation.

EXAMPLE 11.10: The subordinate theme retains the same structure as that of the exposition (cf. ex. 8.3a) but is transposed instead into

the home key of C major. To keep the music in an appropriate register, the melody is at first transposed down a fifth (while the accompaniment is moved a fourth higher). At the upbeat to measure 65, the melody is then transposed up a fourth (compared with the exposition) so that it will not descend too low. The cadential phrase (mm. 67–71) witnesses ornamental changes in harmony and rhythm, with the goal of creating greater intensity for the cadential arrival. The pre-dominant II[6] is prolonged by VII[7]/V, and the sixteenth notes in measure 69 help make the following trill all the more climactic.

Standard Additions and Deletions

Like the main theme and transition, the subordinate theme in the recapitulation may delete material that is stated more than once in the exposition.[19] But it is also typical for the cadential area of the subordinate theme to undergo greater expansion than it received in the exposition. As a result, the most powerful cadential emphasis in the form is accorded the confirmation of the home key instead of the subordinate key. This procedure is especially characteristic of the concerto (and related genres), in which the dramatic cadential peroration brings passage-work in a "brilliant" style.

EXAMPLE 11.11: The final cadential phrase, beginning at measure 210, is expanded from five measures in the exposition (cf. ex. 8.8, mm. 108–12) to seven in the recapitulation. The passage gives the soloist the opportunity of displaying virtuosic technique by having to negotiate the very highest tessitura in the movement.[20]

Major Alterations

Although the subordinate theme usually appears in the recapitulation similar to how it did in the exposition, the composer occasionally alters the thematic structure in more

EXAMPLE 11.10 Mozart, Piano Sonata in C, K. 545, i, 58–73

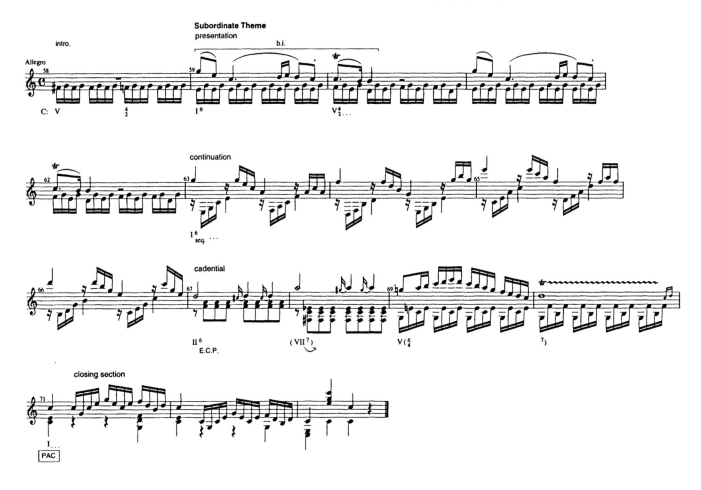

EXAMPLE 11.11 Mozart, Violin Concerto in A, K. 219, i, 209–16

substantial ways. Sometimes the changes are made for expressive and dramatic goals unique to the individual work. But some compositional situations arising in the exposition regularly lead to major alterations in the recapitulation.[21]

"Monothematic" exposition. One such situation involves the so-called monothematic exposition—the use of the same basic idea for both the main theme and the subordinate theme. If the original structure of the subordinate theme is retained in the recapitulation, then the basic idea would occur in the home key twice: first in the main theme and second in the tonally adjusted subordinate theme. To preclude a potential tautology, the composer normally deletes the second appearance of the basic idea. (The first appearance, of course, is needed to articulate the beginning of the recapitulation.) But simply omitting the basic idea at the start of the subordinate theme does not suffice, for a theme cannot necessarily begin logically with, say, the continuation function that formerly followed the basic idea (and its repetition). Therefore, the composer must usually alter the theme more substantially or even eliminate it altogether.[22] Haydn, who writes a large number of monothematic expositions, typically uses these procedures,[23] but some striking examples are found in Mozart as well.

EXAMPLE 11.12: Following the close of the transition, Mozart begins the subordinate theme of the recapitulation with material from the *second* subordinate theme of the exposition (see ex. 8.1, mm. 42ff.). He does so presumably to avoid a redundant appearance of the main theme's basic idea in the home key, which would arise from using the first subordinate theme (ex. 8.1, mm. 28ff.). Some kind of change is especially needed here, because earlier in the recapitulation (ex. 11.12b), the main theme is repeated (and fused with the transition) in an imitative manner that strongly resembles the beginning of the exposition's first subordinate theme.

In the recapitulation, the "second" subordinate theme is now normalized to become a conventional eight-measure period (mm. 122–29). (In the exposition, the consequent was lengthened by means of an expanded cadential progression.) The theme begins to be repeated, but at measure 136, just at the point that the cadential expansion in the exposition occurred (ex. 8.1, m. 48), the music becomes significantly more chromatic and, in the following measure, stops rather abruptly with an air of uncertainty on V^6/VI. Measure 138 then initiates an enormous interpolation of the *first* subordinate theme from the exposition. But again to avoid a redundant home-key statement of the basic idea, Mozart transposes it into VI (thus resolving the previous dominant) and converts what was originally an initiating tonic prolongational passage (ex. 8.1, mm. 28–34) into a fully sequential passage. Indeed, this model–sequence is now suitable as a further continuation of the repeated subordinate theme, begun at measure 130.

To close the theme, Mozart brings at measure 148 the expanded cadential progression from the first subordinate theme (ex. 8.1, mm. 38–41) and, in measures 152–55, appends to it the end of the expanded cadential progression from the second subordinate theme (mm. 50–53). The resulting cadential area is thus more expansive than either two of those in the exposition. Indeed, by interpolating the exposition's first subordinate theme into a repetition of its second subordinate theme, Mozart has fashioned in the recapitulation a single theme of considerably greater complexity and structural scope.

Two-part subordinate theme. The use of a two-part subordinate theme in the exposition can sometimes lead to major structural changes in the recapitulation. In the exposition, an internal half cadence and standing on the dominant often serve to emphasize dominant harmony of the subordinate key, especially if the previous transition is nonmodulating. If the two-part subordinate theme is left intact in the recapitulation, two cadential articulations of home-key dominant will result: the cadence of the transition and the internal half cadence of the two-part subordinate theme. To avoid overemphasizing the home-key dominant, the composer sometimes retains only one of these cadences, usually the internal half cadence. Therefore, either the first part of the subordinate theme is deleted, or portions of it are assimilated into the preceding transition. The second part of the subordinate theme then follows as the actual theme in the recapitulation.

EXAMPLE 11.6: The transition of the recapitulation concludes in measures 126–30 with material that earlier functioned as the internal half cadence and standing on the dominant in the subordinate theme (see ex. 9.14, mm. 30–35). The first part of that theme (ex. 9.14, mm. 23–29) is deleted in the recapitulation, and the second part now functions as the subordinate theme of that section.

According to Rosen, Mozart's deleting the first part of this subordinate theme does not violate the general principle that the subordinate-theme area, or "at least any part of it that has an individual and characteristic aspect, and that does not already have its analogue in the first group [main theme]" must reappear transposed into the home key in the recapitulation. He points out that the deleted passage "has been played in the development section at the subdominant. This is also a clear indication of the role of the subdominant as a substitute tonic in the Viennese classical language."[24] Whether the subdominant is a tonic substitute in this style is, of course, highly debatable, but the appearance of this material in the pre-core of the development (mm. 79–82) unquestionably helps permit its being omitted in the recapitulation.[25]

Modulating subordinate theme. If the exposition contains a modulating subordinate theme, the tonal adjustment in the recapitulation will be more complicated than usual. In some cases, the subordinate theme can still give the impression of modulating by beginning in some other tonal region (of the home key) and eventually returning to emphasize the tonic region. In other cases, the theme begins directly on the home-key tonic and so loses some of its modulatory character.

EXAMPLE 11.13: The transition ends on V/VI, just as in the exposition (see ex. 8.18, mm. 31–34). The subordinate theme begins "off

EXAMPLE 11.12 (a) Mozart, Piano Sonata in D, K. 576, i, 120–55; (b) mm. 107–10

EXAMPLE 11.13 Beethoven, Piano Sonata in E-flat, Op. 31/3, ii, 136–49

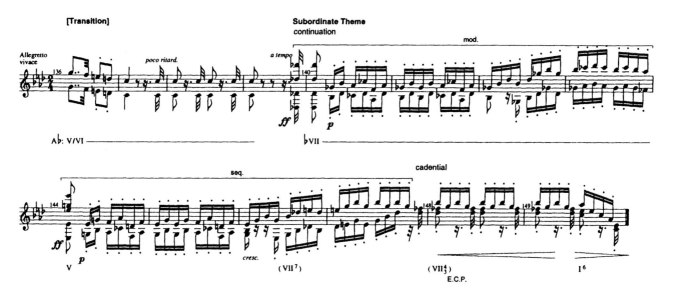

tonic" in the ♭VII region and eventually "modulates" back to the tonic of A♭ by the end of measure 149. (To make a smooth progression from V/VI at the end of the transition to ♭VII at the beginning of the subordinate theme, Beethoven introduces the octave D♭, which sounds at first like a deceptive resolution of the secondary dominant but which then functions as the dominant of ♭VII.)[26]

EXAMPLE 11.14: The subordinate theme begins at measure 178 directly in the major mode of the home key. If no further adjustments were made, the theme would end up modulating from C to E minor, since the subordinate theme in the exposition modulated from E♭ to G minor (cf. ex. 8.9, mm. 52–72). Although E minor is eventually reached at measure 198, Beethoven reorganizes the harmonies in order to arrive on the home-key dominant (m. 206), after which the music continues just as it had in the exposition, but now fully in the home key.[27]

Closing Section, "Retransition"

The closing section of the subordinate theme (group) usually reappears in the recapitulation in much the same way as it did in the exposition. If the recapitulation is followed by a coda, the final codettas of the closing section are sometimes altered or eliminated. In the absence of a genuine coda, the closing section may be extended in order to impart a more decisive sense of conclusion to the movement as a whole.

EXAMPLE 11.15: The closing section is extended, relative to its appearance in the exposition (cf. ex. 1.8, mm. 42–48), to form a complete sentence, whose continuation is stretched to eight measures.[28]

If the exposition closes with a retransition leading back to the home key, the recapitulation may very well bring a similar passage, this time leading to the subdominant re-

gion for the beginning of the coda. This "retransition," however, no longer fulfills its nominal function, since it does not return to the home key. Because this passage modulates to some other region (the subdominant), it functions more as a "transition" to the coda (see in the following chapter ex. 12.1, mm. 230–31, and ex. 12.2, mm. 265–68).

ADDITIONAL FEATURES

Influence of the development. The content and organization of the development section seem at times to influence changes made in the recapitulation. We have already observed two such cases. In example 11.6, the deletion of the first part of the subordinate theme is "explained" by its use in the pre-core of the development. In example 11.2, the added sequence in the main theme (mm. 76–79) is understood to compensate for the lack of core in the development.[29]

EXAMPLE 11.5: The use of explicit model–sequence technique in measures 42–43 is especially fitting in light of the rather brief development section (not shown), in which sequential organization is conspicuously absent (despite the exploration of various tonal regions of the home key).

To speak of the development influencing the recapitulation is not to suggest a causal connection between these sections. What happens in the former does not necessarily determine what will happen in the latter; the literature abounds in counterexamples to disprove such a claim. Rather, it is more a question of the *appropriateness* of occurrence. When we attend carefully to certain events in the development, we may come to believe that it is particularly

EXAMPLE 11.14 Beethoven, Overture to *Coriolanus*, Op. 62, 177–206

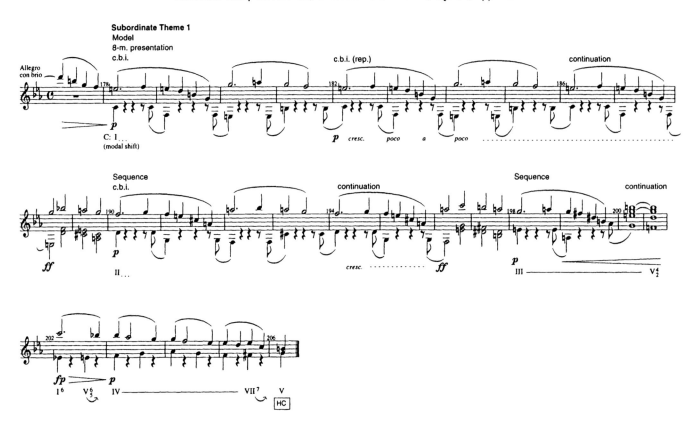

EXAMPLE 11.15 Beethoven, Piano Sonata in F Minor, Op. 2/1, i, 141–52

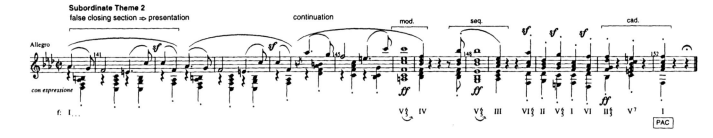

EXAMPLE 11.16 Mozart, Clarinet Trio in E-flat, K. 498, i, 74–83

fitting that some other event does, or does not, occur in the recapitulation. That a given idea is highly exploited in the development, for example, makes it appropriate that the idea be deleted in the recapitulation, without raising expectations that it necessarily will not appear.

Greater rhythmic continuity. The exposition of a movement often contains prominent interruptions in rhythmic activity, such as rests and fermatas, particularly in the main theme and at the end of the transition. The recapitulation often removes such discontinuities in order to foster greater rhythmic momentum. Following an emotionally charged development section, the flow of events may seem too inhibited if the music is continually checked in its progress by too many stops and starts.

EXAMPLE 11.16: The presentation phrase of the main theme in the exposition is marked by rhythmic breaks in each even-numbered measure (see ex. 5.17, mm. 1–8). In the recapitulation, these gaps are filled in (and the grouping structure somewhat extended) by newly added imitations of the initial two-measure basic idea.[30]

EXAMPLE 11.7: By compressing the exposition's two-part transition into a single part, Haydn also eliminates a pronounced pause in the rhythmic momentum arising at the end of the first part (see ex. 9.4, m. 32).[31]

DEVIATIONS FROM THE NORM

The recapitulation can deviate from the norms described throughout this chapter in so many different ways as to preclude an exhaustive discussion here. But the following types of deviations, each of which has multiple occurrences in the repertory, illustrate some of the possibilities that may be encountered.

Deletion of the main-theme opening. Some recapitulations delete the opening material of the main theme or even the entire theme.[32] At times the transition may be eliminated as well, and the recapitulation begins directly with the subordinate-theme area. Although deviant in the high classical style, this procedure is normative in midcentury works and has its roots in baroque binary dance forms.[33] Omitting the main theme at the beginning of the recapitulation is especially associated with the sonata–rondo, since the theme has already had several earlier statements and will eventually be brought back in the coda (see chap. 16).

As a result of deleting the opening of the main theme, the large-scale form of a sonata movement would seem to be analogous more to the small binary than to the small ternary. Indeed, it might be questioned whether we should even speak of a "recapitulation" function when the main theme's basic idea is not brought back. After all, this requirement, above all others, distinguishes the small ternary from the small binary, and in the case of the latter, recapitulation function is not recognized even if material occurring later in the first part is brought back at the end of the second part. But since it is so traditional to label the main section following the development a recapitulation, the practice can still be maintained despite these theoretical concerns. After all, one of the principal functions of a recapitulation—to restore to the home key any material originally presented in the subordinate key—is nevertheless fulfilled even when significant parts of the main theme and transition are eliminated.

If the recapitulation deletes the opening of the main theme, these ideas usually return later in the movement. This procedure is often referred to as a "reversed" recapitulation.[34] Caution must be exercised in speaking in this manner, however, for it suggests that the composer simply shifted around the main and subordinate themes of the recapitulation in an almost mechanical manner. Yet a careful examination of individual cases reveals that main-theme ideas are sometimes incorporated into the actual subordi-

EXAMPLE 11.17 Beethoven, Overture to *Coriolanus*, Op. 62, 148–79

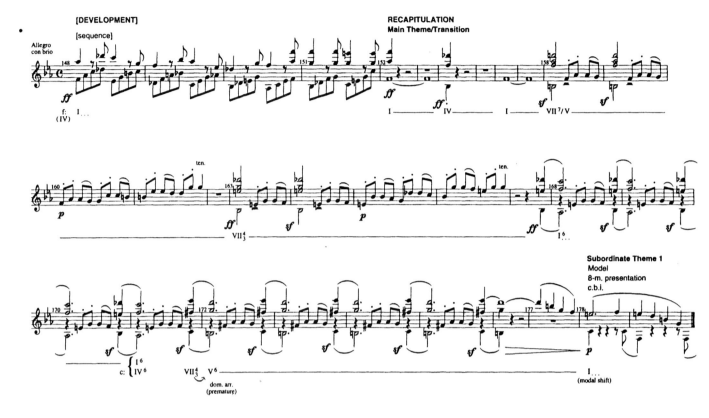

nate-theme area of the recapitulation.[35] At other times, main-theme material does not return in a reversed recapitulation but in a subsequent coda.[36]

Main theme beginning in the subdominant. The "double return" of the main theme and the home key is often cited as a hallmark of classical sonata form. But a few examples from the repertory see the main theme return in the context of subdominant harmony. Like the deletion of opening main-theme ideas just discussed, the use of the subdominant in place of the tonic at this point in the form has antecedents in baroque and preclassical practice.[37] The question of whether a true recapitulation function is at hand is also raised by this tonal procedure. When the recapitulation begins in the subdominant, a tonic setting of the main theme or ideas derived from that theme may appear later in the movement, most likely in the coda.

EXAMPLE 11.17: The relatively short development section of this overture is devoted to a working out of motives from the second subordinate theme (see ex. 8.4, mm. 102ff.). Although the development briefly touches on several tonal regions (VI, ♭II), it is largely centered on the subdominant. In the course of a broad model-sequence plan (mm. 148–51 represent the end of the first sequential repetition), the music from the very opening of the movement suddenly returns at measure 152, still supported by the subdomi-

nant. The listener attentive to tonal relations may not necessarily believe that this moment represents the beginning of the recapitulation, since a subdominant setting of main-theme material occurs now and then in a development section. But as the music continues, fusing with it an adjusted transition and leading to the subordinate-theme area, the listener understands in retrospect that the recapitulation indeed began with measure 152. Main-theme material supported by tonic harmony eventually returns in the coda (see ahead ex. 12.6, m. 276).[38]

Subordinate theme beginning in the subdominant. Another deviation occurs when the tendency for the recapitulation to explore flat-side regions is exploited to the extent that the subordinate theme begins in the subdominant region. To prepare for the theme's entrance, the transition is adjusted to conclude with the dominant of that region. Shortly after the subordinate theme has begun, it is further adjusted in order to remain centered in the home-key tonic.[39]

Minimal correspondence to the exposition. In some highly complex cases, the recapitulation may be altered to the extent that its structure corresponds only minimally to the exposition. Ideas from the earlier section may be incorporated into the later one, but they are shifted about to produce quite a different formal plan. Moreover, new material may appear that is not even derived from the exposition.

EXAMPLE 11.18: To understand the many changes made in the recapitulation, it is necessary first to examine the main theme and transition from the exposition (ex. 11.18b). The construction of the main theme is somewhat ambiguous, although the first phrase is clearly an antecedent, ending in measure 4 with a half cadence in B minor. The second phrase can be construed either as a repetition of that antecedent, ending with another half cadence at measure 8 (notice that the final chord is a triad, not a seventh chord), or as a consequent, whose authentic cadence elides with the beginning of the transition on the downbeat of measure 9. Also ambiguous is the tonality at the very beginning of the piece, for the listener could very well imagine that the movement is in D major until the half cadence at measure 4 confirms B minor.[40] The transition begins in measure 9 with the basic idea of the main theme and modulates, by means of a descending fifth sequence (mm. 11–13), to D major as the subordinate key. The form of the subordinate theme has already been discussed (see exs. 8.15 and 8.6).

The recapitulation (ex. 11.18a) begins at measure 68 with the first phrase of the main theme, now heard unambiguously in B minor because of the preceding dominant from the end of the development. Following the half cadence in measure 71, Haydn deletes both the second phrase of the main theme and the beginning of the transition. Measures 72–73 contain instead material corresponding to the sequential passage from the continuation of the transition (ex. 11.18b, second half of m. 11 to first half of m. 13). In so doing, he gives the impression of letting the music modulate once again to the subordinate key of D major, just as in the exposition. And this impression is reinforced when the subsequent two measures (74–75 of ex. 11.18a) bring back music reminiscent of the continuation of the first subordinate theme (ex. 8.15, mm. 18–19). Just when everything is pointing toward a cadence in D major at the downbeat of measure 76, Haydn extends the music an extra bar and brings about instead a cadence in B minor on the downbeat of measure 77. In so doing, he replays the tonal trick from the opening of the work, namely, suggesting that the music is in D but confirming it at the last moment in B minor.

A thorny question of formal interpretation is raised by the unit's closing with the perfect authentic cadence at measure 77. Is it the main theme or the first subordinate theme? (It could not be a transition because of the authentic cadence.) The latter interpretation is indeed suggested when the subsequent music produces a false closing section, initiating the second subordinate theme of the exposition. But no preceding unit can be construed as a transition (closing with a half cadence or dominant arrival). Yet now, just such a transition-like unit begins at measure 77, when music from the second subordinate theme of the exposition (ex. 8.15, mm. 20–21) leads to a premature dominant arrival, whose subsequent standing on the dominant in measures 80–83 introduces new material having no relation to the exposition.

If the unit of measures 77–83 is understood as the transition of the recapitulation, the resolution to tonic at measure 84 of the long-held dominant represents the beginning of the subordinate theme. There is clear evidence for this view: in this measure Haydn brings back the first subordinate-theme idea (ex. 8.15, mm. 15–16), now unambiguously expressing B minor rather than D major, as it had in the exposition and earlier in the recapitulation (m. 74). The sudden stop in rhythmic momentum in measure 85, however, imparts a tentativeness to the music, undermining its sense as the beginning of a new formal unit. In the following measures, the "first subordinate theme" motive is developed and eventually brought to a perfect authentic cadence on the downbeat of measure 92. (Here, the presence of the dissonant seventh in the dominant chord of measure 91 prohibits us from hearing a half cadence in that measure.)

Haydn then takes the transition music from the exposition and forms a more regular subordinate theme, one whose continuation introduces entirely new material in measures 95–97 and whose cadential area (mm. 98–102) texturally completes the abandoned cadential progression from the exposition (see ex. 8.6, mm. 26–31).[41] (The closing section, not shown, follows the pattern of the exposition.)

From the point of view of motivic ordering and specific formal design, Haydn creates a recapitulation that has little relation to the exposition. Indeed, his procedure calls into question the very idea of adopting the formal labels of the exposition (main theme, transition, subordinate theme) for use in the recapitulation. From the point of view of cadential articulation, however, the recapitulation contains moments of closure that are related to the traditional pattern: measure 77, perfect authentic cadence to close the main theme; measure 80, premature dominant arrival to close the transition; measure 92, perfect authentic cadence to close the first subordinate theme; measure 102, perfect authentic cadence to close the second subordinate theme. Thus Haydn retains the overall shape of a standard recapitulation but distributes the material from the exposition in an entirely different way.[42]

EXAMPLE 11.18 (a) Haydn, String Quartet in B Minor, Op. 64/2, i, 66–102; (b) mm. 1–15; (c) mm. 51–55

EXAMPLE 11.18 (continued)

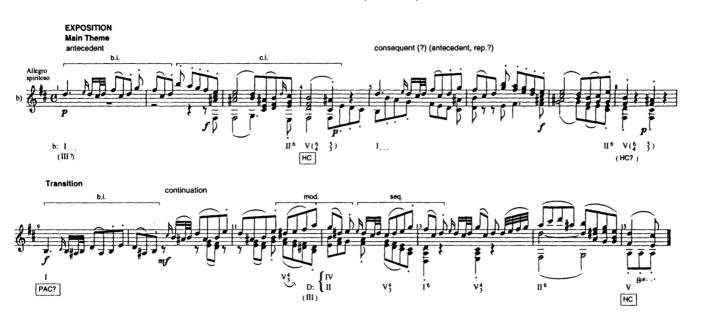

圖 12

Coda

By the end of the recapitulation, the fundamental melodic, harmonic, and tonal processes of a movement have generally achieved closure. Indeed, many movements literally finish at this point. Frequently, however, the composer adds a *coda*, an optional section that follows, and is fully distinct from, the recapitulation.[1] As Schoenberg notes:

> Since many movements have no codas, it is evident that the coda must be considered as an extrinsic addition. The assumption that it serves to establish the tonality is hardly justified; it could scarcely compensate for failure to establish the tonality in the previous sections. In fact, it would be difficult to give any other reason for the addition of a coda than that the composer wants to say something more.[2]

Because a movement's structural close is fulfilled by the recapitulation, the primary function of a coda is to express the temporal quality of "after-the-end." A coda is thus analogous to a closing section—made up of codettas—that follows a perfect authentic cadence ending a theme.

Inasmuch as "coda" and "codetta" are similar both terminologically and functionally, theorists have often had trouble distinguishing one from the other. Despite its diminutive suffix, a codetta is not a "little coda," nor is a coda a large codetta. Rather, the two structures are essentially different in regard to both hierarchical location and formal organization.[3] A codetta follows a perfect authentic cadence and resides on a hierarchical level comparable to that of basic, contrasting, and cadential ideas.[4] A relatively small unit—rarely more than four measures in length—a codetta prolongs root-position tonic and circles melodically around the first scale-degree. By contrast, a coda follows a recapitulation and resides on a hierarchical level comparable to that of an exposition, development, and recapitulation. A coda is a relatively large unit: it contains one or more complete *coda themes*, each ending with a perfect authentic cadence.[5] The coda itself ends with a closing section comprising a series of codettas.

Although Schoenberg speaks rather flippantly about the coda's appearing merely because "the composer wants to say something more," it is nonetheless true that this final section allows the composer to say things that could not have been appropriately said in earlier sections. In this respect, the coda includes a variety of *compensatory functions*, for here the composer can make up for events or procedures that were not fully treated in the main body of the movement. More specifically, the coda often gives the composer an opportunity to impart a circular design to the overall form by recalling main-theme ideas; to restore expositional material deleted from the recapitulation; to recapitulate ideas from the development section; to shape a concluding dynamic curve that differs from (or surpasses) that of the recapitulation; and to realize the implications generated by various compositional processes that have been left unrealized in earlier sections.

To complement the foregoing list of what composers may strive to achieve in a coda, I should mention what they will avoid, namely, introducing new material that calls for further development and initiating new processes that cannot be completed.[6] Both these situations could raise expectations of further continuation and counter the classical aesthetic ideal that once the music finally stops, the listener should have no desire to hear anything more in the movement.

Insofar as the coda wraps up loose ends left hanging from earlier sections, it functions as the movement's genuine conclusion. This characterization would seem to clash with our earlier understanding of a coda expressing an after-the-end. These conflicting functional interpretations can be reconciled by acknowledging that the highly complex organization of a classical instrumental movement gives rise to many compositional processes beyond the fundamental tonal, melodic, and phrase-structural ones initiated by the exposition and ultimately completed by the recapitulation. Whereas the coda does not normally involve these primary processes—and thus appears after-the-end—those other, secondary processes often attain closure only in the coda, thus finally allowing the movement to conclude.

Since the recapitulation brings a fundamental tonal closure to the movement, the coda rarely initiates any changes of tonality that might undermine its primary expression of after-the-end. Instead, the coda tends to remain in the home

EXAMPLE 12.1 Mozart, String Quintet in G Minor, K. 516, i, 230–35

EXAMPLE 12.2 Mozart, Symphony No. 36 in C ("Linz"), K. 425, i, 264–87

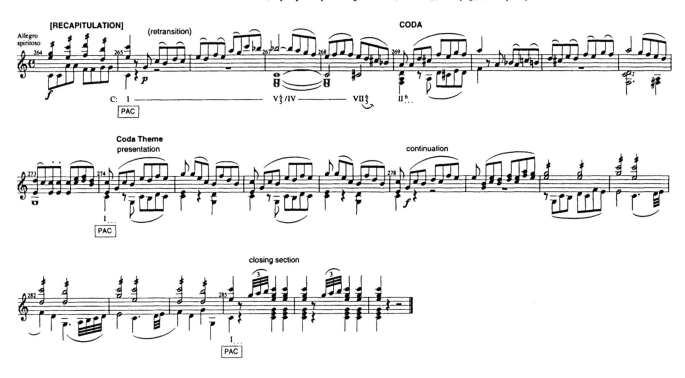

EXAMPLE 12.3 Haydn, Symphony No. 97 in C, i, 236–64

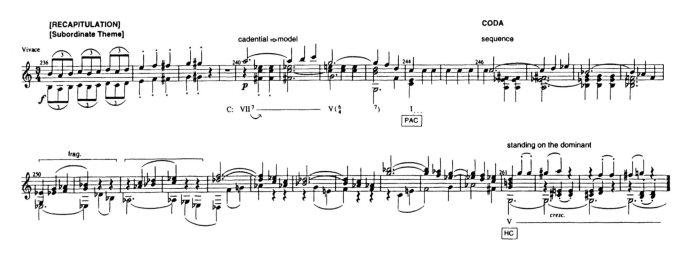

key, although various tonal regions may be briefly explored. Indeed, prominent tonicizations and sequential progressions frequently occur early in a coda to provide harmonic contrast between the end of the recapitulation and the end of the coda, both of which emphasize the home-key tonic.[7]

Even more than with a development section, it is difficult to predict how a given coda will be formally organized, although certain procedures do occur with some degree of regularity. The constituent coda themes are usually built in ways that resemble the loose organization of a subordinate theme, especially because of a highly expanded cadential area. Occasionally, however, a coda theme is structured as a simple tight-knit type (sentence, period, or hybrid). At times, the initial unit of a coda is comparable to a transition, in that its principal harmonic goal is the dominant. Such a unit may also include model–sequence organization suggesting the core of a development, although the sequencing is nonmodulatory and the harmonies remain closely bound to the home key.

START OF THE CODA

Unlike an exposition, development, or recapitulation, whose beginning is usually articulated by a clear initiating function (or, at the very least, by some manifest change in the musical material), the onset of the coda is often not readily perceived. In many cases, the coda is obviously under way before it expresses any sense of formal initiation. For this reason, the "start" of the coda is best located at that moment when the music of the recapitulation no longer corresponds to that of the exposition, even if that moment is not perceived as a structural beginning.

On a few occasions, the start of the coda is unambiguous: the recapitulation is clearly over, rhythmic continuity is broken, the texture changes, and a new initiating unit (such as a basic idea or presentation) begins the coda. Sometimes the notation indicates that the coda starts after the double-bar lines that instruct the performer to repeat the development and recapitulation together.[8] Often, however, the coda begins with a medial, or even a concluding, function, and a true structural beginning is not expressed until later in the coda, if at all. Frequently the coda starts directly with a new model–sequence passage or repeats sequentially the last idea of the recapitulation. If the exposition closes with a retransition leading back to the home key, the recapitulation may conclude with a similar "retransition" leading to the subdominant (or occasionally the supertonic); the coda typically starts somewhere in this passage.[9]

The following discussion treats examples in which the coda's start cannot easily be identified by the listener.

EXAMPLE 12.1: The recapitulation ends at measure 231 with a "retransition" leading to the subdominant region for a repeat of the

development and recapitulation (as indicated by the double bar and repeat signs). The coda starts in the following measure by continuing the retransition material, now adjusted so that the music remains firmly in the home key. A functional beginning, however, is not sensed until measure 235 with the return of the main theme's basic idea. The start of the coda is thus indicated notationally at measure 232, even though this moment is not aurally perceived as a formal beginning.[10]

EXAMPLE 12.2: The recapitulation ends with a reference to the retransition of the exposition (see ex. 10.7, mm. 119–22). This "retransition" begins to move to the subdominant at measure 267 but becomes redirected toward the supertonic in the following measure. Measure 269 then marks the start of the coda, since this is where the music departs from the path of the exposition.[11]

EXAMPLE 12.3: The recapitulation ends at measure 244 with the perfect authentic cadence closing the second subordinate theme. The coda then starts by sequencing up a third (literally down a sixth) the cadential idea, which is fragmented in the following measures. By starting the coda in a broader model–sequence process (already begun at the end of the recapitulation), a functional continuation, not an initiation, is expressed. Indeed, a true sense of structural beginning does not appear until very late in the coda (see ahead ex. 12.9, m. 279), when main-theme material is brought back a final time.[12]

EXAMPLE 12.4: Following a series of deceptive cadences at measures 137 and 139,[13] the final subordinate theme of the recapitulation does not close with an expected perfect authentic cadence (as it did in the exposition, m. 48) but leads instead to a half cadence in measure 141 to prepare for the final return of the rondo refrain at measure 143. Thus according to the rule, the coda starts in the second half of measure 140, that point at which the music of the recapitulation stops corresponding to the exposition. It is almost impossible, of course, to perceive this moment as a "beginning," since it brings neither an initiating function (the music is cadential at this point) nor any change in texture and rhythmic activity. Rather, the return to the main-theme material at measure 143 would seem to be the more functional beginning of the coda.

EXAMPLE 12.5: The closing section of the recapitulation begins at measure 132, just as it did at the corresponding place in the exposition (cf. ex. 8.19, m. 60). Instead of leading into a retransition, as in the exposition, the music at measure 137 brings a new one-measure model, which is repeated sequentially. There follows a brief cadential figure, which locally modulates into the dominant region. The perfect authentic cadence in E♭ at measure 140 and the subsequent codettas now permit the appearance of a real retransition (mm. 142–43), which prepares for the return of the main-theme material at measure 144. (In retrospect, of course, we can understand the authentic cadence and closing section in E♭ [mm. 140–42] to be a reinterpreted half cadence and a standing on the dominant.)

Like the previous example, the recapitulation leads without interruption into the coda, whose literal starting point must be located at measure 137, where the music of the recapitulation departs from the path taken by the exposition. As regards its formal function, however, this moment is a clear continuation following on the codettas of measures 132–35. Consequently, these codettas

EXAMPLE 12.4 Beethoven, Piano Sonata in E-flat, Op. 7, iv, 134–44

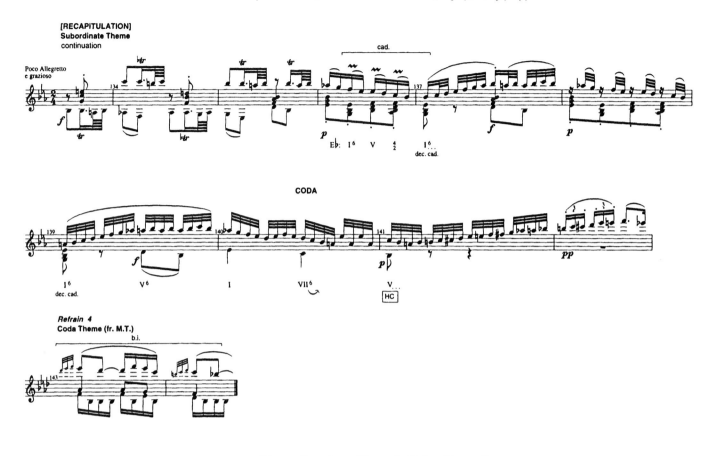

EXAMPLE 12.5 Mozart, Symphony No. 39 in E-flat, K. 543, ii, 132–44

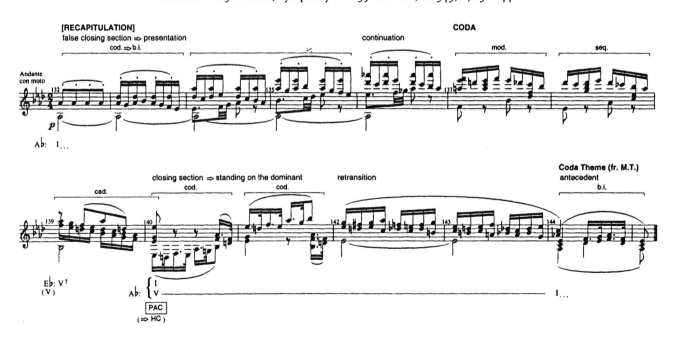

are themselves reinterpreted as basic ideas, and the whole passage is understood to be a false closing section, which initiates a new thematic unit (ending with the perfect authentic cadence in m. 140). That Mozart converts the closing section of the recapitulation into a false closing section is a further consequence of his already having used these same codettas for an earlier false closing section in the subordinate-theme group (see ex. 8.19, mm. 54–57). Thus having written a single false closing section in the exposition, Mozart now writes two—one residing fully in the recapitulation and the other straddling the boundaries of the recapitulation and coda.

PHRASE-STRUCTURAL ORGANIZATION

The themes making up a coda are, in the majority of cases, organized along the lines of a subordinate theme. (The material is occasionally derived from the actual subordinate-theme area but more often than not is taken from other places in the movement.) Any of the loosening devices discussed in connection with subordinate themes can appear in coda themes. The cadential function is especially prone to loosening through extension and expansion. As a result, considerable emphasis can be accorded to the final cadence of the movement. (In the following discussion, specific loosening devices typical of a subordinate theme are highlighted in italics.)

EXAMPLE 12.6: Following a brief introduction, the coda begins at measure 244 in the major mode with a compound basic idea, taken in this case from the subordinate theme as found in the recapitulation (cf. ex. 11.14, m. 178). The idea is repeated with a *modal shift* to make an eight-measure presentation. (This shift to minor, of course, restores the primary modality of the work.) Measure 252 initiates an *extended continuation* featuring an ascending-stepwise sequence. The harmonic acceleration in measures 260–63 can be seen to express the continuation even further, but the harmonies there also serve to prolong a first-inversion tonic, thus suggesting an *expanded cadential progression*. The appearance in measure 264 of pre-dominant harmony prolonged through measure 268 reinforces the idea that a cadential function is under way. The expected cadence is *abandoned*, however, when the dominant appears in first inversion in the following measure 269. An actual cadence to close this theme never does materialize, for what we would want to regard as a second coda theme begins at measure 276 (discussed later in this chapter).

EXAMPLE 12.7: The coda starts at measure 265 when the final cadence of the recapitulation's subordinate-theme group is evaded by VII^6/V, which then leads to a half cadence at measure 267 and eight measures of standing on the dominant. The reduced orchestration and change to piano at the upbeat to measure 276 signal the beginning of the first coda theme. A new presentation (built with material similar to the preceding standing on the dominant) is supported by a *weak tonic prolongation* owing to the metrical placement of the harmonies (dominant on strong measures, tonic on weak measures).[14] The following continuation⇒cadential phrase

(mm. 280–87) is supported by an *expanded cadential progression*, whose pre-dominant is embellished by neighboring chords. The concluding perfect authentic cadence at measure 287 elides with a second coda theme, one that brings a *modal shift* to minor and that *omits an initiating function* by beginning directly with model–sequence technique. The music leads quickly to an *internal dominant arrival* at measure 293; the subsequent standing on the dominant is followed at measure 301 by a new *expanded cadential progression*, whose initial I^6 is prolonged by the conventional V$^4_3$. The theme achieves powerful closure with the perfect authentic cadence at measure 309.[15]

Although coda themes are normally loose in structure, a conventional tight-knit organization appears now and then, particularly in sonata–rondo form. Most often such themes are based on the main theme of the exposition, and sometimes they even duplicate its form.[16] A tight-knit coda theme can also be derived from other material in the movement.[17]

Most coda themes close with a perfect authentic cadence in the home key. Therefore, depending on whether they are constructed in a tight-knit or loose manner, their formal organization will resemble either a main or a subordinate theme. Some units of a coda, however, conclude with a half cadence (or dominant arrival). In such cases, the passage resembles the kinds of structures found in a transition or development. A half cadence usually appears early in a coda, especially when that section starts without any obvious sense of functional beginning.[18]

EXAMPLE 12.3: As mentioned, the initial unit of the coda begins with a sequential repetition of the cadential idea from the end of the second subordinate theme. The coda continues at measure 250 with further model–sequence technique based on this model and eventually arrives on a half cadence at measure 261, followed by a standing on the dominant. The extensive sequential activity in this opening unit is comparable to a transitional or even developmental passage. (The entire unit from m. 246 to m. 267 could also be analyzed as closing with an internal half cadence, thus forming the first part of a two-part coda theme, analogous to a two-part subordinate theme.)

EXAMPLE 12.8: The coda begins at measure 202 by eliding with the final cadence of the recapitulation's second subordinate theme. The music at this point *appears as though it were functioning as a closing section*, but after a fairly extensive tonic prolongation, the dramatic appearance of the F♯ seventh chord in measure 214 throws into doubt the prevailing harmonic–tonal context. When this sonority eventually leads to a dominant arrival of the home key at measure 222 (by means of an intervening B-minor six–four, mm. 218–21), we understand that the F♯ seventh chord functions as an unusual chromatic pre-dominant (built on the raised fourth scale-degree).[19] The resulting dominant arrival at measure 222 is premature, since nothing here suggests the end of any phrase structural process. A subsequent standing on the dominant stretches from measure 226 to measure 237, after which main-theme material returns.

EXAMPLE 12.6 (a) Beethoven, Overture to *Coriolanus*, Op. 62, 238–314; (b) mm. 1–16

EXAMPLE 12.7 Haydn, Symphony No. 104 in D ("London"), iv, 261–312

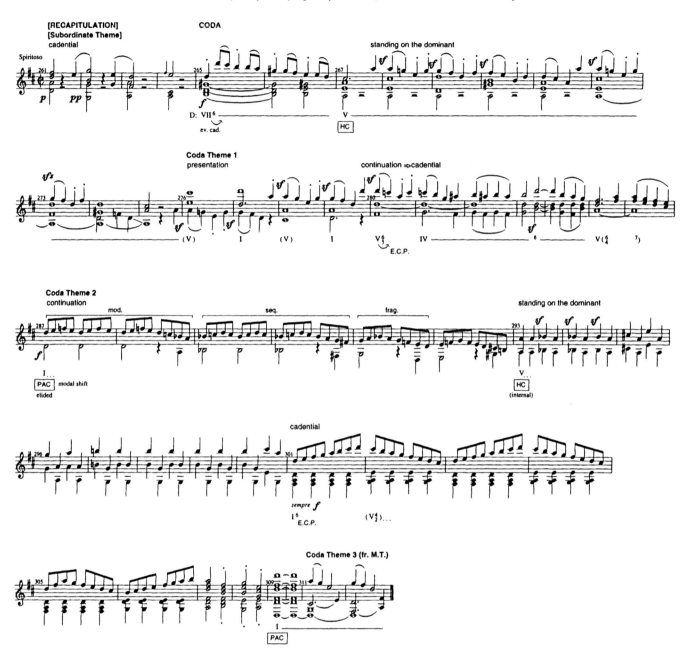

The organization of the standing on the dominant is unusual: with the change of material at measure 226, Haydn reduces the texture to a single voice, thus suggesting the imminent return of a new beginning supported by tonic. When the texture becomes fuller at measure 230, he surprisingly retains the dominant pedal. He eventually reduces the texture again at measure 236, which finally leads to the return of main-theme material at measure 238. The passage of fuller texture (mm. 230–36) is needed, perhaps, to restore more conventional pre-dominant harmonies (♭II, V/V), albeit within the dominant pedal. (Exs. 12.8b and 12.8c are discussed later in this chapter.)

Most codas end with a closing section (made up of codettas) that follows the final perfect authentic cadence of the home key. The melodic–motivic content of this closing section may be new,[20] or it may be based on material appearing earlier in the movement. Sometimes the closing section is extremely short, or it may be omitted altogether.[21]

If the closing section from the recapitulation has been eliminated (because the coda starts immediately after the subordinate-theme group), the coda will likely restore that deleted material as its own closing section (see the discussion of ex. 12.8 in the section on "restoration of deleted material"). When that is the case, the coda can sometimes give the impression of being interpolated in, rather than following on, the recapitulation.

COMPENSATORY FUNCTIONS

In addition to its primary function of expressing an after-the-end, most codas also treat compositional matters not directly implicated in the movement's more fundamental tonal and formal processes (these are generally completed in the recapitulation). Recent studies by Charles Rosen, Joseph Kerman, and Robert P. Morgan have devoted considerable attention to how the coda, respectively, disposes of "unfinished business,"[22] effects "thematic completion,"[23] and achieves the true "culmination" of the movement.[24]

A major reason that the coda takes on these roles is that the preceding recapitulation is relatively constrained in how it can deal with ideas arising earlier in the movement. Since the recapitulation is normally required to bring back material from the exposition in essentially the same order, there is little opportunity, say, for recalling the main theme late in the movement, for referring to ideas arising in the development, or for shaping a new dynamic curve to end the movement. As a result, the coda can be seen to compensate for the inappropriateness of earlier sections to achieve these and other compositional goals. The following five compensatory functions of a coda are regularly observed in the classical repertoire.

Recollection of main-theme ideas.   The notion that the musical material at the beginning of a movement should return

toward its end—thus lending a kind of circularity to the overall form—gained a certain currency in the classical period.[25] In fact, some full-movement forms (large ternary, five-part rondo, and sonata–rondo) require a return of the main theme (or at least a significant portion of it) toward the close of the movement. Other formal types (such as the sonata and minuet), however, see the return of the main theme only at the beginning of the recapitulation. In these forms, if the composers wish to bring back main-theme material late in the movement, they normally have to place it in a coda. Indeed, this is perhaps the coda's principal compensatory function, for most codas refer at some point to main-theme ideas.

Except in the case of the sonata–rondo, main-theme material in a coda is not usually shaped into the same tight-knit form that it took in the exposition. Rather, the material tends to be structured more loosely, along the lines of a subordinate theme. At times, main-theme ideas do not even receive cadential closure and end up instead forming part of the closing section to the coda.

EXAMPLE 12.8: The return at measure 238 of main-theme material imparts a distinctly rondo character to this sonata-form finale. The series of deceptive cadences (mm. 245 and 247) loosens the structure (in the sense of a subordinate theme) and thus creates a greater sense of cadential arrival than originally found in the main theme itself (cf. ex. 4.1).[26]

EXAMPLE 12.9: Main-theme material appears for a final time at measure 279 of the coda. In its original version (see ex. 13.4 in the following chapter), the fanfare opening, with its exclusively tonic support, is eventually followed by a cadential phrase (mm. 22–25) to close the theme. In the coda, the root-position tonic is retained obsessively to the end, thus prohibiting any cadential activity. As a result, material that had functioned as a main theme at the beginning of the exposition (and recapitulation) now functions as a closing section at the end of the coda.[27]

Restoration of deleted material from the recapitulation. To fulfill its own particular formal functions, the recapitulation frequently deletes passages from the exposition. The possibility of "recapitulating" this deleted material is offered by the coda.

EXAMPLE 12.8: The dramatic tonicization of B minor occurring at measures 214–21 was already described as an unusual prolongation of pre-dominant harmony (built on the raised fourth degree in the bass). Beyond the passage's cadential function of leading to a dominant arrival, its appearance here is surely motivated by a similarly dramatic tonicization of B minor (SK: III) following an evaded cadence in the exposition's subordinate theme (ex. 12.8b). If Haydn had used this same continuation in the recapitulation, he would have had to transpose it down a fifth into E minor for the purpose of tonal adjustment. So in order to "recapitulate" a comparable event at its original tonal level, he deleted that continuation from the recapitulation and instead introduced a new B-minor tonicization into the coda.

Another deleted passage from the recapitulation reappears at the end of the coda's closing section (mm. 255–61). This series of reversed "oomp-chink" ideas would ordinarily have been placed at measure 202 to serve as the closing section of the recapitulation, along the lines of the exposition (ex. 12.8c). Instead, Haydn writes a different closing section at m. 202 (ex. 12.8a) that consists of running sixteenth notes (probably to create a greater sense of rhythmic momentum leading up to the dramatic F♯ seventh outburst). At the final cadence of the coda (m. 249), Haydn brings back a new series of running sixteenth notes but eventually restores the closing section deleted from the recapitulation in order to conclude the coda as he had concluded the exposition.[28]

Reference to the development section. Whereas the recapitulation requires the composer to rework the exposition, an opportunity to bring back material from the development section is not necessarily afforded by any of the standard full-movement forms. If the composer wishes to refer to ideas from the development, the logical place to do so is in the coda, especially at its start. Indeed, the opening of that section lends itself well to recalling the opening of the development, because both follow on similar material, namely, the closing section of the exposition and recapitulation.[29] Moreover, the early part of the coda is an appropriate place to destabilize the prevailing emphasis on the home-key tonic, especially through the use of model–sequence technique that may resemble a development.

The analogous formal positions of development and coda—both following on similar sections (exposition and recapitulation)—have led some theorists to view the coda as a "terminal" development, particularly in the hands of Beethoven.[30] Following Kerman's powerful critique, the notion of the coda as a kind of development has fallen into disrepute.[31] In fact, we have seen in this book that these two sections are fundamentally different in tonal and formal organization. So to say that the coda refers to material from the development, as stated in the previous paragraph, is not to claim that the former functions, or structures itself, like the latter.

EXAMPLE 12.2: The opening of the coda clearly derives from the core of the development (cf. ex. 10.7a, mm. 128ff.). Indeed, the rest of the coda (except the last seven measures) "develops" this material, though entirely in the stable context of the home key. Although the original source for the ascending "jagged" line and its subsequent linear descent is the retransition at the end of the exposition (see ex. 10.7a, mm. 119–21), the extensive treatment of this idea in the core gives the impression of its being "new" material, largely unrelated to what happens in the exposition. For this reason, it is appropriate for the material to appear again, this time adjusted back into the home key. The coda provides the logical place for this "recapitulation" of material "exposed" in the development.[32]

Shaping a new dynamic curve. If a movement ends with the closing section of the recapitulation, the final dynamic curve of the movement will conform to that established by the closing section of the exposition. For example, if the exposition's closing section features a recessive dynamic leading to piano and then concludes suddenly with several forte codetta chords, this same dynamic curve will normally reappear at the close of the recapitulation to provide an end for the movement. In some cases, however, the way in which the exposition ends dynamically is not suitable for ending the complete movement, and thus the composer may very well use a coda to shape a new dynamic curve. Some of the most striking examples are in works by Beethoven, in which an extensive passage of progressive dynamic leads to the most powerful climax in the movement.[33] Some of his codas, however, close with a marked recessive dynamic, sometimes leading to a complete dissolution of the texture.[34]

EXAMPLE 12.6: The closing section of the exposition retains the forte dynamic achieved at the end of the subordinate-theme group (see ex. 8.4, mm. 110–18). The end of the recapitulation (mm. 238–40) projects this same dynamic. But for obvious programmatic reasons associated with the tragedy of Coriolanus, Beethoven is not satisfied with this powerful dynamic to close the overture. He thus cuts off the recapitulation even before the appearance of the closing section and suddenly reduces the dynamic to piano (m. 242). Following another buildup to fortissimo at measure 264, the return of main-theme material at measure 276 sustains this dynamic until measure 290, at which point there begins a gradual decrescendo, leading down to pianissimo string pizzicati at the very end of the movement. The systematic deceleration of the eighth-note motive from measure 297 to measure 310 is especially effective in helping project the recessive dynamic.[35]

Realization of unrealized implications. Many of the compositional processes initiated in a work imply particular modes of continuation. Some of these implications are realized immediately; others are realized only much later in the movement; and still others may never be realized at all.[36] The coda gives the composer the last opportunity of realizing an earlier implication, often one that would not have found an appropriate realization earlier in the movement. These implications usually arise in relation to the main theme, particularly a "problem" or "disturbance" that is not resolved until the coda.[37]

EXAMPLE 12.6: The reappearance of main-theme material in the coda (mm. 276ff.) realizes several implications arising earlier in the movement. First, the recapitulation of the main theme in the subdominant (discussed in connection with ex. 11.17, m. 152) implies that the theme will receive tonal adjustment at some later point. This implication is realized when measure 276 brings the first home-key restatement of the main theme since the very beginning of the work.

Second, a cadential ambiguity at the close of the main theme in the exposition (ex. 12.6b)—is it a half cadence at measure 13 or an elided perfect authentic cadence at measure 15?—implies the later realization of a clearer cadential goal.[38] In the coda, the theme unequivocally closes at measure 296 with a perfect authentic cadence,

EXAMPLE 12.8 (a) Haydn, Piano Trio in C, Hob. XV:27, iii, 199–261; (b) mm. 66–75; (c) mm. 88–93

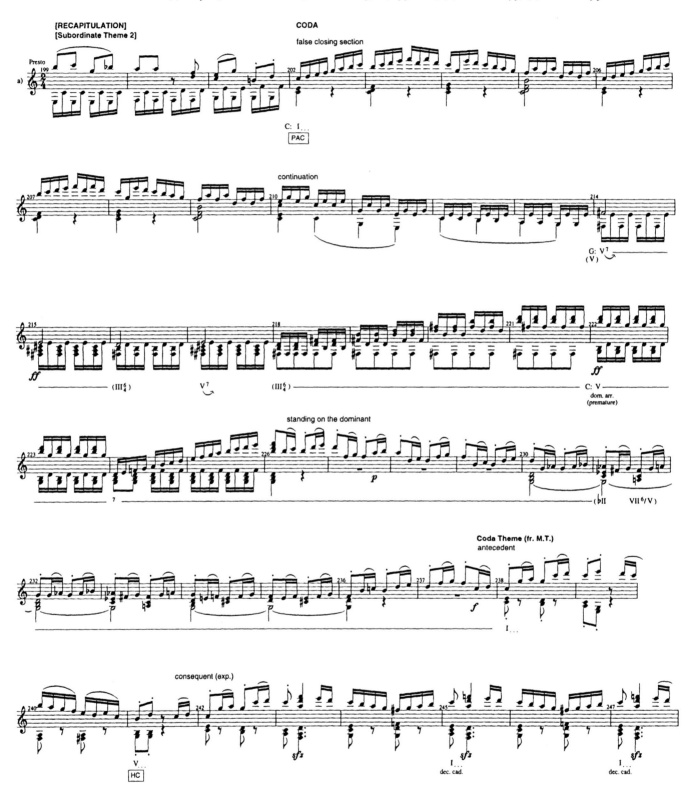

EXAMPLE 12.8 (continued)

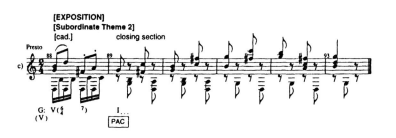

EXAMPLE 12.9 Haydn, Symphony No. 97 in C, i, 279–93

EXAMPLE 12.11 Beethoven, Piano Sonata in C Minor, Op. 10/1, ii, 89–112

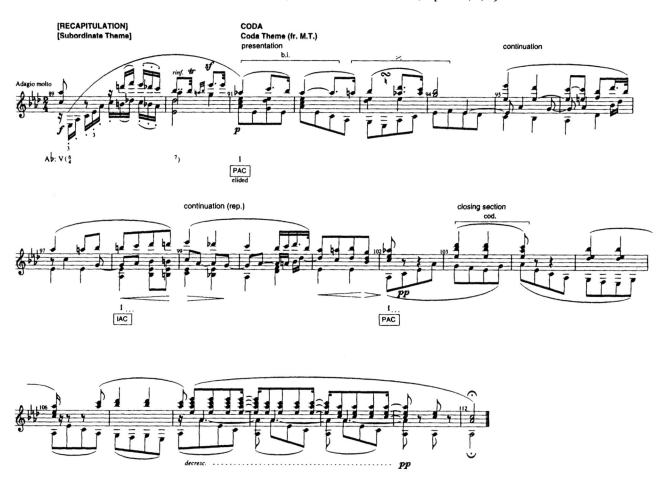

even though the cadential progression itself (a simple I–V–I) is somewhat unconventional. (The more typical cadential I⁶ and II⁶ are missing from the cadential progression, perhaps because they had already been sufficiently exploited in the earlier abandoned cadential progression of measures 260–69. In this connection it is interesting to note that Beethoven brings, in measures 288–90, another reference to the harmonic progression of that abandoned cadence just before the real cadence in the following measures.)

EXAMPLE 12.10: The return to main-theme ideas in the coda (m. 144) realizes an interesting implication engendered by the expressive turn to minor at measures 22–25 of the exposition's main theme (ex. 12.10b). Since a modal shift is most unusual in a main theme, its use here implies that the theme may return later, expunged of this minor-mode disturbance. Indeed, an explicit modal shift is eliminated in the coda's version of the theme, although Mozart continues to make oblique reference to the minor mode by means of the C♭s in the lower voice of measures 151 and 155.

A different implication is realized when the coda version of the theme closes with a perfect authentic cadence (m. 158), which had been eliminated in the recapitulation (ex. 12.10c). There, the modal shift at measure 91 leads the music into the remote region of C♭ minor (notated as B minor). (The appearance of C♭ minor at

measure 96 is itself a realization of the implication that the pitch C♭ in measures 22–25 [ex. 12.10b] may later be exploited as a significant tonal region.)

EXAMPLE 12.11: The coda begins with an explicit reference to the main theme. In the exposition, this theme is constructed as a compound period (see ex. 5.10), whose constituent antecedent and consequent units are simple sentences. In the coda, the four-measure presentation is brought back intact (mm. 91–94), but the continuation is markedly different from either of the two versions of the exposition (ex. 5.10, mm. 5–8 and mm. 13–16). There the continuations bring striking intensifications in both rhythm and melody (the use of the double-dotted eighth and thirty-second figure and the rapid ascents leading first to the high A♭ in m. 6 and then to F in m. 14). This prominent increase in rhythmic and melodic activity is appropriate enough for the beginning of a movement, where the composer strives to "open up" a variety of compositional processes. The implication for a simpler continuation is ultimately realized in the coda (mm. 95–101), where the continuation phrases (and the subsequent codettas) have a decidedly "closing down" character, owing to the linear descent from the fifth scale-degree in generally even note values.

IV

FULL-MOVEMENT FORMS

Sonata Form

Sonata form is the most important large-scale formal type in instrumental music of the classical period. Almost every multimovement work (except the concerto) contains at least one movement written in this form.[1] But sonata form is important not only because of its frequency of use: many historians and theorists consider it to be the period's most highly developed and complex compositional design, the one in which composers reveal their greatest technical skill and expressive potential. Moreover, sonata form continued to exert enormous influence over compositional practice in later musical styles, and it remained a viable form, albeit highly modified, at least until the middle of the twentieth century.

Sonata form consists of three large-scale functions—exposition, development, and recapitulation. Two additional functions are sometimes included: the exposition may be preceded by an introduction (in a slow tempo), and the recapitulation may be followed by a coda. Because the development, recapitulation, and coda, as well as the exposition's constituent functions (main theme, transition, and subordinate theme), were treated at length in parts II and III of this book, it remains the task of this chapter to summarize the essential characteristics of the form and to examine a number of issues left undiscussed. These include the sonata's overall tonal organization, the relation of interthematic functions to cadential goals within the exposition, various issues associated with main themes (including the possibility of their nonconventional organization), difficulties in determining the boundary between the transition and the subordinate theme, and the structure of the slow introduction.

In its large-scale tonal and form-functional organization, sonata form is analogous to the small ternary form. The sonata's three principal functions correspond in many respects to the three functions of that smaller theme-type. More specifically, sonata form resembles the rounded binary version, since the exposition is normally repeated (as indicated by double-bar lines) and the development and recapitulation are sometimes repeated together (almost always in works written before 1780).[2]

Just as theorists and historians have debated whether the small ternary is essentially two parts or three parts, so too have they disagreed over the fundamental partitioning of sonata form. The arguments on each side are largely the same as with the small ternary,[3] and the dispute is likewise founded on a false dichotomy, since differing modes of organization generate both bipartite and tripartite characteristics in sonata form. This book, with its focus on formal functionality, emphasizes the ternary aspects of the sonata, but without thereby meaning to devalue its manifestly binary traits.

OVERALL TONAL ORGANIZATION

In one major respect, sonata form differs fundamentally from the small ternary: whereas an A section may or may not remain in the home key, a sonata exposition necessarily modulates to a subordinate key. This tonal requirement gives rise to a central characteristic of sonata form highly emphasized in recent literature—the dramatic establishment in the exposition of two contrasting tonal regions. The second region (the subordinate key) is understood to create a structural dissonance in relation to the first (the home key), one that is intensified throughout the development and is eventually resolved (in favor of the home key) in the recapitulation.[4]

A view of sonata form that focuses primarily on the initial dramatic conflict of two keys and its eventual resolution is clearly attractive. But this *tonal-polarity model* is deficient in several respects. First, the notion of a structural dissonance in the exposition may be evident enough in major-mode movements, in which the subordinate key is the dominant region. But in most minor-mode movements, in which home and subordinate keys share the same basic scale, the sense of genuine tonal polarity is less palpable. Second, this view says little about the tonal plan of the development. At most, the various keys and regions explored in that section are considered, following Schenker,

TABLE 13.1 Cadential goals and form-functional patterns

	Cadences				
	One Required		Optional		Required
Pattern	HC in HK	PAC in HK	HC in HK	HC in SK	PAC in SK
1	—ᵃ	MT	—	Tr mod	ST
2	MT	—	—	Tr mod	ST
3	MT ant	Mt cons	—	Tr mod	ST
4	—	MT	Tr non-mod	—	ST
5	(MT)ᵇ	MT	Tr non-mod	ST pt 1	ST pt 2
6	(MT)ᵇ	MT	Tr pt 1	Tr pt 2	ST
7	(MT A)ᵇ	MT A	MT B	MT A'⇒Tr	ST
8	MT	—	—	—	Tr/ST

Abbreviations: *A* = small ternary exposition; *A'* = small ternary recapitulation; *ant* = antecedent; *B* = small ternary contrasting middle; *cons* = consequent; *HC* = half cadence; *HK* = home key; *mod* = modulating; *MT* = main theme; *non-mod* = nonmodulating; *PAC* = perfect authentic cadence; *pt* = part; *SK* = subordinate key; *ST* = subordinate theme; *Tr* = transition; *Tr/ST* = fusion of transition and subordinate theme; ⇒ = "becomes"

a. A dash indicates that the cadence is omitted from the pattern.

b. A half cadence at the end of an optional antecedent phrase of the main theme.

to prolong a more fundamental dominant achieved in the exposition.

To complement our understanding of sonata form's tonal organization, a second view should be recognized, one that is derived from earlier baroque practice. This *tour-of-keys model* sees the subordinate key in the exposition as the first of various keys to be explored throughout the entire movement.[5] Compositions written in the first half of the eighteenth century typically present one fundamental melodic idea (i.e., a fugue subject or ritornello theme) in the home key and then proceed to explore systematically the expressive and developmental possibilities of that idea by setting it in a variety of related keys. In the second half of the century, the tonal-polarity model gained ground and eventually came to dominate tonal organization in the sonata (and other full-movement forms). But the tour-of-keys model continued to have an effect. Its influence can be seen most clearly when the movement confirms one or more development keys by an authentic cadence.[6] The model is particularly evident when extensive material from the exposition reappears (transposed) in the development, as occurs frequently with Haydn (see the discussion of ex. 10.18). A vestige of the model can also be found when the recapitulation emphasizes the subdominant, notably when material from the main or subordinate themes is set into this region.[7]

Taken together, these two models provide a fairly complete picture of the large-scale tonal design of the classical sonata form. The tonal-polarity model emphasizes the oppositional nature of two primary keys, and the tour-of-keys model emphasizes the diversity of tonal expression arising throughout the movement.

CADENTIAL GOALS IN THE EXPOSITION

In a sonata exposition, the establishment of two primary keys is articulated by a succession of cadential goals. In its complete form, this series of cadences projects a tonal curve that (1) partially confirms the home key by means of a half cadence, (2) fully confirms that key by a perfect authentic cadence, (3) destabilizes the home key by a half cadence or dominant arrival, (4) partially confirms the subordinate key by a half cadence or dominant arrival, and (5) fully confirms the new key by a perfect authentic cadence.

These cadential goals can relate to the exposition's constituent interthematic functions in a variety of ways. Eight such patterns are shown in table 13.1. (Other patterns seen now and then can usually be understood as variants of those presented.) Note that any one of the first four cadences can be omitted, as indicated by the dashes; however, the perfect authentic cadence of the subordinate key must always appear.[8] The exposition must also contain at least one cadence confirming the home key.

1. In this common pattern, the main theme, usually built as a sentence (or sentential hybrid), closes with a perfect authentic cadence. The home key is thus fully confirmed early in the form. A transition then modulates to the subordinate key, which is confirmed when the subordinate theme concludes with a perfect authentic cadence.

2. This pattern is like the preceding one, except that the main theme (again, sentential) ends with a half cadence. The home key is only partially confirmed,

full confirmation being postponed until much later in the movement (most likely toward the end of the recapitulation).

3. This pattern combines features of the two previous ones. Here, the main theme is more or less periodic: an antecedent first brings partial confirmation of the home key, and a following consequent (or continuation) achieves full confirmation of the key.

4. The main theme fully confirms the home key, which is then destabilized by a nonmodulating transition. The subordinate key is fully confirmed without any prior partial confirmation.[9]

5. In this pattern, the home key is destabilized in two stages. First, a nonmodulating transition brings a half cadence in that key, and then the subordinate theme brings an internal half cadence in the new key. Full confirmation occurs at the end of the subordinate theme.[10] A variant arises if the main theme is periodic, in which an antecedent brings a half cadence before the perfect authentic cadence ending the theme.[11] In this form, all five of the primary cadential goals occur in the exposition.[12]

6. Here, the two stages of home-key destabilization take place in a two-part transition.[13]

7. In this pattern, the main theme is constructed as an incomplete small ternary. The close of the A section brings a perfect authentic cadence in the home key, and the B section brings a half cadence (or dominant arrival). An expected A' section begins to sound but eventually fails to reach completion as the music modulates to the new key. As a result, we retrospectively understand this section as a transition.[14]

8. Following a half-cadential articulation of the home key at the end of the main theme, the functions of transition and subordinate theme are fused into a single unit, a situation discussed and illustrated later in this chapter.[15]

MAIN THEME

General Issues

The main theme of a sonata exposition is most often constructed as one of the conventional theme-types described in part II of this study—sentence, period, hybrid, small ternary, or small binary. A significant minority of main themes are nonconventional in their organization, as discussed in the next section.

To fulfill its principal tonal function, the main theme must reside primarily in the home key. The theme may bring a transient modulation, but the home key eventually returns at the close. Most main themes end with a perfect authentic cadence, rarely with an imperfect one. A sonata's main theme may also end with a half cadence as long as

there has not been an internal modulation. Such partial confirmation is acceptable in the exposition because ample opportunity will be afforded later in the recapitulation to reconfirm the home key with authentic cadential closure. Main themes in a minor mode often close with a half cadence, since the resulting degree of tonal instability matches the unsettled emotional quality typically expressed by movements in this mode. Unlike subordinate themes, which frequently shift from major to minor (or vice versa), main themes normally remain in a single mode throughout. The few exceptions in the literature create a striking effect (see chap. 8, n. 64).

Many main themes exhibit a certain hesitancy or uncertainty in the course of their unfolding, often bringing sudden, striking changes in texture and marked discontinuities in rhythmic momentum. In fact, it often is not until the beginning of the transition that the movement seems finally to "get under way."[16] As a result, the main theme itself may seem to possess an "introductory" character. Such a main theme, however, must not be confused with an actual introduction. Despite the theme's textural, dynamic, and rhythmic instabilities, it still contains sufficient tonal, cadential, and phrase-structural solidity to function as the true formal beginning of the exposition.

If the main theme ends with a perfect authentic cadence, a closing section made up of codettas may be appended. Main themes closing with a half cadence may be followed by a postcadential standing on the dominant.[17] A main theme ending with a perfect authentic cadence may also be immediately followed by a second main theme to create a *main-theme group* (analogous to a subordinate-theme group).[18] It is important to note that both themes in the group end with a perfect authentic cadence in the home key. If a presumed second main theme were to end with a half cadence, it would destabilize the home key and thus express transition function (as either a single nonmodulating transition or the first part of a two-part transition).

Nonconventional Forms

The main themes of some sonatas have a nonconventional formal organization; that is, they cannot be easily accommodated by such standard categories as sentence, period, and hybrids. A nonconventional theme should, in principle, be distinguished from a conventional one that "deviates from the norm." The distinction is not always so facile, however, and even some of the examples here may be understood as extreme deviants of a particular conventional type.

Although thematic nonconventionality is a criterion of loose formal organization, a nonconventional main theme is usually more tightly knit than the subsequent thematic units of the movement. Indeed, many nonconventional main themes are eight measures in length. Sometimes, however, a main theme may be sufficiently loose in organization to

EXAMPLE 13.1 Haydn, String Quartet in G Minor ("Rider"), Op. 74/3, iv, 1–8

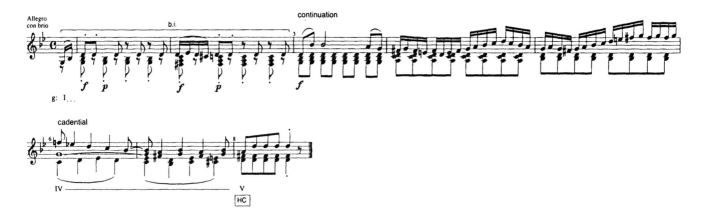

EXAMPLE 13.2 Mozart, Symphony No. 38 in D ("Prague"), K. 504, i, 37–45

EXAMPLE 13.3 Haydn, Piano Sonata in E Minor, Hob. XVI:34, i, 1–8

EXAMPLE 13.4 Haydn, Symphony No. 97 in C, i, 14–25

resemble a subordinate theme. In such cases, comparison with the actual subordinate theme of the movement reveals the former theme to be more tightly knit.

If we cannot generalize about typical characteristics of nonconventional themes (if we could, they would no longer be nonconventional!), it usually is possible to situate many of them in one (or more) of the following groups.

Eight-measure themes. Some main themes are organized in a nonconventional manner but still occupy eight measures, just like the simple sentence, period, or hybrid. As a result, the nonconventional theme retains a distinct sense of tight-knit organization despite its formal irregularities. Most often, the grouping structure of the eight measures is asymmetrical, yet the internal units express definite intrathematic functions.

EXAMPLE 13.1: The grouping structure of this eight-measure theme is 2 + 3 + 3. The opening two measures contain a standard basic idea (itself subdivided 1 + 1). The following three measures are continuational in expression, as the bass line rises from the first to the third scale-degree and the surface rhythmic activity of the melodic line increases significantly. The final three measures bring cadential function to close the theme with a half cadence. Although this main theme is clearly more sentential than periodic, the lack of a presentation and the presence of separate continuation and cadential units discourage us from classifying it as a genuine sentence, even a highly deviant one.

EXAMPLE 13.2: The lack of melodic profile in measure 37 implies introductory function. In the following measures, harmonic instability, fragmentation, and increased surface rhythm project a strong continuational quality, which is maintained up to the imperfect authentic cadence at measure 43. (The authentic cadence is imperfect, because the violin line in measure 43 ends on F♯, the third scale-degree. The tonic scale-degree sounding above on the downbeat of that measure belongs to the winds and brass.) Eliding with the cadence is a two-measure codetta containing fanfare motives.[19]

The direct move from an introduction to a continuation, thereby circumventing any clearly defined initiating unit, makes this theme highly nonconventional. Yet despite its irregularities, it occupies the standard eight measures. Note that the codetta, which fills out the eight-measure span, emphasizes root-position tonic and thus compensates for the minimal expression of this harmony at the opening of the theme.

EXAMPLE 13.3: The opening three measures are supported by root-position tonic, and the move to VI in measure 4 can be seen to prolong this harmony. But the change in surface harmony combined with a marked change in articulation (from staccato to legato) permits measure 4 to group with the following measure, supported by V⁶. A half cadence on the second beat of measure 6 marks the structural end of the theme, and the dominant is further prolonged by the twofold repetition of the half-cadence idea in measures 7 and 8. The resulting grouping structure (3 + 3 + 2) creates an asymmetrical subdivision of the eight-measure theme.

(Measure 6 could also be seen to group with its following two measures, thus yielding a 3 + 2 + 3 structure.)

From a form-functional point of view, measures 1–3 are clearly initiating, yet interpreting these measures as either an expanded basic idea or a compressed presentation seems somewhat unconvincing. Measures 4–6 bring continuation and cadential functions, and measures 7–8 are postcadential. The theme is clearly related to the sentence, but that theme-type remains insufficiently expressed.[20]

Tonic pedal, fanfare gestures. Some main themes begin with a long tonic pedal, over which may be found gestures that evoke a heraldic, fanfare style. Such powerful passages are ideal for projecting a strong opening, but they often obscure a clear sense of basic idea and its repetition, or its juxtaposition with a contrasting idea. The lack of a conventional initiating function thus makes it difficult to classify such a theme as one of the standard types.

EXAMPLE 13.4: All the orchestral forces combine in unisons and octaves to sound out a series of fanfare-like gestures. The texture becomes more chordal beginning at measure 21, and the move to I⁶ in the following measure initiates a cadential progression leading to closure at measure 25. The internal grouping structure of the opening eight measures is ambiguous enough to make it almost impossible to demarcate a conventional basic idea and contrasting idea. To be sure, the theme has a general sentential quality about it: the cadential function is obvious, and there is a general acceleration of rhythmic activity in the course of the opening eight measures. But it is difficult to distinguish clearly between presentation and continuation functions. The theme is thus best regarded as nonconventional in organization.[21]

Omission of initiating function. Some main themes are nonconventional because they lack a clear sense of functional initiation. In such cases, the theme seems to start "in the middle" or "toward the end," that is, with continuation or cadential functions.[22] This formal anomaly has already been seen in connection with example 13.2, in which after a one-measure introduction, the instability of the material immediately expresses continuation function. A main theme that begins even more obviously "toward the end" has already been seen in example 8.13b, in which an initiating tonic harmony is entirely absent.

EXAMPLE 13.5: The slow introduction ends, unusually, on a predominant VII♯/V,[23] whose resolution to V⁶ (along with the change of tempo) marks the beginning of the main theme. The first four-measure unit is characteristic of a continuation phrase, ending with a perfect authentic cadence in measure 20. The following material, with metrical emphasis on the subdominant (albeit in a tonic prolongation), suggests either a series of codettas or the beginning of a contrasting middle.[24] As the music continues, these measures (21–24) are understood as a false closing section, and further continuational material leads to measure 29, where the initial continuation phrase returns to create a second cadence (m.

EXAMPLE 13.5 Haydn, Symphony No. 90 in C, i, 14–33

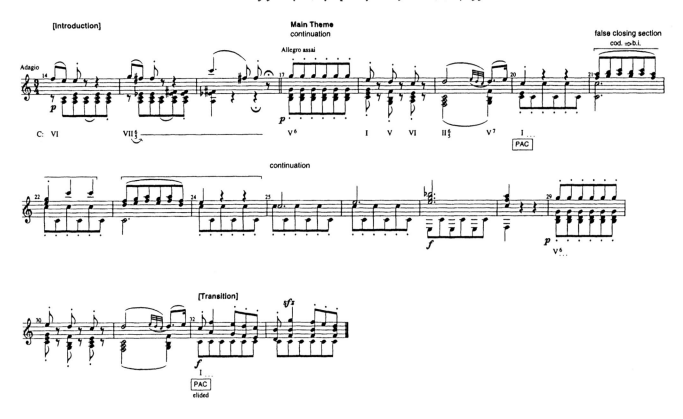

EXAMPLE 13.6 Beethoven, Piano Sonata in A, Op. 2/2, i, 1–33

32), one that elides with the beginning of the transition. The entire thematic complex (mm. 17–32) is highly nonconventional, even though a logical succession of intrathematic functions is clearly expressed.[25]

Loose organization. Some main themes are constructed in a manner considerably less tightly knit than would ordinarily be expected. At times, the loosening techniques resemble those associated with a subordinate theme, such as redundant repetitions, cadential extensions and expansions, and internal dominant arrivals. Although the main theme's form-functional characteristics may be like those of a subordinate theme, the melodic, rhythmic, and textural aspects usually are typical of a main theme (especially in the use of "opening up" gestures and marked discontinuities of rhythm and texture). As a rule, a loosely organized, nonconventional main theme is still more tightly knit than the subordinate theme appearing later in the exposition.

EXAMPLE 13.6: The opening eight measures give the initial impression of being a simple sentence, but the absence of harmonic activity in the "continuation" (mm. 5–8) and the resulting lack of cadence disallows this interpretation. Instead, the entire eight-measure group, supported by a single harmonic progression, can be seen as the primary initiating unit of the theme. The following measures have a definite continuational quality, although the actual grouping organization is somewhat obscured by various imitations and recombinations of the scalar motives first presented in measures 9–12. At measure 16, a sudden modulation to the dominant region (E major) brings an imperfect authentic cadence, which is extended postcadentially to measure 20.

When the initial basic idea returns in the home key, we recognize the previous authentic cadence in E to be a reinterpreted half cadence in A and so can view the entire first part of the theme as a highly expanded antecedent. The rest of the consequent is made up of the antecedent's continuation (somewhat extended), which leads to a perfect authentic cadence at measure 32. Although the theme has a certain periodic structure, the various repetitions, expansions, and extensions render it quite loose relative to most main themes in the classical repertory. But if we compare this theme with the subsequent subordinate theme (see ex. 8.12), we will readily perceive that the latter—with its omission of initiating function, modal shift, chromatic sequences, and expanded cadential progressions—expresses a decidedly looser organization.[26]

OBSCURED BOUNDARY BETWEEN TRANSITION AND SUBORDINATE THEME

The structure and function of the transition and subordinate theme were treated in detail in chapters 8 and 9. One important issue, however, has not yet been covered sufficiently, namely, those expositions in which the boundary between these functions is obscured. Such situations often pose difficulties of analysis, and in extreme cases, it may not

be possible to distinguish with certainty where one function ends and the other begins.

In most late-eighteenth-century sonata expositions, this important boundary is demarcated clearly, not only through appropriate form-functional devices (an obvious ending for the transition and a distinct initiation for the subordinate theme), but also through a marked change in melody, rhythm, and texture. In some cases, however, the music flows without interruption from the transition into the subordinate theme. If sufficient form-functional cues are present—a distinct half cadence and standing on the dominant (in the subordinate key) followed by new material in a firm tonic prolongation—then the beginning of the subordinate theme can still be well articulated.

In a few works, such cues are considerably weaker, or even missing, and the listener only gradually becomes aware that the subordinate theme is indeed under way. Two different conditions are responsible for promoting confusion about this boundary: the transition lacks a concluding function, and the subordinate theme lacks an initiating function and thereby fuses with the transition (which may also lack a normal ending) to form a single thematic unit.[27]

Transition Lacking a Concluding Function

The location of the boundary between the transition and the subordinate theme can be confusing if the former is not closed by means of a half cadence or a dominant arrival. Readily identifying the beginning of the subordinate theme therefore depends on a decisive melodic change in the context of a strong initiation (such as occurs in ex. 9.13, m. 30, and ex. 9.14, m. 23). If these conditions are not met, then perceiving a clear boundary between the two functions is considerably more difficult.

EXAMPLE 13.7: The transition begins in measure 64 with a four-measure presentation, whose constituent basic idea is taken directly from that of the main theme. The phrase is then repeated, but in the context of dominant harmony of the subordinate key, C minor. The phrase is repeated again (mm. 72–75), now supported by root-position tonic of the new key. The melodic material finally changes at measure 76, where a new two-measure idea embellishes tonic in first inversion (by means of neighboring ♭II⁶ and VII⁶ chords, which suggest a potential descending stepwise sequence). After a repetition of this new idea, the implied sequence is fully realized in measures 80–83. The sequence gives way to a cadential idea that is evaded at measure 86, at which a repetition of the sequence finally leads to the perfect authentic cadence at measure 96, marking the end of a subordinate theme.

But where exactly did this theme begin? From a harmonic point of view, the root-position tonic at measure 72 is the only likely possibility, and indeed, a four-measure presentation could be said to begin at that moment. From a melodic, rhythmic, and textural point of view, however, measure 72 stands right in the middle

EXAMPLE 13.7 Beethoven, Piano Sonata in F Minor ("Appassionata"), Op. 57, iii, 64–96

of various processes begun at measure 64, and the first real change to something new does not occur until measure 76. Indeed, the phrase beginning at that point can also be regarded as a presentation. In a conflict between harmonic considerations on the one hand and melodic, textural, and rhythmic ones on the other, preference should normally be given to the powerful, form-defining role of harmony.[28] Thus the root-position tonic prolongation of measures 72–75 projects a greater sense of formal initiation than does the first-inversion prolongation of measures 76–79. Moreover, since no point in this passage can be seen to articulate a genuine sense of ending for the transition, it is more logical and consistent to consider the transition to conclude in the subordinate key with dominant harmony (mm. 68–71) rather than with tonic (mm. 72–75). To be sure, an interpretation of measure 72 as the beginning of the subordinate theme (with m. 76 marking the continuation function) emerges only in retrospect, for in the "real time" experience of this passage, little besides the harmony suggests that this moment represents a structural beginning.[29]

Transition/Subordinate-Theme Fusion

Some expositions witness the fusion of transition and subordinate theme functions into a single thematic unit. This unit not only modulates to the subordinate key—a prime constituent of transition function—but also closes with a perfect authentic cadence to confirm that key—a fundamental requirement of the subordinate theme's function. In such cases, it is not possible to find an appropriate initiating function for the subordinate theme, even in retrospect (such as in the previous example).

EXAMPLE 13.8: The home-key dominant of measures 47–52 marks the end of what we might first hear as a simple nonmodulating transition. But when the next passage, beginning at measure 53, continues on in the home key, we reinterpret the previous unit as the first part of a two-part transition. The second part modulates quickly to the subordinate key and would seem to end with the half cadence at measure 61 and the subsequent standing on the dominant. When that harmony resolves to tonic at measure 66, the new music is supported quite clearly by cadential progressions all the way to the perfect authentic cadence at measure 74. Such expanded cadential activity is typical of subordinate-theme function. The question of where that function begins, however, is difficult to answer.

Unlike some subordinate themes that truly begin with a cadential function (see ex. 8.13a, less obviously ex. 8.7), the music from measure 66 onward expresses little, if any, sense of initiation, and thus it is difficult to hear this point as the beginning of a discrete subordinate theme. Rather, this cadential unit seems to arise in a way that strongly resembles an internal half cadence and standing on the dominant, which is then followed by the resumption of a cadential phrase (see chap. 8, p. 117, and ex. 10.7b, m. 68, p. 148). The passage from measure 53 to 74 appears, therefore, as a single thematic unit, one that fuses transition and subordinate-theme functions.[30]

EXAMPLE 13.9: The exposition opens at measure 14 with an eight-measure hybrid (c.b.i. + cont.⇒cad.) that ends with a half cadence

in the home key. Measure 22 sees a return to the opening compound basic idea, but at the upbeat to measure 26, a new continuation modulates to the subordinate key of F major, confirmed by the perfect authentic cadence at measure 29. Although this sixteen-measure unit can be considered a regular modulating period, such a description says nothing about the interthematic functions of the exposition. Therefore, a more complete analysis recognizes that the antecedent (mm. 14–21) serves as the main theme and that the consequent (mm. 22–29) fuses transition and subordinate-theme functions.[31]

Many cases of transition/subordinate-theme fusion, though by no means all, seem on the surface to be transitions that close with a perfect authentic cadence in the subordinate key, instead of the more normal half cadence. Thus in the previous example, it would be simple to claim that the consequent phrase of the period is exclusively transitional, especially since a new and discrete subordinate theme begins at measure 29. To speak in this manner, however, is to recognize authentic cadential closure as a legitimate deviation from the normal ending of a transition. But sanctioning this cadential possibility blurs a theoretical distinction fundamental to this study, namely, that the authentic cadential confirmation of a subordinate key is an essential criterion of the subordinate theme's function. It is thus theoretically more consistent to interpret such passages as cases of fusion than to risk confusing the fundamental characteristics of the interthematic formal functions.

SLOW INTRODUCTION

The exposition of a fast sonata movement is sometimes preceded by a *slow introduction*. This section, which functions as a "before-the-beginning," is optional to the form. A slow introduction typically invokes a solemn, serious tone, and yet it also arouses a strong sense of anticipation of the livelier character expressed by the rest of the movement. Of all the large-scale units of classical form, slow introductions are the least predictable in their organization, and so it is difficult to generalize about their internal phrase structure and formal functionality.

Just as a coda must be distinguished from a codetta, so too must a slow introduction be differentiated from an introduction that precedes a theme, even though both express the formal function of before-the-beginning. And like the difference between coda and codetta, a slow introduction differs from a thematic introduction with respect to both its location in the structural hierarchy and the complexity of its formal organization. A thematic introduction resides on a hierarchical level comparable to that of a basic idea, contrasting idea, cadential idea, and codetta. This short unit is normally supported by a tonic prolongation and generally has no melodic profile (see chap. 1).

Conversely, a slow introduction resides on a level com-

EXAMPLE 13.8 Haydn, Symphony No. 93 in D, i, 46–77

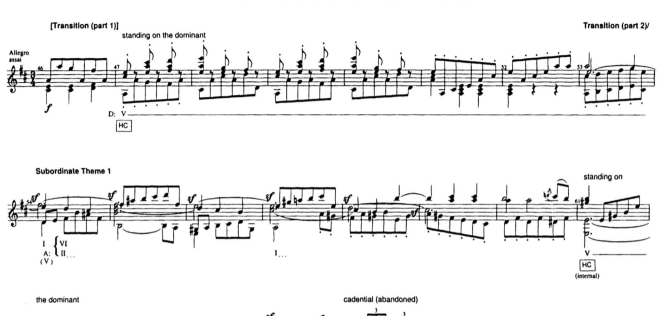

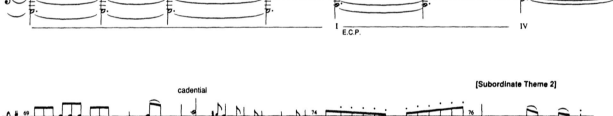

EXAMPLE 13.9 Mozart, Violin Sonata in B-flat, K. 454, i, 14–31

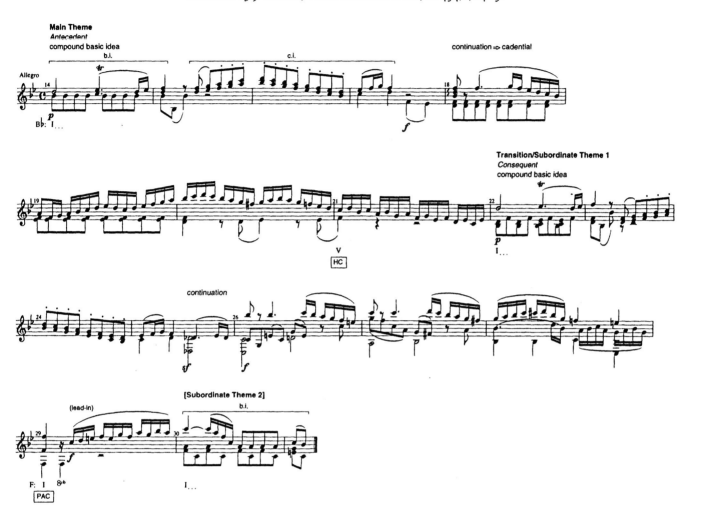

parable to that of an exposition, development, recapitulation, and coda. Whereas some slow introductions are relatively short, others, such as those opening Beethoven's Second and Seventh Symphonies, are so extensive as to occupy a significant proportion of the movement as a whole. Slow introductions usually contain their own prominent melodic–motivic material, supported by a wide variety of harmonic progressions. Finally, a slow introduction itself can even open with a thematic introduction.[32]

A notable characteristic of slow introductions in the classical style is the special way in which they unite the expression of two seemingly incompatible affective worlds: the realm of the stately, heraldic, and solemn is combined with the realm of the anticipatory, uncertain, and unstable. The sense of solemnity is expressed by the slow tempo, fanfare gestures, tutti textures, dotted rhythms, and an initial forte dynamic. The sense of anticipation is created by marked discontinuities in such dimensions as melody, rhythm, texture, and dynamics, instabilities of harmonic progression, minor modality, and chromaticism (at times extreme). To

be sure, some slow introductions play down, or even lack, a stately character, but they almost always contain something of the uncertain and hesitant.[33]

Slow introductions typically begin with tonic harmony of the home key and generally remain in that key throughout. Prominent tonicizations and an emphasis on minor modality (in movements that are otherwise in a major key) are common. In the majority of cases, the harmonic goal is the dominant of the home key, articulated by a half cadence (or dominant arrival) and followed by a standing on the dominant. This harmonic emphasis is most appropriate, of course, for building up a powerful expectation for a home-key tonic at the start of the exposition. Frequently, however, introductions close with an authentic cadence that elides with the beginning of the exposition.[34] As befits their expression of uncertainty and instability, slow introductions are usually loose in formal organization, although tight-knit theme-types do appear now and then. Many introductions are bipartite or tripartite in form (as articulated by cadences), and some larger ones contain four or more distinct parts.[35]

EXAMPLE 13.10 Mozart, Violin Sonata in B-flat, K. 454, i, 1–15

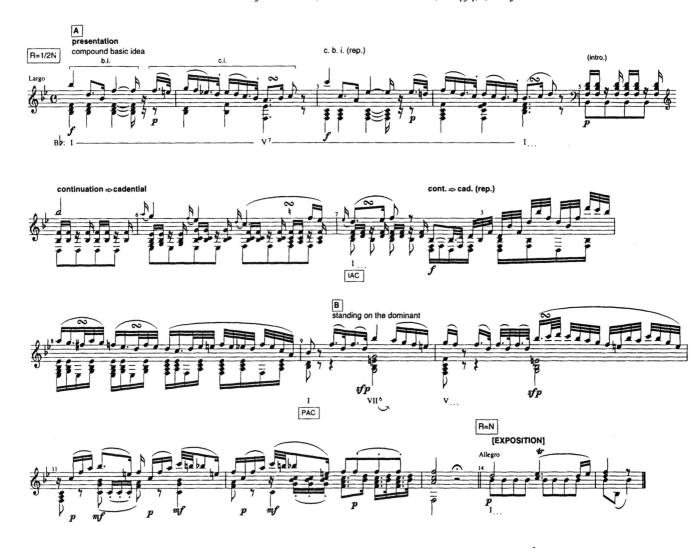

Many slow introductions by Haydn and Mozart present melodic–motivic material having no immediately obvious relation to the rest of the movement. But in some of their late works, and in many by Beethoven, the slow introduction hints at ideas that are more fully realized later on. Such motivic anticipations have been the primary topic of some full-length studies of slow introductions, and thus the issue need not be pursued further here.[36]

EXAMPLE 13.10: The introduction opens with a majestic fanfare-like basic idea. (Each real measure would seem to last one-half a notated measure [R = ½N], although this interpretation is somewhat uncertain, since the introduction does not contain sufficient material for verifying the status of the notation.) A contrasting idea in measure 2, lyrical yet somewhat limping and hesitant, ends on a dominant seventh, thus ruling out a potential half cadence at that point. The resulting compound basic idea is repeated (mm. 3–4) to create a large presentation. The following continuation⇒cadential phrase (itself preceded unusually by an introduction)

brings greater rhythmic continuity than does the presentation, in which each of the constituent ideas is followed by a rest. The imperfect authentic cadence at measure 7 motivates a repetition of the phrase, which eventually closes with a perfect authentic cadence at measure 9.

The remaining music of the introduction brings a standing on the dominant. Since this passage directly follows full cadential closure, it resembles a typical contrasting middle. But the implied small ternary becomes *truncated* when the resolution to tonic at measure 14 initiates the exposition of the movement, rather than bringing a recapitulation of the opening fanfares.[37]

EXAMPLE 13.11: The opening basic idea (R = ½N), a fortissimo fanfare motive sounded by the full orchestra, immediately creates an air of dignified solemnity. Note, however, that a degree of uncertainty is already projected by this idea and its immediate repetition in measure 2: the fermatas prohibit the establishment of rhythmic continuity and metrical definition, and the lack of a harmonic third raises doubt about the mode. The following continuation clarifies the modality and establishes a regular pulse, yet the character of the

EXAMPLE 13.11 Haydn, Symphony No. 104 in D ("London"), i, 1–20

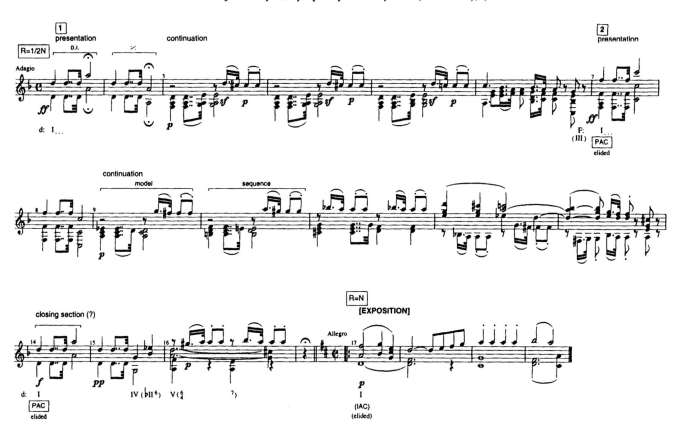

ideas is hesitant and unsure (especially with the leading tone dangling at the end of mm. 3–4). At the same time, the continued use of the fanfare rhythms maintains an impression of the heraldic.

The continuation modulates to the relative major and closes there with a perfect authentic cadence on the downbeat of measure 7. Because of the marked discontinuity of dynamics, texture, and melodic line from the end of measure 6 to the downbeat of measure 7, it is possible to consider the perfect authentic cadence to be evaded. Although such an interpretation is feasible, it is probably not preferred, since a cadential evasion usually motivates a repetition (in the sense of "one more time") and subsequent true authentic cadential closure, neither of which occurs here. (Similar potential evasions arise at mm. 14 and 17.)

The cadence at measure 7 elides with a new thematic unit, one that brings back the opening fanfare motive. This passage clearly parallels the first one but acquires a looser expression because of the model–sequence technique at the beginning of the continuation (mm. 9–10). A modulation back to the home key is confirmed by the perfect authentic cadence at measure 14. A second return of the fanfare idea brings several surprises: measure 15 appears unexpectedly pianissimo, and the descending leap is enlarged by a step, thus reaching down to the subdominant, which initiates a final cadential progression. Note that despite the fermata, the dominant seventh harmony of measure 16 is penultimate and that the resolution to tonic at the beginning of the exposition creates an elided cadence to mark the end of the introduction. (This final cadence could also be heard as evaded.)

The overall form emerges as a highly deviated small binary (part 1 = mm. 1–7, part 2 = mm. 7–14), followed by a closing section (mm. 14–17). Several unusual features of this interpretation, however, must be mentioned. First, the two parts of a real small binary are never elided, as is the case here. Second, the "closing section" brings a stronger sense of closure (due to a more expanded cadential progression) than does the second part. Such irregularities, of course, are not surprising in light of the nonconventional form normally taken by a slow introduction.

EXAMPLE 13.12: The introduction begins with a compound basic idea sounded by the violin alone. The lack of piano accompaniment immediately creates a textural gap, which adds a degree of uncertainty to what is otherwise a stately sarabande-like gesture. The next phrase brings back the basic idea, now played exclusively by the piano, and the immediate shift to minor, typical of an introduction, permits a smooth modulation to the mediant (C major). Subsequent fragmentation, beginning with the upbeat to measure 9, leads to a half cadence in that key (m. 13), followed by a brief standing on the dominant (lasting to the middle of m. 14). The formal situation thus far resembles a sixteen-measure sentence in which the opening compound basic idea and its modified repetition creates a presentation, followed by a continuation leading to the cadence at measure 13. Problematic in this interpretation, of course, is the lack of tonic prolongation at the end of the presentation.

At the downbeat of measure 15, the expected dominant of C

EXAMPLE 13.12 Beethoven, Violin Sonata in A Minor ("Kreutzer"), Op. 47, i, 1–27

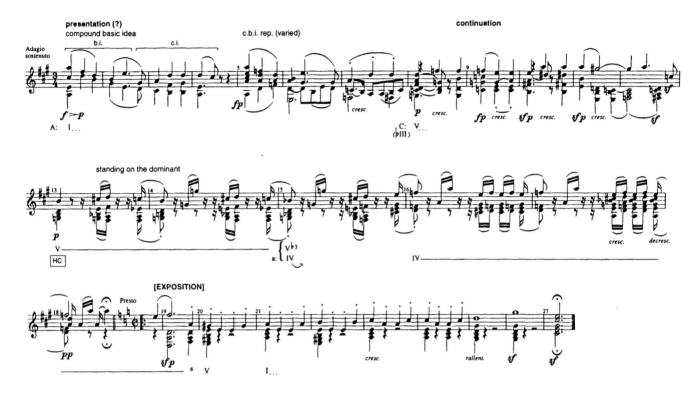

major is modally inflected to become a G-minor triad. This har-mony provides a means of allowing the music to tonicize D minor, and the introduction literally ends on this sonority, which is then understood to be IV in A minor, the home key of the movement as a whole. Ending an introduction on a minor triad is unusual, since that chord cannot be construed as a dominant, the more conventional ending harmony. But the logic of Beethoven's strat-egy immediately becomes clear when we hear the exposition's basic idea (mm. 19–20), supported at first by the pre-dominant IV (the D-minor harmony) and then leading to the dominant. Rather than choosing a harmony whose resolution would bring the pre-dominant at the start of the exposition, Beethoven intro-duces this harmony in advance, toward the end of the introduc-tion, and simply sustains it for the new beginning. In addition to anticipating the opening harmony of the main theme, the end of the introduction also anticipates the main theme's melody, since the violin part repeatedly sounds the opening motive E–F from the beginning of measure 16 onward.

Slow-Movement Forms

Most instrumental cycles in the classical period contain at least one movement to be performed in a slow tempo (Adagio, Largo, Andante).[1] This movement normally occupies an interior position in the cycle and contrasts in tonality (or at least in modality) with its surrounding movements.[2] Slow movements commonly employ one of the following formal types: sonata, sonata without development, large ternary, theme and variations, or five-part rondo.[3] The first four of these forms are treated in this chapter; the five-part rondo will be discussed together with the other rondo forms in chapter 16.

If all the movements of an instrumental cycle were constructed with the same degree of formal complexity, the slow movement would last considerably longer than the other movements, because of the slower pacing of its events. Thus to maintain a relatively consistent length among movements, composers often select a formal type for the slow movement that is inherently simpler than those used for fast movements. Compared with the highly elaborate schemes of the sonata, sonata–rondo, and concerto (the most common fast-movement forms), the large ternary, sonata without development, and theme and variations are considerably less complex. The five-part rondo is somewhat more complicated, but less so than other rondo forms. If composers choose to write a slow movement in sonata form, they normally do not exploit all its resources, so as to prevent the movement from becoming excessively long.

In addition to adopting a simpler formal type, a slow movement typically employs phrase-structural procedures that either produce compressions or inhibit expansions. For example, an exposition of a slow movement usually contains a single subordinate theme, often one that is relatively tight knit (though still looser than the main theme). Standings on the dominant are generally held in check, and form-functional fusion (especially of a transition and subordinate theme) is regularly employed.

As a remnant of standard high-baroque practice, a number of slow movements, particularly by Haydn, end with dominant harmony. The resolution to tonic occurs only at the beginning of the following movement. Such weaker closure forges a stronger bond between the movements yet may undermine the slow movement's independence.[4] A variety of formal contexts and procedures can produce an ending on the dominant. Sometimes the movement closes regularly with a perfect authentic cadence, but then an appended passage leads to a final dominant.[5] At other times, the music finds itself "stuck" rather unexpectedly on the dominant, which becomes de facto the ending harmony.[6] More frequently, an expected closing authentic cadence fails to materialize, and a half cadence or dominant arrival appears instead (usually after a deceptive cadence).[7]

SONATA FORM IN SLOW MOVEMENTS

Many slow movements are constructed in conventional sonata form. A number of modifications are frequently employed, however, to effect the kinds of formal compressions typically found in slow movements of any form. Most notably, a slow-movement sonata often fuses the transition and subordinate-theme functions, eliminates the entire transition (a technique favored by Mozart), or reduces the size of the development section (favored by Haydn).[8]

Transition/subordinate-theme fusion. The idea of fusing the transition and subordinate theme into a single grouping unit was explained in the previous chapter with respect to fast-movement sonatas (see exs. 13.8 and 13.9). In fact, the technique occurs with greater frequency in slow movements.[9] Such fusion permits these interthematic functions to be traversed more rapidly than when they occupy their own distinct groups. The process of fusion compresses the form by eliminating a number of phrase-functional elements—the half cadence (and the subsequent standing on the dominant) for the transition and an initiating unit for the subordinate theme.

EXAMPLE 14.1: The transition begins after the close of the main theme in measure 9. Model–sequence technique starting in the second half of measure 11 brings a modulation to C major, the first of two subordinate keys.[10] The new key is partially confirmed by

EXAMPLE 14.1 Beethoven, Piano Sonata in D, Op. 10/3, ii, 9–17

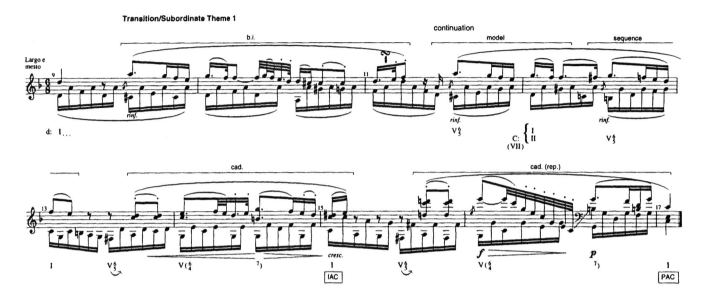

EXAMPLE 14.2 Haydn, Piano Sonata in E, Hob. XVI:31, ii, 1–8, 33–49

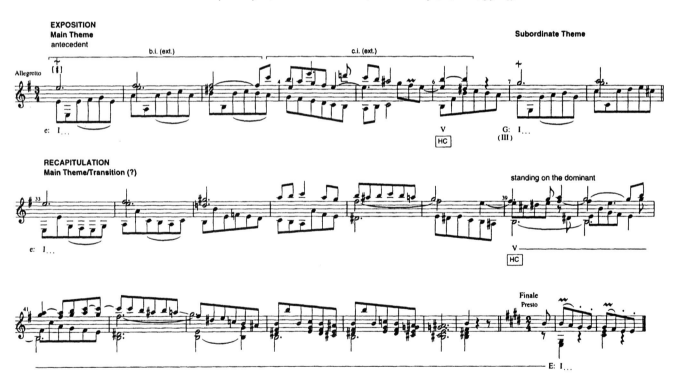

the imperfect authentic cadence at measure 15 and then is fully confirmed by the perfect authentic cadence two measures later. (A second subordinate theme in the dominant minor follows immediately thereafter.)

In this single thematic unit, it is feasible to identify the opening basic idea as well as the model–sequence activity with transition function and the cadential units with subordinate-theme function. The middle of measure 13 thus stands as a formal boundary. Yet this moment is recognizable as such only after the fact, for it clearly lies very much "in the middle" and fails to be associated with a sense of either "ending" (of the transition) or "beginning" (of the subordinate theme).[11]

Elimination of the transition. In some sonata expositions, the form becomes compressed when the final cadence of the main theme is immediately followed by the subordinate theme. The lack of transition often results in the emphasis on dominant of the new key becoming shifted into the subordinate theme proper (usually through an internal half cadence and standing on the dominant). Although the transition is eliminated from the exposition most often in slow movements, it may also be omitted in fast-movement rondo forms.[12]

EXAMPLE 14.2: The main theme closes with a half cadence in measure 6.[13] The next unit begins directly in the subordinate key of G major with main-theme material, thus bypassing any semblance of transition function. Because Haydn's "monothematicism" brings the subordinate theme so close to the main theme, we can already predict that the recapitulation will be significantly rewritten in order to avoid a redundant, twofold succession of main-theme ideas in the home key.

The recapitulation begins at measure 33 with a recomposed version of the main theme, which, like the exposition, closes with a half cadence (m. 39). There follows, however, a long standing on the dominant, suggestive of the main-theme/transition fusion often found in recapitulations. Our expectation for a recapitulation of the subordinate theme is then thwarted when the standing on the dominant emerges as the actual end of the movement. In light of the close proximity of the main and subordinate themes in the exposition, it would not be surprising if the first part of the subordinate theme were eliminated (or at least modified), but that the entire subordinate theme is discarded is astonishing, indeed. (And perhaps somewhat disappointing as well, for the subordinate theme in the exposition contains a glorious passage featuring a long stepwise descent in the bass, above which a series of motives reach over one another to create a striking climax [mm. 15–18, not shown].)[14]

Reduction of the development. One way of limiting the length of a slow-movement sonata is to reduce the scope of the development. In such cases, the composer forgoes a full-fledged core (although there may be some brief model–sequence activity) and normally does not allow a development key to be cadentially confirmed. At times, the

development may be so simple as to resemble a contrasting middle of the small ternary form.[15]

EXAMPLE 14.3: Whereas the development section in a fast-movement sonata form by Haydn tends to be roughly the same length as the surrounding exposition and recapitulation, the development from this slow-movement sonata form is less than one-third as long as the exposition. In these eight measures, Haydn briefly touches on three tonal regions (VI, IV, and II) by means of a descending third sequential pattern. The final dominant in measure 34 is so weakly articulated that it is unlikely to be perceived as an "ending" harmony.[16]

LARGE TERNARY

The full-movement *large ternary* form is used almost exclusively in slow movements.[17] This form is employed most often by Haydn, but a number of large ternaries are found in the works of Mozart and Beethoven as well. The name of the form makes explicit its tripartite structure and suggests that it is formally analogous to the small ternary.[18] As I shall show, however, small and large ternaries are fundamentally different forms, whose corresponding parts are comparable to one another in only the most superficial ways.

Like the small ternary, the first part of the large ternary is a relatively stable unit that achieves closure by means of a perfect authentic cadence; the second part is contrasting in nature; and the third part essentially restates the first. In light of these similarities, we might be tempted to apply the functional labels of the small ternary and recognize the presence in a large ternary of an exposition, contrasting middle, and recapitulation. But further investigation into the harmonic, tonal, and phrase-structural organization of its three parts dissuades us from extending this set of functional labels to the larger form. Whereas the A section of a small ternary may modulate and close in a subordinate key, the first part of a large ternary always begins and ends in the home key, even if there has been an internal modulation. Consequently, the third part has no need to make any tonal adjustments. Instead, it usually follows the basic tonal and formal plan of the first part (with the likelihood of ornamental changes, of course). Unlike the B section of a small ternary, which, with few exceptions, ends with dominant of the home key, the second part of a large ternary frequently closes with tonic harmony (though not usually of the home key). Moreover, a B section often highlights dominant harmony throughout, whereas the middle part of a large ternary may bring no such dominant emphasis, except at its very end.

An alternative view of formal functionality in the large ternary is suggested by Ratz, who identifies the first and third parts as a main theme and considers the second part to be a subordinate theme.[19] This view has considerable merit, for the outer parts of the large ternary are indeed normally

EXAMPLE 14.3 Haydn, Piano Trio in A, Hob. XV:9, i, 26–36

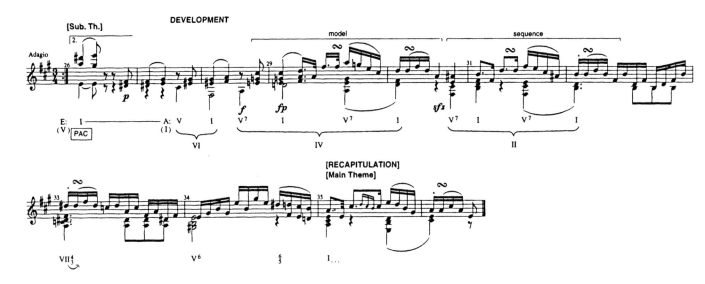

EXAMPLE 14.4 Haydn, Piano Trio in A-flat, Hob. XV:14, ii, 31–35

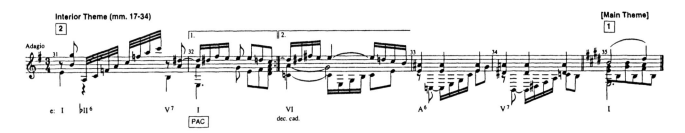

structured as one of the standard main theme forms (usually a small ternary or small binary). But Ratz's notion that the middle part is a subordinate theme is not convincing, since in the majority of cases, this part is not organized in that manner (i.e., as described in chap. 8).

Ratz's position can be somewhat modified by recognizing that the second part of the large ternary is constructed as a different kind of theme, which I term an *interior theme*. As its name suggests, an interior theme occupies a central position in the overall form, always standing between statements of a main theme. (An interior theme appears in a similar location in a number of rondo forms, to be discussed in chap. 16.) The harmonic, tonal, and formal plans of an interior theme can vary considerably, but a number of standard procedures are frequently found. As a general rule, an interior theme resides in the home key, but in its opposite modality. That it does not reside in the conventional subordinate key of the movement distinguishes an interior theme from a subordinate theme. The form of an interior theme is usually related in some way to the small ternary (or small binary), one that is often altered, truncated, or left incomplete in some way.

First Part, Main Theme

As mentioned, the main theme of a large ternary begins in the home key and always ends there with a perfect authentic cadence. Most often the theme is constructed as a small ternary, occasionally as a small binary. The exposition of this small ternary (or the first part of the binary) usually modulates to a subordinate key and closes there with a perfect authentic cadence. But sometimes the A section does not modulate, and a subordinate key is confirmed in the subsequent contrasting middle.[20] In a few cases, the small ternary (or binary) remains exclusively in the home key.[21] A minority of main themes have other conventional, or even nonconventional, designs.[22] There is no need to illustrate main themes of a large ternary, since their formal organization so rarely deviates from the norms established in part II of this book.[23]

Second Part, Interior Theme

The interior theme contrasts with the preceding main theme in a variety of ways. Most obviously, it usually changes the melodic–motivic material, texture, and accompanimental figurations, although the opening basic idea is sometimes derived from that of the main theme. A striking source of contrast comes from an immediate change in modality, for in the great majority of cases, an interior theme is initially set in the minor mode (often labeled *minore* in the score).[24] In the relatively few movements whose main theme is minor, the interior theme shifts to major (*maggiore*).[25]

Although an interior theme usually shifts mode, its tonality generally remains the same as that of the main theme. On occasion, however, the theme resides in a related tonal region, such as the submediant,[26] the lowered submediant,[27] and the subdominant.[28] The use of ♭VI or IV results in those few instances when the mode does not change to minor.[29] It is especially worth emphasizing that an interior theme is never set primarily in the standard subordinate key of the movement, and in this respect, an interior theme is fundamentally different from a subordinate theme.

The formal organization of an interior theme can usually be related more or less to the basic plan of the small ternary (or occasionally the small binary), more specifically, one whose A section modulates to a subordinate key of the *minore* (usually the relative major but sometimes the [minor] dominant or the submediant).[30] In some cases, the small ternary (or binary) follows the norm and ends with a perfect authentic cadence in the home key. This procedure is likely to occur when the theme is set in a nontonic region (VI, ♭VI, IV). The closing authentic cadence is then followed by a brief retransition leading to the home-key dominant in preparation for the return of the main theme.

More frequently, however, the small ternary at the basis of the interior theme is left structurally incomplete, often in ways that significantly distort the form. Sometimes the lack of authentic cadence leaves the theme open-ended. At other times, the entire A' section is deleted, and the form becomes truncated by ending with dominant harmony of the contrasting middle. And even more extreme, though by no means rare, the contrasting middle of the small ternary may be eliminated, and the modulating A section is followed directly by a retransition, often substantial in scope. As a result of these distortions, the final harmony of the interior theme is usually the dominant of the home key, to motivate the main theme's return.

The prominence of minor modality in an interior theme can be likened to the same modal emphasis in the development section of sonata form. Indeed, an interior theme often brings a *Sturm und Drang* affect within highly active and rhythmically continuous accompanimental patterns. Although these secondary characteristics recall a developmental core, the primary characteristics of harmony, tonality, and phrase structure make the interior theme an entirely different formal entity.

It is not necessary here to illustrate interior themes that end with authentic cadences, since the resulting structures simply follow the norms for the small ternary or small binary.[31] Instead, the following examples illustrate progressively distorted versions organized according to a number of regularly recurring techniques.

A' section (or second part of small binary) initially closed, then reopened.

EXAMPLE 14.4: The interior theme (mm. 17–34) is built as a small binary, whose first part modulates to III. (The main theme of this large ternary is also a small binary, shown in ex. 7.3.) The second part returns to the home key and achieves structural completion with a perfect authentic cadence in the first ending of measure 32. After repeating the second part, however, Haydn reopens the form by bringing a deceptive cadence in the second ending for measure 32. Additional music leads to a return of the main theme at measure 35 without any further cadential activity.[32]

A' section (or second part) lacks cadential closure.

EXAMPLE 14.5: The A' section of this interior theme begins at measure 29 and leads through a chromatic descent to the dominant on the third beat of measure 31. The music then seems to get "stuck" on this harmony. When the main theme returns at measure 33, we understand that the interior theme "ended" with a premature dominant arrival.[33]

A' section eliminated, truncated small ternary.

EXAMPLE 14.6: The interior theme begins with the usual shift to the minor mode of the home key and modulates to the relative major, closing there with a perfect authentic cadence in measure 40 (not shown). The resulting structure thus forms a unit that could easily function as the exposition of a small ternary (or the first part of a small binary), especially when the entire passage is then repeated (in the sense of a rounded binary) to close again with a perfect authentic cadence in measure 48 (shown at the beginning of the example). The subsequent section (mm. 49–56) has the typical characteristics of a contrasting middle, namely, a modulation back to the home dominant and a standing on that dominant. But instead of leading to a recapitulation, the B section is followed by the main theme of the large ternary. The interior theme thus takes the form of a *truncated small ternary*, consisting of an exposition and a contrasting middle only.[34]

B and A' sections (or second part) eliminated.

EXAMPLE 14.7: The interior theme begins at measure 25 in the minor mode of the home key and modulates to the relative major, where it closes with a perfect authentic cadence at measure 32. The repetition of this unit reinforces the impression of its being the A section of a small ternary (rounded binary version). The exposition is not followed by a contrasting middle, however: the cadence in the second ending of measure 32 elides with the beginning of a retransition, which leads to a home-key half cadence in measure 38 to end the interior theme. The main theme returns in the following measure.

EXAMPLE 14.5 Haydn, Piano Sonata in E-flat, Hob. XVI:52, ii, 28–33

EXAMPLE 14.6 Haydn, String Quartet in B-flat, Op. 64/3, ii, 47–58

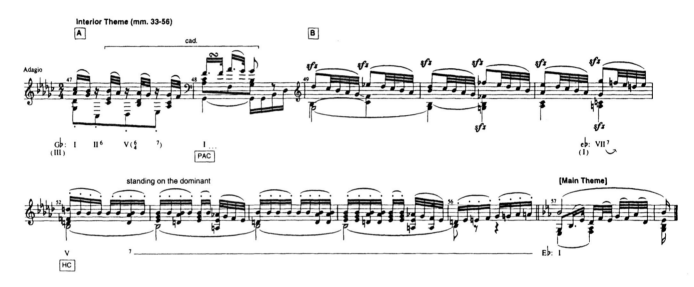

It might be asked why the music in measures 32 (second ending) through 38 could not be considered a contrasting middle rather than a retransition. To be sure, the distinction between these functions can at times be subtle, but it is nonetheless experientially significant. Much of the difference rests on the fact that a contrasting middle does not, in principle, elide with the end of an exposition. A retransition, however, often begins with such an elision and thus seems more directly attached to the exposition, rather than forming an independent section (as would a contrasting middle).[35]

In the two previous examples (as well as the additional works cited in nn. 34 and 35), the structure of the interior theme is by no means as obviously related to the small ternary model as are the earlier examples (exs. 14.4 and 14.5, and those cited in nn. 31, 32, and 33). In fact, an interior theme can sometimes give the impression of being a *subordinate-theme complex* (consisting of a transition, subordinate theme, and retransition) within the tonal framework of the *minore*.[36] In other words, the theme opens in the minor mode of the home key but then quickly modulates to the relative major or minor dominant, as confirmed by a perfect authentic cadence. A later passage (which may or

may not elide with the cadence) leads back to the dominant of the home key. It is indeed occasionally possible to identify distinct units that fulfill the functions of transition, subordinate theme, and retransition.[37] Although such instances might seem to legitimize Ratz's notion that the second part of a large ternary is a "subordinate theme," his view can still be challenged because the new key confirmed by this theme is not the standard subordinate key of the movement as a whole (which would be the regular dominant) but, rather, that of the *minore*. Moreover, such an interior theme includes transition and retransition functions as well as semblance of subordinate-theme function.

Third Part, Return of Main Theme; Coda

Because the main theme of a large ternary essentially resides in the home key, the return of that theme does not require any tonal adjustment. Indeed, the third part of the form is, in the majority of cases, structured the same as the first part, though often with considerable ornamental changes (especially melodic embellishments of the kind found in a

EXAMPLE 14.7 Haydn, String Quartet in E, Op. 54/3, ii, 25–40

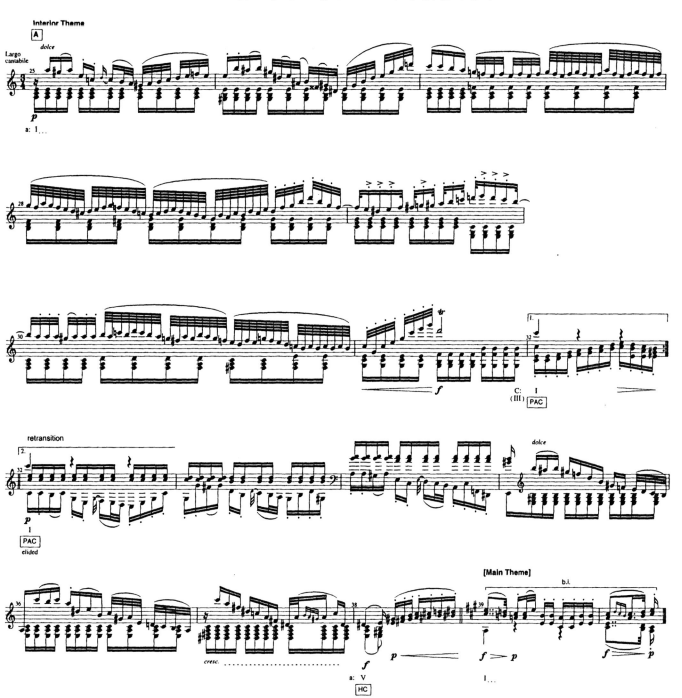

theme-and-variations movement). For these reasons, it is perhaps more appropriate to speak merely of a "return" of the main theme rather than a genuine "recapitulation."

Sometimes when the main theme returns, its structure is changed, and in some cases, a portion of the theme is eliminated.[38] But more commonly, material is added, functioning as an interpolation, extension, or expansion, especially in an A' section.[39]

Some movements in large ternary form conclude with a coda, often of great scope (especially in Beethoven).[40] The coda of a large ternary frequently refers to material from the interior theme, just as the coda of a sonata often "recapitulates" ideas from the development.[41]

SONATA WITHOUT DEVELOPMENT

As its name so baldly indicates, *sonata without development* is a two-part form consisting of a sonata exposition followed immediately by a recapitulation, to which a coda may (optionally) be appended.[42] Although the sonata-without-development form is used most often in slow movements, it is occasionally found in fast movements of an instrumental cycle,[43] and it sometimes serves as the basis of a single-movement overture.[44] The form is employed most often by Mozart, but significant examples appear in the works of Haydn and Beethoven as well.

In its general layout, the exposition of a sonata without development is the same as that of the regular sonata form. Unlike the latter, however, the exposition is never repeated, for at least two reasons. First, such a repetition would likely arouse expectations for a contrasting development section (which is one reason that in a regular sonata, the exposition is usually repeated). Second, the immediate appearance of the recapitulation following a repeated exposition would bring a redundant third run-through of the same basic musical content.

In the regular sonata form, the closing section of the exposition is occasionally followed by a retransition, which helps smooth the connection to the repeated exposition (and thereafter to the development). In a sonata without development, a retransition regularly appears in order to lead the music, without a break, into the recapitulation (see ex. 8.19, mm. 65–67).

The recapitulation of a sonata without development is constructed in essentially the same manner as that of a regular sonata. The main theme and transition are often altered to prepare for the transposition of the entire subordinate-theme area into the home key. And a secondary development frequently appears, in this case to provide harmonic–tonal contrast and motivic manipulation in the absence of a genuine development section.[45] Inasmuch as a fundamental characteristic of any recapitulation is to bring

a *return* following some intervening, contrasting unit, the use of this label in connection with a sonata without development is problematic. If a development is eliminated, then the section following the exposition will seem to function more as a *repetition* than a return.[46] Indeed, the listener hearing the movement for the "first time" would not necessarily know that the appearance of the main theme following the exposition marks the beginning of a recapitulation (of a sonata without development) and could just as likely believe that the exposition is simply being repeated according to the norms of sonata form.[47] Despite this theoretical difficulty, it seems pragmatic to continue using the term recapitulation in connection with the sonata without development. In virtually all respects, the construction of this section is identical to that of a regular sonata. Moreover, since the concept of recapitulation also includes the notion of "resolution of tonal conflict," its use here is additionally justified.

Truncated recapitulation. The principal deviation in sonata-without-development form involves a *truncated recapitulation*. In a number of works by Mozart and Haydn, the exposition is followed only by the main theme, whose structure is the same as that in the exposition.[48] The rest of the recapitulation (transition, subordinate theme, closing section) is eliminated, but a coda may very well be added.

It is interesting to note that with such a truncated recapitulation, the composer creates a form that resembles a large ternary, one whose interior theme has been replaced by a transition and subordinate theme. When the main theme of the sonata without development is built as a small ternary (or small binary), the resemblance to a large ternary is even greater.[49] Despite their similarities, it seems preferable to regard these forms as distinct, especially in light of how we would experience the form. Until the transition and subordinate theme are perceived to be eliminated from the recapitulation, the listener has every reason to believe that the movement is a regular sonata (without development). The possibility of reinterpreting the movement as a deviational large ternary can emerge only after the fact.

List of works. It has not been necessary to illustrate movements in sonata-without-development form, since the ways of organizing the component exposition and recapitulation are essentially the same as in the regular sonata. But for reference, table 14.1 lists selected slow movements written in that form.

THEME AND VARIATIONS

Like so many terms associated with musical form, *theme and variations* can refer to an instrumental genre, a compositional procedure, or a formal category. Theme and varia-

TABLE 14.1 Selected list of movements in sonata-without-development form

Composer	Movement
	Standard Form
Haydn	String Quartet in B-flat, Op. 33/4, iii
	String Quartet in C, Op. 50/2, ii
	String Quartet in B-flat ("Sunrise"), Op. 76/4, ii
Mozart	Symphony No. 39 in E-flat, K. 543, ii
	String Quintet in C, K. 515, iii
	String Quintet in G Minor, K. 516, iii
	String Quartet in G, K. 387, ii
	String Quartet in B-flat ("Hunt"), K. 458, iii
	String Quartet in C ("Dissonance"), K. 465, ii
	String Quartet in B-flat, K. 589, ii
	Piano Quartet in G Minor, K. 478, ii
	Piano Sonata in D, K 311/284c, ii
	Piano Sonata in F, K. 332/300k, ii
Beethoven	Piano Trio in G, Op. 1/2, ii
	Piano Sonata in F Minor, Op. 2/1, ii
	Piano Sonata in C Minor, Op. 10/1, ii
	Piano Sonata in D Minor, Op. 31/2, ii
	Truncated Recapitulation
Haydn	String Quartet in G, Op. 33/5, ii
	String Quartet in D, Op. 33/6, ii
	Piano Trio in E-flat, Hob. XV:30, ii
Mozart	Clarinet Quintet in A, K. 581, ii
	String Quartet in D, K. 575, ii
	Violin Sonata in F, K. 376/374d, ii
	Violin Sonata in B-flat, K. 378/317d, ii

tions is well represented in the works of Haydn, Mozart, and Beethoven, as either independent compositions or individual movements in an instrumental cycle (such as a sonata, quartet, or symphony).[50] Moreover, nearly every movement of a classical work employs variation technique in some way. In slow movements especially, the restatement of a thematic unit is usually subjected to ornamental variations. Thus as both a genre and a compositional procedure, theme and variations provides ample material for study.[51]

As a category of classical form, however, theme and variations requires considerably less treatment. Compared with all other full-movement forms, it is the least complex and presents the fewest problems of formal analysis. The basic plan is simple: a main theme, constructed as either a small ternary or a small binary, is followed by an indefinite number of varied repetitions. A related formal type uses two different themes as the basis for variation. Haydn regularly employs this "double variations" form, or, as Sisman terms it, an "alternating variations" form,[52] and several examples appear in the works of Beethoven.[53] In Haydn's practice, the second theme is a *minore* (or *maggiore*) whose opening idea is often, but not necessarily, derived from that of the first theme. Throughout the movement, the themes alternate with each other and become varied on each reappearance.

The main theme of a variations movement is invariably constructed as a small ternary or small binary, the former appearing only somewhat more frequently than the latter. That the small binary achieves such prominence in themes for variation—in most other formal contexts it is used much less often than the small ternary—is due, no doubt, to the absence of recapitulation within its boundaries. Since theme-and-variations form brings multiple restatements of the initial basic idea, the composer can avoid overexposing it by using the small binary, in which the return of the basic idea then functions exclusively to mark the beginning of each variation.[54]

The variations that follow the main theme normally adhere not only to its overall form (as ternary or binary) but also to its specific arrangement of intrathematic functions. The formal aspect of a theme, however, can occasionally be varied; three standard procedures are typically used. First, the formal structure of the theme may change in one of the variations, usually as a result of changes in the harmonic-tonal scheme of a *minore* variation. Second, passages of extension or interpolation are sometimes added, most often immediately before the final variation. Third, the final variation may have appended to it a brief closing section or may be followed by a full-fledged coda.

Minore. A classical variations movement normally includes one variation written in a modality opposite from the others. This *minore* variation (or *maggiore*, in the rarer case of a minor-mode theme) often changes the original harmonic–tonal organization of the theme. In some cases, simply shifting the harmonies into the minor mode can result in nonsyntactical progressions, and thus new ones must be written. In other cases, the modal shift provides an opportunity for exploring different tonal realms as part of the variation technique per se. As a result of these changes in harmony and tonality, the internal phrase functions are sometimes altered even while the overall form is retained.[55] At other times, the small ternary at the basis of the theme is restructured to become a small binary for the *minore*, or vice versa.[56] In more extreme cases, the *minore* can take on a distinctly looser organization, resembling at times the interior theme of a large ternary (also often labeled *minore*).[57] Finally, the *minore* can be altered to such an extent that it gives the impression of being a variation of an entirely different theme.[58]

Extensions and interpolations. In addition to creating structural changes in a given variation, the composer can alter the general formal plan by adding passages that function as extensions, interpolations, or links from one variation to the next. Such an addition typically occurs just before the final variation, thus breaking the regular succession of variations and drawing attention to the final one by preceding it with something entirely new. The added material is often short,[59] but it can be a more lengthy, developmental passage.[60]

Coda. To provide greater tonal stability for the end of the movement, the final variation is often followed by a closing section or a coda. Besides serving its usual formal functions, the coda in a variations set has the particular function of breaking the pattern of formal symmetry created by the regular succession of more or less equal-size units (i.e., the theme and its variations). Thus the coda provides the only real opportunity for creating the kinds of structural expansion typically found toward the ends of classical movements (such as the enormous cadential expansions in the final subordinate theme of a recapitulation). The coda also permits the composer to create a circular effect for the overall form, by bringing back the theme (or parts of it) in its original, unvaried version at the very end of the movement.[61]

15

Minuet/Trio Form

The minuet is the premier dance type of the classical period. Whereas many instrumental works of the baroque contain a wide variety of dance movements—allemande, courante, sarabande, gigue, bourrée, gavotte, to name the most popular—only the minuet survived the major style shift of the mid-eighteenth century to become incorporated into classical instrumental cycles.

Like baroque practice, the classical minuet movement pairs together two different minuets. The second is traditionally termed *trio*, although the labels "Minuet II" or "*alternativo*" are found now and then. The trio contrasts with the first minuet in a variety of ways, such as melodic–motivic content, rhythmic configurations, and texture. Most trios reside in the same key as the first minuet but frequently shift into the opposite mode or change to a related tonality.

The use of two minuets in one movement creates a thorny problem of terminology, for *minuet* can be used in at least three different ways: as a generic term applicable to either of the two minuets of the movement ("all minuets are in triple meter"); as a more specific term for the first minuet ("the minuet is in major; the trio, in minor"); or as a term for the movement as a whole ("this serenade contains two minuet movements"). In most situations, the context of the discussion makes it clear how the word is being used, but at times it is useful to speak of the *minuet proper* when referring to the first minuet, as opposed to the trio.

The problem of terminology becomes somewhat more acute with respect to form, because "minuet form" can refer to that of the individual minuets (minuet proper and trio) or to that of the whole movement. In this book, I restrict the term *minuet form* to the former definition and use the expression *minuet/trio form* for the latter.[1]

Scherzo

The *scherzo* is a variant style of the minuet and features a faster tempo and a livelier character. The question of whether or not the scherzo is a unique form, different from the minuet, is raised by Schoenberg, who argues that scherzos "differ from smaller ternary forms and the minuet in that the middle section is more modulatory and more thematic. In some cases, there is a special type of *modulatory contrasting middle section* which approaches the elaboration (*Durchführung*) of the Sonata Allegro."[2] Ratz follows Schoenberg's lead by identifying a specific *Scherzoform*, one characterized by the use of a model–sequence technique in the sense of a core.[3]

But we encounter a number of problems when trying to differentiate the minuet from the scherzo. First, it is difficult to determine exactly which pieces from the repertoire are to be regarded as one type or the other. The use of labels in the scores is no help at all, for many works designated as scherzo seem no different from minuets as regards style and character. Moreover, a number of movements specifically entitled "Menuetto" are clearly in a scherzo style.[4] Most problematic, of course, are the many movements that are not labeled either way and that may or may not be considered scherzos.

A second problem with respect to Schoenberg's proposal is that a "modulatory contrasting middle section" featuring model–sequence technique is often found in pieces that would normally be considered minuets, not scherzos. Indeed, Schoenberg himself seems to recognize that fact when shortly after the passage just quoted, he completely reverses his position: "It is generally held that the B-section of a scherzo should be an elaboration (*Durchführung*). But in fact it often resembles the B-section of the minuet, while many minuets possess a modulatory contrast."[5]

Given the problems of distinguishing a minuet from a scherzo, I treat in this book the two styles as a single movement type. In regard to formal organization, it is impossible to differentiate them. I refer to the scherzo only in those situations in which a given movement is undoubtedly in that style, and speaking of it as a minuet would be awkward.

Minuet/Trio Form

Although a minuet movement contains two different minuets (i.e., minuet proper and trio), the full-movement *minuet/trio form* is tripartite, because continuing the baroque practice, the minuet is performed again after the trio. This re-statement of the minuet is not usually written out (unless the composer wishes to introduce ornamental variations). Instead, the expression "Menuet da capo" (or some variant thereof) is indicated in the score. We can thus refer to this restatement as the *da capo* of the minuet. In a few cases, the da capo is followed by a coda to conclude the movement as a whole.[6]

The individual minuets in minuet/trio form conform to one of two different formal schemes. Most are structured in ways that resemble the small ternary (more specifically, the rounded binary); a small number (about 10 percent) resemble the small binary. The minuet proper begins in the home key and modulates to a subordinate key at some point in the form (just where that modulation occurs is an important topic for discussion in the later section on "minuet form"). The minuet always closes in the home key with a perfect authentic cadence.

Most trios follow this same tonal plan, although they more often stay entirely in one key. On occasion, the trio remains open on dominant harmony, which resolves to the tonic on a restatement of the minuet. In approximately one-half of minuet movements, the trio continues in the same key and mode as the preceding minuet. In about one-quarter of cases, the trio shifts to the opposite mode, and in the re-maining quarter, it resides in a different key, usually the subdominant or lowered submediant.

The tripartite scheme of minuet, trio, and da capo is highly suggestive of an overall ternary structure, in which the trio is a "contrasting" element standing in the "middle" of the form, and the da capo represents a "return" of the minuet proper. To employ the functional labels of exposi-tion, contrasting middle, and recapitulation, however, proves unsatisfactory, since the structure of the trio bears no rela-tion to a B section or a development and since the da capo neither tonally adjusts nor structurally alters the original minuet. It would be misleading, therefore, to relate this full-movement form to either the small ternary or the sonata.

Minuet/trio form would seem to have a stronger rela-tionship to the large ternary, especially since the compo-nent parts of each are largely modeled on the small ternary (or small binary). Indeed, if the trio resides in a contrasting mode or tonality, and especially if it remains open on domi-nant harmony, this middle part will function much like an interior theme standing between the statements of a main theme (the minuet proper). We must be cautious, however, not to equate the two full-movement forms, despite their obvious similarities. For often the trio is not at all like an interior theme, especially when it resides in the same key and mode as the minuet and is fully closed both formally and tonally. In such cases, the complete "movement" seems more like a stringing together of parts rather than a true in-tegration of those parts into a single form.[7] Between these two extremes—the trio's total subordination versus its com-

plete independence—lies a spectrum of possibilities, in which the trio stands in a more or less dependent relation to the minuet. For this reason, it is not possible to identify consistent functional relations among the three parts of minuet/trio form, and thus they remain labeled by the rela-tively neutral terms minuet, trio, and da capo.

MINUET FORM

The vast majority of component minuets in minuet/trio form are organized along lines that closely resemble the small ternary (rounded binary version). *Minuet form* thus contains the three fundamental functions of exposition (A), contrasting middle (B), and recapitulation (A'). Most of the formal procedures discussed in connection with the small ternary apply without further comment to minuet form. In-deed, many minuets are virtually identical to that theme-type. Yet whereas some aspects of the small ternary appear regularly in minuet form, others are less often found there. Moreover, some procedures of the minuet are rarely, if ever, associated with the small ternary.

Since a small ternary functions primarily as a main theme in some larger-scale form, its component functions (exposition, contrasting middle, and recapitulation) are es-sentially *intrathematic* (thus somewhat comparable to, say, presentation, antecedent, continuation, and consequent). Conversely, minuet form itself functions as a high-level sec-tion in the full-movement minuet/trio form.[8] Thus atten-tion must be directed to the *interthematic* functions of main theme, transition, subordinate theme, development, reca-pitulation, and coda, which may be expressed.[9] Of particu-lar importance is whether or not a subordinate key is con-firmed, and if so, where and how that confirmation takes place.

Exposition (A)

Like the exposition of a small ternary, the A section of the minuet is usually constructed as a relatively tight knit, con-ventional form (i.e., sentence, period, or hybrid) (see exs. 3.7, 3.9, 3.15, 4.10, 5.4, 5.6, and 5.8). At times, the A section is highly expanded and embraces more than one thematic unit, each ending with a perfect authentic cadence.[10] In the most extreme cases, the A section is complex enough to re-semble an entire sonata-form exposition.[11]

The A section of the minuet, like that of the small ternary, may either remain entirely in the home key or mod-ulate to a closely related subordinate key. Whether or not the exposition of a small ternary modulates is of relatively minor concern. Because that form normally serves as a main theme within a movement, the issue of subordinate-key es-tablishment arises primarily in connection with later formal units (such as a transition and a subordinate theme). In the case of the minuet, however, the appearance of a subordinate key in the A section may well represent the principal tonal conflict of the movement, and thus the presence or absence of a new key is of particular importance. If the modulation does occur there, it is interesting to observe the extent to which subordinate-theme function is expressed. If the A section does not modulate, strong expectations will be aroused for the B section to bring some semblance of that function.[12]

When the A section of the minuet remains entirely in the home key, its interthematic expression is exclusively one of main theme. In such cases, the section is relatively short and compact (formal expansion in that section tends to be associated with a modulation). In almost all cases, the section closes with a perfect authentic cadence.[13]

When the A section modulates to a subordinate key, interthematic functionality is more complex. Not only will a main-theme function appear (at least in a rudimentary way), but a subordinate-theme function also will come to the fore. The sense of transition may be present as well. The extent to which these functions are expressed—the strength of their articulation—depends on a number of factors: the nature of the harmonic progressions in the various keys, the cadences, and the relative degree of tight-knit or loose organization.

A main-theme function in a modulating A section always arises by virtue of initial tonic-stabilizing progressions of the home key. If the music modulates before any home-key cadence, main-theme expression will be minimal, and the form of the section is likely to be sentential, with its first (and usually final) cadence being an authentic one in the subordinate key. Main-theme function will be expressed more strongly if the opening music leads to a home-key half cadence, in which case the form of the section is likely to be periodic, with a matching authentic cadence in the subordinate key.

The sense of main-theme function is strongest when the music residing in the home key closes with a perfect authentic cadence before the end of the section. This *early authentic cadence*, as it can be called, is followed by another thematic unit, one that begins again in the home key and then modulates or one that begins directly in the subordinate key.[14] An early authentic cadence usually closes either a single phrase of exclusively cadential function or a phrase that has the formal characteristics of a consequent. Sometimes the A section is sufficiently complex to yield a complete "main theme" consisting of several phrases, the last one of which closes with an early authentic cadence.

Subordinate-theme function in a modulating A section is always expressed, at least minimally, by a cadential confirmation of the subordinate key. Transition function also emerges if the modulation occurs by means of a harmonic pivot within a phrase. (If a new phrase begins immediately in the subordinate key, the resulting *direct* modulation will not bring any sense of transition).

The expression of transition and subordinate theme is more palpable when the change of key is accompanied by loosening devices typical of these functions. Frequently, the modulation and the cadential confirmation occur in the same phrase, thus creating transition/subordinate-theme fusion. At other times, these functions may occupy their own distinct groups. Occasionally, a perfect authentic cadence in the subordinate key is followed by a second thematic unit residing in the same key and confirmed by another cadence, a situation that produces multiple subordinate themes.

The final cadence of a minuet exposition is sometimes followed by a closing section. In most cases, its content is entirely new; however, sometimes the closing section consists of prior cadence ideas, thus somewhat obscuring the distinction between cadential and postcadential functions. This happens especially in a scherzo, in which a sudden change of material for the closing section could disrupt the intensity of the prevailing rhythmic drive.

The following examples illustrate some of the ways in which interthematic functionality can be expressed by a modulating A section.

EXAMPLE 3.9 (see p. 40): In this sentence form, it is possible to recognize the functional elements of main theme, transition, and subordinate theme. Main-theme function is expressed solely by means of the presentation phrase, supported by a firm tonic prolongation in the home key. The lack of any cadential articulation for the key makes the function weak indeed. The extension of the continuation by means of a harmonic sequence is understandable in light of the phrase serving both transition and subordinate-theme functions. Here, the two functions are fused into a single unit.

EXAMPLE 15.1: The opening eight measures form a hybrid (c.b.i. + cont.) closing with a half cadence in the home key.[15] The unit thus functions as an antecedent in the A section yet can also be seen to express main-theme function in the minuet as a whole. The consequent begins in the home key at measure 9, but the end of the opening compound basic idea resolves deceptively to VI (m. 12), which pivots for the modulation into the subordinate key. The rest of the A section is devoted to reinforcing and confirming this key. The functions of transition and subordinate theme are clearly expressed in this passage, although they are fused together, since it is difficult to find a decisive ending for the former and a beginning for the latter.

The A section closes with a cadential idea beginning on the upbeat to measure 19 and closing on the downbeat of measure 21. The rhythmic momentum generated by the running eighth notes is maintained when this idea is immediately repeated and extended.[16] Where, then, is the cadence? If it is understood to be on the downbeat of measure 23, the downbeat of measure 21 would have to be heard as an evaded cadence. But this interpretation is rather unlikely, since the first beat of that measure is easily heard as the goal of the phrase. Thus it is better to recognize measure 21 as the moment of cadential closure and to view the repeated idea as a codetta, in line with the idea that the closing section of a scherzo often employs the immediately preceding cadential material.

EXAMPLE 15.1 Beethoven, Piano Sonata in E-flat, Op. 7, iii, 1–24

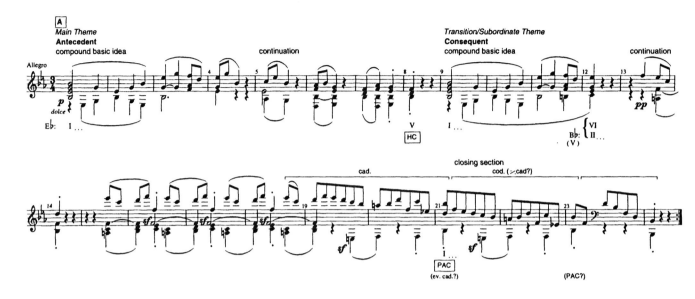

EXAMPLE 15.2 Beethoven, Violin Sonata in F ("Spring"), Op. 24, iii, 1–8

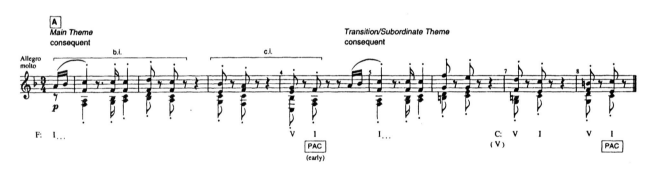

EXAMPLE 15.3 Haydn, Symphony No. 98 in B-flat, iii, 1–20

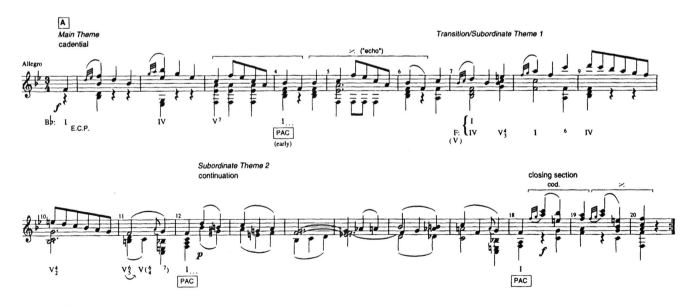

EXAMPLE 15.4 Mozart, Piano Sonata in A, K. 331/300i, ii, 1–18

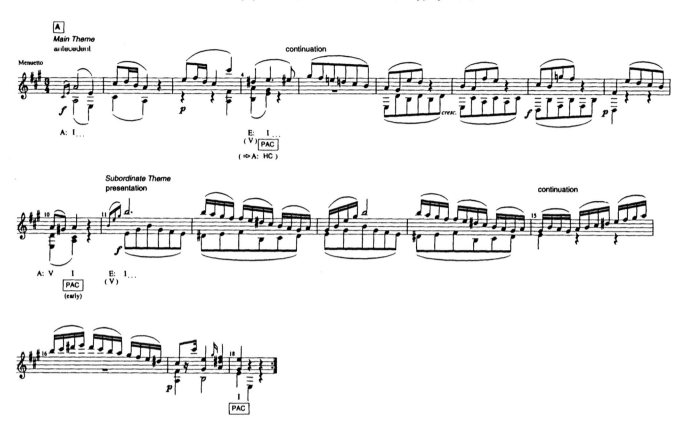

EXAMPLE 15.2: The first phrase is built like a simple four-measure consequent, that is, a basic idea followed by a contrasting idea that ends with a perfect authentic cadence. (That this "initiating" phrase is interpreted here as a consequent can perhaps be more readily understood if the listener imagines its being preceded by an antecedent phrase ending melodically on A, thus implying an imperfect authentic cadence.) The second phrase begins in measure 5, as the first does, but then modulates to the dominant region and closes there with another perfect authentic cadence (m. 8). (Because of its V–I progression, measure 7 could qualify as the cadential arrival, but the strong rhythmic correspondence between the two phrases makes it difficult to hear that measure as the goal of the theme.) The two phrases taken together strongly resemble a modulating period, but this interpretation is flawed, since the cadences closing the phrases are of equal weight (despite their differing tonal expressions). Therefore, rather than finding the intrathematic relation of antecedent–consequent between these two phrases, it is preferable to identify their interthematic expression. The first phrase, with its *early* authentic cadence, brings the main-theme function, and the second phrase fuses (in a highly compressed manner) the transition and subordinate-theme functions.

EXAMPLE 15.3: The A section opens with a four-measure phrase supported by an expanded cadential progression. An early authentic cadence in the home key is thus created on the downbeat of measure 4.[17] The end of the cadential idea is then echoed in the winds (mm. 5–6), after which the music modulates to the domi-

nant region, confirmed cadentially at measure 12. The sense of subordinate-theme function is reinforced when the cadential progression is briefly abandoned at measure 9 (the pre-dominant IV moves to an inverted dominant), after which the cadential progression resumes with V$^6_5$/V at the downbeat of measure 11.

An additional thematic unit, albeit a rather short one, begins on the second beat of measure 12 and continues until the perfect authentic cadence at measure 18. This unit gives the impression of being a "second" subordinate theme, one that starts directly with continuation function. The A section concludes with a brief closing section in measures 19–20.

EXAMPLE 15.4: The opening of the A section resides in the home key and closes with an early authentic cadence in measure 10. Unlike the previous examples, in which main-theme function is expressed by a single phrase, the music here is sufficiently broad to be considered a complete theme, one that takes the form of an expanded hybrid (ant. + cont.). A subordinate theme then begins directly in the new key, thus bypassing any sense of transition function.

EXAMPLE 15.5: The first part of this A section, an eight-measure sentence closing with an imperfect authentic cadence (see ex. 3.15), functions as the main theme in the minuet as a whole. The following four-measure unit (mm. 9–12) accomplishes the modulation and ends with dominant harmony of the subordinate key. This phrase thus functions exclusively as a transition. A subordinate theme then begins at measure 13 and exhibits many of the loosen-

EXAMPLE 15.5 Mozart, String Quartet in A, K. 464, ii, 9–28

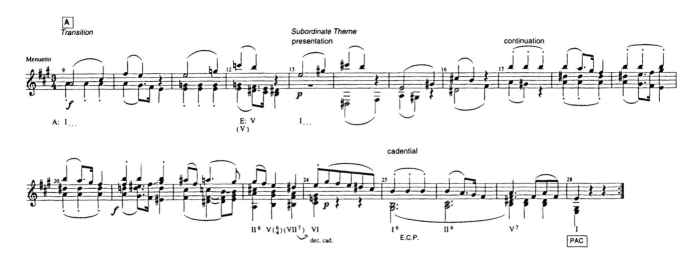

EXAMPLE 15.6 Haydn, Symphony No. 98 in B-flat, iii, 21–41

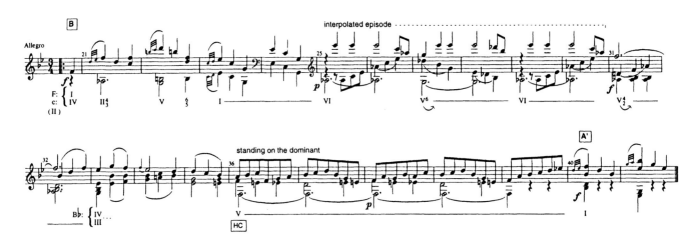

EXAMPLE 15.7 Mozart, Piano Sonata in A, K. 331/300i, ii, 19–32

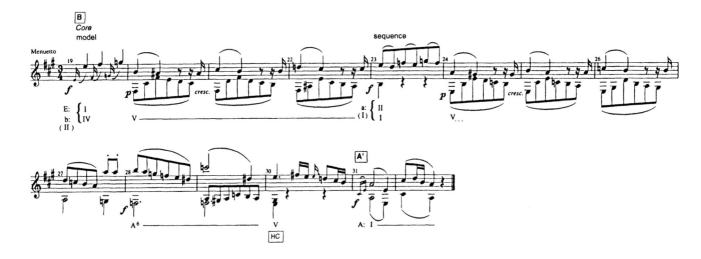

ing devices typical of that function. A presentation in measures 13–16 is followed by an extended continuation, which leads to a deceptive cadence at measure 24. A new cadential unit (based on the second half of the main theme but also alluding to the continuation of the subordinate theme) brings complete closure at measure 28.

Contrasting Middle (B)

The B section of the minuet brings many of the same harmonic, tonal, and formal characteristics of a contrasting middle in small ternary form—loose nonconventional organization, emphasis on the home-key dominant, sequential harmonies, closure in the home key with a half cadence or dominant arrival. But whereas the B section of the small ternary is relatively simple and short, that of a minuet is usually more complex and often lasts considerably longer than the preceding A section. Thus certain techniques appear there that rarely find a place in the smaller scope of the small ternary. For example, the contrasting middle of a minuet might bring an *interpolated episode* of new material in a relatively remote tonal region. Or a false recapitulation may appear toward the end of the B section. In some cases, the section may even feature model–sequence technique in a manner reminiscent of a developmental core.

An important consideration for the B section's organization and functional expression is whether or not its preceding exposition modulates. If the A section has presented main-theme, transition, and subordinate-theme functions, the B section has the opportunity of expressing a rudimentary sense of development by exploring additional tonal regions. If the earlier A section is exclusively a main theme, the B section usually provides the fundamental tonal conflict of the minuet by modulating to, and confirming, a subordinate key.[18]

Following a modulating A section. In cases in which the exposition of a minuet is modulatory, the B section is free either to touch on other tonal regions or, as is often the case, to return to the home key and conclude there with dominant harmony. The phrase-structural organization tends to be loose and nonconventional, with an emphasis on continuational traits (fragmentation, model–sequence, harmonic acceleration). Brief tonicizations of various regions occur frequently, although it is uncommon for the section to confirm a development key. In the simplest cases, the B section consists entirely of a standing on the dominant.

EXAMPLE 15.6: The B section quickly tonicizes the supertonic region using motivic material from the beginning of the minuet (see ex. 15.3). Measure 25 brings an interpolated episode, marked by a new melodic idea, an abrupt shift from forte to piano, and an immediate move into the remote region of A♭ major (VI of the supertonic, C minor). Measure 31 restores the forte dynamic and initiates a return back to the home key, as confirmed by the half

cadence at measure 36. A standing on the dominant concludes the contrasting middle and prepares the way for the recapitulation at measure 40.

EXAMPLE 15.7: Like the previous example, the B section begins by tonicizing II. But here, Mozart establishes a four-measure model (mm. 19–22), which is then repeated sequentially down a step (mm. 23–26). A subsequent move to the augmented sixth in measure 28 prepares for the concluding half cadence. The overall formal organization resembles the core of a development, although the section is relatively short, displays little sense of fragmentation, and lacks the emotional restlessness typical of a core.

Following a nonmodulating A section. If the A section does not modulate, the B section can assume the role of introducing transition and subordinate-theme functions into the minuet. Shifting these expositional functions into the contrasting middle is not, however, required of the form: a number of minuets in the literature remain effectively in the home key throughout, although there may be a prominent tonicization of the subordinate-key region.[19] In cases in which the entire minuet is nonmodulatory, the companion minuet (either the minuet proper or the trio) usually expresses subordinate-theme function.[20] Rarely is a subordinate key not established somewhere in the complete minuet/trio form.[21]

Following a nonmodulating exposition, the contrasting middle most often moves to the subordinate key by employing phrase-structural processes typical of transition and subordinate-theme functions. In some cases, the B section begins immediately in the subordinate key, thereby omitting a transition. The section may include both an interpolated episode and significant model–sequence technique in the manner of a core.

EXAMPLE 15.8: The nonmodulating exposition was discussed in connection with period form (see ex. 4.10a). The B section begins with new material organized into a compound basic idea supported by submediant harmony. This sudden shift to VI, a standard signal for transition function, is found at the start of many contrasting middles.[22] A brief model–sequence pattern (mm. 15–16) brings a modulation to the dominant, which is confirmed as a subordinate key by an expanded cadential progression in measures 17–20. A short closing section turns into a retransition when the tonic pedal of the subordinate key becomes dominant of the home key at measure 23.

EXAMPLE 15.9: Following the home-key cadence closing the A section (shown in ex. 5.8), the B section begins with a four-measure phrase that quickly modulates to the subordinate key as initially confirmed by the dominant in measures 11–12. This phrase thus serves as the transition, after which a genuine subordinate theme begins in measure 13 with a new presentation, followed by a continuation⇒cadential phrase in measures 17–20. A brief retransition brings back the home key and prepares for the recapitulation at measure 25.

EXAMPLE 15.8 Haydn, String Quartet in G, Op. 54/1, iii, 11–26

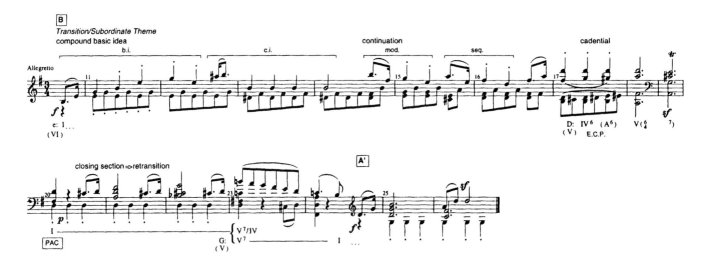

EXAMPLE 15.9 Haydn, Symphony No. 87 in A, iii, 9–26

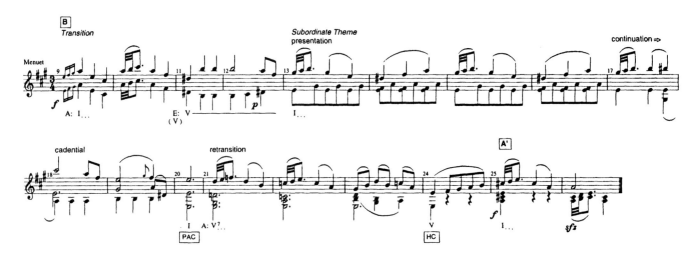

EXAMPLE 15.10 Haydn, String Quartet in G, Op. 54/1, iii, 33–44

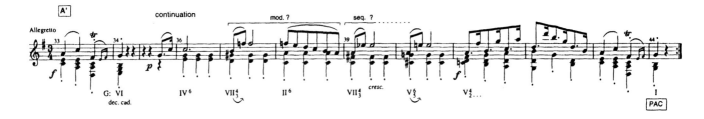

Recapitulation (A')

The A' section of minuet form recapitulates the material initially presented in the A section. In many minuets, this section retains the basic phrase-structural design of the exposition. Unlike the small ternary, which frequently contains a compressed recapitulation, that of a minuet is seldom shorter than the earlier section.[23] In fact, the minuet's recapitulation is much more likely to be significantly expanded. In addition, it frequently includes a new closing section, one not found in the exposition.[24]

The substantial expansion in the recapitulation is created by loosening devices typically associated with a subordinate theme. New material may also appear in an interpolated episode. The deceptive cadence is a particularly favorite device for extending the form; indeed, this technique is perhaps found more often in a minuet than in a sonata, in which evaded cadences are more commonly used to extend cadential function.

The tendency to expand the recapitulation can be explained on a number of grounds. If the A section is shorter than the B section, as is often the case, then bringing an equally short A' section might not give the home key enough space to win the battle of conflicting tonalities. And so an expanded recapitulation, one that features the cadential reinforcements typical of a subordinate theme, might be necessary to restore tonal stability to the form. The addition of a new closing section (and even a coda, as pointed out in the next section) also helps in this struggle for home-key predominance.

Another, somewhat related, explanation sees the expansion of the A' section as providing a kind of "recapitulation of the subordinate theme" to match the expression of that function in an earlier B section. In other words, if a nonmodulating exposition represents main-theme function and the contrasting middle brings a subordinate theme, then simply bringing back the main theme once again in the A' section will leave the latter theme unrecapitulated. An expansion in the A' section does not literally recapitulate the earlier subordinate theme, for the section must model itself on the exposition, not on the B section. But the looser phrase-structural techniques can suggest such a recapitulation nonetheless.

EXAMPLE 15.10: The A' section follows a course identical to that of the A section (see ex. 4.10a) until the deceptive cadence at measure 34.[25] What comes next is a newly inserted development of exposition motives with a hint of sequential organization; the section closes with the expected perfect authentic cadence at measure 44. Had the recapitulation finished with an authentic cadence at measure 34, home-key expression would not have been sufficient to overcome the more powerful subordinate-key confirmation in the B section (see ex. 15.8).

EXAMPLE 15.11: The recapitulation opens with the eight-measure antecedent of the exposition (see ex. 15.1). At measure 51, the music suddenly shifts to minor, and the deceptive resolution at measure 54 brings ♭VI. A subsequent development of this harmony into a tonicized region, using the gesture of measures 13–14 (ex. 15.1), eventually leads into an interpolated episode whose imperfect authentic cadence at measure 62 actually confirms ♭VI as a development key (in the recapitulation!). A retransitional passage (still part of the episode) returns the music to the home key, as articulated by the half cadence at measure 70. The sense of this half cadence as a rhythmic goal is undermined, however, by the pause immediately preceding it: it is as though the music has withered away, and thus the dominant sounds more like a new beginning than an end. (The gesture of the dramatic pause is itself a hallmark of this scherzo; see m. 54 and ex. 15.1, mm. 4, 5, 12.)

A new presentation, beginning with the upbeat to measure 72, is given a modified repetition at measure 76. A continuation⇒cadential phrase follows (m. 80), which is extended by a series of deceptive cadences. The concluding cadence at measure 86 (no longer ambiguous as in the exposition, ex. 15.1, m. 21) is reinforced by an entirely new closing section. From the point of view of interthematic functionality, the recapitulation is expanded in such a way that transition and subordinate-theme functions are no longer fused (as they were in the A section) but, rather, are given their own distinct thematic units (transition, mm. 51–71; subordinate theme, mm. 72–86).[26]

Coda

As part of its expansionist tendencies, the recapitulation can include a new closing section, as just illustrated in the previous example. The expansion is even greater if the material following the final cadence is organized in a manner sufficiently complex to require cadential closure. We then can speak of a *coda* to the minuet itself. Codas are most likely to appear when the recapitulation is modeled closely on the exposition. The coda then can take over the role of expanding the form, for the same purposes discussed in connection with an enlarged A' section.

For the most part, codas in minuet form display the same basic features and functions as those described in chapter 12. But unlike most other forms, in which the coda is entirely separate from the recapitulation, the coda in minuet form is more intimately linked to the latter, since it is included in the repetition of the B and A' sections together (i.e., the coda precedes the double-bar and repeat signs).

EXAMPLE 15.12: The A' section is structurally identical to the A section (see ex. 5.8). As pointed out with respect to example 15.9, the contrasting middle brings transition and subordinate-theme functions, the latter closed by an expanded cadential progression. Thus the cadence confirming the subordinate key (ex. 15.9, mm. 17–20) is considerably stronger than that confirming the home key in the recapitulation (ex. 15.12, mm. 31–32). Consequently, Haydn follows the end of the A' section with a coda made up of a new six-measure unit, which is repeated identically (mm. 39–44). The principal compensatory function of this coda is to give greater

EXAMPLE 15.11 Beethoven, Piano Sonata in E-flat, Op. 7, iii, 51–95

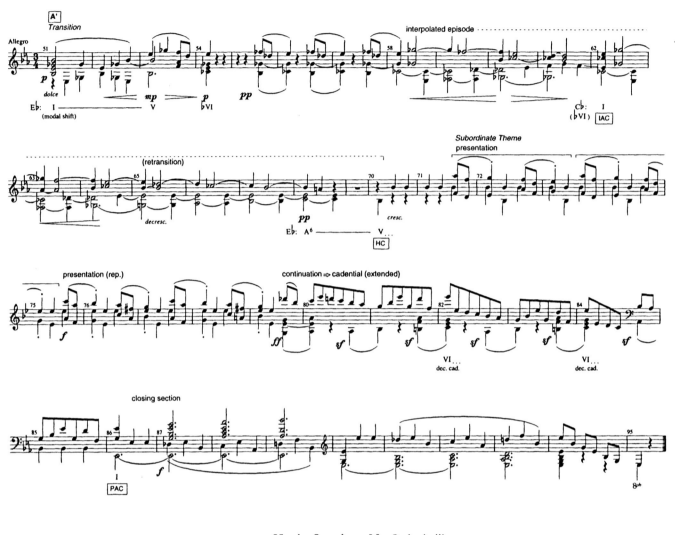

EXAMPLE 15.12 Haydn, Symphony No. 87 in A, iii, 31–44

cadential weight to the home key by means of an expanded cadential progression.

Binary Minuet Form

Whereas most minuets (and trios) are constructed according to minuet form just described, a few are built along lines that resemble the small binary form. This *binary minuet form* contains two parts, each of which is repeated. In most respects, part 1 resembles the A section of regular minuet form, except that it more frequently closes with a half cadence. The second part often contains material that functions like a contrasting middle, but this part does not include a recapitulatory articulation (a return of the opening basic idea in the home key). Although the opening does not come back in the normal boundaries of the form, this material may well appear again in a closing section to the second part or even in a coda, thereby fulfilling an obvious compensatory function.

EXAMPLE 15.13: The minuet opens with a four-measure phrase supported by an expanded cadential progression. The "early" authentic cadence at measure 4 marks the end of main-theme function. The next phrase continues in the home key, and a strongly continuational passage at measure 9 directs the music to the dominant, which is confirmed as the subordinate key by the cadence at measure 12.[27] The first part of this binary minuet ends with a brief closing section, whose melody reopens by rising strangely up to the fifth scale-degree.

The second part starts out with a contrasting middle made up exclusively of a standing on the dominant (which lasts until the end of m. 24), after which the music of measures 5–8 returns in measures 25–28. The subsequent continuation (m. 29) is adjusted to remain in the home key, and the second part concludes with the perfect authentic cadence at measure 32. The earlier closing section then brings its strange rise to the fifth degree at measure 36. But rather than letting this degree "hang in the air," as Mozart did at the end of the first part, he uses it as a springboard to recapture the minuet's opening phrase. The relocation of this phrase to a final position is particularly fitting here, not only because it makes up for its not having been recapitulated, but also because it now finds its more natural location as a cadential unit that closes the preceding material (rather than being the opening phrase of the minuet).[28]

TRIO

Most of what we have observed about minuet form holds for the trio as well. This part of the movement, however, can exhibit some stylistic and formal characteristics that distinguish it from the minuet proper. First and foremost, a trio must provide a distinct element of contrast while still maintaining the same meter and tempo. But whereas the concept of "contrast" in classical form usually entails greater structural complexity and emotional intensification, the trio of a minuet movement generally brings a quality of simplification and re-

laxation.[29] In most of its musical parameters, a trio is usually simpler than its preceding minuet: the harmonic vocabulary is more diatonic; the rhythmic patterns are more uniform and continuous; and the texture is less dense.

With respect to formal organization, the trio generally follows the norms of minuet form but differs from the minuet proper in a number of ways. The trio tends to be shorter and more symmetrically formed; expansions are more likely to be kept under control; and codas occur less often. Many trios, in fact, assume the highly symmetrical proportions of the basic small ternary and small binary forms, for instance, 8 (A) + 4 (B) + 4 (A').

The most important formal distinction occurs when the composer attempts to forge a stronger sense of overall minuet/trio form by making the trio more dependent on the minuet proper. The methods used to achieve this structural dependence include changing the trio's mode or tonality, adding a retransition, and leaving the trio formally incomplete. By varying the modality or tonality (or both), the trio becomes somewhat dependent on its surrounding minuets, for the change motivates a restoration of the original mode or key somewhere later in the overall form (namely, in the da capo). If the tonality changes, and especially if the tonal region is relatively remote, the composer may add a passage linking the end of the trio with the beginning of the da capo. This retransition, which often anticipates motives of the minuet, aids considerably in integrating the form.[30]

The trio can become even more dependent by remaining structurally incomplete. This situation is very similar to what typically happens at the end of an interior theme in large ternary form. And like that theme, a variety of techniques can be employed to inhibit closure of the trio. For example, the A' section may initially cadence but, when repeated, remain open on dominant harmony (sometimes following a deceptive cadence).[31] Or the recapitulation can begin normally but then get stuck on a dominant, which eventually marks the trio's harmonic end.[32] Sometimes the trio is truncated (thus consisting of the A and B sections only), with the dominant of the B section leading back to the da capo.[33] If the trio is set in a key different from that of the minuet, then the harmony ending the structurally incomplete trio normally is dominant of the minuet's home key.[34]

EXAMPLE 15.14: After a minuet in C major, the trio shifts to the minor mode. The music leading up to the double bar ends with a half cadence in the home key. (This half cadence suggests that the section could be interpreted as the first part of a binary minuet form.) A contrasting middle begins with model–sequence technique and closes with a premature dominant arrival at measure 77 and a subsequent standing on the dominant. But rather than bringing a recapitulation of some kind (or some other continuation) and eventual closure in C minor, the marking "Menuetto D.C." instructs the performers to return to the minuet proper. The truncated trio thus remains structurally subordinate to its surrounding minuets.

EXAMPLE 15.13 Mozart, Serenade in D ("Haffner"), K. 250/248b, iii, 1–40

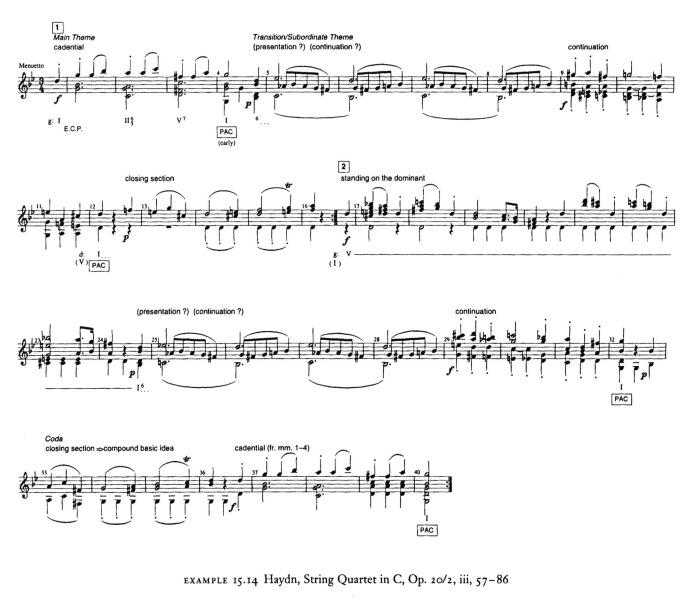

EXAMPLE 15.14 Haydn, String Quartet in C, Op. 20/2, iii, 57–86

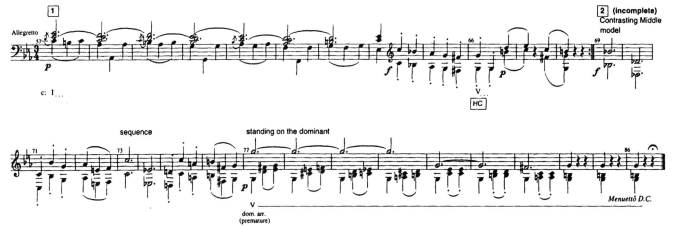

Rondo Forms

All *rondo forms* in Western art music display a basic pattern of formal organization. A principal thematic idea — the "rondo theme" or "refrain" — alternates regularly with two or more contrasting passages, termed "couplets," "episodes," or "digressions." Letters of the alphabet traditionally describe a variety of rondo forms, such as ABACA, ABACADA, ABACABA (where "A" stands for the refrain, and the remaining letters, for couplets of differing material). In the classical era, however, most rondos can be situated in one of two main categories — the *five-part rondo* (ABACA) and the *sonata–rondo* (ABACABA). Variants of each type create a number of other formal designs (e.g., ABACADA, ABACBA).[1]

Labeling the rondo's component parts poses a number of theoretical difficulties. The standard use of letters, for example, is deficient in several respects. First, like all such schemes, the letters indicate little about formal function. Second, they can be confused with the same letters representing other forms, especially the small ternary (and its allied minuet form). For these reasons, it is better to adopt terminology that not only relates more specifically to the rondo but also can reveal the form-functional attributes of its parts. Since there is no single group of expressions that serves both purposes, I use two sets of terms in this book. In the first set, *refrain* and *couplet* refer to the rondo's component parts generally. Each refrain and couplet is numbered according to its position in the form. All the refrains contain essentially the same material; the various couplets contrast with the refrain and usually (though not always) with one another. A second set of terms uses the standard labels of interthematic functionality (e.g., main theme, subordinate theme, interior theme, development) to specify the formal role played by the various refrains and couplets.

FIVE-PART RONDO

In the *five-part rondo* (traditionally ABACA), an opening refrain returns twice, alternating with two couplets of contrasting musical content and organization. A coda is sometimes appended to the form. The refrain appears at all times in the home key, and the two intervening couplets are set in different tonal regions. The first couplet may be constructed in one of two ways, first, as a thematic region consisting of a transition, subordinate theme (group), closing section, and retransition, henceforth termed *subordinate-theme complex*; or, second, as an *interior theme*, like that found in the second part of a large ternary. The second couplet is most often an interior theme differing from the earlier couplet in its melodic–motivic material, tonal region, and formal plan. At times, the second couplet assumes a development-like organization. Table 16.1 summarizes the formal plan.

Refrain 1, Main Theme

The first refrain functions as the main theme of the rondo. The refrain is almost always a conventional, tight-knit theme closing in the home key with a perfect authentic cadence. In the majority of cases, it is built as a small ternary (or rounded binary) or, less often, a small binary. The refrain may also have a simpler form, such as a period or hybrid. A closing section is sometimes added after the cadence closing the refrain, and even a second main theme in the home key may appear.[2]

As a general tendency, main themes in rondo forms are more tightly knit than those in sonata form. For example, a rondo theme always closes with a perfect authentic cadence, never a half cadence. Moreover, rondo refrains tend to be conventional and symmetrical, whereas the looser, noncon-

TABLE 16.1 Five-part rondo form

Rondo Term	Formal Function	Tonal Region
refrain 1 (A)	main theme	I
couplet 1 (B)	subordinate-theme complex *or* interior theme	V *or minore,* (VI)
refrain 2 (A)	first return of main theme	I
couplet 2 (C)	interior theme; development-like unit	*minore,* IV, (VI)
refrain 3 (A)	final return of main theme	I
(—)	(coda)	I

EXAMPLE 16.1 Mozart, Piano Sonata in C, K. 545, iii, 9–22

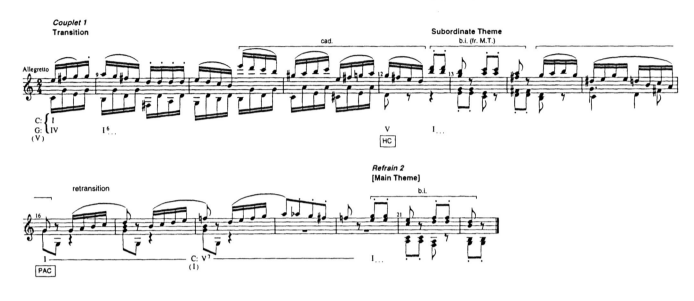

EXAMPLE 16.2 Haydn, Piano Sonata in G, Hob. XVI:39, i, 17–34

ventional themes frequently found in a sonata rarely appear in a rondo.

Couplet 1, Subordinate-Theme Complex or Interior Theme

The first couplet is normally organized as either a subordinate-theme complex (consisting of a transition, subordinate-theme group, closing section, and retransition) or an interior theme. In the first case, the first refrain and couplet constitute a sonata exposition, and in the second case, the refrain and couplet resemble the first two parts of a large ternary.

Subordinate-theme complex.   With this option, the one preferred by Mozart, the end of refrain 1 is followed by a transition (modulating or nonmodulating) and one or more subordinate themes. A closing section then leads directly into a retransition, which prepares for the return of the refrain.

The establishment and confirmation of a subordinate key in a rondo are often less emphatic than they are in a sonata. Thus a rondo frequently eliminates a distinct transition[3] or else fuses it with the subordinate theme.[4] And whereas a sonata's subordinate theme must always close with a perfect authentic cadence, this requirement may sometimes be waived (especially by Beethoven). In sonata form, the subordinate-theme group tends to be formally complex and highly expansive in relation to the main theme. In a rondo, the subordinate theme, like the refrain, can be relatively compressed and simple. In short, the tonal conflict of home and subordinate keys—so often dramatized in sonata form—tends to be tempered in rondo forms.

EXAMPLE 16.1: Following a short main theme (built as a simple period), the transition begins in the middle of measure 8 and consists of a single four-measure phrase leading to the dominant of the subordinate key, G major. The subordinate theme, based on the main theme, is equally short and concludes with a perfect authentic cadence at measure 16. A four-measure retransition leads to the return of the main theme. Such a highly compressed subordinate-theme complex would be extremely rare in a regular sonata exposition (cf. ex. 8.3, the subordinate theme of the first movement of this sonata). Note that the arrangement of cadences generates antecedent and consequent functions for the transition and the subordinate theme, respectively. But the musical content does not permit us to hear the latter as a repetition of the former, and thus a standard period does not result.[5]

Dramatic intensification in the rondo is generally associated more with the various returns of the refrain than with the appearance of the contrasting couplets. Thus the retransition leading back to refrain 2 is usually longer and more elaborate than what might be found at the end of a

sonata exposition, and motives anticipating the refrain's basic idea are often included in order to heighten expectations for its eventual return.

Interior theme.   With this option, favored especially by Haydn, the rondo refrain is followed directly by an interior theme.[6] The interior theme in the second couplet is most likely to be a *minore* (or *maggiore* for minor-mode movements),[7] but sometimes it resides in the submediant. The subdominant is rarely used at this point in the form.[8]

Even more than with the large ternary, an interior theme of a rondo can be structured in diverse ways. Most often the theme is modeled on the small ternary (or small binary). Usually that form is complete, after which a retransition leads back to the home key in preparation for the return of the main theme. Sometimes, however, the small ternary underlying an interior theme is incomplete or truncated. For example, an originally closed theme may be reopened when the A′ section is repeated, or the recapitulation may be eliminated so that the theme ends with the contrasting middle. On occasion, the interior theme cannot be assimilated to the small ternary (or binary) model and is best seen as nonconventional.[9]

EXAMPLE 16.2: The first couplet is a *minore* interior theme constructed as a truncated small ternary. As expected, the A section modulates to the relative major. The B section then begins at measure 25 with model–sequence technique and arrives on the home-key dominant at measure 28. After a four-measure extension, the dominant resolves to the tonic major to initiate the return of the main theme (m. 33).

Refrain 2, First Return of Main Theme

The first return of the opening refrain usually brings back the theme's complete structure, sometimes with ornamental changes (such as melodic embellishment and textural enrichment).[10] Often, however, an *abridged refrain* brings back just the A (or A′) section of an original ternary, and therefore the form still concludes with a perfect authentic cadence in the home key.[11] Less frequently, the refrain is shortened to the extent that it lacks cadential closure or concludes with a cadence in some other tonal region. Both these situations result in an *incomplete refrain.*[12]

On "first hearing," refrain 2 can elicit quite different formal interpretations, depending on the structure of the first couplet. Following a subordinate-theme complex, the return of the main theme appears to mark the repeat of a sonata exposition or the beginning of a recapitulation in a sonata without development. Following an interior theme, the return suggests the third part of a large ternary. In both cases, the rondo form is not confirmed until the appearance of the subsequent couplet.[13]

Refrain 2 typically ends with a home-key authentic ca-

EXAMPLE 16.3 Haydn, Piano Sonata in E-flat, Hob. XVI:49, iii, 58–64

EXAMPLE 16.4 Beethoven, Symphony No. 3 in E-flat ("Eroica"), Op. 55, ii, 105–15

dence, after which couplet 2 starts immediately. In the case of an incomplete refrain, the couplet may start after an internal cadence, or the refrain may be extended to become a transitional passage leading to the new key of the following couplet.

EXAMPLE 16.3: The second refrain is incomplete because it consists only of its modulating A section (the complete refrain, a small ternary, was seen in ex. 6.6). Although the final cadence (m. 60) of the incomplete refrain 2 is initially understood as authentic in the new key of Bb, it can be heard as a reinterpreted half cadence in the home key of Eb when the second couplet, a *minore*, begins at measure 61.

EXAMPLE 16.4: Refrain 2 remains incomplete when the music moves toward the subdominant region at measure 111 and cadences there at measure 114. The beginning of couplet 2, a development-like fugal passage, elides with the end of the second refrain.

Couplet 2, Interior Theme or Development-like Organization

The second couplet of the five-part rondo is usually organized as an interior theme, especially when the first couplet

is a subordinate-theme complex. If couplet 1 is an interior theme, the second couplet may also have that form (in a different tonal region). For the sake of contrast, however, it may instead resemble a development.

An interior theme for couplet 2 can reside in any of the standard tonal regions: *minore* (favored by Haydn), subdominant (favored by Mozart), and submediant.[14] Although an interior theme for couplet 2 can be formed as a complete small ternary (or small binary), frequently—indeed more often than with couplet 1—the theme remains incomplete in some way. In addition, it may be based on one of the other tight-knit forms.[15] Like the first couplet, the end of the second one brings a retransitional passage, which either follows the close of the interior theme or makes up its last phrase.

Couplet 2 is sometimes organized in a manner that cannot be easily assimilated to the category of interior theme. Such a wide variety of formal procedures can be found at this point in the form that generalizations are difficult to make. Most such cases have a certain development-like quality about them. Indeed, a few are organized along the lines of a true development section.[16]

Refrain 3, Final Return of Main Theme; Coda

The final return of the rondo refrain usually brings back the original structure of the main theme, although an abridged or incomplete version occasionally appears instead.[17] We might be tempted to consider the final return of the main theme as a functional "recapitulation" of some sorts. It is interesting to note, however, that except for the general sense of *return* (defined as a restatement following an intervening contrast), few other recapitulatory aspects—such as tonal adjustment or secondary development—are normally found when the rondo refrain comes back for the last time. Here, therefore, as in the case of the third part of the large ternary, it is perhaps best to characterize the reappearance of the main theme as a functional return rather than as a full-fledged recapitulation.

Following the close of refrain 3, the rondo may end with a new closing section or even a full coda. (If the refrain is incomplete, the coda usually follows without a break in texture or rhythm.)[18] The coda, which may be quite extensive,[19] often has strong developmental qualities, introduces new material, makes reference to earlier couplets, or even brings additional statements of the refrain.

Seven-Part Rondo

The five-part rondo can be enlarged by adding a third couplet and a fourth refrain. Only a few works in the classical repertory follow this procedure, which creates what is traditionally termed a *seven-part rondo* (ABACADA). The additional couplet is usually constructed as an interior theme, one whose tonal region and formal organization contrasts with those of earlier interior themes. The following works demonstrate various possibilities for the three couplets of a seven-part rondo:[20]

Haydn, Piano Trio in D, Hob. XV:16, iii:
    couplet 1: interior theme, *minore*, small ternary
    couplet 2: interior theme, VI, small binary
    couplet 3: interior theme, IV, small ternary

Mozart, Clarinet Trio in E-flat, K. 498, iii:
    couplet 1: subordinate-theme group (no transition)
    couplet 2: interior theme, VI, small ternary
    couplet 3: interior theme, IV, small ternary

Beethoven, Violin Sonata in A Minor, Op. 23, iii:
    couplet 1: transition/subordinate-theme fusion
    couplet 2: interior theme, *maggiore*, incomplete form
    couplet 3: interior theme, VI, small binary

SONATA–RONDO

The majority of rondos in the classical repertoire are written in *sonata–rondo form*. Most of these are by Mozart and Beethoven, with only a small number by Haydn.[21] Because of their complex organization, sonata–rondos are used almost exclusively for fast finale movements, rarely for slow movements.[22] As its label suggests, the sonata–rondo combines features of the five-part rondo (with its regular alternation of refrains and couplets) and the sonata (with its tripartite organization of exposition, development, and recapitulation). The resulting structure, summarized in table 16.2, is perhaps the most complex of the classical forms.

The rondo aspects of sonata–rondo form are fairly obvious. The sonata aspects, however, require additional comment. First, the initial refrain and couplet constitute a sonata exposition, except that this exposition is never repeated, as it is in regular sonata form; the third refrain and couplet constitute a complete recapitulation of the prior exposition. Second, when couplet 2 is organized as a development rather than an interior theme, the overall form is considerably more like a sonata than a rondo. Finally, unlike a regular sonata, the coda is a required element of sonata–rondo, because that section includes the final return of the main theme.

TABLE 16.2 Sonata–rondo form

Rondo Term	Formal Function	Tonal Region
refrain 1 (A)	exposition of main theme	I
couplet 1 (B)	exposition of subordinate-theme complex	V
refrain 2 (A)	first return of main theme	I
couplet 2 (C)	development *or* interior theme	various *or* IV, VI, *minore*
refrain 3 (A)	recapitulation of main theme	I
couplet 3 (B)	recapitulation of subordinate-theme complex	I
refrain 4 (A)	coda (including final return of main theme)	I

EXAMPLE 16.5 Beethoven, Piano Sonata in D, Op. 10/3, iv, 15–26

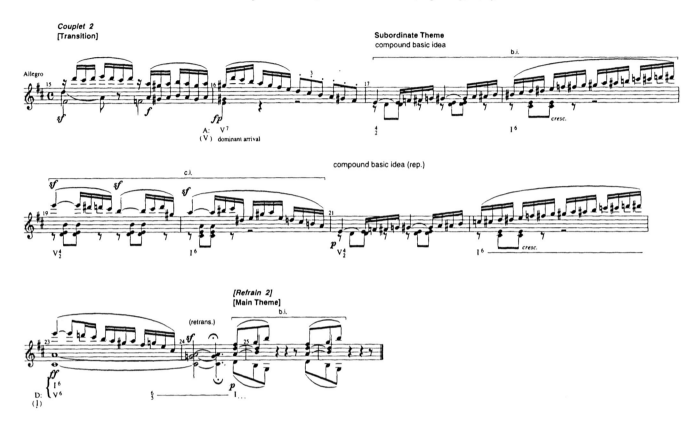

EXAMPLE 16.6 Beethoven, Violin Sonata in D, Op. 12/1, iii, 58–71

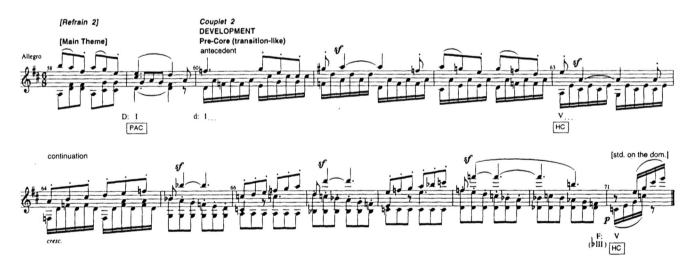

Refrain 1, Exposition of Main Theme

Much of what we observed in connection with the main theme of the five-part rondo holds for the sonata–rondo as well, especially the requirement that the theme close with a perfect authentic cadence. Sonata–rondo forms, however, generally employ a wider variety of main-theme types, although the small ternary and the sixteen-measure period tend to be favored. Frequently, the refrain proper is followed by additional themes, all ending in home-key authentic cadences, thus making up a main-theme group.[23]

Couplet 1, Exposition of Subordinate-Theme Complex

In many sonata–rondos, the initial refrain and couplet 1 together form a regular sonata exposition. The main theme is followed by a transition, usually modulating (but sometimes nonmodulating), and one or more subordinate themes.[24] The closing section of the subordinate theme is always followed by a retransition leading back to the home key for the first return of the rondo refrain. In many cases, this retransition is relatively long and anticipates the basic idea of the main theme.

As in the five-part rondo, the establishment and confirmation of the subordinate key in a sonata–rondo exposition are sometimes significantly weaker than the sharp dramatization that this tonal event usually achieves in a regular sonata. Thus the transition is frequently eliminated or else fused together with the subordinate theme. In addition, the subordinate theme may be relatively short or incomplete in various ways. In a number of rondos by Beethoven, the subordinate theme lacks cadential closure (a strict requirement of sonata form) while the music moves without interruption into the retransition.[25]

EXAMPLE 16.5: The transition ends at measure 16 with a dominant arrival in the new key of A major. The subordinate theme begins in the following measure and consists of a compound basic idea supported by the progression V^6_5–I^6. The phrase begins to be repeated at measure 21, but following the melodic high point at measure 23, I^6 of the subordinate key is converted into a V^6_5 of the home key, which, following the fermata, leads to a return of the rondo refrain. This extremely incomplete subordinate theme consists essentially of a weak initiating function (weak because the prolonged tonic is inverted) followed by a brief retransition. Continuation and cadential functions are eliminated from the form.

Refrain 2, First Return of Main Theme

The return of the refrain after couplet 1 is a conventional signal for rondo form, although at first this return can be heard to mark the repetition of a sonata exposition. Thus it is only when the music begins to depart from the plan laid out in the exposition that the listener can confirm an interpretation of rondo form. In the majority of cases, the refrain returns intact, but abridged and incomplete versions are common also.[26]

Couplet 2, Development or Interior Theme

The second couplet of a sonata–rondo normally takes the form of a development section or an interior theme. In addition, it is possible to identify a deviation that is employed exclusively by Mozart and that I term a *double-region couplet* (because of its being set in both the subdominant and submediant tonal regions).

Development. When the second couplet is organized as a development, it normally contains a transition-like pre-core followed by one or more cores. In place of a core, the composer may substitute a pseudo-core or some other loosely organized thematic unit. In some couplets, the pre-core is omitted, and the development begins directly with a core (or core substitute). The development usually ends with a standing on the dominant of the home key in preparation for the recapitulation of the rondo refrain.

The development can follow on refrain 2 in a number of ways. If the refrain is complete, the development will begin with a unit that functions as a pre-core, one whose organization resembles a transition. That is, the unit opens in the home key and modulates to a new tonal region for the start of the core (or substitute thereof). This transition-like pre-core is usually based on prior ideas, but also possibly on new material. One logical strategy brings back the original transition (from the beginning of couplet 1), which eventually moves to a new tonal region.[27] Another common procedure is for the refrain (or some part of it) to start over again but then lead into new material. In both these techniques, a shift to minor typically signals that the previous exposition will not be repeated and that a new couplet is under way.

EXAMPLE 16.6: The rondo's main theme (see ex. 5.3) reappears intact as refrain 2. The theme begins to be repeated at measure 60, although the immediate shift to minor reveals that we are not hearing the repeat of a sonata exposition but, rather, the second refrain and couplet of a rondo. At measure 66, the music departs from the plan of the refrain and modulates to ♭III, the key in which a core begins (at m. 77, not shown). The unit in measures 60–76 thus functions as a transition-like pre-core.

If the second rondo refrain is incomplete, the development typically begins in one of two ways. First, refrain 2 consists of an antecedent unit; a presumed consequent begins to sound but then departs from the course laid out by

EXAMPLE 16.7 Mozart, Piano Trio in B-flat, K. 502, iii, 86–103

the antecedent in order to become a transition-like pre-core. Second, the refrain fails to achieve any cadential closure and merges instead with transitional material.[28] Sometimes it is difficult to discern a clear dividing line between the end of the refrain and the beginning of the couplet.

EXAMPLE 16.7: The antecedent unit of the refrain closes at measure 87 with a reinterpreted half cadence. The consequent follows the plan of the antecedent until the second half of measure 93, at which point the music develops sequentially the motive of the continuation phrase. The consequent thus becomes a transition-like pre-core ending at measure 99, albeit without a sense of dominant closure. A core begins with the upbeat to the next measure.[29]

A number of sonata–rondo developments by Beethoven contain near their end a false recapitulation, in which material from the rondo refrain reappears first in some other tonal region.[30] Indeed, false recapitulations are more common in rondo movements than in sonata movements. Since a rondo places its dramatic emphasis on the return of the refrain, an initial appearance in the "wrong" key, corrected shortly thereafter in the right key, is a particularly effective device.[31]

Interior theme. The second couplet of sonata–rondo form is often organized as an interior theme.[32] This theme is most likely to reside in the subdominant region but ap-

pears frequently in the submediant or as a *minore*. The formal organization of the interior theme is the same as that described for the five-part rondo, especially the more loosely constructed themes that appear in couplet 2 of that form. Like most couplets containing interior themes, a retransition either follows its closing cadence or emerges out of an incomplete theme. In the sonata–rondo, this retransition can be highly developmental, even to the extent of resembling a core.[33]

Like the five-part rondo, an interior theme in sonata-rondo form typically begins immediately after the close of refrain 2. Sometimes, however, greater continuity between refrain and couplet is created by means of a distinct transition, analogous to a pre-core, to prepare for the beginning of the interior theme proper.[34]

Double-region couplet. In a number of Mozart's sonata-rondos, couplet 2 emphasizes two tonal regions—submediant and subdominant. The phrase-structural organization of the material, however, does not result in two interior themes, as might be suggested by the use of these particular regions. It is difficult to generalize about the organization of such a *double-region couplet* because Mozart employs a wide variety of formal possibilities. Typically, however, each of the two regions is associated with a distinct thematic unit, only one of which may be an interior theme. In some cases, both the units are constructed as simpler main-theme types (sentence, period, or hybrid), which may be more or less tight knit and may even be left incomplete. Most often, the submediant region precedes the subdominant, but the reverse order occurs now and then. The two regions are sometimes linked by a transition, which may range from a short phrase to a lengthy developmental passage.[35]

EXAMPLE 16.8: Refrain 2 closes at measure 56, after which appears material from the transition that opens couplet 1. At measure 61 the music departs from the path taken by the exposition and continues on to the dominant of VI. The first thematic unit of this double-region couplet (beginning at m. 65) is an eight-measure sentence ending with a half cadence at measure 72 in the submediant. A brief transitional passage leads to the subdominant region, where a second sentential unit, much more loosely constructed than the first, begins at measure 76. A promised cadence is evaded at measure 88 and then again two measures later. Indeed, the theme never achieves cadential closure, since measure 90 initiates a retransition leading back to the home-key dominant at measure 102.[36]

Refrain 3, Recapitulation of Main Theme

The return of the rondo's main theme following couplet 2 corresponds to the beginning of the recapitulation in sonata form.[37] At this point, the complete structure of the rondo refrain is usually brought back, sometimes including the entire main-theme group from the exposition. But like any return, an abridged or incomplete version may appear instead.[38]

One standard deviation, adopted frequently by Mozart, eliminates refrain 3 from the form. Since a full sonata-rondo brings four statements of the refrain, omitting one of them does not significantly impair the rondo effect. When refrain 3 is left out, couplet 3 usually begins directly with the subordinate-theme group. In such cases, the end of couplet 2 usually brings material from the transition of couplet 1 to prepare for the recapitulation of the subordinate theme in couplet 3.[39]

Couplet 3, Recapitulation of Subordinate-Theme Complex

Couplet 3 recapitulates the subordinate-theme complex, which in most cases simply follows the norms established for the recapitulation of a regular sonata. Unlike a sonata, however, the subordinate theme (or the final theme of a subordinate-theme group) may not receive authentic cadential closure. In cases in which such closure was lacking in the exposition, the recapitulation usually follows the same course and omits the cadence. But in some cases, a subordinate theme that was closed in the exposition is left open in the recapitulation and then merges into the beginning of the coda.[40]

One interesting deviation in Beethoven occurs when the subordinate-theme complex is not recapitulated in the home key but, instead, in some other tonal region, usually IV.[41] Such a situation is clearly related to the tendency of a sonata recapitulation to emphasize the flat side of the tonal spectrum, and it recalls the type of deviation in which the subordinate theme first begins in the subdominant but then is adjusted into the home key.[42] In the context of the sonata–rondo, a subdominant recapitulation also relates to the notion that a "pure" rondo couplet would reside in a tonal region contrasting with that of the refrain.

Refrain 4, Coda and Final Return of Main Theme

Following the norms of rondo forms in general, the last couplet of a sonata–rondo leads to a final restatement of the refrain. In addition, sonata–rondos include a coda that appears after the recapitulation of the subordinate-theme complex.[43] The relation of the final refrain to the coda is somewhat problematic, with most theorists tending to see the coda as a separate section following the final refrain.[44] To be sure, this position is reasonable in those many cases in which refrain 4 appears directly after the closing section of the recapitulation. But sometimes the recapitulation leads into music that is already best understood as belonging to a coda, and the rondo refrain returns only somewhat later.[45] It would seem, then, that there is no consistent relation between the beginning of the coda and the beginning of the final refrain. For that reason, it is perhaps best to say that the former embraces the latter. In other words, the coda of a sonata–rondo can be said to start at the same place as it does in a regular sonata, namely, at that point where the music of the recapitulation stops corresponding to the exposition. In this view, the rondo refrain always appears somewhere in the coda, often at its very beginning, but sometimes only after the coda is under way.

Like all subsequent appearances of the rondo refrain, the final restatement may be complete but may also be abridged or remain incomplete. In a number of cases, the basic structure of the refrain fails to appear at all, and only its initial motives are used.[46] This procedure represents a deviation from the norm comparable to the elimination of refrain 3 already discussed. In fact, if Mozart retains refrain 3 in his sonata–rondo forms, then he usually eliminates refrain 4, although its opening motives may pervade the texture of the coda.[47]

Nine-Part Sonata–Rondo

Just as the five-part rondo can be expanded into a seven-part rondo through an additional refrain and couplet, so too can the sonata–rondo be expanded into a *nine-part sonata–rondo* in the same way. At least three examples in the classical repertoire, all by Mozart, feature this elaborate for-

EXAMPLE 16.8 Mozart, Piano Sonata in B-flat, K. 333/315c, iii, 55–102

mal design.[48] In all three cases, the extra refrain and couplet are inserted between couplet 2 and the recapitulation. And in each of these nine-part rondos, both couplet 2 and the added couplet are organized as interior themes.

Mozart's Rondo for Piano in F, K. 494 (which was eventually published as the last movement of the Piano Sonata in F, K. 533), is a particularly impressive example. Couplet 1 is a subordinate theme (without a transition); couplet 2 contains a double-region couplet (VI followed by IV); and the added couplet before the recapitulation is a *minore*. Thus all three of the standard tonal regions used for interior themes are explored in this nine-part sonata–rondo. The last couplet recapitulates the subordinate theme, and, as a coup de grâce, Mozart interpolates an elaborate, written-out cadenza before the close of that couplet.[49] With the exception of a true development, this movement features all the standard options for couplets in the classical rondo.

17

Concerto Form

Throughout the eighteenth century, the concerto stood alongside opera (and, later in the century, the symphony) as one of the principal "public" genres of musical composition. Whereas the high baroque cultivated various kinds of concertos, including the concerto grosso, ripieno concerto, double concerto, and solo concerto, the high classical period saw the solo concerto—for single instrument and orchestra—emerge as the preeminent concerto type. A defining feature of this classical concerto is its employment of a formal scheme derived from the baroque "ritornello form" and strongly infused with elements of the sonata. This *concerto form* is used in the first movement of all classical concertos.[1] The form is sometimes found in slow movements, but rarely in finales.[2]

Unlike the private instrumental genres (such as the solo sonata and the quartet) and the public symphony, whose participating forces are roughly equal, the classical concerto pits a single instrumentalist against a full orchestra. Because of this inherent inequality, ways must be found to make certain that the soloist can compete effectively against the larger forces of the orchestra while not allowing the latter to be so subordinate that it becomes a mere accompaniment. Throughout the eighteenth century, various compositional devices were developed for realizing these aesthetic goals. Some of the techniques used to highlight the solo include the following: assigning it musical ideas not previously sounded by the orchestra, permitting the solo part to have the principal modulatory action in the movement, and throwing special light on the solo by means of an unaccompanied cadenza interpolated into the form. To ensure that the orchestra is not reduced to an exclusively accompanimental role, the orchestra alone provides a textural "frame" for the opening and closing of the movement. In addition, the orchestra is permitted to appear by itself at least one other time in order to assert its own identity in relation to the solo part.[3]

Early in the eighteenth century, these compositional devices were embraced in *ritornello form*, in which passages performed by the full orchestra, each termed a "ritornello" (little return), alternate with passages played by the solo instrument. A relatively long "opening ritornello" brings the primary melodic–motivic content of the movement, and subsequent ritornellos typically transpose parts of this opening into related tonal regions. A "closing ritornello" brings back the content and structure of the opening ritornello to create a frame for the movement as a whole.

Later in the century, ritornello form was transformed into concerto form through the incorporation of classical formal functions, especially those associated with the sonata. Indeed, concerto form has often been seen as derivative of the latter and has thus been described as containing three parts—exposition, development, recapitulation—in which the first part is preceded by an orchestral introduction (not to be confused with a slow introduction). The orchestral introduction itself resembles the exposition of a sonata in that it contains a distinct main theme, transition, and subordinate-theme group. Unlike a sonata exposition, however, the introduction largely resides in the home key. When the orchestral introduction is followed by a genuine exposition, a kind of "double exposition" is created, one that corresponds to the repeated exposition of sonata form.

This view of the concerto *cum* sonata has its attractions but is misleading in a number of respects. In particular, it ignores the historical development of the classical concerto out of sources distinct from those of the sonata. Moreover, it fails to take into account a number of compositional procedures that clearly are vestiges of the older ritornello form.[4] Thus an alternative view of concerto form sees it as composed of six principal sections: (1) an opening ritornello for orchestra alone, (2) a solo section (with orchestral accompaniment) that functions like a sonata exposition by modulating from the home to the subordinate key, (3) a subordinate-key ritornello for orchestra that reinforces the modulation, (4) a solo section functioning as a sonata development, (5) a solo section functioning as a sonata recapitulation, and (6) a closing ritornello for orchestra (usually interrupted by a solo cadenza) that completes the structural frame.[5] From this perspective, concerto is viewed as an independent form, one that is a variant of neither the baroque ritornello form nor the classical sonata form but one that incorporates form-functional elements associated with both.

EXAMPLE 17.1 Mozart, Piano Concerto in E-flat, K. 482, i, 50–76

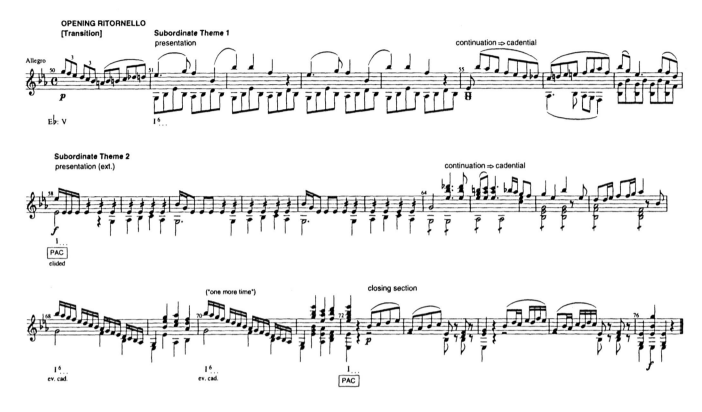

OPENING RITORNELLO

The *opening ritornello*, played by the orchestra alone,[6] initiates the textural frame for the concerto and brings much, but rarely all, the fundamental melodic–motivic material of the movement. For the orchestra to assume an independent identity in relation to the solo and at the same time to build up expectations for the solo's entrance, the opening ritornello is often relatively long and filled with a variety of musical ideas. In fact, the ritornello distributes these ideas as discrete thematic units in a way that strongly suggests the interthematic functions of a sonata exposition.

The opening ritornello begins with a tight-knit main theme closing with a perfect authentic cadence.[7] The sixteen-measure sentence is particularly favored for a concerto main theme (see chap. 5, n. 26), but other conventional types (and the occasional nonconventional theme) are found there as well. The main theme is followed by a more loosely organized thematic region ending with a home-key half cadence, in other words, a unit that resembles a nonmodulating transition. Unlike sonata expositions, in which the transition can begin like the main theme, the transition of a concerto ritornello almost always begins with new material.[8] The next thematic unit continues to reside in the home key but, because of its placement following a transition, gives the impression of being a subordinate theme. Indeed, this theme effects a modest degree of formal loosen-

ing in relation to the main theme. Additional subordinate themes may follow, and the ritornello eventually ends with a closing section made up of codettas.

If the opening ritornello strongly resembles a sonata-form exposition, it lacks one of its principal characteristics—a genuine tonal conflict between home and subordinate keys. In most cases, the ritornello remains entirely in the home key. In this way, the solo part can be given the opportunity to produce one of the major tonal events of the work, namely, the establishment of the subordinate key. If the orchestra alone does not depart from the home key, then strong expectations are generated for the solo to accomplish this task. Occasionally the unit following the ritornello's transition begins in the subordinate key but then returns, usually rather quickly, to the home key without cadencing in the new key.[9] Only seldom does a modulating transition lead to a theme that confirms the subordinate key.[10]

The opening ritornello differs from a regular sonata exposition not only in tonality but also in phrase structure. More specifically, the "subordinate theme" (or themes) is generally more tight knit than would ordinarily be expected in a sonata exposition of a comparable orchestral movement, such as a symphony or overture. Formal loosening is kept to a minimum for a number of reasons. First, the home key, in which the subordinate theme resides, does not require any particular emphasis, especially of the cadential kind typically used to consolidate a subordinate key. Second, long extensions of continuation function usually call for sequential treatment, whose developmental potential might undermine the solo part as the bearer of prominent harmonic activity in the movement. Third, major cadential expansions normally bring in material of a virtuosic character, best reserved for the solo part.

EXAMPLE 17.1: The transition of this opening ritornello ends on dominant of the home key, after which a new thematic unit, the first of two subordinate themes, begins at measure 51. A simple presentation leads to a continuation⇒cadential phrase to close this tight-knit theme. A second subordinate theme (mm. 58–72) is more extensive, due to the evaded cadences in measures 68 and 70. Yet even this theme, together with the first, would unlikely be found as the complete subordinate-theme group in a symphonic sonata-form exposition, especially with the lack of any substantial cadential expansion.

Up to this point, we have considered the opening ritornello largely in terms of its allowing the orchestra to express its own material while building strong expectations for the entrance of the solo. An additional role is the ritornello's forging of an initial association between the various musical ideas and their form-functional expression. Since the subsequent sections of the concerto rarely bring back the content of the opening ritornello in the same order, it is always of analytical interest to observe how ritornello ideas are linked to varying formal units throughout the rest of the movement. For example, the main-theme material of the ritornello frequently functions in the solo exposition to begin the transition. Likewise, an idea first presented as a subordinate theme may return only in the development. To be sure, the creation of multiple associations of a given idea with differing formal contexts is a compositional technique found throughout all classical forms. But it is especially prominent in concerto form, in which each of the five subsequent sections has the possibility of granting a new formal interpretation to material originally presented in the opening ritornello.

SOLO EXPOSITION

The entrance of the solo initiates the second major section of concerto form. This section functions in essentially the same way as a sonata exposition does and contains the standard interthematic functions of main theme, transition, and subordinate-theme group (a single subordinate theme is uncommon).[11] Unlike a sonata exposition, however, the solo exposition does not conclude with a closing section but ends instead with the final perfect authentic cadence of the subordinate-theme group. An orchestral ritornello then follows as the formal analogue of a closing section.

The solo exposition rarely represents a repetition of the opening ritornello, as the "double-exposition" model of concerto form suggests. Rather, this section almost always contains new material for the solo part to present on its own.[12] Yet the solo exposition brings back a considerable amount of music presented earlier, thus allowing the composer to vary the ideas or the formal context in which they are situated. Consequently, the solo exposition can already represent a "development" of material previously heard. Indeed, a solo exposition often contains greater sequential activity than that ordinarily found in a regular sonata exposition.[13]

After the relatively long buildup created by the opening ritornello, the entrance of the soloist is a dramatic event. Most often, the musical motion comes to a complete stop at the end of the opening ritornello, thus setting off the solo entrance by a moment of silence. But in some concertos, the solo appears to be overanxious and enters while the orchestra is still in the process of closing the ritornello.[14]

Main Theme

The first unit of the solo exposition usually functions as a main theme. Frequently, this *solo main theme* brings back material of the *ritornello main theme* in the same formal plan.[15] Sometimes, though, the phrase structure is altered, usually by means of loosening devices (such as a cadential extension) or the addition of new material.[16] The ritornello main theme may also be subjected to any number of variation procedures, which, by imbuing it with greater virtuosic character, allows the solo to appropriate the theme for itself.

On occasion, the solo exposition begins with an entirely new theme. This *alternative main theme* tends to appear when the ritornello main theme is highly orchestral in character and not likely to be rendered idiomatically by the soloist. For example, the use of loud, fanfare-like figures for the full orchestra usually are not effective on the piano.[17] In addition, orchestral beginnings that feature a polyphonic texture highlighting different sonorities are not likely to create a similar impression by the homogeneous sound of the solo instrument.[18]

EXAMPLE 17.2: The intensely brooding orchestral opening is shown in measures 1–4. (The same texture continues for another eleven measures, creating a large crescendo.) An alternative main theme, introduced at the beginning of the solo exposition (m. 77), is considerably more pianistic and lyrical in character. Indeed, Mozart never attempts to imitate the texture of the orchestral opening in the piano part at any later point in the movement.

Transition

The choice of material to begin the solo transition seems to be guided, in most cases, by two general principles: (1) the solo section should not reproduce the same succession of

EXAMPLE 17.2 Mozart, Piano Concerto in D Minor, K. 466, i, 1-4, 77-85

EXAMPLE 17.3 Mozart, Piano Concerto in E-flat, K. 482, i, 170-85

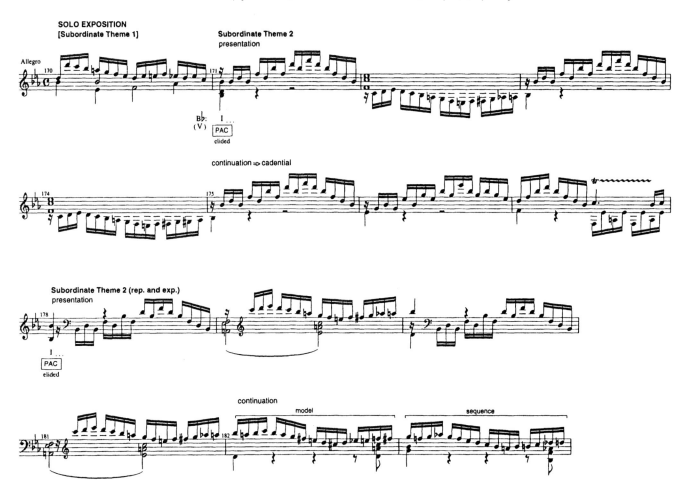

ideas found in the ritornello from the main theme to the transition, and (2) the use of an alternative main theme prompts the immediate reappearance of material from the ritornello main theme. A variety of scenarios can be explained by one or both of these principles:

1. If the solo main theme is based on the ritornello main theme, the solo transition will begin with new material. This scheme, following principle 1, appears in approximately one-half of Mozart's mature concertos.
2. If an alternative main theme is used in the solo section, an immediately following transition will be based on the ritornello main theme, as proposed in principle 2.[19]
3. If, following an alternative main theme, the ritornello main theme is used as a "second" theme making up a main-theme group (according to principle 2), the solo transition will be based on new material (according to principle 1).[20]
4. If the solo exposition brings an alternative main theme, the solo transition can be based on the ritornello transition, since the succession of ideas in the solo exposition will be different from that in the opening ritornello (principle 1).[21]

Although most concerto-form movements follow these principles, a significant few bring a solo main theme and transition that largely restate those of the opening ritornello (with the possibility of structural changes and ornamental variations).[22]

Subordinate-Theme Group

As in a regular sonata exposition, the subordinate-theme group of the solo exposition is responsible for expressing and confirming the subordinate key. The group contains at least two themes (each ending with a perfect authentic cadence), but a group of three is extremely common.[23] One or more of the themes is generally based on ideas from the opening ritornello, but new material is almost always added. In fact, the entire subordinate-theme group can be unrelated to the ritornello.[24]

When the solo subordinate theme draws on material from the opening ritornello, that material typically comes from the ritornello's subordinate-theme group. But it may also derive from the ritornello main theme or, especially, the transition. After all, the latter is often replaced by a new solo transition, and thus ideas from the ritornello transition are free to reappear in the context of the solo subordinate-theme group.

Because each concerto finds its own logical and appropriate way of distributing its material, it is difficult to formulate principles for how various ideas will appear in the subordinate-theme group. One general tendency, however,

is that in the majority of concertos, the first subordinate theme is entirely new, most likely in order to aid the solo part in projecting its own melodic–motivic profile.[25] In those cases, the first ritornello subordinate theme usually reappears in the solo exposition, as either the second subordinate theme or the second part of a two-part subordinate theme. This latter option is particularly effective, since both the new material and the earlier ritornello theme can be preceded by a standing on the dominant—the one ending the solo transition and the one following the internal half cadence.

EXAMPLE 8.17 (see p. 118): Part 1 of the first subordinate theme (mm. 74–80) consists of ideas not previously heard. Part 2, beginning at measure 81, brings back material from the subordinate theme of the opening ritornello. Thus the solo part has the opportunity not only to sound its own subordinate theme but also to bring into the new key the subordinate theme originally sounded by the orchestra in the home key.[26]

As already discussed, the subordinate-theme group of the opening ritornello fails to confirm the subordinate key and also tends to remain relatively tight knit. The solo subordinate-theme group, on the contrary, is largely responsible for substantially loosening the form. Most often, one of the themes prominently extends continuation function by means of harmonic sequence, and the cadential areas, especially in the final theme, are greatly expanded. In fact, enormous expanded cadential progressions are a hallmark of the concerto and an element of its style that permeated other genres of the period.[27] The rhythmic and dynamic climax of the exposition is normally reached during the expansion of the final cadential dominant, in which the shortest durational values culminate in the "cadential trill," the conventional sign for the close of the solo exposition.[28] In addition to their normal roles in loosening the structure, the use of extended sequences and expanded cadential progressions opens up considerable structural space for the soloist to display his or her virtuosic abilities. These places in the form are usually filled with figurational passage-work that explores the extreme ranges of the instrument and shows off the performer's technique.

The final subordinate theme is often written in a "bravura" style featuring continuous sixteenth notes. Typically, this *bravura theme* is first presented in a relatively compressed form. The effect of cutting short such hustle and bustle raises expectations that more of the theme will have to appear. And indeed, the theme is then repeated and significantly expanded in accord with the nature of its material.

EXAMPLE 17.3: The second subordinate theme begins at measure 171 with sixteenth-note arpeggiations (which continue the sixteenth-note runs found at the end of the previous subordinate theme). This bravura theme takes the form of a simple eight-measure sentence, which, in light of the energy accumulated by

EXAMPLE 17.4 Haydn, Trumpet Concerto in E-flat, Hob. VIIe:1, i, 81–94

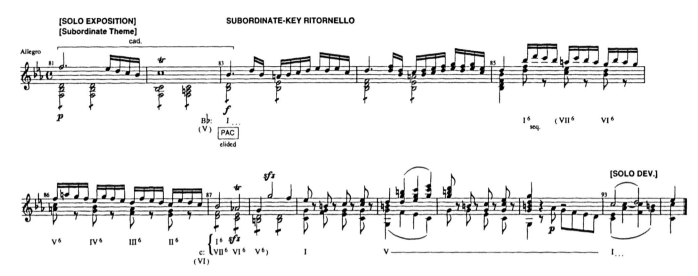

the rhythmic motion, seems all too short. Therefore the theme is repeated (m. 178) and expanded by means of model–sequence technique and a cadential progression, whose dominant is stretched to ten measures (not shown in the example).[29]

SUBORDINATE-KEY RITORNELLO

In a sonata-form exposition, the final perfect authentic cadence is followed by a closing section, in which a recessive dynamic frequently helps dissipate the energy accumulated in reaching the cadential goal. At the corresponding place in concerto form, the final cadence is invariably followed by a section for orchestra alone, with the solo remaining silent until the beginning of the development. This orchestral passage is clearly the formal analogue of a closing section, but in the majority of cases it is not organized as a series of codettas. Moreover, the dynamic intensity reached by the solo's climax is seldom, if ever, lessened during this section. Thus even though this passage is located where a closing section might be expected, it displays few characteristics of that formal function.

In a baroque concerto, a similarly placed orchestral passage serves as an internal ritornello, which would reside in a new key and bring back many of the ideas of the opening ritornello, especially those from the beginning of the work. Invoking the notion of an orchestral ritornello following the solo exposition seems to be appropriate for the classical concerto as well. This *subordinate-key ritornello*, as it can be termed, always begins in the new key and consists of material taken from the opening ritornello, although unlike the baroque concerto, the ideas are rarely drawn from the main theme.[30]

The subordinate-key ritornello fulfills a variety of func-

tions. First, it gives the orchestra another opportunity for sounding its "own" music, now in the context of the subordinate key. As a result, the orchestra is allowed to participate in the tonal conflict lying at the heart of the form, if not as an equal partner, then at least as more than a mere accompaniment. Second, the subordinate-key ritornello frequently brings back ideas from the opening ritornello that were eliminated from the solo exposition. For example, the "second subordinate theme" (including the closing section) from the opening ritornello of example 17.1, measures 58–76, is eliminated from the solo exposition (and replaced by the bravura theme shown in example 17.3). This material then reappears to make up the entire subordinate-key ritornello, transposed, of course, into the new key.

A third function of this ritornello is to sustain, and often to intensify, the dynamic level attained by the solo. After all, a climax created by a single instrument, no matter how forceful, can always be superseded by the full orchestral mass.[31] Finally, the subordinate-key ritornello offers the solo a chance to rest following the virtuosic workout of the exposition and to reappear as a fresh sonority at the beginning of the development section.

To fulfill its dynamic function of sustaining, if not surpassing, the solo's climax, the subordinate-key ritornello usually contains forte material of powerful rhythmic vitality and forward drive; soft, lyrical, and tentative gestures are not found in this ritornello, at least not at its beginning.[32] A favorite passage to reappear at the start of the subordinate-key ritornello is the one beginning the transition in the opening ritornello, which typically projects a vigorous, brilliant style. As already pointed out, this material is often eliminated in the solo exposition for a variety of reasons.[33]

The subordinate-key ritornello is usually structured as a complete thematic unit ending with a perfect authentic cadence in the subordinate key. Its form is often nonconventional, yet it stays rather tight knit and compressed in relation to the final subordinate theme of the solo exposition. A brief closing section may follow the final cadence of the ritornello. In some cases, this closing section veers off and modulates to a new tonal region for the beginning of the development.[34] At other times, the ritornello itself fails to close cadentially before heading off to the development.

EXAMPLE 17.4: The subordinate-key ritornello elides with the end of the cadential trill closing the solo exposition (m. 83). The content of this ritornello is taken from the subordinate theme of the opening ritornello, material that is deleted in the solo exposition in order to give the trumpet part its own subordinate theme (based on the main theme, as is typical with Haydn). Following the descending-stepwise sequence in measures 85–86, the arrival on I^6 in measure 87 might very well signal the beginning of a cadential progression to close the ritornello in the subordinate key. The cadence does not materialize, however, because the sequence is continued further in order to modulate to the development key of C minor (HK: VI). Consequently, the subordinate-key ritornello does not receive cadential closure.[35]

SOLO DEVELOPMENT

The formal organization of a concerto development is, for all intents and purposes, the same as that of sonata form. Only two stylistic and textural features typical of the concerto need be mentioned here. First, since the solo development of concerto form corresponds to the "second solo" of ritornello form, this section usually begins with a reappearance of the solo part, which was silent during the subordinate-key ritornello. Second, the development of a concerto tends to be less a working-out of prominent motivic material from the exposition than a rhapsodic improvisation, often employing conventional passage-work (scales, arpeggiations, and the like).[36] Indeed, the *motivische Arbeit* typical of a symphony by Haydn or Beethoven would likely employ polyphonic instrumental textures that might direct attention more to the orchestra than to the solo. Conversely, the use of figurational patterns fosters a greater display of virtuosity from the soloist while the orchestra remains largely in the background.

SOLO RECAPITULATION

The recapitulation of concerto form fulfills some of the same basic functions as that of a sonata recapitulation, namely, to project a large-scale *return* and to resolve the dramatic conflict of tonalities created by the exposition (and prolonged by the development). Thus, from the perspective of sonata form, one would expect that the organization of a concerto recapitulation would be modeled largely on that of the solo exposition, except, of course, for the necessary adjustments of tonality (as well as eliminating

redundancies, adding a secondary development, etc.). And to be sure, a number of concerto movements follow this course.[37]

But to the extent that a concerto brings two different "expositions"—here, the double-exposition model of concerto form comes more into its own—the recapitulation has an additional function: elements of both the opening ritornello and the solo exposition must somehow be "recapitulated" in a single section of the movement. Sometimes this makes the solo recapitulation, especially at its start, resemble more the opening ritornello than the solo exposition.[38] More often, however, the recapitulation is organized differently from either of the earlier "expositions." In particular, the recapitulation is likely to reintroduce ideas from the opening ritornello that were not used in the solo exposition and that find no place in the subsequent subordinate-key ritornello or development section. As a result, the formal placement of various passages as defined by each of the expositions is significantly altered.

Main Theme

In most cases, the recapitulation begins with main-theme material from the opening ritornello, since the sense of large-scale return is most effectively projected when music from the very beginning of the movement is reintroduced.[39] As in a sonata recapitulation, the form of the theme may be altered and even left unclosed, in which case the main-theme and transition functions may fuse (see ex. 11.8).

If the solo exposition has introduced an alternative main theme, this new theme will seldom be used to begin the recapitulation.[40] More often, the theme is used elsewhere in the movement, such as at the start of the development section (thus making it easier for the composer to dispense with it at the beginning of the recapitulation)[41] or following the original main theme in the recapitulation to make a theme group.[42] In some cases, the alternative main theme never appears again.[43]

Transition

Since the transition of the solo exposition often differs from that of the opening ritornello, usually one or the other is chosen for the recapitulation, although in at least one case both are used.[44] Sometimes a completely new transition is written instead.[45]

Subordinate-Theme Group

The subordinate-theme group usually offers several opportunities for altering the structure of the recapitulation in relation to the earlier expositions. In most concertos, the solo exposition introduces one, if not two, new subordinate themes and thus does not use one or more of those from

EXAMPLE 17.5 Mozart, Piano Concerto in E-flat, K. 482, i, 128–31, 152–54, 312–15, 328–30

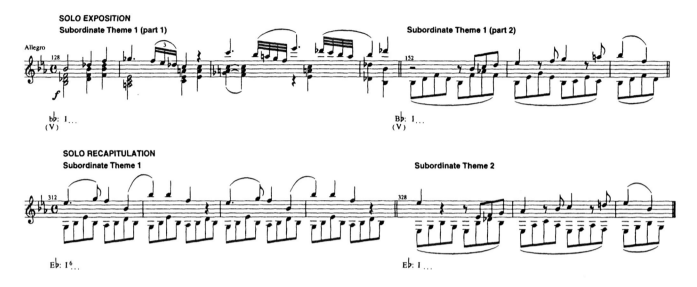

EXAMPLE 17.6 Mozart, Piano Concerto in E-flat, K. 482, i, 357–67

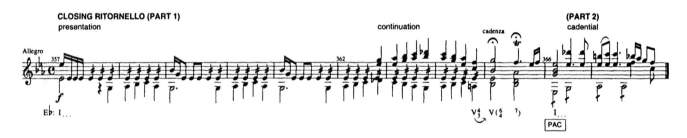

the opening ritornello. Consequently, the recapitulation frequently incorporates into its subordinate-theme group some material from the opening ritornello that is not found in the solo exposition.

The first subordinate theme from the opening ritornello is, for a number of reasons, especially likely to be brought back for the first time in the recapitulation. This theme is often eliminated from the solo exposition so as to allow the solo to have its own, new subordinate theme. Moreover, the ritornello's first subordinate theme tends to be soft and lyrical in character and thus is generally not appropriate for use in the subordinate-key ritornello. Consequently, this theme cries out to reappear and be performed by the solo at some point in the recapitulation. And so it may come back in the recapitulation (1) in its original position at the beginning of the subordinate-theme group,[46] (2) immediately after the opening of the first solo subordinate theme,[47] or (3) at the start of a second subordinate theme.[48] It *does not normally return later than this*, because a lyrical theme is unlikely to help build the climax needed for the end of the recapitulation.

EXAMPLE 17.5: The first subordinate theme in the opening ritornello (see ex. 17.1) begins at measure 51 with a quiet and peaceful melody. This theme is then eliminated in the solo exposition, whose subordinate-theme group begins at measure 128 with a bold, dramatic shift to the minor mode. Following an internal half cadence and standing on the dominant, a new lyrical melody for the solo initiates the second part of this theme (m. 153).

In the recapitulation, the ritornello's first subordinate theme returns to begin the subordinate-theme group and is played at first by the solo piano (m. 312). The lyrical theme from the solo exposition (m. 153) then returns at measure 328 to initiate a second subordinate theme.

CLOSING RITORNELLO

The end of the solo recapitulation is normally marked by a "cadential trill" in the solo part and a subsequent perfect authentic cadence. The *closing ritornello*, performed by the orchestra alone (except for the interrupting cadenza) elides with this cadence to complete the textural frame initiated by the opening ritornello.

Like the subordinate-key ritornello, the closing ritornello is the formal analogue of a closing section in a sonata recapitulation. In addition, the closing ritornello fulfills some of the same functions as that of the earlier subordinate-key ritornello: it gives the orchestra a final opportunity for sounding its own music, now, of course, fully rooted in the home key; it sustains or intensifies the dynamic climax attained by the solo at the end of the recapitulation; and it provides one last chance to bring back ideas from the opening ritornello that found no place in the other sections of the movement.

In most of Mozart's concertos, and all of Beethoven's, the closing ritornello brings a cadenza for the solo.[49] (Haydn follows the mid-eighteenth-century convention of having the cadenza mark the end of the recapitulation, after which comes the closing ritornello.) Thus the closing ritornello divides itself into a *first part* before the cadenza and a *second part* after the cadenza.[50] The first part closes with a cadential progression leading to a six–four embellishment of the dominant. The cadenza brings a large-scale prolongation of this dominant and eventually completes the cadential progression.[51] The second part always ends with a closing section, usually the same one as that of the opening ritornello.

EXAMPLE 17.6: The closing ritornello beginning at measure 357 is drawn directly from the second subordinate theme of the opening ritornello (see ex. 17.1, mm. 58–76), just like the earlier subordinate-key ritornello. Here, however, the opening presentation (mm. 357–62) is followed by a new continuation leading to the cadential six–four. Following the cadenza, the rest of the opening ritornello's subordinate theme returns. The movement concludes with the same closing section used to end the earlier ritornellos.

Inasmuch as the closing ritornello follows the end of the recapitulation, we might think that it functions as the coda of the movement. For a number of reasons, however, this ritornello should not be confused with a genuine coda. First, the ritornello generally brings back material in much the same way that it appeared earlier in the work, whereas a coda almost always sets earlier ideas in a fresh formal context. Moreover, a closing ritornello does not normally feature loosening devices typical of a coda, such as sequential extensions and cadential expansions. And whereas most codas refer to main-theme ideas for purposes of formal circularity, a closing ritornello rarely contains material from the main theme, preferring instead to create its sense of formal frame through matching closing sections, in the sense of a rhyme. Finally, the notion that a closing ritornello is not a coda is confirmed when we encounter a genuine coda at the end of the first movement of Beethoven's *Emperor* Concerto and thus observe how unlike it is from a regular closing ritornello.

GLOSSARY OF TERMS

abandoned cadence The failure to realize an implied authentic cadence by eliminating the cadential dominant in root position or by inverting that harmony before *its resolution.*

abridged refrain In rondo form, a restatement of the refrain that consists of the A or A' section of an original small ternary (compare **incomplete refrain**).

accompanimental overlap The simultaneous appearance of the cadential arrival of one thematic unit with a change in the accompanimental pattern of the next unit, whose structural beginning, as defined by its initial downbeat, occurs in the following measure (compare **elision**).

adjustment In a recapitulation, altering material that originally appeared in a subordinate key in such a way as to remain entirely in the home key.

alternative main theme In concerto form, a new main theme appearing at the start of the solo exposition.

antecedent An initiating intrathematic function consisting of a unit that closes with a weak cadence, thus implying a repetition (a consequent) to bring stronger cadential closure.

antecedent phrase The first phrase of an eight-measure period, containing a basic idea followed by a contrasting idea, which leads to a weak cadence.

authentic cadence A cadential arrival articulated by the final tonic of an authentic cadential progression.

authentic cadential progression A cadential progression whose complete form brings, in order, the harmonic functions of tonic (usually in first inversion), pre-dominant, dominant (in root position), and tonic (in root position).

basic idea An initiating function consisting of a two-measure idea that usually contains several melodic or rhythmic motives constituting the primary material of a theme.

binary minuet A large-scale bipartite form modeled largely on the small binary theme-type.

bravura theme In concerto form, a solo subordinate theme featuring continuous rhythmic activity in sixteenth notes.

cadential A concluding intrathematic function that produces the requisite conditions for thematic closure. It is supported exclusively by one or more cadential progressions.

cadential arrival A moment in time marking the structural end of a theme or themelike unit.

cadential idea A concluding function consisting of a two-measure (or shorter) unit, supported exclusively by a cadential progression, that effects (or implies) a cadence.

cadential phrase A phrase supported exclusively by an expanded

cadential progression. It does not usually exhibit continuational characteristics.

cadential progression A progression that confirms a tonality by bringing its fundamental harmonic functions.

characteristic material Melodic and rhythmic configurations used to define a theme as unique (compare **conventional material**).

closing ritornello The final section of concerto form. It fulfills a similar function as the subordinate-key ritornello, except that it resides entirely in the home key and is usually interrupted by a solo cadenza.

closing section A postcadential intrathematic function following a perfect authentic cadence. It consists of a group of codettas, often featuring fragmentation and a recessive dynamic.

coda A large-scale framing function that follows on a recapitulation. It contains one or more coda themes to reinforce further the home key and to serve various compensatory functions.

coda theme In a coda, a theme that closes with a home-key perfect authentic cadence. It usually features loosening devices typical of a subordinate theme.

codetta A postcadential function following a perfect authentic cadence and ranging in length from a single chord to a four-measure phrase. It is supported by a tonic prolongational (occasionally a cadential) progression (compare **closing section**).

compensatory function In a coda, the function acquired by a compositional procedure or event that compensates for procedures or events not occurring in earlier sections. It may serve to recall main theme ideas, restore material deleted from the recapitulation, reference material from the development, shape a new dynamic curve, or realize unrealized implications.

complete cadential progression A cadential progression that contains all the constituent harmonic functions (compare **incomplete cadential progression**).

complete pre-core A pre-core that contains a full complement of initiating, medial, and concluding intrathematic functions (compare **incomplete pre-core**).

compound basic idea An initiating intrathematic function. It is a four-measure phrase consisting of a basic idea followed by a contrasting idea, which does not lead to cadential closure. It usually is supported by a tonic prolongational progression.

compound theme A more complex version of the simple eight-measure period or sentence (rarely, a hybrid). It is normatively sixteen measures in length.

compression An internal shortening of the constituent members of a formal function.

concerto   A full-movement form containing six sections: opening ritornello, solo exposition, subordinate-key ritornello, solo development, solo recapitulation, and closing ritornello.

concluding function   Any number of functions at various hierarchical levels that express the temporal quality of "ending" (compare **initiating function; medial function**).

consequent   A concluding intrathematic function that repeats a prior antecedent but ends with stronger cadential closure.

consequent phrase   The second phrase of the eight-measure period. It restates the basic idea from the antecedent, followed by a contrasting (or cadential) idea, leading to strong cadential closure (usually a perfect authentic cadence).

continuation   A medial intrathematic function that destabilizes the prevailing formal context by means of fragmentation, harmonic acceleration, faster surface rhythm, and harmonic sequence.

continuation phrase   The second phrase of the sentence. It fuses continuation and cadential functions.

continuation⇒cadential phrase   A phrase supported exclusively by an expanded cadential progression. It fuses continuation and cadential functions.

contrasting idea   A concluding function consisting of a two-measure unit that follows and contrasts with (i.e., is not a repetition of) a basic idea.

contrasting middle (B section)   A medial intrathematic function that loosens the prevailing formal organization, emphasizes the home-key dominant, and closes with a half cadence (or dominant arrival). The second unit of the small ternary form.

conventional material   Melodic and rhythmic configurations widely used in the style and thus potentially interchangeable from piece to piece (compare **characteristic material**).

core   A themelike unit of a development consisting of a relatively large model (4–8 mm.), one or more sequential repetitions, fragmentation, a concluding half cadence (or dominant arrival), and a postcadential standing on the dominant.

core substitute   A themelike unit standing in place of a regular core in a development. It may be a pseudo-core or be organized like a transition or (modulating) subordinate theme.

couplet   In rondo form, a large-scale section situated between, and contrasting with, statements of the refrain.

da capo   The third part of the minuet/trio form, bringing a return of the minuet proper.

deceptive cadence   The failure to realize an implied authentic cadence by replacing the final tonic with another harmony (usually VI, but possibly I⁶), which nonetheless represents the end of the prevailing cadential progression.

deceptive cadential progression   A variant of the authentic cadential progression in which the final tonic is replaced by a related harmony (usually VI).

development   A large-scale medial function standing between an exposition and a recapitulation. It creates the loosest formal expression in the movement, and it may contain a pre-core, one or more cores (or core substitutes), and a retransition.

development key   A tonal region (beside the home or subordinate keys) that is confirmed, usually in a development section, by some cadential function, though not necessarily by an actual cadence: in major-mode movements, VI, III, and II; in minor-mode ones, IV and V.

dominant arrival   A noncadential articulation of formal closure marked by the appearance of a dominant harmony near the end of a themelike unit (especially a contrasting middle, transition, retransition, or development) (compare **premature dominant arrival; half cadence**).

dominant function   Various harmonies whose primary role is to progress to tonic. All dominant functioning harmonies contain the leading-tone.

dominant version   A unit (typically a basic idea) whose initial harmonic support is dominant (compare **tonic version**).

double-region couplet   In Mozart's rondo forms, a couplet that contains thematic units residing in both the subdominant and submediant regions.

dynamic curve   A particular pattern of progressive and recessive dynamics.

early authentic cadence   In minuet form, the appearance of a home-key authentic cadence before the end of the exposition (A section).

elided cadence   A cadential arrival that simultaneously marks the beginning of the next unit.

elision   A moment of time that simultaneously marks the end of one unit and the beginning of the next (compare **accompanimental overlap**).

end   An articulation of formal closure (compare **stop**).

evaded cadence   The failure of an implied authentic cadence to reach its goal harmony. The event appearing in place of the final tonic groups with the subsequent unit and (usually) represents the beginning of a new cadential progression.

exact repetition   A unit (usually a basic idea) immediately restated in the same harmonic context (although the melody may be altered or transposed to different scale-degrees).

expanded cadential progression   An expansion of the cadential progression to the extent of supporting a complete phrase (of at least four measures) or group of phrases.

expansion   An internal lengthening of the constituent members of a formal function (compare **extension**).

exposition (A section)   An initiating intrathematic function consisting of a complete thematic unit ending with an authentic cadence. The first unit of the small ternary form.

exposition (full movement)   A large-scale initiating function consisting of a main theme (group), transition, and subordinate theme (group).

extension   The addition of extra units of similar material in order to stretch out a formal function in time (compare **expansion**).

failed consequent   A unit that follows an antecedent in the sense of a consequent but does not close with the expected stronger cadence.

false closing section   A closing section that is reinterpreted retrospectively as an initiation (usually a presentation) of a subsequent thematic unit.

false recapitulation   Near the end of a development or a rondo couplet, the appearance of main-theme material in a tonal region other than tonic of the home key.

five-part rondo   A full-movement form in which a refrain alternates with two couplets. Couplet 1 is a subordinate-theme complex or an interior theme, and couplet 2 is an interior theme or development-like unit.

formal function   The specific role played by a particular musical passage in the formal organization of a work. It generally expresses a temporal sense of beginning, middle, end, before-the-beginning, or after-the-end. More specifically, it can express a wide variety of formal characteristics and relationships.

fragmentation A reduction in the length of units in relation to the prevailing grouping structure. Fragmented units do not necessarily contain melodic–motivic material derived from the preceding units.

framing function Any number of functions at various hierarchical levels that precede the beginning or follow the end of a formal unit.

fusion The merging of two formal functions within a single unit.

group A general term for any self-contained "chunk" of music, embracing its complete melodic, harmonic, rhythmic, and textural content. More specifically, it refers to multiple themes (e.g., subordinate-theme group).

grouping structure The organization of discrete, perceptually significant time spans (group, unit, part, section, etc.) at any or all hierarchical levels in a movement.

half cadence A cadential arrival articulated by the final dominant of a half-cadential progression (compare **dominant arrival**).

half-cadential progression A cadential progression whose complete form brings, in order, the harmonic functions of tonic (usually in first inversion), pre-dominant, and dominant (triad in root position).

harmonic acceleration An increase in the rate of harmonic change.

harmonic functions The three fundamental harmonies—tonic, dominant, and pre-dominant—that embrace all other harmonic formations in a key.

home key The principal tonality of a movement. The key in which a movement begins and ends and to which all other keys or tonal regions ultimately relate.

hybrid theme A simple eight-measure theme combining functions associated with both the sentence and the period. The four basic patterns are antecedent + continuation, antecedent + cadential, compound basic idea + continuation, and compound basic idea + consequent.

idea Minimally, a two-measure unit.

imperfect authentic cadence An authentic cadence in which the soprano voice ends on the third (or, rarely, the fifth) scale-degree (compare **perfect authentic cadence**).

incomplete cadential progression A cadential progression that omits one or more constituent harmonic functions (compare **complete cadential progression**).

incomplete pre-core A pre-core composed of one or two intrathematic functions. It usually lacks a concluding function (compare **complete pre-core**).

incomplete refrain In rondo form, a restatement of a refrain that lacks a home-key authentic cadence (compare **abridged refrain**).

initiating function Any number of functions at various hierarchical levels that express the temporal quality of "beginning" (compare **medial function; concluding function**).

initiating region A tonicized region (in some key) associated with an initiating intrathematic function (such as a presentation). It does not receive subsequent cadential confirmation.

interior theme A medial interthematic function, standing between statements of a main theme, that is modeled largely on the small ternary or small binary forms. It resides in the contrasting modality of the main theme (*minore* or *maggiore*) or in the subdominant or submediant regions.

internal half cadence A half cadence appearing within the boundaries of a subordinate theme. It can be followed by a new continuation (or cadential) passage or can mark the end of the first part of a two-part subordinate theme.

interpolated episode A passage of strikingly new, unrelated material lying in a relatively remote tonal region and standing apart from the regular succession of formal functions.

interpolation Unrelated material inserted between two logically succeeding functions.

interthematic functions The constituent formal functions of a full-movement form (or the principal sections of such a form) operating above the level of the theme.

intrathematic functions The constituent formal functions of a theme (or themelike unit).

introduction *See* **thematic introduction** or **slow introduction**.

large ternary A tripartite full-movement form consisting of a main theme, an interior theme, and a return of the main theme (compare **small ternary**).

lead-in A melodic link, usually following a cadential articulation, that helps provide rhythmic continuity between two adjacent formal units.

level of the idea unit The level of harmonic activity most directly associated with the basic idea, its repetition, and its fragmented units.

liquidation The systematic elimination of characteristic motives.

loose A formal organization characterized by the use of nonconventional thematic structures, harmonic–tonal instability (modulation, chromaticism), an asymmetrical grouping structure, phrase-structural extension and expansion, form-functional redundancy, and a diversity of melodic–motivic material (compare **tight knit**).

main theme An initiating interthematic function that brings the main melodic–motivic ideas of the movement, establishes and confirms the home key, and defines the standard of tight-knit organization.

main-theme group Two successive main themes, each ending with a perfect authentic cadence.

medial function Any number of functions at various hierarchical levels that express the temporal quality of "being-in-the-middle" (compare **initiating function; concluding function**).

minuet A large-scale tripartite form modeled on the small ternary theme-type. It consists of an exposition (A), contrasting middle (B), and recapitulation (A′).

minuet proper The first part of minuet/trio form. It is constructed in minuet or binary minuet form.

minuet/trio A tripartite full-movement form consisting of a minuet proper, trio, and da capo (of the minuet proper).

modal mixture The use of harmonies containing notes from the opposite modality of the prevailing mode.

modal shift A change of mode within the same tonality.

model A unit established for the purpose of sequential repetition.

model–sequence technique A unit (the model) that is immediately followed by a restatement transposed to a different scale-degree (the sequence); the same as **sequential repetition**.

modulating subordinate theme A subordinate theme that begins in a nontonic region (of either the home key or a subordinate key), thus giving the impression of modulating to the subordinate key.

modulating transition A transition that modulates to the subordinate key, ending on dominant harmony of that key (compare **nonmodulating transition**).

modulation The process of changing tonal focus so that a new tonic, confirmed as such by cadential function, is perceived to displace the previous tonic (compare **tonicization**).

motive A collection of several notes constituting the smallest meaningful melodic or rhythmic configuration.

neighboring chord In a prolongational progression, a subordinate harmony situated between a prolonged harmony that retains its same position (e.g., I–V⁶–I) (compare **passing chord**).

nine-part sonata–rondo A sonata–rondo form extended by an additional refrain and couplet, the latter built as an interior theme.

nonmodulating transition A transition that remains in the home key, ending on dominant harmony of that key (compare **modulating transition**).

notated measure A unit of musical time demarcated by bar lines in the score (compare **real measure**).

"one more time" technique Following an evaded cadence, the repetition of the previous cadential idea or phrase.

opening ritornello The first section of concerto form. It is organized like an exposition but remains in the home key throughout.

ornamental changes In a restatement of any kind, alterations of the melody, durational values, texture, dynamics, and the like of the original unit while retaining its basic tonal, harmonic, and phrase-structural organization (compare **structural changes**).

part A general term for grouping structure, often used in connection with some multipart thematic units (e.g., the first part of a small binary or the second part of a closing ritornello).

passing chord In a prolongational progression, a subordinate harmony situated between a prolonged harmony that changes position (e.g., I–V⁴₃–I⁶) (compare **neighboring chord**).

pedal point In a prolongational progression, the replacement of the bass voice of the subordinate harmonies by the root of the prolonged harmony.

penultimate dominant The root-position dominant harmony of an authentic cadential progression (compare **ultimate dominant**).

perfect authentic cadence An authentic cadence in which the soprano voice ends on the tonic scale-degree (compare **imperfect authentic cadence**).

period (eight-measure) A simple theme consisting of an antecedent phrase and a consequent phrase.

period (sixteen-measure) A compound theme consisting of an eight-measure antecedent (built as either a simple sentence or a hybrid) and an eight-measure consequent.

phrase Minimally, a four-measure unit, often, but not necessarily, containing two ideas.

postcadential One of several framing functions that express the sense of "after-the-end." It follows a cadence and prolongs its final harmony, usually with a recessive dynamic.

pre-core The initial unit of a development section, preceding a core or core substitute.

pre-dominant function Various harmonies whose primary role is to progress to a dominant.

premature dominant arrival A dominant arrival that appears before the end of the prevailing melodic–motivic and phrase-structural processes.

presentation An initiating intrathematic function consisting of a unit (usually a basic idea) and its repetition, supported by a prolongation of tonic harmony.

presentation phrase The first phrase of the eight-measure sentence.

primary development key In the case of multiple development keys, the one that receives the greatest (cadential, textural, durational) emphasis. It usually appears near the end of the development section (compare **secondary development key**).

progressive dynamic A systematic buildup of tension and excitement by various musical means (including intensity, texture, rhythmic activity) (compare **recessive dynamic**).

prolongational progression A progression that sustains the perception of an individual harmony through time despite the presence of an intervening chord of different harmonic meaning.

prolonged harmony The harmony that is prolonged by a prolongational progression.

pseudo-core A themelike unit in a development section that resembles a core as regards dynamics, texture, rhythm, and emotional character but that lacks genuine model–sequence technique.

real measure A unit of musical time corresponding to a listener's perception of a "full measure" of music (compare **notated measure**).

recapitulation (A' section) A concluding intrathematic function that represents a return (often adjusted and altered) of an earlier exposition. The third unit of the small ternary form.

recapitulation (full movement) A large-scale concluding function that brings back, usually modified, an earlier exposition. It resolves tonal conflicts by adjusting all material into the home key.

recessive dynamic A systematic release of tension and excitement by various musical means (including intensity, texture, rhythmic activity) (compare **progressive dynamic**).

refrain The initial section of any rondo form. It functions as a main theme and is usually built as a small ternary or small binary.

reinterpreted half cadence A local authentic cadence in the dominant region that is reinterpreted retrospectively as a half cadence.

repetition The immediate restatement of a unit (compare **return**).

response *See* **dominant version** (compare **statement**).

restatement The reappearance of any formal unit as either a repetition or a return, with or without ornamental or structural changes.

retransition An intrathematic function that effects a modulation from a subordinate key or development key to the home key, thus preparing for the return of a main theme (or A' section). It may range in length from a single chord to a multiphrase unit, and it frequently anticipates motives of the main theme's basic idea.

return A restatement of a unit following an intervening, contrasting unit (compare **repetition**).

ritornello In concerto form, a section written for the orchestra alone.

rondo Any one of a number of full-movement forms in which a single refrain alternates with two or more couplets.

rounded binary A version of the small ternary form that first repeats the exposition and then repeats together the contrasting middle and recapitulation (compare **small binary**).

secondary development In a recapitulation, a newly added passage featuring model–sequence technique and the tonicization of "flat" tonal regions.

secondary development key In the case of multiple development keys, one that receives lesser (cadential, textural, durational) emphasis than does the primary development key. It usually appears early in the development section (compare **primary development key**).

section A general term for grouping structure (e.g., the closing section of a subordinate theme, the development section of a sonata).

sentence (eight-measure) A simple theme consisting of a presentation phrase and a continuation (or continuation⇒cadential) phrase.

sentence (sixteen-measure) A compound theme consisting of an eight-measure presentation (repeated compound basic idea) and an eight-measure continuation.

sequence A sequentially repeated version of a model.

sequential progression A progression that projects a consistent intervallic pattern among the individual voices of the harmonies. It is classified in terms of the intervallic motion of its constituent roots (e.g., descending fifth sequence, ascending second sequence).

sequential repetition A unit that is followed by a restatement transposed to a different scale-degree; the same as **model–sequence technique**.

seven-part rondo A five-part rondo form extended by an additional refrain and couplet, the latter built as an interior theme.

slow introduction A large-scale framing function that expresses the sense of "before-the-beginning." It precedes an exposition (compare **thematic introduction**).

small binary A bipartite theme whose parts are normally repeated. It resembles the rounded binary except that the second part contains no recapitulatory function and the first part may end with a half cadence (compare **rounded binary**).

small ternary A tripartite theme consisting of an exposition (A), contrasting middle (B), and recapitulation (A′) (compare **large ternary**).

sonata A tripartite full-movement form containing an exposition, development, and recapitulation; a slow introduction and a coda may also be added.

sonata–rondo A full-movement form consisting of four statements of a refrain alternating with three couplets. The first refrain and couplet constitute a sonata exposition; the second couplet is either a development section or an interior theme; the third refrain and couplet form a recapitulation; and an obligatory coda brings the final refrain.

sonata without development A bipartite full-movement form consisting of an exposition followed by a recapitulation.

standing on the dominant A postcadential intrathematic function following a half cadence. It may also follow a perfect authentic cadence at the end of a small ternary exposition to initiate a contrasting middle. It consists of one or more ideas supported exclusively by a dominant prolongation.

statement *See* **tonic version** (compare **response**).

statement–response repetition A tonic version of a unit (usually a basic idea) immediately restated by a dominant version.

stop A cessation of musical activity at any point in a formal unit, not necessarily at a moment of cadential arrival (compare **end**).

structural changes In a restatement of any kind, alterations in the basic tonal, harmonic, and phrase-structural organization of the original unit (compare **ornamental changes**).

subordinate harmony In a prolongational progression, a harmony with a meaning different from that of the prolonged harmony.

subordinate key A closely related tonal region confirmed by a perfect authentic cadence as the principal contrasting key to the home key: in major-mode movements, the dominant region of the home key, and in minor-mode ones, the mediant ("relative major").

subordinate-key ritornello The third section of concerto form. It reinforces the confirmation of the subordinate key, is structured as a thematic unit ending with a perfect authentic cadence, and draws on material from the opening ritornello.

subordinate theme An interthematic function that confirms a subordinate key by closing with a perfect authentic cadence. It loosens the formal organization in order to solidify the new key in relation to the home key.

subordinate-theme complex In rondo form, a single couplet consisting of a transition, subordinate theme (group), closing section, and retransition.

subordinate-theme group Two or more successive subordinate themes, each ending with a perfect authentic cadence.

thematic introduction A framing function that expresses the sense of "before-the-beginning." It consists of a brief passage prolonging tonic (sometimes dominant) with a progressive dynamic. It contains minimal melodic activity (so as not to suggest a basic idea) (compare **slow introduction**).

thematic unit A theme or themelike unit.

theme A unit consisting of a conventional set of initiating, medial, and ending intrathematic functions. It must close with a cadence (compare **themelike unit**).

theme and variations A multipart, full-movement form consisting of a main theme followed by an indefinite number of varied repetitions of that theme.

themelike unit A unit that resembles a theme in formal organization but is usually looser and is not required to close with a cadence.

three-key exposition An exposition that contains a modulating subordinate theme, thus suggesting (but rarely confirming) three different keys.

tight knit A formal organization characterized by the use of conventional theme-types, harmonic–tonal stability, a symmetrical grouping structure, form-functional efficiency, and a unity of melodic–motivic material (compare **loose**).

tonal-polarity model A model of overall tonal organization for a movement based on a fundamental opposition of home (tonic) and subordinate (dominant or relative major) keys (compare **tour-of-keys model**).

tonic function The central harmony of a key, the one to which all others ultimately relate and derive their meaning.

tonic version A unit (usually a basic idea) whose initial harmonic support is tonic (compare **dominant version**).

tonicization The process of emphasizing a scale-degree (besides the tonic) so that it is perceived as a local tonic. A tonicized region does not receive cadential confirmation (compare **modulation**).

tour-of-keys model A model of overall tonal organization for a movement based on the home key progressing to a multiplicity of related tonal regions (including the subordinate key and multiple development keys) (compare **tonal-polarity model**).

transition An interthematic function that destabilizes the home key and loosens the formal organization in order for a subordinate key to be established and eventually confirmed.

transition-like pre-core A modulatory thematic unit, usually sentential in form, that leads to dominant harmony of a development key (to begin a core).

transitional introduction A passage built over dominant harmony of a new tonal region. It typically appears at the beginning of a pre-core.

trio The second part of minuet/trio form. It is constructed in minuet or binary minuet form.

truncated recapitulation In sonata-without-development form, a recapitulation consisting of only the main theme (thus omitting the transition and subordinate theme).

truncated small ternary An incomplete theme consisting of an exposition (A) and a contrasting middle (B). The expected recapitulation (A') is eliminated.

two-part subordinate theme A subordinate theme whose first part ends with an internal half cadence and whose second part starts with new, initiating material.

two-part transition A transition whose first part is nonmodulatory and closes with the home-key dominant and whose second part, often beginning with reference to main-theme ideas, modulates to the subordinate key and closes there with dominant harmony.

ultimate dominant The root-position dominant triad of a half-cadential progression (compare **penultimate dominant**).

unit A general term for any self-contained "chunk" of music, embracing its complete melodic, harmonic, rhythmic, and textural content.

NOTES

Introduction

1. Some of the most notable books include V. Kofi Agawu, *Playing with Signs: A Semiotic Interpretation of Classic Music* (Princeton, NJ: Princeton University Press, 1991); Michael Broyles, *Beethoven: The Emergence and Evolution of Beethoven's Heroic Style* (New York: Excelsior, 1987); Carl Dahlhaus, *Ludwig van Beethoven: Approaches to His Music*, trans. Mary Whittall (Oxford: Clarendon Press, 1993); Philip G. Downs, *Classical Music: The Era of Haydn, Mozart, and Beethoven* (New York: Norton, 1992); Robert O. Gjerdingen, *A Classic Turn of Phrase: Music and the Psychology of Convention* (Philadelphia: University of Pennsylvania Press, 1988); Ethan Haimo, *Haydn's Symphonic Forms: Essays in Compositional Logic* (Oxford: Clarendon Press, 1995); Robert S. Hatten, *Musical Meaning in Beethoven: Markedness, Correlation, and Interpretation* (Bloomington: Indiana University Press, 1994); Daniel Heartz, *Haydn, Mozart, and the Viennese School, 1740–1780* (New York: Norton, 1995); Lewis Lockwood, *Beethoven: Studies in the Creative Process* (Cambridge, MA: Harvard University Press, 1992); Elaine R. Sisman, *Haydn and the Classical Variation* (Cambridge, MA: Harvard University Press, 1993); James Webster, *Haydn's "Farewell" Symphony and the Idea of Classical Style: Through-Composition and Cyclic Integration in His Instrumental Music* (Cambridge: Cambridge University Press, 1991); and Gretchen Wheelock, *Haydn's Ingenious Jesting with Art: Contexts of Musical Wit and Humor* (New York: Schirmer, 1992).

2. The "form" of a complete multimovement instrumental cycle lies outside the scope of this book, but see Webster, *Haydn's "Farewell" Symphony*, for an important inquiry into formal processes spanning the movements of a cycle.

3. The analyses accompanying the text are intended in the first instance to illustrate technical points of theory; the analytical commentary is thus partial and highly selective. I regret that limitations of space prohibit more complete analyses, especially of entire movements. For more extensive analytical applications of the theory, see William E. Caplin, "Structural Expansion in Beethoven's Symphonic Forms," in *Beethoven's Compositional Process*, ed. William Kinderman (Lincoln: University of Nebraska Press, 1991), 27–54, and "The 'Expanded Cadential Progression': A Category for the Analysis of Classical Form," *Journal of Musicological Research* 7 (1987): 215–57.

4. Arnold Schoenberg, *Fundamentals of Musical Composition*, ed. Gerald Strang and Leonard Stein (London: Faber & Faber, 1967). Issues of form are also treated in Schoenberg's *Structural Functions of Harmony*, rev. ed., ed. Leonard Stein (New York: Nor-

ton, 1969), and Schoenberg's *The Musical Idea and the Logic, Technique, and Art of Its Presentation*, ed. and trans. Patricia Carpenter and Severine Neff (New York: Columbia University Press, 1995).

5. Erwin Ratz, *Einführung in die musikalische Formenlehre: Über Formprizipien in den Inventionen und Fugen J. S. Bachs und ihre Bedeutung für die Kompositionstechnik Beethovens*, 3rd ed., enl. (Vienna: Universal, 1973), 56.

6. Among the recent studies of late-eighteenth-century music cited in n. 1, only the work of Agawu treats issues of formal function in any detailed manner. With his notion of "introversive semiosis," he advances a "beginning–middle–end paradigm" tied intimately to harmonic organization (*Playing with Signs*, chap. 3).

7. To be sure, the concept of "classical style" is currently regarded with suspicion, especially in light of Webster's recent critique (*Haydn's "Farewell" Symphony*, 347–57). Moreover, defining this style on the works of only three composers obviously distorts the complete music-historical record. These methodological concerns notwithstanding, this book continues the long tradition of establishing general principles of form on the basis of music held in the highest esteem and regularly performed by communities of musicians. Determining the extent to which the theory offered here applies to works by the many *Kleinmeister* of the late eighteenth century must await the results of future research.

8. See especially the seminal works by Leonard G. Ratner, *Classic Music: Expression, Form, and Style* (New York: Schirmer, 1980); and Charles Rosen, *The Classical Style: Haydn, Mozart, Beethoven* (New York: Norton, 1972), and *Sonata Forms*, rev. ed. (New York: Norton, 1988).

9. Fred Lerdahl and Ray Jackendoff, *A Generative Theory of Tonal Music* (Cambridge, MA: MIT Press, 1983), 13–16.

10. This aspect of formal functionality is to be thoroughly investigated by Janet Schmalfeldt, *In the Process of Becoming: Philosophical and Analytical Perspectives on Form in Early Nineteenth-Century Music* (New York: Oxford University Press, forthcoming).

11. For example, Mozart's Rondo for Piano in D, K. 485 (the work is actually in sonata form), uses the same motive, in various transformations, for the beginning of each of its major sections. Yet the functions of main theme, transition, subordinate theme, development, and the like are fully articulated by various harmonic and phrase-structural processes that operate independent of motivic content.

12. Throughout his writings, Schoenberg intermingles principles of formal procedure with concerns of motivic derivation. He surely regarded the two domains as inextricably linked, but in fact his actual *Formenlehre* (especially as developed by Ratz) has little

connection to melody and motive. Moreover, the extensive investigations of these latter ideas by most present-day Schoenbergians have largely bypassed issues of formal functionality. See, for example, Patricia Carpenter, "A Problem in Organic Form: Schoenberg's Tonal Body," *Theory and Practice* 13 (1988): 31–63; David Epstein, *Beyond Orpheus: Studies in Musical Structure* (Cambridge, MA: MIT Press, 1979); Walter Frisch, *Brahms and the Principle of Developing Variation* (Berkeley and Los Angeles: University of California Press, 1984); and Severine Neff, "Schoenberg and Goethe: Organicism and Analysis," in *Music Theory and the Exploration of the Past*, ed. Christopher Hatch and David W. Bernstein (Chicago: University of Chicago Press, 1993), 409–33.

13. On the relation of classical form to durational proportions, see David Smyth, "'Balanced Interruption' and the Formal Repeat," *Music Theory Spectrum* 15 (1993): 76–88, and "Large-Scale Rhythm and Classical Form," *Music Theory Spectrum* 12 (1990): 236–46. Also see Jane Perry-Camp, "Time and Temporal Proportion: The Golden Section Metaphor in Mozart, Music, and History," *Journal of Musicological Research* 3 (1979): 149–53; and Jonathan D. Kramer, *The Time of Music: New Meanings, New Temporalities, New Listening Strategies* (New York: Schirmer, 1988), 355–65.

14. See Miriam Sheer, "Patterns of Dynamic Organization in Beethoven's *Eroica* Symphony," *Journal of Musicology* 10 (1992): 483–504.

15. For an initial step in this direction, see Janet Schmalfeldt, "Towards a Reconciliation of Schenkerian Concepts with Traditional and Recent Theories of Form," *Music Analysis* 10 (1991): 233–87. Recent studies of form from a predominantly Schenkerian perspective include those by Allen Cadwallader, "Form and Tonal Process," in *Trends in Schenkerian Research*, ed. Allen Cadwallader (New York: Schirmer, 1990), 1–21; David Beach, "Phrase Expansion: Three Analytical Studies," *Music Analysis* 14 (1995): 27–47; Joel Galand, "Form, Genre, and Style in the Eighteenth-Century Rondo," *Music Theory Spectrum* 17 (1995): 27–52; John L. Snyder, "Schenker and the First Movement of Mozart's Sonata, K. 545: An Uninterrupted Sonata-Form Movement?" *Theory and Practice* 16 (1991): 51–78; and Norman L. Wick, "Transformations of Middleground Hypermeasures in Selected Mozart Keyboard Sonatas," *Theory and Practice* 16 (1991): 79–102.

16. See, for example, Mark Evan Bonds, *Wordless Rhetoric: Musical Form and the Metaphor of the Oration* (Cambridge, MA: Harvard University Press, 1991); Wolfgang Budday, *Grundlagen musikalischer Formen der Wiener Klassik: An Hand der zeitgenössischen Theorie von Joseph Riepel und Heinrich Christoph Koch dargestellt an Menuetten und Sonatensätzen (1750-1790)* (Kassel: Bärenreiter, 1983); Hermann Danuser, "Vers- oder Prosaprinzip?: Mozarts Streichquartett in d-Moll (KV 421) in der Deutung Jérôme-Joseph de Momignys und Arnold Schönbergs," *Musiktheorie* 7 (1992): 245–63; Siegfried Schmalzreidt, "Charakter und Drama: Zur historischen Analyse von Haydnschen und Beethovenschen Sonatensätzen," *Archiv für Musikwissenschaft* 42 (1985): 37–66; Elaine R. Sisman, "Small and Expanded Forms: Koch's Model and Haydn's Music," *Musical Quarterly* 68 (1982): 444–75.

Chapter 1

1. More philosophically minded musicians might also speculate on the seemingly incompatible meanings of form as (1) the specific shape taken by an individual composition in all its particularity (so that changing even a single detail would mean altering its form) or (2) abstractions or generalizations based on structural uniformities displayed by a multiplicity of works (*New Harvard Dictionary*, 320). For a recent discussion of this "paradox of musical form," see Bonds, *Wordless Rhetoric*, 13.

2. Lerdahl and Jackendoff, *Generative Theory*, 13–16.

3. Schoenberg, *Musical Composition*, 23; Ratz, *Musikalische Formenlehre*, 23.

4. Chap. 3 treats sentences lasting four or sixteen notated measures and irregular-length sentences arising from extensions or compressions. A distinct *sixteen-measure sentence* is discussed in chap. 5.

5. Some readers may object that this presentation is considered a *phrase*, since it neither closes with a cadence nor completes a full linear or tonal progression. Although most theories of form define phrase in relation to varying degrees of melodic and harmonic closure, the notion of phrase in this book does not entail any special pitch requirements. Indeed, many of the problematic issues traditionally associated with the definition of phrase are more comfortably assimilated to the concept of formal function. Thus phrase is used here as a functionally neutral term of grouping structure and refers, in general, to a discrete group approximately four measures in length.

6. A third main feature of continuation function—harmonic sequence—is discussed in connection with the following example.

7. I acknowledge an inconsistency in terminology when the adjectival *cadential* is used along with the nominative *presentation* and *continuation*. The problem arises because in many situations, the nominative form *cadence* is preferably restricted to the "moment" of cadential arrival. When we want to identify "the cadence" of a theme, we traditionally refer to that arrival point, not necessarily to the complete time span that functions to achieve that arrival. See chap. 3 for further discussion of the varying usages of the terms *cadence* and *cadential*.

8. An authentic cadence is *perfect* when the melodic line ends on the first scale-degree. An *imperfect* authentic cadence is defined later in chap. 3.

9. Unlike the earlier example, however, the progression does not end with root-position tonic. Instead, the dominant in m. 6 leads through a passing chord (on the last eighth-note beat of the measure) to a secondary dominant of VI. Nonetheless, it is still possible to recognize a true tonic prolongation even if the progression does not literally conclude with that harmony.

10. Since these dominant chords are subordinate to the framing tonic harmony, they are placed in parentheses. Ellipses (. . .) indicate a gap in the harmonic analysis; they are used in the examples to avoid needless repetitions, as here, or if a complete harmonic analysis is not necessary for the discussion.

11. A specific *sixteen-measure period* (traditionally termed "double period") is defined in chap. 5.

12. We speak of a *return* of the basic idea, not a *repetition*, because intervening material stands between the two statements of the idea. Conversely, the consequent can properly be said to repeat the antecedent because no material stands between the phrases. This useful distinction between repetition and return is made by Leonard B. Meyer, *Explaining Music: Essays and Explorations* (Berkeley and Los Angeles: University of California Press, 1973), 49.

13. The first two labels obviously derive from terminology

traditionally associated with sonata form. The middle section of the sonata, however, is termed *development*.

14. Expositions also typically feature a *hybrid* theme which, as defined in chap. 5, combines the functional characteristics of both the sentence and period.

15. Even when the A section modulates, the final harmony of the perfect authentic cadence is the "tonic" of the subordinate key.

16. See the end of chap. 6 for a fuller discussion of this issue. The distinction between tight-knit and loose formal organization originates with Schoenberg and is developed extensively by Ratz. The terms translate these theorists' use of the German adjectives *fest* and *locker*, respectively. The translation of *fest* as "stable" by Carpenter and Neff (Schoenberg, *Musical Idea*, 445, n. 191), following the lead of Schoenberg (*Musical Composition*, 178, 201), has not been adopted here, since the metaphor of stability is more traditionally associated with matters of harmony and tonality than with form.

17. These low E♭s are merely ornamental and do not represent the genuine bass part, which is found on the first half of each beat (as indicated by the harmonic analysis).

18. For this reason, the "half cadence" in m. 12 is perhaps better understood as a *dominant arrival*, a concept that I define (and distinguish from half cadence) in chap. 6.

19. A thematic introduction should not be confused with another type of introduction, namely, the *slow introduction* that precedes a sonata-form exposition, which is of considerably larger scope; see chap. 13.

20. Wallace Berry, *Structural Functions in Music* (Englewood Cliffs, NJ: Prentice-Hall, 1976), 7. Berry also speaks of a *recessive dynamic*, which brings about a diminution and dissolution of tension and excitement. Recessive dynamic is generally associated with postcadential formal function, to be discussed shortly.

21. There is an unfortunate lack of terminological parallelism between standing on the dominant and closing section, which itself can be considered a kind of "standing on the tonic." But I maintain the distinction in this book in order to conform to the traditional usage of these expressions, especially by Schoenberg and Ratz.

22. Berry, *Structural Functions*, 7. Recessive dynamic is particularly associated with a closing section. In the case of a postcadential standing on the dominant, the situation is more complex: the emphasis given to an inherently unstable harmonic function (one having such a powerful need to resolve to the tonic) often generates a degree of progressive dynamic that counters the recessive character introduced by other musical forces, such as a systematic reduction in texture.

23. Subdominant emphasis in a codetta functions as a dynamic counterweight to the dominant harmony preceding the final tonic of the cadence. Whereas the cadential dominant creates tension for its resolution to the tonic, the subdominant acts as an agent of resolution and relaxation and thus helps create the recessive dynamic so characteristic of codettas.

24. As mentioned, however, a codetta is not usually formed out of immediately preceding ideas. A closing section containing "new" codettas is discussed in connection with ex. 1.8 (mm. 42–48).

25. To be sure, some individual themes of complete subordinate theme groups are extremely tight knit (the first subordinate theme of Beethoven's *Waldstein* Sonata comes quickly to mind). In those cases, the entire group of themes can be seen as looser in relation to the main theme (or theme group).

26. The sequential progression actually begins with the C-minor harmony of mm. 9–10. Since the prevailing tonality is not entirely clear, a harmonic analysis of this sequential progression is given both for C minor (the initial tonality of the transition) and for A♭ major (the goal tonality).

27. The notion of phrase *extension* is defined and discussed later in connection with the subordinate theme.

28. This tonic prolongation is shown in brackets in the harmonic analysis.

29. To say that a given phrase prolongs two opposing harmonic functions (tonic and dominant) "at the same time" may seem contradictory. But such disparities can be resolved when we understand that the prolongations actually occur at different "phenomenological space-times" and thus do not truly conflict with each other. See David Lewin, "Theory, Phenomenology, and Modes of Perception," *Music Perception* 3 (1986): 357–61.

30. Other theorists have proposed somewhat differing distinctions between extension and expansion. See William Rothstein, *Phrase Rhythm in Tonal Music* (New York: Schirmer, 1989), 311, n. 27; and Wick, "Middleground Hypermeasures," 84, 89.

31. A case of phrase extension was also discussed earlier in connection with the continuation of the transition (ex. 1.7, mm. 13–14).

32. Presentation function can also be expanded by lengthening the basic idea, as discussed in chap. 3. Conversely, continuation function, with its characteristic processes of fragmentation and harmonic acceleration, is inherently unsuitable to withstand expansion techniques.

33. Indeed, the dominant pedal first sounds in m. 20 (see ex. 1.7) as an extension of the standing on the dominant at the end of the transition.

34. The development section of Beethoven's piano sonata movement is discussed in chap. 10 (see exs. 10.8 and 10.15).

Chapter 2

1. Most of the paradigms can also appear in minor (with the usual alterations); paradigms associated especially with minor are set in that mode.

2. Hugo Riemann, *Vereinfachte Harmonielehre, oder die Lehre von den tonalen Funktionen der Akkorde* (London: Augener, 1893).

3. The first comprehensive formulation of the *Stufentheorie* appears in the writings of Simon Sechter, *Die Grundsätze der musikalischen Komposition*, 3 vols. (Leipzig, 1853), who built his system on principles developed in the eighteenth century by Jean-Philippe Rameau and Johann Philipp Kirnberger. Sechter's work established a distinctly Austrian tradition of harmonic theory that led directly to the ideas of Bruckner, Schenker, and Schoenberg at the end of the nineteenth century. See Robert W. Wason, *Viennese Harmonic Theory from Albrechtsberger to Schenker and Schoenberg* (Ann Arbor, MI: UMI Research Press, 1985).

4. For modern formulations of a functional theory of harmony, see Eytan Agmon, "Functional Harmony Revisited: A Prototype-Theoretic Approach," *Music Theory Spectrum* 17 (1995): 196–214; Marion Guck, "The Functional Relations of Chords: A Theory of Musical Intuitions," *In Theory Only* 4 (1978): 29–42; and Daniel Harrison, *Harmonic Function in Chromatic Music: A Renewed Dualist Theory and an Account of Its Precedents* (Chicago: University of Chicago Press, 1994).

5. In Riemann's *Funktionstheorie*, subdominant function is primarily conceived (following Rameau) as one of two tonal poles to the tonic (the other pole being dominant function). He eventually proposes that the subdominant leads logically to the dominant but this notion remains secondary to his original polar conception of two dominants ("overdominant" and "underdominant") centering on the tonic. The North American adaptation of the functional theory, which emphasizes a group of pre-dominant harmonies leading to the dominant, has most likely been influenced in this respect by Schenkerian notions (despite Schenker's own adherence to the *Stufentheorie* tradition).

6. In this chapter, *chord* is regularly used in the sense of *harmony*. In theory, the terms should be clearly distinguished, so that the former would refer to a specific vertical sonority and the latter, to a broader range of tonal relations. In practice, however, it is helpful to have chord available as a rough synonym for harmony, especially when the texture is four-voice homophonic and the discussion emphasizes details of chordal formation (such as inversion, doubling, and voice-leading).

7. These three categories are not as mutually exclusive as just presented. For example, prolongational progressions can occur within a broad cadential progression, and some sequential progressions may acquire an overall prolongational function. Moreover, a given progression may sometimes be classified in more than one way.

8. Allen Forte and Steven Gilbert, *An Introduction to Schenkerian Analysis* (New York: Norton, 1982), 142. The concept of prolongation derives, of course, from the theories of Heinrich Schenker. This book adopts a considerably more restricted notion of prolongation than that found in traditional Schenkerian analysis.

9. The paradigms used to illustrate the various harmonic progressions are written (with some exceptions) in four voices and feature an unembellished melody typical of the progression.

10. All the subordinate harmonies in the following paradigms are placed in parentheses in order to highlight the prolonged harmony. In the analysis of actual musical passages, a greater flexibility in the use of parentheses helps differentiate levels of harmonic organization; thus, the harmonic rhythm of a given passage may be more clearly indicated if the subordinate chords are shown without parentheses. With a pedal point, however, the lack of a true bass for the subordinate harmonies prompts us to place these chords in parentheses at all times.

11. The substitute chords in ex. 2.4d–e lie outside parentheses to indicate that the passing chords are even more subordinate in the overall prolongation.

12. The following discussion exclusively involves a particular type of harmonic progression, one associated most often with *cadence* as a category of musical form. The issue of cadential formal function, however, is not raised here but, rather, in subsequent chapters.

13. It is difficult to provide a completely satisfying explanation for the special prominence given to the fourth scale-degree as the bearer of pre-dominant harmony. That this degree serves as a passing tone between the third and fifth scale-degrees, which support the initial tonic and dominant harmonies, is undoubtedly one of a number of reasons that the fourth degree is used so frequently in the bass line of a cadential progression.

14. There is a second, related reason that the initial tonic is often inverted. Most themes open with root-position tonic in order to create a stable harmonic–tonal beginning. The appearance of a prominent cadential I⁶ later in the theme helps lighten the harmonic texture, provide greater dynamic momentum, and motivate a return to the stability of the final cadential tonic.

15. The use of IV in cadential progressions increases with Beethoven and becomes even more favored throughout the nineteenth century. Just why the classical composers prefer II⁶ for the cadential pre-dominant is likely to be explained more by melodic and contrapuntal reasons than by specifically harmonic ones. (This issue is raised again shortly in the discussion of embellishments to the cadential dominant.)

16. The final tonic of the authentic cadential progression, though never harmonically altered, is often melodically ornamented with suspensions or appoggiaturas.

17. Although the cadential six–four is consistently analyzed as dominant harmony throughout this book, a certain "tonic" quality nonetheless remains attached to the chord. In many cadential situations, it is precisely the six–four chord that can bear enormous expansion, no doubt due to the degree of harmonic stability the chord retains by virtue of its also being a second-inversion tonic.

18. To be sure, the presence of the leading-tone (substituting for the seventh of the II⁶₅) lends a certain dominant character to this diminished seventh harmony, but not enough to overturn its more obvious pre-dominant function.

19. As is discussed in later chapters, this progression is particularly associated with the *deceptive cadence*, a specific formal device used to extend a thematic structure. But the progression is occasionally used in other formal contexts as well.

20. These last two forms of the deceptive cadential progression (ex. 2.9d–e) resemble the harmonic situation typically associated with the *evaded cadence*. The central difference between deceptive and evaded cadences concerns whether the event following the cadential dominant is the *goal* of the ongoing phrase (as in the deceptive cadence) or whether this event signals the *beginning* of a new phrase (as in the evaded cadence). In the latter, the I⁶ that typically follows the dominant does not genuinely belong to the cadential progression per se but, rather, initiates a new progression (usually another authentic cadential one). Therefore, it is not quite accurate to speak of a deceptive cadential progression when a genuine cadential evasion occurs.

21. Sometimes V⁷/IV seems to mark a genuine authentic cadential progression, such as at the end of Bach's Prelude in C from the *Well-Tempered Clavier*, bk. 1. In such cases, it is as if a "passing seventh," which would normally follow the tonic triad (as in ex. 2.1b), appeared simultaneously with that triad.

22. The following discussion is highly indebted to the excellent treatment of harmonic sequences given by Edward Aldwell and Carl Schachter, *Harmony and Voice Leading*, 2d ed. (New York: Harcourt Brace Jovanovich, 1989), chap. 17.

23. In the analytical annotation of sequential progressions, the initial, functional chord has appended to it the label *seq.* to signal the nature of the subsequent progression. The following chords are placed in parentheses because of their relatively nonfunctional status, and the final chord of the progression stands outside the parentheses to indicate the regaining of functional meaning.

24. Ascending and descending fourths, sixths, and sevenths are logically accommodated through inversion into one of the six categories.

25. The chromatic version in example 2.11f makes the incipient functionality more palpable. Note, too, the functional progression ♭II–V–I in E embedded in the sequence.

26. It is somewhat anomalous, though, that the tonic goal of the sequence itself can be understood as a "dominant" (of IV).

27. The ascending third sequential progression becomes more prominent in nineteenth-century repertories.

28. The term *stepwise* can also be used for sequential progressions by ascending (and descending) seconds.

29. It might be possible, though, to see an incipient functional relationship among the chords of example 2.15b when compared with a descending fifth progression using diatonic seventh chords (ex. 2.15c). Here, some of the roots would be "implied" because they are not actually present in the chords.

30. The choice of nonsequential upper voices in ex. 2.16e supports the cadential implications of the progression.

31. Just this situation arises in the first movement of Beethoven's *Eroica* Symphony, mm. 123–34. See Caplin, "Structural Expansion," 42–43.

Chapter 3

1. As a distinct theme-type, the sentence (Ger. *Satz*) seems to have been defined with precision and consistency first by Arnold Schoenberg early in this century. His most complete formulation appears in *Fundamentals of Musical Composition* (chaps. 5 and 8), written later in his life. In developing the concept, Schoenberg was likely influenced by Wilhelm Fischer's notion of *Fortspinnungstypus*, "Zur Entwicklungsgeschichte des Wiener klassischen Stils," *Studien zur Musikwissenschaft* 3 (1915): 24–84. The sentence is also discussed by a number of Schoenberg's students, especially Ratz (*Musikalische Formenlehre*, 21–24), but also Anton Webern, *The Path to the New Music*, ed. Willi Reich (Bryn Mawr, PA: Theodore Presser, 1963), 27, 30–31; Erwin Stein, *Form and Performance* (London: Faber & Faber, 1962), 93–95; and Josef Rufer, *Composition with Twelve Notes*, trans. Humphrey Searle (London: Barrie and Rockliff, 1954), 32–33. Carl Dahlhaus's important study of the sentence in relation to the period continues this tradition: "Satz und Periode: Zur Theorie der musikalischen Syntax," *Zeitschrift für Musiktheorie* 9 (1978): 16–26. Seemingly independent of the Schoenberg school, the Hungarian musicologist Dénes Bartha described many sentence types according to his concept of "quaternary stanza structure": "On Beethoven's Thematic Structure," in *The Creative World of Beethoven*, ed. Paul Henry Lang (New York: Norton, 1971), 260–66. Later, Bartha termed this form the "quatrain," "Das Quatrain-Modell in Mozarts Perioden- und Liedform-Strukturen," *Mozart-Jahrbuch 1978/79*, 30–44. In the late eighteenth century, Heinrich Christoph Koch considered some examples of the sentence in connection with his notion of "compound phrase," in *Introductory Essay on Composition: The Mechanical Rules of Melody, Sections 3 and 4*, trans. Nancy Kovaleff Baker (New Haven, CT: Yale University Press, 1983), 57, but the concept remains somewhat peripheral to his thought.

North American theory has only lately come to recognize the sentence form as a distinct theme-type. A brief but influential reference is made by Edward T. Cone in *Musical Form and Musical Performance* (New York: Norton, 1968), 75–76. More recent discussions include those by Michelle Fillion, "Sonata-Exposition Procedures in Haydn's Keyboard Sonatas," in *Haydn Studies*, ed.

Jens Peter Larsen, Howard Serwer, and James Webster (New York: Norton, 1981), 477–78; William E. Benjamin, "A Theory of Musical Meter," *Music Perception* 1 (1984): 363; Frisch, *Developing Variation*, 12–18; Rothstein, *Phrase Rhythm*, 26–27; Janet Schmalfeldt, "Cadential Processes: The Evaded Cadence and the 'One More Time' Technique," *Journal of Musicological Research* 12 (1992): 1–51, and her "Reconciliation."

2. In the arithmetical formula for a grouping structure, × stands for "times" and indicates the number of statements of a given idea lasting a given number of measures. Thus, the formula (2 × 2) + 4 means "a two-measure unit is stated two times and is then followed by a four-measure unit." In the sentence form, the four-measure continuation phrase itself is sometimes grouped (2 × 1) + 2.

3. The notion that the sentence form contains three formal functions is a central innovation of my book. None of the traditional writings on the sentence form makes any such explicit formulation. Fischer's *Fortspinnungstypus* (see n. 1) involves three functional elements, but they differ significantly from those of the sentence, as explained in William E. Caplin, "Funktionale Komponenten im achttaktigen Satz," *Musiktheorie* 1 (1986): 255–58.

4. An alternative expression for this second phrase, "continuation⇒cadential," is introduced later. Recall again that the term *phrase* is functionally neutral and merely refers to a musical unit of approximately four measures (see chap. 1, n. 5).

5. The situation R = 2N may seem to resemble the notion of "hypermeter," as developed by Edward T. Cone, *Musical Form*; William Rothstein, *Phrase Rhythm*; and Carl Schachter, "Rhythm and Linear Analysis: Durational Reduction," in *Music Forum*, ed. Felix Salzer, vol. 5 (New York: Columbia University Press, 1980), 197–232, and "Rhythm and Linear Analysis: Aspects of Meter," in *Music Forum*, ed. Felix Salzer, vol. 6, pt. 1 (New York: Columbia University Press, 1987), 1–59. These theorists do not, however, postulate a distinction between real and notated measures; instead, they understand hypermeter to be any metrical organization lying above the level of the *notated* measure, whether or not that measure is real (in the sense formulated here).

6. For example, the slow introduction to a sonata form's first movement may feature R = ½N, which then becomes R = N (or even R = 2N) at the onset of the exposition. See chap. 13, exs. 13.10 and 13.11.

7. This example is the actual main theme of the movement; the "fate" motives of mm. 1–5 make up a thematic introduction.

8. A genuine *sixteen-measure sentence* is defined in chap. 5.

9. The term *presentation* is new: neither Schoenberg nor his followers introduce a specific label to distinguish the first phrase of the sentence from that of other theme-types. Thus whereas Schoenberg speaks of an "antecedent" of the period, he refers merely to the "beginning" of the sentence (*Musical Composition*, 21). Ratz, who describes the sentence as consisting of three units—*Zweitakter* ("two-measure unit"), *Wiederholung* ("repetition"), and *Entwicklung* ("development")—provides no term for the first phrase containing the basic idea and its repetition (*Musikalische Formenlehre*, 21). Dahlhaus uses *Vordersatz* ("antecedent") to label the first phrase of both the sentence and period ("Satz und Periode").

10. Hugo Leichtentritt, *Musical Form* (Cambridge, MA: Harvard University Press, 1951), 5; Ellis B. Kohs, *Musical Form* (Boston: Houghton Mifflin, 1976), 7; Wallace Berry, *Form in Music*, 2d ed. (Englewood Cliffs, NJ: Prentice-Hall, 1986), 2.

11. Traditional formal theory lacks a satisfactory English term for the initial two measures of a classical theme. Schoenberg's use of "phrase" for this unit (*Musical Composition*, 3–7) runs counter to the usual English practice of regarding the phrase as, minimally, four measures in length. The terms "subphrase" and "half phrase" are occasionally encountered, but they misleadingly imply that the unit is merely a subordinate component of a more fundamental, higher-level structure, namely, the phrase. Finally, German theory does not provide much help in finding an English term. Ratz, for example, refers to the opening unit of a sentence simply as a *Zweitakter* ("two-measure unit") (*Musikalische Formenlehre*, 21).

I chose the term *basic idea* here in deliberate reference to Schoenberg's famous *Grundgestalt*. Although Schoenberg never achieved a definitive and unambiguous formulation of this problematical concept, his student Josef Rufer reports one meaning that is compatible with my notion of basic idea: "In my very full notes of his [Schoenberg's] teaching between 1919 and 1922 I find these definitions: a *motif* is the smallest musical form, consisting of at least one interval and one rhythm. The next sized form is the *Grundgestalt* or phrase, 'as a rule 2 to 3 bars long' . . . and consisting of the 'firm connection of one or more motifs and their more or less varied repetitions'" (*Composition with Twelve Notes*, viii).

Note that Schoenberg here regards the motive as the "smallest musical form." In his *Musical Composition*, he revised his view and refers to the two-measure "phrase" as the "smallest structural unit" (3).

12. Metrical reasons may also account for the two-measure size of the basic idea. To perceive a measure as a complete metrical unit, it is necessary to hear two downbeats: the second downbeat both marks the end of the first measure and initiates the second measure. Thus a basic idea not only provides the principal melodic–motivic content in a stable harmonic context but also helps define the metrical organization of the theme.

13. See also ahead exs. 3.4 and 3.10 for basic ideas supported exclusively by tonic harmony.

14. Despite the foregoing generality, a significant minority of classical themes begin with conventional, cadence-like gestures. (The opening of the trio in Mozart's Symphony No. 41 in C ["Jupiter"], K. 551, is a well-known example, although the initial idea is probably better heard as a codetta rather than as a cadence.) In such cases, the composer uses a variety of strategies to make sure that the theme properly expresses a sense of beginning and leads appropriately to a true cadence at its end.

15. See ahead ex. 4.12, m. 2, in which the slur in the first violin embraces all three quarter notes. However, the basic idea most likely ends with the note B, and the following C initiates the brief contrasting idea. Whereas slurring marks and other signs of articulation are of obvious importance to the performer, they must not be taken as analytical imperatives. Neither is the performer obliged to realize in performance any particular analytical interpretation. In certain situations, indeed, a performer may very well want to create continuities of "phrasing" (in the performative sense) that cross over the boundaries of the work's grouping structure.

16. Ex. 4.6, considered in the next chapter, also contains a basic idea that consists of a repeated one-measure unit.

17. I describe sequential repetition in greater detail when discussing continuation function.

18. See also ahead ex. 3.9 for a case of an exact repetition of the basic idea with a changed melodic component.

19. See also ahead exs. 3.10 and 3.14.

20. See also ahead exs. 3.13, 3.15, and 3.16. The "1–7 . . . 4–3" melodic schema, which is embedded in the first four measures of ex. 3.3a, is examined in detail by Gjerdingen (*Classic Turn of Phrase*). This schema arises in the vast majority of cases within a presentation phrase containing a statement–response repetition of a basic idea.

21. See also ahead ex. 3.12.

22. See Mozart, Piano Sonata in C, K. 309/284b, iii, 1–4; Beethoven, String Quartet in C Minor, Op. 18/4, i, 1–4; Beethoven, Violin Sonata in A Minor, Op. 23, i, 1–4.

23. If the melody is transposed by an ascending fifth (or descending fourth), the repetition is more like a sequence than a response.

24. Other examples: Mozart, String Quartet in F, K. 590, ii, 1–4; Beethoven, Violin Sonata in A, Op. 30/1, ii, 1–8; Beethoven, Piano Sonata in C ("Waldstein"), Op. 53, i, 1–8. Throughout this book, additional illustrations of formal situations and procedures are cited in order to supplement those discussed in the musical examples.

25. Deviations from the norms of formal organization are mentioned regularly throughout this book. Needless to say, the notion of formal deviation must be understood to carry no pejorative connotations. On the contrary, many deviations are of special aesthetic and compositional interest.

26. A case of an *extended* presentation in the loose organization of a subordinate theme is examined in connection with ex. 8.1, mm. 28–33.

Identifying techniques of phrase alterations (extension, expansion, compression) as deviations from the norms of a symmetrical grouping structure (2 + 2, 4 + 4, etc.) has a long and distinguished history in the theory of musical form (and rhythm). Riepel, Kirnberger, and Koch initiated the practice in the eighteenth century, and it found even greater expression in the metrical theories of Hugo Riemann and the formal theories of Schoenberg (*Musical Composition* frequently refers to various techniques of phrase alteration). Rothstein's excellent study (*Phrase Rhythm*, esp. chaps. 2 and 3) discusses many of the same issues, particularly in relation to a Schenkerian viewpoint (but also a Riemannian one). The treatment of the topic here, though similar to others of its kind, emphasizes the form-functional contexts in which the standard techniques of phrase alteration arise.

27. The label *Main Theme* (and the subsequent italicized labels) refer to interthematic functions discussed in chap. 15.

28. Other examples: Mozart, Piano Concerto in F, K. 413/387a, ii, 1–6 (R = ½N); Beethoven, Symphony No. 1 in C, Op. 21, i, 13–24; Beethoven, String Quartet in C, Op. 59/3, i, 30–40; Beethoven, Piano Sonata in C ("Waldstein"), Op. 53, i, 1–8. References to "other examples" that appear following the discussion of a musical example pertain to the general formal technique or principle illustrated by the example as a whole, not necessarily to a specific technique mentioned toward the end of the discussion.

29. In addition to speaking of this phrase as a "continuation," Schoenberg also calls it a "development" (*Musical Composition*, 58), as does Ratz, when he exclusively refers to this phrase as an *Entwicklung* (*Musikalische Formenlehre*, 21, 24). Since "development" has more specific meanings in traditional formal theory (develop-

ment of a motive, development section of sonata form), the expression is not used here in connection with the sentence.

30. An important exception to the prominence of continuation function over cadential function is discussed later in connection with a "continuation⇒cadential" phrase.

31. Schoenberg refers to this procedure as "reduction" (*Musical Composition*, 59), but I have avoided that expression here because of its different meaning in connection with a Schenkerian representation of harmonic–contrapuntal phenomena.

32. For an insightful discussion of Mozart's tendency to increase surface rhythmic activity toward the end of themes, see Edward E. Lowinsky, "On Mozart's Rhythm," in *The Creative World of Mozart*, ed. Paul Henry Lang (New York: Norton, 1963), 31–55.

33. See also ahead ex. 3.16.

34. See Ann Blombach, "Phrase and Cadence: A Study of Terminology and Definition," *Journal of Music Theory Pedagogy* 1 (1987): 225–51, for a summary of widely divergent definitions of cadence (and phrase) given in standard theory texts.

35. This last point requires further elaboration and some major modifications when we consider situations in which a thematic unit appears to begin, paradoxically, with cadential function; see chap. 8, p. 113.

36. The foregoing generalization must be qualified by those many cases in which the cadential material directly relates to earlier ideas, even the basic idea itself.

37. Thus Schoenberg's definition: "*Liquidation* consists in gradually eliminating characteristic features, until only uncharacteristic ones remain, which no longer demand a continuation. Often only residues remain, which have little in common with the basic motive. In conjunction with a cadence or half cadence, this process can be used to provide adequate delimitation for a sentence" (*Musical Composition*, 58).

38. Melodic closure need not occur precisely at the same time as harmonic closure. Indeed, the melodic line is often embellished (e.g., by suspensions) so that it concludes later than the onset of the final cadential harmony.

39. Additional cadential variants include the *evaded cadence* and the *abandoned cadence*. Since these types rarely occur in tight-knit main themes, I reserve a detailed discussion of them for chap. 8.

40. In light of the rest of the movement, this example may be interpreted as R = ½ N, in which case it would be a sixteen-measure sentence, as defined in chap. 5.
Other examples: Haydn, String Quartet in B-flat, Op. 50/1, i, 3–12; Beethoven, String Quartet in C Minor, Op. 18/4, i, 8 (a I⁶ substitutes for the final tonic).

41. Plagal cadences perhaps arise in works from the nineteenth century. But even in some of those cases, the progression from IV to I seems to omit an implied penultimate dominant of an authentic cadence.

42. Thus the concept of plagal cadence is one of many manifestations of a chronic confusion between cadential and postcadential functions.

43. The complete sentence is sometimes then repeated to close with a perfect authentic cadence, thus creating a sixteen-measure period, as discussed in chap. 5 (see exs. 5.9 and 5.10).

44. The useful term *lead-in* is introduced by Rothstein, *Phrase Rhythm*, 51–52.
See also ex. 3.5, where the closing imperfect authentic ca-

dence motivates a repetition of the continuation phrase (not shown). Other examples: Haydn, Piano Sonata in D, Hob. XVI:33, i, 1–12; Mozart, Horn Quintet in E-flat, K. 407/386c, i, 1–12.

45. Refer again to the discussion in chap. 1 of the subordinate theme of Beethoven's Piano Sonata in F Minor, Op. 2/1, i (ex. 1.8).

46. In other contexts, the same symbol indicates retrospective reinterpretations of harmony, tonality, and cadence. I thank Janet Schmalfeldt for recommending the use of this symbol for these many purposes.

47. Other examples: Haydn, Symphony No. 83 in G Minor ("The Hen"), ii, 1–8; Haydn, Piano Sonata in D, Hob. XVI:33, i, 1–8; Mozart, Violin Sonata in C, K. 403/385c, ii, 1–12; Mozart, Piano Sonata in B-flat, K. 333/315c, ii, 14–21; Beethoven, Violin Sonata in D, Op. 12/1, i, 5–13.

48. The final cadence of this theme is somewhat ambiguous. Hearing a perfect authentic cadence here is not out of the question, but it is probably best interpreted as an imperfect authentic cadence, since the principal melodic tone in measure 8 is C♯ (resolving the repeated Ds of the previous measure). The motion down to A would thus be a melodic embellishment, like that described by Koch as an "overhang" (*Überhang*), *Essay on Composition*, 24. See also the discussion in chap. 4 of ex. 4.16.

49. Other examples: Haydn, Piano Trio in E Minor, Hob. XV:12, iii, 1–8 (exposition of small ternary); Beethoven, Thirty-Three Variations for Piano ("Diabelli"), Op. 120, 1–8 (first part of small binary).

50. Frequently, the alterations take place in a repetition of an original four-measure continuation.

51. For the definition of *extension* and a discussion of how this process differs from *expansion*, see chap. 1.

52. Other examples: Mozart, Piano Sonata in A Minor, K. 310/300d, i, 1–9; Mozart, Piano Sonata in B-flat, K. 333/315c, i, 1–10; Beethoven, Piano Sonata in F, Op. 10/2, i, 1–12; Beethoven, Piano Sonata in B-flat ("Hammerklavier"), Op. 106, i, 1–17.

53. *Musical Composition*, 30, and ex. 45(I), p. 38.

54. Other example: Haydn, String Quartet in G Minor ("The Rider"), Op. 74/3, ii, 1–10.

55. Other examples: Haydn, String Quartet in F Minor ("The Razor"), Op. 55/2, iv, 1–6; Haydn, Piano Trio in F, Hob. XV:2, i, 1–7.

Chapter 4

1. *Period* has long been used as a term for formal organization. In the eighteenth century, the term broadly described various phrase-structural patterns ending with a relatively strong cadence. Nineteenth-century theorists began to characterize the period as a symmetrical, two-phrase structure with differentiated cadential weight, a notion that has remained largely intact to the present. See Carl Dahlhaus, "Periode," *Riemann Musiklexikon*, 12th ed., vol. 3, *Sachteil* (Mainz: B. Schott, 1967), 721–22.

Schoenberg and his followers restrict the concept of period to what is frequently called the "parallel period" (i.e., where the beginning of the consequent is the same as the beginning of the antecedent), and this tradition is continued here. The so-called contrasting period is better understood as a *hybrid theme* (see chap. 5).

2. In a small ternary to be discussed in chap. 6, we will observe the same basic idea used to begin a period and, later in the form, a sentence (see ex. 6.11).

3. See Piano Concertos in C, K. 415/387b, in D, K. 451, in G, K. 453, and in B-flat, K. 456.

4. See also ahead ex. 6.5, mm. 1–8. Other examples: Haydn, Piano Sonata in D, Hob. XVI:37, i, 1–4; Mozart, Piano Concerto in B-flat, K. 456, ii, 1–4.

5. Some theorists introduce a wide range of factors for defining various degrees of cadential weight. See Kohs, *Musical Form*, 26–27; and Douglass M. Green, *Form in Tonal Music*, 2d ed. (New York: Holt, Rinehart and Winston, 1979), 8–9. To be sure, many individual cadences of the same type (either half, imperfect authentic, or perfect authentic) can give the impression of having differing amounts of perceptual salience. But for the definition of form, all cadences of the same type are considered to have the same structural weight.

6. An exception to the principle that an antecedent cannot close with a perfect authentic cadence is raised toward the end of this chapter in connection with the *reinterpreted half cadence*.

7. Other examples: Mozart, Violin Sonata in A, K. 526, iii, 4–5; Mozart, Piano Sonata in G, K. 283/189h, ii, 2–3 (R = ½ N).

8. Likewise, "start" and "beginning" are similarly distinct. See the discussion on "start of the coda" in chap 12. For more on this topic, see Kramer, *Time of Music*, 202–3.

9. The terms *elision* and *elided cadence* are widely found in modern formal theory (Berry, *Form in Music*, 9; Green, *Form in Tonal Music*, 15; Kohs, *Musical Form*, 22). For this reason, their use is retained here. Koch, writing late in the eighteenth century, evokes the more colorful image of a "suffocation" or "choking" of a measure (*Tacterstickung*) (*Essay on Composition*, 54–56). More recently, the term "overlap" has been employed in connection with this phenomenon (Rothstein, *Phrase Rhythm*, 44; Lerdahl and Jackendoff, *Generative Theory*, 55–62).

It may be objected that "elision" is incorrectly used in this context, since neither the end of one phrase nor the beginning of the next is suppressed or omitted. Both these structural events are present but are sounding simultaneously. Yet the literal sense of elision can still be maintained when we recognize that the procedure is not one of omitting a structural event but, rather, a unit of time. In other words, the end of a phrase and the beginning of a new phrase normally occupy two distinct measures. In the case of phrase elision, however, one of these measures is omitted. For further discussion of these issues, see Schmalfeldt, "Cadential Processes," 46–47, n. 11, and 48–49, n. 14.

10. An elided antecedent and consequent would also result in an asymmetrical rhythmic structure—a five-measure antecedent overlapping with a four-measure consequent.

11. See Mozart, Piano Concerto in D Minor, K. 466, ii, 1–8.

12. See also ahead ex. 4.12. Other examples: Haydn, String Quartet in C, Op. 50/2, iii, 1–8; Beethoven, Piano Sonata in E-flat ("Lebewohl"), Op. 81a, ii, 1–8.

13. Other examples: Haydn, Piano Trio in D, Hob. XV:24, i, 2–13; Beethoven, String Quartet in B-flat, Op. 18/6, iii, 1–8; Beethoven, Piano Sonata in D ("Pastoral"), Op. 28, ii, 1–8.

14. Occasionally, the contrasting idea of the antecedent is also harmonized exclusively by a cadential progression (see ex. 4.1, mm. 3–4).

15. Schoenberg correctly observes that the term "symmetry" is not entirely applicable to musical form: "Former theorists and aestheticians called such forms as the period symmetrical. The term symmetry has probably been applied to music by analogy to the forms of the graphic arts and architecture. But the only really symmetrical forms in music are the mirror forms, derived from contrapuntal music. Real symmetry is not a principle of musical construction. Even if the consequent in a period repeats the antecedent strictly, the structure can only be called 'quasi-symmetrical'" (*Musical Composition*, 25).

Ratz also admits that "the concept of symmetry in music is not applicable in the strictest sense because of its [music's] temporal dimension," but he nevertheless prefers "this idea to all others because of its direct vividness and usefulness" (*Musikalische Formenlehre*, 24, n.; this and all subsequent translations of Ratz are mine). This book follows Ratz in using the term "symmetrical" in reference to grouping structures involving equal-length units.

16. The D♯ in the melody of m. 7 suggests a local tonicization of the submediant degree, but the subsequent E ends up functioning as an appoggiatura to D within tonic harmony. The VI harmony implied here, however, is eventually realized in interesting ways later in the minuet (see chap. 15, nn. 22, 25).

Other examples: Haydn, Piano Sonata in C, Hob. XVI:48, ii, 1–12; Haydn, Piano Trio in D, Hob. XV:24, i, 2–13; Mozart, Piano Sonata in F, K. 533, iii, 1–12; Beethoven, Piano Sonata in A-flat, Op. 26, iv, 1–12.

17. Interpolations rarely occur within a sentence; thus they were not treated in chap. 3. For an example, see Mozart, Violin Sonata in C, K. 403/385c, ii, 3 and 6.

18. Other examples: Haydn, Piano Trio in E, Hob. XV:28, iii, 1–12 (4 + 8); Haydn, Variations for Piano in F Minor, Hob. XVII:6, 30–39 (4 + 6); Mozart, Piano Concerto in D Minor, K. 466, iii, 1–13 (4 + 9); Mozart, Piano Sonata in C, K. 279/189d, iii, 1–10 (4 + 6).

19. Other examples: Haydn, String Quartet in D ("The Frog"), Op. 50/6, iv, 1–8; Haydn, String Quartet in D Minor ("Fifths"), Op. 76/2, ii, 1–4 (R = ½ N); Beethoven, Piano Sonata in A-flat, Op. 26, ii, 1–8.

20. See ex. 3.15 for a similar ambiguity of cadence type.

Chapter 5

1. *Musikalische Formenlehre*, 24.

2. Indeed, Ratz admits that "in practice, of course, we will frequently meet themes that cannot be attributed clearly to one or the other type." He then states his fundamental attitude toward the establishment and employment of formal categories, an attitude that also underlies this book: "But only when we have correctly comprehended the contrasting nature of these two kinds of construction [the sentence and period] (both of which, however, represent *tight-knit* organization) can we find our way about in the great variety of their appearances. We first have to establish clearly a type that exists as a norm and can be considered as such according to its nature, in order to be able to recognize eventual deviations. And it cannot be disputed that what we have described as the period and the sentence in the sense of opposing, extreme cases is present in the works of the masters, indeed, not only in Beethoven, but in Bach, Haydn, and Mozart as well. Although we understand the concepts of period and sentence as more narrow (and consequently more definite) than has otherwise been the case in the theory of form, we believe that we have helped to clarify these concepts and to emerge from the vague circumstance where different phenomena are designated by the same term" (pp. 24–25).

3. Such nonconventional theme-types are discussed and illustrated in chap. 13 in connection with main themes of sonata form.

4. See also ahead ex. 5.13, mm. 1–8, and ex. 15.4, mm. 1–10. Other examples: Haydn, String Quartet in F, Op. 74/2, ii, 1–8; Haydn, Piano Trio in G, Hob. XV:25, i, 1–10; Mozart, Piano Concerto in B-flat, K. 456, ii, 1–8; Mozart, Piano Trio in B-flat, K. 502, ii, 1–8; Beethoven, String Quartet in F, Op. 59/1, iii, 1–8; Beethoven, Piano Sonata in A, Op. 2/2, ii, 1–8.

5. See also ahead ex. 7.5, mm. 1–8, and ex. 7.8, mm. 1–8. Other examples: Mozart, Symphony No. 35 in D ("Haffner"), K. 385, iii, 1–8; Beethoven, Violin Sonata in E-flat, Op. 12/3, ii, 1–8, iii, 1–8; Beethoven, Piano Sonata in C Minor, Op. 111, ii, 1–8.

6. The choice of this term will become clearer when we examine the sixteen-measure sentence and observe that a four-measure compound basic idea is repeated to make an eight-measure presentation.

7. See also ahead ex. 5.11, mm. 1–8, ex. 5.14, mm. 1–8, ex. 6.7, mm. 27–34, and ex. 15.1, mm. 1–8. Other examples: Haydn, String Quartet in F, Op. 77/2, i, 1–8; Mozart, Horn Quintet in E-flat, K. 407/386c, ii, 1–8; Mozart, String Quartet in D, K. 499, ii, 1–8; Beethoven, Violin Sonata in D, Op. 12/1, ii, 1–8; Beethoven, Bagatelle in E-flat, Op. 126/3, 1–8.

8. See also ahead ex. 5.12, mm. 1–8, ex. 6.6, mm. 1–8, ex. 6.8, mm. 9–16, and ex. 13.9, mm. 14–21. Other examples: Beethoven, String Quartet in A, Op. 18/5, ii, 82–89; Beethoven, Bagatelle in E-flat, Op. 126/3, 9–16.

9. See also ahead ex. 6.7, mm. 1–8, ex. 6.9, mm. 67–74, and ex. 7.6, mm. 1–8. Other examples: Haydn, Symphony No. 103 in E-flat ("Drumroll"), ii, 27–34; Haydn, String Quartet in C ("The Bird"), Op. 33/3, ii, 1–10; Mozart, String Quartet in B-flat, K. 589, iii, 1–8; Beethoven, Piano Sonata in G, Op. 49/2, ii, 1–8.

10. Of the hybrids illustrated in this chapter, exs. 5.3, 5.4, 5.5, and 5.8 function independently as the main theme of a movement. Exs. 5.1 and 5.2 form the first part of a small binary; ex. 5.7, the A' section of a small ternary; and ex. 5.6, the antecedent of a sixteen-measure period.

11. The small ternary form and the strophic song form are additional contexts suitable for the use of a hybrid whose basic idea appears only once. See William E. Caplin, "Hybrid Themes: Toward a Refinement in the Classification of Classical Theme Types," *Beethoven Forum* 3 (1994): 163–64.

12. Thus a sixteen-measure compound theme must be distinguished from a simple eight-measure theme consisting of sixteen notated measures (R = 2N), such as exs. 3.2 and 4.7.

13. Compound hybrid themes appear seldom in the literature and thus require no special treatment here. See Beethoven, Piano Sonata in G, Op. 79, i, 1–12, for a compound sentential hybrid (8-m. compound basic idea + 4-m. continuation).

14. A reinterpreted half cadence (see chap. 4) is frequently used to end the large-scale antecedent, which often gives the strong impression of having modulated to the dominant region. See Mozart, Piano Trio in B-flat, K. 502, i, 1–20; Mozart, Violin Sonata in B-flat, K. 454, ii, 1–16.

15. What is defined here as a sixteen-measure period is frequently termed a "double period" in a number of standard textbooks (see Berry, *Form in Music*, 22–23; Green, *Form in Tonal Music*, 63–65; Kohs, *Musical Form*, 66–67). Unfortunately, double period implies a form made up of two periods or of a period within

a period. Since that situation rarely occurs in classical themes (for an exception, see n. 22), the term is not used in this book.

16. As will be discussed later, the "return of the basic idea" associated with a four-measure consequent would obscure the articulation of a higher-level consequent.

17. Other examples: Haydn, String Quartet in E, Op. 54/3, iv, 1–16; Mozart, Piano Trio in E, K. 542, iii, 1–16; Beethoven, Violin Sonata in A Minor, Op. 23, iii, 1–20.

18. The notion of abandoning a cadence is explained and illustrated in chap. 8.

Other example: Haydn, Symphony No. 83 in G Minor ("The Hen"), ii, 1–16.

19. Other examples: Haydn, Symphony No. 104 in D ("London"), i, 1–16; Mozart, Piano Sonata in B-flat, K. 333/315c, i, 23–38; Beethoven, Bagatelle in E-flat, Op. 126/3, 1–16.

20. Other example (of a significantly altered consequent): Haydn, String Quartet in F, Op. 77/2, i, 1–16.

21. Other examples: Mozart, String Quartet in C ("Dissonance"), K. 465, iv, 1–16; Mozart, Piano Sonata in F, K. 332/300k, i, 41–56.

22. For one such exception, see Mozart, Violin Sonata in E-flat, K. 481, i, 69–84.

23. It is not immediately clear why hybrid type 2 (antecedent + cadential) rarely appears as a constituent of the sixteen-measure period (except occasionally in the consequent unit). Perhaps the reason lies in the tendency for the cadential phrase of this hybrid to close with an authentic cadence (with its four principal harmonies), rather than with a half cadence, which is typically used for projecting a large-scale antecedent function.

24. Other example: Mozart, Symphony No. 36 in C ("Linz"), K. 425, i, 20–42.

25. With the sixteen-measure sentence, the term compound basic idea comes entirely into its own. The function of a repeated compound basic idea within that form is identical to the repeated simple idea of an eight-measure sentence.

26. Other examples: Mozart, Symphony No. 41 in C ("Jupiter"), K. 551, iii, 1–16; Mozart, String Quartet in A, K. 464, i, 1–16; Mozart, Piano Quartet in G Minor, K. 478, i, 1–16. The sixteen-measure sentence seems to be a favorite theme-type for beginning a classical concerto. Mozart uses the form at the start of four of his mature piano concertos (in B-flat, K. 450, in G, K. 453, in D Minor, K. 466, and in C, K. 503). Beethoven uses the compound sentence to open his first three piano concertos and also his violin concerto.

27. The same ratio is also seen frequently in the simple eight-measure sentence, in which the two-measure basic idea is fragmented into one-measure units at the beginning of the continuation phrase.

28. Other examples: Haydn, String Quartet in C ("Emperor"), Op. 76/3, iv, 1–12; Haydn, Piano Sonata in E-flat, Hob. XVI:49, i, 1–12.

29. Other example: Beethoven, Piano Concerto No. 2 in B-flat, Op. 19, i, 1–16.

Chapter 6

1. The small ternary form as defined in this study has been described by theorists and historians in a wide variety of ways. Some understand the form to be essentially tripartite and use such

terms as "small ternary" (Schoenberg, *Musical Composition*, 119–25) or "three-part song form" (*dreiteiliges Lied*) (Ratz, *Musikalische Formenlehre*, 25–28). Others see the form as essentially bipartite, such as Leonard Ratner's concept of the "small two-reprise form" (*Classic Music*, 209–16). Many theorists employ both binary and ternary labels, such as Berry (*Form in Music*, 41, 48) and Kohs (*Musical Form*, 111–19), who view the "rounded binary" and the "incipient ternary" as roughly the same form (see also Green, *Form in Tonal Music*, 87). Dénes Bartha, "Liedform-Probleme," in *Festskrift Jens Peter Larsen*, ed. Nils Schiørring, Henrik Glahn, and Carsten E. Hatting (Copenhagen: Wilhelm Hansen, 1972), 317–37, summarized in "Song Form and the Concept of 'Quatrain,'" in *Haydn Studies*, ed. Jens Peter Larsen, Howard Serwer, and James Webster, 353–55 (New York: Norton, 1981), sees the form as a four-part structure and describes it using his concept of "quatrain,'" which he also uses for the sentence form (see chap. 3, n. 1).

2. *Interior theme* is first defined in connection with the large ternary form (chap. 14) and further discussed in connection with the various rondo forms (chap. 16).

3. As briefly discussed in chap. 1, tight-knit organization arises from harmonic–tonal stability, clear-cut cadences, motivic unity, functional efficiency, and symmetrical groupings. The companion concept of loose organization arises from harmonic–tonal instability, lack of cadence, motivic diversity, functional inefficiency or ambiguity, and asymmetrical groupings. I develop these general criteria more fully toward the close of this chapter.

4. Some theorists identify fundamentally different forms based on whether the first section modulates or else remains in the home key (e.g., Green's distinction between "continuous" and "sectional" forms [*Form in Tonal Music*, 74]). To be sure, the tonal organization of the A section—be it modulating or not—has major consequences (both tonal and phrase structural) for the remainder of the theme. Nevertheless, I recognize the small ternary as a single formal type because of the many other functional features that do not depend on this tonal distinction.

5. The only exception to this rule is found in a small number of ternaries by Haydn, in which the A section ends with a half cadence. See Symphony No. 92 in G ("Oxford"), ii, 7–8; String Quartet in E-flat, Op. 76/6, i, 7–8. As discussed in chap. 7, an apparent A section ending with a half cadence is more typical of a small binary than a small ternary.

6. See ahead exs. 6.5 and 6.8 for A sections built as a non-modulating period. The exposition of ex. 6.9 is best analyzed as a periodic hybrid (compound basic idea + consequent) because the implied half cadence in m. 70 is undermined by the tonic pedal, which continues until just before the final cadence.

7. See ahead exs. 6.2 and 6.11 for cases of modulating A sections.

8. See ahead ex. 6.4 for an A section constructed as a regular eight-measure sentence. The exposition of ex. 6.6 is a sentential hybrid made up of a compound basic idea followed by a continuation.

9. The sixteen-measure period of ex. 5.14, for instance, serves as the A section of a small ternary. See also Haydn, String Quartet in D ("The Lark"), Op. 64/5, ii, 1–16.

10. See ex. 6.7, examined later in the section on "compressed recapitulation."

11. For an exposition of a small ternary built as an incomplete theme, see Haydn, Symphony No. 76 in E-flat, iv, 1–4.

12. Since this idea has the same harmony and rhythm of mm. 1–2, it is interpreted here as a repetition of the basic idea, but because of its differing contour, it could also be heard as a contrasting idea.

13. Note how the accumulating melodic ascents in m. 3 compensate for the cadential nature of the basic idea. Thus, although an interpolation may not relate functionally to its surrounding material, it still can contribute important elements of functionality to a theme (cf. ex. 4.11, upbeats to mm. 3 and 8). This interpolation also has a certain "introductory" quality about it, as if the repeated basic idea were having trouble getting started again.

14. See ahead ex. 6.10, m. 9, for another case of a closing section (consisting of a single codetta) at the end of a small-ternary exposition.

15. In some highly exceptional cases in Beethoven, the contrasting middle emphasizes tonic and even ends with that harmony. See String Quartet in A, Op. 18/5, ii, 9–12; Rondo for Piano in C, Op. 51/1, i, 9–13.

16. That the B section of a small ternary can sometimes be built as an eight-measure sentence, but not as an eight-measure period, suggests that the former is, in principle, looser than the latter.

17. Ratz, *Musikalische Formenlehre*, 25.

18. This rather colloquial term is a direct translation of Ratz's *Stehen auf der Dominante* (*Musikalische Formenlehre*, 25). It is important in this connection to distinguish dominant prolongation, which is a type of harmonic progression, from standing on the dominant, which is a label of formal function.

19. Other examples: Haydn, Piano Trio in E-flat, Hob. XV:30, ii, 11–14; Mozart, String Quintet in E-flat, K. 614, ii, 9–12 (very similar to the *Eine kleine Nachtmusik* theme just discussed); Beethoven, Piano Sonata in G, Op. 14/2, iii, 9–16; Beethoven, Piano Sonata in D ("Pastoral"), Op. 28, ii, 9–16 (features fragmentation and liquidation following the repeated new idea).

20. Ratz sees the third statement of the idea as a departure from the norm (namely, that the B section usually features a single repetition of a new idea), and he claims that this extra repetition motivates further deviations in the recapitulation. The discussion of ex. 6.4 here owes much to Ratz's insightful analysis of this theme (*Musikalische Formenlehre*, 26–28).

21. Other examples: Haydn, Symphony No. 101 in D ("The Clock"), ii, 11–23; Mozart, Clarinet Quintet in A, K. 581, iv, 9–12; Beethoven, Violin Sonata in C Minor, Op. 30/2, ii, 17–20.

22. Other examples: Haydn, Symphony No. 76 in E-flat, iv, 9–12; Haydn, Symphony No. 104 in D ("London"), ii, 9–16; Mozart, Piano Sonata in D, K. 284/205b, iii, 9–12; Beethoven, Cello Sonata in G Minor, Op. 5/2, ii, 9–12.

23. Other examples: Haydn, String Quartet in E-flat ("The Joke"), Op. 33/2, iv, 9–16; Haydn, Piano Sonata in C, Hob. XVI:48, ii, 13–20; Mozart, Piano Concerto in C, K. 467, iii, 9–20.

24. Other examples: Haydn, String Quartet in E-flat ("The Joke"), Op. 33/2, iv, 17–28; Haydn, String Quartet in C, Op. 50/2, i, 13–20; Beethoven, Piano Concerto No. 3 in C Minor, Op. 37, iii, 22–26.

25. Thus the modulation to the dominant in the B section of ex. 6.11 (appearing later in the chapter) is somewhat unusual, since the A section has already confirmed that region as a subordinate key.

26. A similar procedure occurs at m. 14 in ex. 6.4, where the dominant region is only tonicized. The seventh introduced at the

end of the section prohibits us from hearing the final harmony as a temporary tonic but, rather, reinforces its exclusively dominant function.

27. Other examples: Haydn, Symphony No. 74 in E-flat, ii, 9–12; Haydn, String Quartet in E-flat, Op. 50/3, ii, 9–16; Mozart, Rondo for Piano in A Minor, K. 511, 9–22; Beethoven, Piano Trio in E-flat, Op. 1/1, ii, 9–12.

28. Other examples: Haydn, String Quartet in F, Op. 74/2, ii, 9–16; Beethoven, String Quartet in G, Op. 18/2, iv, 9–20.

29. As I discuss in later chapters, a dominant arrival also occurs at the end of other loosely organized units, such as a transition (chap. 9) or a *core* of a development (chap. 10).

30. Other examples: Haydn, Piano Trio in E Minor, Hob. XV:12, iii, 21–22; Beethoven, Bagatelle in D, Op. 33/6, 12.

31. Other example: Beethoven, String Quartet in E-flat ("Harp"), Op. 74, iv, 13–16.

32. The dominant of the submediant is strongly related to the dominant of the home key because both harmonies contain the leading-tone (in this instance, G). Thus just as the sixth scale-degree functions as a tonic substitute, so can the dominant of this degree be understood as a substitute for the home-key dominant.

33. In the transition that immediately follows this main theme (see ex. 9.8), the opening material of the B section appears again. This time, however, the implied resolution to the submediant is realized, and a sudden fortissimo F-major chord initiates the subordinate theme.

34. Additional cases of tonal adjustment can be seen in the A' sections of exs. 6.1, 6.2, 6.7, and (ahead) 6.11.

35. Other examples: Haydn, String Quartet in D ("The Lark"), Op. 64/5, ii, 23–34; Beethoven, Piano Sonata in A, Op. 2/2, ii, 13–19; Beethoven, Piano Sonata in D ("Pastoral"), Op. 28, ii, 17–22.

36. Other examples: Haydn, Symphony No. 84 in E-flat, ii, 13–16; Beethoven, Cello Sonata in G Minor, Op. 5/2, ii, 13–16.

37. Other example: Mozart, Piano Sonata in D, K. 284/205b, iii, 14–17.

38. Ratz, *Musikalische Formenlehre*, 27. Further in connection with this example, Ratz notes that writing a simple four-measure consequent-like phrase for the recapitulation is not easy when the exposition is constructed as a sentence: "The structure of the third part [of a small ternary] is significantly more complicated when the first is built as an eight-measure sentence. Here, the fundamental difference between the two types of structure [period and sentence] is especially clear. Since the consequent phrase of the period represents a varied repetition of the antecedent phrase, the third part of the small ternary can be confined to the stating of the antecedent or consequent or some analogous combination of the two that suits the harmonic requirements. On the contrary, the two parts of the eight-measure sentence (2 × 2) + 4 are not similar: the two-measure basic idea and its repetition give the premises to which conclusions are drawn in the continuation phrase. Therefore, it is not possible simply to use only one of the two halves; rather, another course must be followed" (p. 26).

39. By developing one motive of the basic idea in the A section and another in the A' section, Beethoven realizes one of Ratz's "laws of artistic economy": "if one of two possibilities is employed at a given place, then one endeavors to employ the other possibility at an analogous place" (*Musikalische Formenlehre*, 28).

40. Other examples: Haydn, Symphony No. 104 in D ("Lon-

don"), ii, 17–37; Haydn, Piano Trio in E-flat Minor, Hob. XV:31, i, 17–32; Haydn, Piano Sonata in E-flat, Hob. XVI:49, ii, 27–36.

41. This generalization is perhaps open to debate. Since the recapitulation minimally demands a return of the basic idea and a closing perfect authentic cadence, one may argue that anything else is functionally redundant. Thus, paradoxically, a recapitulation organized exactly like its preceding exposition might be considered looser than that exposition, and a compressed version of the recapitulation might be understood as equally tight knit as the exposition.

Chapter 7

1. Moreover, many theorists resist drawing a categorical distinction between binary and ternary. Indeed, some find it possible to analyze a given theme as both a "rounded binary" and an "incipient ternary" (see chap. 6, n. 1).

2. The notion of a specific small binary (*zweiteiliges Lied*) derives largely from Ratz (*Musikalische Formenlehre*, 30), who, even more than Schoenberg, establishes this theme-type as conceptually distinct from, but strongly related to, the small ternary. (Schoenberg likely recognized and taught the small binary, but he does not discuss the form in either *Musical Composition* or *Structural Functions*.)

3. For exceptions to this rule, see chap. 6, n. 5.

4. Ratz, *Musikalische Formenlehre*, 30.

5. Letter labels cannot satisfactorily represent the form. The combination A–B would suggest, in regard to their meaning in the small ternary, a structure consisting of an exposition and a contrasting middle. Likewise, A–A' would suggest an exposition followed by a recapitulation.

6. Of the examples discussed in this chapter, only ex. 7.5 deviates from the norm.

7. Exs. 7.3, 7.5, 7.6, and 7.8 begin with conventional theme-types.

8. See ahead exs. 7.4 and 7.7 for first parts that end with a half cadence.

9. Hybrid type 1 (antecedent + continuation) usually closes with an authentic cadence but may sometimes close with a half cadence, especially when serving as the antecedent of a compound period.

10. In this respect I disagree with Ratz, who holds that "the small binary (8 + 8) is differentiated from the small ternary above all by the absence of a functionally contrasting middle section" (*Musikalische Formenlehre*, 30). Rather, these forms differ on the presence or absence of a recapitulation function.

11. See ahead exs. 7.2, 7.4, and 7.8 for second parts that begin with contrasting material.

12. Other examples: Haydn, Symphony No. 84 in E-flat, iv, 1–16; Mozart, Piano Sonata in B-flat, K. 570, ii, 32–39 (R = ¼N).

13. See the remarks by Ratz, chap. 6, n. 38.

14. Other examples: Mozart, Piano Sonata in D, K. 284/205b, iii, var. 7 (*minore*), 14–17; Beethoven, Seven Variations for Piano on "God Save the King," WoO 78, var. 5 (*minore*), 12–14.

15. See chap. 2, ex. 2.7h, for a discussion of the unusual function of this diminished seventh chord.

16. Other examples: Haydn, Piano Sonata in E Minor, Hob. XVI:34, iii, 1–18; Beethoven, Violin Sonata in D, Op. 12/1, ii, 17–24; Beethoven, Piano Sonata in C Minor, Op. 111, ii, 13–16.

17. Other examples: Haydn, Piano Trio in G, Hob. XV:15, ii, 1–16; Mozart, Piano Trio in G, K. 564, ii, 1–16; Mozart, Piano Sonata in C, K. 330/300h, ii, 1–20.

The second part of ex. 7.2 might also be seen to belong to this category, since the phrase following the contrasting middle begins with dominant harmony (m. 21). But this dominant resolves directly to the tonic in the following measure, thereby giving the impression that the entire two-measure idea is supported essentially by tonic harmony. As a result, the sense of a "consequent" for the phrase as a whole seems more compelling for this example than for ex. 7.6, whose dominant is salient throughout the first two-measure idea of the final phrase (mm. 13–14).

18. For an example of a periodic second part, see Haydn, Piano Sonata in D, Hob. XVI:33, iii, 9–16.

19. Other examples: Beethoven, Violin Sonata in G, Op. 96, iii, 1–32; Beethoven, Thirty-Three Variations for Piano ("Diabelli"), Op. 120, theme.

Chapter 8

1. In major-mode works, the subordinate key is normally the dominant region; in minor-mode works, it is the relative major, occasionally the minor dominant. From his middle period on, Beethoven sometimes used mediant relations, such as III or ♭VI, to produce the subordinate key in major-mode works.

2. Rosen, *The Classical Style*, 70.

3. The term *subordinate theme* is taken from Schoenberg (*Musical Composition*, 183) and is a translation of the standard German expression *Seitensatz*. English writing on sonata form more frequently speaks of a "second theme" or "second subject." This terminology, however, suggests a numbering scheme starting from the "first theme" (i.e., main theme) that often cannot be sustained in analysis. A given subordinate theme is not necessarily the literal "second" theme of a movement. The notion of a "subordinate" theme— which, needless to say, does not imply a theme of inferior aesthetic value—has the advantage of relating directly to the expression "subordinate" key, the tonal region confirmed by this theme.

4. Carl Czerny, *School of Practical Composition*, trans. John Bishop, 3 vols. (ca. 1848; reprint, New York: Da Capo, 1979), 1:35; Adolph Bernhard Marx, *Die Lehre von der musikalischen Komposition*, 5th ed., 3 vols. (Leipzig: Breitkopf und Härtel, 1879), 3:282.

5. Ratner, *Classic Music*, 217–21; James Webster, "Sonata Form," *The New Grove Dictionary of Music and Musicians*, 17:497–98.

6. The notion that the subordinate key creates a large-scale dissonance is noted prominently by Rosen, but the idea largely derives from Schenker's understanding of fundamental tonal organization.

7. Schoenberg, *Musical Composition*, 184; Ratz, *Musikalische Formenlehre*, 30–32.

8. Subordinate theme function in a minuet is not discussed here but is treated in detail in chap. 15.

9. The rare use of ternary functions in subordinate themes cannot be easily explained. It would seem to be almost a general principle for the classical composers that once melodic material is abandoned in the subordinate-theme area, that material is not brought back (as could happen with a ternary recapitulation). On the contrary, romantic composers frequently reintroduce subordinate-theme ideas in this part of the form, and thus their subordinate themes often have a ternary design. On occasion, subordinate themes display a tripartite structure recalling elements of the small

ternary form, as in Haydn, Piano Sonata in F, Hob. XVI:23, iii, 17–40. See also the discussion of Beethoven's First, Third, and Ninth Symphonies in Caplin, "Structural Expansion."

10. The subordinate theme of Haydn's String Quartet in G Minor ("The Rider"), Op. 74/3, i, ends with an imperfect authentic cadence (m. 54). A series of codettas continues to prolong the third scale-degree in the soprano, with melodic closure to the tonic achieved only with the final codetta of the exposition (m. 78). The immense first subordinate theme in the opening movement of Beethoven's Piano Sonata in B-flat ("Hammerklavier"), Op. 106, also ends exceptionally with an imperfect authentic cadence (see Caplin, "Expanded Cadential Progression," 237–42, ex. 6a). As explained in chap. 16, a number of subordinate themes in Beethoven's rondo forms fail to close with any cadence.

11. For most instrumental genres, the upper limit for the group is three subordinate themes. With the concerto, however, the appearance of four or five themes is not out of the question. See the first movement of Beethoven's Piano Concerto No. 1 in C, Op. 15, for a group containing five different subordinate themes (the third of which is even repeated and highly expanded). The presence of large subordinate-theme groups in concertos is due most likely to the need for providing sufficiently contrasting material to set up a variety of oppositions between the solo part and the orchestral accompaniment.

12. A similar extension of presentation within a I–II–V progression appears at the beginning of the subordinate theme in the first movement of Mozart's String Quartet in D, K. 575, 32–44, and in his Overture to *Don Giovanni*, K. 527, 56–61, both of which are in the same key as the sonata. In addition, the extended presentation in all three works is preceded by a *nonmodulating transition* (see chap. 9) and is followed by a continuation phrase that delays fragmentation (see the later discussion of this issue in connection with the sonata). Further similarities between the quartet, K. 575, and the sonata, K. 576, are cited in n. 57.

13. Beethoven particularly favors this loosening device in his piano sonatas. See Sonata in C Minor, Op. 10/1, i, 56–71, and ii, 24–31; Sonata in E, Op. 14/1, i, 23–38; Sonata in B-flat ("Hammerklavier"), Op. 106, i, 47–62 (the last is examined in Caplin, "Expanded Cadential Progression," 237–42).

14. Other examples: Mozart, Piano Sonata in B-flat, K. 333/315c, iii, 25–28; Beethoven, Piano Sonata in C Minor, Op. 10/1, ii, 24–27.

15. Other examples: Beethoven, Symphony No. 9 in D Minor, Op. 125, i, 120–27 (Caplin, "Structural Expansion," 50–51); Beethoven, Piano Sonata in D Minor, Op. 31/2, i, 42–55; Beethoven, Piano Sonata in B-flat ("Hammerklavier"), Op. 106, i, 47–62 (Caplin, "Expanded Cadential Progression," 237–42).

16. See ex. 8.15, mm. 18–20, discussed later in the section on "beginning with standing on the dominant."

17. Some nonconventional main themes also have individual phrases devoted to continuation and cadential function; see ahead ex. 13.1. See also Beethoven, Piano Sonata in C Minor, Op. 10/1, i, 1–22.

18. Theoretically, a sequential progression can continue indefinitely. In practice, however, most sequences lead toward a conventional harmonic goal, one that varies according to the particular sequential pattern and the formal context in which it occurs.

19. See also ahead ex. 8.6, mm. 22–26, ex. 8.14, mm. 46–49, and ex. 8.16, mm. 44–48.

20. Other example: Haydn, Piano Sonata in A, Hob. XVI:26, i, 11–17.

21. Rarely, if ever, does an initiating function (presentation or compound basic idea) follow directly on an unrealized perfect authentic cadence.

22. This same procedure was already discussed in chap. 3 as a deviation technique in connection with tight-knit main themes; see ex. 3.13, m. 8.

23. Other examples: Mozart, Piano Sonata in B-flat, K. 333/ 315c, iii, 32; Beethoven, Piano Sonata in C Minor, Op. 10/1, ii, 76.

24. If the final chord of the progression groups with the subsequent material and thus represents not a goal but, rather, a new beginning, then the potential authentic cadence is *evaded*, a situation to be discussed shortly.

25. For a deceptive cadence that substitutes for an imperfect authentic cadence, see Haydn, Piano Sonata in A, Hob. XVI:26, i, 18.

26. A number of theorists describe the phenomenon of evaded cadence: some use the identical term (Kohs, *Musical Form*, 49–50), and others speak of an "avoided cadence" (Berry, *Form in Music*, 9). Schmalfeldt, "Cadential Processes," provides extensive treatment of the phenomenon.

27. If a melodic closure truly brings the end of the prevailing phrase-structural processes, then the effect is one of deceptive cadence (assuming a substitute for the final tonic), not evaded cadence.

28. Sometimes, however, a I⁶ replacing a final cadential tonic groups with the ongoing cadential progression, thus creating a genuine deceptive cadence, not an evaded cadence; see ahead ex. 12.4, mm. 137 and 139, as discussed in chap. 12, n. 13. Schmalfeldt, on the contrary, characterizes this situation as an evaded cadence, albeit of the "deceptive type" ("Cadential Processes," 13–14).

29. For example, see Beethoven, Symphony No. 1 in C, Op. 21, i, 68–69 (discussed in Caplin, "Expanded Cadential Progression," 234–36).

30. Schmalfeldt, "Cadential Processes."

31. See ahead ex. 8.12, m. 88, for an additional case of cadential evasion involving a root-position tonic and the "one more time" technique. In such situations, the performer can be decisive in helping project the cadential evasion by making sure not to allow the event following the cadential dominant to sound like the goal of the prevailing phrase. Instead, a slight breath (*Luftpause*) before this event can help make the event sound like a new beginning.

32. One exception involves the occasional use of a V⁴₂ immediately preceding the I⁶ of either a deceptive or an evaded cadence (see ex. 2.9e). But even here, the chordal seventh in the bass voice of the inverted dominant can be explained as a passing tone, and the V⁴₂ can be understood as an embellishment of a root-position dominant.

33. The phenomenon of abandoned cadence seems not to be discussed in the theoretical literature. In my "Expanded Cadential Progression," 243, I call this cadential situation a "foiled" cadence. The idea of foiling, however, suggests the interposition of some outside force standing in the way of the cadence. But the cadential weakening brought about by inverting (or omitting) the dominant suggests more the notion of that harmony's "giving up" its promised cadential function. For this reason, I now prefer the term abandoned cadence as a more apt characterization of this loosening procedure.

34. Other examples: Mozart, Piano Concerto in F, K. 459, iii, 179–83; Beethoven, Symphony No. 3 in E-flat ("Eroica"), Op. 55,

i, 127–44 (see Caplin, "Structural Expansion," 42–43); Beethoven, Piano Sonata in C, Op. 2/3, i, 61–69.

35. A subordinate theme may, however, include an expanded cadential progression supporting a continuation⇒cadential phrase.

36. A number of the most interesting and impressive examples of cadential expansion are discussed in Caplin, "Expanded Cadential Progression," and "Structural Expansion." To avoid redundancy and save space, these passages are not reproduced again in this book but are cited where appropriate.

37. The cadential six-four has the same intervallic structure and scale-degree content as the more consonant "tonic six-four." Thus, despite its broader dissonant function (in a prolongation of V), the cadential six-four possesses a moderate degree of harmonic stability to sustain prominent expansion.

38. Other examples: Mozart, Piano Concerto in C, K. 467, i, 188–93; Beethoven, Symphony No. 3 in E-flat ("Eroica"), Op. 55, i, 77–82 (see Caplin, "Structural Expansion," 41); Beethoven, Piano Sonata in C Minor, Op. 10/1, i, 82–93.

39. See ahead ex. 8.14, mm. 50–54, for a case of pre-dominant expansion (II⁶, further embellished by VII⁷/V) within a cadential phrase. Other examples: Haydn, Piano Sonata in A, Hob. XVI: 26, i, 19–22 (see Caplin, "Expanded Cadential Progression," 228); Mozart, Violin Sonata in E Minor, K. 304/300c, i, 53–56; Beethoven, String Quartet in F, Op. 18/1, i, 78–81.

40. Even when the cadential progression begins with tonic in root position, there is often a prominent move to first inversion shortly thereafter. For a discussion of "conventionalized signs," see Janet M. Levy, "Texture as Sign in Classic and Early Romantic Music," *Journal of the American Musicological Society* 35 (1982): 482–531.

41. See also ahead ex. 8.18, mm. 43–50, in which the I⁶ is prolonged by neighboring VII⁴₃ chords substituting for the more conventional V⁴₃. Other examples: Haydn, String Quartet in F, Op. 77/2, i, 48–51; Mozart, Violin Sonata in B-flat, K. 454, i, 44–45.

42. See Beethoven, Symphony No. 1 in C, Op. 21, i, 69–77; Beethoven, Piano Sonata in B-flat ("Hammerklavier"), Op. 106, i, 75–100 (see Caplin, "Expanded Cadential Progression," 237–42).

43. Other examples: Mozart, Violin Sonata in E-flat, K. 481, i, 37–68; Beethoven, Symphony No. 1 in C, Op. 21, i, 53–77, and Piano Sonata in B-flat ("Hammerklavier"), Op. 106, i, 63–74.

44. When conflicting musical characteristics make for functional ambiguity, we must, of course, consider the actual temporal location as a cue for formal interpretation.

45. The issue of how a particular passage can express a formal function independent of its actual temporal location is complicated and worthy of considerably greater study than that attempted here. Jonathan Kramer's discussion ("Beginnings, Ending, and Temporal Multiplicity," chap. 6 in *Time of Music*) is particularly valuable. See also Agawu, *Playing with Signs*, 103; and Janet M. Levy, "Gesture, Form, and Syntax in Haydn's Music," in *Haydn Studies*, ed. Jens Peter Larsen, Howard Serwer, and James Webster (New York: Norton, 1981), 355–62.

46. Other example: Haydn, String Quartet in G, Op. 54/1, ii, 35–52. The unusual ascending minor third sequence featured at the beginning of this theme is an interesting precedent for the Beethoven example (8.12) just discussed.

47. Other example: Mozart, Piano Sonata in B-flat, K. 333/315c, iii, 24–29.

48. Other example: Beethoven, Cello Sonata in A, Op. 69, iii, 46–61.

49. An excellent study by Bathia Churgin, "Harmonic and Tonal Instability in the Second Key Area of Classic Sonata Form," in *Convention in Eighteenth- and Nineteenth-Century Music: Essays in Honor of Leonard G. Ratner*, ed. Wye J. Allanbrook, Janet M. Levy, and William P. Mahrt (Stuyvesant, NY: Pendragon, 1992), 23–57, treats subordinate themes beginning on dominant harmony along with some of the other issues of harmonic–tonal loosening discussed here (such as modal shift, tonicization of remote regions, and modulating subordinate theme).

50. In some particularly ambiguous cases, it is difficult to tell whether the standing on the dominant belongs to the transition or to the subordinate theme. This issue is raised again in chap. 13.

51. That this formal reading yields a very short transition is not problematic. Rondo forms typically de-emphasize transition function, sometimes even omitting it from the exposition entirely (see chap. 16).

52. Perhaps because he is resistant to the idea that a subordinate theme could begin with a standing on the dominant, Leo Treitler reads this entire passage as a "kind of transition" and the new material at m. 54 as a "second subject." See his "Mozart and the Idea of Absolute Music," chap. 7 in *Music and the Historical Imagination* (Cambridge, MA: Harvard University Press, 1989), 208. Donald Francis Tovey suggests a similar view in *Essays in Musical Analysis*, 7 vols. (London: Oxford University Press, 1935–39), 1:190.

53. An additional difficulty arises from the question of whether each real measure equals a notated measure or one-half a notated measure. From a purely formal perspective, the former seems to be the preferred interpretation. Rothstein, however, gives a convincing analysis of hypermeter in this movement *within* the measure, thus effectively understanding that R = ½ N (*Phrase Rhythm*, 170–73). Moreover, at one point, the music shifts by half a notated measure (cf. second half of m. 15 with first half of m. 17), as so often happens when R = ½ N.

54. As defined in chap. 6, a dominant arrival can be said to occur when the final dominant harmony of a passage is inverted, contains a dissonant seventh, or precedes the moment in time representing the end of the prevailing melodic, rhythmic, and grouping processes (the last case being a "premature" dominant arrival).

55. To simplify the rest of the discussion, all further references to internal half cadences assume the possibility of that cadence's being replaced by a dominant arrival.

56. Other example: Mozart, Piano Sonata in C Minor, K. 457, iii, 69.

57. Other examples: Haydn, Trumpet Concerto in E-flat, Hob. VIIe:1, i, 60–83; Haydn, Piano Trio in E-flat, Hob. XV:29, iii, 91–121; Beethoven, Piano Sonata in F, Op. 10/2, i, 19–55; Beethoven, Piano Sonata in C Minor ("Pathétique"), Op. 13, iii, 37–43. A subordinate theme organized along lines almost identical to ex. 8.16 can be found in the last movement of the same composer's String Quartet in D, K. 575, 32–58. The identity of key, the close dates of composition, and the similarities of form, harmonic progression, and rhythmic configurations (the new continuation features triplet arpeggiations in an alternation of I⁶ and V⁴₂) suggest overwhelmingly that one of these works served as the model for the other. (Other similarities between the two works were mentioned in n. 12.)

58. Some reasons for the rule requiring perfect authentic clo-sure for a subordinate theme have already been brought forward, including the notion that the theme needs to confirm fully the subordinate key. In addition, it can be observed in the repertory that a movement containing a single subordinate theme never ends with a half cadence. Perhaps the best reason, though, is a pragmatic one: by holding on to the idea that a subordinate theme must end with a perfect authentic cadence, it is possible to delineate precisely and consistently a wide range of form-functional situations that can arise in an exposition. Allowing a subordinate theme to end with a half cadence raises considerable difficulties, particularly in trying to clarify the relation of a subordinate theme to its prior transition.

59. The idea that the boundaries of a subordinate theme can be defined in reference to a "catchy tune" or a "lyrical melody" runs counter to the basic premises of this study. To be sure, melodic salience is an important aesthetic category, and the location of such a melody in relation to its formal context has been, and continues to be, significant for the history of style. But basing a category of musical form on such melodic criteria creates a host of problems, both theoretical and analytical.

60. See also ex. 9.14. Other examples: Haydn, Symphony No. 85 in B-flat ("La reine"), i, 62–96; Mozart, Violin Sonata in F, K. 547, ii, 32–64; Beethoven, String Quartet in C Minor, Op. 18/4, i, 34–70.

61. See Haydn, Piano Trio in E-flat, Hob. XV:29, iii, 55–58.

62. An extensive literature has grown around the rhythmical problems that ensue from Mozart's preceding the actual start of the theme (a sixteen-measure sentence) with an introductory measure (see Lerdahl and Jackendoff, *Generative Theory*, 22–25).

63. In those relatively few cases in the classical literature in which both the main and subordinate themes reside in the minor mode, a modal shift to major in the subordinate theme is not normally encountered.

64. One case of modal shift in a main theme is discussed ahead in connection with ex. 12.10b. Other examples of modal shift in main themes can be found in Mozart's Piano Concerto in C, K. 503, i, 17, and his String Quintet in C, K. 515, i, 21. Both these works, especially the latter, feature long and loosely organized main themes. A startling example appears in the opening of the slow movement of Mozart's Violin Sonata in A, K. 526, where the main theme not only shifts from major to minor but also cadences in that mode at the end of the theme. The main theme from the opening movement of Beethoven's *Waldstein* sonata also begins in major and closes in minor, signaling from the start a conflict between major and minor that pervades the movement, only to be resolved toward the end of the coda (esp. mm. 291–94).

65. Unfortunately, the examples chosen for this chapter do not illustrate the wide variety of formal situations in which a modal shift can appear. Other contexts can include a repetition of a basic idea in a presentation (Haydn, Piano Sonata in F, Hob. XVI:23, iii, 19), the beginning of a continuation (Beethoven, Symphony No. 3 in E-flat ["Eroica"], Op. 55, i, 91), and an internal dominant arrival and subsequent continuation (Mozart, Piano Concerto in B-flat, K. 456, i, 117).

66. Other examples: Haydn, Symphony No. 85 in B-flat ("La reine"), i, 62; Haydn, Symphony No. 102 in B-flat, ii, 9; Mozart, Piano Concerto in D Minor, K. 466, iii, 92; Mozart, Piano Sonata in F, K. 332/300k, iii, 50; Beethoven, Piano Sonata in C Minor ("Pathétique"), Op. 13, i, 41. Rosen considers the use of the minor

dominant at the opening of the second key as a stereotype of the mid-eighteenth century that quickly died out in the high classical style (*Sonata Forms*, 153–54 and 246, n. 3). Yet some prominent examples in Haydn, Mozart, and Beethoven suggest that the technique continued to be an important way of introducing a modal shift in a subordinate theme throughout the classical period. See also Churgin, "Harmonic and Tonal Instability," 35–37.

67. In Mozart's Piano Concerto in F, K. 459, ii, the second of two subordinate themes resides entirely in minor until the final tonic of the cadence (m. 74) shifts the music back to major.

68. The expression is coined by Ratz, who considers the *modulierender Seitensatz* to be one of two principal categories, the other being subordinate themes that reside in the dominant but that feature a different construction from the main theme (*Musikalische Formenlehre*, 30–31). With such a fundamental distinction, Ratz surely exaggerates the importance and frequency of appearance of modulating subordinate themes. Moreover, the two examples that he discusses (the slow movements of Beethoven's Piano Sonatas in A, Op. 2/2, and in E-flat, Op. 7) should not even be considered subordinate themes, since they function more as development sections.

69. But see the modulating subordinate themes in Haydn, Symphony No. 45 in F-sharp Minor ("Farewell"), i, and Mozart, Piano Sonata in A Minor, K. 310/300d, iii.

70. James Webster, "Schubert's Sonata Form and Brahms' First Maturity," *Nineteenth-Century Music* 2 (1978): 18–35, and 3 (1979): 52–71; Rosen, *Sonata Forms*, 246–61; Rey M. Longyear and Kate R. Covington, "Sources of the Three-Key Exposition," *Journal of Musicology* 6 (1988): 448–70; Churgin, "Harmonic and Tonal Instability," 24–25, 49–53.

71. For an exception, see ahead ex. 14.1, in which the first of two subordinate keys is confirmed cadentially at m. 17.

72. Rosen gives an excellent account of how the "second key" often represents an "inner expansion" of some tonal region on the road toward the dominant (*Sonata Forms*, 246–61).

73. By contrast, there is little need for an internal half cadence in the modulating theme of ex. 8.18, because the dominant harmony is emphasized sufficiently as both the second link in the sequential chain (mm. 39–42) and the accented neighbor to the cadential I^6.

74. Other examples: Beethoven, Symphony No. 8 in F, Op. 93, i; Beethoven, Piano Concerto No. 5 in E-flat ("Emperor"), Op. 73, i; Beethoven, Piano Sonata in D, Op. 10/3, i.

75. As discussed on several occasions already, a half cadence does not bring sufficient confirmation of the subordinate key to create closure for a subordinate theme (see n. 58).

76. A detailed investigation of how loosening devices can be distributed in a group of subordinate themes and the nature of the ensuing overall form exceeds the bounds of this study.

77. An extreme case is seen ahead in ex. 8.19, where the bassoon in m. 53 provides an upbeat figure to the elided m. 54.

78. Here, the term *overlap* is preferable to *elision*, since neither a formal event nor a measure of time is being omitted; see chap. 4, n. 9. Hypermetrical conflicts that can arise from accompanimental overlaps are studied by Roger Kamien in "Conflicting Metrical Patterns in Accompaniment and Melody in Works by Mozart and Beethoven: A Preliminary Study," *Journal of Music Theory* 37 (1993): 311–48.

79. For an example of a tight-knit theme occupying a medial position in a group, see Mozart, Piano Concerto in F, K. 459, iii, 203–18.

80. Other examples: Mozart, Piano Sonata in F, K. 332/300k, i, 41–56; Beethoven, Piano Sonata in C ("Waldstein"), Op. 53, i, 35–50.

81. Other example: Haydn, Piano Trio in C, Hob. XV:27, i, 82–89.

82. Rothstein is one of the few theorists to propose a consistent concept of closing theme, namely, all the material of an exposition "following the first strongly articulated perfect cadence in the goal key" (*Phrase Rhythm*, 116). Using this definition, however, he frequently identifies as closing themes units that are defined in this study as genuine subordinate themes.

83. The analytical application of "closing theme" has often created confusion between cadential function (which closes a theme) and postcadential function (which follows that structural close). Consider, for example, one part of Rosen's "textbook" definition of sonata form: "At the end of the second group, there is a *closing theme* (or several closing themes) with a cadential function. The final cadence of the exposition, on the dominant, may be followed by an immediate repetition of the exposition, or by a short transition leading back to the tonic" (*Sonata Forms*, 2). What Rosen describes as a "cadential function" is usually postcadential, and his "final cadence" is most likely a codetta. Another instance of this confusion can be found in the labeling system devised by Jan LaRue, *Guidelines for Style Analysis*, 2d ed. (Warren, MI: Harmonie Park Press, 1992), chap. 7, and followed by many subsequent historians (e.g., Eugene Wolf, Bathia Churgin, A. Peter Brown, Beth Shamgar) when the functions of "cadential" and "closing" are typically combined without differentiation into a single *K* region at the end of an exposition.

84. One thematic situation previously described, however, resembles somewhat the traditional notion of a closing "theme," namely, the case in which the final subordinate theme of a group acquires a relatively tight knit organization, so that its sense of being a subordinate theme, with a markedly loose organization, is minimally expressed (see exs. 8.2 and 8.4).

85. The closing section following the subordinate theme is often referred to as a "cadence theme" or a "cadence phrase," especially by writers following in the tradition of Donald Francis Tovey, who uses these terms to translate the traditional German *Schlussgruppe*; see Tovey, *The Forms of Music* (New York: Meridian, 1956), 210. See also his analysis of the first movement of Beethoven's *Eroica* Symphony, ibid., 223, mm. 144–47). To be sure, *Schluss* has among its technical meanings that of "cadence," but it also is a common word meaning "end" or "conclusion." As with "closing theme," this usage of "cadence theme" confuses cadential with postcadential function.

86. For an exception, see Beethoven, Piano Sonata in C Minor, Op. 10/1, ii, 44 (ex. 12.11, m. 91, shows the corresponding end of the recapitulation). In rondo forms, a closing section is sometimes replaced by a retransition (see ex. 8.5, m. 48). In concerto form, the final subordinate theme is followed not by a closing section but by an orchestral ritornello (see chap. 17).

87. As an exception, it may contain a single codetta or one that is repeated (often with some variation).

88. The closing section of ex. 8.11, mm. 66–79, is thus exceptional in that upon repetition, the first four-measure codetta is expanded to six measures.

89. As discussed in chap. 1 in connection with thematic introduction, the notion of "dynamic" refers to more than just the intensity (loudness and softness) of the musical content.

90. Surprising, too, is the fact that this moment (m. 35) is indeed the beginning of the theme; see the earlier discussion of its modulating structure.

91. One of Beethoven's favorite tricks, however, is to pull away from the climax just at the moment of cadential arrival; see ex. 8.2, m. 104, and his Piano Sonata in B-flat ("Hammerklavier"), Op. 106, i, 100.

Chapter 9

1. This formal unit is often termed "bridge" in the theoretical literature. The image of a bridge spanning two shores of a river (the main and subordinate themes) has its attractions yet is also somewhat flawed. The term suggests a structural symmetry—two ends of a bridge being anchored in the same firm soil—not entirely compatible with musical reality, in which the main theme is considerably more tightly knit than the loosely organized subordinate theme. The expression "transition" emphasizes instead the process of moving from one function to the next, without any implications about the relative stability of the surrounding functions.

2. Indeed, in an exposition, the transition can be seen as a kind of "contrasting middle" between the main and subordinate themes.

3. See Beethoven, Piano Sonata in D ("Pastoral"), Op. 28, iv, 17–20.

4. Robert Batt, "Function and Structure of Transitions in Sonata-Form Music of Mozart," *Canadian University Music Review* 9 (1988): 157–201, also speaks of loosening techniques in the transition.

5. Ex. 9.8, examined later in the chapter, is exceptional in this respect because its beginning with dominant harmony is a reference back to the B section of the main theme (see ex. 6.10, mm. 10ff.). See also Mozart, String Quartet in D Minor, K. 421/417b, i, 9ff.

6. See ex. 8.5, mm. 28–32. Other examples: Haydn, String Quartet in F, Op. 50/5, i, 25–28; Mozart, Violin Sonata in G, K. 379/373a, ii, 25–28; Beethoven, Piano Sonata in F, Op. 10/2, i, 13–18.

7. Main themes themselves, of course, do not necessarily have tuneful melodies.

8. Ratner, *Classic Music*, 19–20; see ahead ex. 9.13.

9. Ratner, *Classic Music*, 223–24, and Rosen, *Sonata Forms*, 229–38, extensively treat such modulation techniques. On differences between Haydn's and Mozart's modulatory practices, see John Harutunian, "Haydn and Mozart: Tonic–Dominant Polarity in Mature Sonata-Style Works," *Journal of Musicological Research* 9 (1990): 273–98.

10. See ahead ex. 9.7, m. 18, and ex. 9.10, m. 18, for instances of this type of modulation.

11. See ahead ex. 9.2, m. 9, ex. 9.11, m. 59, and ex. 9.15, m. 38.

12. See ahead ex. 9.12, mm. 89–92.

13. See ahead ex. 9.3, m. 12.

14. Robert Winter describes in detail the foregoing procedure as a "bifocal close" and discusses its historical antecedents and subsequent influence. See "The Bifocal Close and the Evolution of the Viennese Classical Style," *Journal of the American Musicological Society* 42 (1989): 275–337.

15. Ex. 9.5, mm. 16–17, discussed later in the chapter, shows a rare instance of the technique in a minor-mode movement.

16. Other examples: Haydn, Piano Sonata in E-flat, Hob. XVI:38, i, 8–12; Mozart, String Quartet in E-flat, K. 428/421b, i, 12–24; Beethoven, Symphony No. 1 in C, Op. 21, i, 33–52. Winter ("Bifocal Close") cites many more examples.

17. Exceptions, however, are found in some slow movements, such as Haydn, Piano Trio in E, Hob. XV:28, ii, 7–14; Mozart, String Quartet in E-flat, K. 428/421b, ii, 6–10.

18. The possibility of an exposition's including a *main-theme group* embracing more than one main theme is discussed in chap. 13.

19. See also ahead ex. 9.10. The transition of the first movement of Beethoven's Symphony No. 4 in B-flat, Op. 60, is thus somewhat unusual because the basic idea of the main theme returns in the lower voice at m. 81 (shown ahead in ex. 9.12) after the transition has already begun with new material (m. 65, not shown).

20. This well-known procedure is described at least as early as Marx's notion of "dissolved consequent" (*aufgelöster Nachsatz*) (*Lehre von der musikalischen Komposition*, 3:259).

21. Other examples: Haydn, Piano Trio in F-sharp Minor, Hob. XV:26, i, 5; Mozart, Symphony No. 40 in G Minor, K. 550, i, 22; Beethoven, Piano Sonata in C ("Waldstein"), Op. 53, i, 14.

22. See ahead ex. 9.14, m. 19. Other examples: Haydn, String Quartet in G, Op. 77/1, i, 15–26; Beethoven, Piano Sonata in D, Op. 10/3, i, 17–22.

23. The terms "inverted period" and "antiperiod" (Webster, *Haydn's "Farewell" Symphony*, 44) are also sometimes encountered.

24. Other examples: Haydn, String Quartet in F, Op. 50/5, iv, 13–24; Mozart, Violin Sonata in A, K. 526, ii, 9–16.

25. See ahead ex. 9.6, mm. 21–23, for such a rhythmic break between the closing section of the main theme and the beginning of the transition.

26. Other examples: Mozart, Clarinet Trio in E-flat, K. 498, i, 16–19; Beethoven, Piano Sonata in E-flat, Op. 7, i, 17.

27. Other examples: Haydn, String Quartet in G, Op. 76/1, i, 33; Mozart, Piano Concerto in D ("Coronation"), K. 537, iii, 65; Beethoven, Piano Sonata in C Minor, Op. 10/1, i, 32.

28. Other example: Mozart, String Quartet in G, K. 387, iv, 31–51.

29. Other examples: Haydn, String Quartet in C, Op. 50/2, i, 30–42; Beethoven, Symphony No. 7 in A, Op. 92, i, 97–112.

30. In this particular formal situation, it is not possible, even in retrospect, to identify a convincing end point for the main theme.

Other examples: Haydn, String Quartet in C, Op. 50/2, iv, 23–32; Haydn, Piano Sonata in A, Hob. XVI:30, i, 17–21.

31. Other examples: Haydn, Symphony No. 98 in B-flat, iv, 32; Beethoven, Piano Trio in E-flat, Op. 1/1, i, 26.

32. Other examples: Mozart, String Quartet in A, K. 464, iv, 33; Beethoven, Cello Sonata in A, Op. 69, i, 29.

33. See Mozart, Symphony No. 31 in D, K. 297/300a, iii, 33; Mozart, Clarinet Trio in E-flat, K. 498, i, 24.

34. Other examples: Haydn, Symphony No. 93 in D, iv, 66; Beethoven, Symphony No. 5 in C Minor, Op. 67, iv, 36; Beethoven, Piano Concerto No. 2 in B-flat, Op. 19, i, 115.

35. Chap. 13 considers more problematic cases of an obscured boundary between a transition and a subordinate theme.

36. Other examples: Haydn, Symphony No. 95 in C Minor,

iv, 53; Mozart, Piano Trio in D Minor, K. 442, i, 24; Beethoven, Symphony No. 6 in F ("Pastoral"), Op. 68, v, 41.

37. Other examples: Haydn, String Quartet in D Minor, Op. 42, i, 9–12; Haydn, Piano Sonata in F Minor, Hob. XVI:34, i, 13; Beethoven, Piano Sonata in C Minor ("Pathétique"), Op. 13, iii, 18–24. This is one of many points of similarity between the *Pathétique* and Mozart's Piano Sonata in C Minor, K. 457, discussed in ex. 9.14.

38. Other examples: Haydn, String Quartet in F, Op. 74/2, i, 28, 40; Beethoven, Symphony No. 2 in D, Op. 36, iv, 13, 26; Beethoven, Piano Sonata in C Minor ("Pathétique"), Op. 13, i, 19, 35.

39. The passage shown in this example is perhaps not by Mozart, but rather by M. Stadler.

Other examples: Mozart, Symphony No. 35 in D ("Haffner"), K. 385, i, 13, 40; Beethoven, Symphony No. 3 in E-flat ("Eroica"), Op. 55, i, 15, 37; Beethoven, Piano Sonata in E-flat, Op. 31/3, i, 18, 33; Beethoven, Piano Sonata in B-flat ("Hammerklavier"), Op. 106, i, 17, 35.

Chapter 10

1. "Working out," "elaboration," and "free fantasia" are also frequently found in the theoretical literature. The traditional German term *Durchführung* literally translates as "leading-through." Some full-movement forms (five-part rondo, minuet) contain a development now and then. Other forms (large ternary, theme and variations) use it only rarely, and the sonata without development, not at all.

2. Many writers also speak of development as a "series of techniques of thematic transformation," which may take place anywhere in a movement (Rosen, *Sonata Forms*, 262). I also will occasionally use this sense of the term to speak informally about the "development" of a particular motive or idea.

3. See the discussion of ex. 10.18 later in the section on "subordinate themelike unit."

4. Berry, *Form in Music*, 166–69; Leichtentritt, *Musical Form*, 134–48.

5. Heinrich Schenker, *Free Composition*, ed. and trans. Ernst Oster (New York: Longman, 1979), 136–37. One of Oster's notes (pp. 139–41) considerably augments Schenker's own position. A more detailed investigation into middle-ground tonal plans for development sections lies beyond the scope of this study. But see David Bushler, "Harmonic Structure in Mozart's Sonata-Form Developments," *Mozart-Jahrbuch 1984/85*, 15–24; Steven B. Jan, "X Marks the Spot: Schenkerian Perspectives on the Minor-Key Classical Development Section," *Music Analysis* 11 (1992): 37–54; and Joseph C. Kraus, "Mozart's Chromatic Third Relations: Evidence from the Late Quartets and Quintets," *Journal of Musicological Research* 9 (1990): 229–54. Significant work in this direction has also been undertaken by Edward Laufer; his paper "Voice-Leading Procedures in Development Sections" (presented at the conference "Music Theory Canada 1990," London, Ontario) unfortunately has not yet been published.

6. In a minor key, the dominant is minor because tonicizable regions are based on the "natural" minor scale.

7. Carl Schachter's recent reexamination of these issues, though, has helped rehabilitate the notion of modulation in Schenkerian theory. See his "Analysis by Key: Another Look at Modulation," *Music Analysis* 6 (1987): 289–318.

8. The tendency for the classical development section to confirm the submediant as a prominent tonal center is well known. See Rosen, *Sonata Forms*, 263; Harold L. Andrews, "The Submediant in Haydn's Development Sections," in *Haydn Studies*, ed. Jens Peter Larsen, Howard Serwer, and James Webster (New York: Norton, 1981), 465–71. A Schenkerian view is offered by David Beach, "A Recurring Pattern in Mozart's Music," *Journal of Music Theory* 27 (1983): 1–29, who interprets the typical arrival on V/VI as III♯.

9. See ahead ex. 10.18, mm. 58–68.

10. See ahead ex. 10.6, m. 90ff.

11. See ahead ex. 10.11, where the tonal regions of ♭III and ♭VI are emphasized within the development section.

12. See ahead ex. 10.8. See also Mozart, Piano Concerto in A, K. 488, i; Mozart Piano Sonata in C Minor, K. 457, i.

13. See Beethoven, Piano Sonata in D, Op. 10/3, i, 133 (♭VI).

14. Cases of exceptional harmonic endings to developments are also discussed by Heino Schwarting, "Ungewöhnliche Repriseneintritte in Haydns späterer Instrumentalmusik," *Archiv für Musikwissenschaft* 17 (1960): 168–82; Webster, *Haydn's "Farewell" Symphony*, 142–43; and Jan LaRue, "Bifocal Tonality in Haydn Symphonies," in *Convention in Eighteenth- and Nineteenth-Century Music: Essays in Honor of Leonard G. Ratner*, ed. Wye J. Allanbrook, Janet M. Levy, and William P. Mahrt (Stuyvesant, NY: Pendragon, 1992), 59–73.

15. Other examples: Haydn, Symphony No. 94 in G ("The Surprise"), i, 153–54; Haydn, String Quartet in C ("The Bird"), Op. 33/3, i, 108–9; Beethoven, Violin Sonata in A Minor ("Kreutzer"), Op. 47, i, 343; Beethoven, Piano Sonata in E-flat, Op. 31/3, i, 130–37.

16. Such textural reduction, as part of a broader liquidation process, is a common feature of developments, even when ending with the home-key dominant.

17. Other examples: Haydn, Symphony No. 90 in C, i, 137ff. (V/VI); Haydn, Symphony No. 104 in D ("London"), iv, 187ff. (V/III); Haydn, Concertante in B-flat, Hob. I:105, i, 159–62 (V/VI).

18. *Musikalische Formenlehre*, 33. The following discussion of pre-core/core technique is highly inspired by Ratz, although I introduce many refinements, as well as some differences. For example, Ratz does not consider the standing on the dominant to belong to the core proper. Schoenberg's treatment of the development (which he calls an "elaboration") attends more to issues of tonal flux and motivic play than to conventional techniques of phrase structure (*Fundamentals*, 206–9).

19. See ahead ex. 10.10. See also Haydn, Piano Trio in C, Hob. XV:27, iii; Haydn, Piano Sonata in E-flat, Hob. XVI:49, i (first core shown in ex. 10.4); Beethoven, Symphony No. 1 in C, Op. 21, i; Beethoven, Piano Concerto No. 5 in B-flat ("Emperor"), Op. 73, i (three cores).

20. In this sense, the beginning of the core resembles the beginning of a transition. Likewise, the rhythm and texture of the pre-core are often similar to that generally found in a main theme (though not necessarily to the actual main theme of the movement).

21. See Mozart, Violin Sonata in F, K. 377/374e, i, 75–76; Beethoven, String Quartet in F, Op. 18/1, i, 150–51.

22. In the case of a premature dominant arrival, the subsequent dominant prolongation does not necessarily seem like a

postcadential standing on the dominant, because the sense of structural end appears later than the dominant arrival itself (see ahead ex. 10.9, mm. 93-98).

23. Other example (prolongational progressions at the basis of fragmentation): Beethoven, Symphony No. 2 in D, Op. 36, i, 159-70.

24. Other example (sequential repetition in the model): Mozart, Piano Sonata in C Minor, K. 457, i, 83-87.

25. Other examples (core ends with perfect authentic cadence): Haydn, Piano Trio in A, Hob. XV:18, i, 118; Mozart, Piano Quartet in G Minor, K. 478, i, 133; Beethoven, Violin Sonata in A Minor ("Kreutzer"), Op. 47, i, 258.

26. This region can be heard readily enough as the subdominant of the home key, but it actually arises out of a deceptive resolution of V/VI in the short pre-core (mm. 87-89). Thus A♭ can also be understood as VI/VI, especially when the submediant region returns prominently again at m. 104.

27. Other example (sentential model): Mozart, Piano Trio in B-flat, K. 502, i, 98-103.

28. Other example (harmonic alteration within the sequence): Mozart, Piano Sonata in C Minor, K. 457, i, 83-91.

29. Other example (incomplete sequence): Mozart, Symphony No. 39 in E-flat, K. 543, iv, 115-26.

30. Other examples (new model within the fragmentation): Mozart, Symphony No. 39 in E-flat, K. 543, iv, 125-32; Mozart, Piano Sonata in B-flat, K. 570, i, 117-23.

31. Other examples (core ends with premature dominant arrival): Haydn, Piano Trio in E-flat, Hob. XV:22, i, 143; Mozart, Piano Sonata in B-flat, K. 333/315c, ii, 48; Mozart, Piano Sonata in C Minor, K. 457, i, 93; Beethoven, Symphony No. 1 in C, Op. 21, i, 130.

32. For exceptions, see Haydn, Concertante in B-flat, Hob. I:105, i; Mozart, Piano Concerto in C, K. 503, i; Mozart, Violin Sonata in F, K. 377/374e, i; Beethoven, Violin Sonata in A Minor ("Kreutzer"), Op. 47, i.

33. *Musikalische Formenlehre*, 33.

34. Transitional introductions are discussed in greater detail later in the chapter in connection with exs. 10.6, 10.7, 10.14, and 10.18.

35. See also ahead exs. 10.13, 10.14, 10.15, and 10.17. Jack Adrian, "The Function of the Apparent Tonic at the Beginning of Development Sections," *Intégral* 5 (1991): 1-53, discusses development sections that feign starting with tonic of the home key.

36. The pre-cores of exs. 10.6 and 10.18 also begin with material from their preceding closing sections (not shown).

37. Mozart's practice here is one of many manifestations of his tendency to introduce a greater variety of motivic content in a single movement than do Haydn and Beethoven. See Rudolf Kelterborn, *Zum Beispiel Mozart: Ein Beitrag zur musikalischen Analyse* (Basel: Bärenreiter, 1981), 69-80, a study directly influenced by Ratz's *Formenlehre*.

38. Unfortunately, none of the excerpts chosen for this chapter illustrates a pre-core beginning with new material. For examples, see the following works by Mozart: Quintet for Piano and Winds in E-flat, K. 452, ii, 44; Piano Trio in B-flat, K. 502, i, 83; Piano Sonata in G, K. 283/189h, i, 54; Piano Sonata in A Minor, K. 310/300d, ii, 32.

39. A pre-core does not normally feature loosening techniques associated with a subordinate theme.

40. Other examples: Haydn, Piano Sonata in A-flat, Hob. XVI:43, i, 56-61; Mozart, Piano Concerto in A, K. 488, i, 143-49; Mozart, Piano Sonata in F, K. 332/300k, i, 94-101; Beethoven, String Quartet in C Minor, Op. 18/4, i, 78-90. See also ahead ex. 10.17, in which the pre-core has the same basic structure as the main theme except that it is set in the development key of A♭ (HK: ♭III).

41. *Classic Music*, 23.

42. The four-measure presentation phrase that follows the standing on the dominant also technically belongs to the pre-core as a whole, as explained in connection with the section "multiple thematic units."

43. Other examples: Haydn, Piano Trio in E-flat, Hob. XV:22, i, 87-103; Mozart, String Quartet in C ("Dissonance"), K. 465, i, 107-21; Mozart, Piano Sonata in B-flat, K. 570, i, 80-100.

44. Other examples: Mozart, Piano Sonata in F, K. 332/300k, iii, 91-95; Beethoven, String Quartet in F, Op. 18/1, i, 115-28.

45. Other examples: Mozart, Piano Concerto in C Minor, K. 491, i, 283-301, 302-8; Beethoven, String Quartet in D, Op. 18/3, i, 108-22, 122-34.

46. For cores that are directly preceded by a presentation phrase, see Mozart, Piano Sonata in F, K. 332/300k, i, 109-12; Mozart, Piano Sonata in C Minor, K. 457, i, 79-82; Beethoven, Piano Sonata in D, Op. 10/3, i, 133-40.

47. A sense of descending fifth sequence, however, is suggested by the roots of the harmonies at m. 73 (G), m. 75 (C), and m. 77 (F).

48. Other examples: Haydn, Piano Sonata in A-flat, Hob. XVI:43, i, 64-83; Mozart, String Quartet in B-flat, K. 589, i, 77-104; Beethoven, Piano Sonata in E, Op. 14/1, i, 65-75.

49. The very slow tempo and compressed scope of the thematic material suggest that each notated measure contains more than one real measure of music. The main theme in the exposition (and thus the pre-core) takes place in four notated measures, and the entire exposition only lasts sixteen measures (it then has a written-out repeat). Likewise, mm. 36-38 give the impression of being a full presentation phrase. But since the notated 3/4 meter cannot be divided into two equal parts, the formula R = ½N cannot literally apply.

50. Other examples: Haydn, String Quartet in G, Op. 33/5, i, 114-31; Haydn, Piano Sonata in C, Hob. XVI:50, i, 73-94.

51. See Haydn, Symphony No. 94 in G ("The Surprise"), i, 125-48; Haydn, Piano Trio in C, Hob. XV:21, i, 64-82.

52. The sense of cadential abandonment arises because of our uncertainty about the position of the dominant on the downbeat of m. 84, due to the reduction of texture to a single part in the previous measure. Another interpretation would not recognize an abandoned cadence here but instead would understand all of m. 84 to be supported by an implied root-position dominant, in which I^6 and II^6_5 would be subordinate harmonies prolonging that dominant.

53. Having the development run through material of the exposition in roughly the same order occurs now and then in Haydn's compositional practice. See his Symphony No. 89 in F, i, and Piano Sonata in A-flat, Hob. XVI:43, i.

Other examples (subordinate themelike unit): Haydn, String Quartet in C ("The Bird"), Op. 33/3, i; Haydn, String Quartet in G, Op. 33/5, i, 132-70; Haydn, String Quartet in C, Op. 74/1, i, 74-84.

54. Kohs, *Musical Form*, 266; Rosen, *Sonata Forms*, 95.

55. This is largely the practice of Beth Shamgar, "On Locating the Retransition in Classic Sonata Form," *Music Review* 42 (1981): 130–43, in connection with Haydn and Mozart. With Beethoven, however, she generally recognizes the retransition beginning with the arrival of the home-key dominant.

56. Other examples: Haydn, String Quartet in G, Op. 33/5, i, 171–81; Haydn, Piano Sonata in E Minor, Hob. XVI:34, i, 71–79; Mozart, Piano Concerto in G, K. 453, i, 207–26; Mozart, Piano Quartet in G Minor, K. 478, i, 133–40.

57. Other examples: Mozart, Piano Sonata in F, K. 332/300k, i, 127–32; Beethoven, Symphony No. 1 in C, Op. 21, i, 174–77; Beethoven, Symphony No. 2 in D, Op. 36, i, 215.

58. There is little consensus in the theoretical literature on the meaning of *false recapitulation*, also termed *false return* or *false reprise*. For Berry, it includes an appearance, before the genuine recapitulation, of main-theme ideas in the "wrong" key, but also possibly in the home key (*Form in Music*, 166, 188; see also Webster, "Sonata Form," 502). Rosen insists that a genuine false reprise occurs only in the home key or its subdominant region (*Sonata Forms*, 276–82). Mark Evan Bonds further restricts it to the home key only ("Haydn's False Recapitulations and the Perception of Sonata Form in the Eighteenth Century," Ph.D. diss., Harvard University, 1988, 229). Green sees a false reprise occurring in the rondo form, where a couplet first starts out in the wrong key but then immediately corrects itself into the home key (*Form in Tonal Music*, 159). Kohs' false recapitulation is entirely different in that it involves motivic anticipations of the main theme in the standing on the dominant (*Musical Form*, 266).

59. Other examples: Haydn, Symphony No. 102 in B-flat, i, 185; Haydn, Piano Trio in E, Hob. XV:28, i, 44; Beethoven, Piano Sonata in F, Op. 10/2, i, 118.

Chapter 11

1. The minuet form has a recapitulation organized similar to the A' section of a small ternary (discussed in chap. 15). Whether or not we can speak of a recapitulation in connection with the large ternary and the five-part rondo forms is a complex issue, to be addressed in chaps. 14 and 16. Theme and variations form does not include a recapitulation.

2. To minimize confusion throughout the rest of this chapter, the term "recapitulation" is restricted to a large full-movement section, and the third section of the small ternary is called an A' section exclusively.

3. For a discussion of registral changes in Mozart's recapitulations, see Esther Cavett-Dunsby, "Mozart's 'Haydn' Quartets: Composing Up and Down Without Rules," *Journal of the Royal Musical Association* 113 (1988): 57–80.

4. This practice is rooted in the traditional notion that formal units are defined primarily by their melodic content and not necessarily by their formal function.

5. I speak of a "local" harmonic resolution here, because, in line with the Schenkerian view of sonata form (applicable as well to the allied forms), the dominant at the end of the development interrupts the progression of the fundamental *Ursatz*, which is then repeated and fully closed in the recapitulation. As a result, the dominant of the development is not structurally resolved by the beginning of the recapitulation but, rather, by its end, when the final tonic of the *Ursatz* arrives.

6. See Haydn, Symphony No. 90 in C, iv; Haydn, Piano Sonata in C, Hob. XVI:35, i; Mozart, Clarinet Quintet in A, K. 581, i.

7. See Mozart, Violin Sonata in E Minor, K. 304/300c, i.

8. *Sonata Forms*, 289. The term is useful as an informal description but is potentially misleading: the new sequential passage does not usually resemble the way in which sequences are organized in a real development. Unlike in a core, the model of a secondary development is generally short, and the sequential activity is rarely modulatory.

9. The reasons for this shift to the flat side are explained in connection with the transition, which, even more than the main theme, tends to feature this structural change.

10. In the development, a unit resembling a pre-core is followed directly by a standing on the dominant (Kelterborn, *Zum Beispiel Mozart*, 17).

11. See, for example, Mozart, Violin Concerto in A, K. 219, i; Beethoven, Piano Sonata in C Minor, Op 10/1, iii. The subordinate theme then usually begins directly in the home key, this time resolving the home-key dominant. (In the exposition, this same dominant is retained to become the tonic of the new key.) Winter discusses this situation as the realization of a "complementary bifocal close" ("Bifocal Close," 278).

12. See Haydn, Symphony No. 90 in C, iv; Haydn, Piano Sonata in A, Hob. XVI:26, i.

13. Eugene K. Wolf also mentions this point in his important study of Haydn's recapitulatory practice: "The Recapitulations in Haydn's London Symphonies," *Musical Quarterly* 52 (1966): 76–77.

14. But Nicholas Marston proposes that such passages are sometimes more truly "recapitulatory" than "developmental." See his "The Recapitulation Transition in Mozart's Music," *Mozart-Jahrbuch 1991*, pt. 2, 799.

15. Other examples: Beethoven, Piano Sonata in C Minor ("Pathétique"), Op. 13, i, 193–210; Beethoven, Piano Sonata in E-flat, Op. 31/3, i, 154–69.

16. Rarely do the main theme and transition fuse within the exposition; Mozart's Piano Sonata in C, K. 545, i, 1–12, is highly exceptional in this respect.

17. See also ahead ex. 11.17, mm. 152–77. Other example: Beethoven, Symphony No. 2 in D, Op. 36, i.

18. Other examples: Haydn, Piano Sonata in F, Hob. XVI:23, iii; Haydn, Piano Sonata in B Minor, Hob. XVI:32, i; Beethoven, Symphony No. 1 in C, Op. 21, i.

19. See Haydn, Piano Sonata in E-flat, Hob. XVI:49, i, 172–75 (cf. mm. 42–49); Mozart, Clarinet Trio in E-flat, K. 498, i, 98–113 (cf. mm. 25–47).

20. Other examples: Mozart, Piano Concerto in C, K. 467, i, 370–84; Mozart, Piano Sonata in B-flat, K. 333/315c, iii, 155–63.

21. For important discussions of major alterations in subordinate themes of Haydn's recapitulations, see Wolf, "Recapitulations"; and Ethan Haimo, "Haydn's Altered Reprise," *Journal of Music Theory* 32 (1988): 335–51.

22. The latter option is possible in the case of multiple subordinate themes, in which the second (or third) theme can then be recapitulated as usual. See Haydn, String Quartet in G, Op. 54/1, ii (the first subordinate theme in the exposition begins like the B section of the main theme and is thus deleted in the recapitulation).

23. See Symphony No. 100 in G ("Military"), i (discussed in

Haimo, "Haydn's Altered Reprise," 341–43); String Quartet in E-flat, Op. 50/3, i; String Quartet in C, Op. 64/1, i.

24. *Sonata Forms*, 287–88.

25. Other examples: Haydn, Symphony No. 85 in B-flat ("La reine"), i; Mozart, Symphony No. 41 in C ("Jupiter"), K. 551, ii.

26. Other example: Beethoven, Piano Sonata in D, Op. 10/3, i.

27. Other example: Mozart, Piano Sonata in A Minor, K. 310/300d, iii.

28. Other examples: Haydn, String Quartet in G, Op. 54/1, ii; Haydn, String Quartet in F, Op. 77/2, i.

29. Another case of the development influencing changes in the recapitulation is seen ahead in connection with ex. 11.18c; see n. 41.

30. Other example: Beethoven, Piano Sonata in B-flat ("Hammerklavier"), Op. 106, i, 227–34.

31. Other examples: Haydn, String Quartet in F, Op. 77/2, i, 145–46; Haydn, Piano Sonata in E-flat, Hob. XVI:49, i, 156–58.

32. See Haydn, String Quartet in E-flat, Op. 50/3, i (discussed in Rosen, *Sonata Forms*, 158–61); Mozart, String Quartet in G, K. 387, iv.

33. Rosen, *Sonata Forms*, 144–45.

34. Rosen, *Sonata Forms*, 286; Berry, *Form in Music*, 172; Green, *Form in Tonal Music*, 214.

35. See Haydn, String Quartet in E-flat, Op. 50/3, i; Mozart, Violin Sonata in D, K. 306/300l, i; Mozart, Piano Sonata in D, K. 311/284c, i.

36. See Mozart, *Eine kleine Nachtmusik*, K. 525, iv; Mozart, Piano Sonata in E-flat, K. 282/189g, i.

37. And as Rosen points out, subdominant recapitulations became even more of a "lazy mannerism" after 1800 (*Sonata Forms*, 144).

38. Other example: Mozart, Piano Sonata in C, K. 545, i.

39. See Beethoven, Piano Sonata in C Minor, Op. 10/1, i; Beethoven, Piano Sonata in C Minor ("Pathétique"), Op. 13, i.

40. Many critics have noted this tonal ambiguity and have related it to a similar one at the opening of Haydn's String Quartet in B Minor, Op. 33/1, i.

41. That Haydn fills out the texture of this cadential phrase is due most likely to an event that occurs in the development section, shown in ex. 11.18c. In m. 53, Haydn suddenly reduces the texture to a single voice with octave doublings, just like the abandoned cadential passage within the second subordinate theme of the exposition (see ex. 8.6, mm. 28–30). This dramatic and somewhat mysterious effect does not recur within the recapitulation, most likely because a third appearance of such a "characteristic" event would have been redundant. Instead, a related passage beginning at m. 98 sees the ascending leaps accompanied by a fully chordal texture.

42. Other example: Haydn, String Quartet in D Minor ("Fifths"), Op. 76/2, i.

Chapter 12

1. The only form in which this section is not optional is the sonata–rondo, in which an obligatory coda brings a final reference to the main theme (see chap. 16). If a full-movement form does not contain a genuine recapitulation (such as a theme and variations or a large ternary), then a section following the final appearance of the main theme will sometimes function as a coda.

2. *Musical Composition*, 185.

3. Even theorists who acknowledge that a coda and a codetta are different sometimes base their distinction on criteria unrelated to a given unit's musical content and formal organization. Green (*Form in Tonal Music*, 142), for instance, understands the final part of a piece to be a coda if it can be construed as an appendage to the entire piece or movement, whereas it would be a codetta if it were construe as an appendage to the last part of the piece. As a result, he allows for a "coda" to consist of a single phrase prolonging the final tonic by a pedal (p. 140), precisely the kind of structure that I define here as a codetta.

4. Codettas group together to form a closing section, which operates at a level comparable to such fundamental phrase functions as presentation, continuation, and cadential.

5. The term *coda theme* is introduced primarily for purposes of identification and labeling rather than of defining a new and unique formal function (such as *main theme* and *subordinate theme*).

6. The rare appearance of new material in a coda—such as the funereal music in the first movement of Beethoven's Ninth Symphony—suggests extramusical or programmatic references transcending the strictly internal relationships in the movement.

7. The ascending-stepwise pattern seems to be the most popular sequence in codas.

8. Esther Cavett-Dunsby, "Mozart's Codas," *Music Analysis* 7 (1988): 32, refers to this moment as the start of the "formal coda," as distinguished from the "structural coda," which begins after the completion of the "fundamental line" (Schenker's *Urlinie*).

On occasion, a genuine coda is included in the repeat of the development and recapitulation. See Mozart, Violin Sonata in B-flat, K. 454, i, 146; Mozart, Piano Sonata in F, K. 332/300k, iii, 227.

9. As discussed in the previous chapter, this "retransition" of the recapitulation more accurately serves a transitional function, because it leads the music into a nontonic region.

10. Other examples: Mozart, String Quintet in E-flat, K. 614, i, 215; Mozart, String Quartet in C ("Dissonance"), K. 465, i, 227; Beethoven, Violin Sonata in A Minor, Op. 23, i, 222.

11. Other examples: Mozart, String Quartet in D, K. 575, iv, 168; Beethoven, Symphony No. 1 in C, Op. 21, i, 260.

12. Other example: Beethoven, Piano Sonata in C Minor, Op. 10/1, iii, 102.

13. These are not evaded cadences, as their underlying harmonic support might suggest. We can easily perceive the I^6 harmonies as goals of the cadential ideas, not as new beginnings.

14. This hypermetrical interpretation assumes that odd-numbered measures from the beginning of a grouping unit are, in general, metrically stronger (accented) than even-numbered measures. See Rothstein, *Phrase Rhythm*, 8–9.

15. Other examples: Mozart, String Quartet in D, K. 575, iv, 200ff.; Mozart, Piano Sonata in B-flat, K. 570, iii, 71ff.; Beethoven, Piano Sonata in C ("Waldstein"), Op. 53, i, 249–84.

16. See Haydn, String Quartet in B-flat, Op. 50/1, iv, 226–33; Mozart, Violin Sonata in E Minor, K. 304/300c, i, 193.

17. The coda of the finale of Mozart's Piano Concerto in D Minor, K. 466, largely consists of three relatively tight knit themes, each of which is immediately repeated (mm. 356–70, 371–94, 395–410). The material for these themes is drawn from different places in the movement, but not from the actual main theme.

18. Such early-appearing half cadences have already been

seen in ex. 12.4, m. 141, ex. 12.5, m. 140 (reinterpreted half cadence), and ex. 12.7, m. 267.

19. More technically, the F♯ seventh sonority can be interpreted as G: V⁷/III, a relatively rare dominant substitute. As a dominant (V/III) of the dominant (V), its broader function is a pre-dominant of C. The B-minor six–four sonority is wonderfully ambiguous here. On the one hand, it can be seen to prolong the F♯ seventh. On the other hand, its appearance in mm. 218–21 can be understood already to express the dominant harmony of C major (by the common tones B and D, the F♯ in the bass being a retardation).

20. See ahead ex. 12.11, mm. 103–12.

21. See Beethoven, Violin Sonata in F ("Spring"), Op. 24, i; Beethoven, Piano Sonata in C ("Waldstein"), Op. 53, i.

22. Rosen, *Sonata Forms*, 324.

23. Joseph Kerman, "Notes on Beethoven's Codas," in *Beethoven Studies 3*, ed. Alan Tyson (Cambridge: Cambridge University Press, 1982), 151.

24. Robert P. Morgan, "Coda as Culmination: The First Movement of the 'Eroica' Symphony," in *Music Theory and the Exploration of the Past*, ed. Christopher Hatch and David W. Bernstein (Chicago: University of Chicago Press, 1993), 357–76. Other important studies dealing with similar issues include Cavett-Dunsby, "Mozart's Codas"; and Robert G. Hopkins, "When a Coda Is More Than a Coda: Reflections on Beethoven," in *Explorations in Music, the Arts, and Ideas: Essays in Honor of Leonard B. Meyer*, ed. Eugene Narmour and Ruth Solie (Stuyvesant, NY: Pendragon, 1988), 393–410.

25. Circularity of melodic–motivic organization, however, is not essential to the aesthetics of classical form. In many works of this style, material from the main theme is confined exclusively to the beginning of the exposition and recapitulation. As the content of the main theme, especially its basic idea, becomes more memorable—more "characteristic"—classical composers take a greater opportunity to present this material in various guises throughout the movement, especially in the development section but also in the coda. Inasmuch as a circular organization is more central to nineteenth-century forms, its use in the classical period is a "progressive" trait. It is not surprising, therefore, that formal circularity appears in works of Beethoven more regularly than in those of Haydn and Mozart.

26. See also ahead ex. 12.10.

27. See Kerman, "Notes on Beethoven's Codas," 147–49, for a discussion of this coda that emphasizes its influence on Beethoven, especially his Symphony No. 1 in C, Op. 21, i, 277ff.

28. Other examples: Mozart, Symphony No. 41 in C ("Jupiter"), K. 551, ii, 95–99 (from the main theme); Mozart, String Quartet in G, K. 387, iv, 282–87 (from the main theme); Mozart, Piano Sonata in F, K. 332/300k, iii, 232–45 (from the closing section in the exposition).

29. See Haydn, Piano Sonata in E-flat, Hob. XVI:49, i, 190; Mozart, String Quartet in G, K. 387, iv, 268; Beethoven, Symphony No. 7 in A, Op. 92, i, 391; Beethoven, Violin Sonata in F ("Spring"), Op. 24, i, 211.

30. See Berry, *Form in Music*, 175; Green, *Form in Tonal Music*, 226.

31. Kerman, "Notes on Beethoven's Codas," 151–53. Hopkins, however, revives the notion of a second development (fol-

lowed by a second recapitulation) in his analysis of the finale of Beethoven's Eighth Symphony ("Coda," 394–98).

32. The idea that the development section can take on a degree of "expository" function is raised by Rosen, *Sonata Forms*, 274.

Other example: Beethoven, Symphony No. 3 in E-flat ("Eroica"), Op. 55, i, 581ff. Morgan ("Coda as Culmination") sees the coda of this movement as not only referring to the development section proper but also actually continuing powerful developmental processes.

33. The first-movement codas in the Third and Seventh Symphonies feature well-known examples of enormous orchestral crescendos.

34. Kerman points to the *"calando* effect" found at the end of Mozart's Piano Concerto in C Minor, K. 491, i, as a probable influence on Beethoven ("Notes on Beethoven's Codas," 143–44).

35. This rhythmic technique, rarely found in Haydn and Mozart and only sporadically used by Beethoven, became commonplace in the nineteenth century.

Other example: Beethoven, Symphony No. 3 in E-flat ("Eroica"), Op. 55, ii.

36. The "implication–realization" model of musical process is advanced by Leonard B. Meyer, *Explaining Music*, pt. 2, and developed further by Eugene Narmour, *The Analysis and Cognition of Basic Melodic Structures: The Implication-Realization Model* (Chicago: University of Chicago Press, 1990). These theorists concern themselves primarily with melodic implications, but their general approach lends itself to harmonic, formal, rhythmic, and dynamic implications as well.

37. Kerman's notion that the codas in Beethoven's sonata forms represent the last chapter in the "story of a [main] theme" is thus applicable to Haydn and Mozart as well ("Notes on Beethoven's Codas," 150).

38. It is also possible to hear an evaded cadence at measure 15 of ex. 12.6b because of the sudden change from fortissimo to piano. The interpretation of a half cadence is least plausible, especially for hypermetrical reasons. The harmonic goal of dominant (as a cadential six–four) arises "too early" at the seventh hypermeasure of the theme (each hypermeasure consisting of two notated measures). A perfect authentic cadence, on the contrary, appears more conventionally at hypermeasure eight.

Chapter 13

1. In a concerto, movements that would ordinarily be written in sonata form (namely, the first movement but sometimes also the second) are usually written in *concerto form* (see chap. 17).

2. After 1780, composers began to stop repeating the development and recapitulation together so that by 1800 the practice seemed "archaic." See Michael Broyles, "Organic Form and the Binary Repeat," *Musical Quarterly* 66 (1980): 341.

3. See chap. 6; also Ratner, *Classic Music*, 217–21.

4. These ideas were developed (and their supporting secondary literature cited) in chaps. 8–11.

5. Ratner, *Classic Music*, 217; Ratner also speaks of a "circular" or "solar" arrangement of many keys in relation to the home key (tonic), as opposed to the "contrasting" or "polar" arrangement of two keys in a movement (tonic and dominant, or tonic and relative major) (48).

6. Weaker cadential confirmation—half cadence, dominant arrival, evaded and abandoned cadence—reveals the model's declining influence.

7. See ex. 11.3. In baroque compositions, the subdominant is often the last key to be explored before the return home.

8. Additional perfect authentic cadences in the subordinate key will appear if the exposition contains multiple subordinate themes.

9. See Mozart, Violin Sonata in C, K. 403/385c, i (see ex. 9.1); Mozart, Piano Sonata in G, K. 283/189h, i; Beethoven, Symphony No. 1, Op. 21, i; Beethoven, Piano Sonata in C Minor, Op. 10/1, iii (see ex. 9.5).

10. See Haydn, Piano Sonata in E-flat, Hob. XVI:38, i; Mozart, String Quartet in D, K. 575, i.

11. This option is indicated in the table by "MT" placed in parentheses under the first "HC in HK." Patterns 6 and 7 can also include this option.

12. See Mozart, String Quartet in D, K. 575, iv; Mozart, Piano Sonata in D, K. 576, iii (see ex. 8.16).

13. See Haydn, Piano Trio in E-flat, Hob. XV:30, i (see ex. 9.4); Mozart, Symphony No. 35 in D ("Haffner"), K. 385, i; Mozart, Piano Trio in D Minor, K. 442, iii (see ex. 9.15); Beethoven, Symphony No. 3 in E-flat ("Eroica"), Op. 55, i; Beethoven, Piano Sonata in E-flat, Op. 31/3, i; Beethoven, Piano Sonata in B-flat ("Hammerklavier"), Op. 106, i.

14. See Haydn, String Quartet in C, Op. 50/2, iv; Haydn, Piano Sonata in A, Hob. XVI:30, i; Beethoven, Piano Sonata in C, Op. 2/3, iv (see ex. 9.9).

15. See Haydn, String Quartet in G Minor ("The Rider"), Op. 74/3, i; Mozart, Violin Sonata in C, K. 303/293c, ii; Mozart, Violin Sonata in B-flat, K. 454, i (see ahead ex. 13.9).

16. In a well-known comedy sketch, Peter Schikele (P. D. Q. Bach) satirizes this effect in connection with the opening main theme (including the introduction) of Beethoven's Fifth Symphony: a radio announcer describing a performance of the work as though it were a football match exclaims that he "doesn't know whether it's slow or fast yet, because it keeps stopping; it doesn't seem to be able to get off the ground!" ("New Horizons in Music Appreciation," *Report from Hoople: P. D. Q. Bach on the Air*, Vanguard VSD-79268-A).

17. This technique is frequently found with minor-mode movements, in which the dominant emphasis helps reinforce a *Sturm und Drang* affect; see ex. 5.18.

18. Whereas a subordinate-theme group can, in extreme cases, contain up to five distinct themes, the number of main themes in a group would seem to be limited to two. See Haydn, String Quartet in B-flat, Op. 64/3, i, 8; Haydn, Piano Sonata in D, Hob. XVI:51, i, 11; Mozart, Piano Sonata in F, K. 332/300k, i, 13; Beethoven, String Quartet in G, Op. 18/2, i, 9.

19. For more discussion of the intricate motivic play in this theme, with an emphasis on the differing roles of leading line and accompanying figuration, see Rosen, *Sonata Forms*, 201.

20. Other examples: Haydn, Symphony No. 74 in E-flat, i, 1-8; Mozart, Violin Sonata in E-flat, K. 302/293b, i, 1-8; Mozart, Piano Sonata in D, K. 284/205b, i, 1-8.

21. Other examples: Beethoven, String Quartet in A, Op. 18/5, i, 1-15; Beethoven, Piano Sonata in B-flat, Op. 22, i, 1-11.

22. The same situation in respect to subordinate themes was considered in chap. 8.

23. As will be discussed in the last section of this chapter,

slow introductions normally end with dominant, or occasionally tonic, harmony.

24. Ex. 6.9, mm. 75-80, illustrates a B section whose beginning emphasizes subdominant harmony.

25. Other examples: Haydn, Symphony No. 101 in D ("The Clock"), i, 23-32; Mozart, Piano Sonata in C, K. 279/189d, ii, 1-6.

26. Other examples: Haydn, String Quartet in G, Op. 54/1, ii, 1-20; Mozart, Serenade for Eight Winds in C Minor, K. 388/384a, i, 1-22; Mozart, String Quintet in C, K. 515, i, 1-46.

27. Jens Peter Larsen treats this general issue somewhat differently with his notion of a "three-part" sonata exposition typical of Haydn: "Sonata Form Problems," in *Handel, Haydn, and the Viennese Classical Style*, trans. Ulrich Krämer (Ann Arbor, MI: UMI Research Press, 1988), 274-75. According to Larsen, the first part of such an exposition contains the main theme. The second part, an "elaboration section," embraces the transition and subordinate theme up to and including an internal half cadence and standing on the dominant (Larsen does not use this terminology, of course). The third part, a "closing section," brings the cadential function of the theme. See Fillion, "Sonata-Exposition Procedures," for further treatment of Larsen's ideas.

28. Martha Frohlich would seem to privilege melody over harmony by considering the subordinate theme to begin at m. 76. See her *Beethoven's "Appassionata" Sonata* (Oxford: Clarendon Press, 1991), 35.

29. Other examples: Haydn, Piano Trio in C, Hob. XV:27, iii (subordinate theme begins in m. 54); Mozart, Symphony No. 36 in C ("Linz"), K. 425, i (subordinate theme begins in m. 53); Beethoven, Piano Sonata in G, Op. 79, i (subordinate theme begins in m. 24).

30. Other examples: Haydn, String Quartet in E-flat, Op. 50/3, iv, 25-47; Haydn, String Quartet in G Minor ("The Rider"), Op. 74/3, i, 11-54; Mozart, String Quartet in D Minor, K. 421/417b, i, 9-24.

31. This passage is also discussed by Batt ("Function and Structure," 177-78).
Other example: Mozart, Violin Sonata in C, K. 303/293c, ii, 13-24.

32. See Haydn, Symphony No. 93 in D.

33. In the baroque period, on the contrary, an introductory section to an instrumental movement can very well be serious and heraldic without arousing a marked anticipatory effect. This is usually the case, for example, in the first part of a French overture.

34. See Haydn, Symphony No. 97 in C, i; Mozart, Symphony No. 39 in E-flat, K. 543, i; Mozart, Overture to *Don Giovanni*, K. 527; Beethoven, Symphony No. 1 in C, Op. 21, i; Beethoven, Piano Sonata in C Minor ("Pathétique"), Op. 13, i. In some cases, the moment representing the structural end of the introduction actually occurs somewhat after the exposition has begun; see Beethoven, Piano Sonata in E-flat ("Lebewohl"), Op. 81a, i, 21. The introduction to Haydn's Symphony No. 90 in C could also be seen to "end" after the exposition has already begun (see ex. 13.5, m. 20).

35. See Mozart, Quintet for Piano and Winds in E-flat, K. 452, i (four parts); Beethoven, Symphony No. 7 in A, Op. 92, i (five parts).

36. See Rudolf Klinkhammer, *Die langsame Einleitung in der Instrumentalmusik der Klassik und Romantik: ein Sonderproblem in der*

Entwicklung der Sonatenform (Regensburg: Bosse, 1971); and Marianne Danckwardt, *Die langsame Einleitung: Ihre Herkunft und ihr Bau bei Haydn und Mozart*, 2 vols. (Tutzing: Schneider, 1977).

37. A *truncated small ternary* thus lacks an A' section.

Chapter 14

1. Andante is more rightly considered a moderate tempo, but movements indicated by this marking usually follow the formal plans of a "slow" movement.

2. The key of the slow movement is typically the subdominant of the cycle's overall tonality.

3. A small number of slow movements are built as simple small ternaries. See Haydn, Piano Trio in D, Hob. XV:24, ii; Mozart, Piano Sonata in C, K. 309/284b, ii; Beethoven, Piano Sonata in E-flat, Op. 27/1, iii. Haydn's Piano Trio in E-flat, Hob. XV:29, ii, is in small binary form. Three slow movements in violin sonatas by Mozart (in G, K. 379/373a, i; in A, K. 402/385e, i; and in C, K. 403/385c, ii) are effectively sonata forms in which the recapitulation is eliminated. The end of the development is followed instead by the beginning of the next movement.

4. In extreme cases, the slow movement can seem like an introduction to the next movement. See Haydn, Piano Sonata in D, Hob. XVI:37, ii. The slow movement of Beethoven's *Waldstein* Sonata is even specifically designated *Introduzione*.

5. See Haydn, Piano Trio in D, Hob. XV:16, ii; Beethoven, Piano Sonata in E-flat, Op. 27/1, iii.

6. See ex. 14.2, discussed shortly; see also Beethoven, String Quartet in F, Op. 59/1, iii.

7. See Haydn, String Quartet in C, Op. 54/2, ii; Haydn, Piano Trio in E-flat, Hob. XV:30, ii; Haydn, Piano Sonata in E Minor, Hob. XVI:34, ii.

8. Rather than reducing the development, Mozart tends to delete it, thus creating a sonata without development form.

9. Transition/subordinate-theme fusion is also regularly observed in minuet form; see chap. 15.

10. The use of ♭VII as the first of two subordinate keys is somewhat unusual. Here, it surely functions more as the relative major of the goal subordinate key, A minor. Another case of ♭VII as a subordinate key occurs in the scherzo of Beethoven's Ninth Symphony. There, however, Beethoven uses C major as the only subordinate key of a D-minor movement.

11. Other examples: Haydn, Piano Sonata in E Minor, Hob. XVI:34, ii, 9–18; Mozart, Serenade in D ("Haffner"), K. 250/248b, ii, 30–37; Mozart, Serenade for Eight Winds in C Minor, K. 388/384a, ii, 17–24; Beethoven, Piano Sonata in F Minor, Op. 2/1, ii, 17–27 (sonata without development); Beethoven, Piano Sonata in B-flat, Op. 22, ii, 13–18.

12. See chap. 16. For a fast-movement sonata that eliminates the transition from the exposition, see Haydn, Piano Sonata in E, Hob. XVI:22, i, 9.

13. The form of the main theme is nonconventional. It is perhaps best analyzed as an antecedent consisting of extended basic and contrasting ideas.

14. Other examples: Haydn, Piano Sonata in F, Hob. XVI:23, ii, 5; Mozart, Symphony No. 35 in D ("Haffner"), K. 385, ii, 17 (the unit preceding the subordinate theme may perhaps be considered a fusion of main-theme and transition functions); Mozart, Symphony No. 40 in G Minor, K. 550, ii, 20 (main theme ends

with perfect authentic cadence); Mozart, Piano Concerto in C, K. 503, ii, 35; Mozart, Piano Sonata in F, K. 280/189e, ii, 9.

15. Indeed, the development section in the slow movement of Mozart's Piano Sonata in B-flat, K. 281/189f, consists exclusively of a standing on the dominant.

16. Other examples: Haydn, String Quartet in C ("The Bird"), Op. 33/3, iii, 59–66; Haydn, Piano Sonata in G, Hob. XVI:39, ii, 23–30; Mozart, Symphony No. 35 in D ("Haffner"), K. 385, ii, 36–49.

17. See Haydn's Piano Trio in E-flat, Hob. XV:29, i, and his Piano Sonata in B-flat, Hob. XVI:41, ii, for rare instances of large ternary form in a fast opening movement and a fast finale, respectively.

18. The secondary literature yields no consistent terminology for this form. Most theorists adopt a label indicating that it consists of three parts: "three-part Adagio form" (Ratz, *Musikalische Formenlehre*, 35); "full sectional ternary" (Green, *Form in Tonal Music*, 93); "simple ternary" (Ebenezer Prout, *Musical Form* [London: Augener, 1893], chap. 10); and "compound ternary" (Berry, *Form in Music*, 68). Others classify it in the family of rondo forms: Schoenberg, *Musical Composition*, 190; Percy Goetschius, *The Larger Forms of Musical Composition* (New York: Schirmer, 1915), 94.

19. *Musikalische Formenlehre*, 35. Goetschius recognizes a similar scheme for what he calls the "first rondo form": principal theme, subordinate theme, principal theme (*Larger Forms*, 94). That he (along with Schoenberg) considers the large ternary to belong to the "rondo" family undoubtedly relates to the idea that this formal type brings a recurring main theme.

20. See Haydn, Symphony No. 92 in G ("Oxford"), ii; Haydn, Symphony No. 100 in G ("Military"), ii; Mozart, Piano Sonata in C, K. 545, ii.

21. See Haydn, Symphony No. 101 in D ("The Clock"), ii; Beethoven, String Quartet in B-flat, Op. 18/6, ii.

22. For instance, the main theme from the slow movement of Beethoven's Piano Sonata in C, Op. 2/3, is built as a simple eight-measure period (whose consequent is somewhat extended). In the second movement of Haydn's Piano Trio in C, Hob. XV:27, the first part of the form consists of three distinct thematic units, each ending with a perfect authentic cadence in the home key.

23. Exs. 6.1, 6.4, 7.3, and 7.8 are main themes of large ternary forms.

24. See Haydn, Symphony No. 92 in G ("Oxford"), ii; Haydn, Symphony No. 96 in D ("The Miracle"), ii; Haydn, Piano Trio in C, Hob. XV:27, ii.

25. See Haydn, Piano Trio in A, Hob. XV:18, ii; Beethoven, Piano Sonata in D ("Pastoral"), Op. 28, ii.

26. See Haydn, Piano Trio in C, Hob. XV:21, ii (in this movement, Haydn already uses the parallel minor prominently in the B section of the main theme); Mozart, Piano Sonata in D, K. 576, ii.

27. See Beethoven, Violin Sonata in A, Op. 12/2, ii; Beethoven, Piano Sonata in G, Op. 79, ii.

28. See Haydn, Piano Trio in G, Hob. XV:25, ii.

29. Placing an interior theme in a new key is more typical of the various rondo forms than of the large ternary. The greater formal complexity of the rondo makes more pressing the need for tonal contrast among its principal parts.

30. To be sure, VI is not a normal subordinate key but, rather, is more a development key. See Haydn, String Quartet in G

Minor ("The Rider"), Op. 74/3, ii; Beethoven, Piano Sonata in G, Op. 31/1, ii.

31. See Haydn, Symphony No. 100 in G ("Military"), ii; Haydn, Piano Trio in A, Hob. XV:18, ii; Mozart, Piano Sonata in C, K. 330/300h, ii; Mozart, Piano Sonata in C, K. 545, ii; Beethoven, Piano Sonata in D ("Pastoral"), Op. 28, ii.

32. Other example: Beethoven, String Quartet in B-flat, Op. 18/6, ii, 32.

33. Other examples: Haydn, Symphony No. 89 in F, ii, 45-46; Haydn, String Quartet in G, Op. 64/4, iii, 62; Haydn, Piano Trio in G, Hob. XV:15, ii, 46-47.

34. Other examples: Haydn, String Quartet in D ("The Lark"), Op. 64/5, ii; Haydn, String Quartet in G Minor ("The Rider"), Op. 74/3, ii; Beethoven, Violin Sonata in C Minor, Op. 30/2, ii; Beethoven, Piano Sonata in G, Op. 31/1, ii.

35. Other examples: Haydn, Symphony No. 96 in D ("The Miracle"), ii; Haydn, Symphony No. 101 in D ("The Clock"), ii; Haydn, Symphony No. 104 in D ("London"), ii; Haydn, String Quartet in E-flat, Op. 64/6, ii; Haydn, Piano Sonata in E-flat, Hob. XVI:49, ii.

36. The notion of a *subordinate-theme complex* is explained more fully in connection with couplet 2 of the five-part rondo and the sonata-rondo (chap. 16).

37. See, for example, the interior theme of Haydn's Symphony No. 101 ("The Clock"), ii, where mm. 35-39 are transitional, mm. 40-50 are like a subordinate theme (with a brief internal half cadence), and mm. 50-62 are retransitional.

38. Such as when Mozart, in the second movement of his Piano Sonata in C, K. 545, omits from the main theme, originally built as a small ternary, both the B and A' sections.

39. See Haydn, Symphony No. 104 in D ("London"), ii, 103-21; Haydn, String Quartet in D Minor ("Fifths"), Op. 76/2, ii, 51-61; Beethoven, Violin Sonata in A, Op. 12/2, ii, 100-19.

40. See Beethoven, Violin Sonata in C Minor, Op. 30/2, ii; Beethoven, Piano Sonata in A, Op. 2/2, ii; Beethoven, Piano Sonata in E-flat, Op. 7, ii. In Beethoven's Piano Sonata in C, Op. 2/3, ii, a large section beginning at m. 53 functions very much like a coda, but because the main theme has not truly ended (m. 53 is a deceptive cadence), the section can ultimately be seen as an enormous interpolation within the main theme proper.

41. See Beethoven, Violin Sonata in A, Op. 12/2, ii; Beethoven, Piano Sonata in C, Op. 2/3, ii; Beethoven, Piano Sonata in E-flat, Op. 7, ii.

42. The precise, but inelegant, term *sonata without development* appears often enough in the theoretical literature to warrant its use here (Tovey, *The Forms of Music*, 229; Webster, "Sonata Form," 506). A number of texts refer to "sonatina form" (Berry, *Form in Music*, 197-98; Green, *Form in Tonal Music*, 230-31; Kohs, *Musical Form*, 291-96), but this usage is problematic, since the form is not particularly associated with actual pieces labeled "sonatina." Rosen (*Sonata Forms*, 120-21) speaks of the "slow-movement" form (or the "overture" or "cavatina" form) and notes, contrary to the theoretical view presented here, that this "is not a first-movement form with the development omitted but the reworking of an earlier and independent pattern," what he calls "aria" form, from earlier in the eighteenth century. Schoenberg identifies two different "Andante" forms, the second one, labeled ABAB, corresponding to a sonata without development (*Musical Composition*, 190). For the same form, Ratz employs the unhelpful

expression "two-part Adagio form" but nonetheless clearly identifies its constituent formal functions (*Musikalische Formenlehre*, 36).

43. See Haydn, Piano Trio in A, Hob. XV:18, iii; Mozart, String Quartet in E-flat, K. 428/421b, iv; Mozart, Violin Sonata in C, K. 303/293c, i; Mozart, Violin Sonata in D, K. 306/300l, iii.

44. See Mozart, Overture to *The Marriage of Figaro*, K. 492.

45. See Rosen, *Sonata Forms*, 108-12.

46. On the distinction between repetition and return, see chap. 1, n. 12.

47. To speak of a "first-time" listening experience is not necessarily to refer literally to the initial hearing of the piece. Even a well-known work can be experienced by a listener as if it were being heard for the first time.

48. Beethoven does not seem to use this deviation.

49. See Haydn, Piano Trio in E-flat, Hob. XV:30, ii; Mozart, Violin Sonata in B-flat, K. 378/317d, ii.

50. In an instrumental cycle, theme-and-variations form serves most often as the basis of a slow movement, although the form is frequently used for a fast finale. Thus the works cited here are not restricted to slow movements.

51. Elaine R. Sisman's *Haydn and the Classical Variation* offers the most comprehensive and up-to-date treatment of the topic. Other important studies include those by Esther Cavett-Dunsby, *Mozart's Variations Reconsidered: Four Case Studies (K. 613, K. 501, K. 421/417b, K. 491)* (New York: Garland, 1989); and Nicholas Marston, "Analysing Variations: The Finale of Beethoven's String Quartet Op. 74," *Music Analysis* 8 (1989): 303-24. The major English-language study of variation procedure in general is that by Robert U. Nelson, *The Technique of Variation* (Berkeley and Los Angeles: University of California Press, 1948).

52. Elaine R. Sisman, "Tradition and Transformation in the Alternating Variations of Haydn and Beethoven," *Acta Musicologica* 62 (1990): 152-82.

53. See his Symphony No. 5 in C Minor, Op. 67, ii, and Piano Trio in E-flat, Op. 70/2, ii. Mozart did not adopt this type of variation form (Sisman, "Alternating Variations," 160).

54. Most of the examples of small binary in chap. 7 are themes for variation. See exs. 7.1, 7.2, 7.4, 7.5, and 7.7.

55. See Haydn, String Quartet in F, Op. 74/2, ii; Mozart, Piano Trio in G, K. 496, iii.

56. See Haydn, Symphony No. 97 in C, ii (binary to ternary); Mozart, Piano Sonata in D, K. 284/205b, iii (ternary to binary).

57. See Haydn, Symphony No. 94 in G ("The Surprise"), ii; Haydn, Symphony No. 95 in C Minor, ii.

58. See Haydn, Symphony No. 81 in G, ii; Haydn, Symphony No. 91 in E-flat, ii.

59. See Mozart, Clarinet Quintet in A, K. 581, iv, 81-84, 91-95; Mozart, Violin Sonata in E-flat, K. 481, iii, 141-49; Beethoven, Piano Sonata in G, Op. 14/2, ii, 61-64.

60. See Beethoven, Violin Sonata in A, Op. 30/1, iii, 128-51.

61. See Mozart, String Quartet in A, K. 464, iii, 164; Beethoven, String Quartet in A, Op. 18/5, iii, 130 (a work frequently claimed to be modeled on the preceding quartet by Mozart; see Jeremy Yudkin, "Beethoven's 'Mozart' Quartet," *Journal of the American Musicological Society* 45 [1992]: 30-74); Beethoven, Piano Sonata in F Minor ("Appassionata"), Op. 57, ii, 81; Beethoven, Piano Sonata in E, Op. 109, ii, 188.

Chapter 15

1. The idea of even speaking of "minuet form" derives from Ratz, who specifically invokes the notion of *Scherzoform* (*Musikalische Formenlehre*, 33–35). Schoenberg does not refer to "minuet form" as such but devotes an entire chapter to this dance type, as well as a chapter to the scherzo (*Musical Composition*, chaps. 15 and 16). Rosen (*Sonata Forms*, 112–23) develops the concept of "minuet sonata form" as a subcategory of sonata form but then refers more colloquially to "minuet form" (114). For all these writers, the form being discussed is that of the minuet proper or the trio, not the form of the minuet movement as a whole.

2. *Musical Composition*, 150–51.

3. *Musikalische Formenlehre*, 33–35. Unlike Schoenberg, Ratz does not discuss the minuet as a separate movement type (probably because he primarily studies the music of Bach and Beethoven).

4. See Beethoven, Symphony No. 4 in B-flat, Op. 60, iii.

5. *Musical Composition*, 151. It is hard to reconcile the contradictory positions expressed here, except to recall that the published version of *Musical Composition* represents an edition compiled by Leonard Stein from (at least) five versions of the text (see "Editor's Preface," xiii).

6. See Haydn, Piano Trio in B-flat, Hob. XV:8, ii; Beethoven, Piano Sonata in C, Op. 2/3, iii; Beethoven, Piano Sonata in E, Op. 14/1, ii.

7. Another important difference between minuet/trio form and large ternary form concerns the restatement of the first part: the da capo almost always has the identical structure as the original minuet, whereas the return of the large ternary's main theme is more readily altered.

8. And as suggested, the minuet and trio themselves often seem to function as relatively independent "movements."

9. A number of historians have observed striking relationships between minuet form and sonata form: Rosen directly assimilates the former to the latter with his notion of "minuet sonata form" (*Sonata Forms*, 112–23). James Webster views some minuets as "miniature sonata-form movements." See his "Freedom of Form in Haydn's Early String Quartets," in *Haydn Studies*, ed. Jens Peter Larsen, Howard Serwer, and James Webster (New York: Norton, 1981), 523. The notion propounded in this study is that the minuet and sonata are similar forms because they express some of the same interthematic functions, not because the minuet is a (smaller) version of the sonata.

10. This situation is rare in the small ternary, but see ex. 6.7.

11. See Mozart, String Quartet in G, K. 387, ii.

12. Charles Rosen is perhaps the first writer to point out an "anomaly—or what ought to be an anomaly: the fact that it makes so little difference whether the first period [of the minuet] has a cadence on I or V. . . . If the harmonic structure is as important as we suspect it to be for the eighteenth century, then the cadence of the first part of a binary [i.e., minuet] form ought to count for a great deal" (*Sonata Forms*, 114). What Rosen is alluding to here is that minuet form, unlike sonata form, does not require the exposition to modulate. He notes that this anomaly can be explained largely by the brevity of the former compared with the latter and further notes that if the modulation does not take place in the first part of the minuet, then it will likely occur in the next part.

13. On occasion, however, the A section ends with a half cadence (see ex. 3.7), as is also sometimes the case for the small ternary (see chap. 6, n. 5).

14. The appearance of an early authentic cadence is typical of the minuet form but is only rarely found in the small ternary. The juxtaposition of two strong cadences—one in the home key, the other in the subordinate key—would create too great a dramatic conflict so early in a form that functions as a main theme in a larger formal context.

15. This movement can also be interpreted as R = 2N without changing the basic purport of the analysis. In that case, the compound basic idea and continuation would be understood as a simple basic idea and contrasting idea. (The other formal labels of the movement could be easily adjusted as well.)

16. Other example: Beethoven, Symphony No. 7 in A, Op. 92, iii, 17–22.

17. As regards a formal unit "beginning" with cadential function (or even consequent function, as in the preceding example), see chap. 8.

18. Rosen, *Sonata Forms*, 114.

19. See, for example, the minuet from Beethoven's Symphony No. 8 in F, Op. 93, whose B section brings the dominant as an initiating region but fails to confirm it by any subsequent cadence.

20. In two works by Mozart, the minuet proper remains nonmodulatory in the home key, but the trio expresses the subordinate key by residing entirely in the dominant region. See *Eine kleine Nachtmusik*, K. 525, iii, and Symphony No. 35 in D ("Haffner"), K. 385, iii.

21. But see Haydn, Symphony No. 85 in B-flat ("La reine"), iii; Haydn, String Quartet in D, Op. 71/2, iii; Beethoven, Piano Sonata in C-sharp Minor ("Moonlight"), Op. 27/2, ii.

22. In addition to signaling a transition, the submediant is particularly appropriate here, for it realizes an earlier implication (see ex. 4.10a) that the diminished seventh chord (over the tonic pedal) in m. 7 wants to resolve to VI, even though it moves to I instead; see chap. 4, n. 16.

23. See Haydn, String Quartet in B-flat, Op. 50/1, iii; Mozart, *Eine kleine Nachtmusik*, K. 525, iii; Mozart, String Quartet in A, K. 464, ii; Beethoven, Violin Sonata in F ("Spring"), Op. 24, iii.

24. See Nors S. Josephson, "Veränderte Reprisen in Mozarts späten Menuetten," *Mozart-Jahrbuch 1976/77*, 59–69, for a detailed examination of changes in the recapitulations of some Mozart minuets.

25. Besides fulfilling its specific formal purposes, the deceptive cadence gives Haydn a final chance to play on the potential of the diminished seventh chord in measure 31 (not shown, but cf. ex. 4.10a, m. 7) to resolve to VI rather than to I; see n. 22.

26. In discussing this scherzo, Ratz notes that the expansion of the A' section is motivated by the relatively "unsatisfying" nature of the B section, which does not bring the emotional climax of the scherzo as might be expected. Thus the sense of "development" is transferred instead to the recapitulation in the guise of the ♭VI episode (*Musikalische Formenlehre*, 35).

27. The functional expression of the phrase in mm. 5–8 is ambiguous. Following the cadence, it can be considered a new presentation to begin the transition/subordinate-theme fusion. But the nature of the musical material hardly suggests the sense of a new beginning. In addition, the phrase is supported by a weak tonic prolongation (I^6), and the new grouping units of two measures represent fragmentation in relation to the previous four-

measure cadential unit. Thus the phrase also projects a strong degree of continuation function.

28. Other example: Mozart, Symphony No. 36 in C ("Linz"), K. 425, iii.

29. That the "contrasting" middle of the small ternary tends to be more complex and intense than the outer parts is fairly obvious. And at a lower level of formal organization, a "contrasting" idea tends to exhibit greater intensity regarding harmony and rhythm in relation to the preceding basic idea. As a general rule, a "middle" function at any level of structure is more intense than a beginning function (e.g., continuation vs. presentation, development vs. exposition, interior theme vs. main theme, etc.). The main exception to this principle is the trio of minuet/trio form.

30. See Webster, *Haydn's "Farewell" Symphony*, 160–62. The minuet proper is rarely linked by a transitional passage to the trio. For an exception, see Haydn, Symphony No. 99 in E-flat, iii.

31. See the second ending of the trio in Mozart's String Quartet in D, K. 499, ii.

32. See Beethoven, String Quartet in D, Op. 18/3, iii.

33. See Beethoven, Piano Sonata in E, Op. 14/1, ii.

34. An exceptional situation arises in Haydn's String Quartet in E-flat, Op. 20/1, ii, in which the ending harmony is neither the dominant of the key of the trio (A♭) nor that of the minuet (E♭) but, rather, the dominant of F minor, a key related to both.

Chapter 16

1. The theoretical literature offers a variety of terms for labeling and classifying the different rondo types. Most terminologies refer to the number of parts and thus include such expressions as "five-part," "seven-part," and even "nine-part" rondo. A favorite scheme originating in the nineteenth century (also based on the number of parts) establishes "first" (ABA, the large ternary), "second" (ABACA), and "third" (ABACADA) rondo forms. The term "sonata–rondo" is used by many writers, but its precise definition varies considerably.

2. See Haydn, Piano Trio in G, Hob. XV:25, iii, 35.

3. See Mozart, Violin Sonata in F, K. 547, i, 17; Mozart, Piano Sonata in C Minor, K. 457, ii, 8; Beethoven, Piano Trio in E-flat, Op. 1/1, ii, 21.

4. See Mozart, Violin Sonata in E-flat, K. 481, ii, 17–28; Beethoven, Piano Sonata in C Minor, Op. 13 ("Pathétique"), ii, 17–23.

5. Other example: Mozart, Piano Trio in E, K. 542, ii, 33–47.

6. Given that Haydn privileges the large ternary for slow movements, it is not surprising that he tends to fashion the second couplet of the five-part rondo as an interior theme. Likewise, Mozart's regular use of a subordinate-theme complex for this couplet relates to his preference for the sonata-without-development form. (Beethoven regularly employs both options.)

7. All subsequent references to a *minore* assume the possibility of a *maggiore* as well.

8. For an exception, see Haydn, Symphony No. 89 in F, iv.

9. See Beethoven, Piano Sonata in G, Op. 14/2, iii, 23–42.

10. Indeed, refrain 2 (and any subsequent return) may seem like a "variation" of refrain 1, giving rise to what some writers call a "variation rondo" (Green, *Form in Tonal Music*, 113); Sisman, following hints by Koch, prefers to see such movements as "hybrid"

forms of the variation, not of the rondo, and so prefers the term "rondo-variation" (*Classical Variation*, 72, 150).

11. See Mozart, *Eine kleine Nachtmusik*, K. 525, ii, 31; Mozart, Violin Sonata in E-flat, K. 380/374f, iii, 28; Mozart, Piano Sonata in B-flat, K. 570, ii, 27; Beethoven, Rondo for Piano in C, Op. 51/1, 44.

12. See Haydn, Symphony No. 97 in C, iv, 114; Haydn, String Quartet in G, Op. 54/1, iv, 66; Haydn, String Quartet in F, Op. 77/2, iii, 40.

13. There is an exception for fast movements, in which the appearance of an interior theme for couplet 1 would immediately suggest a rondo, because large ternary form is used almost exclusively for slow movements.

14. An exceptional case is Haydn's String Quartet in G, Op. 54/1, iv, in which an interior theme appears in III.

15. See Mozart, Piano Sonata in C, K. 545, iii; Beethoven, Piano Sonata in G, Op. 49/2, ii.

16. For example, the second movement of Beethoven's Piano Trio in E-flat, Op. 1/1, mm. 51ff., establishes a genuine core (model, sequence, fragmentation, half cadence, standing on the dominant), whose final harmony (V/VI) leads directly to refrain 3. Haydn's Piano Trio in D, Hob. XV:7, iii, mm. 129ff., brings a pseudo-core in fantasia style, and the finale of his Piano Trio in E Minor, Hob. XV:12, mm. 95ff., contains a lengthy core substitute typical of his development sections in sonata form. The second couplet in the funeral march of Beethoven's *Eroica* Symphony (see ex. 16.4, m. 114) features a fugato passage that begins in IV and modulates to V, a standard tonal progression for the development section of a minor-mode movement.

17. See Haydn, Piano Sonata in C, Hob. XVI:48, i (abridged).

18. See Beethoven, Rondo for Piano in C, Op. 51/1.

19. See Haydn, Piano Sonata in A-flat, Hob. XVI:43, iii; Mozart, Horn Quintet in E-flat, K. 407/386c, iii; Beethoven, Piano Sonata in G, Op. 14/2, iii.

20. See also Mozart, Piano Trio in G, K. 564, iii; Beethoven, String Quartet in C Minor, Op. 18/4, iv.

21. Precisely which works of Haydn should be considered sonata–rondos and the extent of Mozart's influence on these works have been hotly debated by Malcolm S. Cole, "The Rondo–Finale: Evidence for the Mozart–Haydn Exchange?" *Mozart-Jahrbuch 1968–70*, 242–56, and "Haydn's Symphonic Rondo Finales: Their Structure and Stylistic Evolution," *Haydn Yearbook* 13 (1982): 113–42; and Steven C. Fisher, ("Sonata Procedures in Haydn's Symphonic Rondo Finales of the 1770s," in *Haydn Studies*, ed. Jens Peter Larsen, Howard Serwer, and James Webster (New York: Norton, 1981), 481–87, and "Further Thoughts on Haydn's Symphonic Rondo Finales," *Haydn Yearbook* 17 (1992): 85–107.

22. Exceptions include Mozart, Piano Trio in D Minor, K. 442, ii; Beethoven, Symphony No. 4 in B-flat, Op. 60, ii; Beethoven, String Quartet in D, Op. 18/3, ii.

23. The main-theme group from Mozart's Serenade in D ("Posthorn"), K. 320, iv, is particularly large, containing at least three distinct themes.

24. Indeed, the discussions of subordinate theme and transition in chaps. 8 and 9 include some examples of sonata–rondo form. See exs. 8.5, 8.16, and 9.10.

25. In the finale to Beethoven's Symphony No. 2 in D, Op.

36, the cadential progression of the theme is abandoned and never completed (see also Symphony No. 6 in F ["Pastoral"], Op. 68, v; Piano Sonata in G, Op. 31/1, iv; Piano Sonata in E Minor, Op. 90, ii). In the finale of his Symphony No. 8 in F, Op. 93, a cadential unit to close the theme is missing entirely (see also Violin Sonata in D, Op. 12/1, iii; Piano Sonata in A, Op. 2/2, iv). And in his Piano Sonata in C, Op. 2/3, iv, a relatively tight knit subordinate theme initially closes with a perfect authentic cadence, but is then repeated, significantly expanded, and left open without cadential closure.

26. Abridged second refrains are rarely used before a second couplet built as a development section (but see Haydn, Symphony No. 94 in G ["The Surprise"], iv). However, they do appear now and then when they precede a second couplet built as an interior theme. See Mozart, Violin Sonata in A, K. 526, iii, 168; Mozart, Piano Trio in C, K. 548, iii, 62; Beethoven, Piano Sonata in C, Op. 2/3, iv, 69–76.

27. See Haydn, Symphony No. 94 in G ("The Surprise"), iv, 112.

28. See Haydn, Symphony No. 88 in G, iv; Haydn, String Quartet in E-flat, Op. 64/6, iv; Beethoven, Symphony No. 8 in F, Op. 93, iv; Beethoven, Piano Sonata in E-flat, Op. 7, iv.

29. Other example: Mozart, Symphony No. 35 in D ("Haffner"), K. 385, iv, 80.

30. See Symphony No. 8 in F, Op. 93, iv, 151; Piano Sonata in D, Op. 10/3, iv, 46. A false recapitulation at the end of the second couplet can also be constructed as an interior theme. See Violin Sonata in F ("Spring"), Op. 24, iv, 112; Cello Sonata in G Minor, Op. 5/2, ii, 159.

31. Beethoven's technique of the false recapitulation is not confined to the sonata–rondo. See his Rondo for Piano in C, Op. 51/1, and Piano Sonata in G, Op. 14/2, iii (five-part rondos), and his Violin Sonata in G, Op. 30/3, iii (seven-part rondo). The technique can also be found preceding refrain 2 of any rondo form. See Haydn, Piano Trio in D, Hob. XV:7, iii, 91 (a five-part rondo whose first couplet is highly developmental); Beethoven, Cello Sonata in F, Op. 5/1, ii, 60 (sonata–rondo).

32. For some theorists, a sonata–rondo must contain a development section, and thus the appearance of an interior theme at this point in the form would yield a different rondo type (e.g., a "seven-part rondo" for Kohs [*Musical Form*, 296–97], a "large Rondo" for Schoenberg [*Musical Composition*, 190]). On the contrary, I consider the essential "sonata" component of the sonata–rondo form to be the recapitulation of the subordinate-theme complex, not the presence of a development section.

33. See Mozart, String Quintet in G Minor, K. 516, iv; Mozart, Violin Sonata in B-flat, K. 454, iii; Beethoven, Piano Sonata in C, Op. 2/3, iv.

34. See Mozart, Piano Quartet in E-flat, K. 493, iii; Mozart, Piano Sonata in C, K. 309/284b, iii; Beethoven, Symphony No. 6 in F ("Pastoral"), Op. 68, v.

35. Double-region couplets are almost always found in sonata–rondos, but at least one five-part rondo (Mozart, Piano Sonata in C Minor, K. 457, ii) also features this procedure. Although genuine double-region couplets seem to appear in works by Mozart only, Beethoven wrote one couplet that represents a variant on the Mozartian type. In Beethoven's Piano Sonata in C, Op. 2/3, iv, the second couplet is in two parts—a development leading to a perfect authentic cadence in VI, and a true interior theme in IV.

36. Other examples: Piano Quartet in E-flat, K. 493, iii, 170, 200; Piano Trio in D Minor, K. 442, ii, 112, 141; Piano Trio in E, K. 542, iii, 93, 121; Violin Sonata in C, K. 296, iii, 70, 92; Violin Sonata in A, K. 526, iii, 185, 216; Piano Sonata in D, K. 311/284c, iii, 119, 139.

37. Despite the correspondence to a sonata recapitulation, it is still questionable whether this return should be considered a true "recapitulation" of the rondo refrain. See the earlier discussion of refrain 3 in the five-part rondo form.

38. See Haydn, Symphony No. 102 in B-flat, iv (incomplete).

39. See Mozart, String Quintet in C, K. 515, iv; Mozart, Piano Quartet in E-flat, K. 493, iii.

40. See ex. 12.4, m. 140; see also Mozart, Piano Trio in C, K. 548, iii; Mozart, Piano Sonata in C, K. 309/284b, iii; Mozart, Piano Sonata in C Minor, K. 457, iii; Beethoven, Piano Sonata in C Minor ("Pathétique"), Op. 13, iii.

41. See Beethoven, Piano Sonata in E, Op. 14/1, iii. On at least one occasion, the couplet appears in ♭VII. See his Violin Sonata in F ("Spring"), Op. 24, iv.

42. See chap. 11. The sonata–rondo finale of the Piano Trio in B-flat ("Archduke"), Op. 97, brings the final couplet first in the subdominant, but then readjusts it into the home key.

43. Exceptions include Haydn, Symphony No. 88 in G, iv; Beethoven, Piano Sonata in A-flat, Op. 26, iv. In such cases, the form resembles a sonata more than a rondo.

44. See Green, *Form in Tonal Music*, 163–64. Berry is not explicit on this point, but his one complete analysis of a classical sonata–rondo places the coda after the refrain (*Form in Music*, 213). Tovey's views are inconsistent: in the entry "Rondo" (in *The Forms of Music*, 193), he discusses sonata–rondo form in which "the coda may contain a final return of the rondo-theme" but then refers to situations in which the coda occurs after the final refrain. Throughout *A Companion to Beethoven's Pianoforte Sonatas* (London: Associated Board, 1935), Tovey invariably analyzes the coda according to this latter view.

45. See Mozart, String Quartet in D, K. 575, iv, 168, 182; Mozart, Piano Sonata in C Minor, K. 457, iii, 211, 221.

46. See Haydn, Symphony No. 103 in E-flat ("Drumroll"), iv; Beethoven, String Quartet in F, Op. 18/1, iv; Beethoven, Violin Sonata in E-flat, Op. 12/3, iii.

47. See Piano Trio in D Minor, K. 442, ii; Piano Trio in B-flat, K. 502, iii; Violin Sonata in B-flat, K. 454, iii.

48. See Serenade in D ("Haffner"), K. 250/248b, iv; Piano Sonata in B-flat, K. 281/189f, iii; Rondo for Piano in F, K. 494.

49. Written-out cadenzas appear in a number of other sonata–rondos in the repertory. See Mozart, Quintet for Piano and Winds in E-flat, K. 452, iii; Mozart, Piano Sonata in D, K. 311/284c, iii; Mozart, Piano Sonata in B-flat, K. 333/315c, iii; Beethoven, Piano Sonata in G, Op. 31/1, iii.

Chapter 17

1. With the exception of Green's informative treatment of "concerto–sonata form" (*Form in Tonal Music*, 241–50), few of the standard theory texts, such as those by Berry and Kohs, recognize a specific "concerto form" as such. Likewise, both Schoenberg and Ratz are silent on the topic. Unlike theorists, however, historians have actively investigated the formal organization of the classical concerto, especially as handled by Mozart. Among the more im-

portant recent studies are those by Shelly Davis, "H. C. Koch, the Classic Concerto, and the Sonata-Form Retransition," *Journal of Musicology* 2 (1983): 45–61; Robert Forster, "Zur Funktion von Anfangsritornell und Reprise in den Kopfsätzen einiger Klavierkonzerte Mozarts," *Mozart-Jahrbuch 1986*, 74–89; Konrad Küster, *Formale Aspekte des ersten Allegros in Mozarts Konzerten* (Kassel: Bärenreiter, 1991); Daniel Leeson and Robert D. Levin, "On the Authenticity of K. Anh. C 14.01 (297b), a Symphonia Concertante for Four Winds and Orchestra," *Mozart-Jahrbuch 1976/77*, 70–96; Charles Rosen, *Sonata Forms*, chap. 5; David Rosen, "The Composer's 'Standard Operating Procedure' as Evidence of Intention: The Case of a Formal Quirk in Mozart's K. 595," *Journal of Musicology* 5 (1987): 79–90; and Jane R. Stevens, "Patterns of Recapitulation in the First Movements of Mozart's Piano Concertos," in *Musical Humanism and Its Legacy: Essays in Honor of Claude Palisca*, ed. Nancy Kovaleff Baker and Barbara Russano Hanning (Stuyvesant, NY: Pendragon, 1992), 397–418. This chapter treats many of the same issues explored in these studies but situates them in a more specifically form-functional approach.

2. The slow movement of a classical concerto may also be written as a sonata, a sonata without development, or a five-part rondo. The finale is usually a rondo of some kind, either a standard sonata–rondo or one containing prominent concerto-form elements. See Green's discussion of "concerto–rondo" form (*Form in Tonal Music*, 250–53). For convenience, all subsequent citations to individual works refer to their first movement.

3. This summary of the aesthetics of concerto form owes much to Tovey ("The Classical Concerto," in *Essays in Musical Analysis*, 3: 3–27); and Rosen (*The Classical Style* and *Sonata Forms*).

4. Terminological problems associated with concerto form in relation to ritornello form, on the one hand, and sonata form, on the other hand, are summarized in Küster, *Formale Aspekte*, 3–7.

5. Most modern views of concerto form present a similar scheme, although the number and placement of the ritornellos vary. For example, David Rosen ("Standard Operating Procedure," 81) follows Leeson and Levin ("Authenticity," 79) in recognizing for Mozart's concertos two distinct ritornellos toward the end of the movement—one that precedes the cadenza and one that follows it. A number of historians also identify for some concertos an additional ritornello (or remnants of such a ritornello) standing between the solo development and the solo recapitulation. See Eugene K. Wolf, "Concerto," *The New Harvard Dictionary of Music*, 189; Davis, "Classic Concerto," 49–56; and Stevens, "Patterns of Recapitulation," 409–15.

6. Very exceptionally, the soloist participates briefly with the orchestra at the beginning of the opening ritornello. See Mozart, Piano Concerto in E-flat, K. 271; and Beethoven, Piano Concerto No. 4 in G, Op. 58.

7. Like a rondo, but unlike a sonata, a concerto's main theme does not close with a half cadence.

8. Exceptions include Mozart, Piano Concerto in C Minor, K. 491; Beethoven, Piano Concertos No. 1 in C, Op. 15, and No. 2 in B-flat, Op. 19.

9. See Mozart, Piano Concerto in F, K. 413/387a; Mozart, Piano Concerto in D Minor, K. 466. In both cases, the transition is nonmodulating, and the subordinate key first appears at the very beginning of the subordinate theme. In Beethoven's Piano Concerto No. 2 in B-flat, Op. 19, the transition of the opening ritornello modulates to the subordinate key. The subsequent subordi-

nate theme begins in the ♭VI region of that key and returns quickly back to the home key. The opening of Beethoven's Piano Concerto No. 3 in C Minor, Op. 37, also modulates to the subordinate key, but the return to the home key is considerably delayed well into the subordinate theme.

10. See Mozart, Piano Concerto in E-flat, K. 449; Mozart, Piano Concerto in C, K. 503.

11. See Haydn, Piano Concerto in D, Hob. XVIII:11; Beethoven, Piano Concerto No. 5 in E-flat ("Emperor"), Op. 73; both of these movements contain a single, albeit two-part, subordinate theme. Three of the four horn concertos by Mozart (in D, K. 412/386b, in E-flat, K. 447, and in E-flat, K. 495) have a single, relatively short, subordinate theme.

12. Mozart's Piano Concerto in A, K. 488, is exceptional for having the solo exposition largely reproduce the content and organization of the opening ritornello.

13. Cuthbert Girdlestone, *Mozart and His Piano Concertos* (1958; reprint, New York: Dover, 1964), 27.

14. See Mozart, Piano Concertos in E-flat, K. 271, in F, K. 413/387a, and in B-flat, K. 450; Beethoven, Piano Concertos No. 4 in G, Op. 58, and No. 5 in E-flat ("Emperor"), Op. 73; Beethoven, Violin Concerto in D, Op. 61.

15. The terms *ritornello* and *solo* can now be used as adjectives to distinguish between the main theme, transition, and subordinate themes of the opening ritornello and those of the solo exposition.

16. See Mozart, Piano Concertos in G, K. 453, and in D ("Coronation"), K. 537.

17. See Mozart, Piano Concertos in F, K. 413/387a, and in C, K. 503.

18. See Mozart, Piano Concertos in C, K. 415/387b, and in E-flat, K. 482; Beethoven, Piano Concerto No. 2 in B-flat, Op. 19.

19. See Mozart, Piano Concertos in C, K. 415/387b, in D Minor, K. 466, in C Minor, K. 491, and in C, K. 503; Beethoven, Piano Concertos No. 1 in C, Op. 15, and No. 2 in B-flat, Op. 19.

20. See Mozart, Piano Concertos in F, K. 413/387a, and in E-flat, K. 482.

21. See Beethoven, Piano Concertos No. 4 in G, Op. 58, and No. 5 in E-flat ("Emperor"), Op. 73.

22. See a group of four piano concertos written by Mozart, one after the other in 1784 (in D, K. 451, in G, K. 453, in B-flat, K. 456, and in F, K. 459). See also Haydn, Piano Concerto in D, Hob. XVIII:11; Haydn, Trumpet Concerto in E-flat, Hob. VIIe:1; Beethoven, Piano Concerto No. 3 in C Minor, Op. 37.

23. Four different themes can also appear. See Mozart, Piano Concerto in C Minor, K. 491; Beethoven, Piano Concerto No. 1 in C, Op. 15.

24. See Mozart, Piano Concerto in E-flat, K. 482 (parts are shown in exs. 17.3 and 17.5).

25. In Mozart's mature piano concertos (those written in Vienna), there are only three instances when the first solo subordinate theme draws on material from the first ritornello subordinate theme (see Piano Concertos in D, K. 451, in D Minor, K. 466, and in A, K. 488).

26. Other examples: Mozart, Piano Concertos in E-flat, K. 449, in G, K. 453, and in B-flat, K. 595.

27. Rosen, *Sonata Forms*, 79–80.

28. Lowinsky, "On Mozart's Rhythm," 44.

29. Other examples: Mozart, Piano Concertos in F, K. 413/387a, in G, K. 453, in B-flat, K. 456, and in C, K. 467;

Mozart, Sinfonia Concertante for Violin and Viola in E-flat, K. 364/320d; Beethoven, Piano Concerto No. 3 in C Minor, Op. 37.

30. In the scholarly literature, this ritornello is usually identified by number as the "second" ritornello (or tutti). The term *subordinate-key ritornello* seeks to provide a degree of functional interpretation to this section of the concerto, since, as will be discussed shortly, the transposing of opening ritornello material into the subordinate key is central to its function.

31. Tovey, "The Classical Concerto," 9-10.

32. David Rosen, "Standard Operating Procedure," 82-83.

33. See Mozart, Piano Concertos in D Minor, K. 466, and in D ("Coronation"), K. 537; Mozart, Clarinet Concerto in A, K. 622.

34. See Mozart, Piano Concerto in B-flat, K. 595; Mozart, Sinfonia Concertante for Violin and Viola in E-flat, K. 364/320d.

35. Other examples: Mozart, Piano Concerto in C, K. 467; Beethoven, Piano Concerto No. 3 in C Minor, Op. 37.

36. Rosen, *Sonata Forms*, 89-95.

37. See Haydn, Piano Concerto in D, Hob. XVIII:11; Mozart, Piano Concerto in B-flat, K. 595; Mozart, Clarinet Concerto in A, K. 622.

38. See Mozart, Piano Concertos in G, K. 453, and in E-flat, K. 482.

39. Given that the beginning of the recapitulation often brings the full orchestra alone, historians have sometimes recognized a formal "ritornello" at this point, one that harks back to earlier midcentury models of concerto. See Stevens, "Patterns of Recapitulation," for an interesting discussion of the different ways in which tutti and solo textures can interact at the start of Mozart's concerto recapitulations.

40. Exceptions include Mozart, Piano Concertos in F, K. 413/387a, and in C, K. 415/387b.

41. See Mozart, Piano Concertos in D Minor, K. 466, and in C Minor, K. 491; Beethoven, Piano Concertos No. 2 in B-flat, Op. 19, and No. 4 in G, Op. 58.

42. See Mozart, Horn Concerto in E-flat, K. 417; Mozart, Sinfonia Concertante for Violin and Viola in E-flat, K. 364.

43. See Mozart, Piano Concertos in E-flat, K. 482, and in C, K. 503; Beethoven, Piano Concerto No. 1 in C, Op. 15.

44. See Mozart, Piano Concerto in B-flat, K. 450.

45. See Mozart, Piano Concertos in E-flat, K. 271, and in F, K. 459.

46. See Mozart, Piano Concerto in E-flat, K. 482.

47. See Mozart, Horn Concerto in D, K. 412/386b.

48. See Mozart, Piano Concerto in B-flat, K. 450.

49. Cadenzas are omitted in Mozart's Clarinet Concerto in A, K. 622, as well as his Horn Concertos in D, K. 412/386b, and in E-flat, K. 417.

50. As mentioned, some historians recognize these parts as separate ritornellos (see n. 5).

51. A form-functional examination of Mozart's and Beethoven's written-out cadenzas must be postponed for a later study. For now, see Joseph Swain, "Form and Function of the Classical Cadenza," *Journal of Musicology* 6 (1988): 27-59, for an important step in this direction.

BIBLIOGRAPHY

Adrian, Jack. "The Function of the Apparent Tonic at the Beginning of Development Sections." *Intégral* 5 (1991): 1–53.

Agawu, V. Kofi. *Playing with Signs: A Semiotic Interpretation of Classic Music.* Princeton, NJ: Princeton University Press, 1991.

Agmon, Eytan. "Functional Harmony Revisited: A Prototype-Theoretic Approach." *Music Theory Spectrum* 17 (1995): 196–214.

Aldwell, Edward, and Carl Schachter. *Harmony and Voice Leading.* 2d ed. New York: Harcourt Brace Jovanovich, 1989.

Andrews, Harold L. "The Submediant in Haydn's Development Sections." In *Haydn Studies,* ed. Jens Peter Larsen, Howard Serwer, and James Webster, 465–71. New York: Norton, 1981.

Bartha, Dénes. "Liedform-Probleme." In *Festskrift Jens Peter Larsen,* ed. Nils Schiørring, Henrick Glahn, and Carsten E. Hatting, 317–37. Copenhagen: Wilhelm Hansen, 1972.

———. "On Beethoven's Thematic Structure." In *The Creative World of Beethoven,* ed. Paul Henry Lang, 257–76. New York: Norton, 1971. First published in *Musical Quarterly* 61 (1970): 759–78.

———. "Das Quatrain-Modell in Mozarts Perioden- und Liedform-Strukturen." *Mozart-Jahrbuch 1978/79,* 30–44.

———. "Song Form and the Concept of 'Quatrain.'" In *Haydn Studies,* ed. Jens Peter Larsen, Howard Serwer, and James Webster, 353–55. New York: Norton, 1981.

Batt, Robert. "Function and Structure of Transitions in Sonata-Form Music of Mozart." *Canadian University Music Review* 9 (1988): 157–201.

Beach, David. "Phrase Expansion: Three Analytical Studies." *Music Analysis* 14 (1995): 27–47.

———. "A Recurring Pattern in Mozart's Music." *Journal of Music Theory* 27 (1983): 1–29.

Benjamin, William E. "A Theory of Musical Meter." *Music Perception* 1 (1984): 355–413.

Berry, Wallace. *Form in Music.* 2d ed. Englewood Cliffs, NJ: Prentice-Hall, 1986.

———. *Structural Functions in Music.* Englewood Cliffs, NJ: Prentice-Hall, 1976.

Blombach, Ann. "Phrase and Cadence: A Study of Terminology and Definition." *Journal of Music Theory Pedagogy* 1 (1987): 225–51.

Bonds, Mark Evan. "Haydn's False Recapitulations and the Perception of Sonata Form in the Eighteenth Century." Ph.D. diss., Harvard University, 1988.

———. *Wordless Rhetoric: Musical Form and the Metaphor of the Oration.* Cambridge, MA: Harvard University Press, 1991.

Broyles, Michael. *Beethoven: The Emergence and Evolution of Beethoven's Heroic Style.* New York: Excelsior, 1987.

———. "Organic Form and the Binary Repeat." *Musical Quarterly* 66 (1980): 339–60.

Budday, Wolfgang. *Grundlagen musikalischer Formen der Wiener Klassik: An Hand der zeitgenössischen Theorie von Joseph Riepel und Heinrich Christoph Koch dargestellt an Menuetten und Sonatensätzen (1750–1790).* Kassel: Bärenreiter, 1983.

Bushler, David. "Harmonic Structure in Mozart's Sonata-Form Developments." *Mozart-Jahrbuch 1984/85,* 15–24.

Cadwallader, Allen. "Form and Tonal Process." In *Trends in Schenkerian Research,* ed. Allen Cadwallader, 1–21. New York: Schirmer, 1990.

Caplin, William E. "The 'Expanded Cadential Progression': A Category for the Analysis of Classical Form." *Journal of Musicological Research* 7 (1987): 215–57.

———. "Funktionale Komponenten im achttaktigen Satz." *Musiktheorie* 1 (1986): 239–60.

———. "Hybrid Themes: Toward a Refinement in the Classification of Classical Theme Types." *Beethoven Forum* 3 (1994): 151–65.

———. "Structural Expansion in Beethoven's Symphonic Forms." In *Beethoven's Compositional Process,* ed. William Kinderman, 27–54. Lincoln: University of Nebraska Press, 1991.

Carpenter, Patrica. "A Problem in Organic Form: Schoenberg's Tonal Body." *Theory and Practice* 13 (1988): 31–63.

Cavett-Dunsby, Esther. "Mozart's Codas." *Music Analysis* 7 (1988): 31–51.

———. "Mozart's 'Haydn' Quartets: Composing Up and Down Without Rules." *Journal of the Royal Musical Association* 113 (1988): 57–80.

———. *Mozart's Variations Reconsidered: Four Case Studies (K. 613, K. 501, K. 421/417b, K. 491).* New York: Garland, 1989.

Churgin, Bathia. "Harmonic and Tonal Instability in the Second Key Area of Classic Sonata Form." In *Convention in Eighteenth- and Nineteenth-Century Music: Essays in Honor of Leonard G. Ratner,* ed. Wye J. Allanbrook, Janet M. Levy, and William P. Mahrt, 23–57. Stuyvesant, NY: Pendragon, 1992.

Cole, Malcolm S. "Haydn's Symphonic Rondo Finales: Their Structure and Stylistic Evolution." *Haydn Yearbook* 13 (1982): 113–42.

———. "The Rondo-Finale: Evidence for the Mozart–Haydn Exchange?" *Mozart-Jahrbuch 1968–70,* 242–56.

Cone, Edward T. *Musical Form and Musical Performance*. New York: Norton, 1968.

Czerny, Carl. *School of Practical Composition*, trans. John Bishop. 3 vols., ca. 1848. Reprint, New York: Da Capo, 1979.

Dahlhaus, Carl. *Ludwig van Beethoven: Approaches to His Music*, trans. Mary Whittall. Oxford: Clarendon, 1993.

———. "Periode." *Riemann Musiklexikon*. 12th ed., vol. 3, *Sachteil*, 721–22. Mainz: B. Schott, 1967.

———. "Satz und Periode: Zur Theorie der musikalischen Syntax." *Zeitschrift für Musiktheorie* 9 (1978): 16–26.

Danckwardt, Marianne. *Die langsame Einleitung: Ihre Herkunft und ihr Bau bei Haydn und Mozart*. 2 vols. Tutzing: Schneider, 1977.

Danuser, Hermann. "Vers- oder Prosaprinzip?: Mozarts Streichquartett in d-Moll (KV 421) in der Deutung Jérôme-Joseph de Momignys und Arnold Schönbergs." *Musiktheorie* 7 (1992): 245–63.

Davis, Shelley. "H. C. Koch, the Classic Concerto, and the Sonata-Form Retransition." *Journal of Musicology* 2 (1983): 45–61.

Downs, Philip G. *Classical Music: The Era of Haydn, Mozart, and Beethoven*. New York: Norton, 1992.

Epstein, David. *Beyond Orpheus: Studies in Musical Structure*. Cambridge, MA: MIT Press, 1979.

Fillion, Michelle. "Sonata-Exposition Procedures in Haydn's Keyboard Sonatas." In *Haydn Studies*, ed. Jens Peter Larsen, Howard Serwer, and James Webster, 475–81. New York: Norton, 1981.

Fischer, Wilhelm. "Zur Entwicklungsgeschichte des Wiener klassischen Stils." *Studien zur Musikwissenschaft* 3 (1915): 24–84.

Fisher, Steven C. "Further Thoughts on Haydn's Symphonic Rondo Finales." *Haydn Yearbook* 17 (1992): 85–107.

———. "Sonata Procedures in Haydn's Symphonic Rondo Finales of the 1770s." In *Haydn Studies*, ed. Jens Peter Larsen, Howard Serwer, and James Webster, 481–87. New York: Norton, 1981.

Forster, Robert. "Zur Funktion von Anfangsritornell und Reprise in den Kopfsätzen einiger Klavierkonzerte Mozarts." *Mozart-Jahrbuch 1986*, 74–89.

Forte, Allen, and Steven Gilbert. *An Introduction to Schenkerian Analysis*. New York: Norton, 1982.

Frisch, Walter. *Brahms and the Principle of Developing Variation*. Berkeley and Los Angeles: University of California Press, 1984.

Frohlich, Martha. *Beethoven's "Appassionata" Sonata*. Oxford: Clarendon, 1991.

Galand, Joel. "Form, Genre, and Style in the Eighteenth-Century Rondo." *Music Theory Spectrum* 17 (1995): 27–52.

Girdlestone, Cuthbert. *Mozart and His Piano Concertos*. 1958. Reprint, New York: Dover, 1964.

Gjerdingen, Robert O. *A Classic Turn of Phrase: Music and the Psychology of Convention*. Philadelphia: University of Pennsylvania Press, 1988.

Goetschius, Percy. *The Larger Forms of Musical Composition*. New York: Schirmer, 1915.

Green, Douglas M. *Form in Tonal Music*. 2d ed. New York: Holt, Rinehart and Winston, 1979.

Guck, Marion. "The Functional Relations of Chords: A Theory of Musical Intuitions." *In Theory Only* 4 (1978): 29–42.

Haimo, Ethan. "Haydn's Altered Reprise." *Journal of Music Theory* 32 (1988): 335–51.

———. *Haydn's Symphonic Forms: Essays in Compositional Logic*. Oxford: Clarendon, 1995.

Harrison, Daniel. *Harmonic Function in Chromatic Music: A Renewed Dualist Theory and an Account of Its Precedents*. Chicago: University of Chicago Press, 1994.

Harutunian, John. "Haydn and Mozart: Tonic–Dominant Polarity in Mature Sonata-Style Works." *Journal of Musicological Research* 9 (1990): 273–98.

Hatten, Robert S. *Musical Meaning in Beethoven: Markedness, Correlation, and Interpretation*. Bloomington: Indiana University Press, 1994.

Heartz, Daniel. *Haydn, Mozart, and the Viennese School, 1740–1780*. New York: Norton, 1995.

Hopkins, Robert G. "When a Coda Is More Than a Coda: Reflections on Beethoven." In *Explorations in Music, the Arts, and Ideas: Essays in Honor of Leonard B. Meyer*, ed. Eugene Narmour and Ruth Solie, 393–410. Stuyvesant, NY: Pendragon, 1988.

Jan, Steven B. "X Marks the Spot: Schenkerian Perspectives on the Minor-Key Classical Development Section." *Music Analysis* 11 (1992): 37–54.

Josephson, Nors S. "Veränderte Reprisen in Mozarts späten Menuetten." *Mozart-Jahrbuch 1976/77*, 59–69.

Kamien, Roger. "Conflicting Metrical Patterns in Accompaniment and Melody in Works by Mozart and Beethoven: A Preliminary Study." *Journal of Music Theory* 37 (1993): 311–48.

Kelterborn, Rudolf. *Zum Beispiel Mozart: Ein Beitrag zur musikalischen Analyse*. Basel: Bärenreiter, 1981.

Kerman, Joseph. "Notes on Beethoven's Codas." In *Beethoven Studies 3*, ed. Alan Tyson, 141–59. Cambridge: Cambridge University Press, 1982.

Klinkhammer, Rudolf. *Die langsame Einleitung in der Instrumentalmusik der Klassik und Romantik: ein Sonderproblem in der Entwicklung der Sonatenform*. Regensburg: Bosse, 1971.

Koch, Heinrich Christoph. *Introductory Essay on Composition: The Mechanical Rules of Melody, Sections 3 and 4*, trans. Nancy Kovaleff Baker. New Haven, CT: Yale University Press, 1983.

Kohs, Ellis B. *Musical Form*. Boston: Houghton Mifflin, 1976.

Kramer, Jonathan D. *The Time of Music: New Meanings, New Temporalities, New Listening Strategies*. New York: Schirmer, 1988.

Kraus, Joseph C. "Mozart's Chromatic Third Relations: Evidence from the Late Quartets and Quintets." *Journal of Musicological Research* 9 (1990): 229–54.

Küster, Konrad. *Formale Aspekte des ersten Allegros in Mozarts Konzerten*. Kassel: Bärenreiter, 1991.

Larsen, Jens Peter. "Sonata Form Problems." In *Handel, Haydn, and the Viennese Classical Style*, trans. Ulrich Krämer, 269–79. Ann Arbor, MI: UMI Research Press, 1988. First published as "Sonatenform-Probleme," in *Festschrift Friedrich Blume zum 70. Geburtstag*, ed. Anna Amalie Abert and Wilhelm Pfannkuch, 221–30. Kassel: Bärenreiter, 1963.

LaRue, Jan. "Bifocal Tonality in Haydn Symphonies." In *Convention in Eighteenth- and Nineteenth-Century Music: Essays in Honor of Leonard G. Ratner*, ed. Wye J. Allanbrook, Janet M. Levy, and William P. Mahrt, 59–73. Stuyvesant, NY: Pendragon, 1992.

———. *Guidelines for Style Analysis*. 2d ed. Warren, MI: Harmonie Park Press, 1992.

Laufer, Edward. "Voice-Leading Procedures in Development Sections." Paper presented at the conference "Music Theory Canada 1990," London, Ontario, March 1990.

Leeson, Daniel, and Robert D. Levin. "On the Authenticity of K. Anh. C 14.01 (297b), a Symphonia Concertante for Four Winds and Orchestra." *Mozart-Jahrbuch 1976/77*, 70–96.

Leichtentritt, Hugo. *Musical Form*. Cambridge, MA: Harvard University Press, 1951.

Lerdahl, Fred, and Ray Jackendoff. *A Generative Theory of Tonal Music*. Cambridge, MA: MIT Press, 1983.

Levy, Janet M. "Gesture, Form, and Syntax in Haydn's Music." In *Haydn Studies*, ed. Jens Peter Larsen, Howard Serwer, and James Webster, 355–62. New York: Norton, 1981.

———. "Texture as Sign in Classic and Early Romantic Music." *Journal of the American Musicological Society* 35 (1982): 482–531.

Lewin, David. "Theory, Phenomenology, and Modes of Perception." *Music Perception* 3 (1986): 327–92.

Lockwood, Lewis. *Beethoven: Studies in the Creative Process*. Cambridge, MA: Harvard University Press, 1992.

Longyear, Rey M., and Kate R. Covington. "Sources of the Three-Key Exposition." *Journal of Musicology* 6 (1988): 448–70.

Lowinsky, Edward E. "On Mozart's Rhythm." In *The Creative World of Mozart*, ed. Paul Henry Lang, 31–55. New York: Norton, 1963. First published in *Musical Quarterly* 42 (1956): 162–86.

Marston, Nicholas. "Analysing Variations: The Finale of Beethoven's String Quartet Op. 74." *Music Analysis* 8 (1989): 303–24.

———. "The Recapitulation Transition in Mozart's Music." *Mozart-Jahrbuch 1991*, pt. 2, 793–809.

Marx, Adolph Bernhard. *Die Lehre von der musikalischen Komposition*. 5th ed., 3 vols. Leipzig: Breitkopf und Härtel, 1879.

Meyer, Leonard B. *Explaining Music: Essays and Explorations*. Berkeley and Los Angeles: University of California Press, 1973.

Morgan, Robert P. "Coda as Culmination: The First Movement of the 'Eroica' Symphony." In *Music Theory and the Exploration of the Past*, ed. Christopher Hatch and David W. Bernstein, 357–76. Chicago: University of Chicago Press, 1993.

Narmour, Eugene. *The Analysis and Cognition of Basic Melodic Structures: The Implication–Realization Model*. Chicago: University of Chicago Press, 1990.

Neff, Severine. "Schoenberg and Goethe: Organicism and Analysis." In *Music Theory and the Exploration of the Past*, ed. Christopher Hatch and David W. Bernstein, 409–33. Chicago: University of Chicago Press, 1993.

Nelson, Robert U. *The Technique of Variation*. Berkeley and Los Angeles: University of California Press, 1948.

Perry-Camp, Jane. "Time and Temporal Proportion: The Golden Section Metaphor in Mozart, Music, and History." *Journal of Musicological Research* 3 (1979): 133–76.

Prout, Ebenezer. *Musical Form*. London: Augener, 1893.

Ratner, Leonard G. *Classic Music: Expression, Form, and Style*. New York: Schirmer, 1980.

Ratz, Erwin. *Einführung in die musikalische Formenlehre: Über Formprizipien in den Inventionen und Fugen J. S. Bachs und ihre Bedeutung für die Kompositionstechnik Beethovens*. 3d ed., enl. Vienna: Universal, 1973.

Riemann, Hugo. *Vereinfachte Harmonielehre, oder die Lehre von den tonalen Funktionen der Akkorde*. London: Augener, 1893.

Rosen, Charles. *The Classical Style: Haydn, Mozart, Beethoven*. New York: Norton, 1972.

———. *Sonata Forms*. Rev. ed. New York: Norton, 1988.

Rosen, David. "The Composer's 'Standard Operating Procedure' as Evidence of Intention: The Case of a Formal Quirk in Mozart's K. 595." *Journal of Musicology* 5 (1987): 79–90.

Rothstein, William. *Phrase Rhythm in Tonal Music*. New York: Schirmer, 1989.

Rufer, Josef. *Composition with Twelve Notes*, trans. Humphrey Searle. London: Barrie and Rockliff, 1954.

Schachter, Carl. "Analysis by Key: Another Look at Modulation." *Music Analysis* 6 (1987): 289–318.

———. "Rhythm and Linear Analysis: Aspects of Meter." In *Music Forum*, ed. Felix Salzer, vol. 6, pt. 1, 1–59. New York: Columbia University Press, 1987.

———. "Rhythm and Linear Analysis: Durational Reduction." In *Music Forum*, ed. Felix Salzer, vol. 5, 197–232. New York: Columbia University Press, 1980.

Schenker, Heinrich. *Free Composition*, ed. and trans. Ernst Oster. New York: Longman, 1979.

Schikele, Peter. "New Horizons in Music Appreciation." *Report from Hoople: P. D. Q. Bach on the Air*. Vanguard VSD-79268-A.

Schmalfeldt, Janet. "Cadential Processes: The Evaded Cadence and the 'One More Time' Technique." *Journal of Musicological Research* 12 (1992): 1–51.

———. *In the Process of Becoming: Philosophical and Analytical Perspectives on Form in Early Nineteenth-Century Music*. New York: Oxford University Press, forthcoming.

———. "Towards a Reconciliation of Schenkerian Concepts with Traditional and Recent Theories of Form." *Music Analysis* 10 (1991): 233–87.

Schmalzreidt, Siegfried. "Charakter und Drama: Zur historischen Analyse von Haydnschen und Beethovenschen Sonatensätzen." *Archiv für Musikwissenschaft* 42 (1985): 37–66.

Schoenberg, Arnold. *Fundamentals of Musical Composition*, ed. Gerald Strang and Leonard Stein. London: Faber & Faber, 1967.

———. *The Musical Idea and the Logic, Technique, and Art of Its Presentation*, ed. and trans. Patricia Carpenter and Severine Neff. New York: Columbia University Press, 1995.

———. *Structural Functions of Harmony*. Rev. ed., ed. Leonard Stein. New York: Norton, 1969.

Schwarting, Heino. "Ungewöhnliche Repriseneintritte in Haydns späterer Instrumentalmusik." *Archiv für Musikwissenschaft* 17 (1960): 168–82.

Sechter, Simon. *Die Grundsätze der musikalischen Komposition*. 3 vols. Leipzig, 1853.

Shamgar, Beth. "On Locating the Retransition in Classic Sonata Form." *Music Review* 42 (1981): 130–43.

Sheer, Miriam. "Patterns of Dynamic Organization in Beethoven's Eroica Symphony." *Journal of Musicology* 10 (1992): 483–504.

Sisman, Elaine R. *Haydn and the Classical Variation*. Cambridge, MA: Harvard University Press, 1993.

———. "Small and Expanded Forms: Koch's Model and Haydn's Music." *Musical Quarterly* 68 (1982): 444–75.

———. "Tradition and Transformation in the Alternating Variations of Haydn and Beethoven." *Acta Musicologica* 62 (1990): 152–82.

Smyth, David. " 'Balanced Interruption' and the Formal Repeat." *Music Theory Spectrum* 15 (1993): 76–88.

———. "Large-Scale Rhythm and Classical Form." *Music Theory Spectrum* 12 (1990): 236–46.

Snyder, John L. "Schenker and the First Movement of Mozart's Sonata, K. 545: An Uninterrupted Sonata-Form Movement?" *Theory and Practice* 16 (1991): 51–78.

Stein, Erwin. *Form and Performance.* London: Faber & Faber, 1962.

Stevens, Jane R. "Patterns of Recapitulation in the First Movements of Mozart's Piano Concertos." In *Musical Humanism and Its Legacy: Essays in Honor of Claude Palisca*, ed. Nancy Kovaleff Baker and Barbara Russano Hanning, 397–418. Stuyvesant, NY: Pendragon, 1992.

Swain, Joseph. "Form and Function of the Classical Cadenza." *Journal of Musicology* 6 (1988): 27–59.

Tovey, Donald Francis. *A Companion to Beethoven's Pianoforte Sonatas.* London: Associated Board, 1935.

———. *Essays in Musical Analysis.* 7 vols. London: Oxford University Press, 1935–39.

———. *The Forms of Music.* New York: Meridian, 1956.

Treitler, Leo. "Mozart and the Idea of Absolute Music." Chap. 7 in Leo Treitler, *Music and the Historical Imagination.* Cambridge, MA: Harvard University Press, 1989.

Wason, Robert W. *Viennese Harmonic Theory from Albrechtsberger to Schenker and Schoenberg.* Ann Arbor, MI: UMI Research Press, 1985.

Webern, Anton. *The Path to the New Music*, ed. Willi Reich. Bryn Mawr, PA: Theodore Presser, 1963.

Webster, James. "Freedom of Form in Haydn's Early String Quartets." In *Haydn Studies*, ed. Jens Peter Larsen, Howard Serwer, and James Webster, 522–30. New York: Norton, 1981.

———. *Haydn's "Farewell" Symphony and the Idea of Classical Style: Through-Composition and Cyclic Integration in His Instrumental Music.* Cambridge: Cambridge University Press, 1991.

———. "Schubert's Sonata Form and Brahms' First Maturity." *Nineteenth-Century Music* 2 (1978): 18–35, and 3 (1979): 52–71.

———. "Sonata Form." *The New Grove Dictionary of Music and Musicians*, vol. 17, 497–508.

Wheelock, Gretchen. *Haydn's Ingenious Jesting with Art: Contexts of Musical Wit and Humor.* New York: Schirmer, 1992.

Wick, Norman L. "Transformations of Middleground Hypermeasures in Selected Mozart Keyboard Sonatas." *Theory and Practice* 16 (1991): 79–102.

Winter, Robert S. "The Bifocal Close and the Evolution of the Viennese Classical Style." *Journal of the American Musicological Society* 42 (1989): 275–337.

Wolf, Eugene K. "Concerto." *The New Harvard Dictionary of Music*, 186–91.

———. "The Recapitulations in Haydn's London Symphonies." *Musical Quarterly* 52 (1966): 71–89.

Yudkin, Jeremy. "Beethoven's 'Mozart' Quartet." *Journal of the American Musicological Society* 45 (1992): 30–74.

INDEX OF CLASSICAL COMPOSITIONS

References to musical examples in the text appear in parentheses following the citation of work and movement. Pages in italics refer to substantive discussions of the compositions.

GENERAL INDEX

formal functions of, 19, 125, 161–63
half cadence, ending with, 181
imperfect authentic cadence, ending
    with, 270n.10
as interthematic function, 17
lacking cadential closure, 237
and large ternary, 211
loose organization of, 97
vs. main theme, 97, 122
major alterations of, 167–71
in minuet, 221, 225, 227
modulating, 119–21, 131, 169–71,
    272n.49
multiple, 221, 277n.22
obscured boundary with transition,
    113, 114, 201–3
in recapitulation, 167–71, 169
rondo vs. sonata, 233, 237
second, 223
in slow movement, 97, 209
terminology for, 270n.3
tight-knit, 209, 261n.25
two-part, 117, 169, 183, 247, 286n.11
subordinate-theme complex, 214,
    231–33, 237, 239
subordinate-theme group, 97, 121, 247,
    270n.11, 280n.18
substitute chords, 25
subtonic (♭VII), 281n.10, 285n.41
supertonic, 24, 141
surface rhythmic activity, 129, 142
symmetrical grouping structure, 9, 20,
    55, 69, 85, 87
vs. asymmetrical, 5, 91
symmetry, 13, 266n.15 (see also symmet-
    rical grouping structure)
syntax, formal, 17, 59–61, 97, 129

ternary form. See large ternary; small
    ternary
texture, 49, 75, 161, 197, 201, 275n.20
marking new beginning, 103, 119
polyphonic, 75, 142, 153, 245, 249
reduction of, 79, 114, 131, 141, 186
thematic functions, 129, 203 (see also
    interthematic functions)
thematic introduction, 15, 117–19, 125,
    183, 203–5, 206
to main theme, 15, 83, 199, 272n.62
theme and variations, 71, 87, 216–18
themelike unit, 125, 139

three-key exposition, 119–21
tight-knit organization
    and conventional form, 85
    criteria of, 17
    and interthematic functions, 17
    in main theme, 17, 42, 99, 197
    and nonconventional form, 73, 197
    in pre-core, 153, 157
    in small ternary, 13
    in subordinate-key ritornello, 249
    in subordinate-theme group, 97, 121
tight knit vs. loose, 17
    general criteria, 84–85, 269n.3
    main vs. subordinate theme, 97,
        197–99, 201
    opening ritornello, 244–45
    A section, minuet, 221
    sentence vs. period, 268n.16
    small ternary, 85–86
    subordinate-theme group, 121
toccata, 155
tonal closure, 53–55
tonal conflict, 125, 227, 233, 244, 249
tonal hierarchy, 139–40
tonality, 17, 84–85, 196
tonal-polarity model, 195–96
tonic. See final tonic; initial tonic
tonic emphasis, 13, 15, 37, 75, 129,
    268n.15
tonic function, 23, 262n.17
tonicization, 119, 140, 181, 225
tonicized region, 140, 141, 144, 227
tonic prolongation, 16, 61, 165, 260n.9
    ending in continuation, 40, 61–63
    in presentation, 10, 19, 39, 49
    vs. sequential, 169
    vs. standing on the dominant, 77
    undermined by dominant pedal,
        19–20, 99
    weak, 99, 183, 237
tonic version, 10, 39, 53, 93
tour-of-keys model, 196
Tovey, Donald Francis, 272n.52,
    273n.85, 282n.42, 285n.44, 286n.3,
    287n.31
transition (see also nonmodulating transi-
    tion; transitional introduction)
    in A section, minuet, 221
    in B section, small ternary, 91
    basic functions of, 17–19, 125, 161
    beginning of, 131, 137, 274n.5

concluding function, lack of, 135,
    201–3
destabilizing home key, 125, 127, 129,
    197
in double-region couplet, 239
eliminated, 165, 173, 211, 233, 235,
    237, 272n.51, 281n.12
ending with perfect authentic
    cadence, 203
in exposition vs. in recapitulation, 161
extended, 19
in five-part rondo, 233
obscured boundary with subordinate
    theme, 113, 114, 201–3
in recapitulation, 163–65
in rondo, 211, 233, 235, 237, 272n.51
single harmony in, 131
in sonata–rondo, 113, 237
texture of, 275n.20
two-part, 165, 197, 203
transitional introduction, 147, 153, 155,
    157
Treitler, Leo, 272n.52
trill, cadential, 109, 123, 167, 247, 249,
    250
trio, 219, 220, 229, 284n.34
truncated recapitulation, 216
truncated small ternary, 206, 212, 213,
    233
two-part subordinate theme, 117, 169,
    183, 247, 286n.11
two-part transition, 165, 197, 203
two-reprise form, small, 267n.1

ultimate dominant, 29, 45, 53, 117, 133

variation rondo, 284n.10

Weber, Max, 4
Webster, James, 259n.1, 284n.30
    classical style, critique of, 259n.7
    ending of development, 275n.14
    false recapitulation, 277n.58
    minuet form vs. sonata form, 283n.9
    multimovement cycle, 259n.2
    reversed period, 274n.23
    subordinate theme, 270n.5
    three-key exposition, 273n.70
Winter, Robert, 274nn.14, 16, 277n.11
Wolf, Eugene K., 273n.83, 277nn.13,
    21, 286n.5

CPSIA information can be obtained at www.ICGtesting.com
Printed in the USA
BVOW05s0949301013

335006BV00003B/6/P